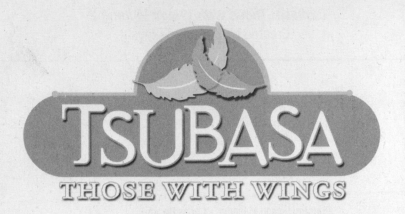

TSUBASA
THOSE WITH WINGS

Volume: 2
By Natsuki Takaya

12-28-10

HAMBURG // LONDON // LOS ANGELES // TOKYO

Tsubasa: Those with Wings Volume 2
Created by Natsuki Takaya

Translation - Adrienne Beck
English Adaptation - Soo-Kyung Kim
Retouch and Lettering - Star Print Brokers
Production Artist - Rui Kyo
Graphic Designer - Louis Csontos

Editor - Bryce P. Coleman
Print Production Manager - Lucas Rivera
Managing Editor - Vy Nguyen
Senior Designer - Louis Csontos
Associate Publisher - Marco F. Pavia
President and C.O.O. - John Parker
C.E.O. and Chief Creative Officer - Stu Levy

A  Manga

TOKYOPOP and ☯ are trademarks or registered trademarks of TOKYOPOP Inc.

TOKYOPOP Inc.
5900 Wilshire Blvd. Suite 2000
Los Angeles, CA 90036

E-mail: info@TOKYOPOP.com
Come visit us online at www.TOKYOPOP.com

ISBN: 978-1-4278-1429-6

First TOKYOPOP printing: August 2009
10 9 8 7 6 5 4 3 2 1
Printed in the USA

CONTENTS

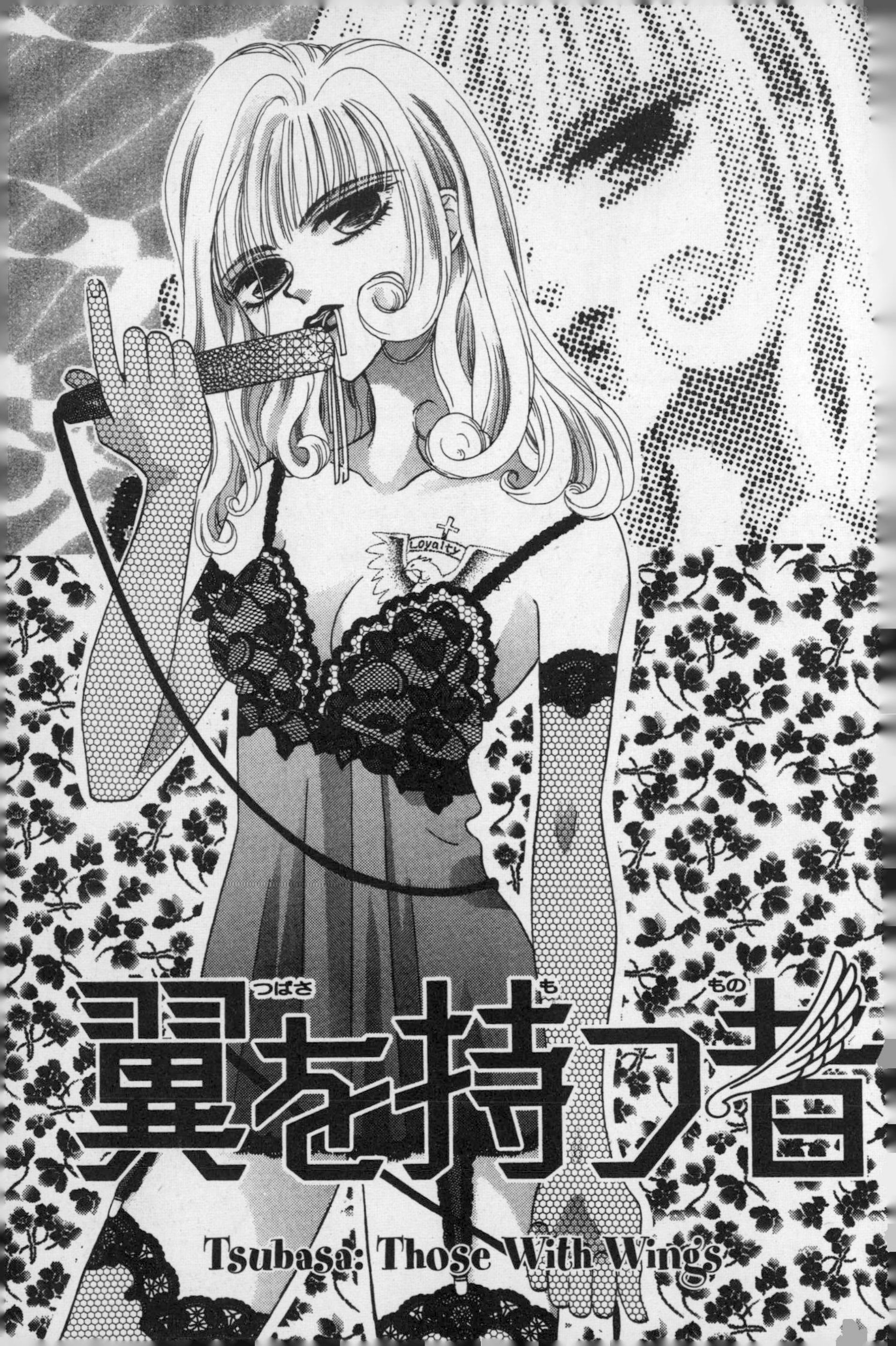
Loyalty
翼(つばさ)を持(も)つ者(もの)
Tsubasa: Those With Wings

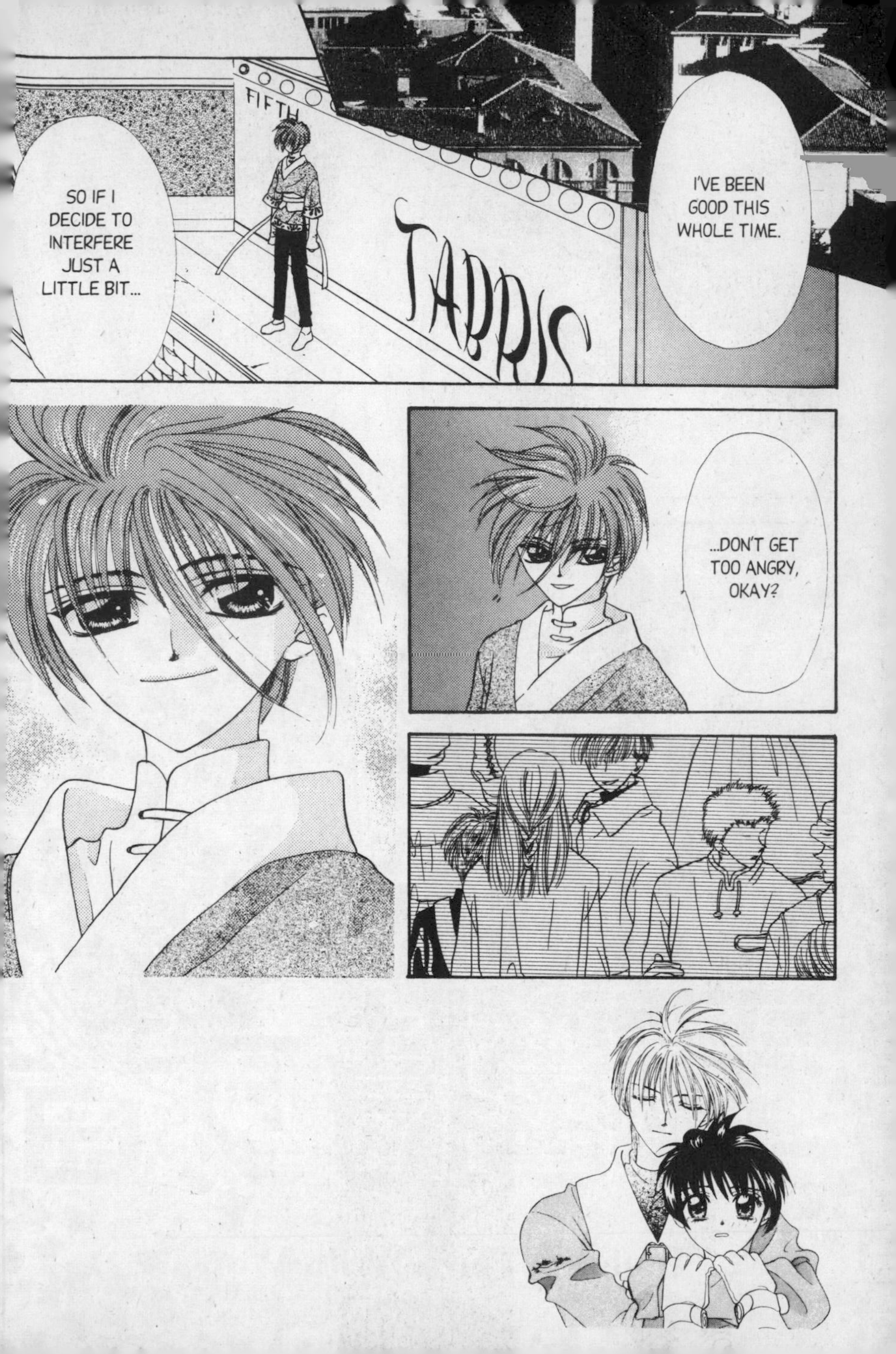
I'VE BEEN GOOD THIS WHOLE TIME.
FIFTH
SO IF I DECIDE TO INTERFERE JUST A LITTLE BIT...
...DON'T GET TOO ANGRY, OKAY?

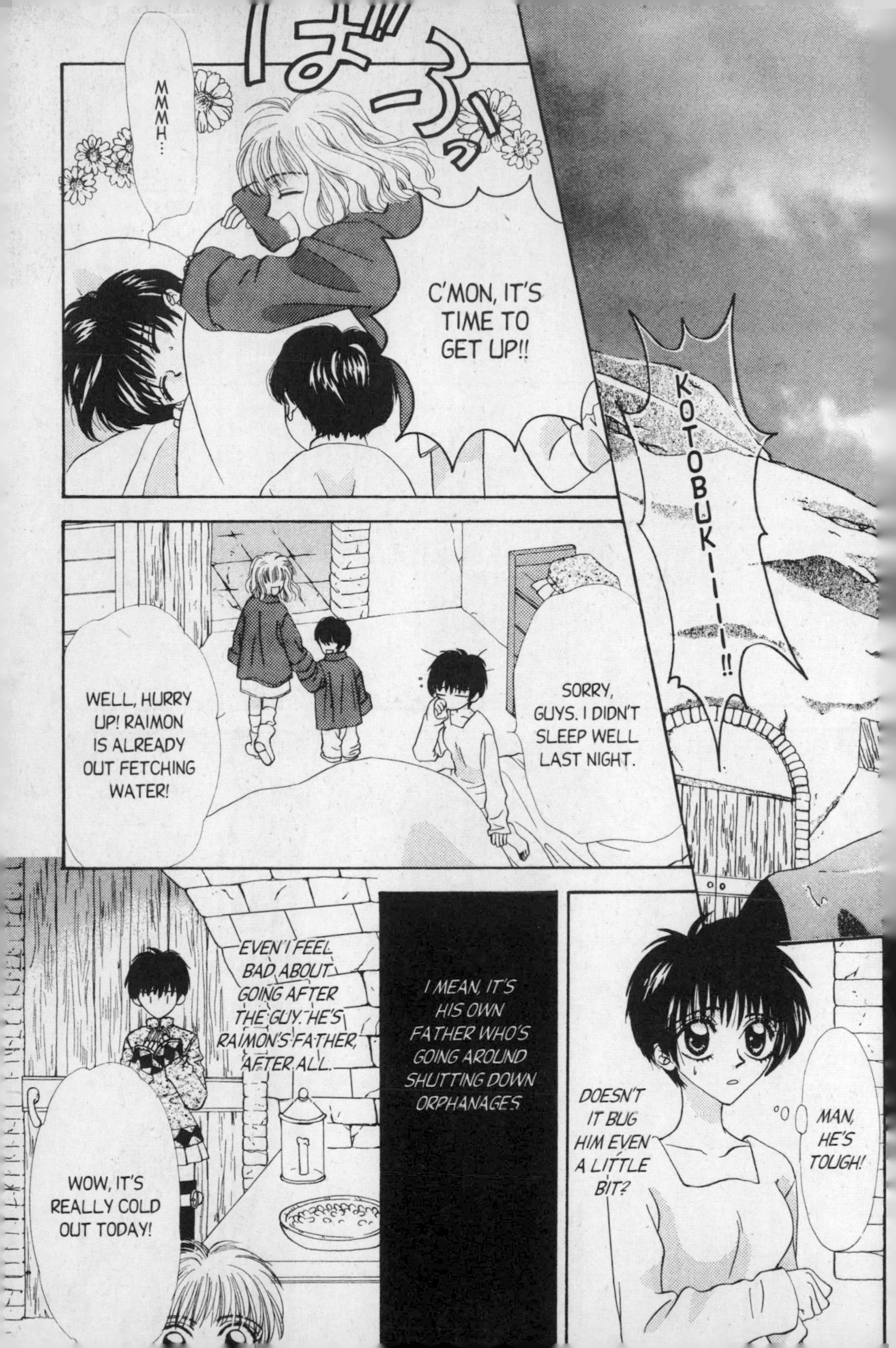

KOTOBUKI---!!
ばーふっ
MMMH...
C'MON, IT'S TIME TO GET UP!!
SORRY, GUYS. I DIDN'T SLEEP WELL LAST NIGHT.
WELL, HURRY UP! RAIMON IS ALREADY OUT FETCHING WATER!
MAN, HE'S TOUGH!
DOESN'T IT BUG HIM EVEN A LITTLE BIT?
I MEAN, IT'S HIS OWN FATHER WHO'S GOING AROUND SHUTTING DOWN ORPHANAGES.
EVEN I FEEL BAD ABOUT GOING AFTER THE GUY. HE'S RAIMON'S FATHER, AFTER ALL.
WOW, IT'S REALLY COLD OUT TODAY!

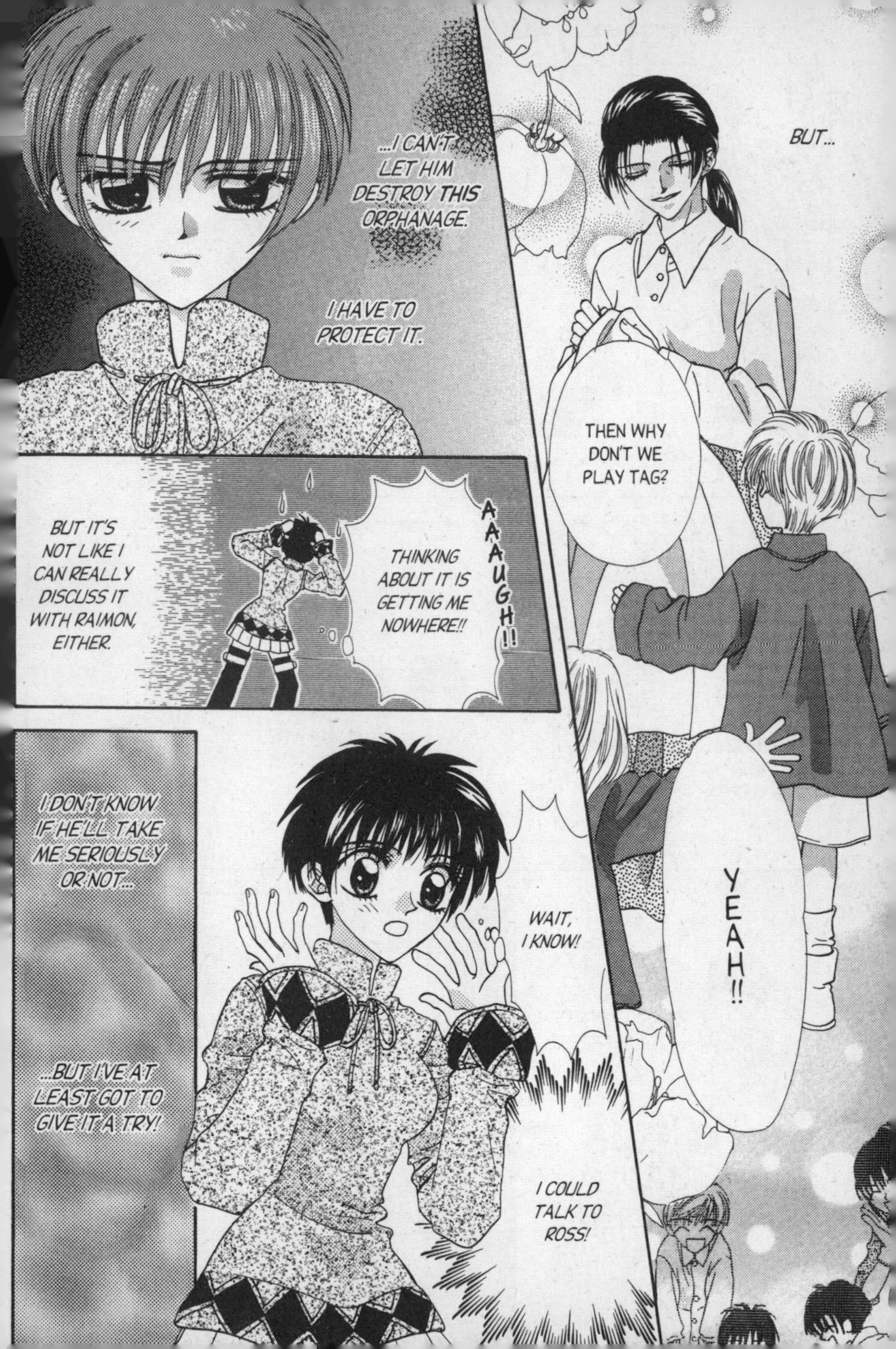
BUT...
THEN WHY DON'T WE PLAY TAG?
YEAH!!
...I CAN'T LET HIM DESTROY THIS ORPHANAGE.
I HAVE TO PROTECT IT.
AAAUGH!!
THINKING ABOUT IT IS GETTING ME NOWHERE!!
BUT IT'S NOT LIKE I CAN REALLY DISCUSS IT WITH RAIMON, EITHER.
WAIT, I KNOW!
I COULD TALK TO ROSS!
I DON'T KNOW IF HE'LL TAKE ME SERIOUSLY OR NOT...
...BUT I'VE AT LEAST GOT TO GIVE IT A TRY!

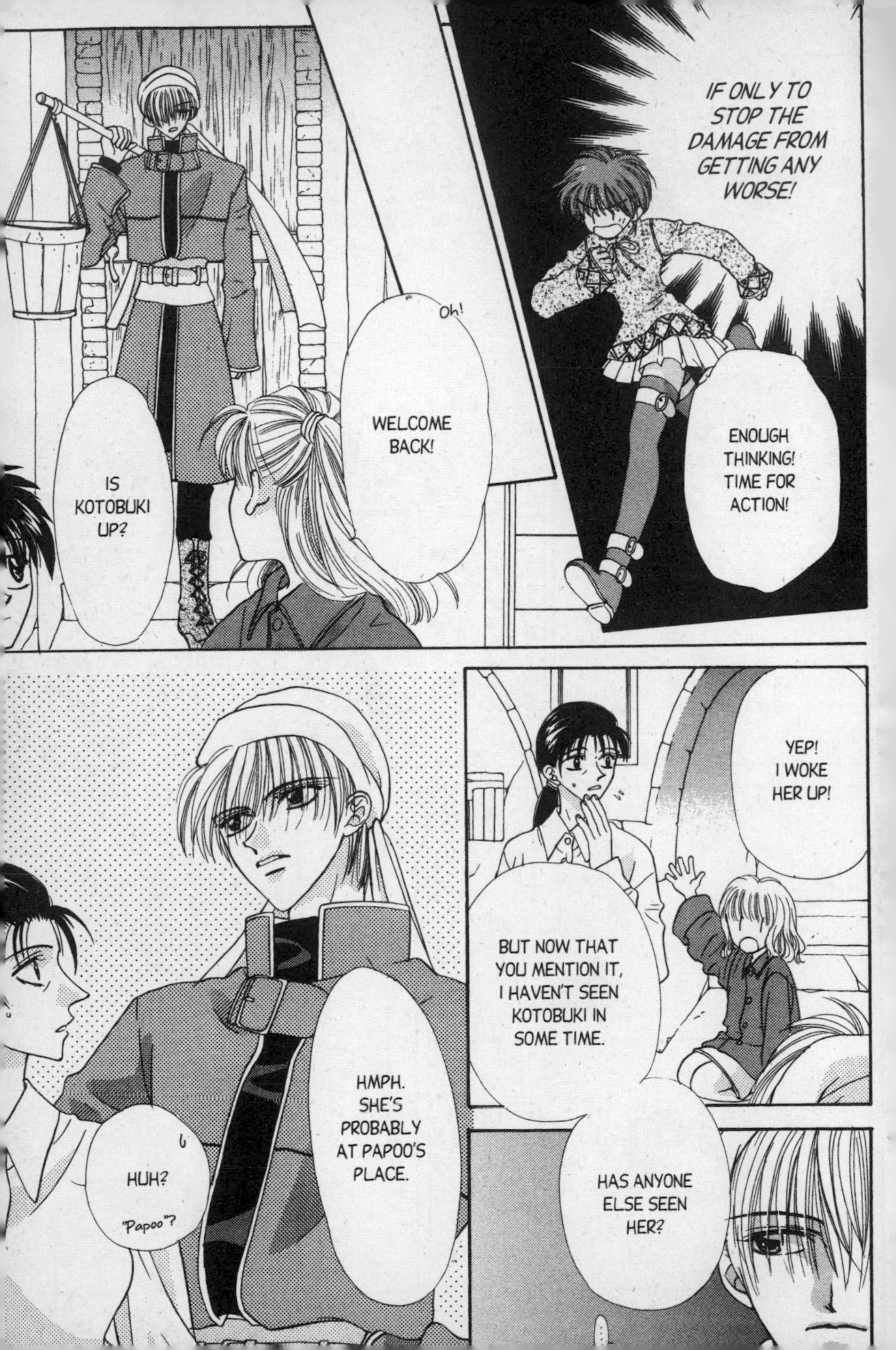
IF ONLY TO STOP THE DAMAGE FROM GETTING ANY WORSE!
ENOUGH THINKING! TIME FOR ACTION!
Oh!
WELCOME BACK!
IS KOTOBUKI UP?
YEP! I WOKE HER UP!
BUT NOW THAT YOU MENTION IT, I HAVEN'T SEEN KOTOBUKI IN SOME TIME.
HAS ANYONE ELSE SEEN HER?
HMPH. SHE'S PROBABLY AT PAPOO'S PLACE.
HUH?
"Papoo"?

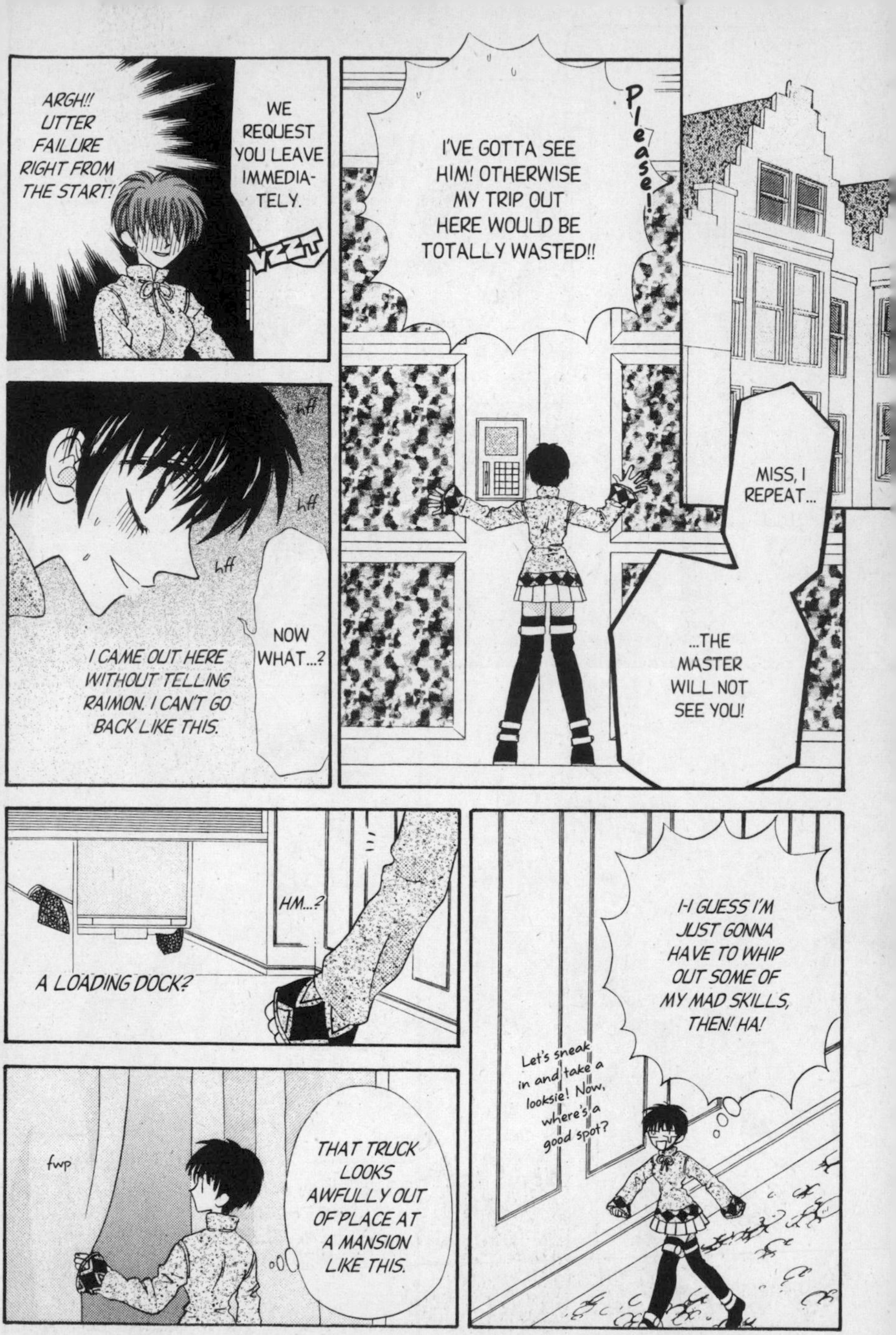
Please!
I'VE GOTTA SEE HIM! OTHERWISE MY TRIP OUT HERE WOULD BE TOTALLY WASTED!!
MISS, I REPEAT...
...THE MASTER WILL NOT SEE YOU!
WE REQUEST YOU LEAVE IMMEDIA-TELY.
VZZT
ARGH!! UTTER FAILURE RIGHT FROM THE START!
hff
hff
hff
NOW WHAT...?
I CAME OUT HERE WITHOUT TELLING RAIMON. I CAN'T GO BACK LIKE THIS.
I-I GUESS I'M JUST GONNA HAVE TO WHIP OUT SOME OF MY MAD SKILLS, THEN! HA!
Let's sneak in and take a looksie! Now, where's a good spot?
HM...?
A LOADING DOCK?
THAT TRUCK LOOKS AWFULLY OUT OF PLACE AT A MANSION LIKE THIS.
fwp

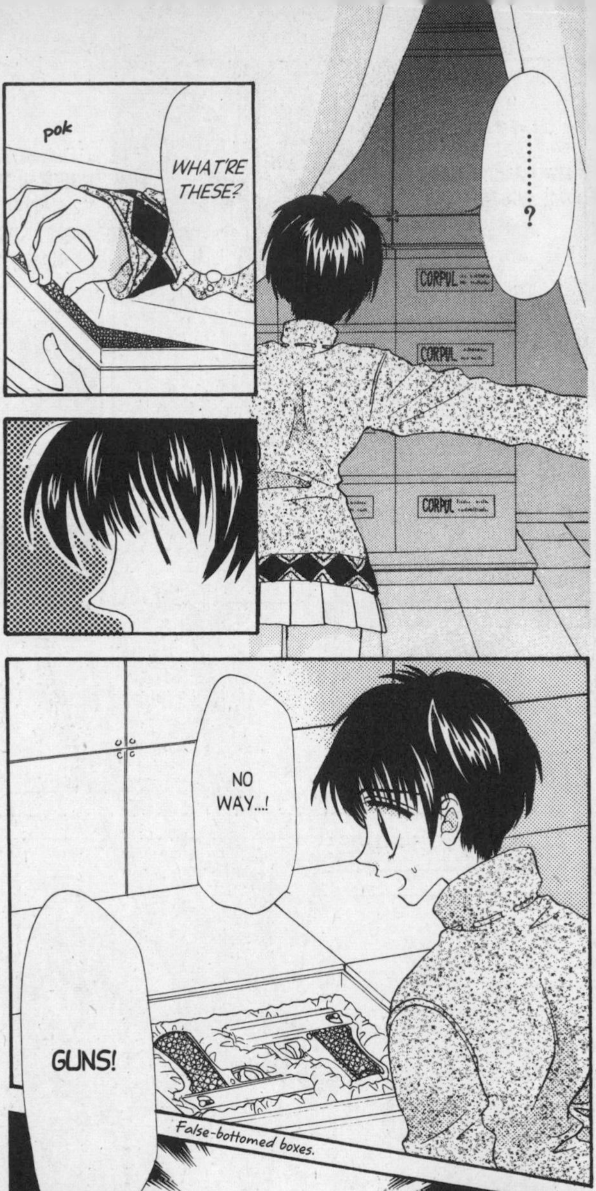
……?
pok
WHAT'RE THESE?
NO WAY...!
GUNS!
False-bottomed boxes.
Ah!
OH YEAH! THAT'S RIGHT! ROSS SMUGGLES MODDED GUNS!
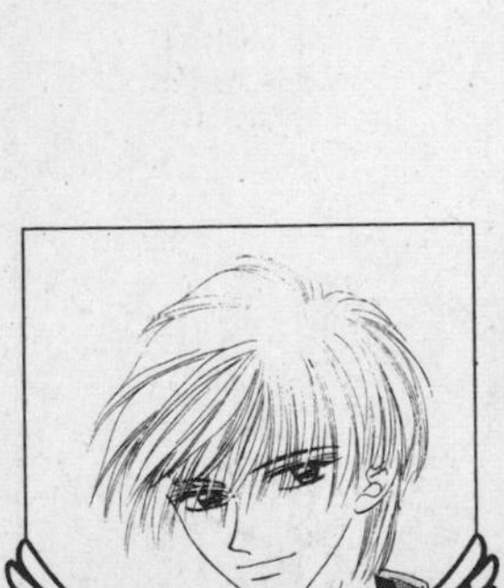

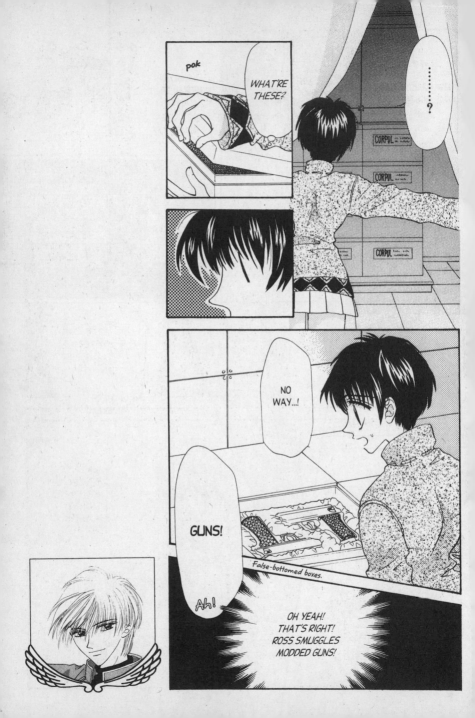

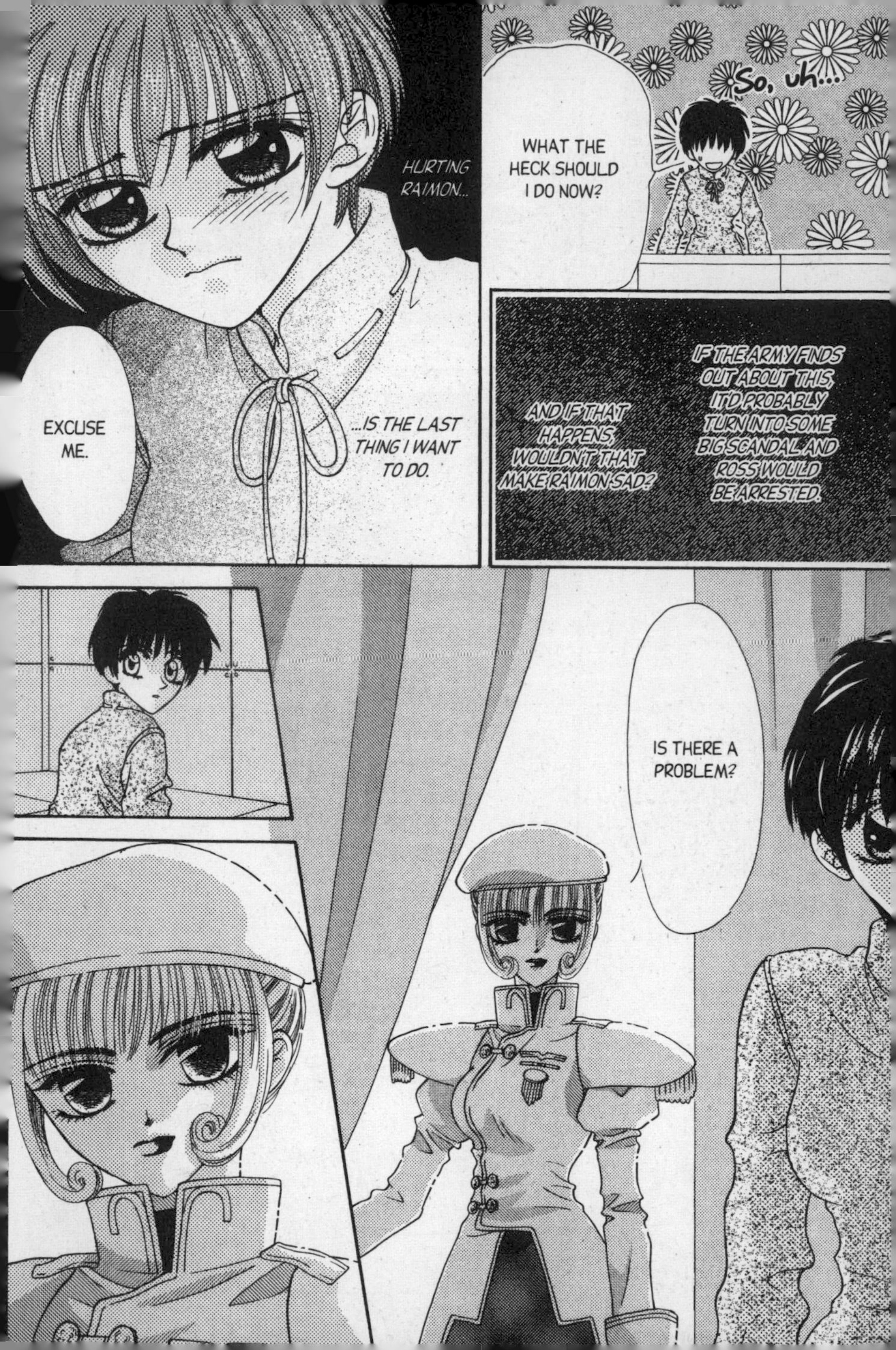
So, uh...
WHAT THE HECK SHOULD I DO NOW?
IF THE ARMY FINDS OUT ABOUT THIS, IT'D PROBABLY TURN INTO SOME BIG SCANDAL AND ROSS WOULD BE ARRESTED.
AND IF THAT HAPPENS, WOULDN'T THAT MAKE RAIMON SAD?
HURTING RAIMON...
...IS THE LAST THING I WANT TO DO.
EXCUSE ME.
IS THERE A PROBLEM?

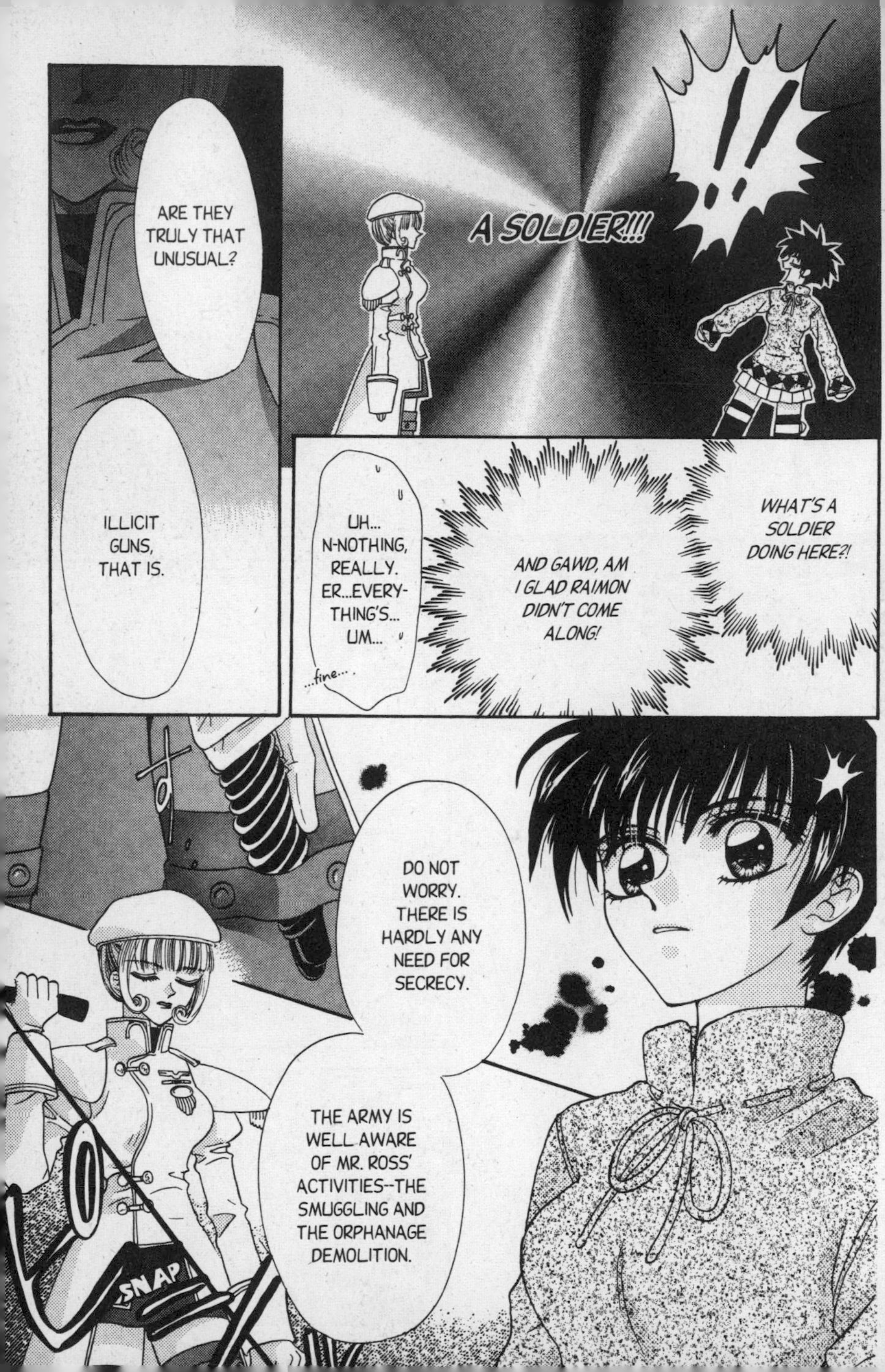
!!
A SOLDIER!!!
WHAT'S A SOLDIER DOING HERE?!
AND GAWD, AM I GLAD RAIMON DIDN'T COME ALONG!
UH... N-NOTHING, REALLY. ER...EVERY-THING'S... UM...
...fine...
ARE THEY TRULY THAT UNUSUAL?
ILLICIT GUNS, THAT IS.
DO NOT WORRY. THERE IS HARDLY ANY NEED FOR SECRECY.
THE ARMY IS WELL AWARE OF MR. ROSS' ACTIVITIES--THE SMUGGLING AND THE ORPHANAGE DEMOLITION.
SNAP

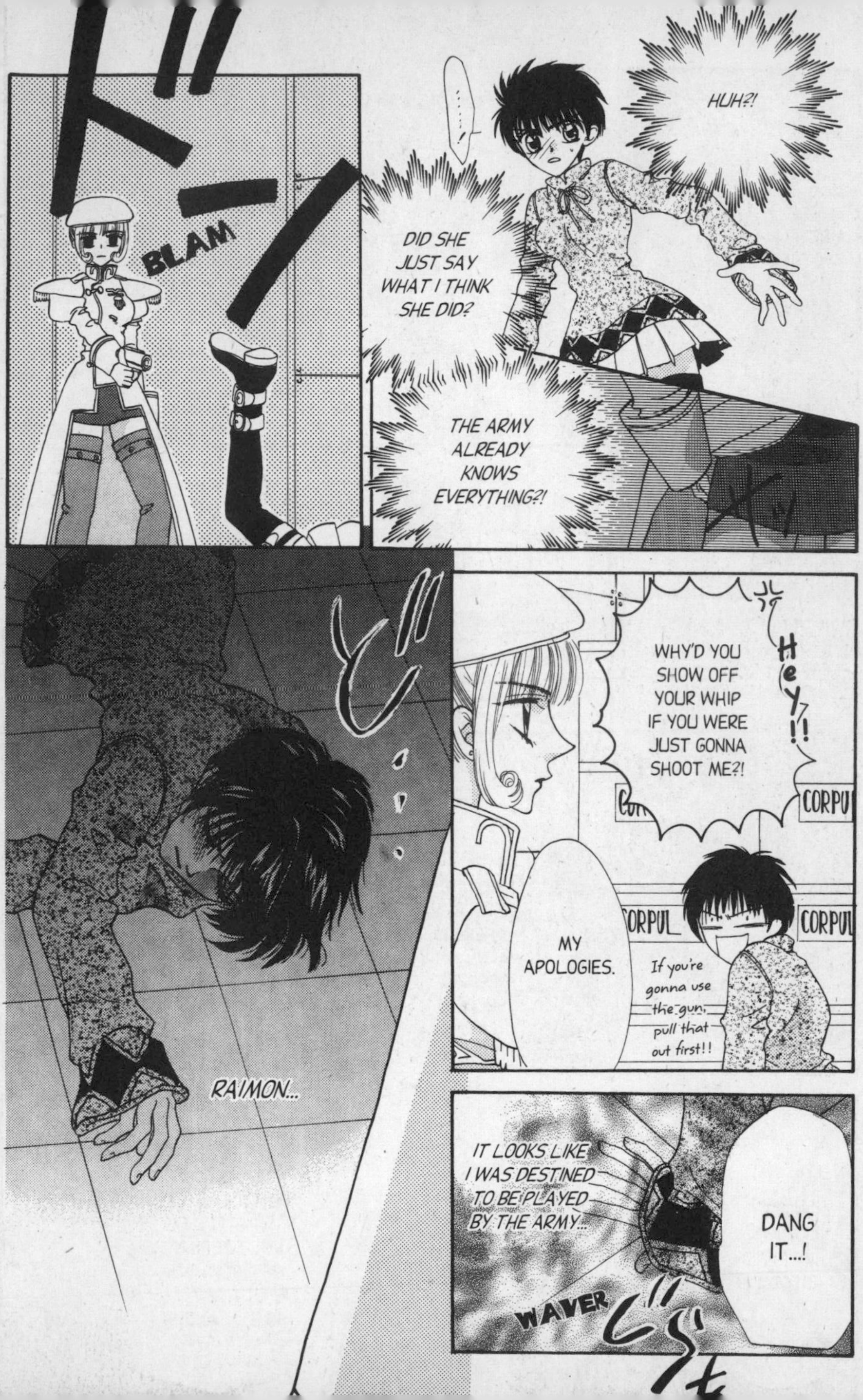
HUH?!
......!
DID SHE JUST SAY WHAT I THINK SHE DID?
THE ARMY ALREADY KNOWS EVERYTHING?!
BLAM
Hey!!
WHY'D YOU SHOW OFF YOUR WHIP IF YOU WERE JUST GONNA SHOOT ME?!
CORPUL
CORPUL
CORPUL
MY APOLOGIES.
If you're gonna use the gun, pull that out first!!
IT LOOKS LIKE I WAS DESTINED TO BE PLAYED BY THE ARMY...
DANG IT...!
WAVER
RAIMON...

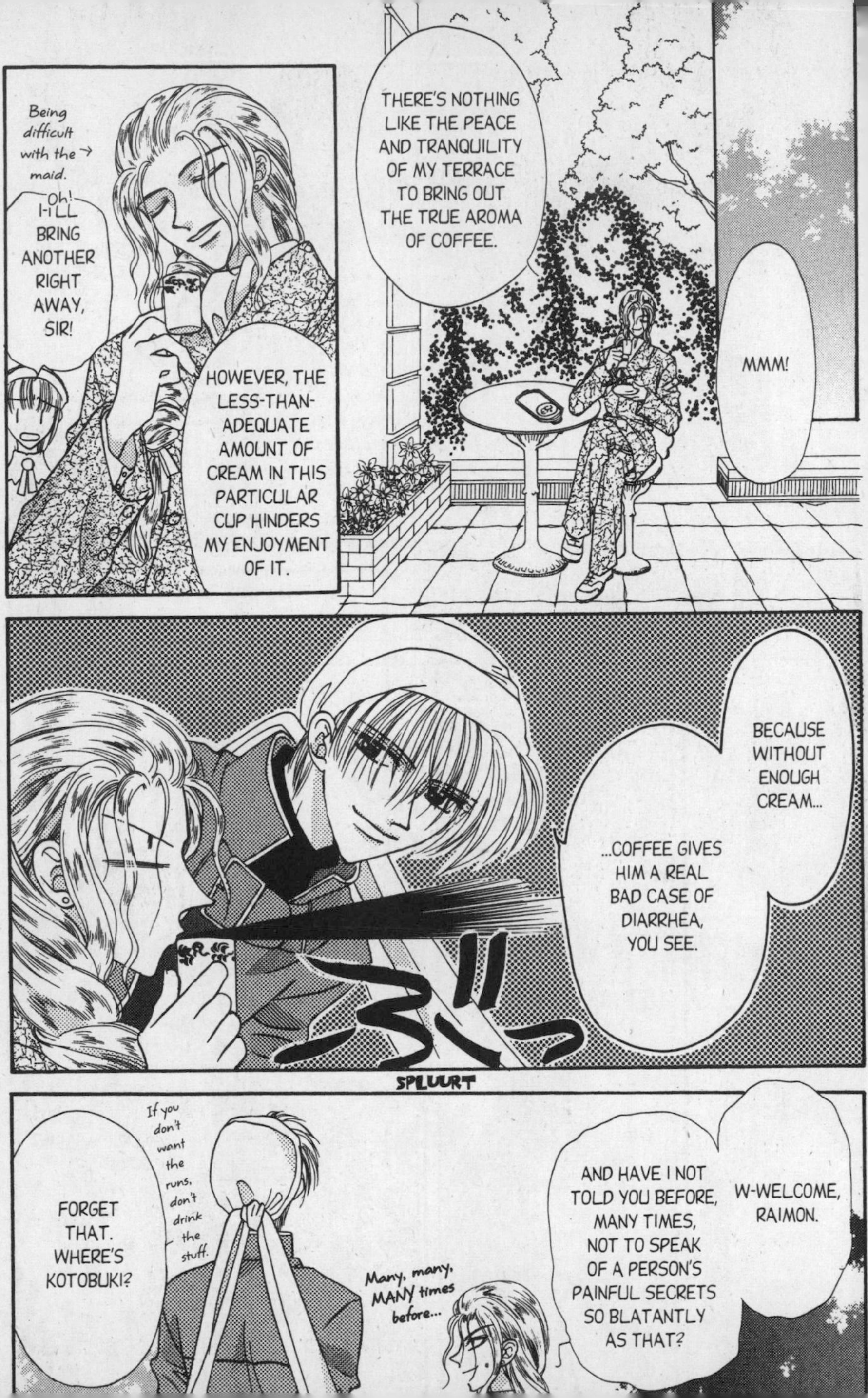
MMM!
THERE'S NOTHING LIKE THE PEACE AND TRANQUILITY OF MY TERRACE TO BRING OUT THE TRUE AROMA OF COFFEE.
HOWEVER, THE LESS-THAN-ADEQUATE AMOUNT OF CREAM IN THIS PARTICULAR CUP HINDERS MY ENJOYMENT OF IT.
Oh! I-I'LL BRING ANOTHER RIGHT AWAY, SIR!
Being difficult with the maid.
BECAUSE WITHOUT ENOUGH CREAM...
...COFFEE GIVES HIM A REAL BAD CASE OF DIARRHEA, YOU SEE.
SPLUURT
W-WELCOME, RAIMON.
AND HAVE I NOT TOLD YOU BEFORE, MANY TIMES, NOT TO SPEAK OF A PERSON'S PAINFUL SECRETS SO BLATANTLY AS THAT?
Many, many, MANY times before...
If you don't want the runs, don't drink the stuff.
FORGET THAT. WHERE'S KOTOBUKI?

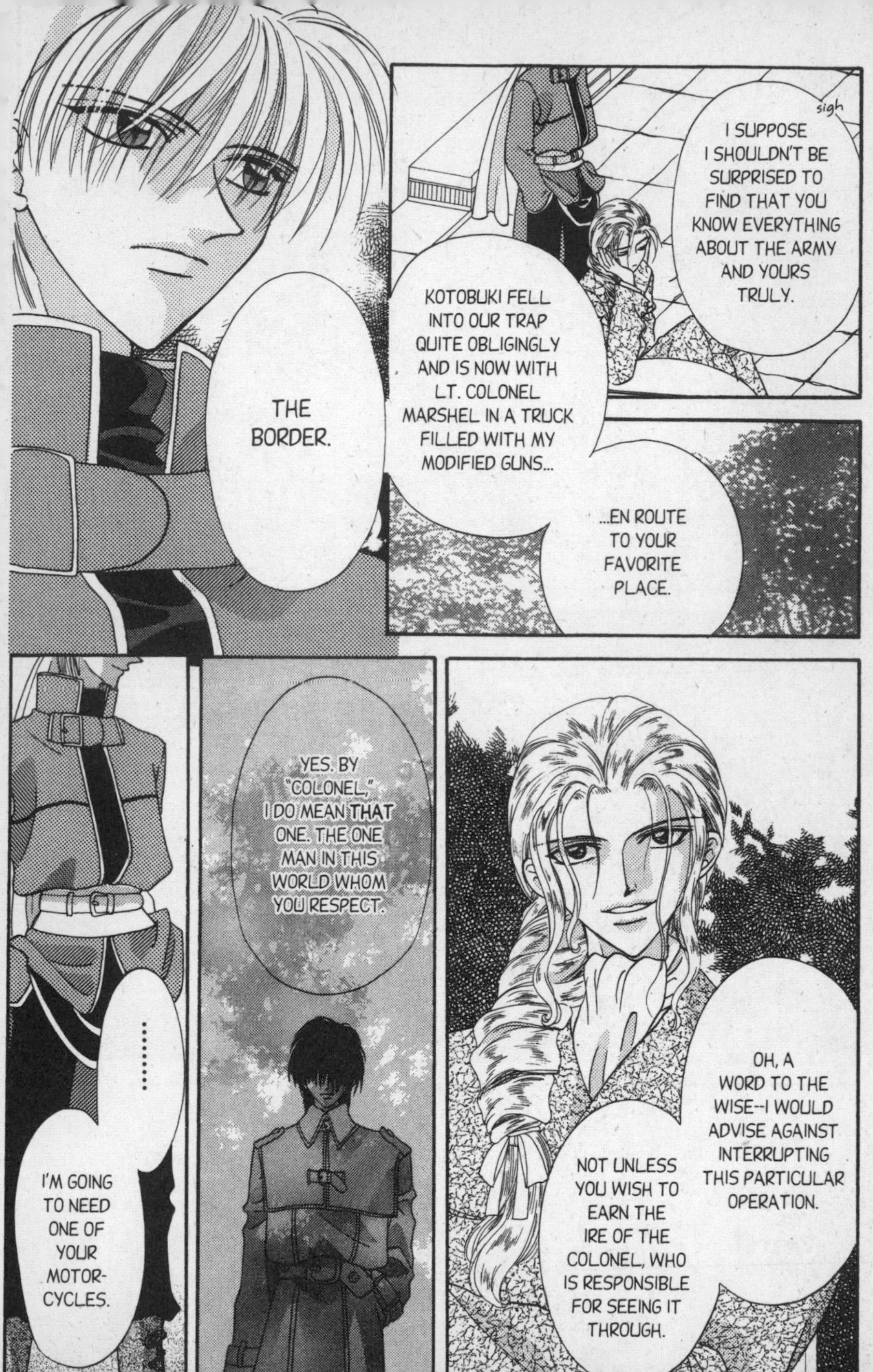
sigh
I SUPPOSE I SHOULDN'T BE SURPRISED TO FIND THAT YOU KNOW EVERYTHING ABOUT THE ARMY AND YOURS TRULY.
KOTOBUKI FELL INTO OUR TRAP QUITE OBLIGINGLY AND IS NOW WITH LT. COLONEL MARSHEL IN A TRUCK FILLED WITH MY MODIFIED GUNS...
...EN ROUTE TO YOUR FAVORITE PLACE.
THE BORDER.
OH, A WORD TO THE WISE--I WOULD ADVISE AGAINST INTERRUPTING THIS PARTICULAR OPERATION.
NOT UNLESS YOU WISH TO EARN THE IRE OF THE COLONEL, WHO IS RESPONSIBLE FOR SEEING IT THROUGH.
YES. BY "COLONEL," I DO MEAN THAT ONE. THE ONE MAN IN THIS WORLD WHOM YOU RESPECT.
......
I'M GOING TO NEED ONE OF YOUR MOTOR-CYCLES.

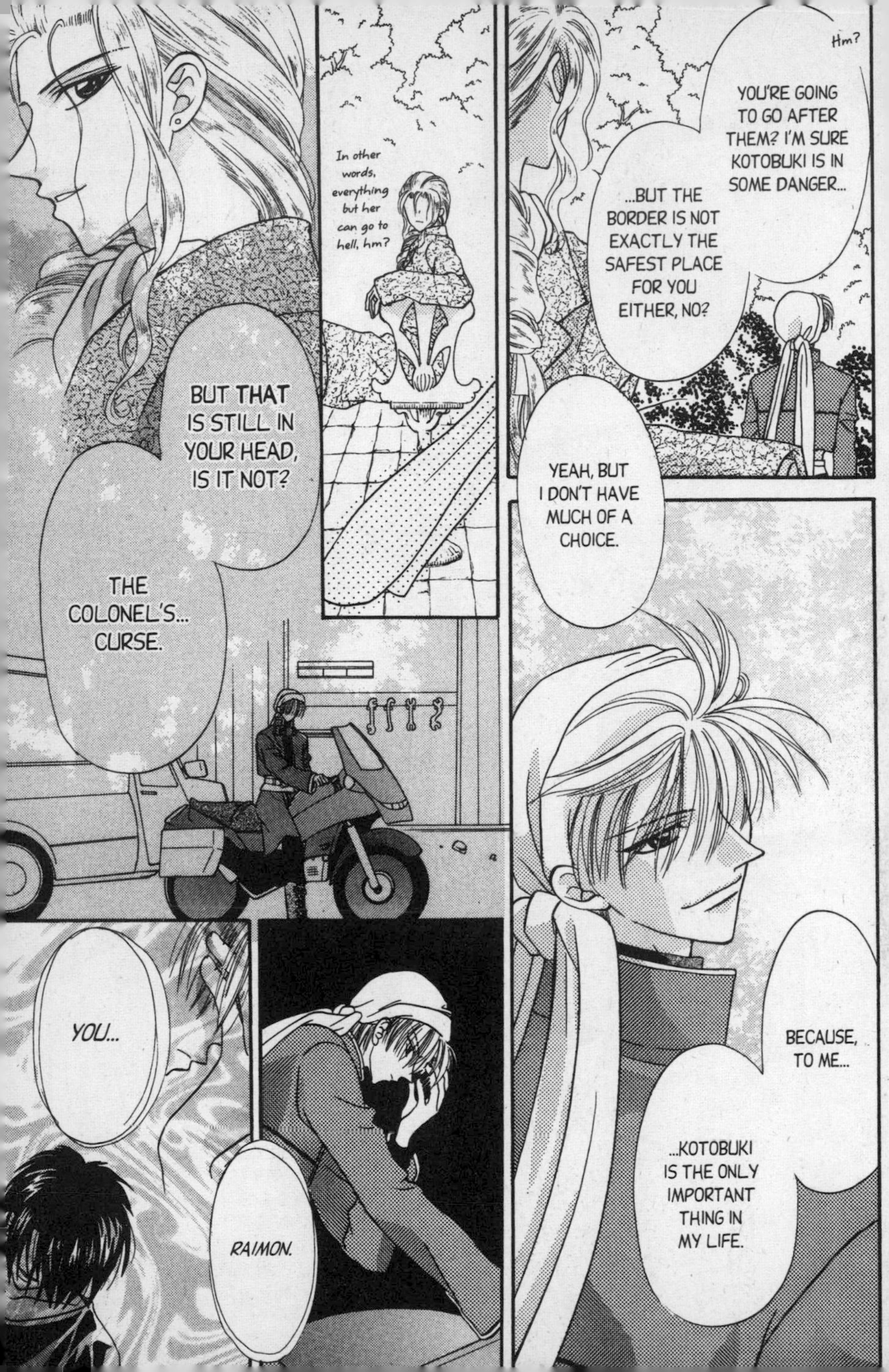
Hm?
YOU'RE GOING TO GO AFTER THEM? I'M SURE KOTOBUKI IS IN SOME DANGER...
...BUT THE BORDER IS NOT EXACTLY THE SAFEST PLACE FOR YOU EITHER, NO?
YEAH, BUT I DON'T HAVE MUCH OF A CHOICE.
BECAUSE, TO ME...
...KOTOBUKI IS THE ONLY IMPORTANT THING IN MY LIFE.
In other words, everything but her can go to hell, hm?
BUT THAT IS STILL IN YOUR HEAD, IS IT NOT?
THE COLONEL'S... CURSE.
YOU...
RAIMON.

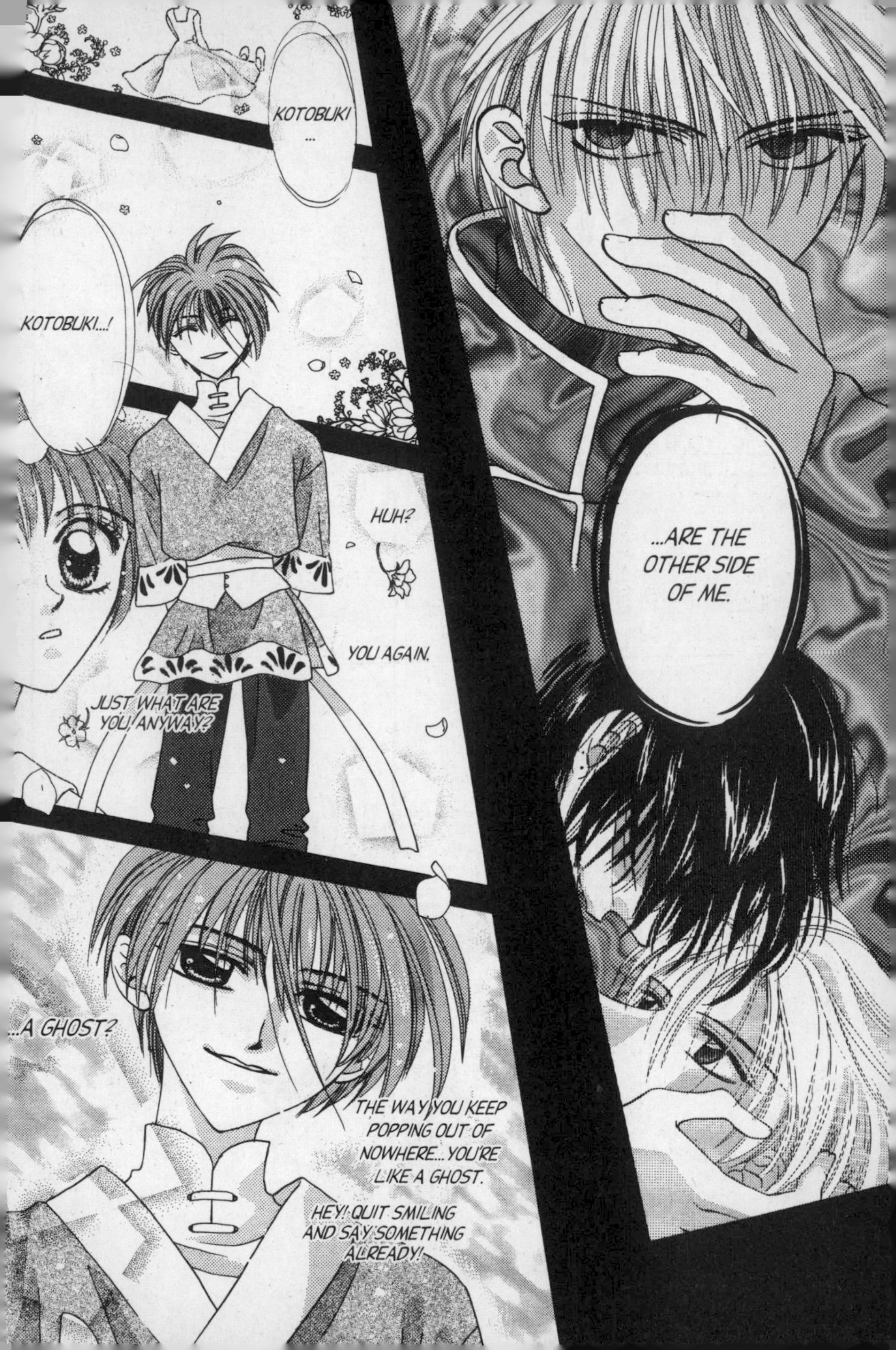
...ARE THE OTHER SIDE OF ME.
KOTOBUKI ...
KOTOBUKI...!
HUH?
YOU AGAIN.
JUST WHAT ARE YOU, ANYWAY?
THE WAY YOU KEEP POPPING OUT OF NOWHERE... YOU'RE LIKE A GHOST.
HEY! QUIT SMILING AND SAY SOMETHING ALREADY!
...A GHOST?

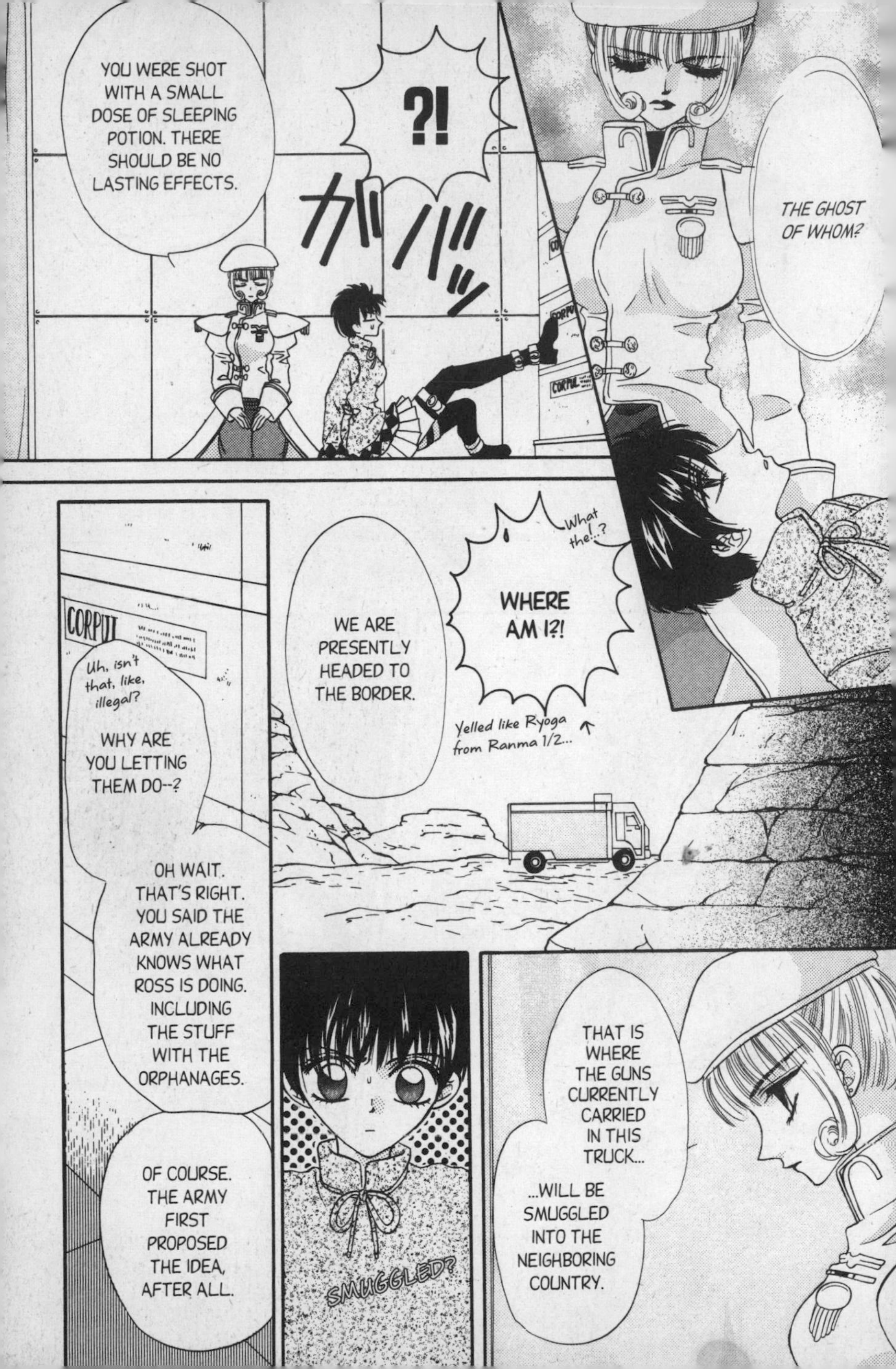
THE GHOST OF WHOM?
?!
ガバッ
YOU WERE SHOT WITH A SMALL DOSE OF SLEEPING POTION. THERE SHOULD BE NO LASTING EFFECTS.
What the!..?
WHERE AM I?!
Yelled like Ryoga from Ranma 1/2...
WE ARE PRESENTLY HEADED TO THE BORDER.
THAT IS WHERE THE GUNS CURRENTLY CARRIED IN THIS TRUCK...
...WILL BE SMUGGLED INTO THE NEIGHBORING COUNTRY.
SMUGGLED?
CORPUI
Uh, isn't that, like, illegal?
WHY ARE YOU LETTING THEM DO--?
OH WAIT. THAT'S RIGHT. YOU SAID THE ARMY ALREADY KNOWS WHAT ROSS IS DOING. INCLUDING THE STUFF WITH THE ORPHANAGES.
OF COURSE. THE ARMY FIRST PROPOSED THE IDEA, AFTER ALL.

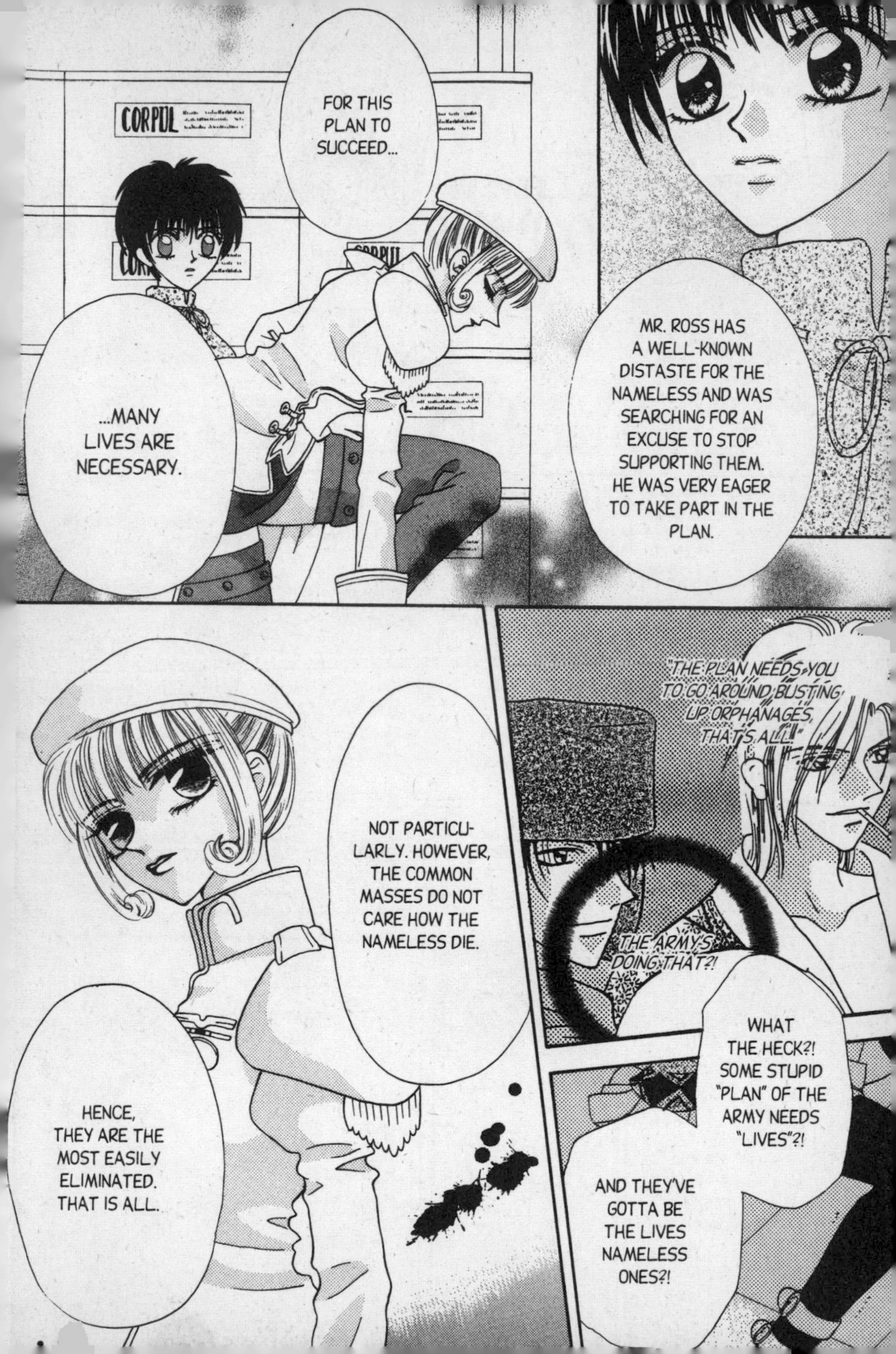
MR. ROSS HAS A WELL-KNOWN DISTASTE FOR THE NAMELESS AND WAS SEARCHING FOR AN EXCUSE TO STOP SUPPORTING THEM. HE WAS VERY EAGER TO TAKE PART IN THE PLAN.
CORPUL
FOR THIS PLAN TO SUCCEED...
...MANY LIVES ARE NECESSARY.
"THE PLAN NEEDS YOU TO GO AROUND BUSTING UP ORPHANAGES, THAT'S ALL."
THE ARMY'S DOING THAT?!
WHAT THE HECK?! SOME STUPID "PLAN" OF THE ARMY NEEDS "LIVES"?!
AND THEY'VE GOTTA BE THE LIVES NAMELESS ONES?!
NOT PARTICU-LARLY. HOWEVER, THE COMMON MASSES DO NOT CARE HOW THE NAMELESS DIE.
HENCE, THEY ARE THE MOST EASILY ELIMINATED. THAT IS ALL.

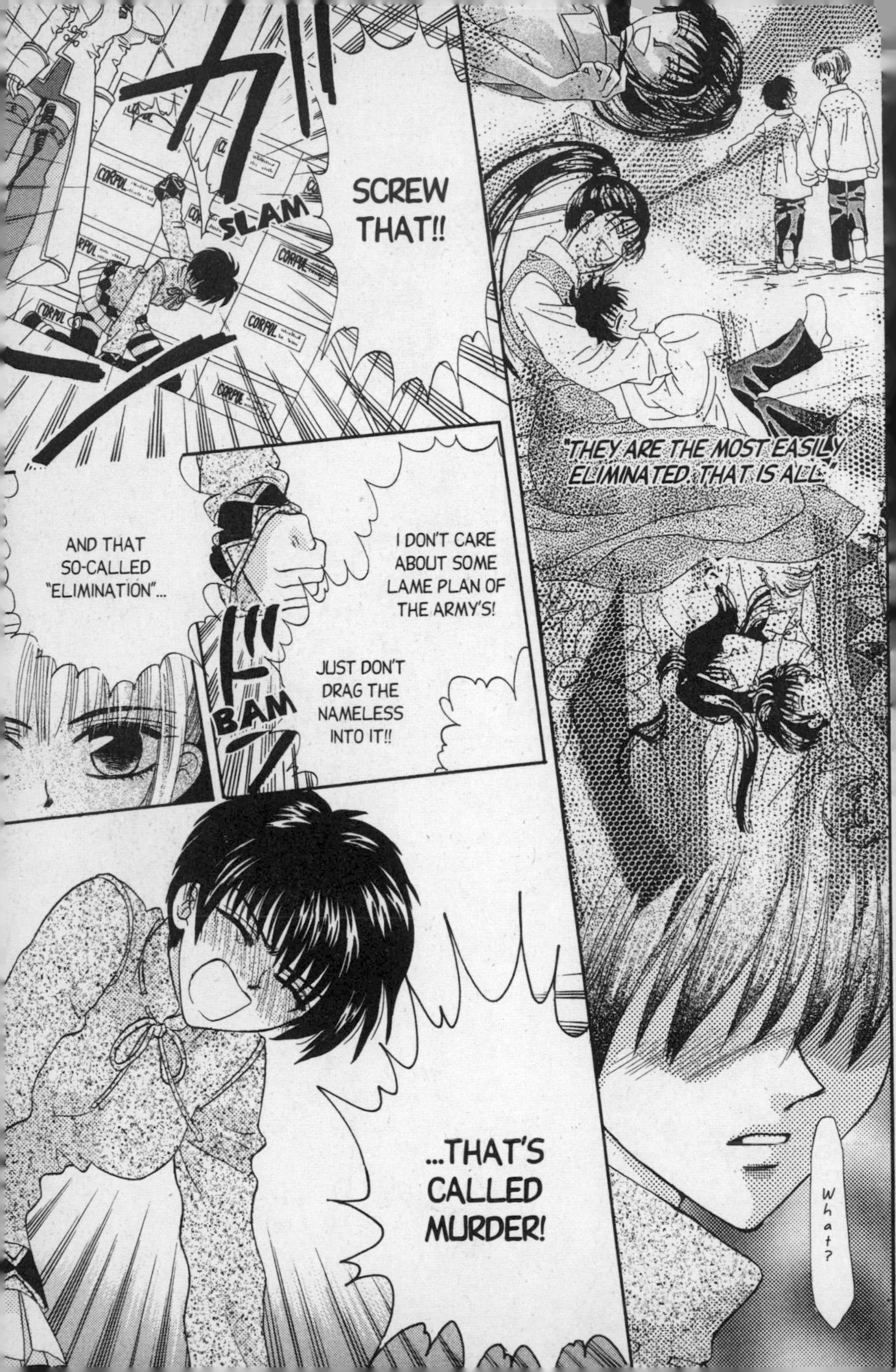
"THEY ARE THE MOST EASILY ELIMINATED. THAT IS ALL."
SLAM
SCREW THAT!!
I DON'T CARE ABOUT SOME LAME PLAN OF THE ARMY'S!
BAM
JUST DON'T DRAG THE NAMELESS INTO IT!!
AND THAT SO-CALLED "ELIMINATION"...
...THAT'S CALLED MURDER!
What?

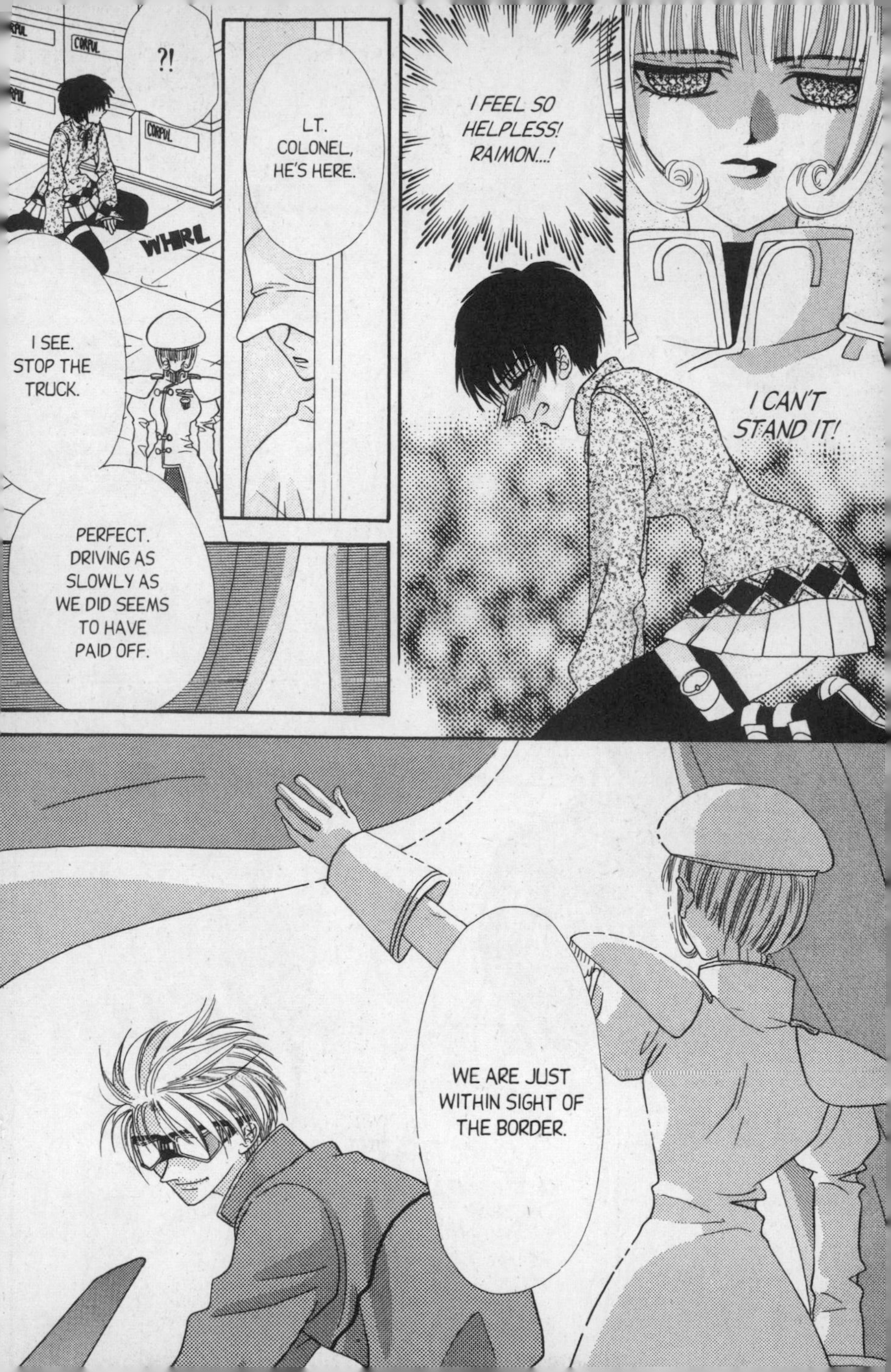
I FEEL SO HELPLESS! RAIMON...!
I CAN'T STAND IT!
LT. COLONEL, HE'S HERE.
?!
WHIRL
I SEE. STOP THE TRUCK.
PERFECT. DRIVING AS SLOWLY AS WE DID SEEMS TO HAVE PAID OFF.
WE ARE JUST WITHIN SIGHT OF THE BORDER.

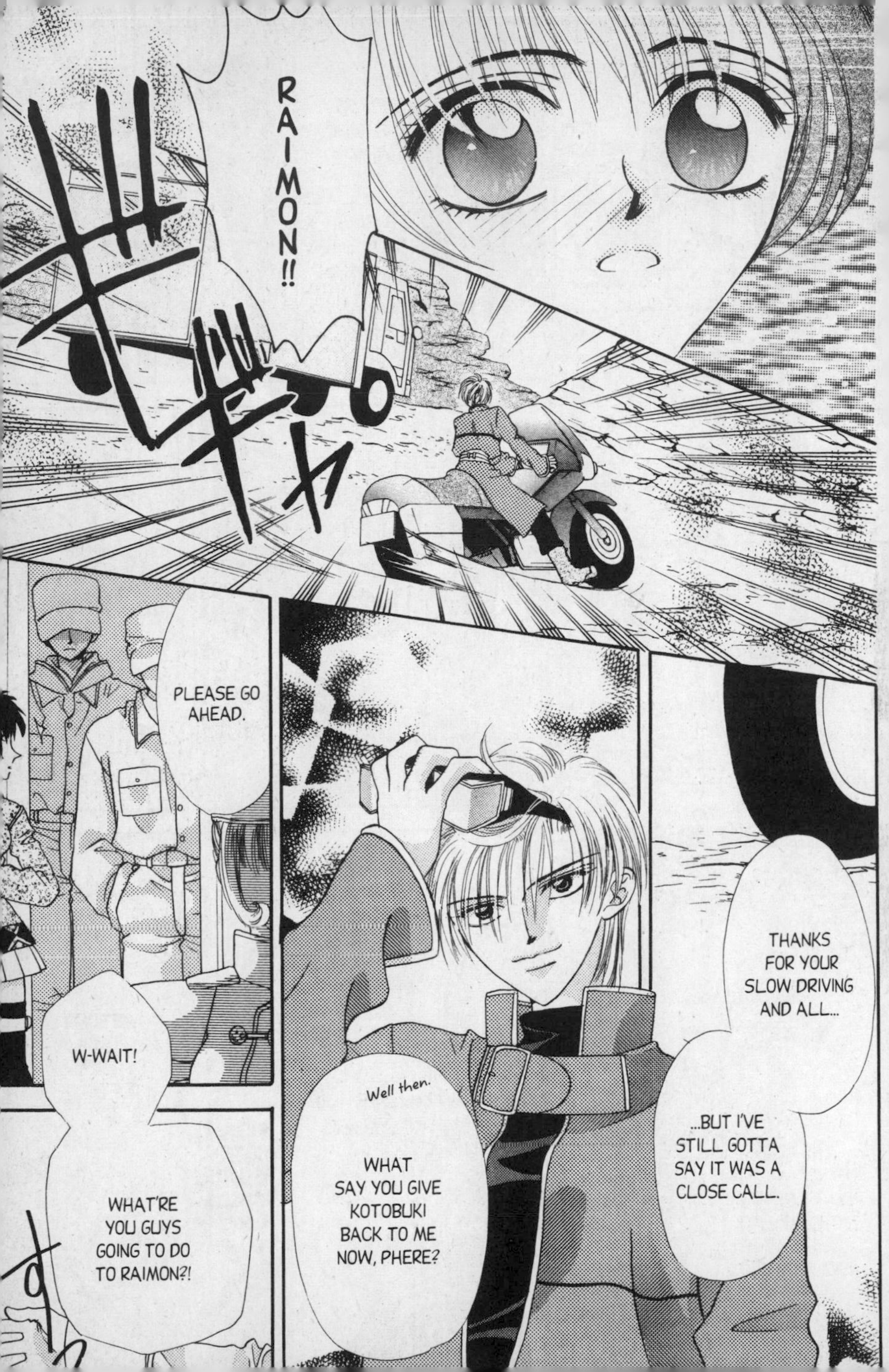
RAIMON!!
THANKS FOR YOUR SLOW DRIVING AND ALL...
...BUT I'VE STILL GOTTA SAY IT WAS A CLOSE CALL.
Well then.
WHAT SAY YOU GIVE KOTOBUKI BACK TO ME NOW, PHERE?
PLEASE GO AHEAD.
W-WAIT!
WHAT'RE YOU GUYS GOING TO DO TO RAIMON?!

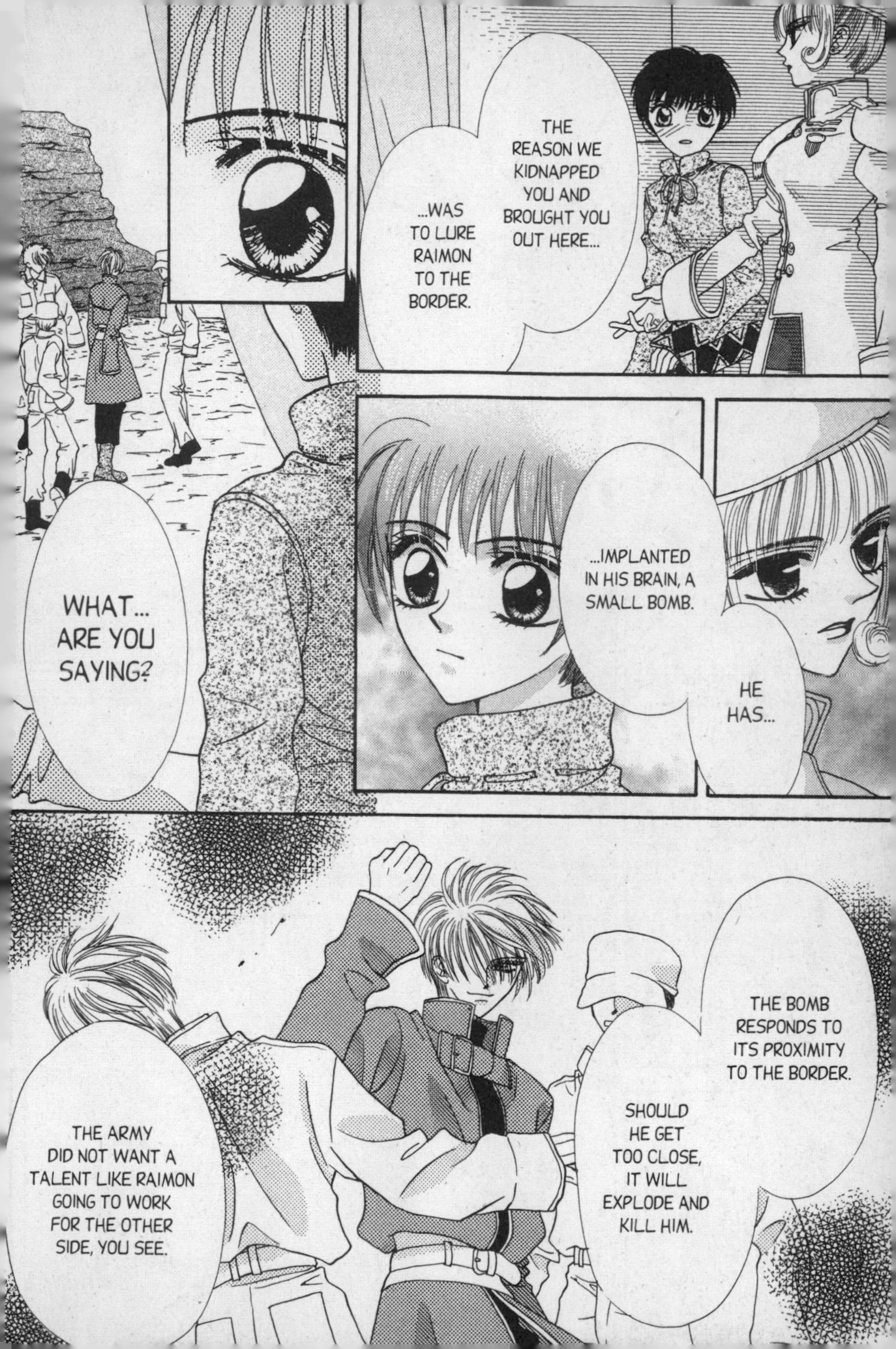

THE REASON WE KIDNAPPED YOU AND BROUGHT YOU OUT HERE...
...WAS TO LURE RAIMON TO THE BORDER.
HE HAS...
...IMPLANTED IN HIS BRAIN, A SMALL BOMB.
WHAT... ARE YOU SAYING?
THE BOMB RESPONDS TO ITS PROXIMITY TO THE BORDER.
SHOULD HE GET TOO CLOSE, IT WILL EXPLODE AND KILL HIM.
THE ARMY DID NOT WANT A TALENT LIKE RAIMON GOING TO WORK FOR THE OTHER SIDE, YOU SEE.

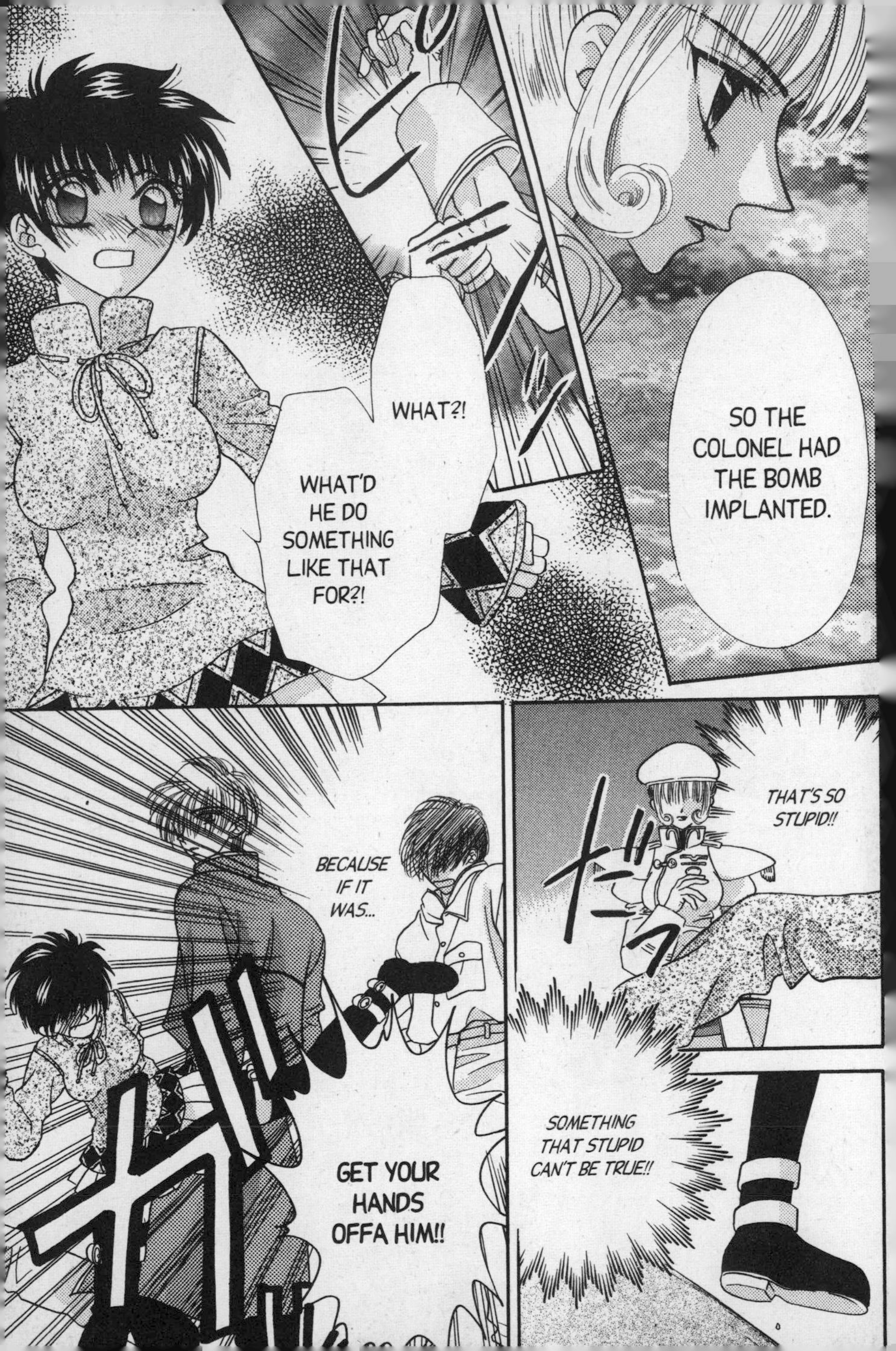
SO THE COLONEL HAD THE BOMB IMPLANTED.
WHAT?!
WHAT'D HE DO SOMETHING LIKE THAT FOR?!
THAT'S SO STUPID!!
SOMETHING THAT STUPID CAN'T BE TRUE!!
BECAUSE IF IT WAS...
GET YOUR HANDS OFFA HIM!!

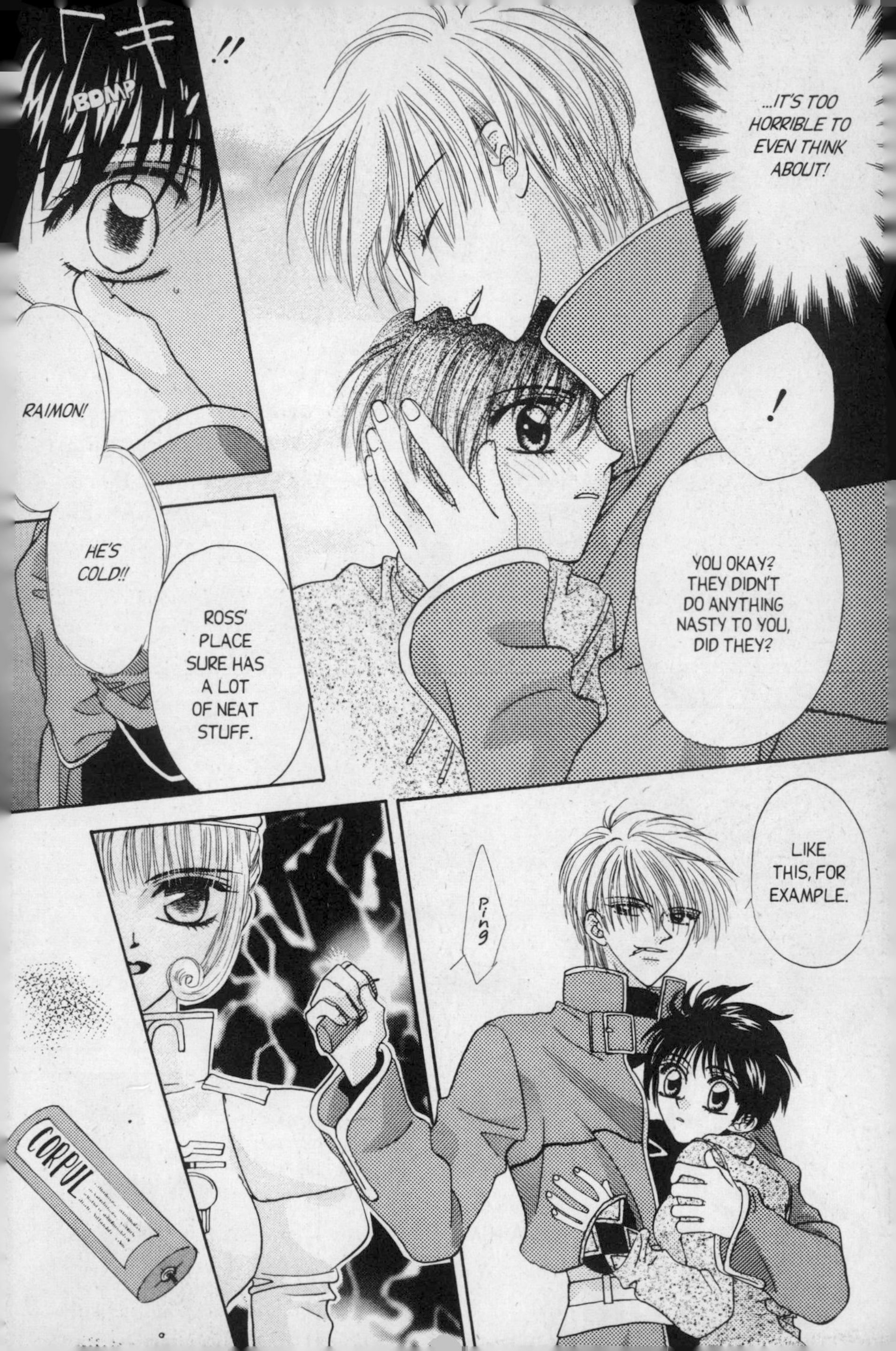

...IT'S TOO HORRIBLE TO EVEN THINK ABOUT!
!
YOU OKAY? THEY DIDN'T DO ANYTHING NASTY TO YOU, DID THEY?
BDMP
!!
RAIMON!
HE'S COLD!!
ROSS' PLACE SURE HAS A LOT OF NEAT STUFF.
LIKE THIS, FOR EXAMPLE.
Ping
CORPUL

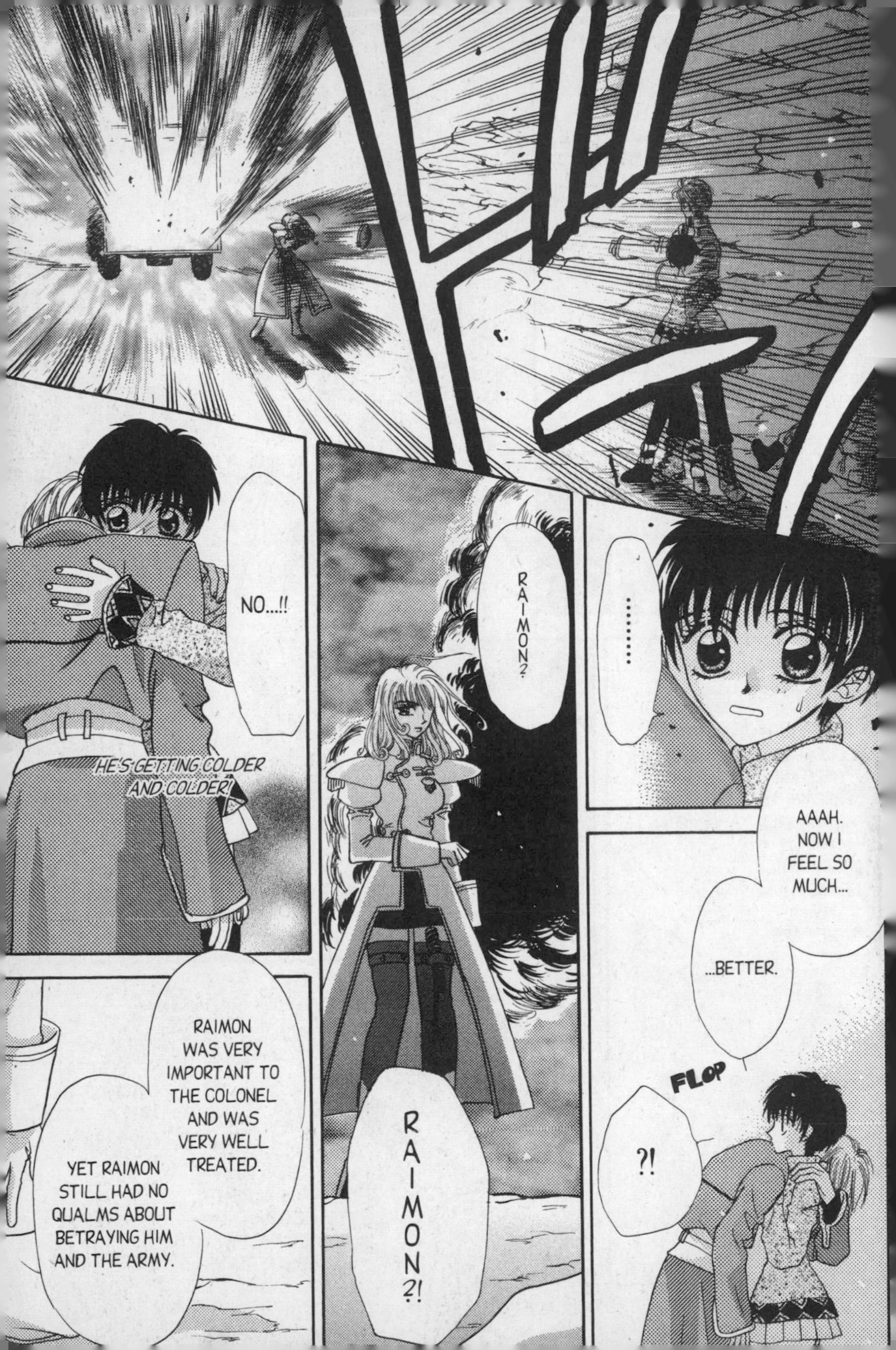

....
AAAH. NOW I FEEL SO MUCH...
...BETTER.
FLOP
?!
RAIMON?
RAIMON?!
NO...!!
HE'S GETTING COLDER AND COLDER!
RAIMON WAS VERY IMPORTANT TO THE COLONEL AND WAS VERY WELL TREATED.
YET RAIMON STILL HAD NO QUALMS ABOUT BETRAYING HIM AND THE ARMY.

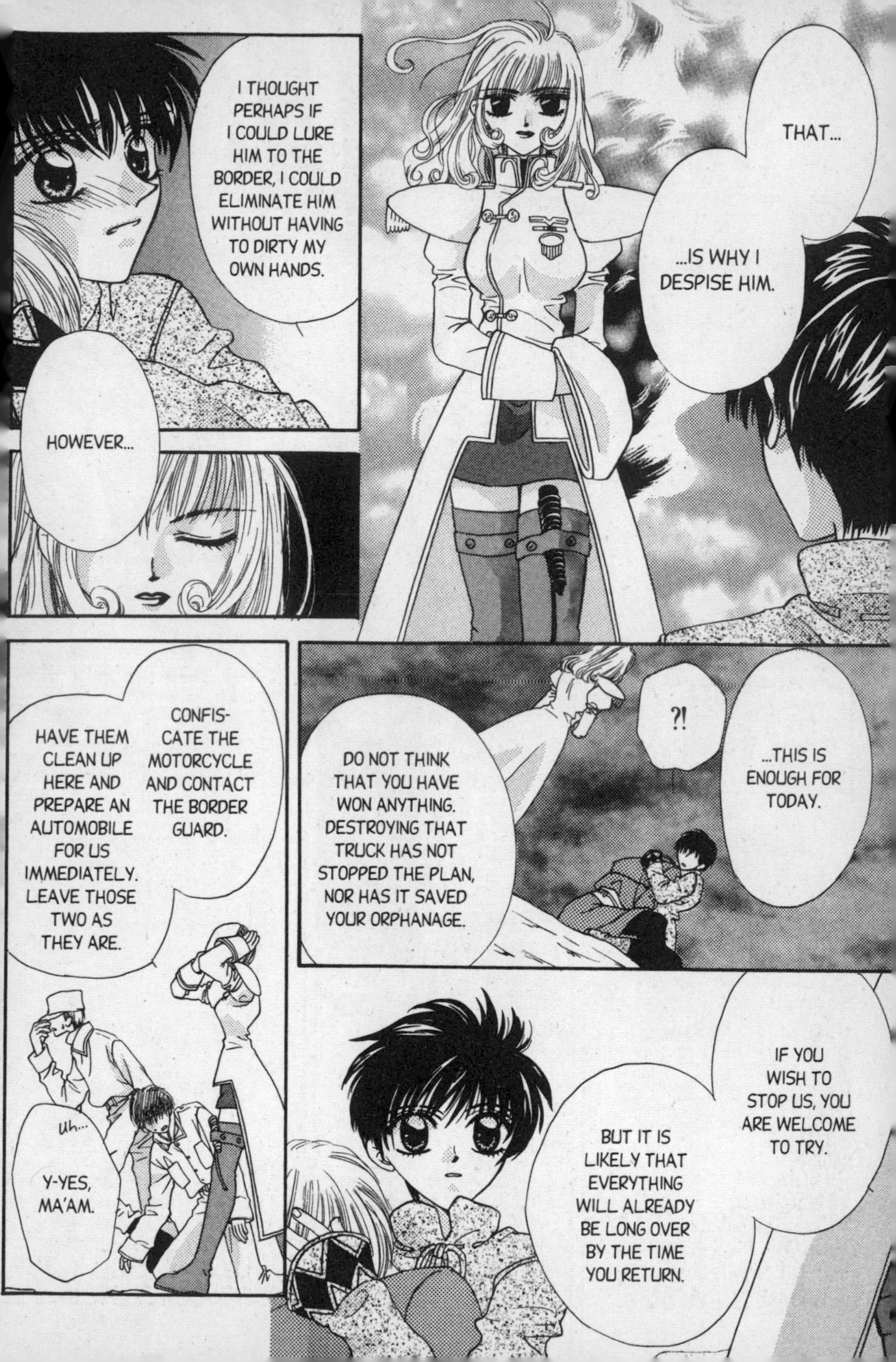
THAT...
...IS WHY I DESPISE HIM.
I THOUGHT PERHAPS IF I COULD LURE HIM TO THE BORDER, I COULD ELIMINATE HIM WITHOUT HAVING TO DIRTY MY OWN HANDS.
HOWEVER...
?!
...THIS IS ENOUGH FOR TODAY.
DO NOT THINK THAT YOU HAVE WON ANYTHING. DESTROYING THAT TRUCK HAS NOT STOPPED THE PLAN, NOR HAS IT SAVED YOUR ORPHANAGE.
IF YOU WISH TO STOP US, YOU ARE WELCOME TO TRY.
BUT IT IS LIKELY THAT EVERYTHING WILL ALREADY BE LONG OVER BY THE TIME YOU RETURN.
CONFIS-CATE THE MOTORCYCLE AND CONTACT THE BORDER GUARD.
HAVE THEM CLEAN UP HERE AND PREPARE AN AUTOMOBILE FOR US IMMEDIATELY. LEAVE THOSE TWO AS THEY ARE.
uh...
Y-YES, MA'AM.

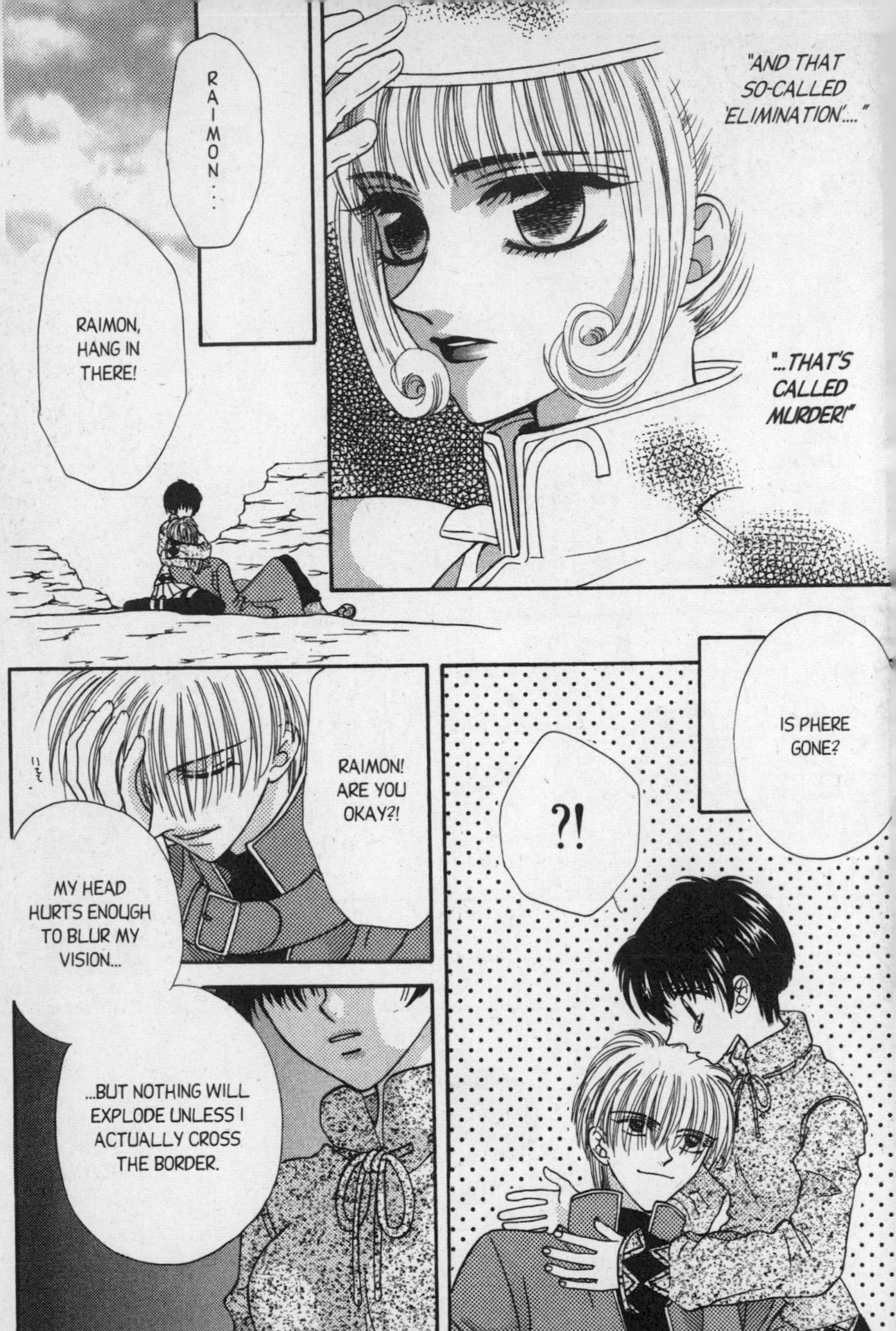
"AND THAT SO-CALLED 'ELIMINATION'...."
"...THAT'S CALLED MURDER!"
RAIMON...
RAIMON, HANG IN THERE!
IS PHERE GONE?
?!
RAIMON! ARE YOU OKAY?!
MY HEAD HURTS ENOUGH TO BLUR MY VISION...
...BUT NOTHING WILL EXPLODE UNLESS I ACTUALLY CROSS THE BORDER.

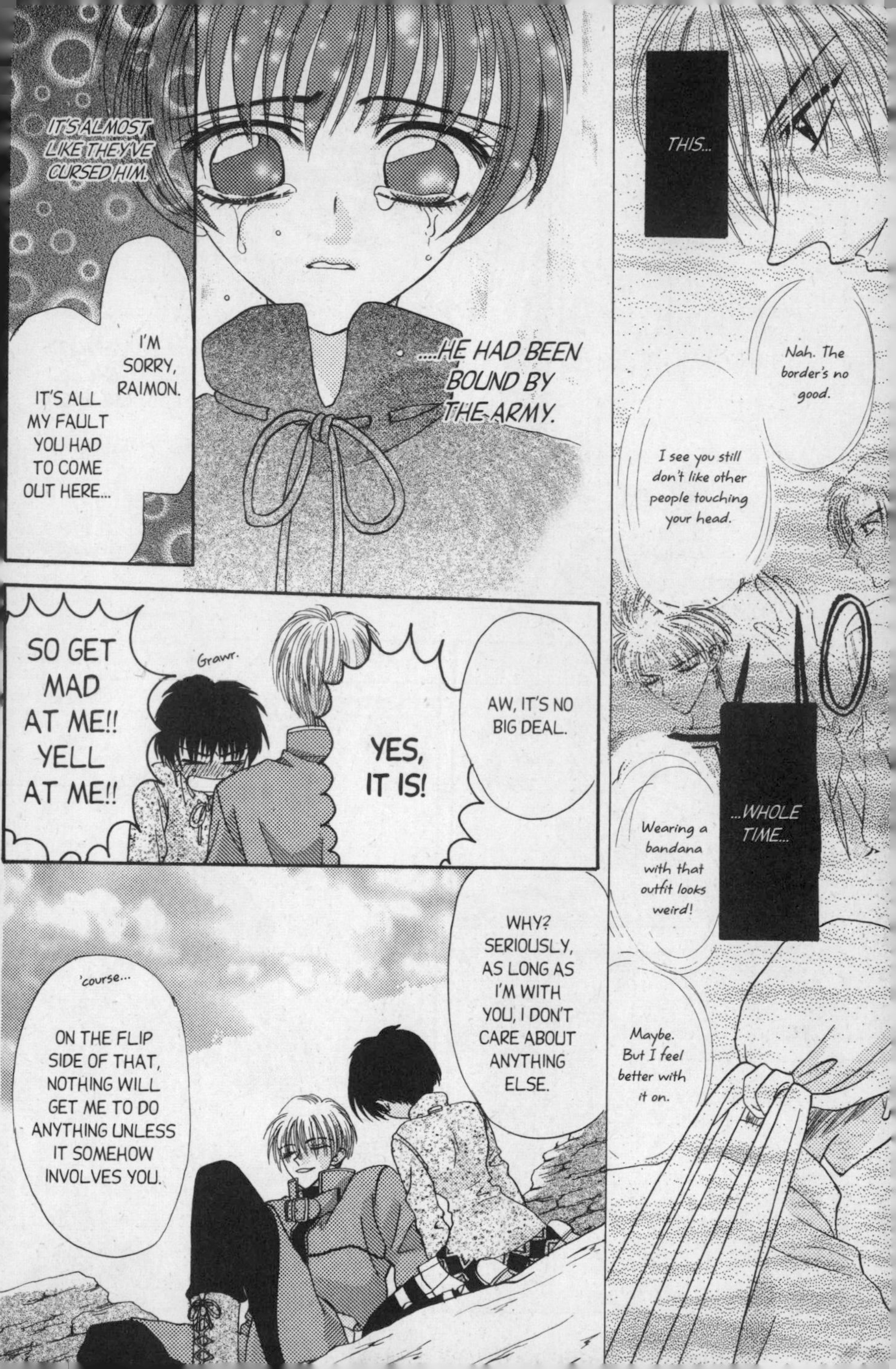
THIS...
Nah. The border's no good.
I see you still don't like other people touching your head.
...WHOLE TIME...
Wearing a bandana with that outfit looks weird!
Maybe. But I feel better with it on.
...HE HAD BEEN BOUND BY THE ARMY.
IT'S ALMOST LIKE THEY'VE CURSED HIM.
I'M SORRY, RAIMON.
IT'S ALL MY FAULT YOU HAD TO COME OUT HERE...
AW, IT'S NO BIG DEAL.
YES, IT IS!
Grawr.
SO GET MAD AT ME!! YELL AT ME!!
WHY? SERIOUSLY, AS LONG AS I'M WITH YOU, I DON'T CARE ABOUT ANYTHING ELSE.
'course...
ON THE FLIP SIDE OF THAT, NOTHING WILL GET ME TO DO ANYTHING UNLESS IT SOMEHOW INVOLVES YOU.

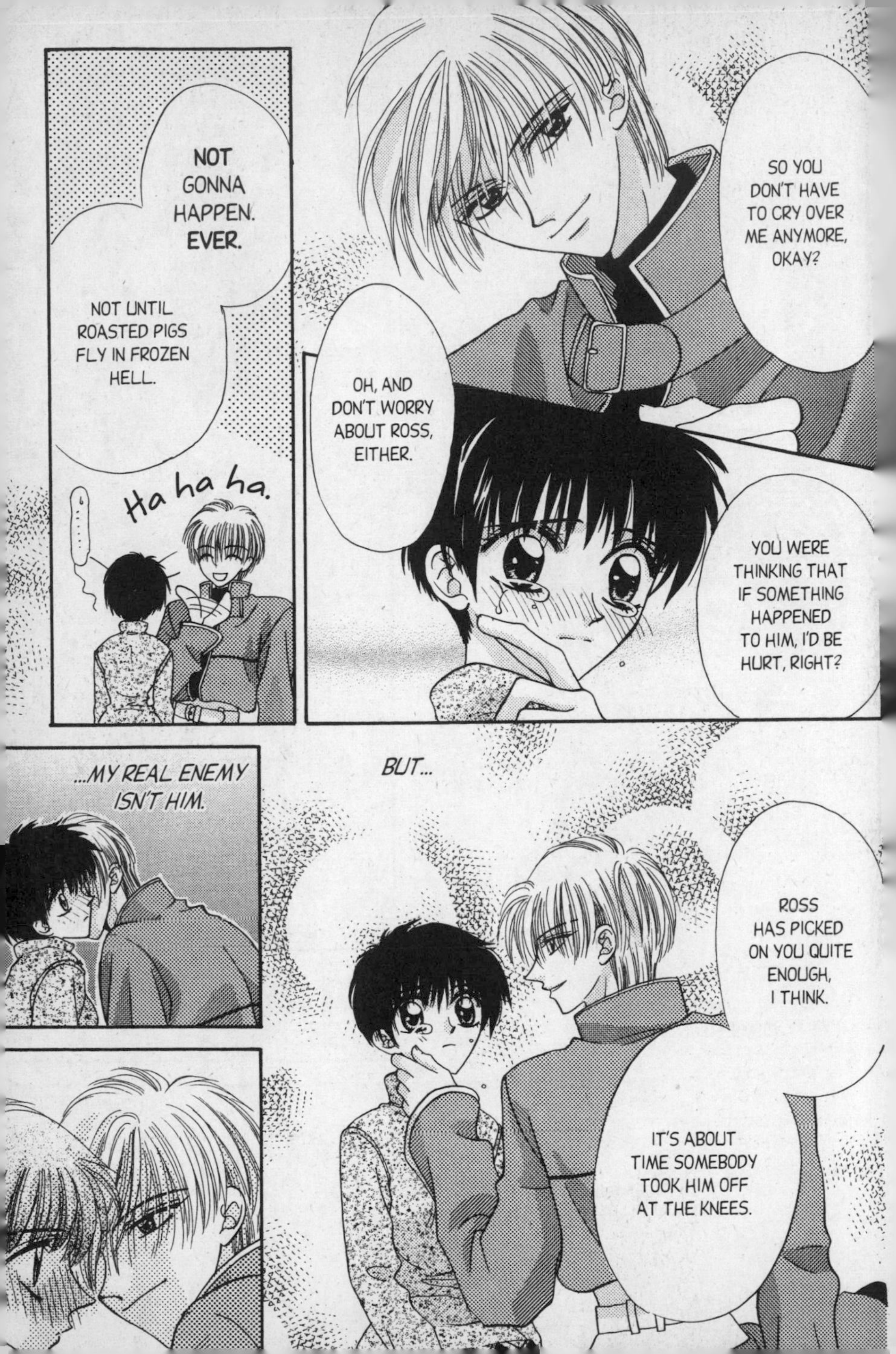
SO YOU DON'T HAVE TO CRY OVER ME ANYMORE, OKAY?
OH, AND DON'T WORRY ABOUT ROSS, EITHER.
YOU WERE THINKING THAT IF SOMETHING HAPPENED TO HIM, I'D BE HURT, RIGHT?
NOT GONNA HAPPEN. EVER.
NOT UNTIL ROASTED PIGS FLY IN FROZEN HELL.
Ha ha ha.
...
BUT...
ROSS HAS PICKED ON YOU QUITE ENOUGH, I THINK.
IT'S ABOUT TIME SOMEBODY TOOK HIM OFF AT THE KNEES.
...MY REAL ENEMY ISN'T HIM.

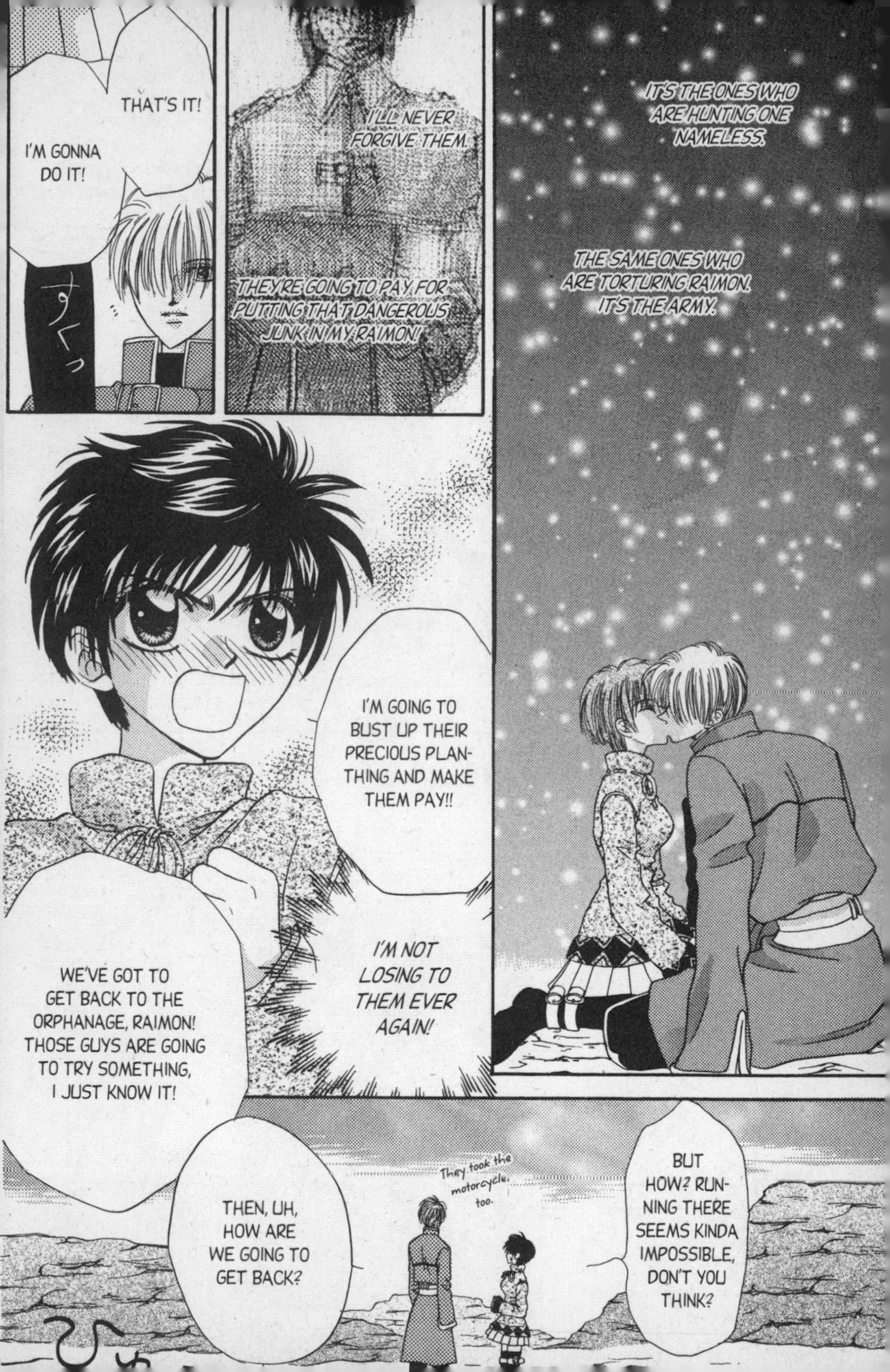
IT'S THE ONES WHO ARE HUNTING ONE NAMELESS.
THE SAME ONES WHO ARE TORTURING RAIMON. IT'S THE ARMY.
I'LL NEVER FORGIVE THEM.
THEY'RE GOING TO PAY FOR PUTTING THAT DANGEROUS JUNK IN MY RAIMON!
THAT'S IT!
I'M GONNA DO IT!
I'M GOING TO BUST UP THEIR PRECIOUS PLAN-THING AND MAKE THEM PAY!!
I'M NOT LOSING TO THEM EVER AGAIN!
WE'VE GOT TO GET BACK TO THE ORPHANAGE, RAIMON! THOSE GUYS ARE GOING TO TRY SOMETHING, I JUST KNOW IT!
BUT HOW? RUN-NING THERE SEEMS KINDA IMPOSSIBLE, DON'T YOU THINK?
They took the motorcycle, too.
THEN, UH, HOW ARE WE GOING TO GET BACK?

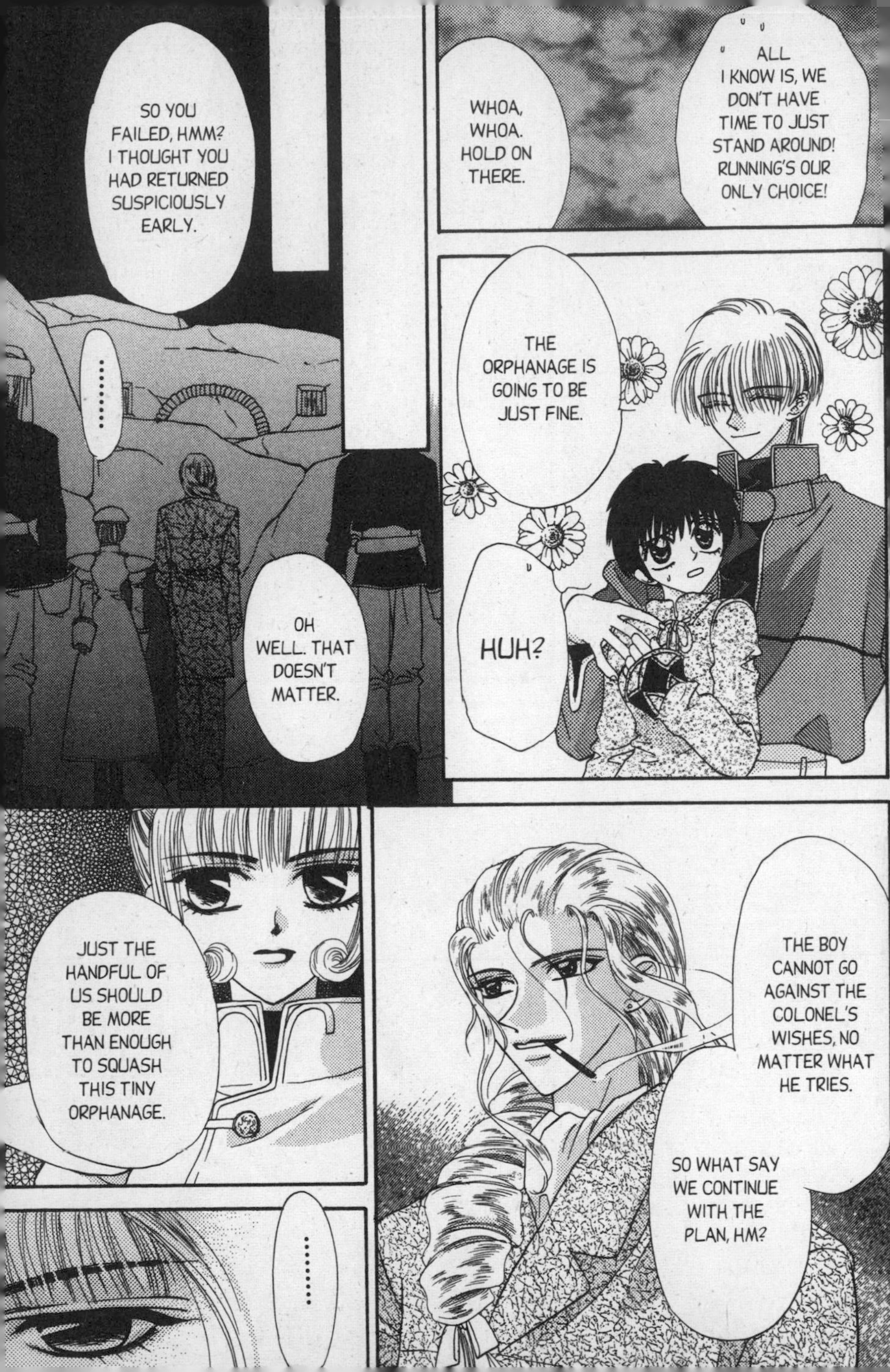
ALL I KNOW IS, WE DON'T HAVE TIME TO JUST STAND AROUND! RUNNING'S OUR ONLY CHOICE!
WHOA, WHOA. HOLD ON THERE.
THE ORPHANAGE IS GOING TO BE JUST FINE.
HUH?
SO YOU FAILED, HMM? I THOUGHT YOU HAD RETURNED SUSPICIOUSLY EARLY.
......
OH WELL. THAT DOESN'T MATTER.
THE BOY CANNOT GO AGAINST THE COLONEL'S WISHES, NO MATTER WHAT HE TRIES.
SO WHAT SAY WE CONTINUE WITH THE PLAN, HM?
JUST THE HANDFUL OF US SHOULD BE MORE THAN ENOUGH TO SQUASH THIS TINY ORPHANAGE.
......

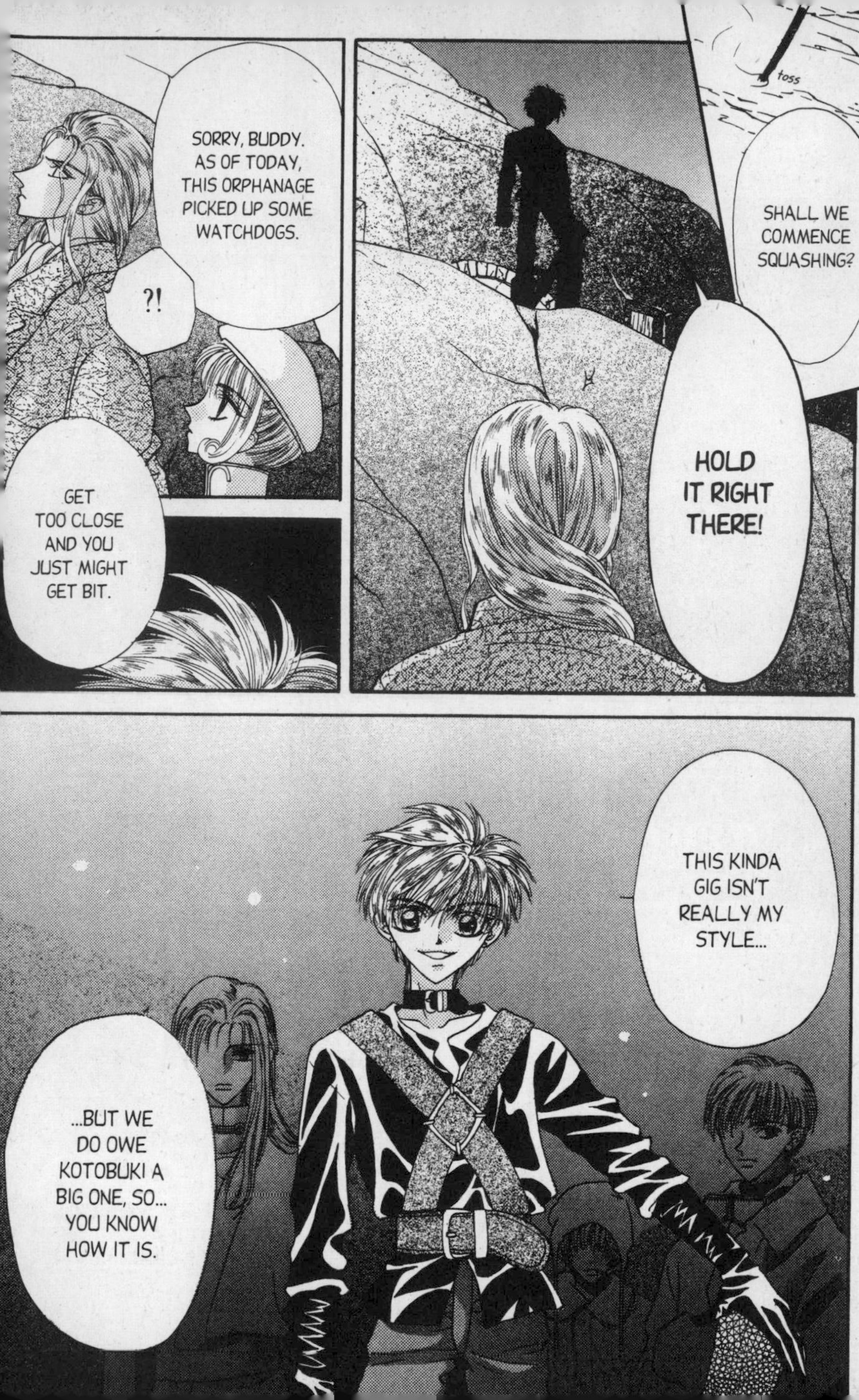
toss
SHALL WE COMMENCE SQUASHING?
HOLD IT RIGHT THERE!
SORRY, BUDDY. AS OF TODAY, THIS ORPHANAGE PICKED UP SOME WATCHDOGS.
?!
GET TOO CLOSE AND YOU JUST MIGHT GET BIT.
THIS KINDA GIG ISN'T REALLY MY STYLE...
...BUT WE DO OWE KOTOBUKI A BIG ONE, SO... YOU KNOW HOW IT IS.

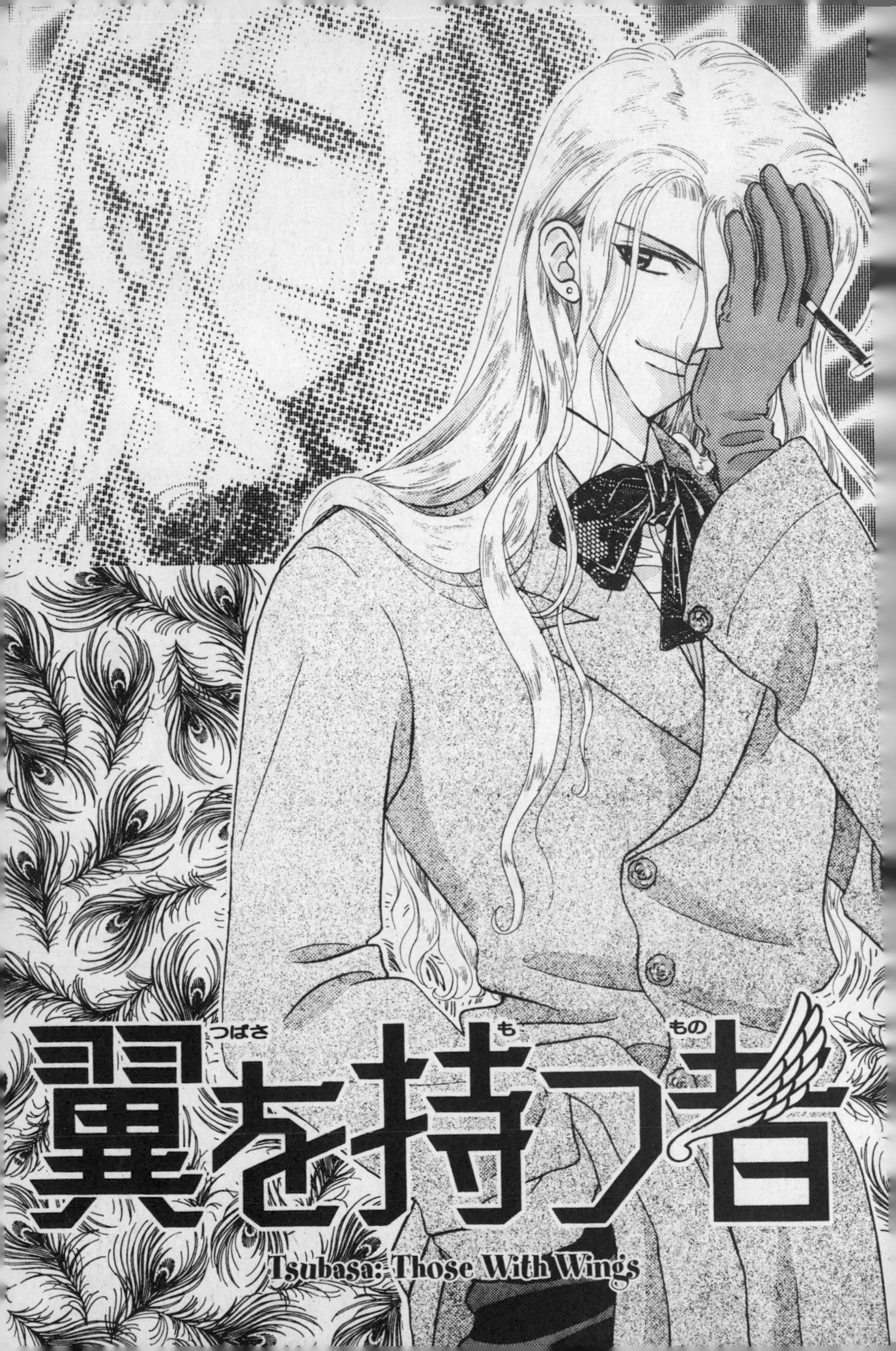
翼(つばさ)を持(も)つ者(もの)
Tsubasa: Those With Wings

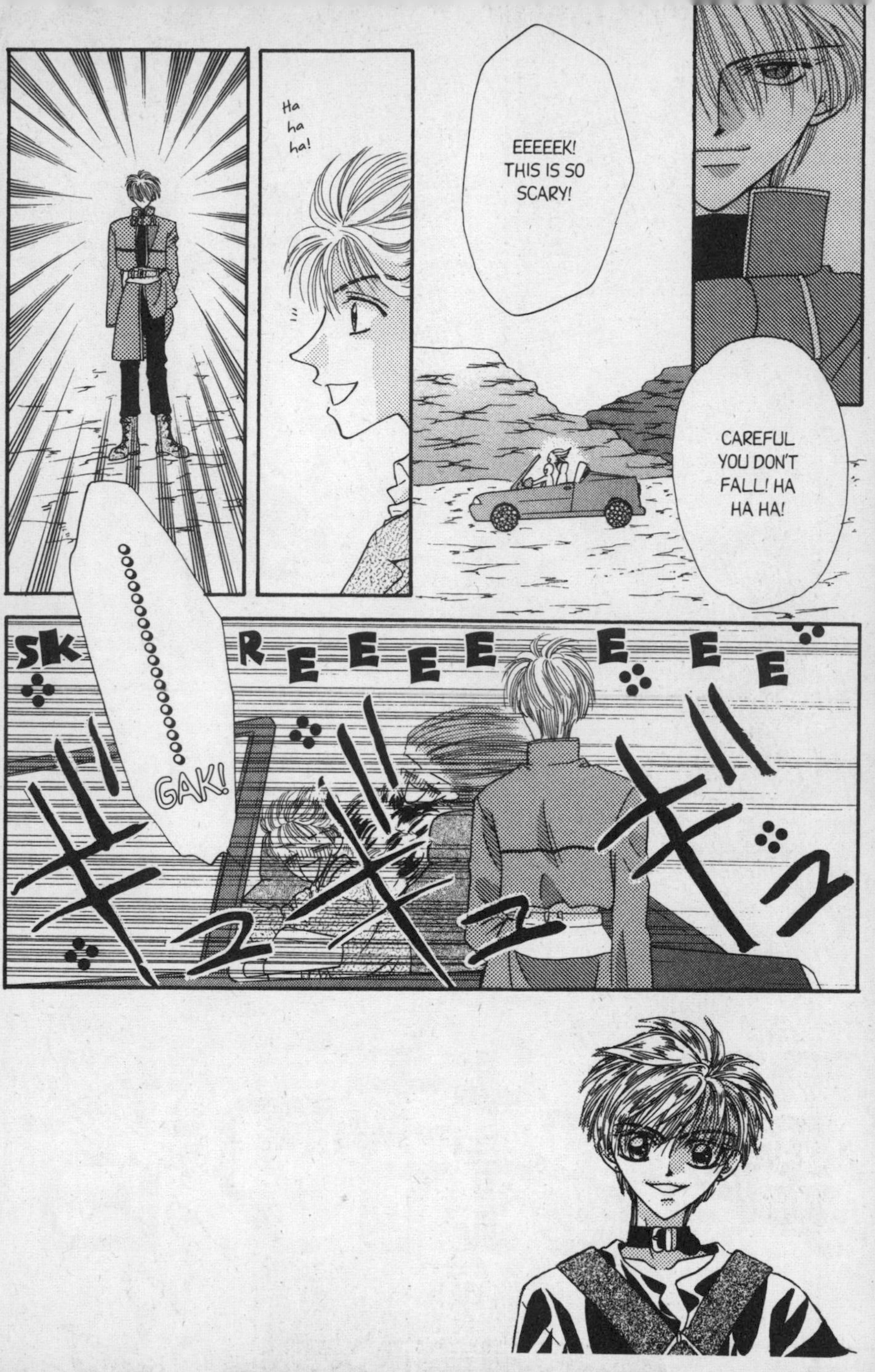
EEEEEK! THIS IS SO SCARY!
CAREFUL YOU DON'T FALL! HA HA HA!
Ha ha ha!
..................GAK!
SKREEEEEEEE

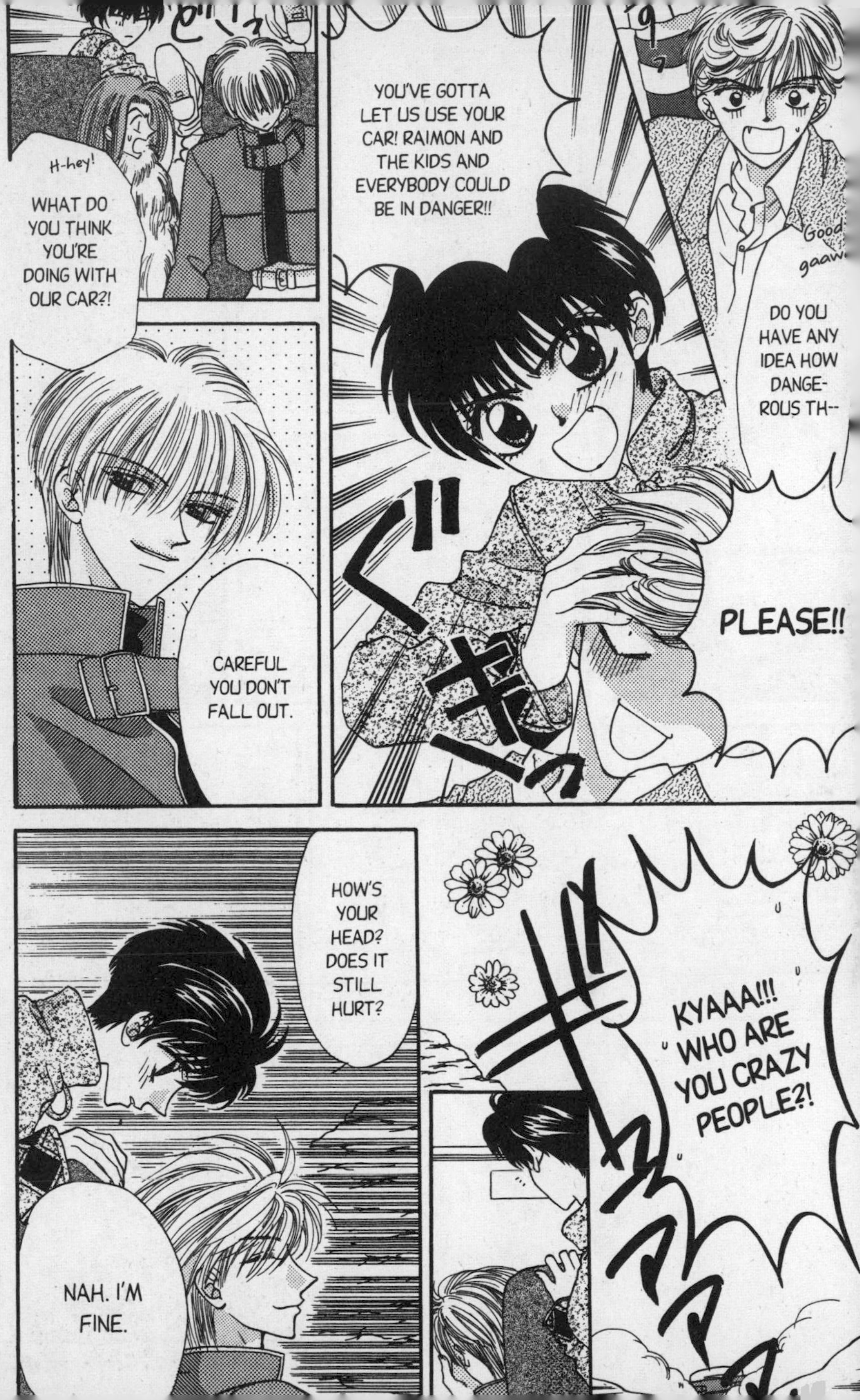
DO YOU HAVE ANY IDEA HOW DANGE-ROUS TH--
YOU'VE GOTTA LET US USE YOUR CAR! RAIMON AND THE KIDS AND EVERYBODY COULD BE IN DANGER!!
PLEASE!!
H-hey!
WHAT DO YOU THINK YOU'RE DOING WITH OUR CAR?!
CAREFUL YOU DON'T FALL OUT.
KYAAA!!! WHO ARE YOU CRAZY PEOPLE?!
HOW'S YOUR HEAD? DOES IT STILL HURT?
NAH. I'M FINE.

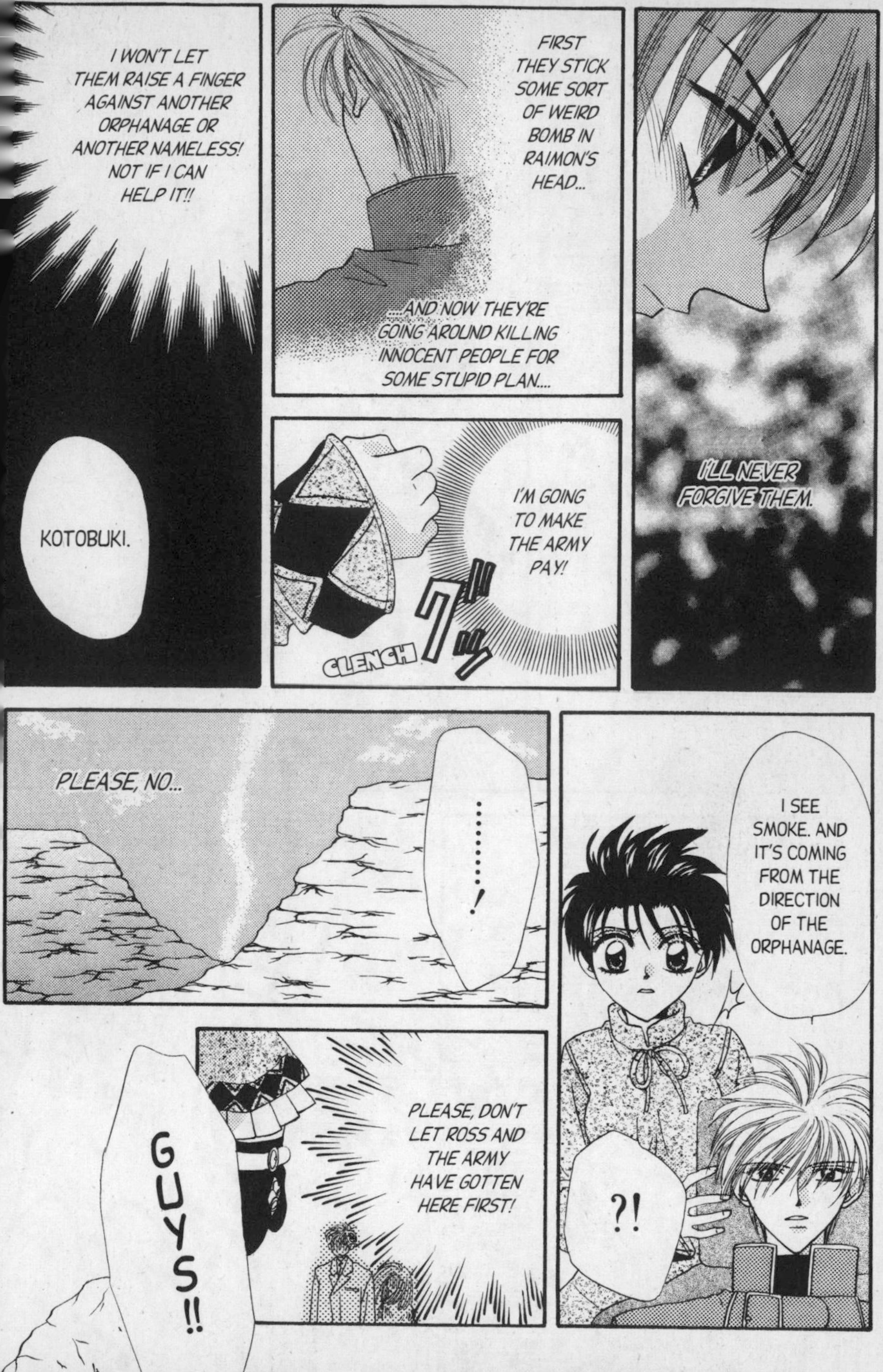
I'LL NEVER FORGIVE THEM.
FIRST THEY STICK SOME SORT OF WEIRD BOMB IN RAIMON'S HEAD...
...AND NOW THEY'RE GOING AROUND KILLING INNOCENT PEOPLE FOR SOME STUPID PLAN....
I'M GOING TO MAKE THE ARMY PAY!
CLENCH
I WON'T LET THEM RAISE A FINGER AGAINST ANOTHER ORPHANAGE OR ANOTHER NAMELESS! NOT IF I CAN HELP IT!!
KOTOBUKI.
I SEE SMOKE. AND IT'S COMING FROM THE DIRECTION OF THE ORPHANAGE.
?!
PLEASE, NO...
......!
PLEASE, DON'T LET ROSS AND THE ARMY HAVE GOTTEN HERE FIRST!
GUYS!!

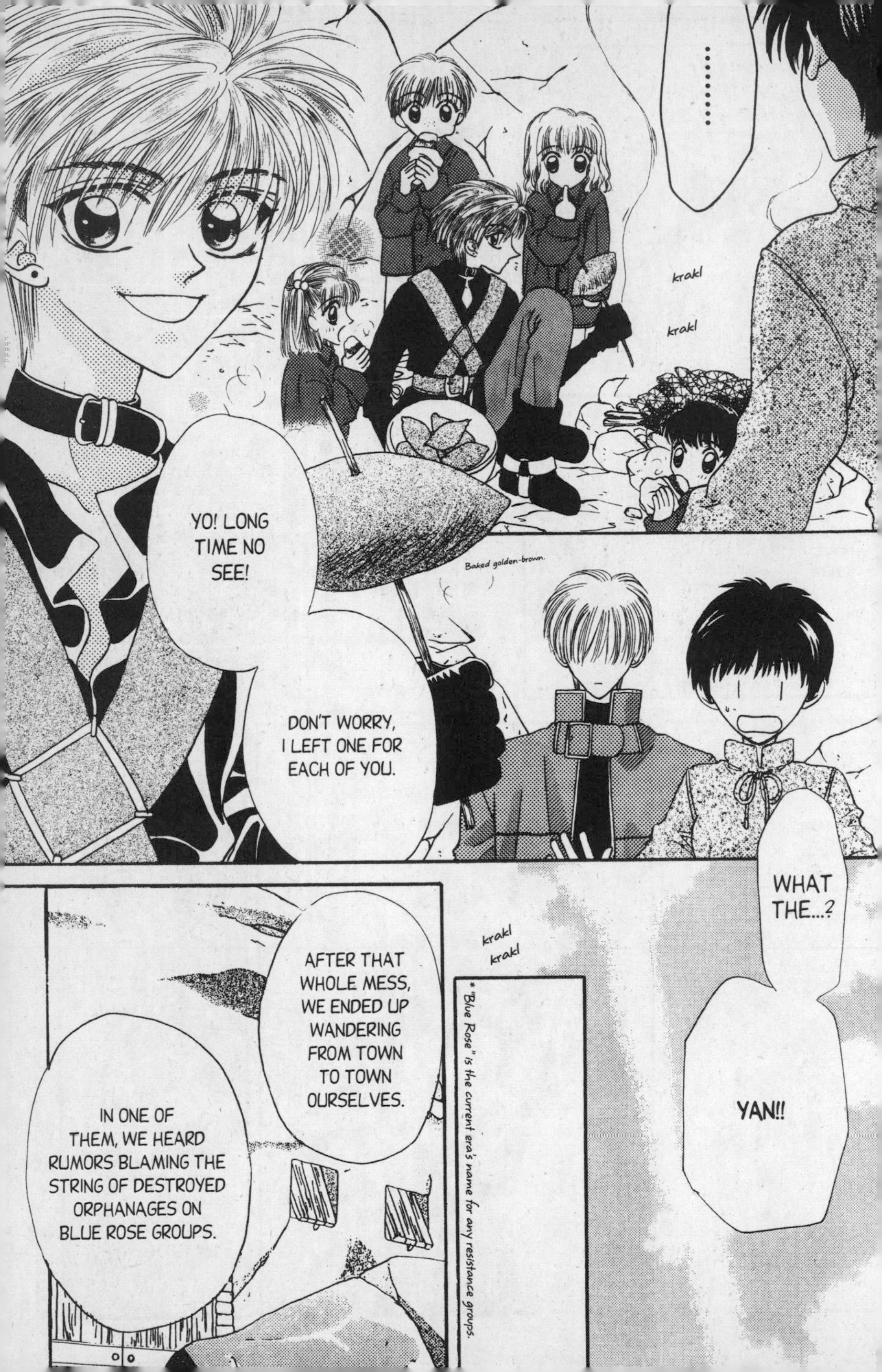
......
krakl
krakl
Baked golden-brown.
WHAT THE...?
YO! LONG TIME NO SEE!
DON'T WORRY, I LEFT ONE FOR EACH OF YOU.
YAN!!
krakl
krakl
AFTER THAT WHOLE MESS, WE ENDED UP WANDERING FROM TOWN TO TOWN OURSELVES.
IN ONE OF THEM, WE HEARD RUMORS BLAMING THE STRING OF DESTROYED ORPHANAGES ON BLUE ROSE GROUPS.
* "Blue Rose" is the current era's name for any resistance groups.

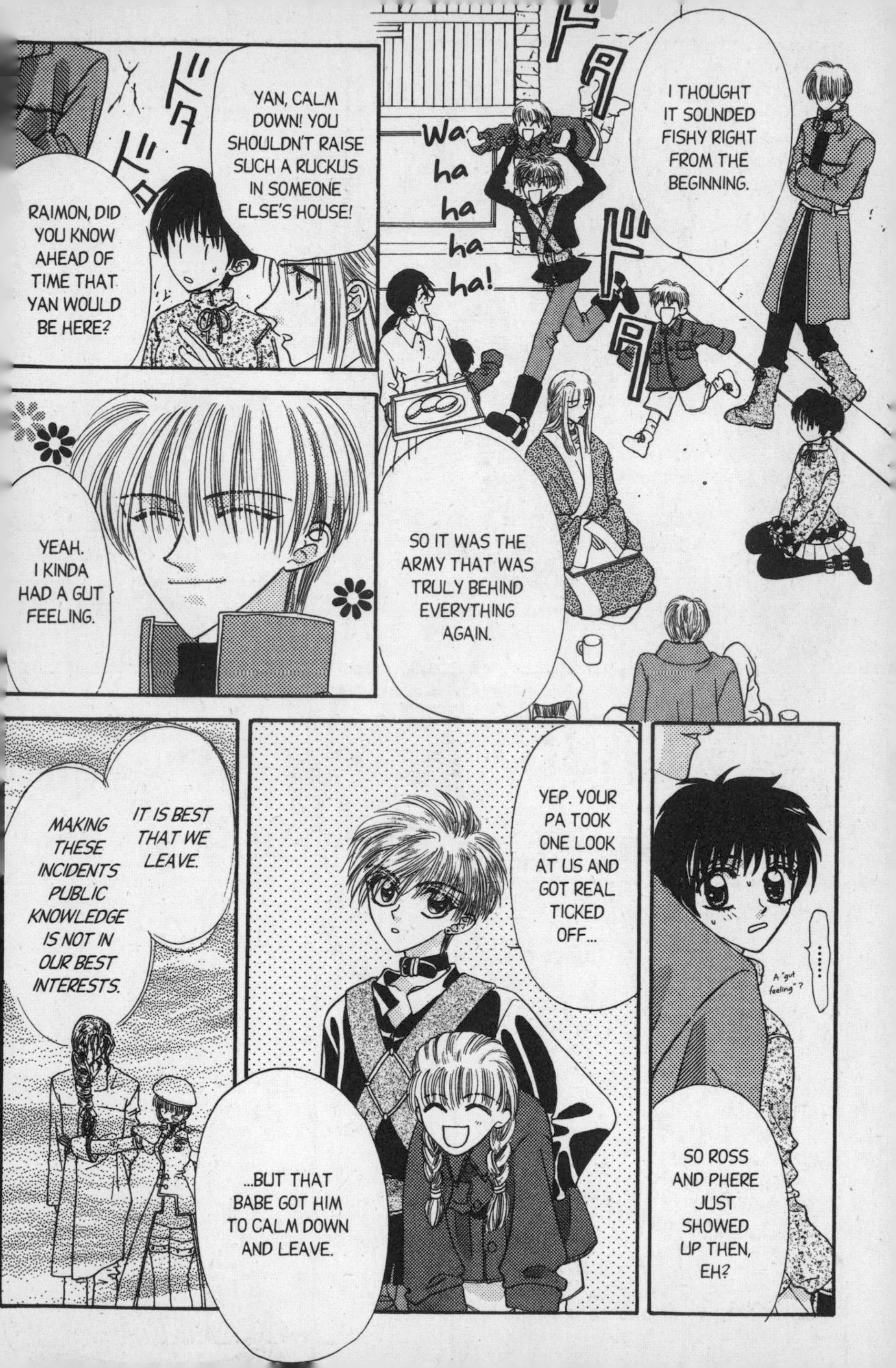
I THOUGHT IT SOUNDED FISHY RIGHT FROM THE BEGINNING.
Wa ha ha ha ha!
SO IT WAS THE ARMY THAT WAS TRULY BEHIND EVERYTHING AGAIN.
YAN, CALM DOWN! YOU SHOULDN'T RAISE SUCH A RUCKUS IN SOMEONE ELSE'S HOUSE!
RAIMON, DID YOU KNOW AHEAD OF TIME THAT YAN WOULD BE HERE?
YEAH. I KINDA HAD A GUT FEELING.
......
A "gut feeling"?
SO ROSS AND PHERE JUST SHOWED UP THEN, EH?
YEP. YOUR PA TOOK ONE LOOK AT US AND GOT REAL TICKED OFF...
...BUT THAT BABE GOT HIM TO CALM DOWN AND LEAVE.
IT IS BEST THAT WE LEAVE.
MAKING THESE INCIDENTS PUBLIC KNOWLEDGE IS NOT IN OUR BEST INTERESTS.

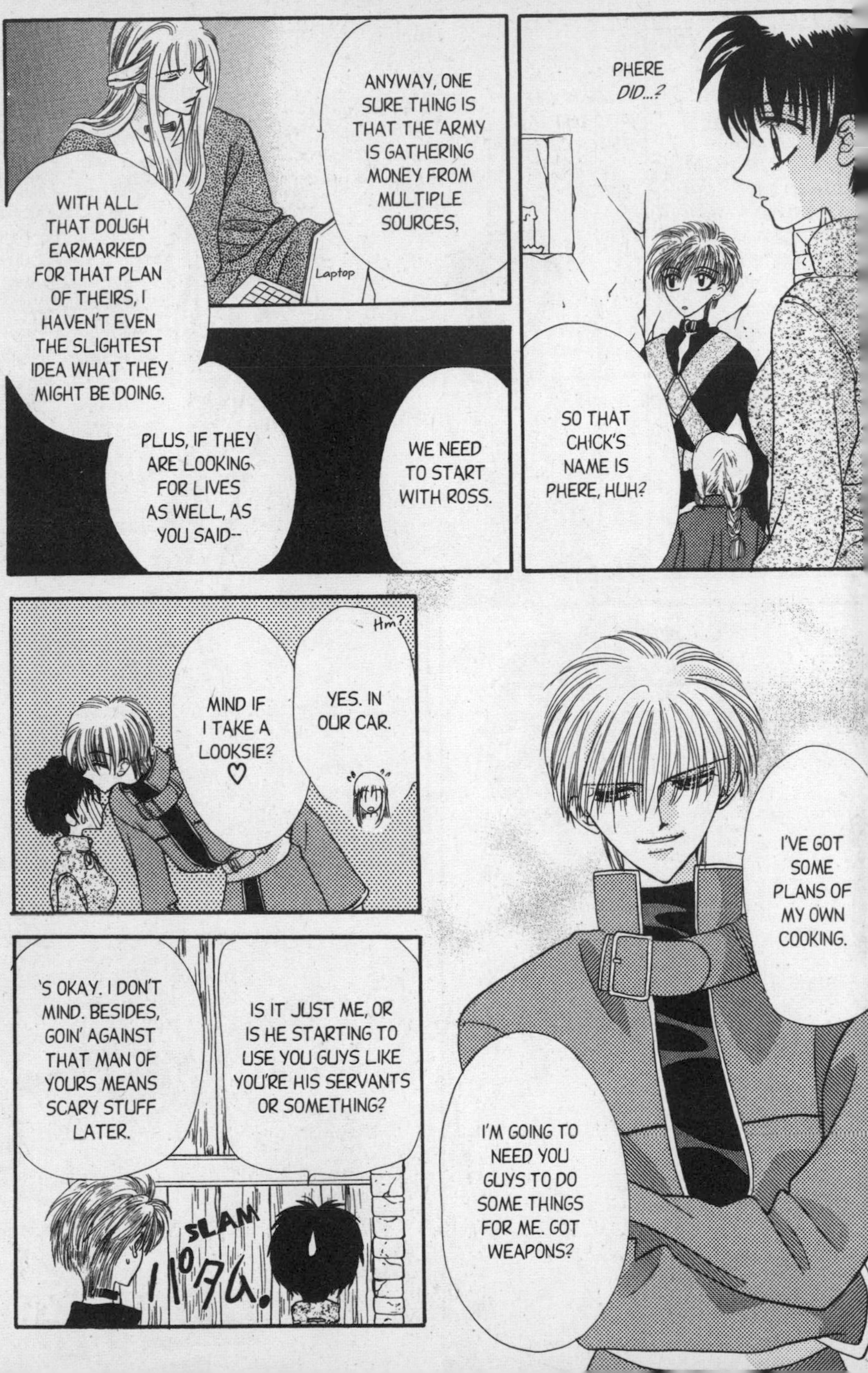
PHERE DID...?
SO THAT CHICK'S NAME IS PHERE, HUH?
ANYWAY, ONE SURE THING IS THAT THE ARMY IS GATHERING MONEY FROM MULTIPLE SOURCES.
WITH ALL THAT DOUGH EARMARKED FOR THAT PLAN OF THEIRS, I HAVEN'T EVEN THE SLIGHTEST IDEA WHAT THEY MIGHT BE DOING.
Laptop
PLUS, IF THEY ARE LOOKING FOR LIVES AS WELL, AS YOU SAID--
WE NEED TO START WITH ROSS.
I'VE GOT SOME PLANS OF MY OWN COOKING.
I'M GOING TO NEED YOU GUYS TO DO SOME THINGS FOR ME. GOT WEAPONS?
Hm?
YES. IN OUR CAR.
MIND IF I TAKE A LOOKSIE? ♡
IS IT JUST ME, OR IS HE STARTING TO USE YOU GUYS LIKE YOU'RE HIS SERVANTS OR SOMETHING?
'S OKAY. I DON'T MIND. BESIDES, GOIN' AGAINST THAT MAN OF YOURS MEANS SCARY STUFF LATER.
SLAM

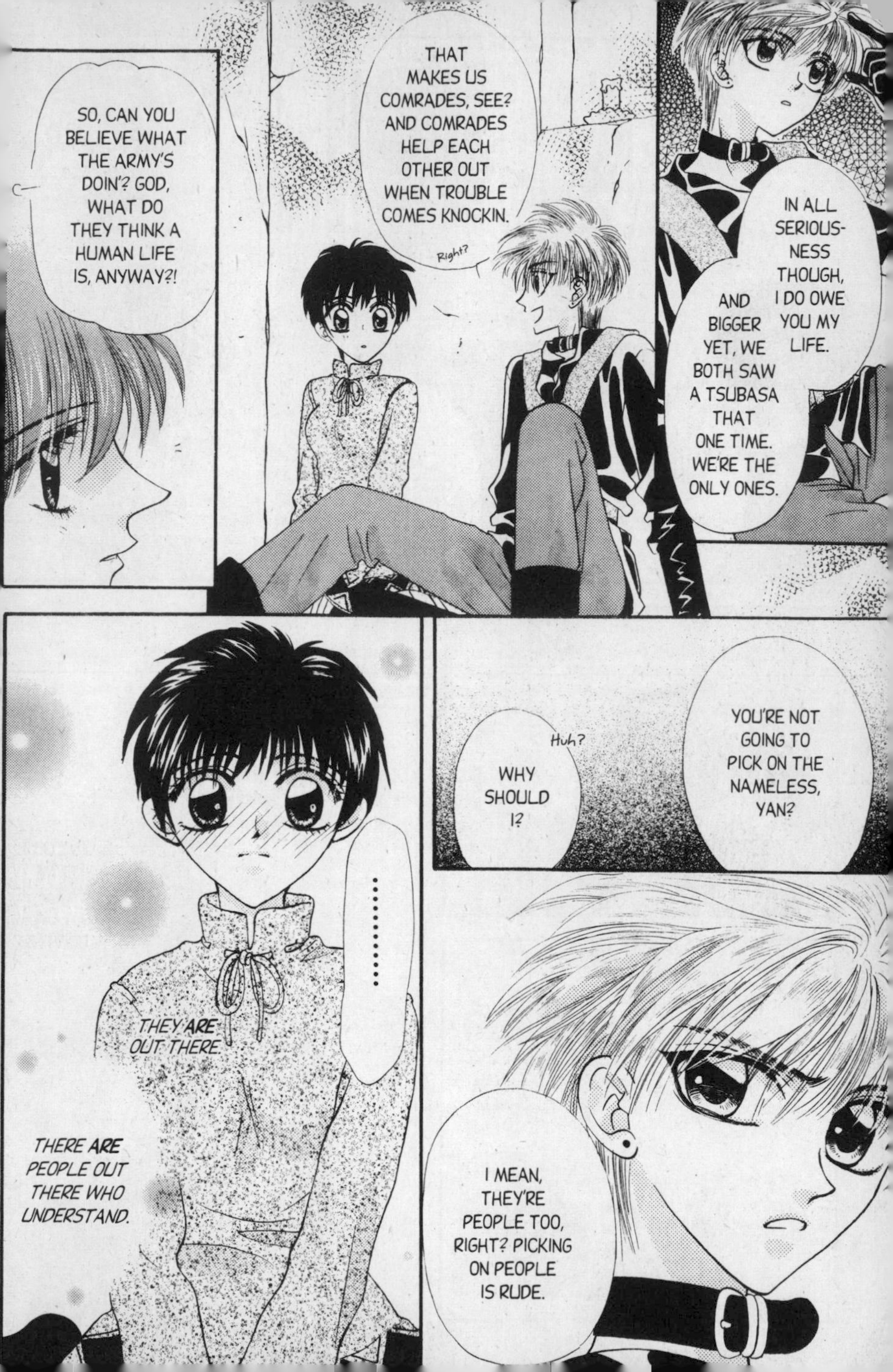
IN ALL SERIOUSNESS THOUGH, I DO OWE YOU MY LIFE.
AND BIGGER YET, WE BOTH SAW A TSUBASA THAT ONE TIME. WE'RE THE ONLY ONES.
THAT MAKES US COMRADES, SEE? AND COMRADES HELP EACH OTHER OUT WHEN TROUBLE COMES KNOCKIN.
Right?
SO, CAN YOU BELIEVE WHAT THE ARMY'S DOIN'? GOD, WHAT DO THEY THINK A HUMAN LIFE IS, ANYWAY?!
YOU'RE NOT GOING TO PICK ON THE NAMELESS, YAN?
Huh?
WHY SHOULD I?
I MEAN, THEY'RE PEOPLE TOO, RIGHT? PICKING ON PEOPLE IS RUDE.
....
THEY ARE OUT THERE.
THERE ARE PEOPLE OUT THERE WHO UNDERSTAND.

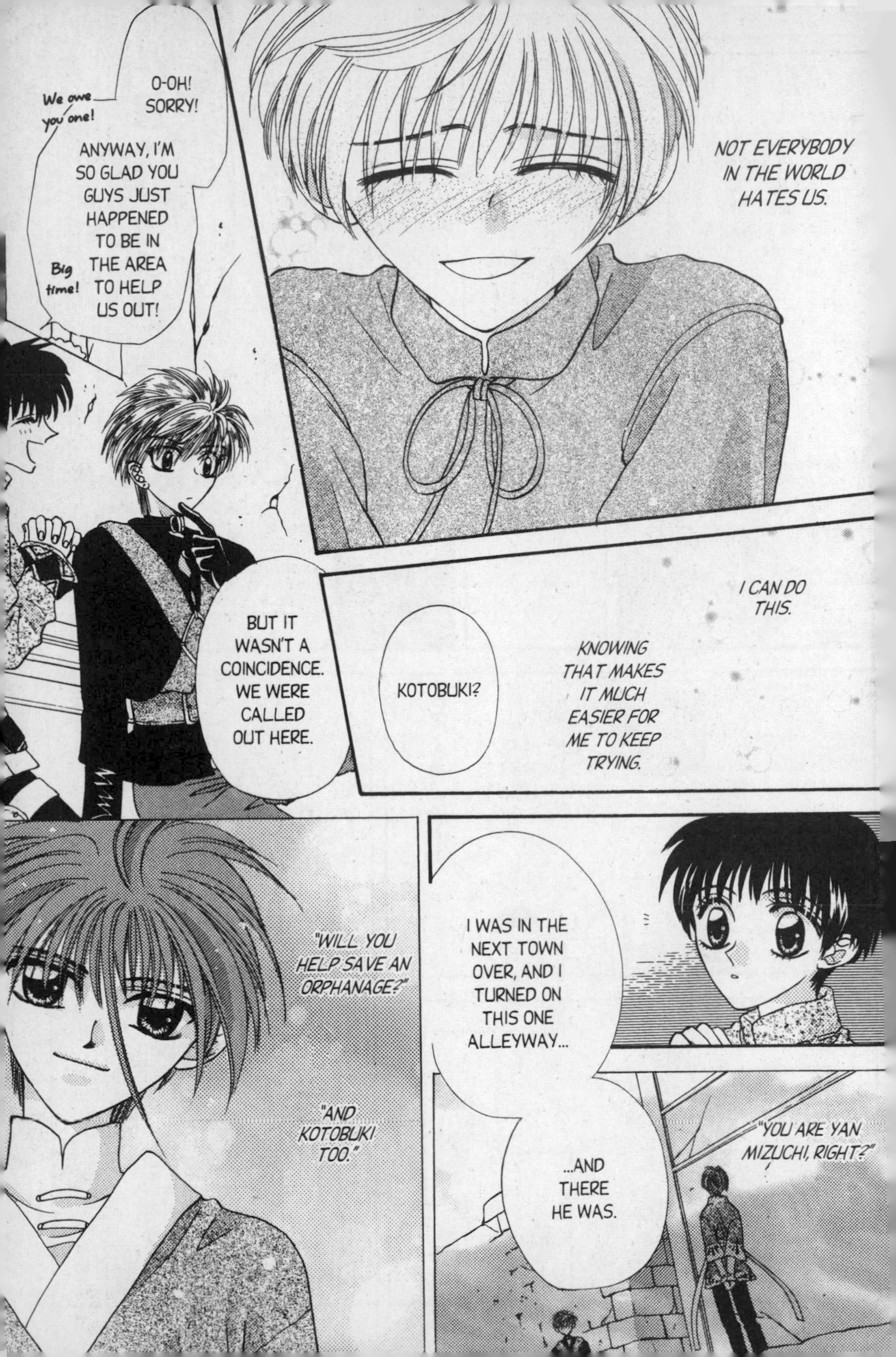
NOT EVERYBODY IN THE WORLD HATES US.
I CAN DO THIS.
KNOWING THAT MAKES IT MUCH EASIER FOR ME TO KEEP TRYING.
KOTOBUKI?
O-OH! SORRY!
We owe you one!
ANYWAY, I'M SO GLAD YOU GUYS JUST HAPPENED TO BE IN THE AREA TO HELP US OUT!
Big time!
BUT IT WASN'T A COINCIDENCE. WE WERE CALLED OUT HERE.
I WAS IN THE NEXT TOWN OVER, AND I TURNED ON THIS ONE ALLEYWAY...
...AND THERE HE WAS.
"YOU ARE YAN MIZUCHI, RIGHT?"
"WILL YOU HELP SAVE AN ORPHANAGE?"
"AND KOTOBUKI TOO."

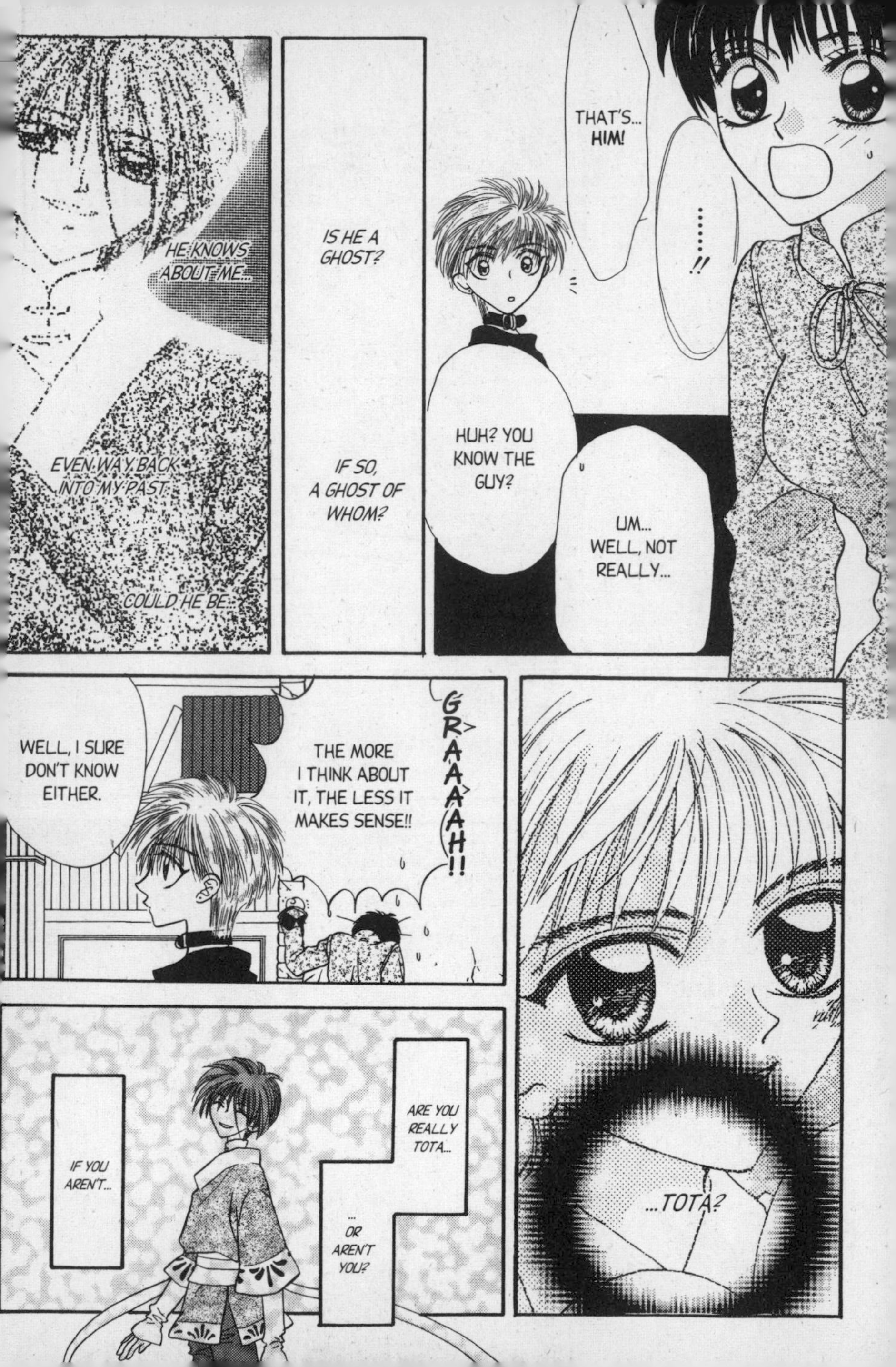
THAT'S... HIM!
......!!
HUH? YOU KNOW THE GUY?
UM... WELL, NOT REALLY...
IS HE A GHOST?
IF SO, A GHOST OF WHOM?
HE KNOWS ABOUT ME...
EVEN WAY BACK INTO MY PAST
COULD HE BE...
...TOTA?
GRAAAAH!!
THE MORE I THINK ABOUT IT, THE LESS IT MAKES SENSE!!
WELL, I SURE DON'T KNOW EITHER.
ARE YOU REALLY TOTA...
...OR AREN'T YOU?
IF YOU AREN'T...

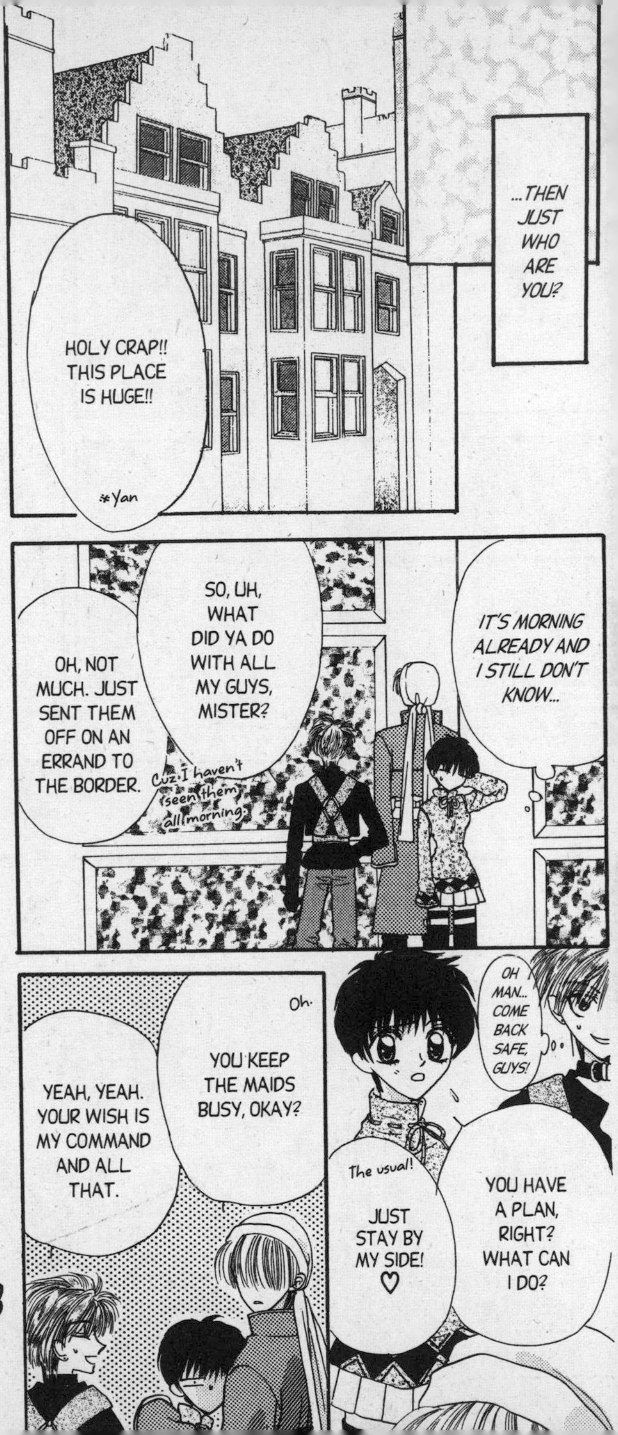
...THEN JUST WHO ARE YOU?
HOLY CRAP!! THIS PLACE IS HUGE!!
*Yan
IT'S MORNING ALREADY AND I STILL DON'T KNOW...
SO, UH, WHAT DID YA DO WITH ALL MY GUYS, MISTER?
OH, NOT MUCH. JUST SENT THEM OFF ON AN ERRAND TO THE BORDER.
Cuz I haven't seen them all morning.
OH MAN... COME BACK SAFE, GUYS!
YOU HAVE A PLAN, RIGHT? WHAT CAN I DO?
The usual!
JUST STAY BY MY SIDE! ♡
Oh.
YOU KEEP THE MAIDS BUSY, OKAY?
YEAH, YEAH. YOUR WISH IS MY COMMAND AND ALL THAT.
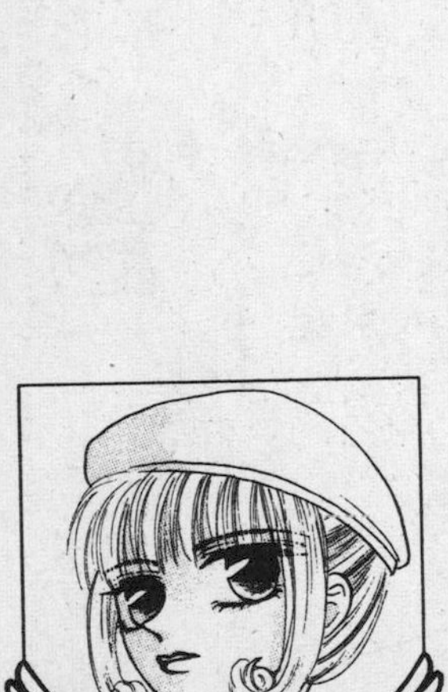

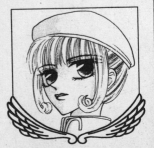

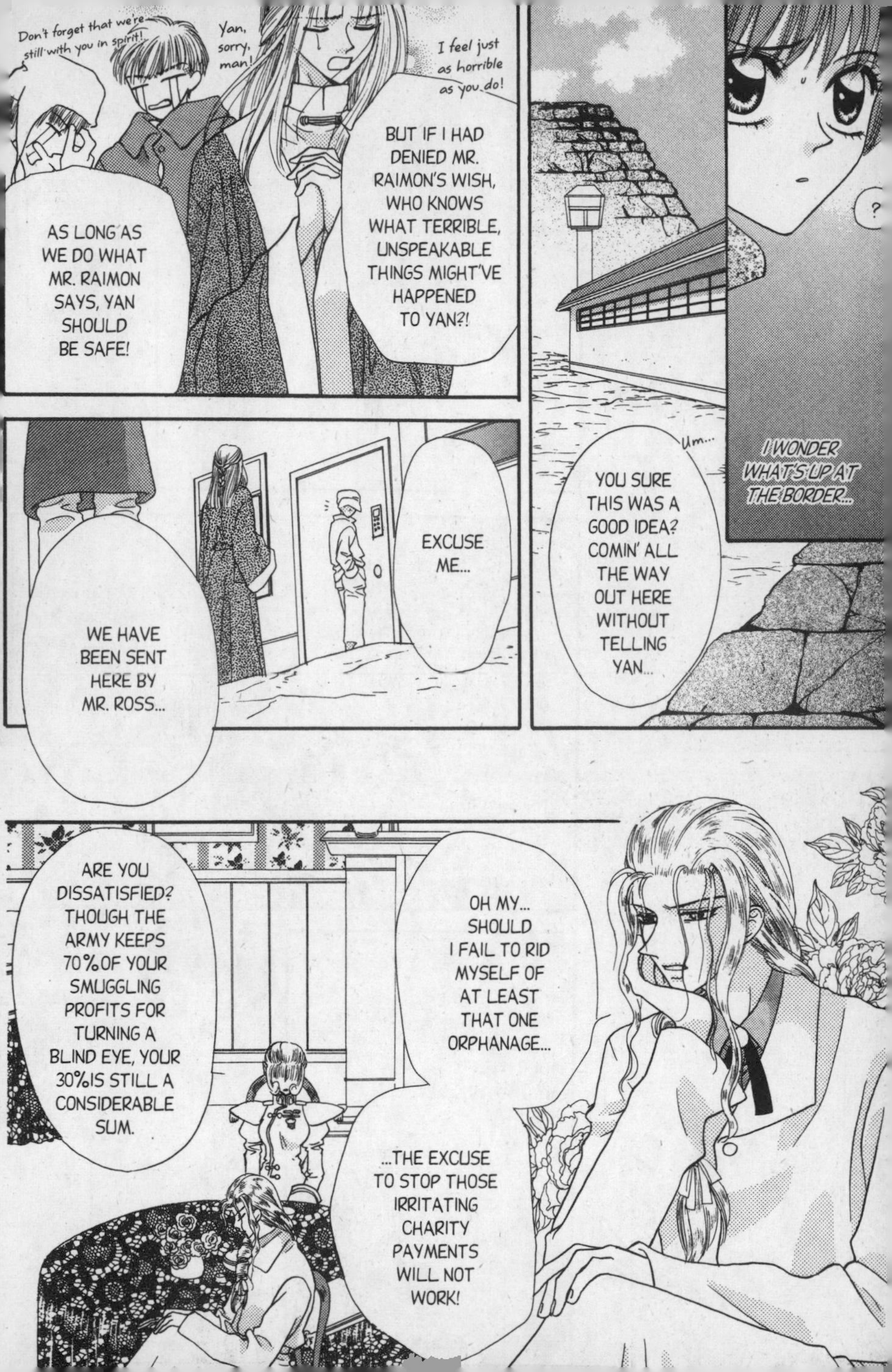
?
I WONDER WHAT'S UP AT THE BORDER...
Um...
YOU SURE THIS WAS A GOOD IDEA? COMIN' ALL THE WAY OUT HERE WITHOUT TELLING YAN...
I feel just as horrible as you do!
BUT IF I HAD DENIED MR. RAIMON'S WISH, WHO KNOWS WHAT TERRIBLE, UNSPEAKABLE THINGS MIGHT'VE HAPPENED TO YAN?!
Yan, sorry, man!
Don't forget that we're still with you in spirit!
AS LONG AS WE DO WHAT MR. RAIMON SAYS, YAN SHOULD BE SAFE!
EXCUSE ME...
WE HAVE BEEN SENT HERE BY MR. ROSS...
OH MY... SHOULD I FAIL TO RID MYSELF OF AT LEAST THAT ONE ORPHANAGE...
...THE EXCUSE TO STOP THOSE IRRITATING CHARITY PAYMENTS WILL NOT WORK!
ARE YOU DISSATISFIED? THOUGH THE ARMY KEEPS 70% OF YOUR SMUGGLING PROFITS FOR TURNING A BLIND EYE, YOUR 30% IS STILL A CONSIDERABLE SUM.

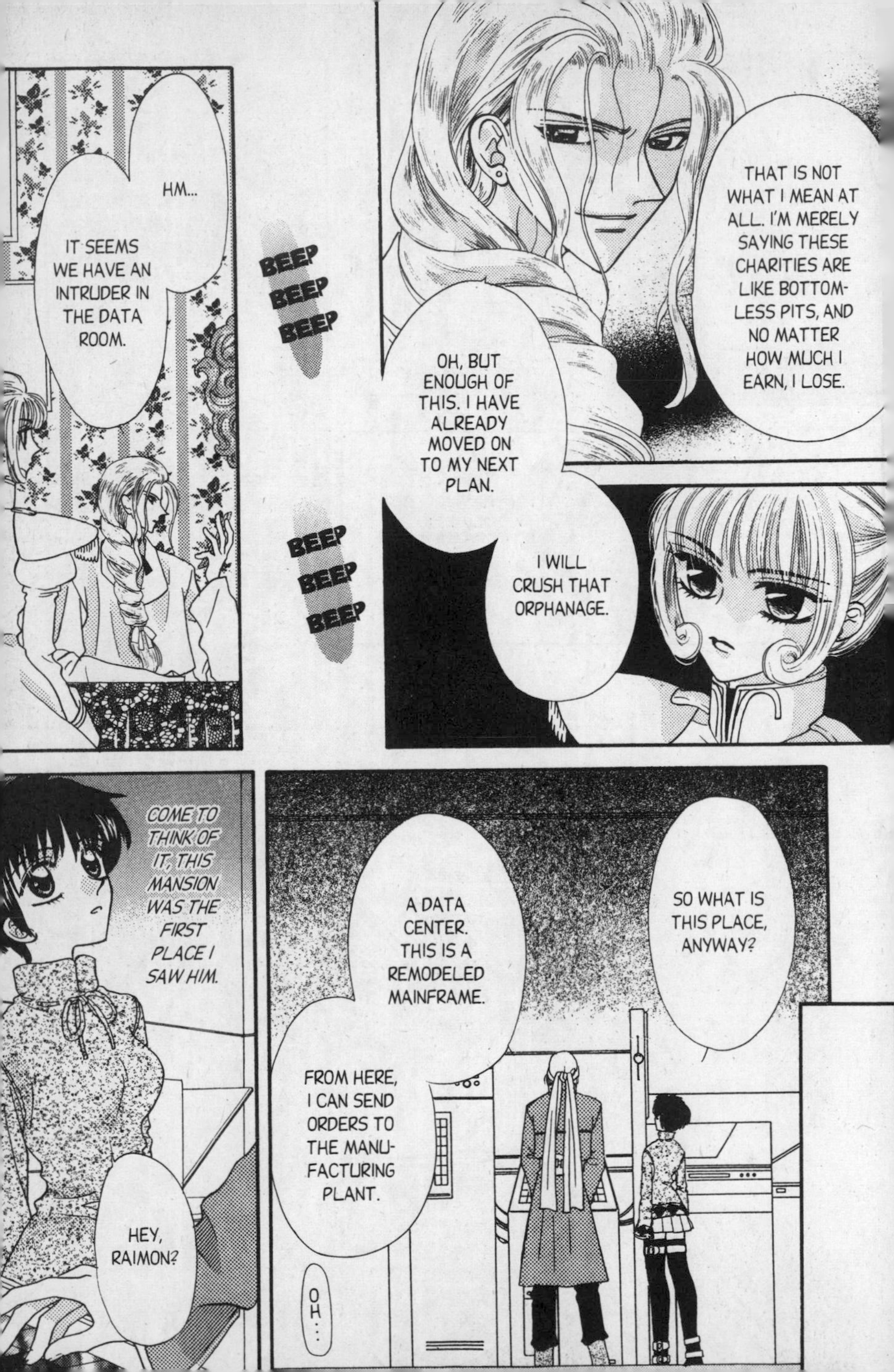
THAT IS NOT WHAT I MEAN AT ALL. I'M MERELY SAYING THESE CHARITIES ARE LIKE BOTTOMLESS PITS, AND NO MATTER HOW MUCH I EARN, I LOSE.
OH, BUT ENOUGH OF THIS. I HAVE ALREADY MOVED ON TO MY NEXT PLAN.
I WILL CRUSH THAT ORPHANAGE.
BEEP BEEP BEEP
BEEP BEEP BEEP
HM...
IT SEEMS WE HAVE AN INTRUDER IN THE DATA ROOM.
SO WHAT IS THIS PLACE, ANYWAY?
A DATA CENTER. THIS IS A REMODELED MAINFRAME.
FROM HERE, I CAN SEND ORDERS TO THE MANUFACTURING PLANT.
OH...
COME TO THINK OF IT, THIS MANSION WAS THE FIRST PLACE I SAW HIM.
HEY, RAIMON?

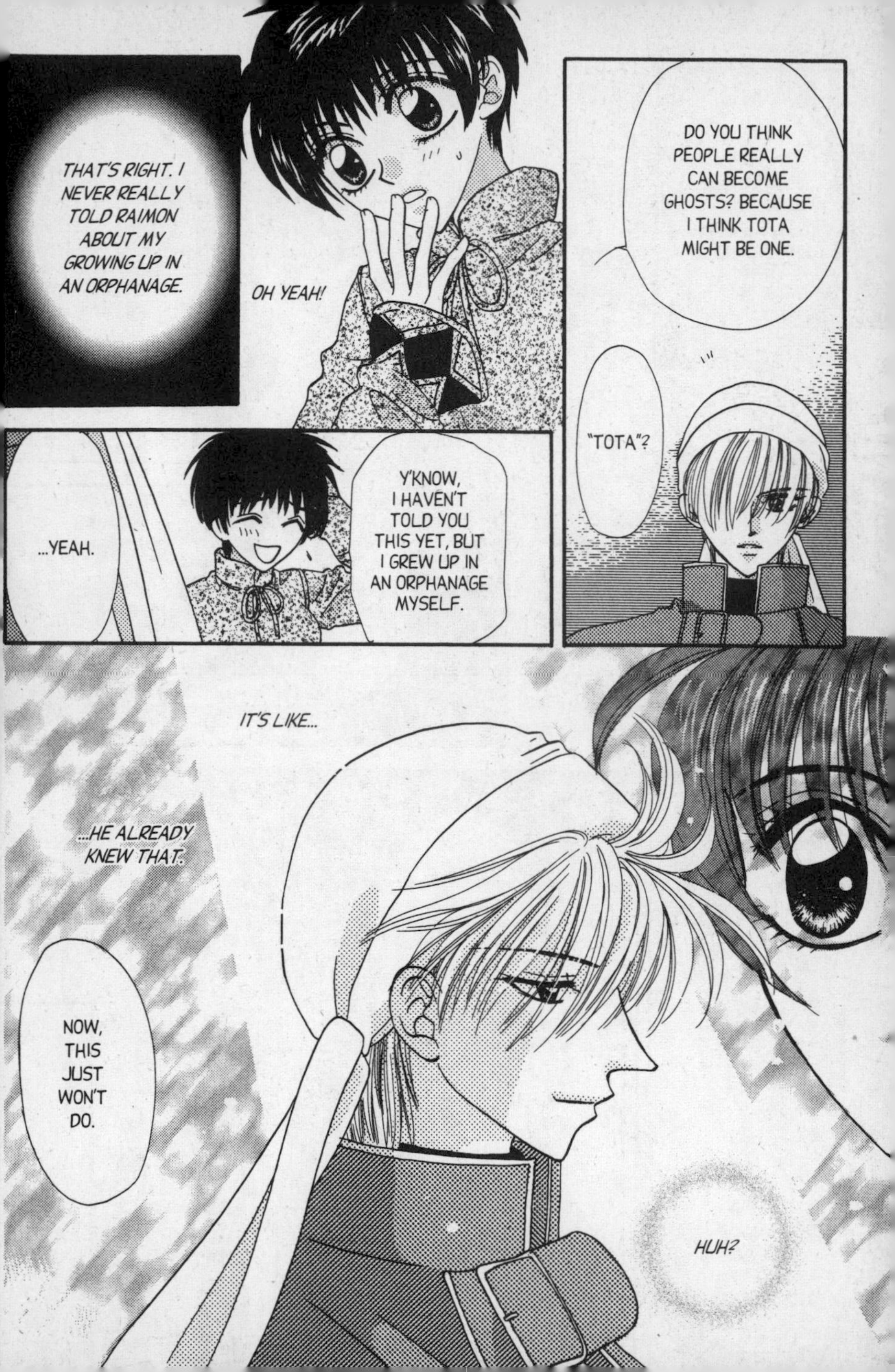

DO YOU THINK PEOPLE REALLY CAN BECOME GHOSTS? BECAUSE I THINK TOTA MIGHT BE ONE.
"TOTA"?
OH YEAH!
THAT'S RIGHT. I NEVER REALLY TOLD RAIMON ABOUT MY GROWING UP IN AN ORPHANAGE.
Y'KNOW, I HAVEN'T TOLD YOU THIS YET, BUT I GREW UP IN AN ORPHANAGE MYSELF.
...YEAH.
IT'S LIKE...
...HE ALREADY KNEW THAT.
NOW, THIS JUST WON'T DO.
HUH?

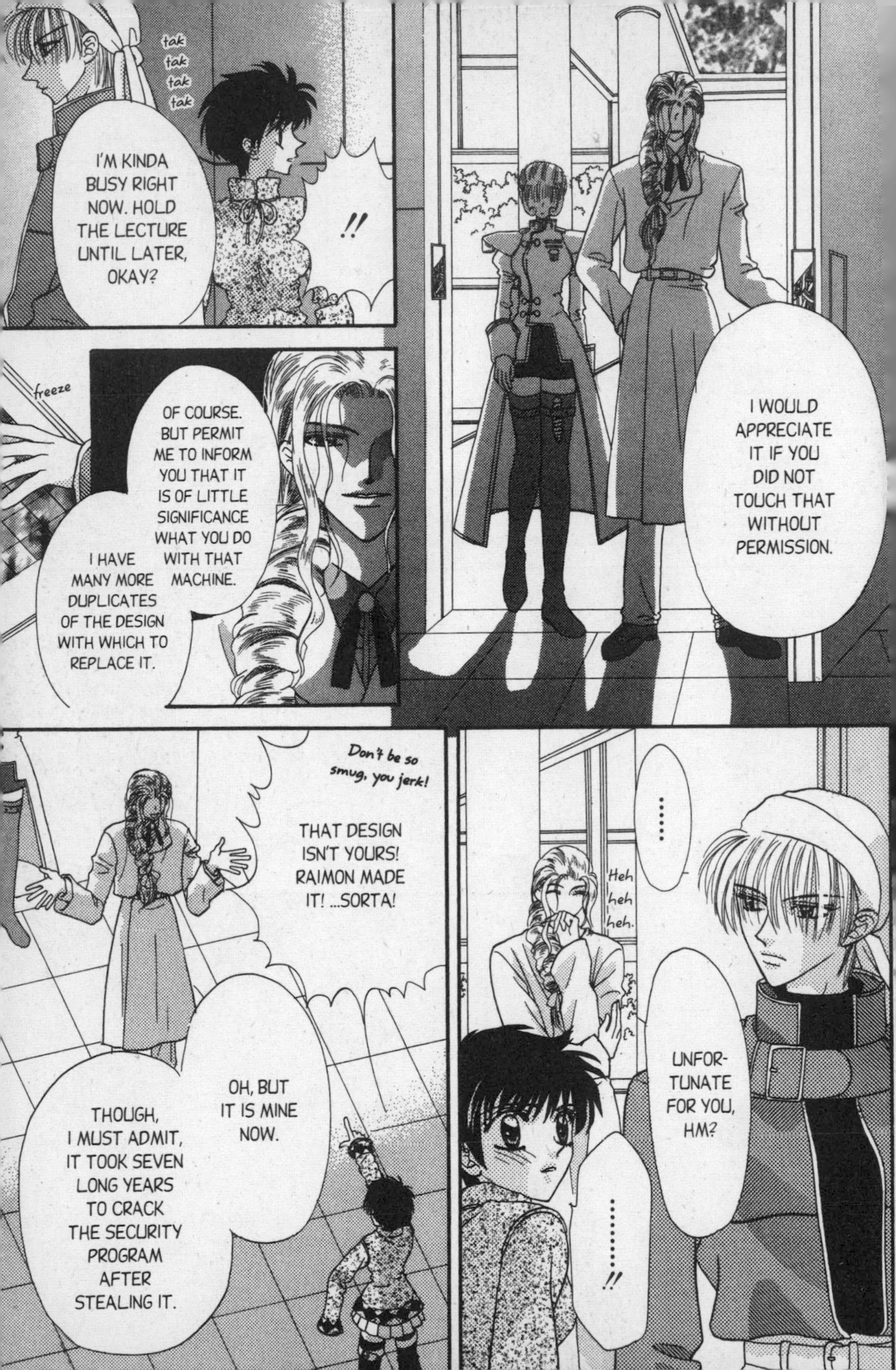
I WOULD APPRECIATE IT IF YOU DID NOT TOUCH THAT WITHOUT PERMISSION.
tak tak tak tak
I'M KINDA BUSY RIGHT NOW. HOLD THE LECTURE UNTIL LATER, OKAY?
!!
freeze
OF COURSE. BUT PERMIT ME TO INFORM YOU THAT IT IS OF LITTLE SIGNIFICANCE WHAT YOU DO WITH THAT MACHINE.
I HAVE MANY MORE DUPLICATES OF THE DESIGN WITH WHICH TO REPLACE IT.
......
Heh heh heh.
UNFOR-TUNATE FOR YOU, HM?
......!!
Don't be so smug, you jerk!
THAT DESIGN ISN'T YOURS! RAIMON MADE IT! ...SORTA!
OH, BUT IT IS MINE NOW.
THOUGH, I MUST ADMIT, IT TOOK SEVEN LONG YEARS TO CRACK THE SECURITY PROGRAM AFTER STEALING IT.

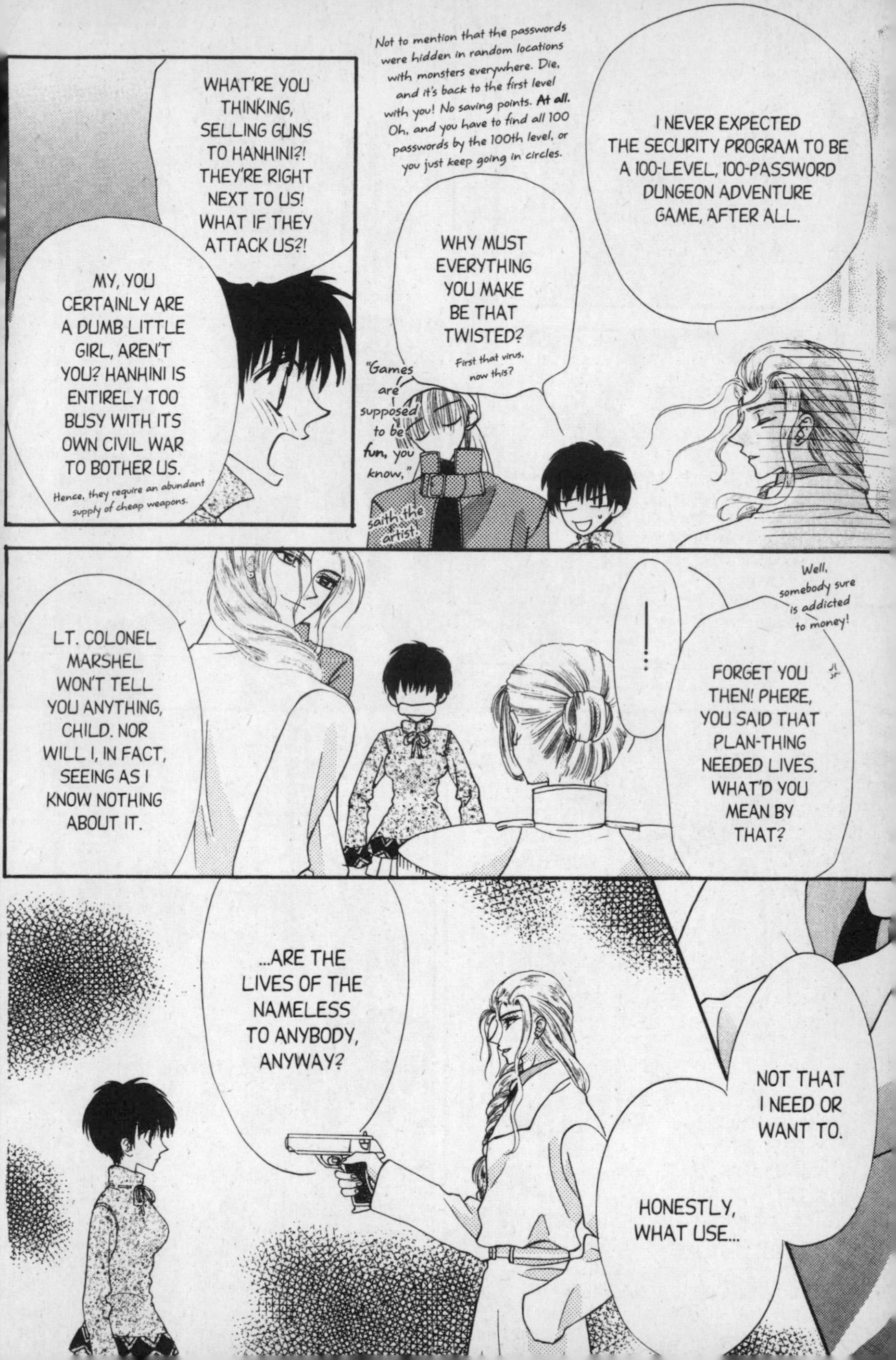
I NEVER EXPECTED THE SECURITY PROGRAM TO BE A 100-LEVEL, 100-PASSWORD DUNGEON ADVENTURE GAME, AFTER ALL.
Not to mention that the passwords were hidden in random locations with monsters everywhere. Die, and it's back to the first level with you! No saving points. At all. Oh, and you have to find all 100 passwords by the 100th level, or you just keep going in circles.
WHY MUST EVERYTHING YOU MAKE BE THAT TWISTED?
First that virus, now this?
"Games are supposed to be fun, you know," saith the artist.
WHAT'RE YOU THINKING, SELLING GUNS TO HANHINI?! THEY'RE RIGHT NEXT TO US! WHAT IF THEY ATTACK US?!
MY, YOU CERTAINLY ARE A DUMB LITTLE GIRL, AREN'T YOU? HANHINI IS ENTIRELY TOO BUSY WITH ITS OWN CIVIL WAR TO BOTHER US.
Hence, they require an abundant supply of cheap weapons.
!
Well, somebody sure is addicted to money!
FORGET YOU THEN! PHERE, YOU SAID THAT PLAN-THING NEEDED LIVES. WHAT'D YOU MEAN BY THAT?
LT. COLONEL MARSHEL WON'T TELL YOU ANYTHING, CHILD. NOR WILL I, IN FACT, SEEING AS I KNOW NOTHING ABOUT IT.
NOT THAT I NEED OR WANT TO.
HONESTLY, WHAT USE...
...ARE THE LIVES OF THE NAMELESS TO ANYBODY, ANYWAY?

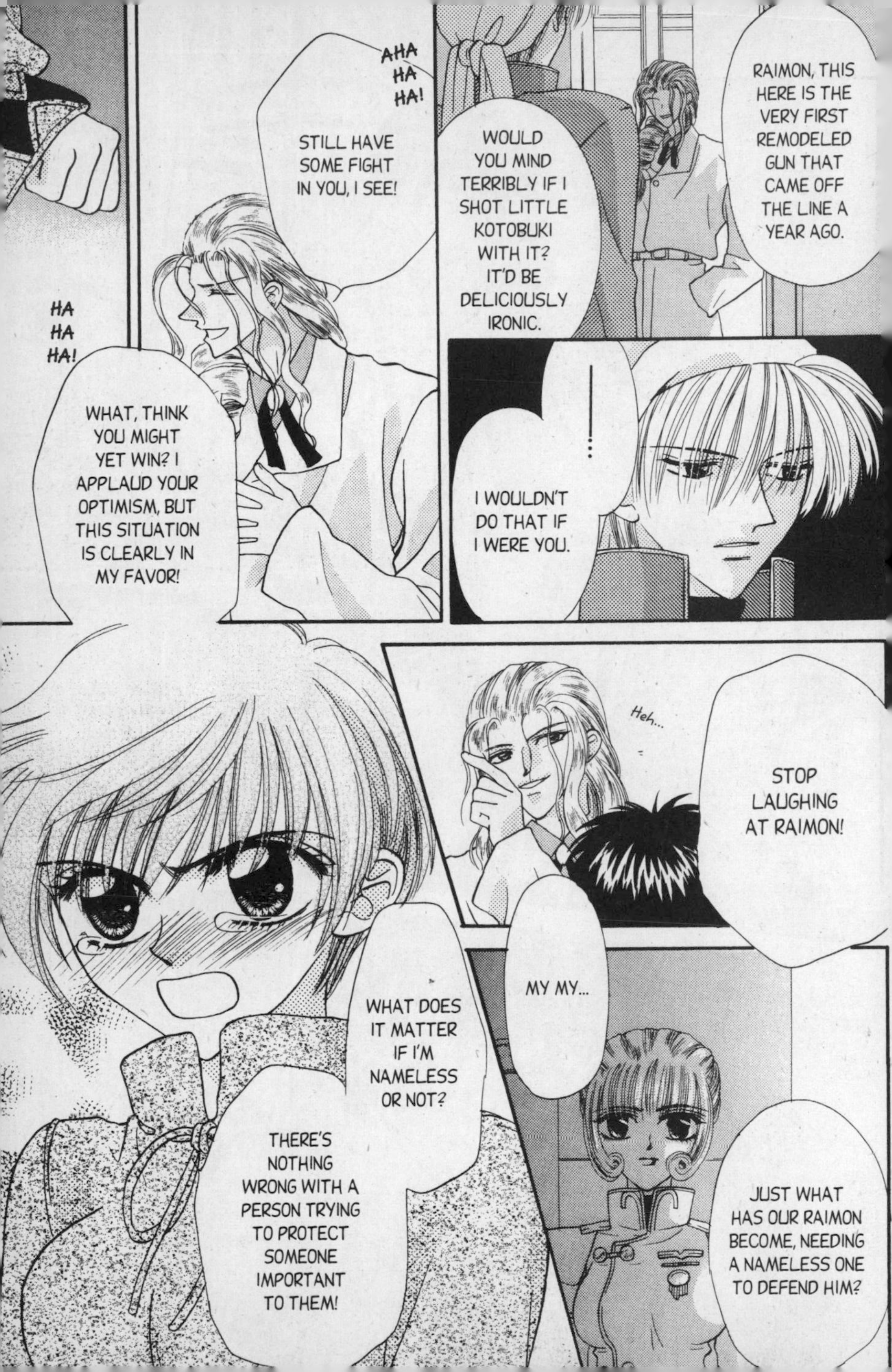
RAIMON, THIS HERE IS THE VERY FIRST REMODELED GUN THAT CAME OFF THE LINE A YEAR AGO.
WOULD YOU MIND TERRIBLY IF I SHOT LITTLE KOTOBUKI WITH IT? IT'D BE DELICIOUSLY IRONIC.
!...
I WOULDN'T DO THAT IF I WERE YOU.
AHA HA HA!
STILL HAVE SOME FIGHT IN YOU, I SEE!
HA HA HA!
WHAT, THINK YOU MIGHT YET WIN? I APPLAUD YOUR OPTIMISM, BUT THIS SITUATION IS CLEARLY IN MY FAVOR!
STOP LAUGHING AT RAIMON!
Heh...
MY MY...
JUST WHAT HAS OUR RAIMON BECOME, NEEDING A NAMELESS ONE TO DEFEND HIM?
WHAT DOES IT MATTER IF I'M NAMELESS OR NOT?
THERE'S NOTHING WRONG WITH A PERSON TRYING TO PROTECT SOMEONE IMPORTANT TO THEM!

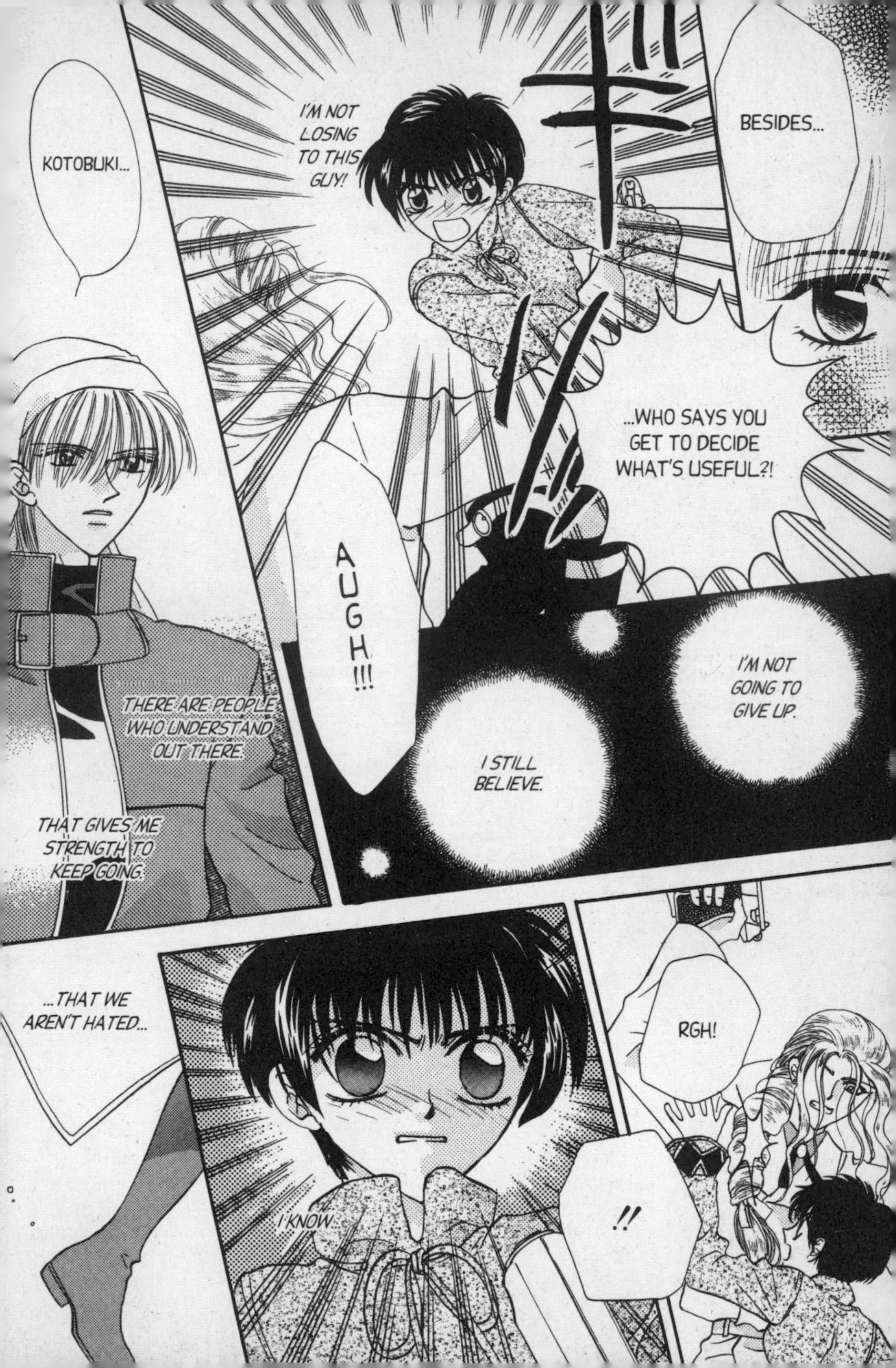
BESIDES...
...WHO SAYS YOU GET TO DECIDE WHAT'S USEFUL?!
I'M NOT LOSING TO THIS GUY!
AUGH!!!
I'M NOT GOING TO GIVE UP.
I STILL BELIEVE.
KOTOBUKI...
THERE ARE PEOPLE WHO UNDERSTAND OUT THERE.
THAT GIVES ME STRENGTH TO KEEP GOING.
RGH!
!!
I KNOW...
...THAT WE AREN'T HATED...

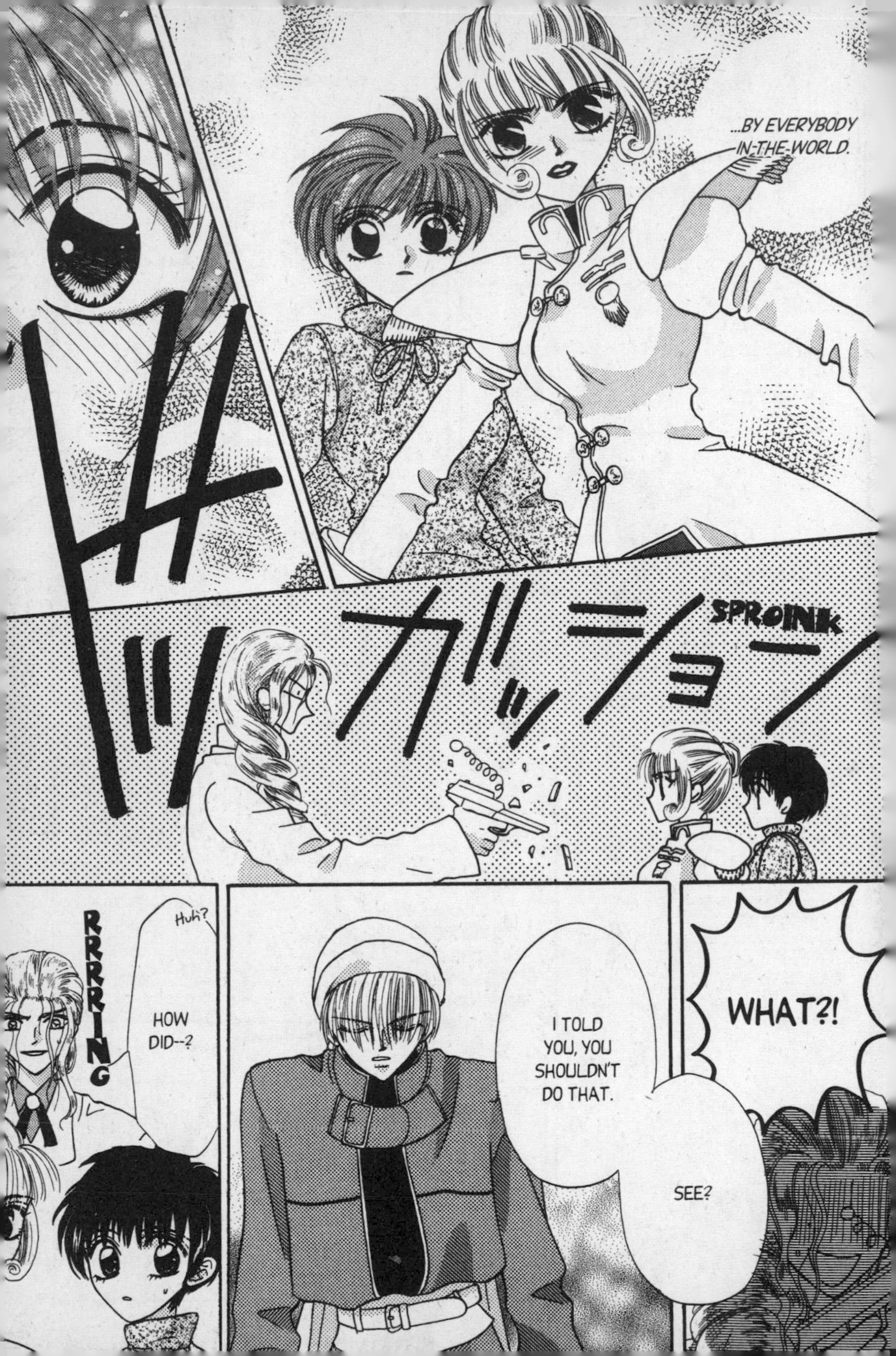
...BY EVERYBODY IN-THE-WORLD.
SPROINK
WHAT?!
I TOLD YOU, YOU SHOULDN'T DO THAT.
SEE?
Huh?
RRRRING
HOW DID--?

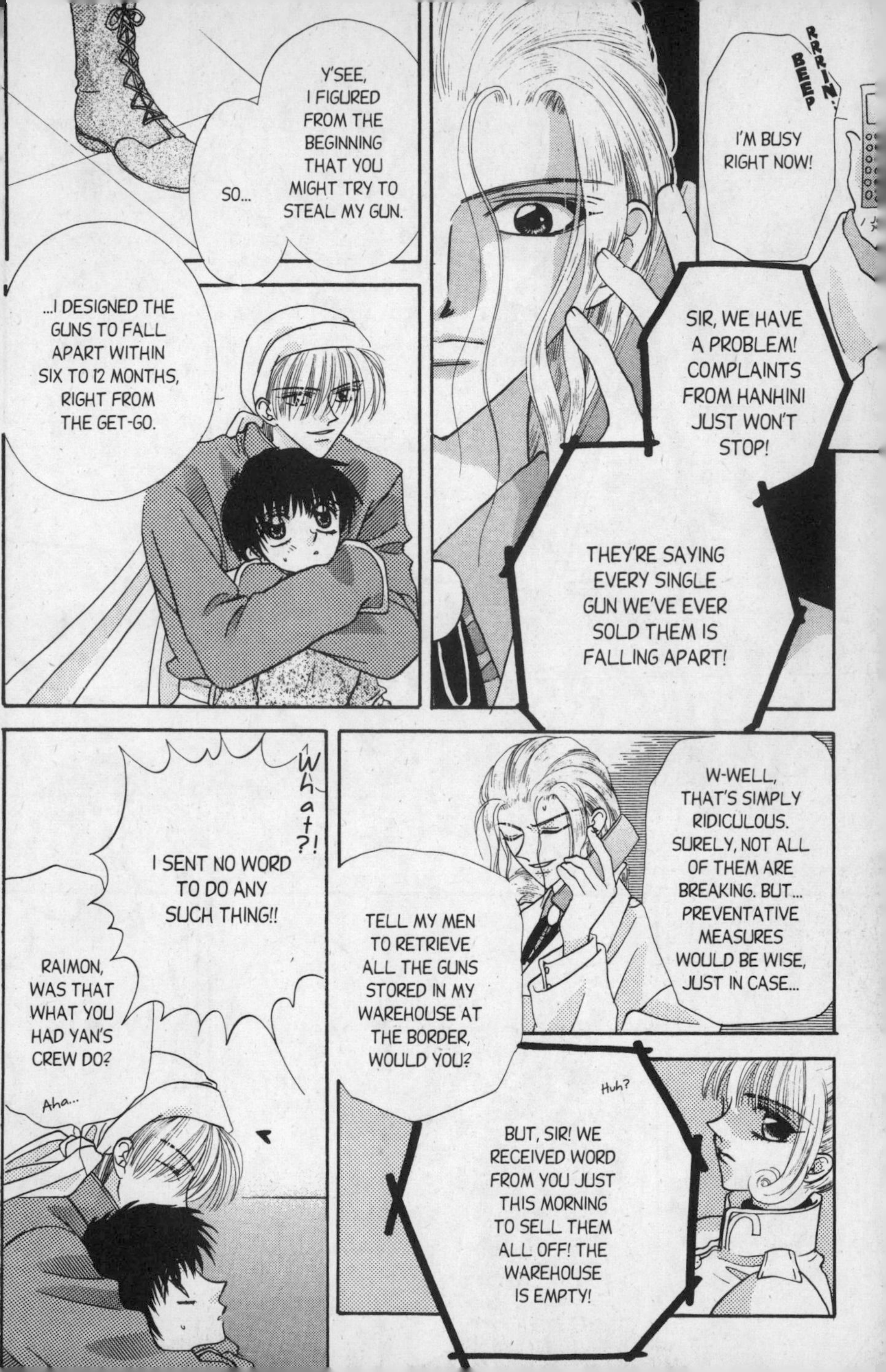
BEEP
RRRIN...
I'M BUSY RIGHT NOW!
SIR, WE HAVE A PROBLEM! COMPLAINTS FROM HANHINI JUST WON'T STOP!
THEY'RE SAYING EVERY SINGLE GUN WE'VE EVER SOLD THEM IS FALLING APART!
Y'SEE, I FIGURED FROM THE BEGINNING THAT YOU MIGHT TRY TO STEAL MY GUN.
SO...
...I DESIGNED THE GUNS TO FALL APART WITHIN SIX TO 12 MONTHS, RIGHT FROM THE GET-GO.
W-WELL, THAT'S SIMPLY RIDICULOUS. SURELY, NOT ALL OF THEM ARE BREAKING. BUT... PREVENTATIVE MEASURES WOULD BE WISE, JUST IN CASE...
TELL MY MEN TO RETRIEVE ALL THE GUNS STORED IN MY WAREHOUSE AT THE BORDER, WOULD YOU?
Huh?
BUT, SIR! WE RECEIVED WORD FROM YOU JUST THIS MORNING TO SELL THEM ALL OFF! THE WAREHOUSE IS EMPTY!
What?!
I SENT NO WORD TO DO ANY SUCH THING!!
RAIMON, WAS THAT WHAT YOU HAD YAN'S CREW DO?
Aha...

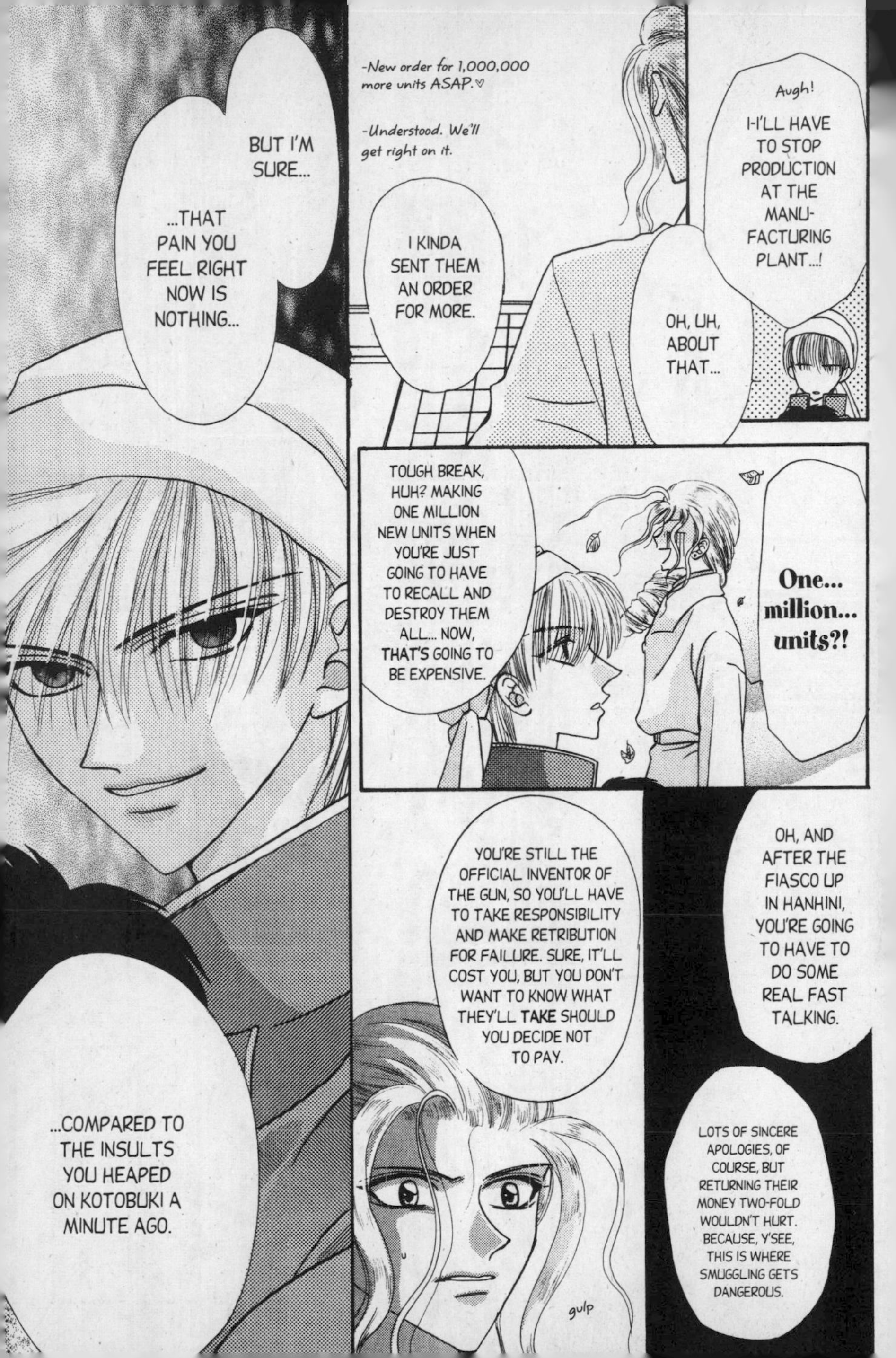
Augh!
I-I'LL HAVE TO STOP PRODUCTION AT THE MANU-FACTURING PLANT...!
OH, UH, ABOUT THAT...
I KINDA SENT THEM AN ORDER FOR MORE.
-New order for 1,000,000 more units ASAP.♡
-Understood. We'll get right on it.
One... million... units?!
TOUGH BREAK, HUH? MAKING ONE MILLION NEW UNITS WHEN YOU'RE JUST GOING TO HAVE TO RECALL AND DESTROY THEM ALL... NOW, **THAT'S** GOING TO BE EXPENSIVE.
OH, AND AFTER THE FIASCO UP IN HANHINI, YOU'RE GOING TO HAVE TO DO SOME REAL FAST TALKING.
LOTS OF SINCERE APOLOGIES, OF COURSE, BUT RETURNING THEIR MONEY TWO-FOLD WOULDN'T HURT. BECAUSE, Y'SEE, THIS IS WHERE SMUGGLING GETS DANGEROUS.
YOU'RE STILL THE OFFICIAL INVENTOR OF THE GUN, SO YOU'LL HAVE TO TAKE RESPONSIBILITY AND MAKE RETRIBUTION FOR FAILURE. SURE, IT'LL COST YOU, BUT YOU DON'T WANT TO KNOW WHAT THEY'LL **TAKE** SHOULD YOU DECIDE NOT TO PAY.
gulp
BUT I'M SURE...
...THAT PAIN YOU FEEL RIGHT NOW IS NOTHING...
...COMPARED TO THE INSULTS YOU HEAPED ON KOTOBUKI A MINUTE AGO.

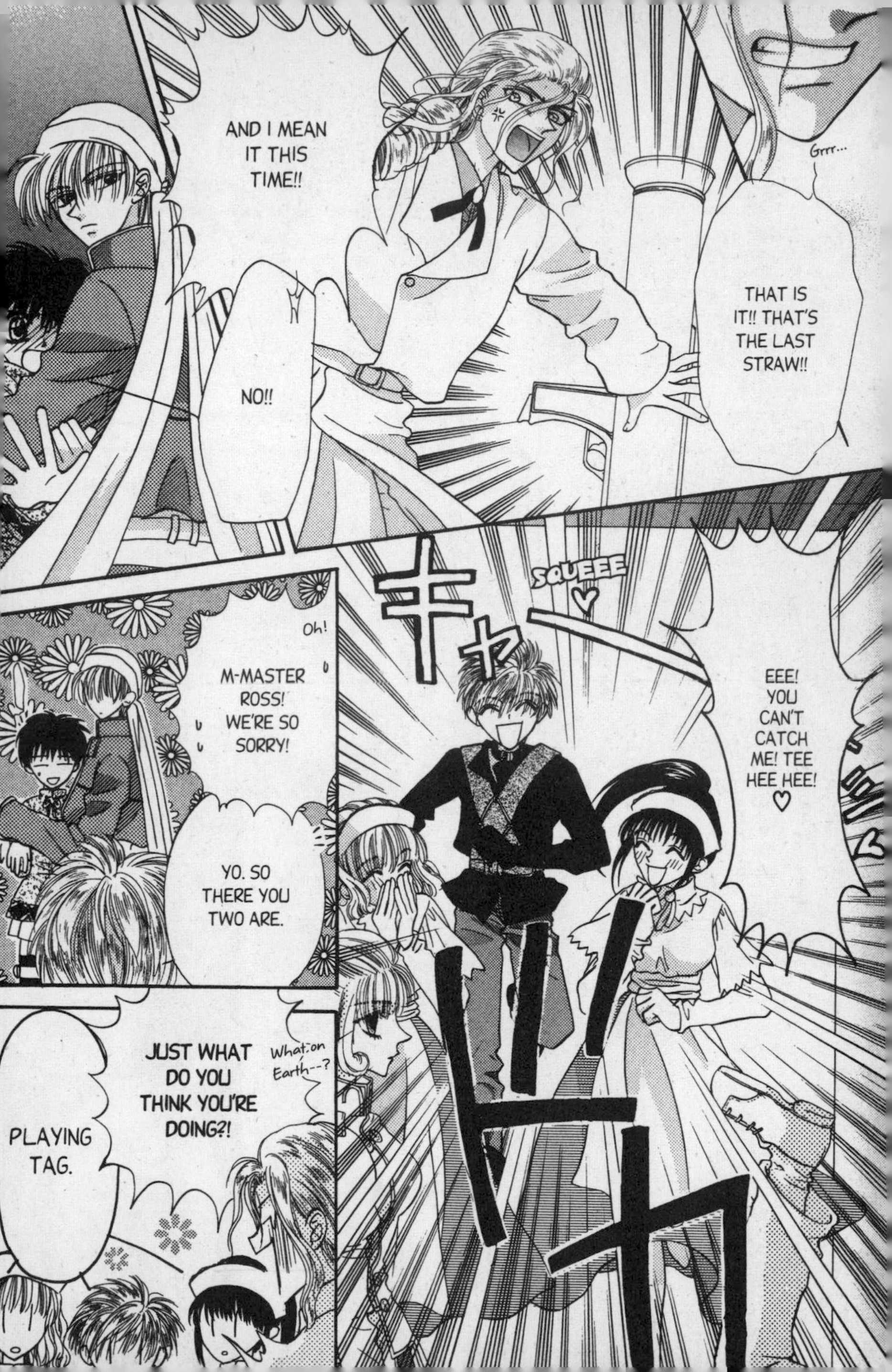
Grrr...
THAT IS IT!! THAT'S THE LAST STRAW!!
AND I MEAN IT THIS TIME!!
NO!!
キャ
SQUEEE ♡
EEE! YOU CAN'T CATCH ME! TEE HEE HEE! ♡
Oh!
M-MASTER ROSS! WE'RE SO SORRY!
YO. SO THERE YOU TWO ARE.
What on Earth--?
JUST WHAT DO YOU THINK YOU'RE DOING?!
PLAYING TAG.

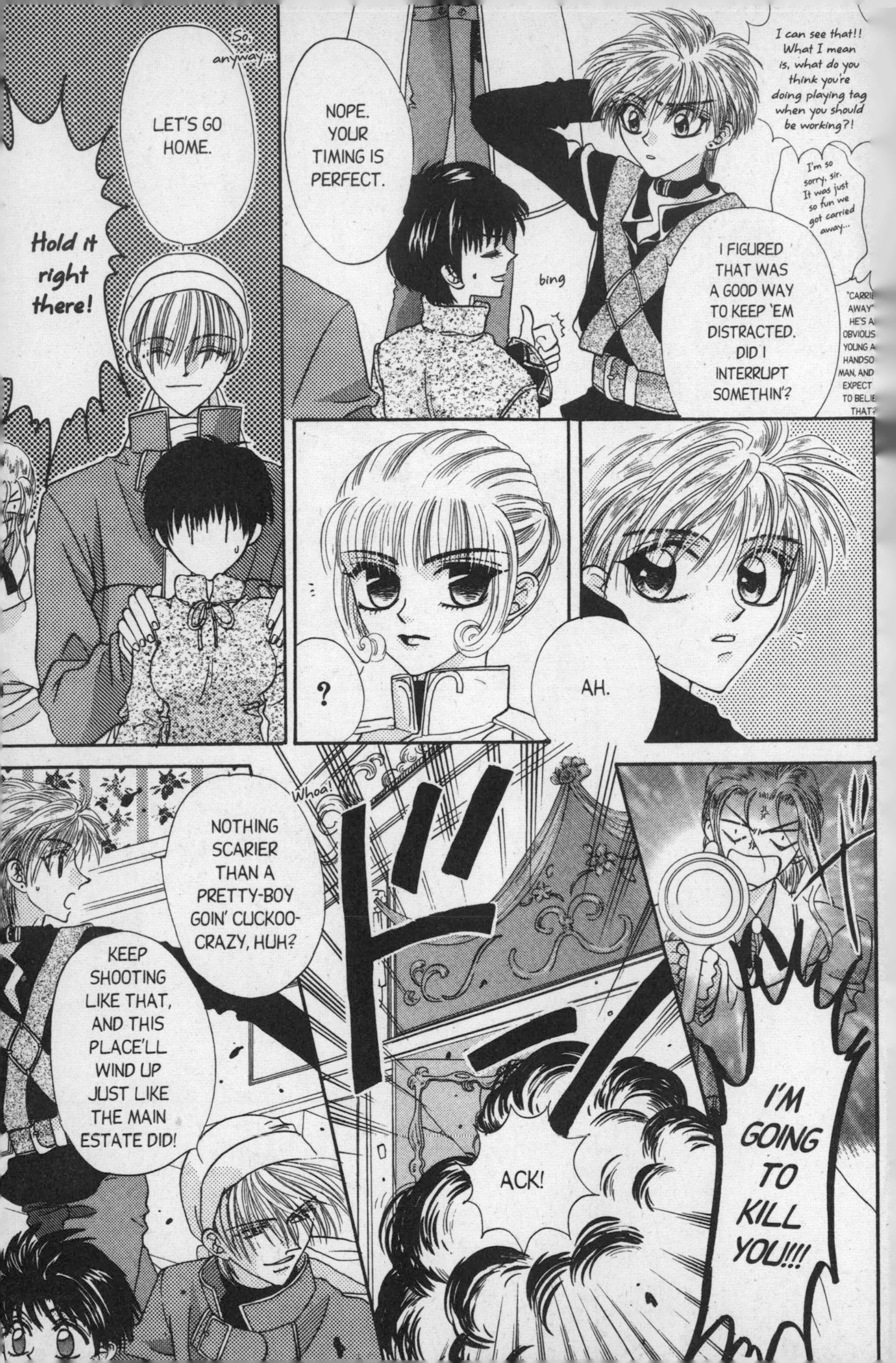

I can see that!! What I mean is, what do you think you're doing playing tag when you should be working?!
I'm so sorry, sir. It was just so fun we got carried away...
I FIGURED THAT WAS A GOOD WAY TO KEEP 'EM DISTRACTED. DID I INTERRUPT SOMETHIN'?
"CARRIE AWAY" HE'S A OBVIOUS YOUNG A HANDSO MAN, AND EXPECT TO BELIE THAT?
bing
NOPE. YOUR TIMING IS PERFECT.
AH.
?
So, anyway...
LET'S GO HOME.
Hold it right there!
I'M GOING TO KILL YOU!!!
ACK!
ドン
Whoa!
NOTHING SCARIER THAN A PRETTY-BOY GOIN' CUCKOO-CRAZY, HUH?
KEEP SHOOTING LIKE THAT, AND THIS PLACE'LL WIND UP JUST LIKE THE MAIN ESTATE DID!

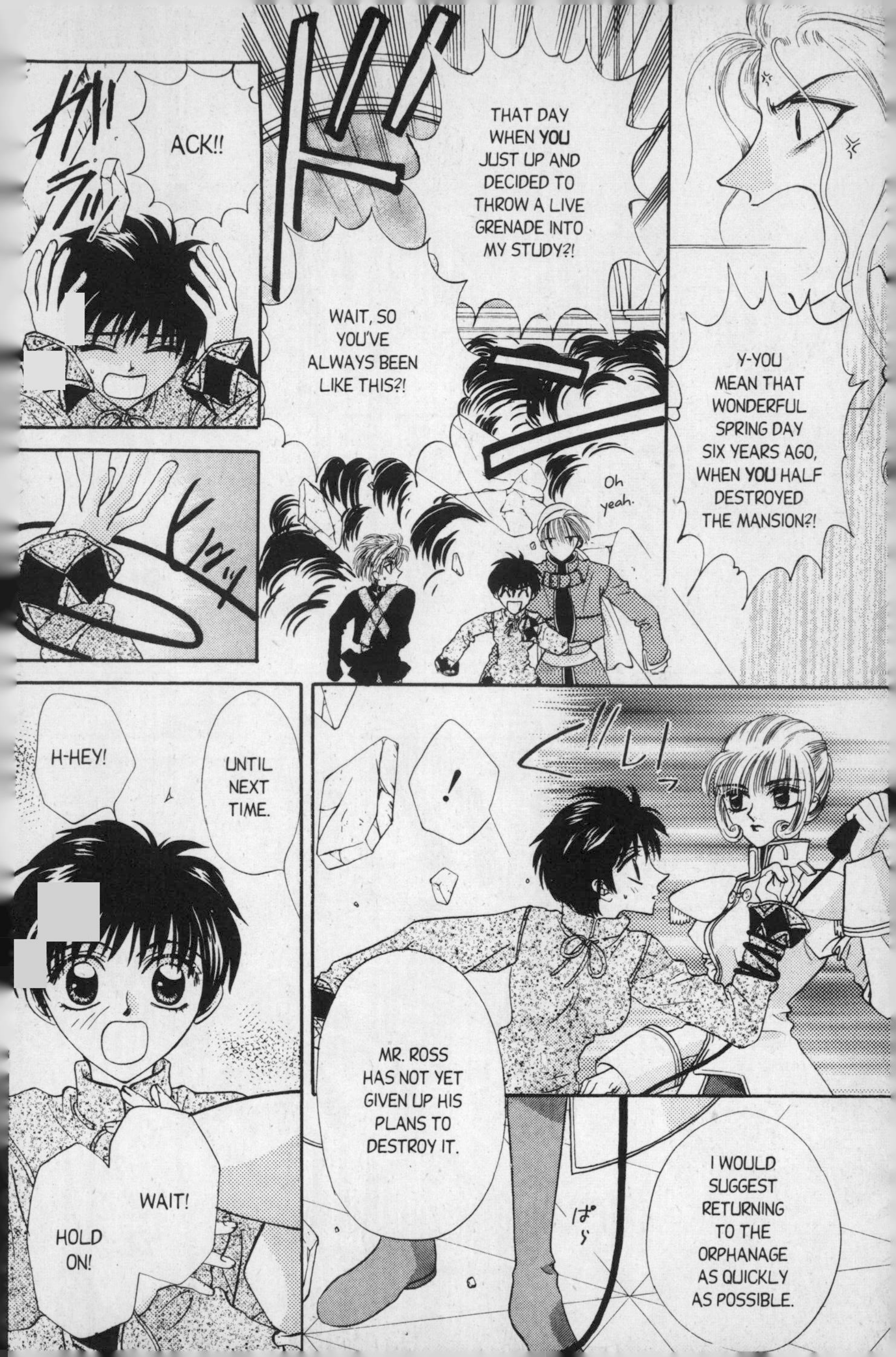
Y-YOU MEAN THAT WONDERFUL SPRING DAY SIX YEARS AGO, WHEN YOU HALF DESTROYED THE MANSION?!
THAT DAY WHEN YOU JUST UP AND DECIDED TO THROW A LIVE GRENADE INTO MY STUDY?!
WAIT, SO YOU'VE ALWAYS BEEN LIKE THIS?!
Oh yeah.
ACK!!
!
MR. ROSS HAS NOT YET GIVEN UP HIS PLANS TO DESTROY IT.
I WOULD SUGGEST RETURNING TO THE ORPHANAGE AS QUICKLY AS POSSIBLE.
UNTIL NEXT TIME.
H-HEY!
WAIT!
HOLD ON!

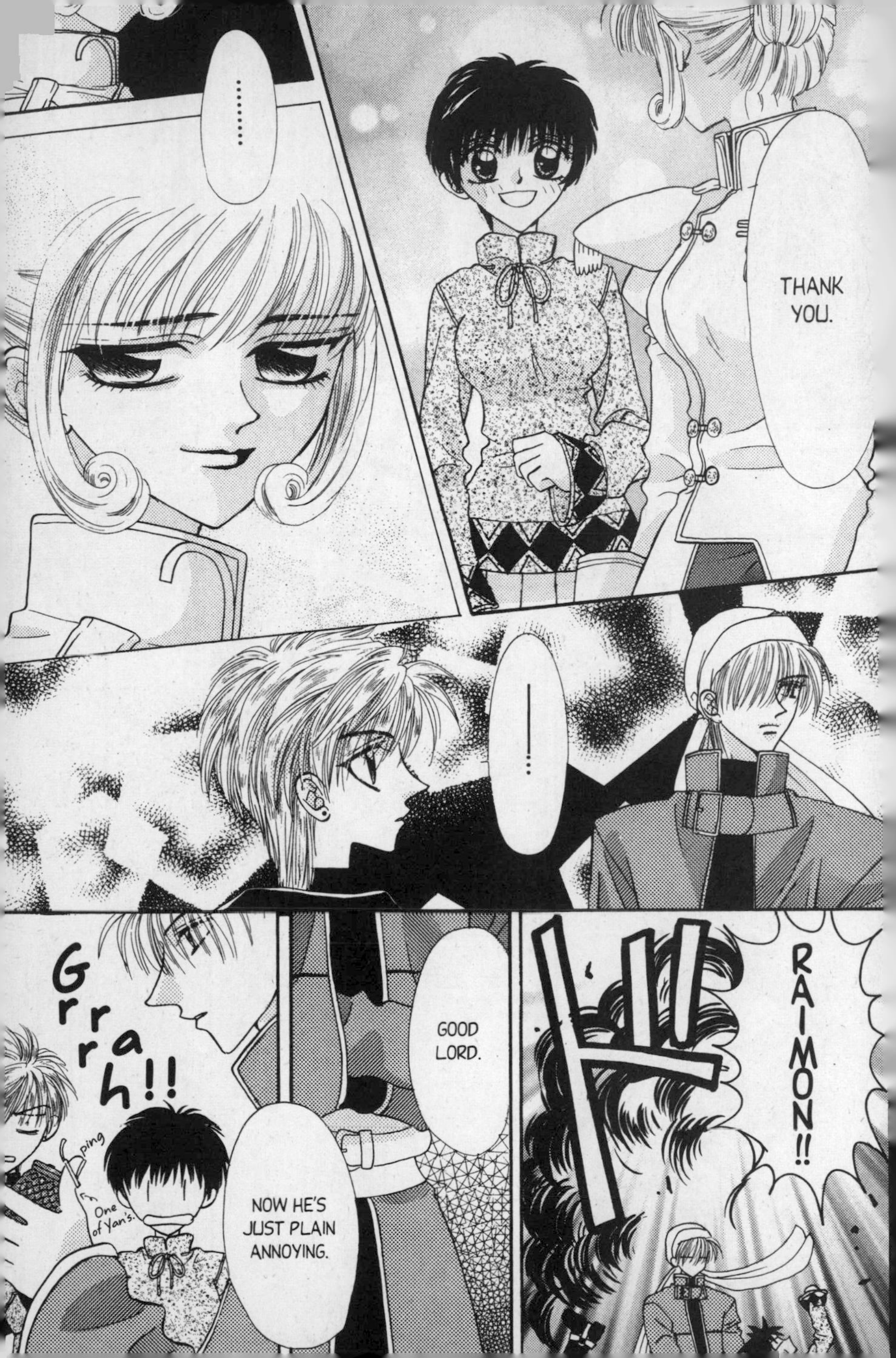

THANK YOU.
......
RAIMON!!
GOOD LORD.
NOW HE'S JUST PLAIN ANNOYING.
Grrrah!!
ping
One of Yan's.

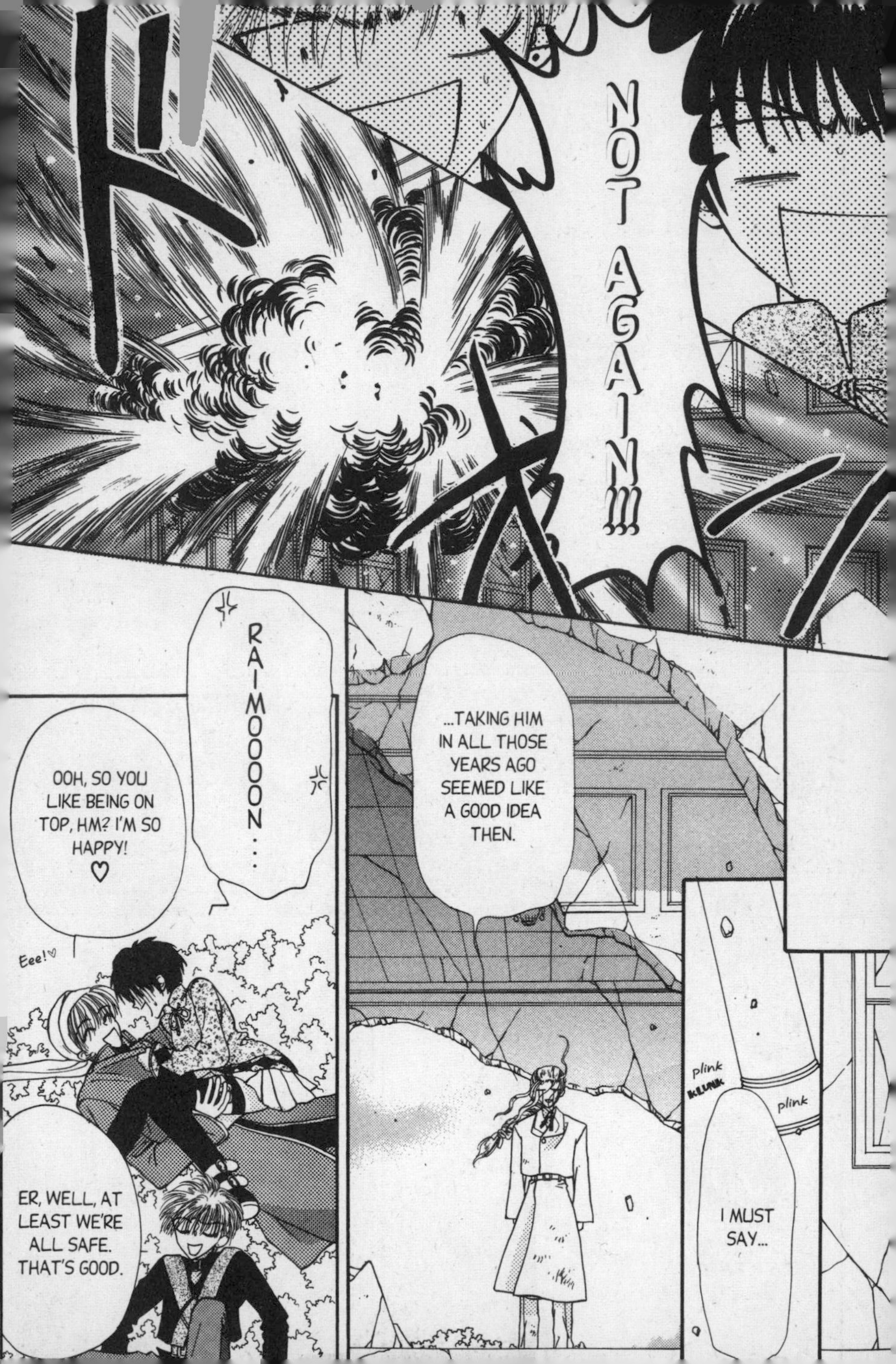
NOT AGAIN!!!
plink
KLUNK
plink
I MUST SAY...
...TAKING HIM IN ALL THOSE YEARS AGO SEEMED LIKE A GOOD IDEA THEN.
RAIMOOOOON...
OOH, SO YOU LIKE BEING ON TOP, HM? I'M SO HAPPY! ♡
Eee!♡
ER, WELL, AT LEAST WE'RE ALL SAFE. THAT'S GOOD.

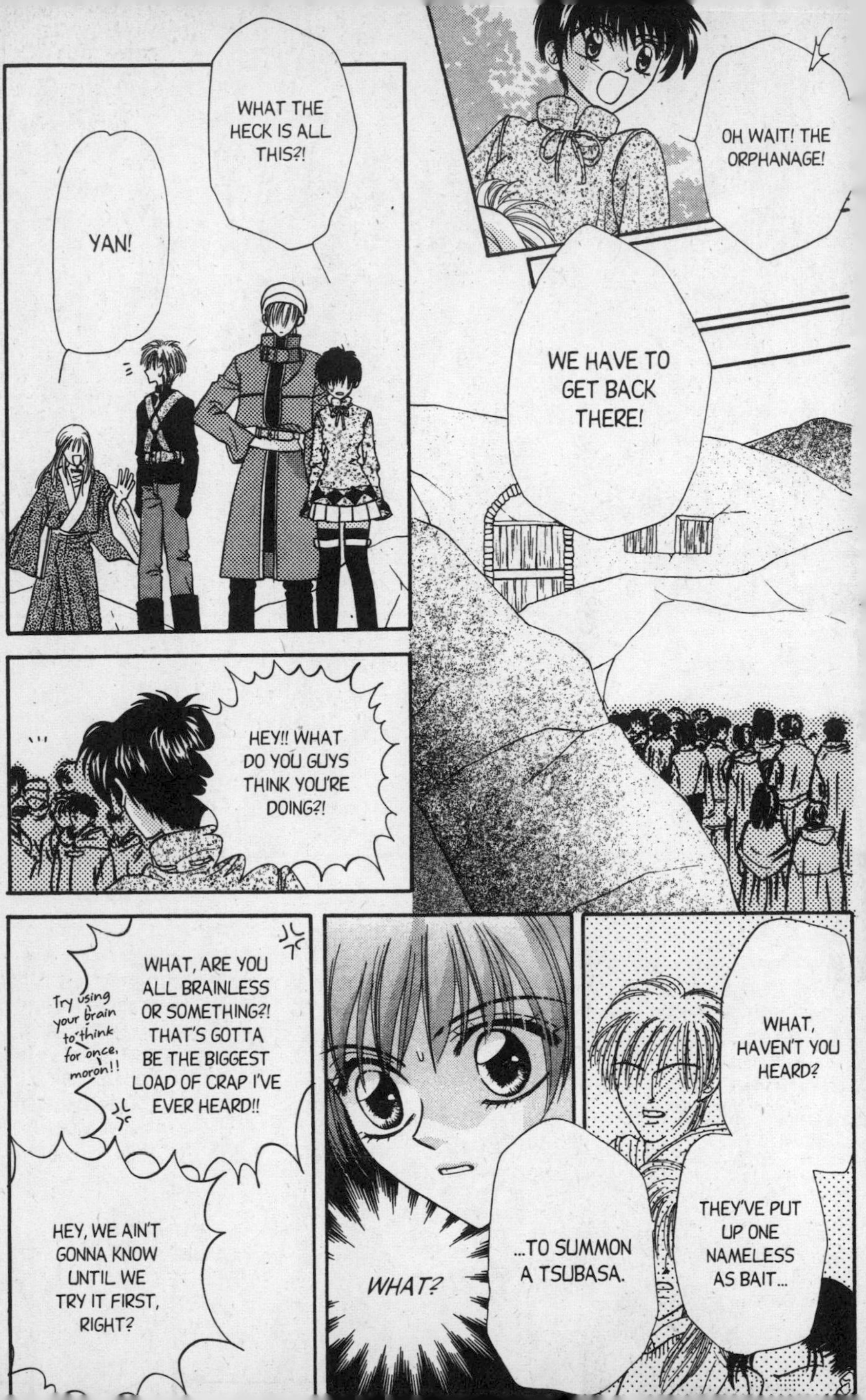

OH WAIT! THE ORPHANAGE!
WE HAVE TO GET BACK THERE!
WHAT THE HECK IS ALL THIS?!
YAN!
HEY!! WHAT DO YOU GUYS THINK YOU'RE DOING?!
WHAT, HAVEN'T YOU HEARD?
THEY'VE PUT UP ONE NAMELESS AS BAIT...
...TO SUMMON A TSUBASA.
WHAT?
WHAT, ARE YOU ALL BRAINLESS OR SOMETHING?! THAT'S GOTTA BE THE BIGGEST LOAD OF CRAP I'VE EVER HEARD!!
Try using your brain to think for once, moron!!
HEY, WE AIN'T GONNA KNOW UNTIL WE TRY IT FIRST, RIGHT?

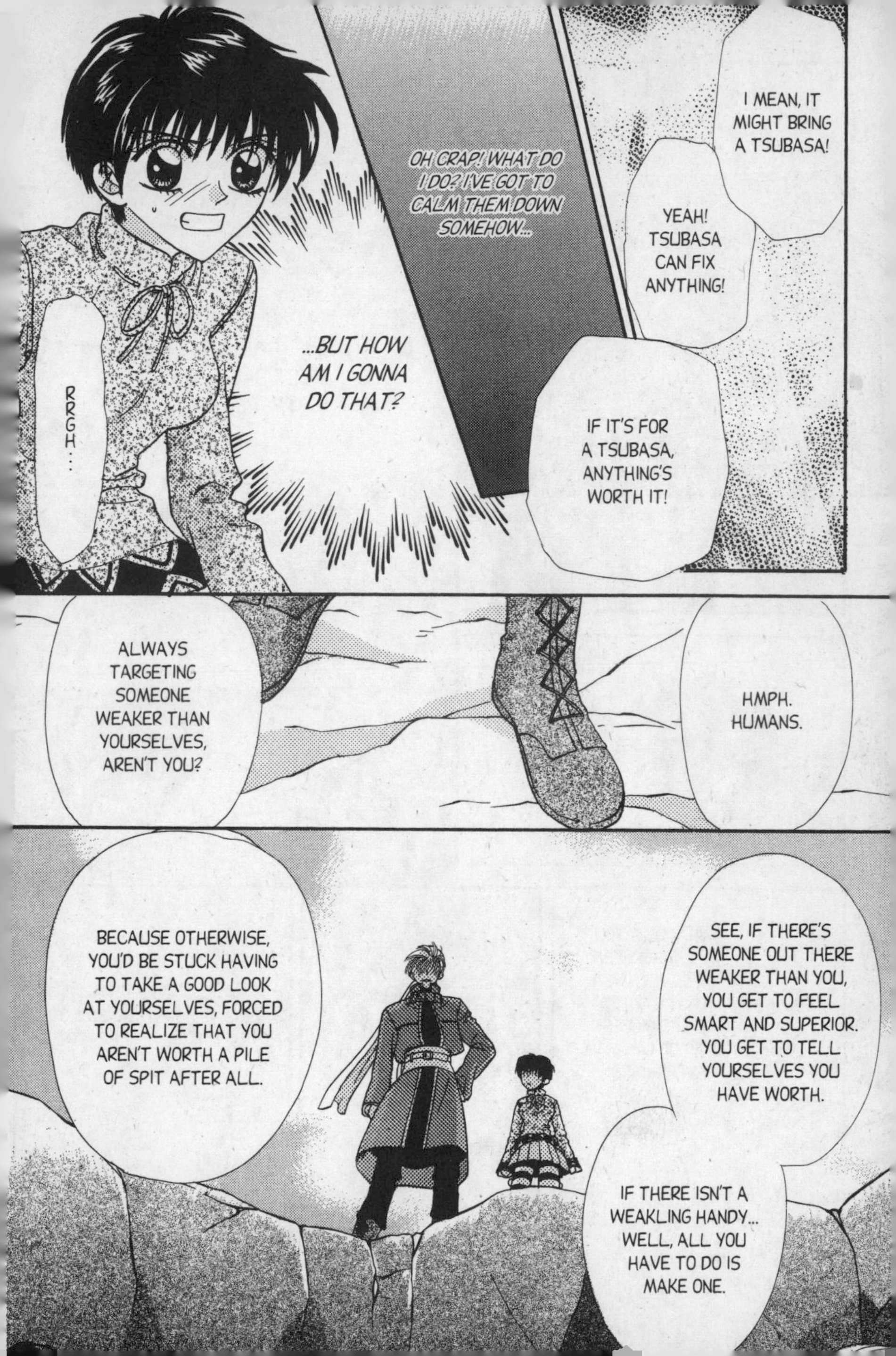
I MEAN, IT MIGHT BRING A TSUBASA!
YEAH! TSUBASA CAN FIX ANYTHING!
IF IT'S FOR A TSUBASA, ANYTHING'S WORTH IT!
OH CRAP! WHAT DO I DO? I'VE GOT TO CALM THEM DOWN SOMEHOW...
...BUT HOW AM I GONNA DO THAT?
RRGH...
HMPH. HUMANS.
ALWAYS TARGETING SOMEONE WEAKER THAN YOURSELVES, AREN'T YOU?
SEE, IF THERE'S SOMEONE OUT THERE WEAKER THAN YOU, YOU GET TO FEEL SMART AND SUPERIOR. YOU GET TO TELL YOURSELVES YOU HAVE WORTH.
IF THERE ISN'T A WEAKLING HANDY... WELL, ALL YOU HAVE TO DO IS MAKE ONE.
BECAUSE OTHERWISE, YOU'D BE STUCK HAVING TO TAKE A GOOD LOOK AT YOURSELVES, FORCED TO REALIZE THAT YOU AREN'T WORTH A PILE OF SPIT AFTER ALL.

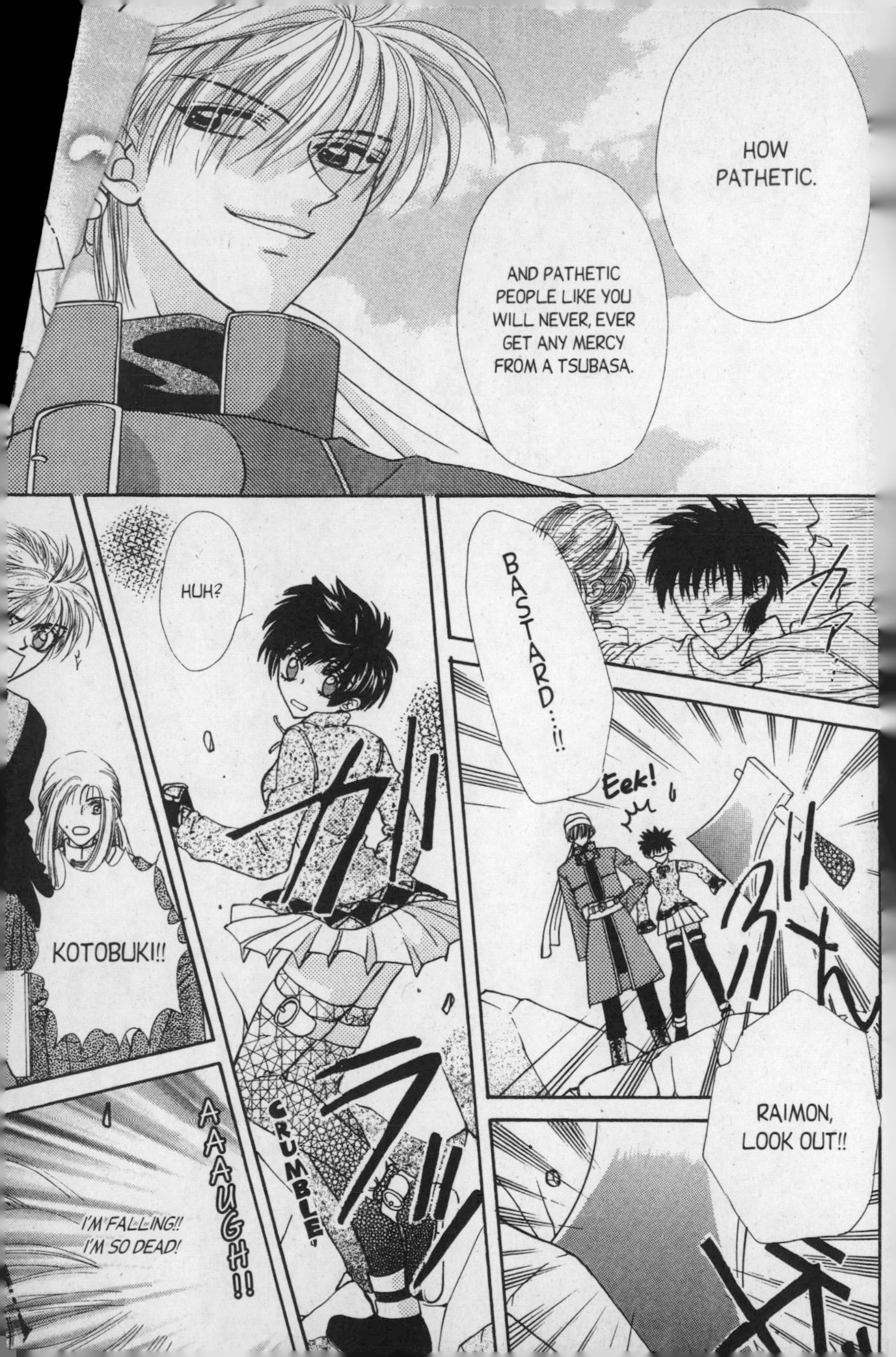
HOW PATHETIC.
AND PATHETIC PEOPLE LIKE YOU WILL NEVER, EVER GET ANY MERCY FROM A TSUBASA.
BASTARD...!!
Eek!
RAIMON, LOOK OUT!!
HUH?
CRUMBLE
AAAUGH!!
KOTOBUKI!!
I'M FALLING!! I'M SO DEAD!

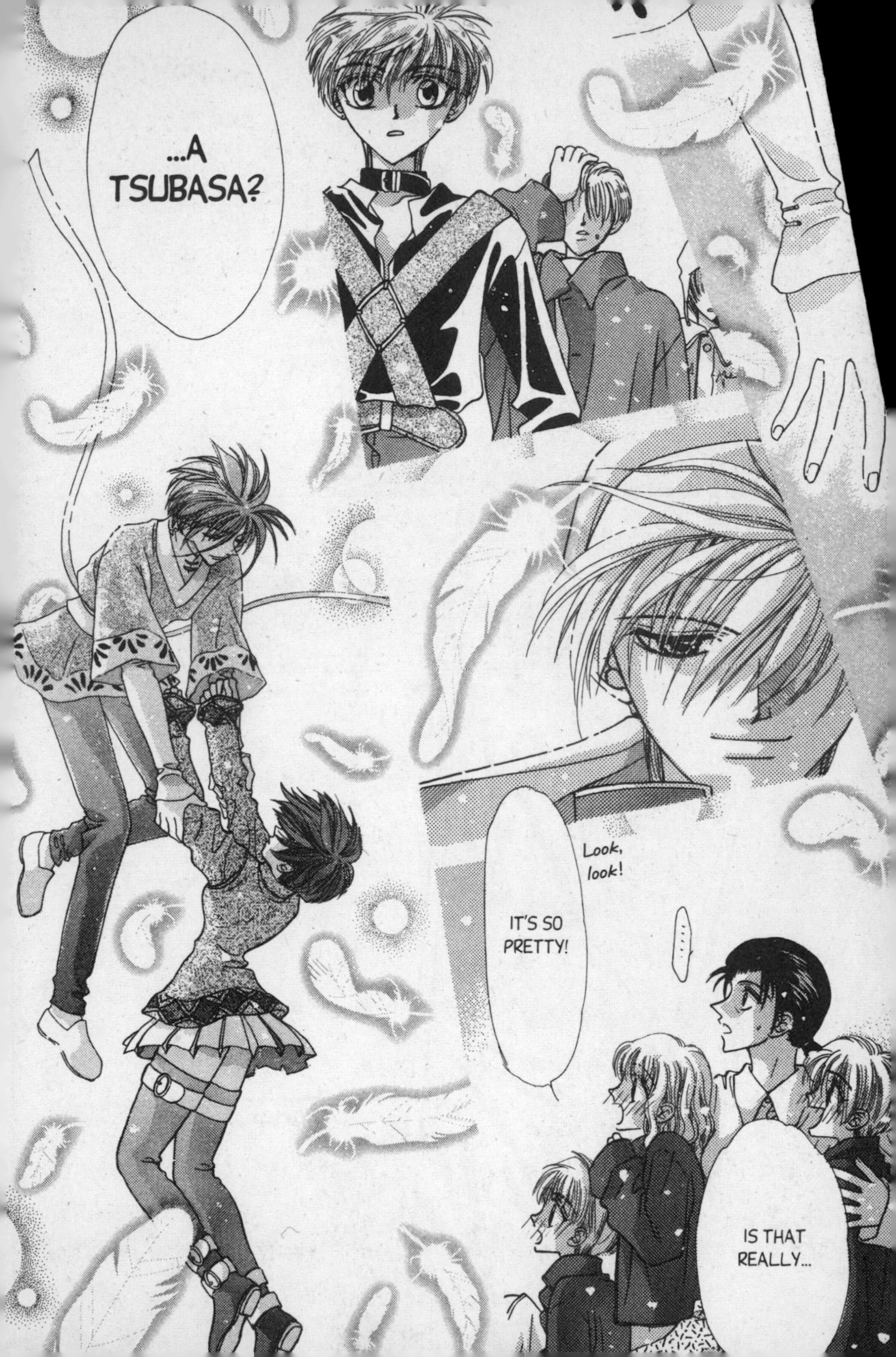

...A TSUBASA?
Look, look!
IT'S SO PRETTY!
......
IS THAT REALLY...

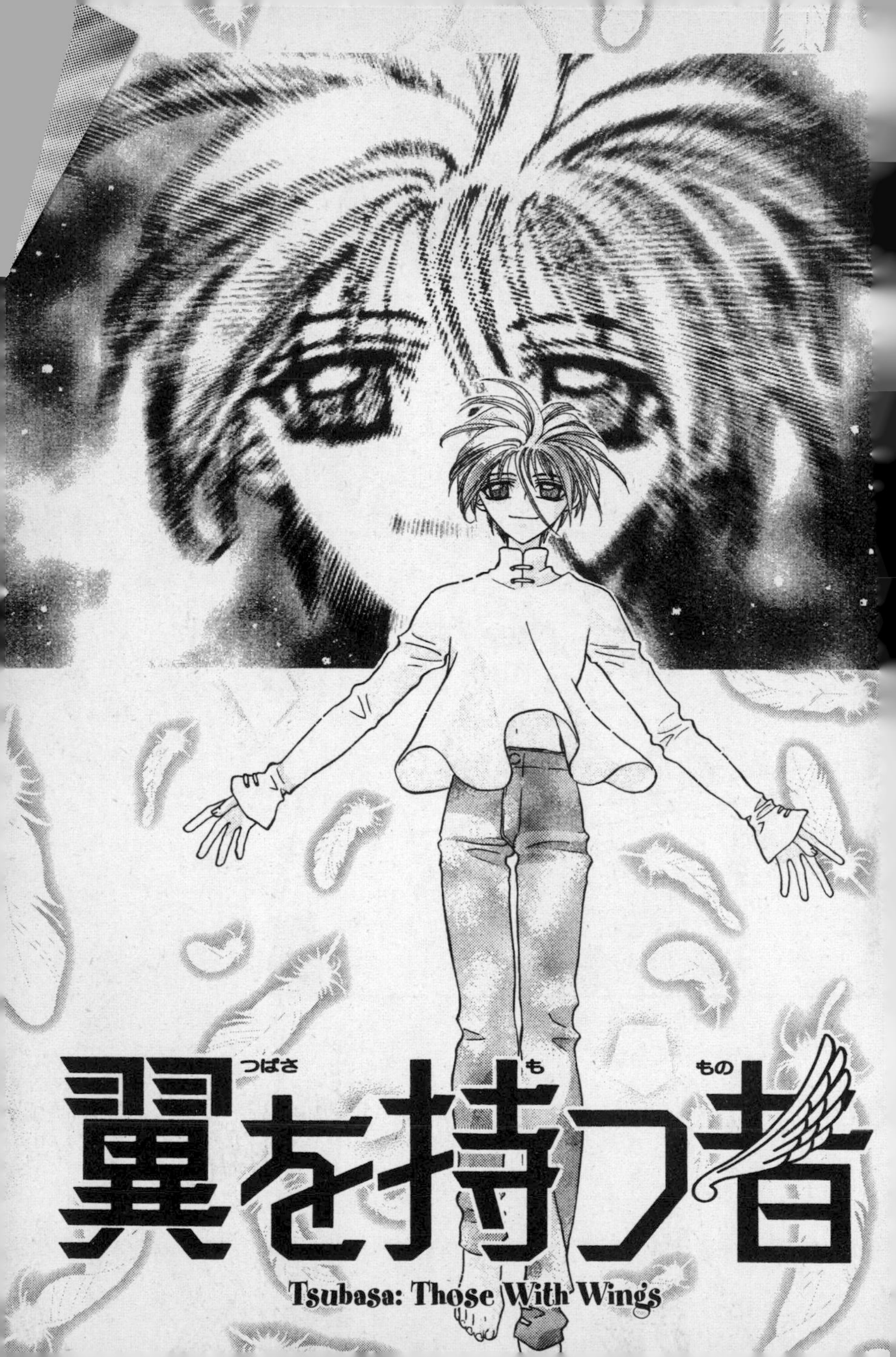
翼(つばさ)を持(も)つ者(もの)
Tsubasa: Those With Wings

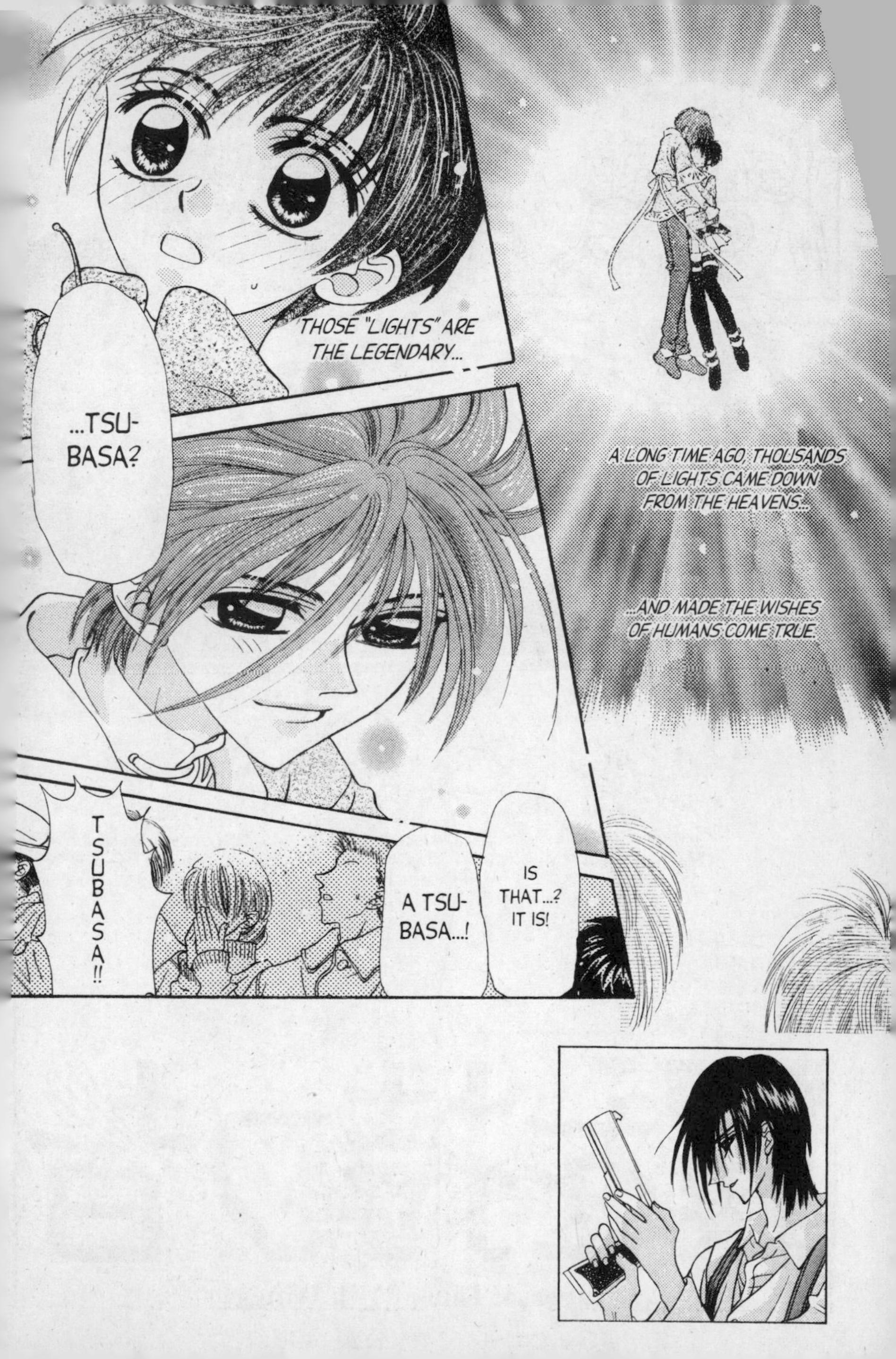
A LONG TIME AGO, THOUSANDS OF LIGHTS CAME DOWN FROM THE HEAVENS...
...AND MADE THE WISHES OF HUMANS COME TRUE.
THOSE "LIGHTS" ARE THE LEGENDARY...
...TSU-BASA?
IS THAT...? IT IS!
A TSU-BASA...!
TSUBASA!!

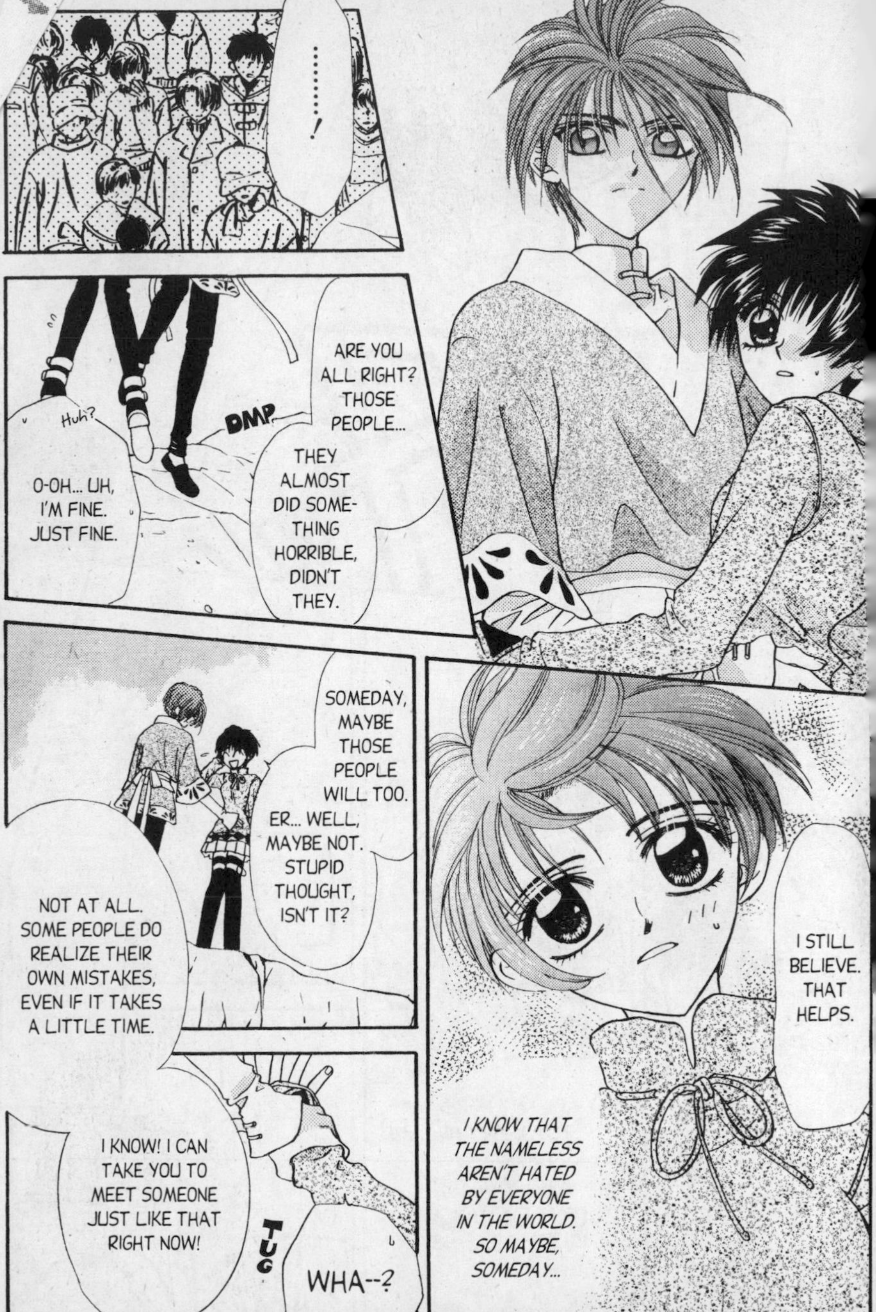
......!
ARE YOU ALL RIGHT? THOSE PEOPLE...
THEY ALMOST DID SOME-THING HORRIBLE, DIDN'T THEY.
DMP
Huh?
O-OH... UH, I'M FINE. JUST FINE.
I STILL BELIEVE. THAT HELPS.
I KNOW THAT THE NAMELESS AREN'T HATED BY EVERYONE IN THE WORLD. SO MAYBE, SOMEDAY...
SOMEDAY, MAYBE THOSE PEOPLE WILL TOO.
ER... WELL, MAYBE NOT. STUPID THOUGHT, ISN'T IT?
NOT AT ALL. SOME PEOPLE DO REALIZE THEIR OWN MISTAKES, EVEN IF IT TAKES A LITTLE TIME.
I KNOW! I CAN TAKE YOU TO MEET SOMEONE JUST LIKE THAT RIGHT NOW!
TUG
WHA--?

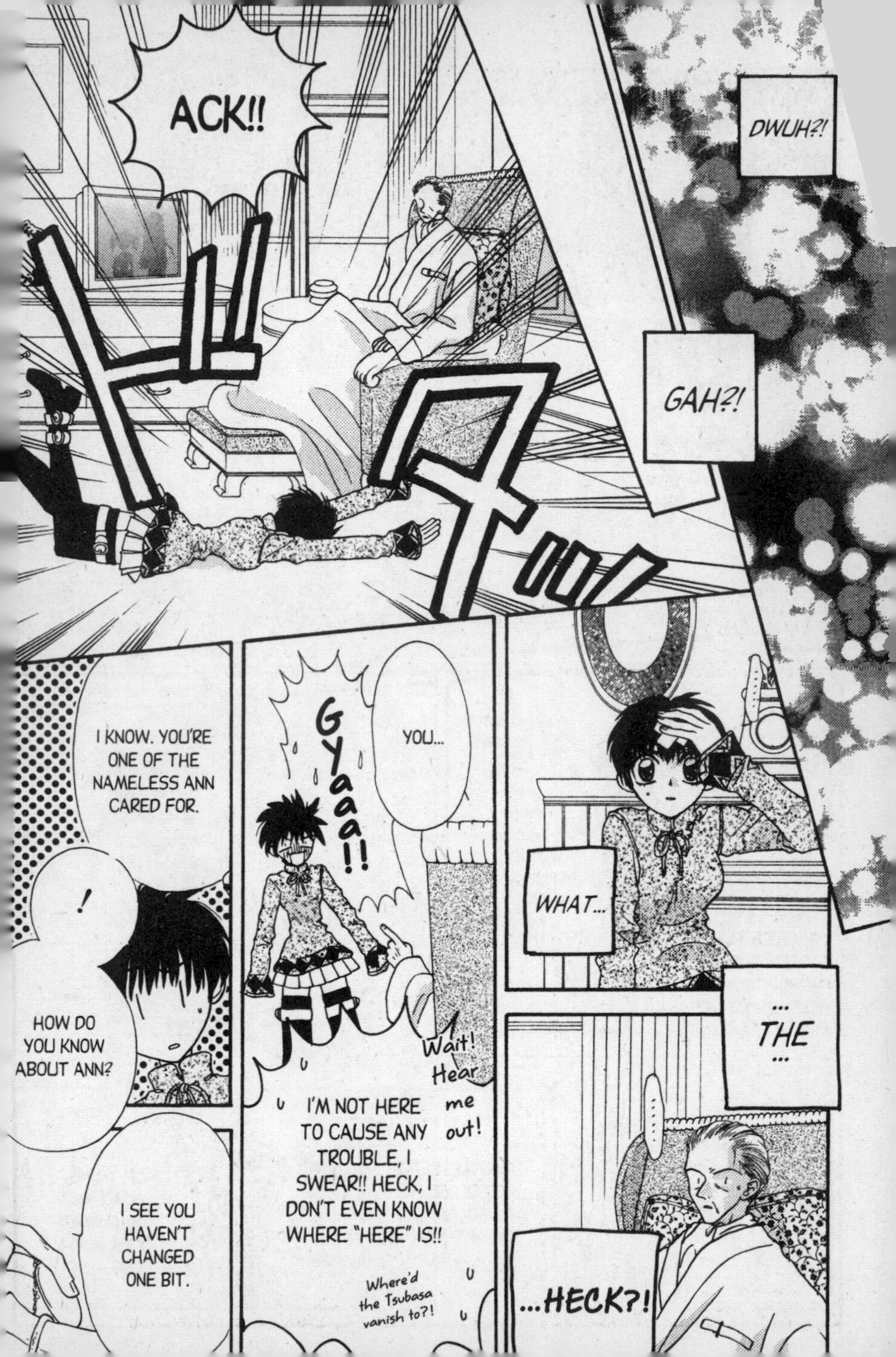
DWUH?!
GAH?!
ACK!!
WHAT...
...THE...
...HECK?!
YOU...
GYaaa!!
Wait! Hear me out!
I'M NOT HERE TO CAUSE ANY TROUBLE, I SWEAR!! HECK, I DON'T EVEN KNOW WHERE "HERE" IS!!
Where'd the Tsubasa vanish to?!
I KNOW. YOU'RE ONE OF THE NAMELESS ANN CARED FOR.
!
HOW DO YOU KNOW ABOUT ANN?
I SEE YOU HAVEN'T CHANGED ONE BIT.

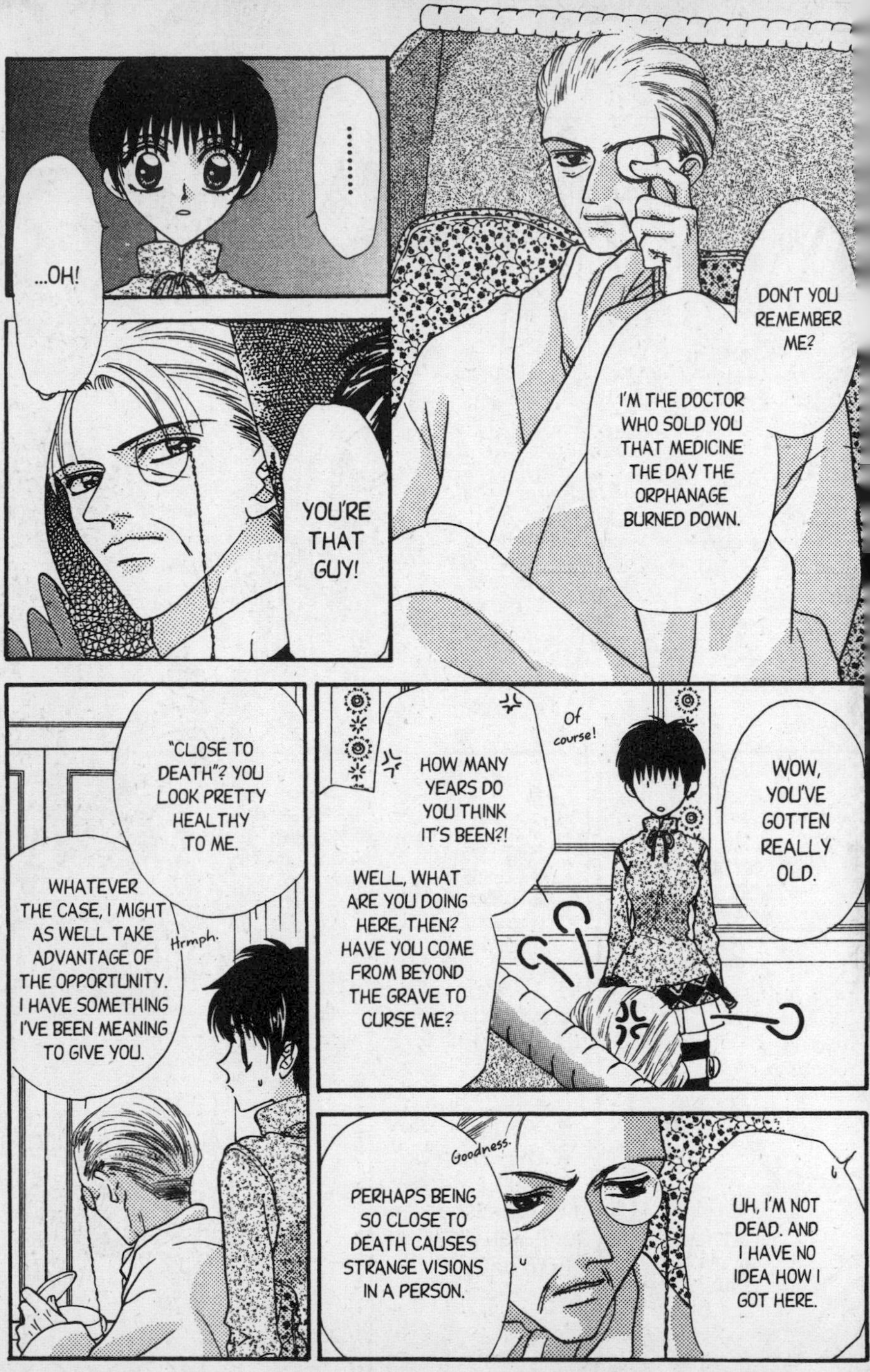
DON'T YOU REMEMBER ME?
I'M THE DOCTOR WHO SOLD YOU THAT MEDICINE THE DAY THE ORPHANAGE BURNED DOWN.
......
...OH!
YOU'RE THAT GUY!
WOW, YOU'VE GOTTEN REALLY OLD.
Of course!
HOW MANY YEARS DO YOU THINK IT'S BEEN?!
WELL, WHAT ARE YOU DOING HERE, THEN? HAVE YOU COME FROM BEYOND THE GRAVE TO CURSE ME?
UH, I'M NOT DEAD. AND I HAVE NO IDEA HOW I GOT HERE.
Goodness.
PERHAPS BEING SO CLOSE TO DEATH CAUSES STRANGE VISIONS IN A PERSON.
"CLOSE TO DEATH"? YOU LOOK PRETTY HEALTHY TO ME.
Hrmph.
WHATEVER THE CASE, I MIGHT AS WELL TAKE ADVANTAGE OF THE OPPORTUNITY. I HAVE SOMETHING I'VE BEEN MEANING TO GIVE YOU.

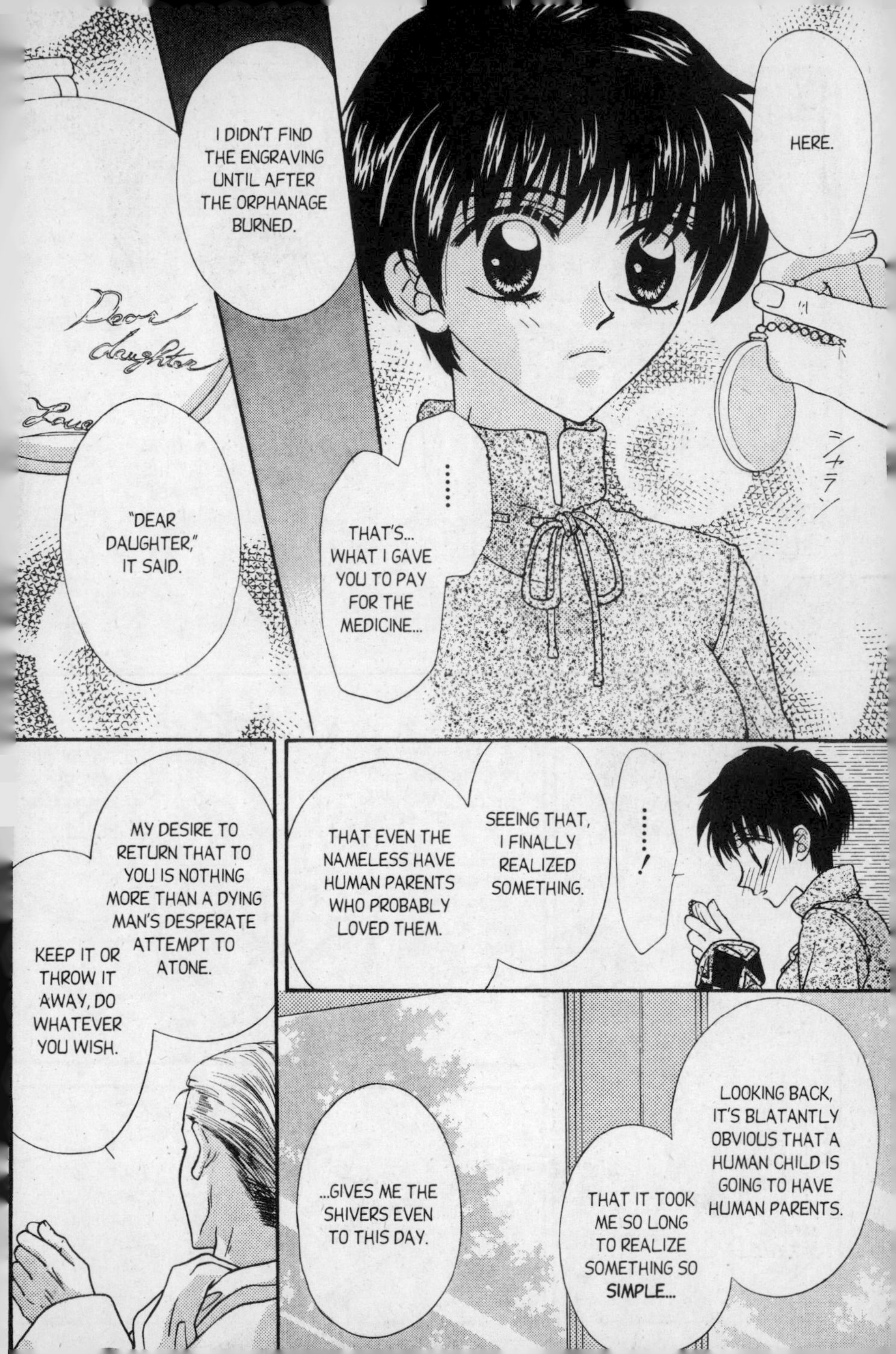
HERE.
......
THAT'S... WHAT I GAVE YOU TO PAY FOR THE MEDICINE...
I DIDN'T FIND THE ENGRAVING UNTIL AFTER THE ORPHANAGE BURNED.
Dear daughter
"DEAR DAUGHTER," IT SAID.
......!
SEEING THAT, I FINALLY REALIZED SOMETHING.
THAT EVEN THE NAMELESS HAVE HUMAN PARENTS WHO PROBABLY LOVED THEM.
LOOKING BACK, IT'S BLATANTLY OBVIOUS THAT A HUMAN CHILD IS GOING TO HAVE HUMAN PARENTS.
THAT IT TOOK ME SO LONG TO REALIZE SOMETHING SO SIMPLE...
...GIVES ME THE SHIVERS EVEN TO THIS DAY.
MY DESIRE TO RETURN THAT TO YOU IS NOTHING MORE THAN A DYING MAN'S DESPERATE ATTEMPT TO ATONE.
KEEP IT OR THROW IT AWAY, DO WHATEVER YOU WISH.

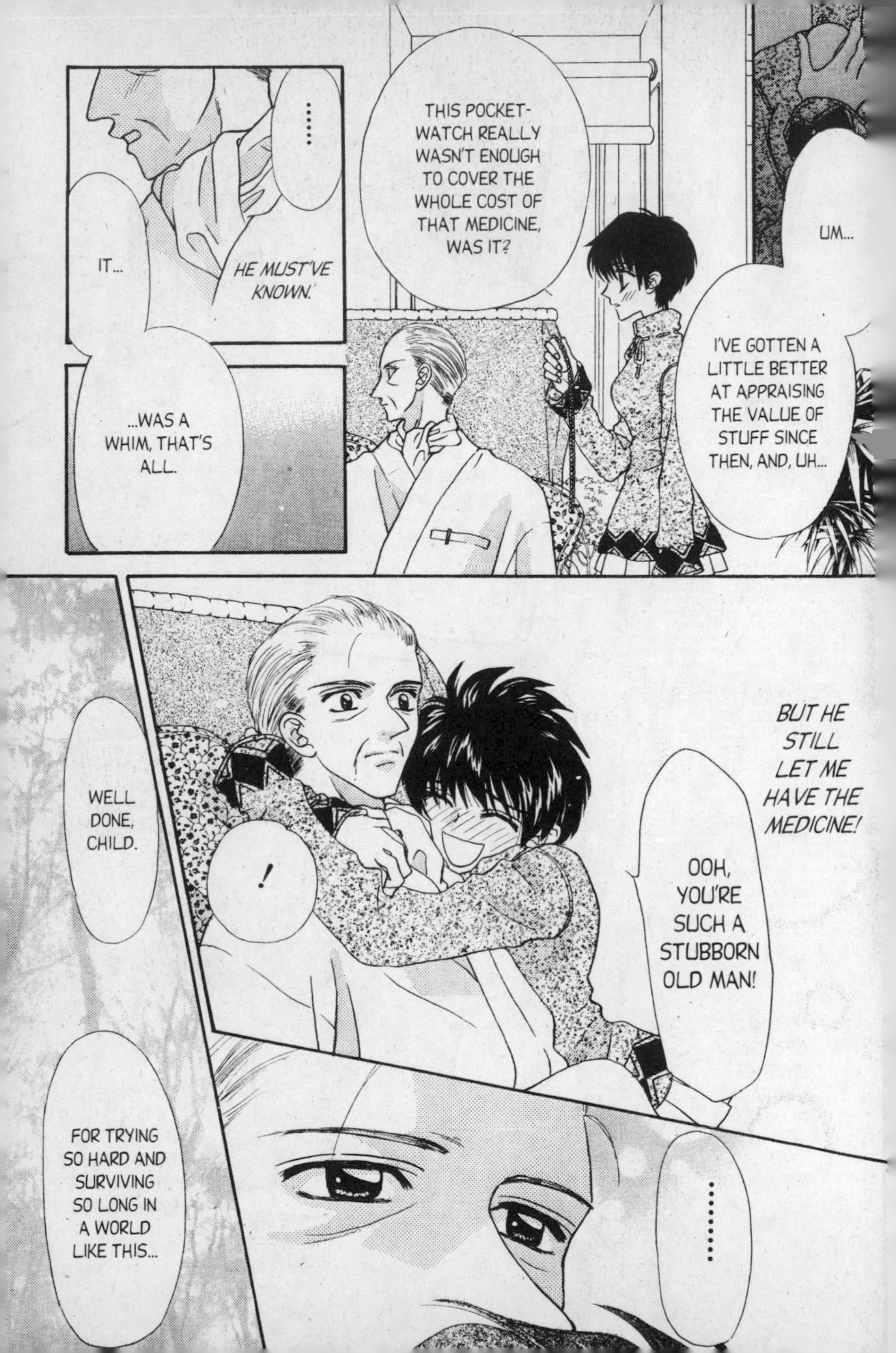
UM...
I'VE GOTTEN A LITTLE BETTER AT APPRAISING THE VALUE OF STUFF SINCE THEN, AND, UH...
THIS POCKET-WATCH REALLY WASN'T ENOUGH TO COVER THE WHOLE COST OF THAT MEDICINE, WAS IT?
......
HE MUST'VE KNOWN.
IT...
...WAS A WHIM, THAT'S ALL.
BUT HE STILL LET ME HAVE THE MEDICINE!
OOH, YOU'RE SUCH A STUBBORN OLD MAN!
!
WELL DONE, CHILD.
......
FOR TRYING SO HARD AND SURVIVING SO LONG IN A WORLD LIKE THIS...

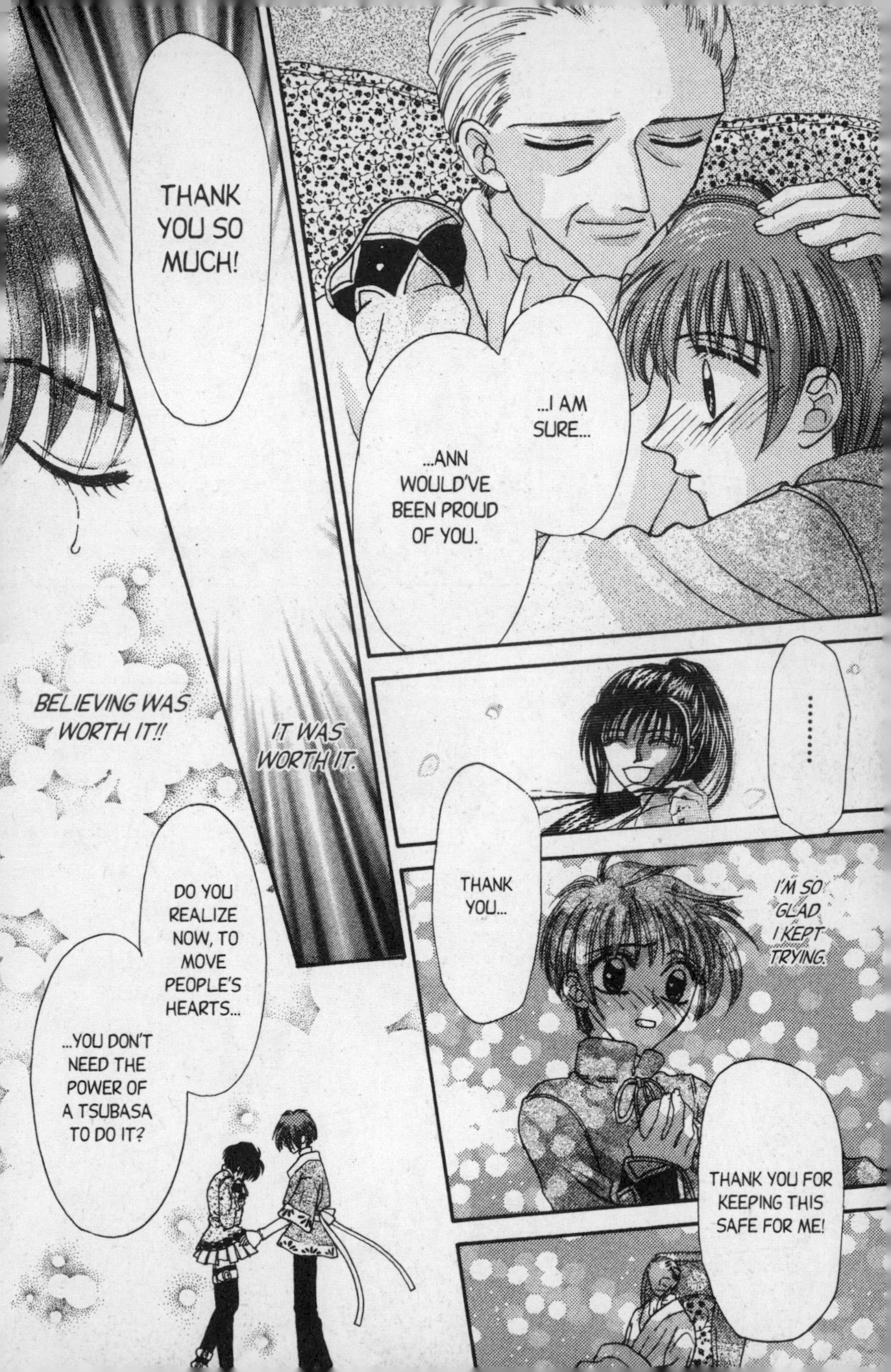
...I AM SURE...
...ANN WOULD'VE BEEN PROUD OF YOU.
THANK YOU SO MUCH!
......
THANK YOU...
I'M SO GLAD I KEPT TRYING.
IT WAS WORTH IT.
BELIEVING WAS WORTH IT!!
THANK YOU FOR KEEPING THIS SAFE FOR ME!
DO YOU REALIZE NOW, TO MOVE PEOPLE'S HEARTS...
...YOU DON'T NEED THE POWER OF A TSUBASA TO DO IT?

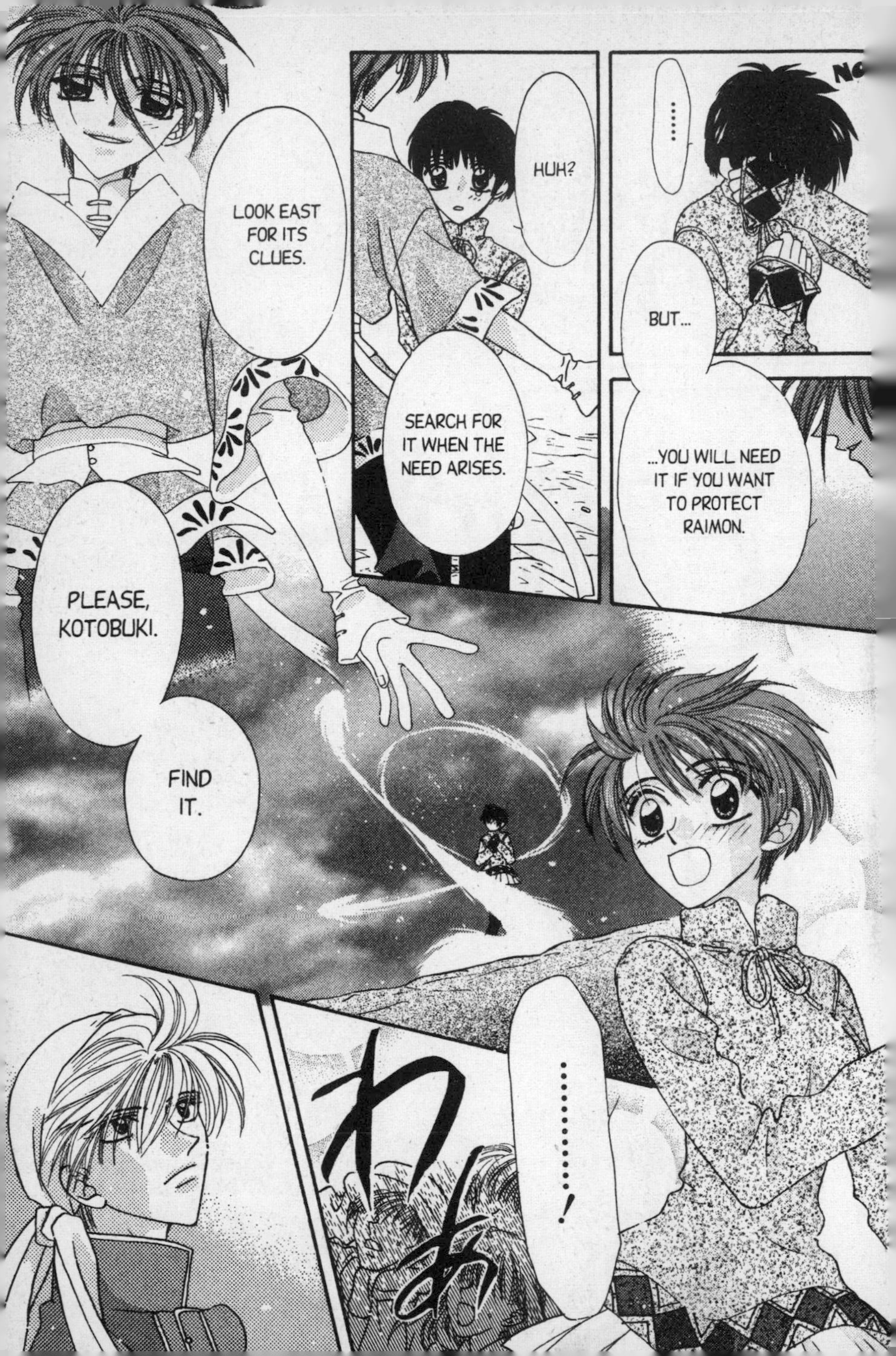
......
BUT...
...YOU WILL NEED IT IF YOU WANT TO PROTECT RAIMON.
HUH?
SEARCH FOR IT WHEN THE NEED ARISES.
LOOK EAST FOR ITS CLUES.
PLEASE, KOTOBUKI.
FIND IT.
......!
わあ

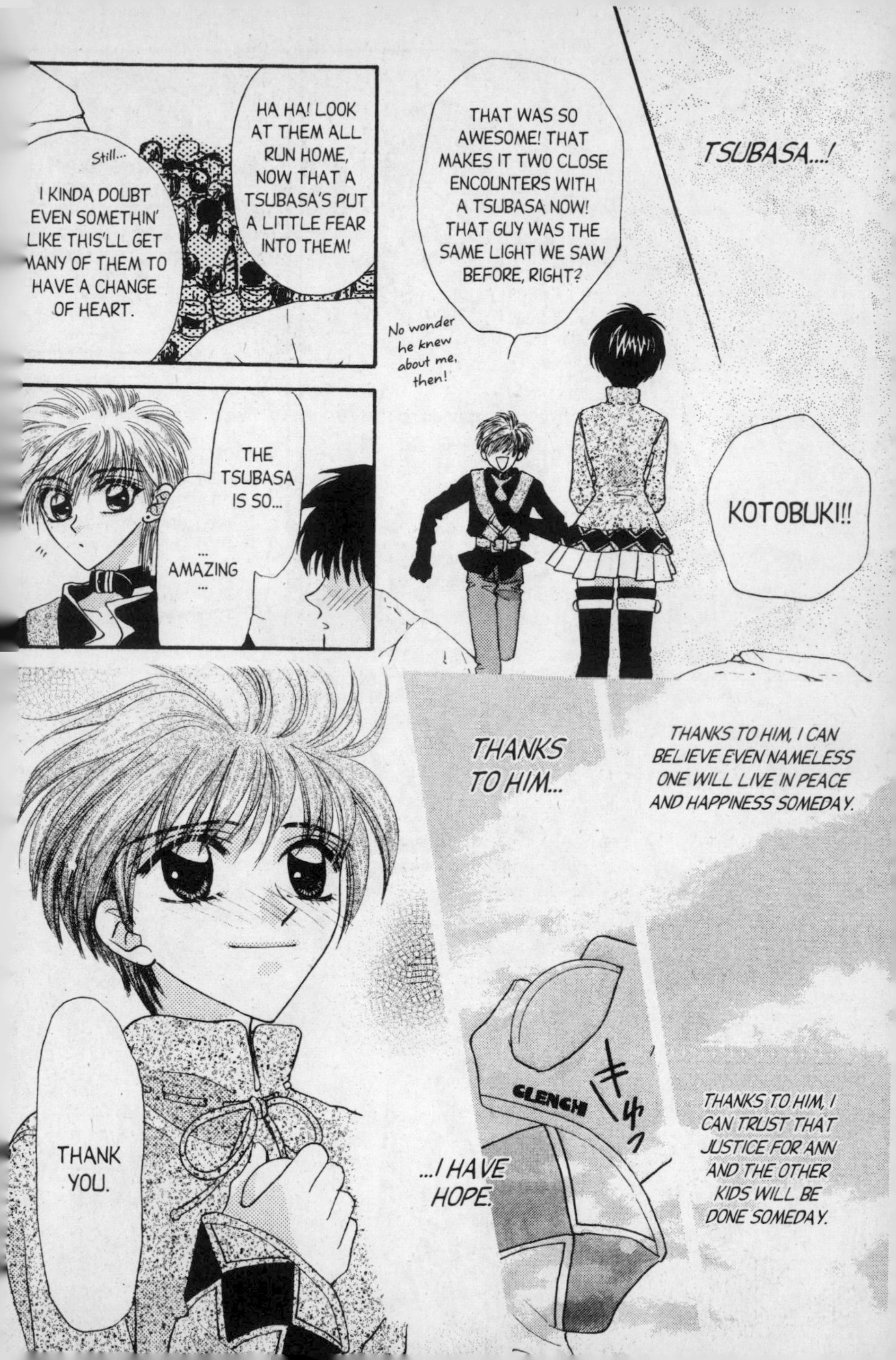
TSUBASA...!
KOTOBUKI!!
THAT WAS SO AWESOME! THAT MAKES IT TWO CLOSE ENCOUNTERS WITH A TSUBASA NOW! THAT GUY WAS THE SAME LIGHT WE SAW BEFORE, RIGHT?
No wonder he knew about me, then!
HA HA! LOOK AT THEM ALL RUN HOME, NOW THAT A TSUBASA'S PUT A LITTLE FEAR INTO THEM!
Still...
I KINDA DOUBT EVEN SOMETHIN' LIKE THIS'LL GET MANY OF THEM TO HAVE A CHANGE OF HEART.
THE TSUBASA IS SO...
...AMAZING...
THANKS TO HIM, I CAN BELIEVE EVEN NAMELESS ONE WILL LIVE IN PEACE AND HAPPINESS SOMEDAY.
THANKS TO HIM...
THANKS TO HIM, I CAN TRUST THAT JUSTICE FOR ANN AND THE OTHER KIDS WILL BE DONE SOMEDAY.
CLENCH
...I HAVE HOPE.
THANK YOU.

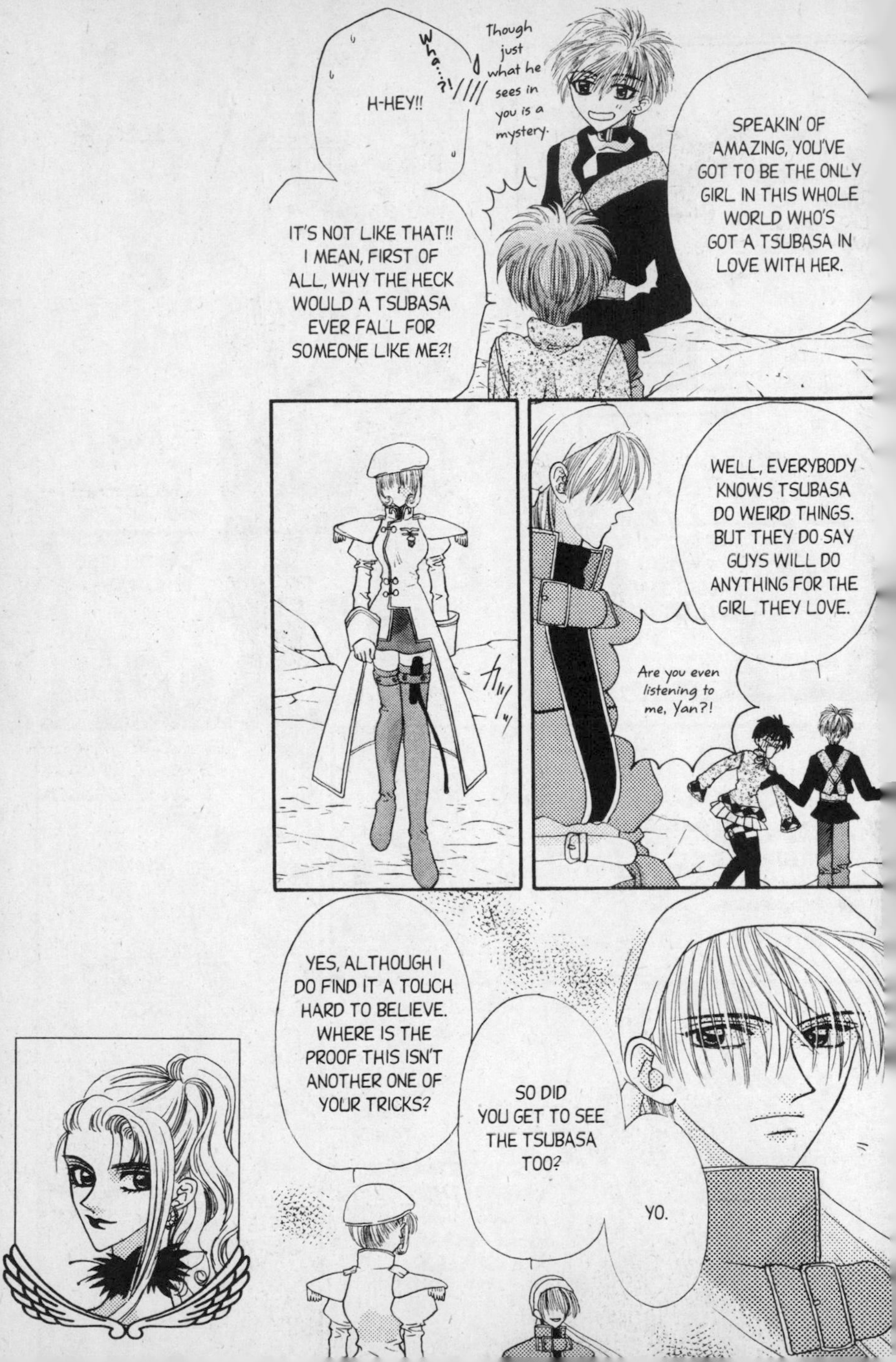
SPEAKIN' OF AMAZING, YOU'VE GOT TO BE THE ONLY GIRL IN THIS WHOLE WORLD WHO'S GOT A TSUBASA IN LOVE WITH HER.
Though just what he sees in you is a mystery.
Wha...?!
H-HEY!!
IT'S NOT LIKE THAT!! I MEAN, FIRST OF ALL, WHY THE HECK WOULD A TSUBASA EVER FALL FOR SOMEONE LIKE ME?!
WELL, EVERYBODY KNOWS TSUBASA DO WEIRD THINGS. BUT THEY DO SAY GUYS WILL DO ANYTHING FOR THE GIRL THEY LOVE.
Are you even listening to me, Yan?!
YO.
SO DID YOU GET TO SEE THE TSUBASA TOO?
YES, ALTHOUGH I DO FIND IT A TOUCH HARD TO BELIEVE. WHERE IS THE PROOF THIS ISN'T ANOTHER ONE OF YOUR TRICKS?

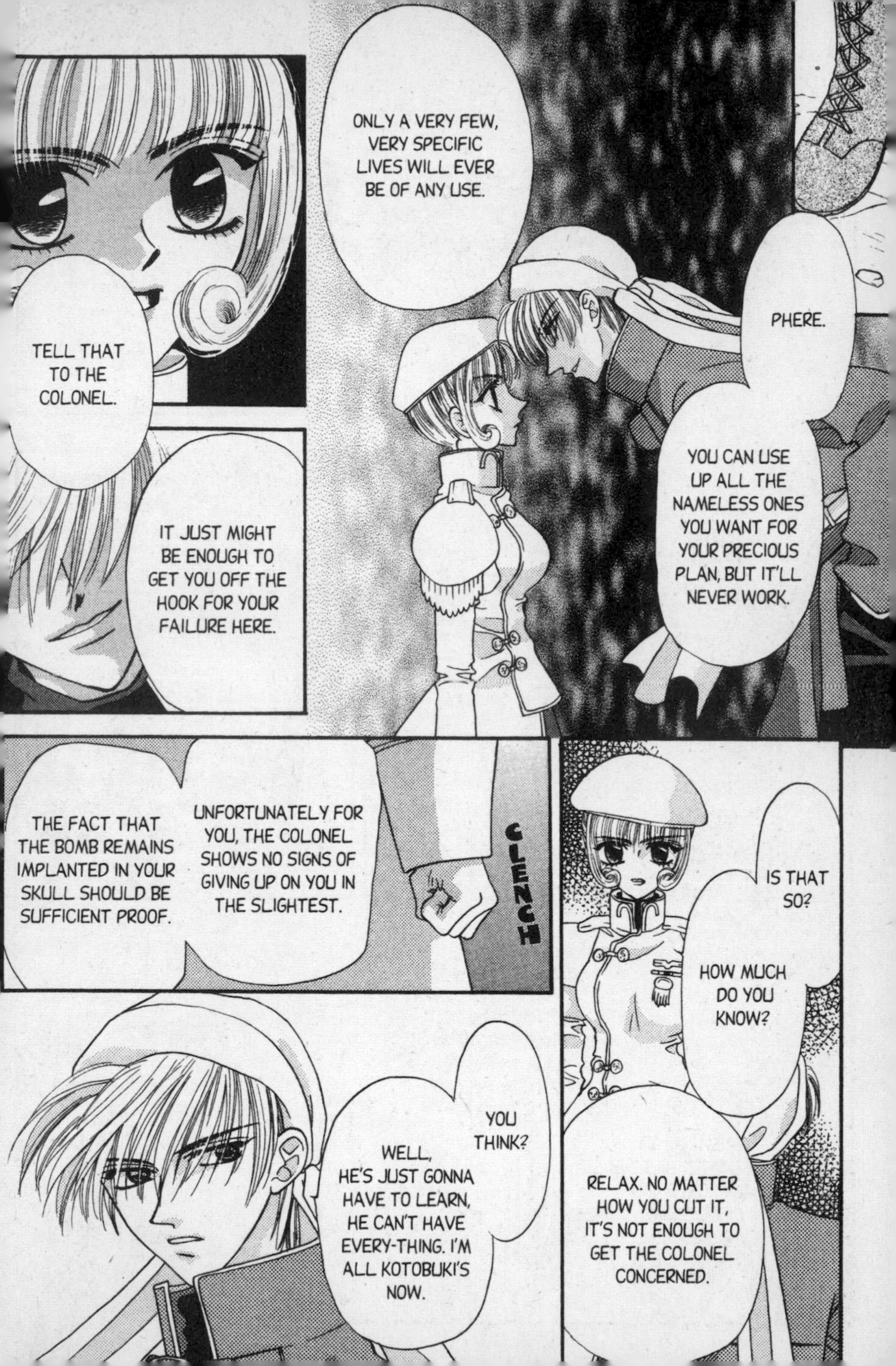
PHERE.
YOU CAN USE UP ALL THE NAMELESS ONES YOU WANT FOR YOUR PRECIOUS PLAN, BUT IT'LL NEVER WORK.
ONLY A VERY FEW, VERY SPECIFIC LIVES WILL EVER BE OF ANY USE.
TELL THAT TO THE COLONEL.
IT JUST MIGHT BE ENOUGH TO GET YOU OFF THE HOOK FOR YOUR FAILURE HERE.
IS THAT SO?
HOW MUCH DO YOU KNOW?
RELAX. NO MATTER HOW YOU CUT IT, IT'S NOT ENOUGH TO GET THE COLONEL CONCERNED.
UNFORTUNATELY FOR YOU, THE COLONEL SHOWS NO SIGNS OF GIVING UP ON YOU IN THE SLIGHTEST.
THE FACT THAT THE BOMB REMAINS IMPLANTED IN YOUR SKULL SHOULD BE SUFFICIENT PROOF.
CLENCH
YOU THINK?
WELL, HE'S JUST GONNA HAVE TO LEARN, HE CAN'T HAVE EVERY-THING. I'M ALL KOTOBUKI'S NOW.

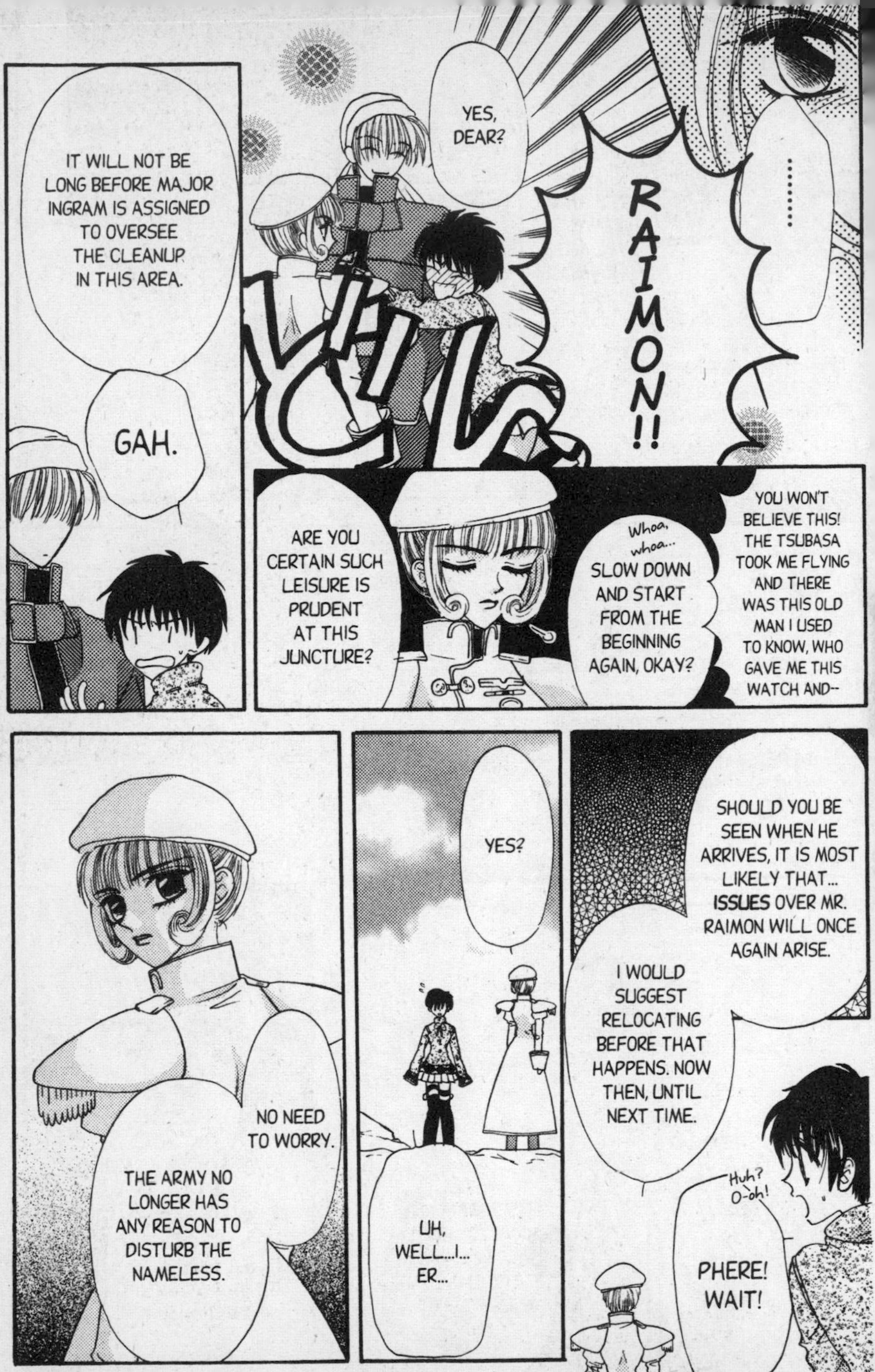
......
RAIMON!!
YES, DEAR?
YOU WON'T BELIEVE THIS! THE TSUBASA TOOK ME FLYING AND THERE WAS THIS OLD MAN I USED TO KNOW, WHO GAVE ME THIS WATCH AND--
Whoa, whoa...
SLOW DOWN AND START FROM THE BEGINNING AGAIN, OKAY?
ARE YOU CERTAIN SUCH LEISURE IS PRUDENT AT THIS JUNCTURE?
IT WILL NOT BE LONG BEFORE MAJOR INGRAM IS ASSIGNED TO OVERSEE THE CLEANUP IN THIS AREA.
GAH.
SHOULD YOU BE SEEN WHEN HE ARRIVES, IT IS MOST LIKELY THAT... ISSUES OVER MR. RAIMON WILL ONCE AGAIN ARISE.
I WOULD SUGGEST RELOCATING BEFORE THAT HAPPENS. NOW THEN, UNTIL NEXT TIME.
Huh? O-oh!
PHERE! WAIT!
YES?
UH, WELL...I... ER...
NO NEED TO WORRY.
THE ARMY NO LONGER HAS ANY REASON TO DISTURB THE NAMELESS.

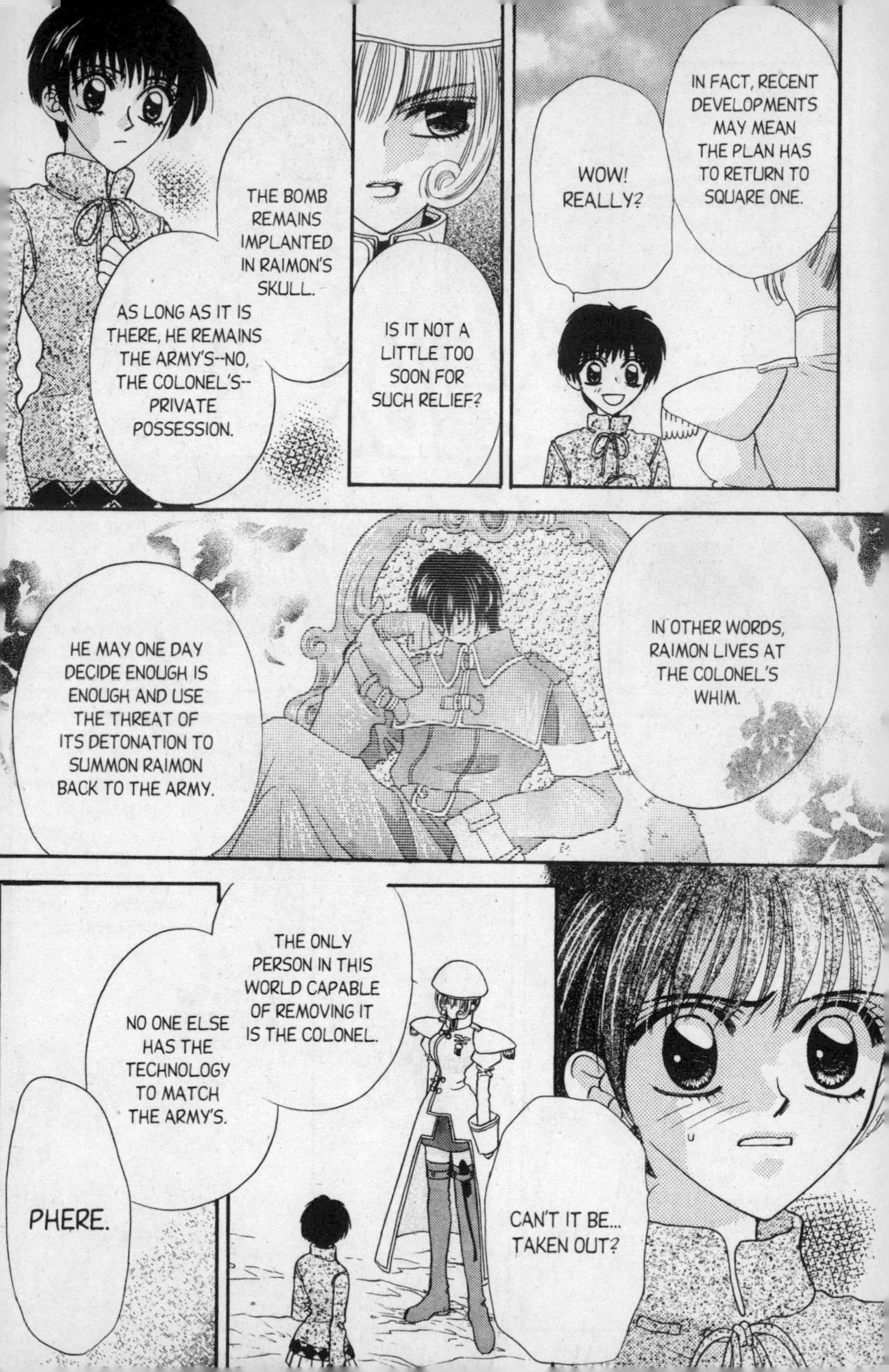
IN FACT, RECENT DEVELOPMENTS MAY MEAN THE PLAN HAS TO RETURN TO SQUARE ONE.
WOW! REALLY?
IS IT NOT A LITTLE TOO SOON FOR SUCH RELIEF?
THE BOMB REMAINS IMPLANTED IN RAIMON'S SKULL.
AS LONG AS IT IS THERE, HE REMAINS THE ARMY'S--NO, THE COLONEL'S--PRIVATE POSSESSION.
IN OTHER WORDS, RAIMON LIVES AT THE COLONEL'S WHIM.
HE MAY ONE DAY DECIDE ENOUGH IS ENOUGH AND USE THE THREAT OF ITS DETONATION TO SUMMON RAIMON BACK TO THE ARMY.
CAN'T IT BE... TAKEN OUT?
THE ONLY PERSON IN THIS WORLD CAPABLE OF REMOVING IT IS THE COLONEL.
NO ONE ELSE HAS THE TECHNOLOGY TO MATCH THE ARMY'S.
PHERE.

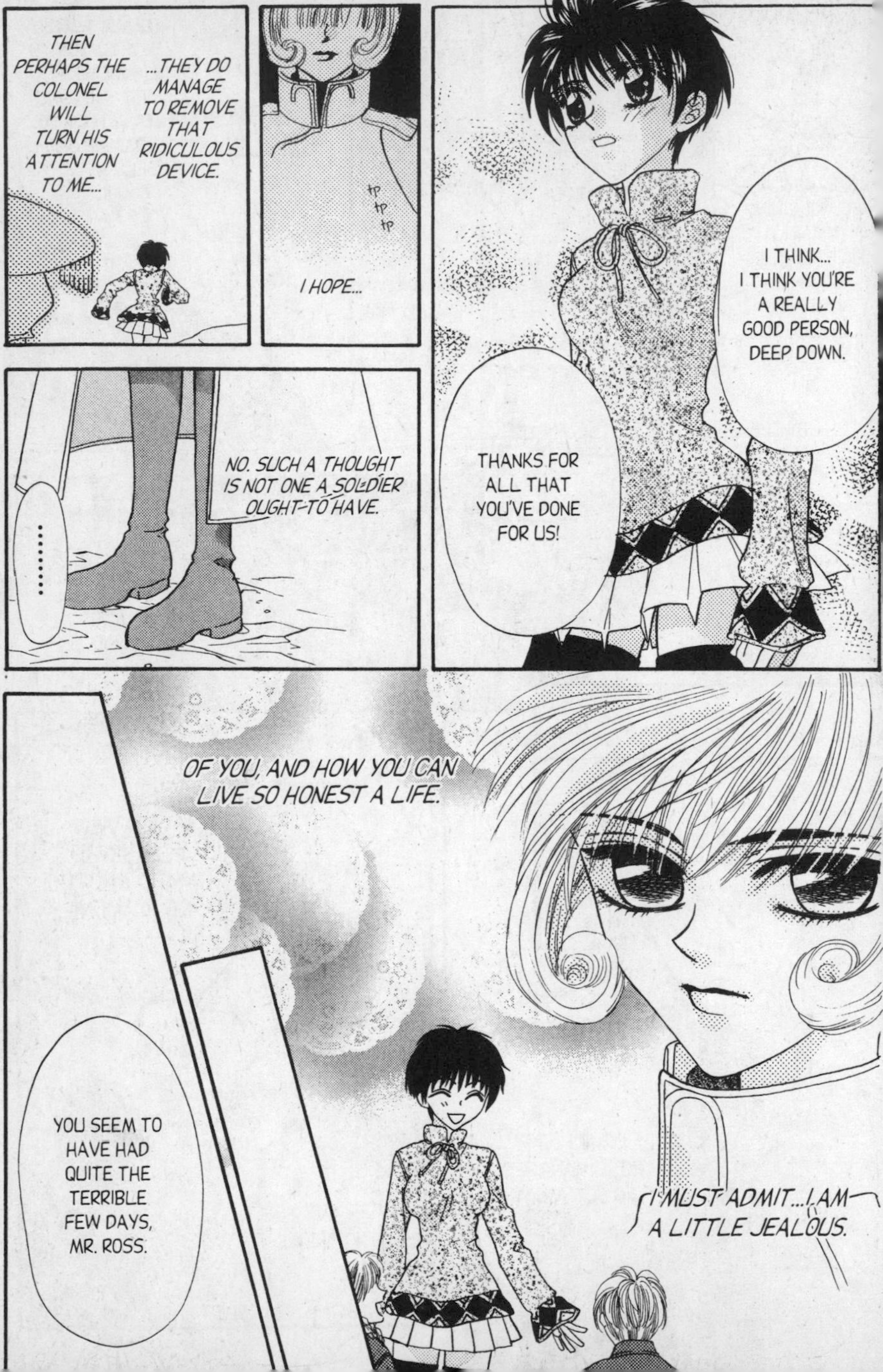
I THINK... I THINK YOU'RE A REALLY GOOD PERSON, DEEP DOWN.
THANKS FOR ALL THAT YOU'VE DONE FOR US!
tp tp tp
I HOPE...
...THEY DO MANAGE TO REMOVE THAT RIDICULOUS DEVICE.
THEN PERHAPS THE COLONEL WILL TURN HIS ATTENTION TO ME...
NO. SUCH A THOUGHT IS NOT ONE A SOLDIER OUGHT TO HAVE.
....
I MUST ADMIT...I AM A LITTLE JEALOUS.
OF YOU, AND HOW YOU CAN LIVE SO HONEST A LIFE.
YOU SEEM TO HAVE HAD QUITE THE TERRIBLE FEW DAYS, MR. ROSS.

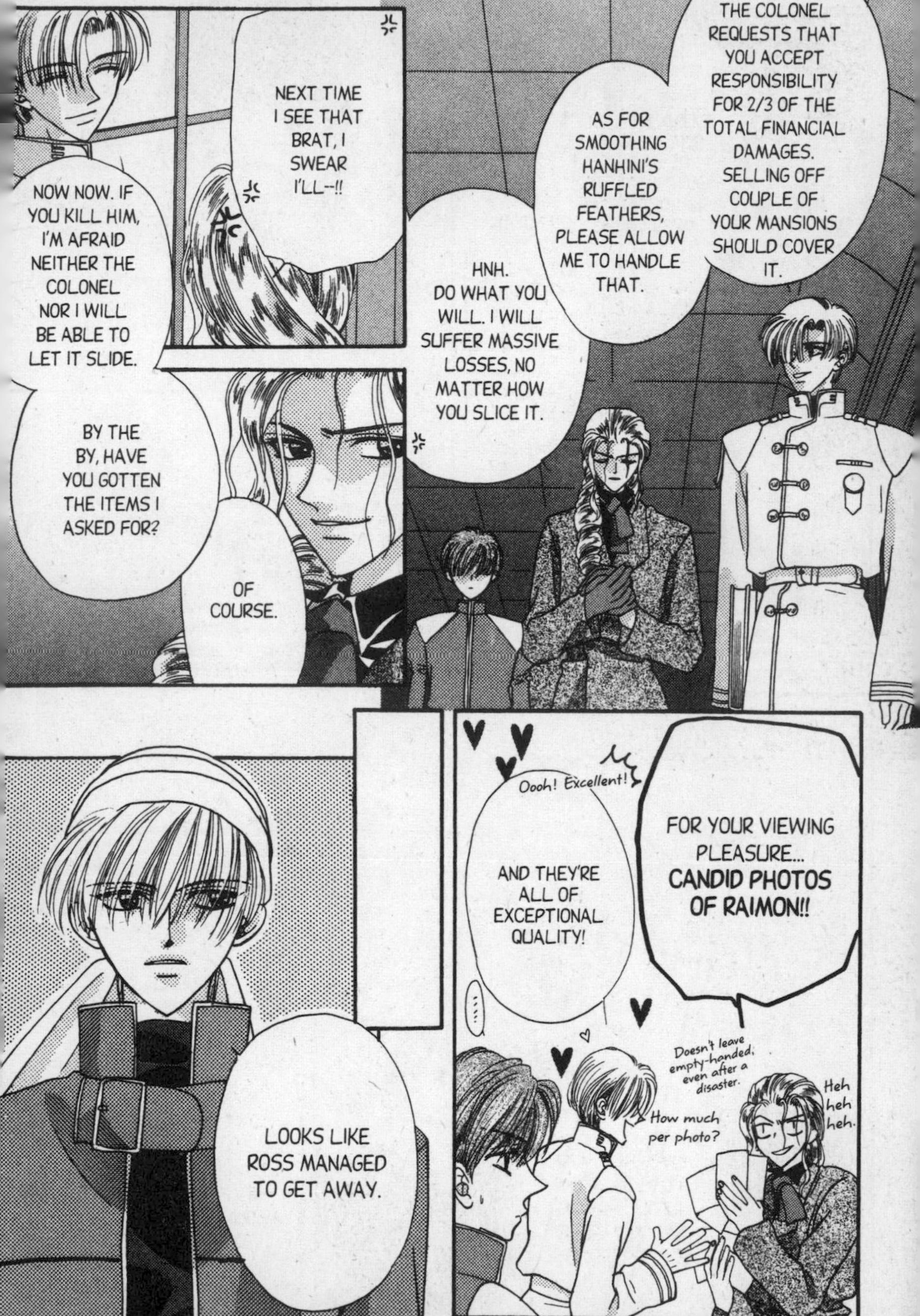
THE COLONEL REQUESTS THAT YOU ACCEPT RESPONSIBILITY FOR 2/3 OF THE TOTAL FINANCIAL DAMAGES. SELLING OFF COUPLE OF YOUR MANSIONS SHOULD COVER IT.
AS FOR SMOOTHING HANHINI'S RUFFLED FEATHERS, PLEASE ALLOW ME TO HANDLE THAT.
HNH. DO WHAT YOU WILL. I WILL SUFFER MASSIVE LOSSES, NO MATTER HOW YOU SLICE IT.
NEXT TIME I SEE THAT BRAT, I SWEAR I'LL--!!
NOW NOW. IF YOU KILL HIM, I'M AFRAID NEITHER THE COLONEL NOR I WILL BE ABLE TO LET IT SLIDE.
BY THE BY, HAVE YOU GOTTEN THE ITEMS I ASKED FOR?
OF COURSE.
FOR YOUR VIEWING PLEASURE... **CANDID PHOTOS OF RAIMON!!**
Oooh! Excellent!
AND THEY'RE ALL OF EXCEPTIONAL QUALITY!
......
Doesn't leave empty-handed, even after a disaster.
Heh heh heh.
How much per photo?
LOOKS LIKE ROSS MANAGED TO GET AWAY.

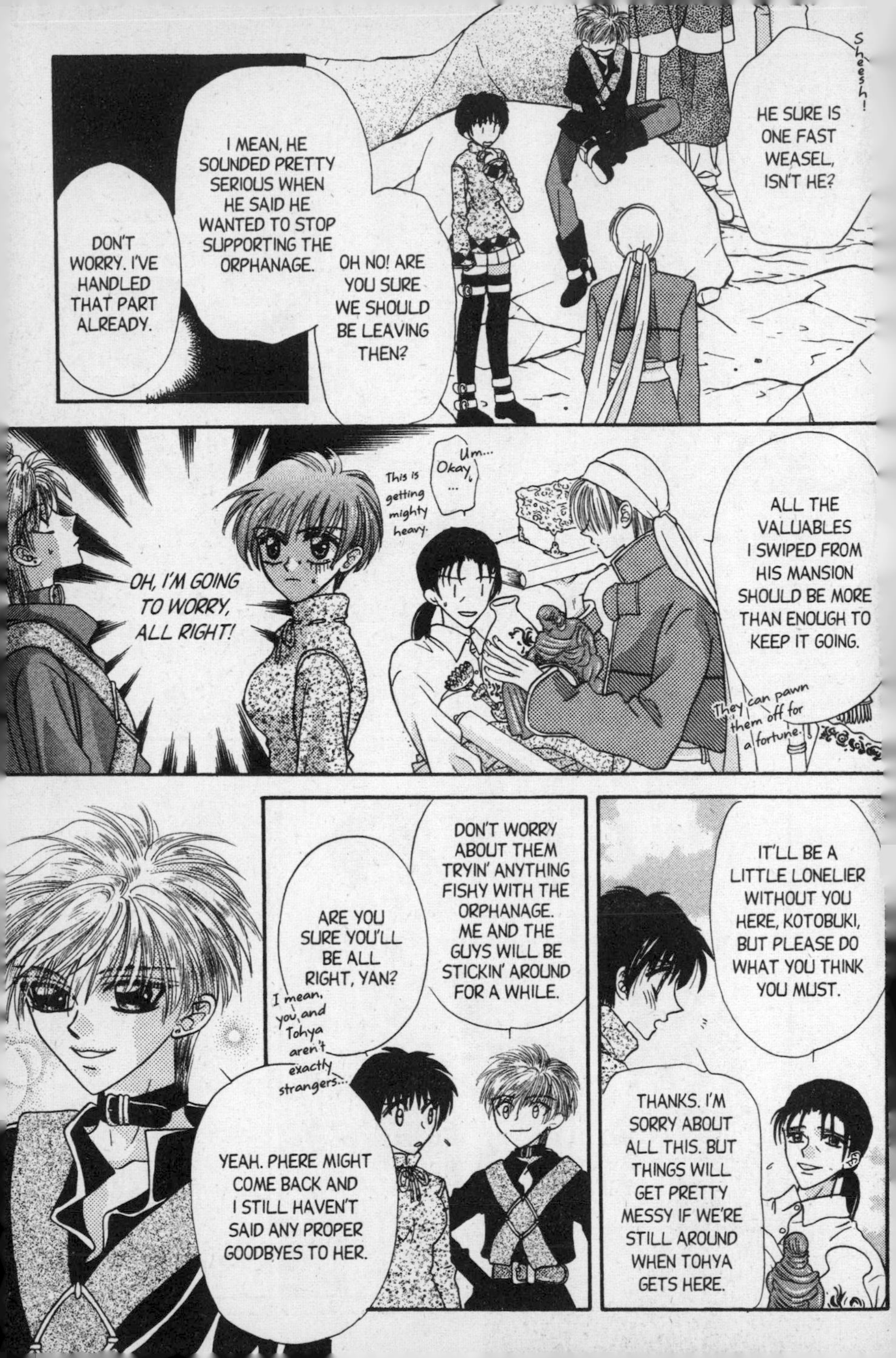
Sheesh!
HE SURE IS ONE FAST WEASEL, ISN'T HE?
OH NO! ARE YOU SURE WE SHOULD BE LEAVING THEN?
I MEAN, HE SOUNDED PRETTY SERIOUS WHEN HE SAID HE WANTED TO STOP SUPPORTING THE ORPHANAGE.
DON'T WORRY. I'VE HANDLED THAT PART ALREADY.
ALL THE VALUABLES I SWIPED FROM HIS MANSION SHOULD BE MORE THAN ENOUGH TO KEEP IT GOING.
They can pawn them off for a fortune.
Um... Okay...
This is getting mighty heavy.
OH, I'M GOING TO WORRY, ALL RIGHT!
IT'LL BE A LITTLE LONELIER WITHOUT YOU HERE, KOTOBUKI, BUT PLEASE DO WHAT YOU THINK YOU MUST.
THANKS. I'M SORRY ABOUT ALL THIS. BUT THINGS WILL GET PRETTY MESSY IF WE'RE STILL AROUND WHEN TOHYA GETS HERE.
DON'T WORRY ABOUT THEM TRYIN' ANYTHING FISHY WITH THE ORPHANAGE. ME AND THE GUYS WILL BE STICKIN' AROUND FOR A WHILE.
ARE YOU SURE YOU'LL BE ALL RIGHT, YAN?
I mean, you and Tohya aren't exactly strangers...
YEAH. PHERE MIGHT COME BACK AND I STILL HAVEN'T SAID ANY PROPER GOODBYES TO HER.

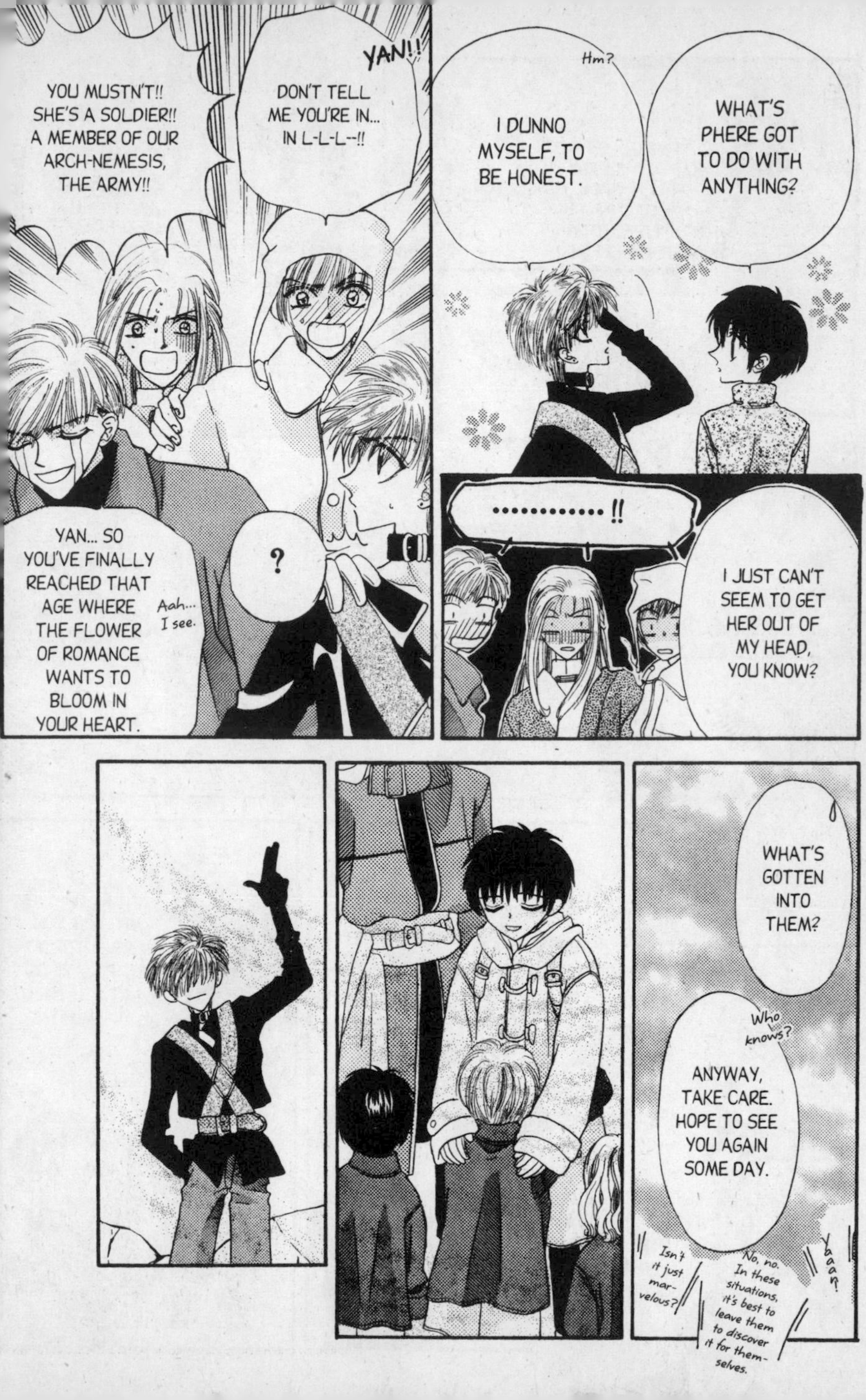
WHAT'S PHERE GOT TO DO WITH ANYTHING?
Hm?
I DUNNO MYSELF, TO BE HONEST.
I JUST CAN'T SEEM TO GET HER OUT OF MY HEAD, YOU KNOW?
.............!!
YAN!!
DON'T TELL ME YOU'RE IN... IN L-L-L--!!
YOU MUSTN'T!! SHE'S A SOLDIER!! A MEMBER OF OUR ARCH-NEMESIS, THE ARMY!!
?
YAN... SO YOU'VE FINALLY REACHED THAT AGE WHERE THE FLOWER OF ROMANCE WANTS TO BLOOM IN YOUR HEART.
Aah... I see.
WHAT'S GOTTEN INTO THEM?
Who knows?
ANYWAY, TAKE CARE. HOPE TO SEE YOU AGAIN SOME DAY.
Yaaan!
No, no. In these situations, it's best to leave them to discover it for them-selves.
Isn't it just mar-velous?

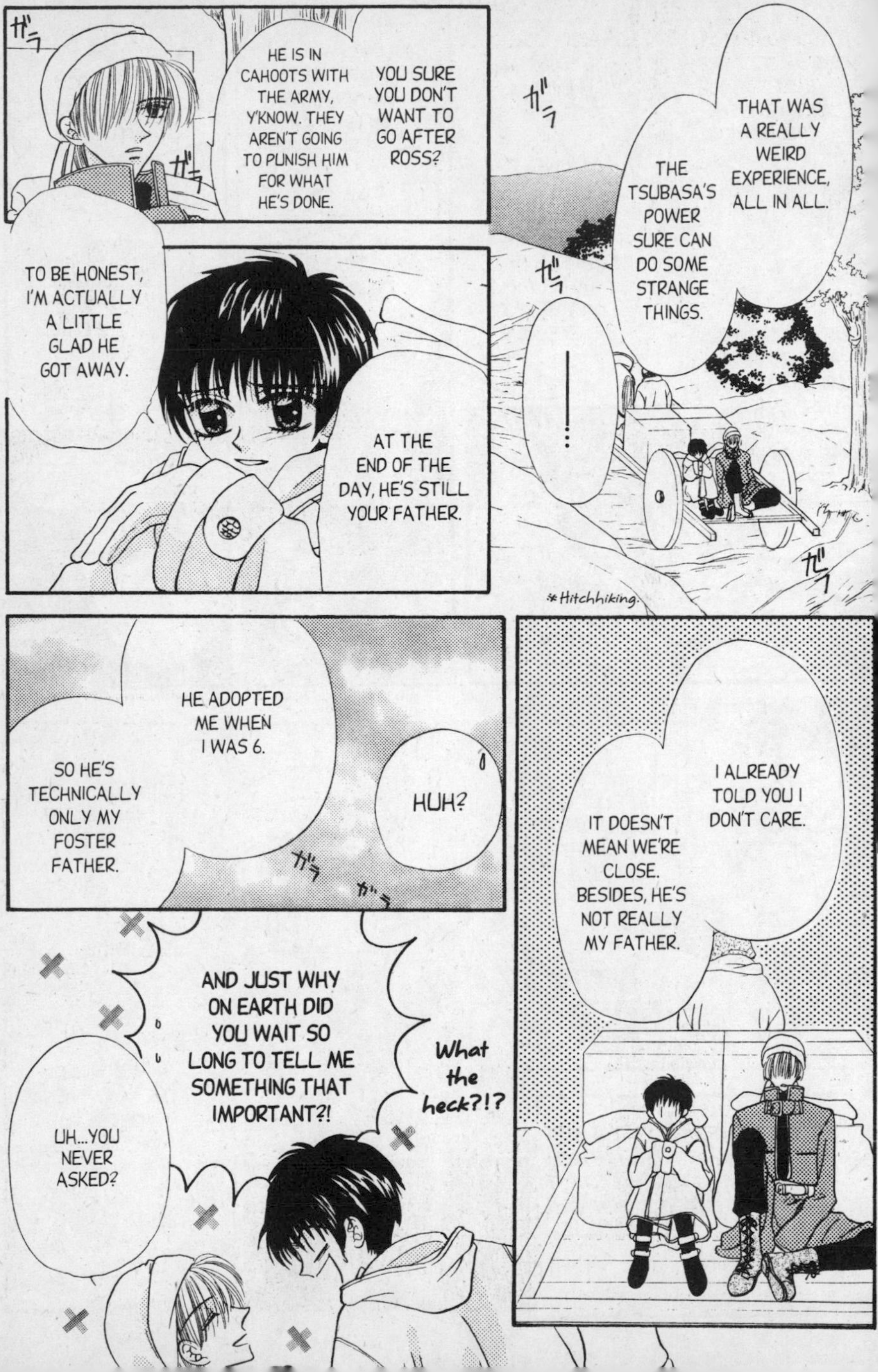
ガラ
THAT WAS A REALLY WEIRD EXPERIENCE, ALL IN ALL.
THE TSUBASA'S POWER SURE CAN DO SOME STRANGE THINGS.
—...
ガラ
ガラ
*Hitchhiking.
ガラ
YOU SURE YOU DON'T WANT TO GO AFTER ROSS?
HE IS IN CAHOOTS WITH THE ARMY, Y'KNOW. THEY AREN'T GOING TO PUNISH HIM FOR WHAT HE'S DONE.
ガラ
AT THE END OF THE DAY, HE'S STILL YOUR FATHER.
TO BE HONEST, I'M ACTUALLY A LITTLE GLAD HE GOT AWAY.
I ALREADY TOLD YOU I DON'T CARE.
IT DOESN'T MEAN WE'RE CLOSE. BESIDES, HE'S NOT REALLY MY FATHER.
HUH?
HE ADOPTED ME WHEN I WAS 6.
SO HE'S TECHNICALLY ONLY MY FOSTER FATHER.
ガラ
ガラ
What the heck?!?
AND JUST WHY ON EARTH DID YOU WAIT SO LONG TO TELL ME SOMETHING THAT IMPORTANT?!
UH...YOU NEVER ASKED?

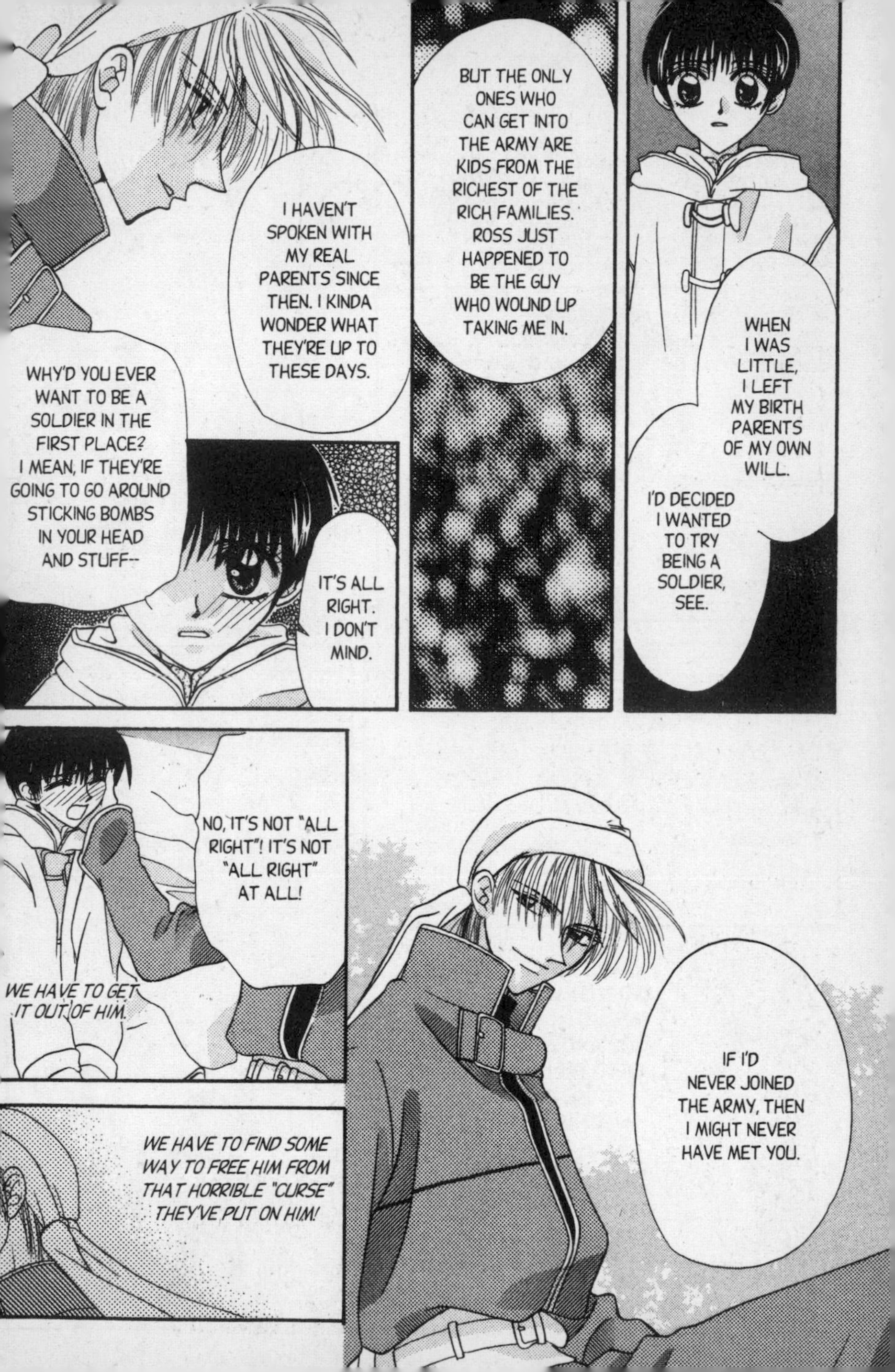
WHEN I WAS LITTLE, I LEFT MY BIRTH PARENTS OF MY OWN WILL.
I'D DECIDED I WANTED TO TRY BEING A SOLDIER, SEE.
BUT THE ONLY ONES WHO CAN GET INTO THE ARMY ARE KIDS FROM THE RICHEST OF THE RICH FAMILIES. ROSS JUST HAPPENED TO BE THE GUY WHO WOUND UP TAKING ME IN.
I HAVEN'T SPOKEN WITH MY REAL PARENTS SINCE THEN. I KINDA WONDER WHAT THEY'RE UP TO THESE DAYS.
WHY'D YOU EVER WANT TO BE A SOLDIER IN THE FIRST PLACE? I MEAN, IF THEY'RE GOING TO GO AROUND STICKING BOMBS IN YOUR HEAD AND STUFF--
IT'S ALL RIGHT. I DON'T MIND.
IF I'D NEVER JOINED THE ARMY, THEN I MIGHT NEVER HAVE MET YOU.
NO, IT'S NOT "ALL RIGHT"! IT'S NOT "ALL RIGHT" AT ALL!
WE HAVE TO GET IT OUT OF HIM.
WE HAVE TO FIND SOME WAY TO FREE HIM FROM THAT HORRIBLE "CURSE" THEY'VE PUT ON HIM!

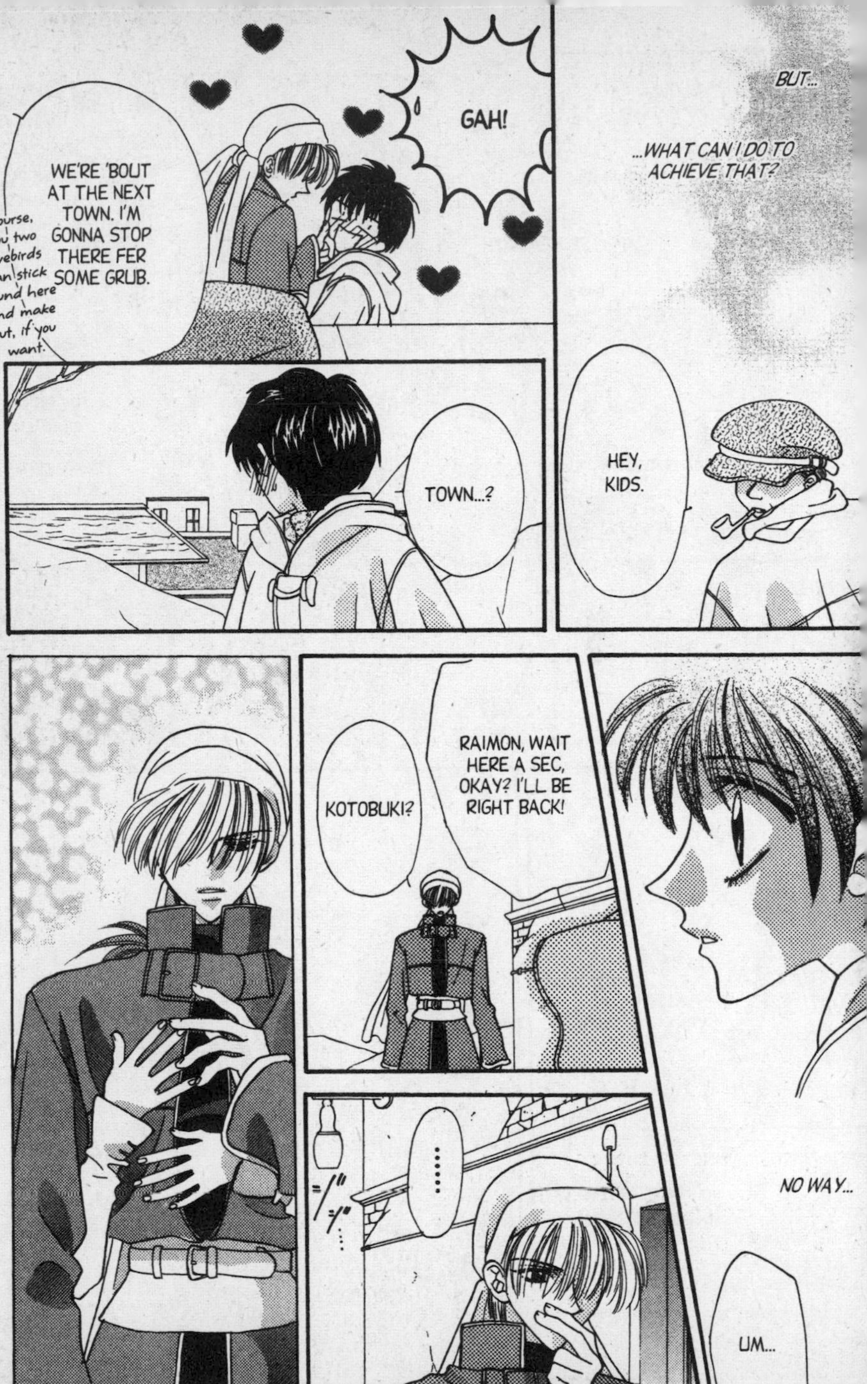
BUT...
...WHAT CAN I DO TO ACHIEVE THAT?
HEY, KIDS.
WE'RE 'BOUT AT THE NEXT TOWN. I'M GONNA STOP THERE FER SOME GRUB.
'Course, you two lovebirds can stick 'round here and make out, if you want.
GAH!
TOWN...?
NO WAY...
UM...
RAIMON, WAIT HERE A SEC, OKAY? I'LL BE RIGHT BACK!
KOTOBUKI?
......

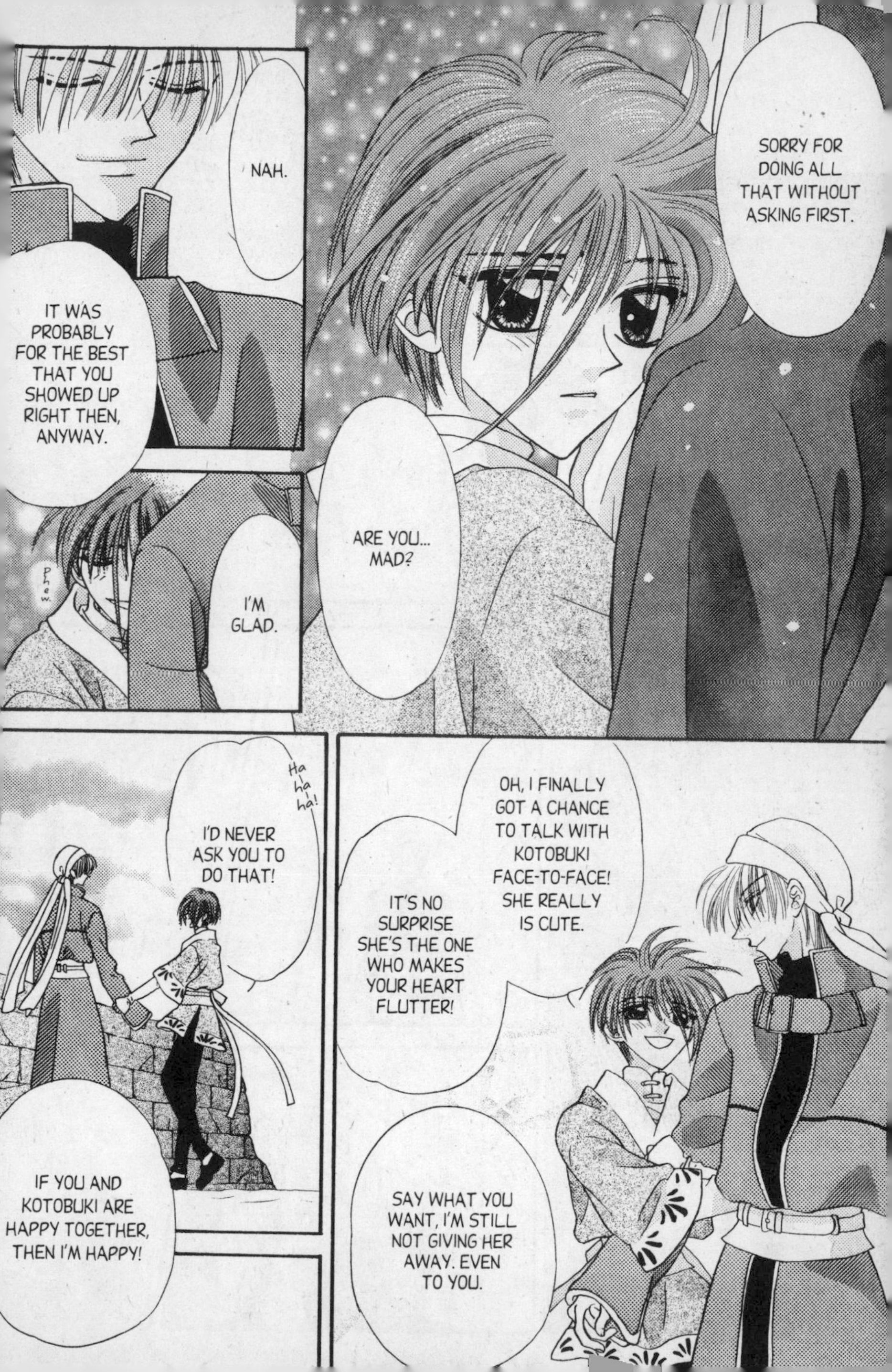
SORRY FOR DOING ALL THAT WITHOUT ASKING FIRST.
ARE YOU... MAD?
NAH.
IT WAS PROBABLY FOR THE BEST THAT YOU SHOWED UP RIGHT THEN, ANYWAY.
Phew
I'M GLAD.
OH, I FINALLY GOT A CHANCE TO TALK WITH KOTOBUKI FACE-TO-FACE! SHE REALLY IS CUTE.
IT'S NO SURPRISE SHE'S THE ONE WHO MAKES YOUR HEART FLUTTER!
SAY WHAT YOU WANT, I'M STILL NOT GIVING HER AWAY. EVEN TO YOU.
Ha ha ha!
I'D NEVER ASK YOU TO DO THAT!
IF YOU AND KOTOBUKI ARE HAPPY TOGETHER, THEN I'M HAPPY!

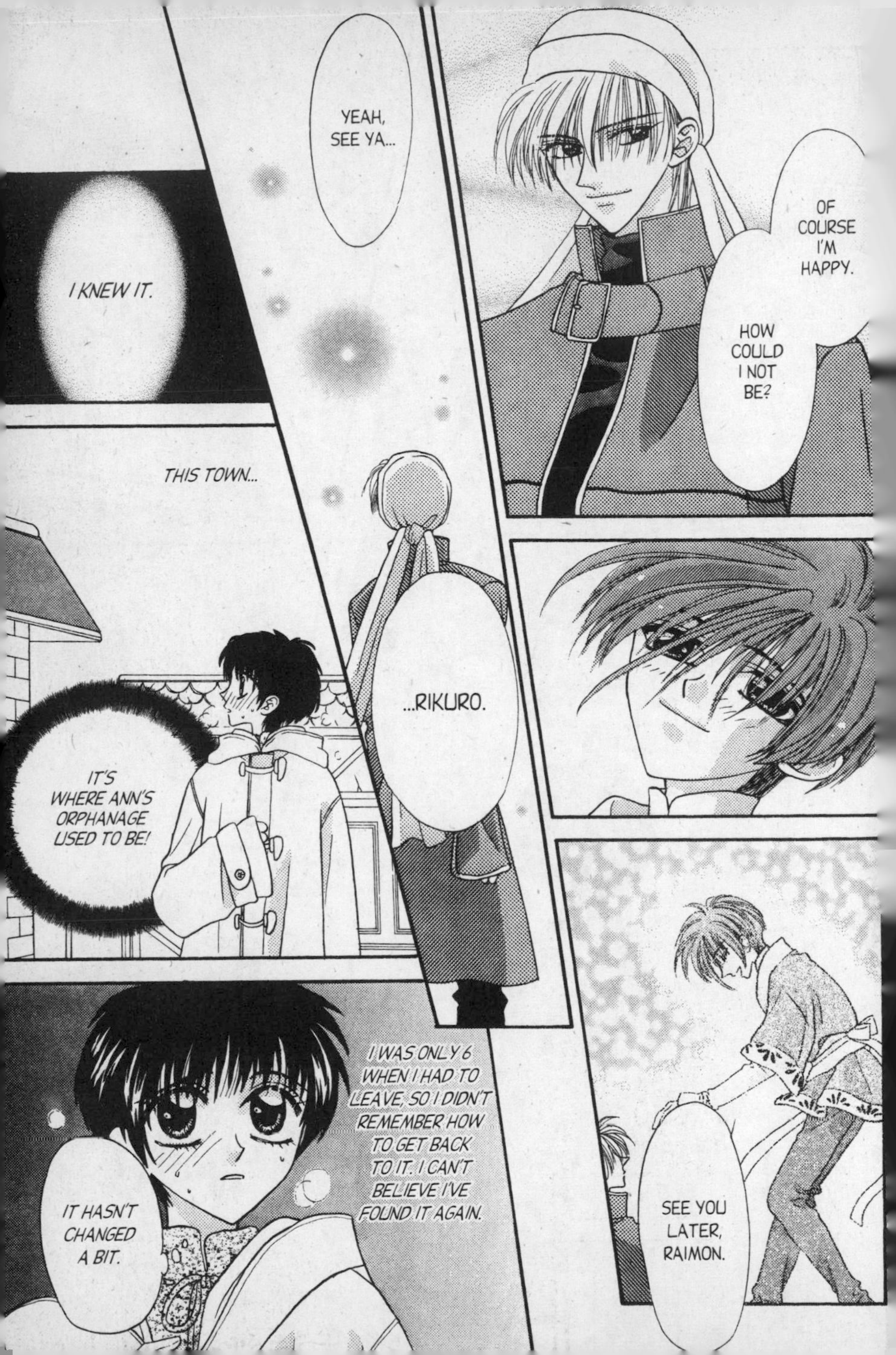
OF COURSE I'M HAPPY.
HOW COULD I NOT BE?
SEE YOU LATER, RAIMON.
YEAH, SEE YA...
...RIKURO.
I KNEW IT.
THIS TOWN...
IT'S WHERE ANN'S ORPHANAGE USED TO BE!
I WAS ONLY 6 WHEN I HAD TO LEAVE, SO I DIDN'T REMEMBER HOW TO GET BACK TO IT. I CAN'T BELIEVE I'VE FOUND IT AGAIN.
IT HASN'T CHANGED A BIT.

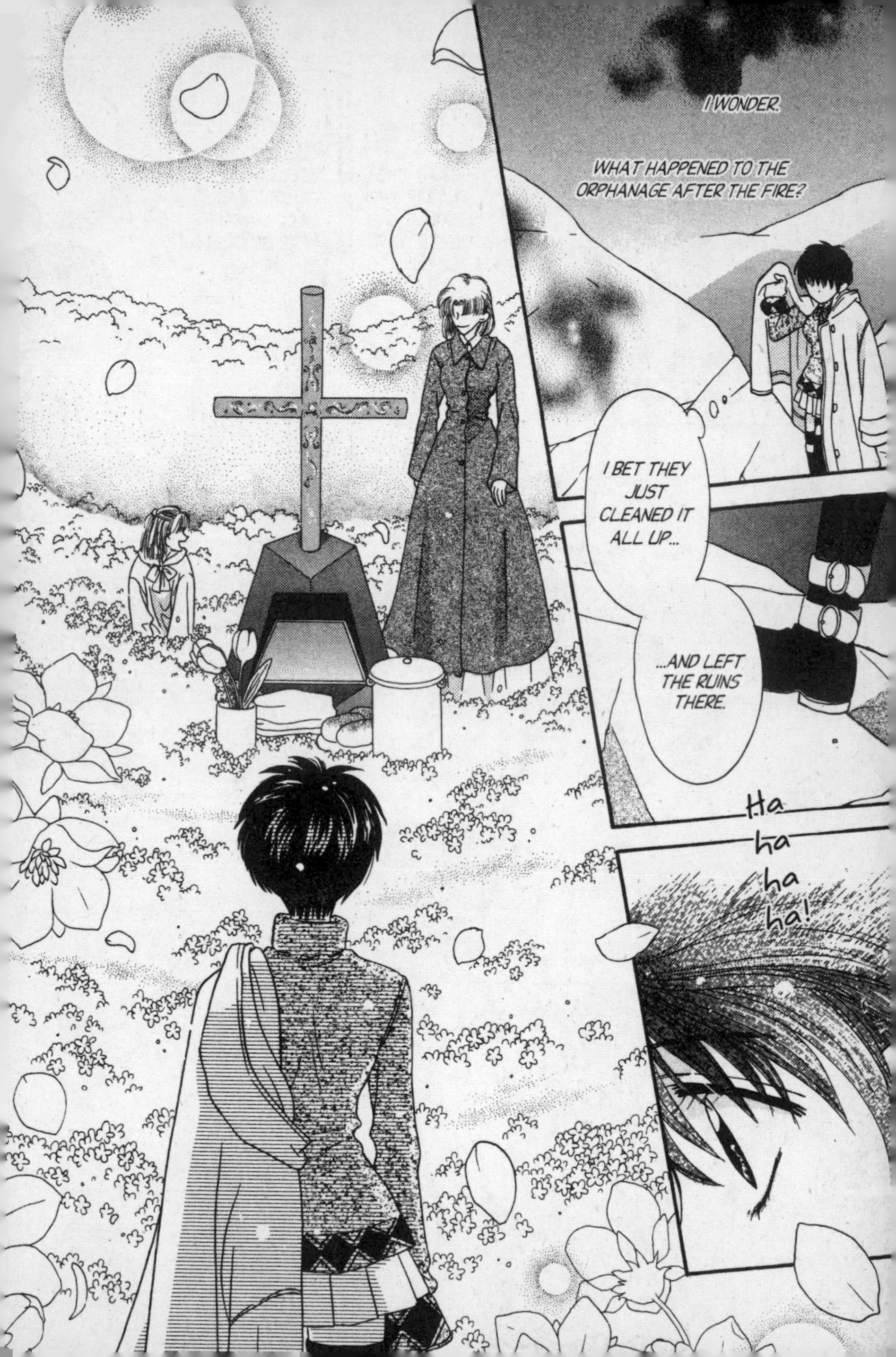
I WONDER.
WHAT HAPPENED TO THE ORPHANAGE AFTER THE FIRE?
I BET THEY JUST CLEANED IT ALL UP...
...AND LEFT THE RUINS THERE.
Ha ha ha ha!

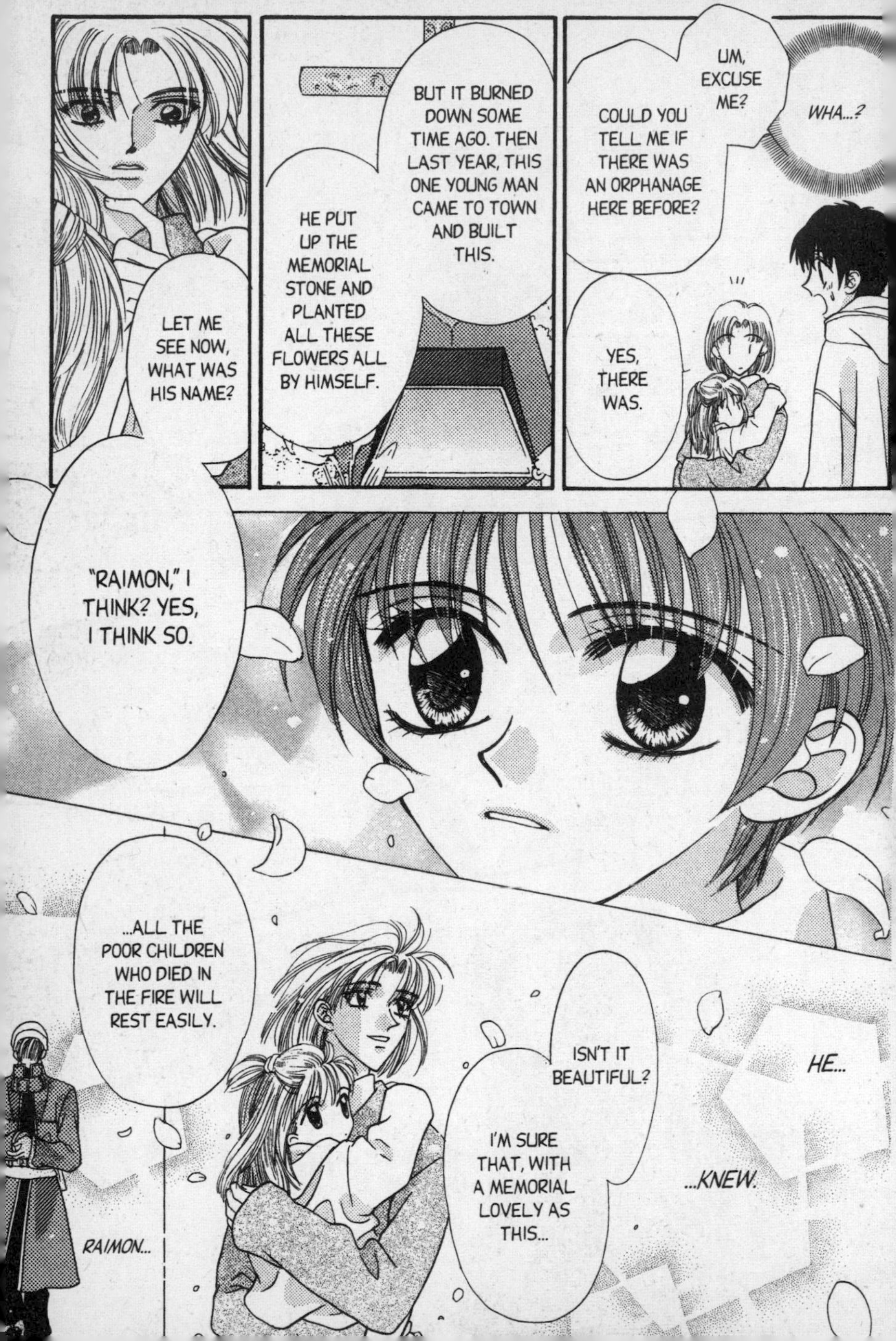
WHA...?
UM, EXCUSE ME?
COULD YOU TELL ME IF THERE WAS AN ORPHANAGE HERE BEFORE?
YES, THERE WAS.
BUT IT BURNED DOWN SOME TIME AGO. THEN LAST YEAR, THIS ONE YOUNG MAN CAME TO TOWN AND BUILT THIS.
HE PUT UP THE MEMORIAL STONE AND PLANTED ALL THESE FLOWERS ALL BY HIMSELF.
LET ME SEE NOW, WHAT WAS HIS NAME?
"RAIMON," I THINK? YES, I THINK SO.
HE...
...KNEW.
ISN'T IT BEAUTIFUL?
I'M SURE THAT, WITH A MEMORIAL LOVELY AS THIS...
...ALL THE POOR CHILDREN WHO DIED IN THE FIRE WILL REST EASILY.
RAIMON...

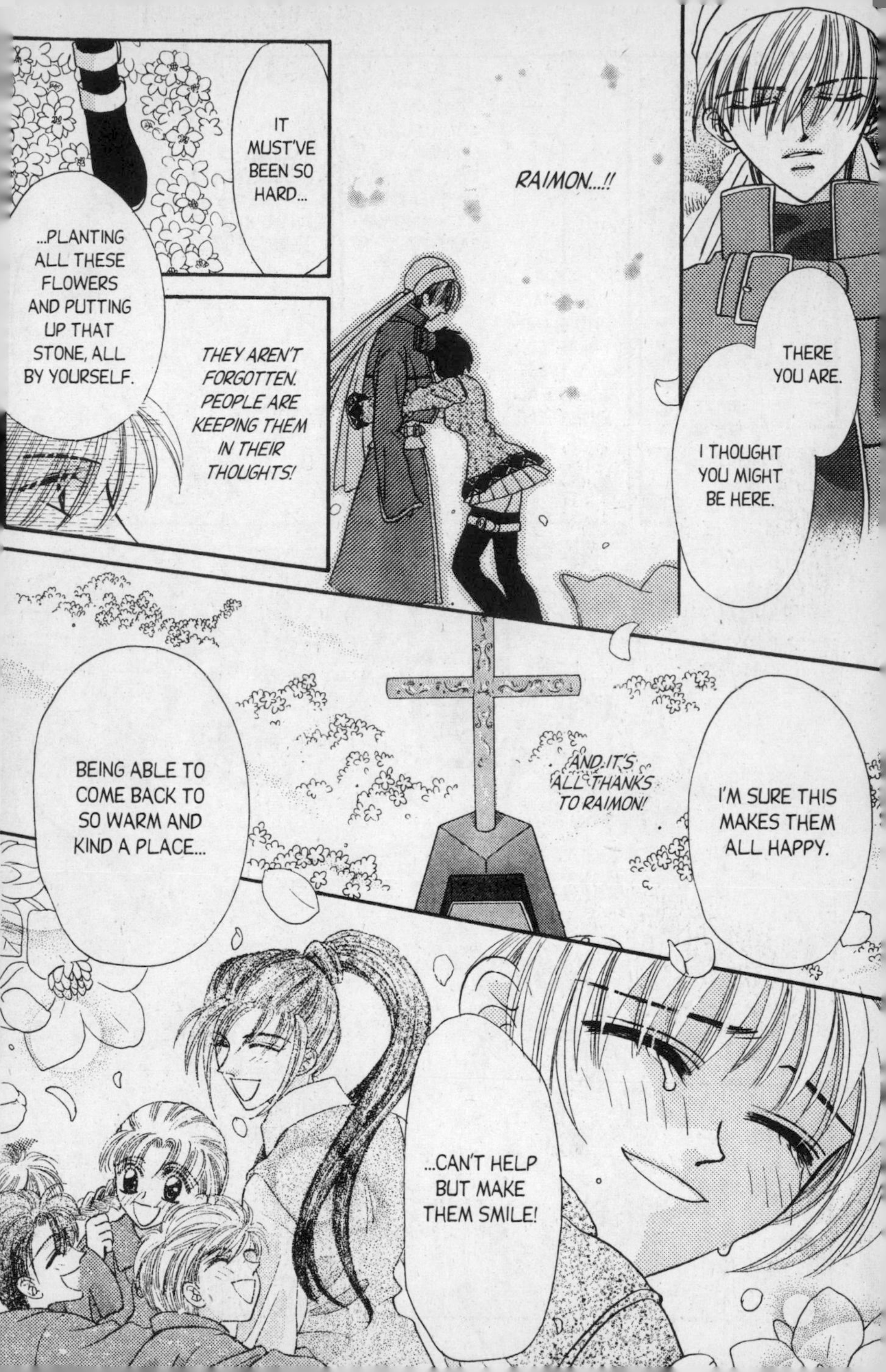
THERE YOU ARE.
I THOUGHT YOU MIGHT BE HERE.
RAIMON...!!
IT MUST'VE BEEN SO HARD...
...PLANTING ALL THESE FLOWERS AND PUTTING UP THAT STONE, ALL BY YOURSELF.
THEY AREN'T FORGOTTEN. PEOPLE ARE KEEPING THEM IN THEIR THOUGHTS!
I'M SURE THIS MAKES THEM ALL HAPPY.
AND IT'S ALL THANKS TO RAIMON!
BEING ABLE TO COME BACK TO SO WARM AND KIND A PLACE...
...CAN'T HELP BUT MAKE THEM SMILE!

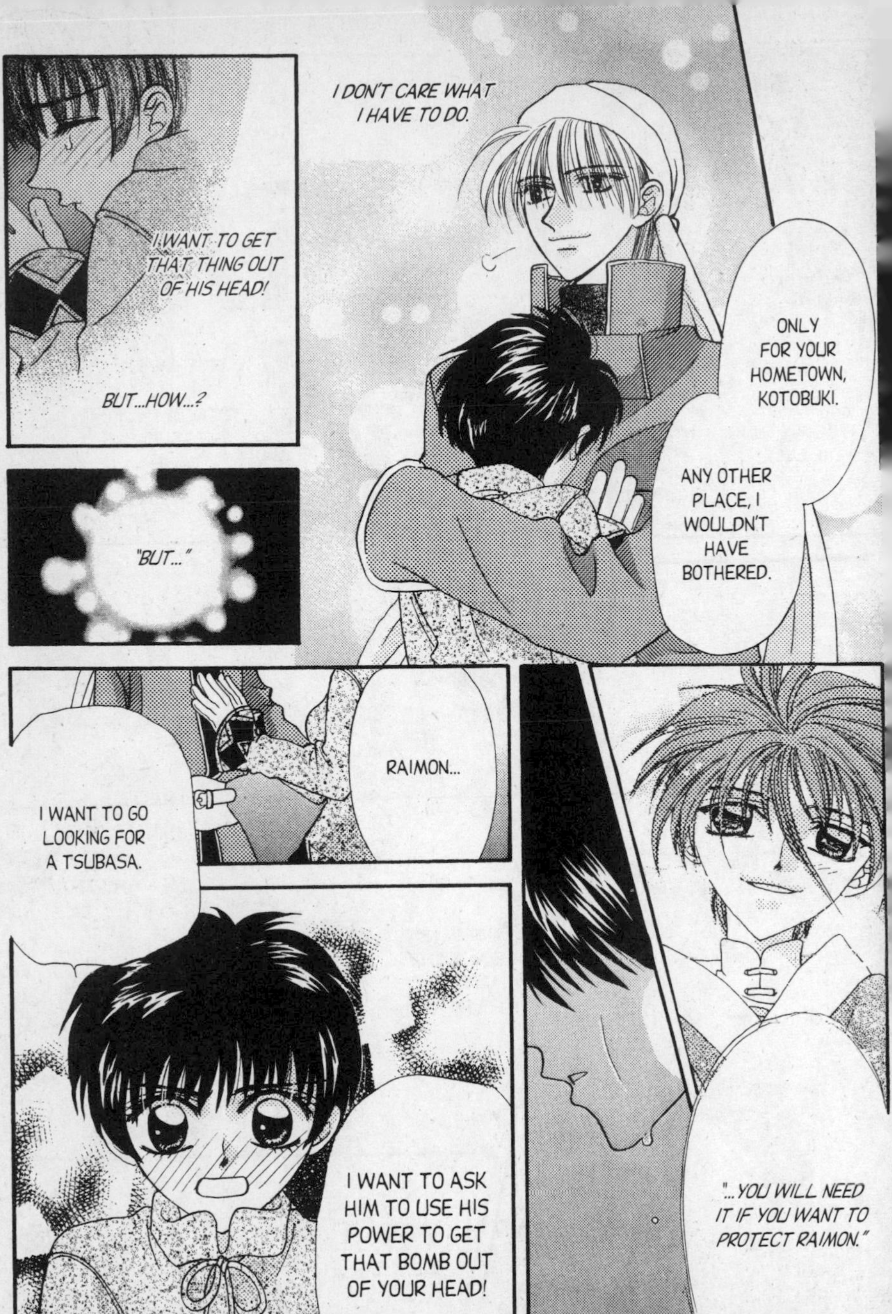
I DON'T CARE WHAT I HAVE TO DO.
ONLY FOR YOUR HOMETOWN, KOTOBUKI.
ANY OTHER PLACE, I WOULDN'T HAVE BOTHERED.
I WANT TO GET THAT THING OUT OF HIS HEAD!
BUT...HOW...?
"BUT..."
"...YOU WILL NEED IT IF YOU WANT TO PROTECT RAIMON."
RAIMON...
I WANT TO GO LOOKING FOR A TSUBASA.
I WANT TO ASK HIM TO USE HIS POWER TO GET THAT BOMB OUT OF YOUR HEAD!

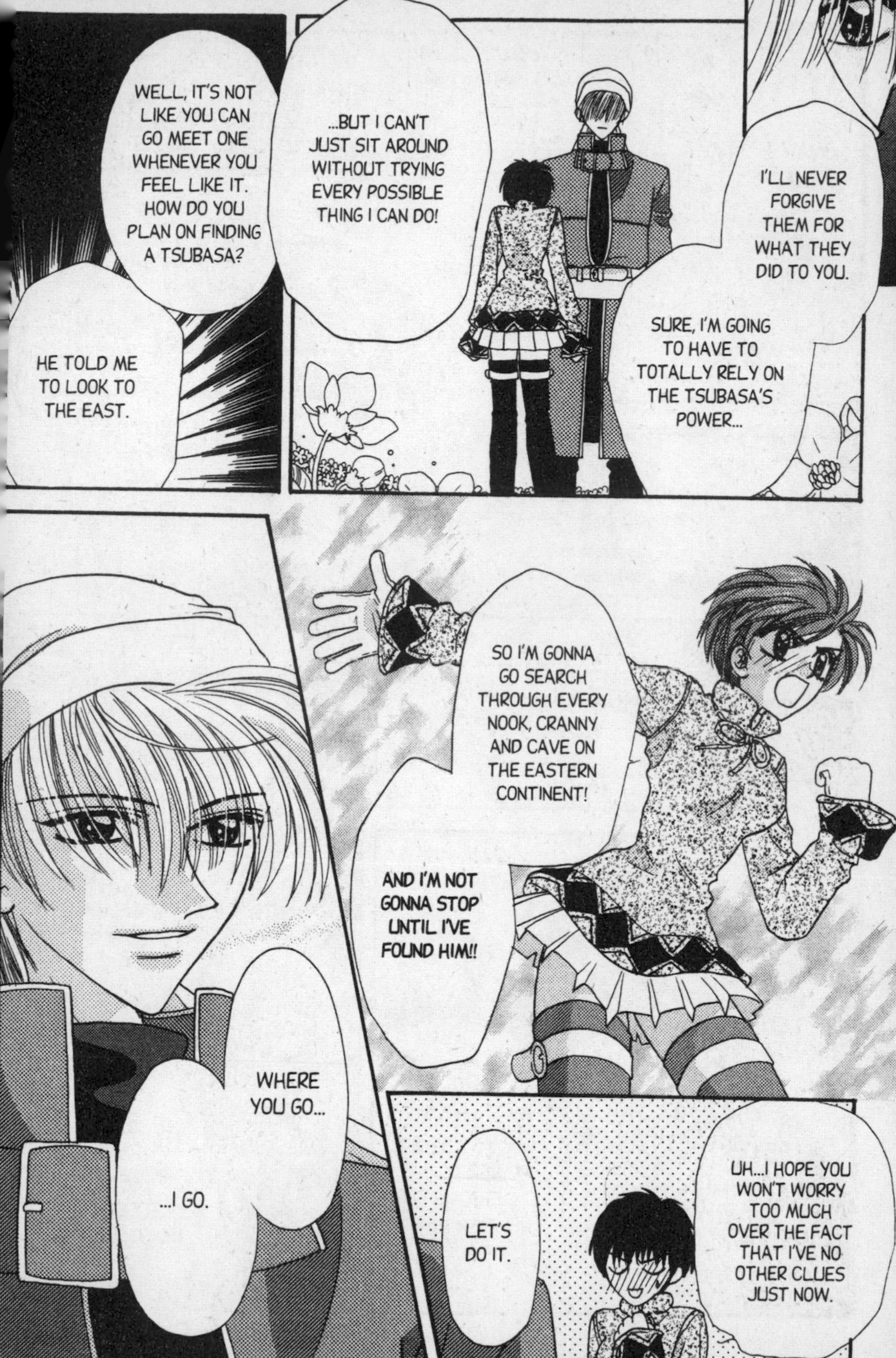
I'LL NEVER FORGIVE THEM FOR WHAT THEY DID TO YOU.
SURE, I'M GOING TO HAVE TO TOTALLY RELY ON THE TSUBASA'S POWER...
...BUT I CAN'T JUST SIT AROUND WITHOUT TRYING EVERY POSSIBLE THING I CAN DO!
WELL, IT'S NOT LIKE YOU CAN GO MEET ONE WHENEVER YOU FEEL LIKE IT. HOW DO YOU PLAN ON FINDING A TSUBASA?
HE TOLD ME TO LOOK TO THE EAST.
SO I'M GONNA GO SEARCH THROUGH EVERY NOOK, CRANNY AND CAVE ON THE EASTERN CONTINENT!
AND I'M NOT GONNA STOP UNTIL I'VE FOUND HIM!!
UH...I HOPE YOU WON'T WORRY TOO MUCH OVER THE FACT THAT I'VE NO OTHER CLUES JUST NOW.
LET'S DO IT.
WHERE YOU GO...
...I GO.

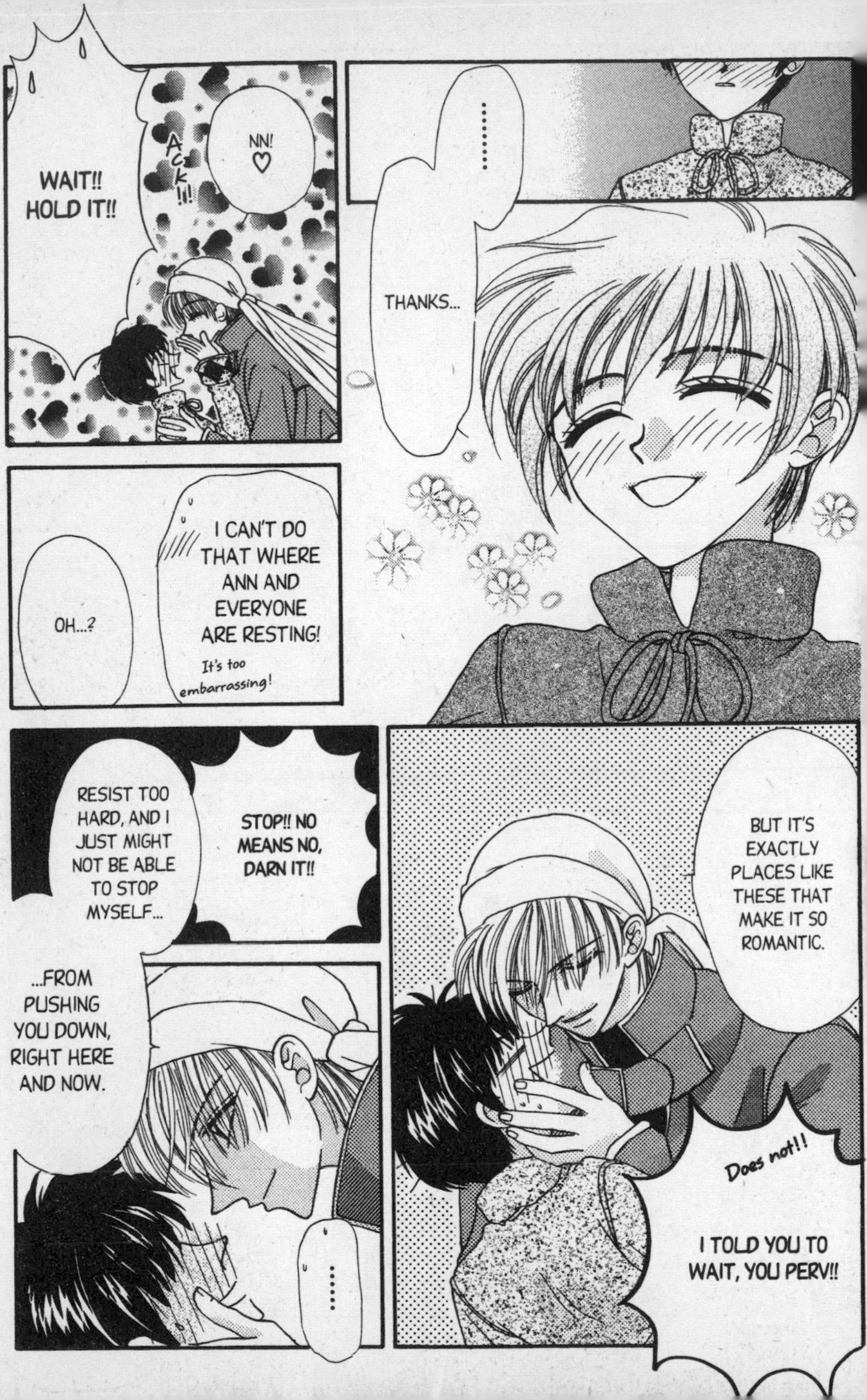

......
THANKS...
NN! ♥
ACK!!
WAIT!! HOLD IT!!
I CAN'T DO THAT WHERE ANN AND EVERYONE ARE RESTING!
It's too embarrassing!
OH...?
BUT IT'S EXACTLY PLACES LIKE THESE THAT MAKE IT SO ROMANTIC.
Does not!!
I TOLD YOU TO WAIT, YOU PERV!!
STOP!! NO MEANS NO, DARN IT!!
RESIST TOO HARD, AND I JUST MIGHT NOT BE ABLE TO STOP MYSELF...
...FROM PUSHING YOU DOWN, RIGHT HERE AND NOW.
......

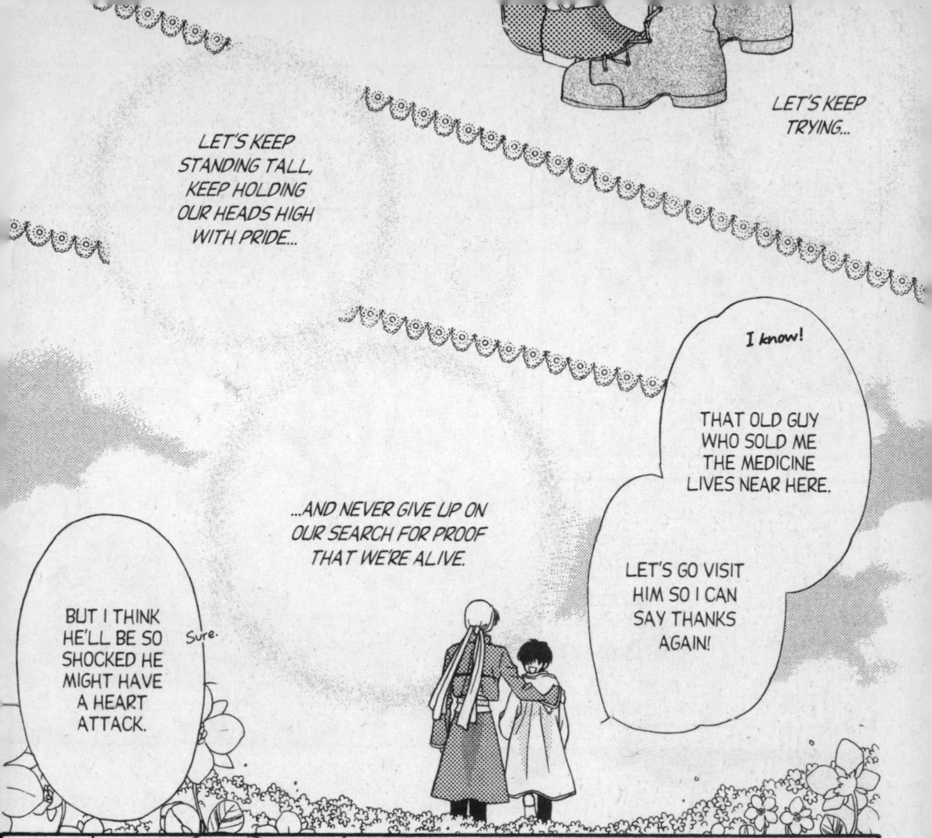
LET'S KEEP TRYING...
LET'S KEEP STANDING TALL, KEEP HOLDING OUR HEADS HIGH WITH PRIDE...
I know!
THAT OLD GUY WHO SOLD ME THE MEDICINE LIVES NEAR HERE.
LET'S GO VISIT HIM SO I CAN SAY THANKS AGAIN!
...AND NEVER GIVE UP ON OUR SEARCH FOR PROOF THAT WE'RE ALIVE.
Sure.
BUT I THINK HE'LL BE SO SHOCKED HE MIGHT HAVE A HEART ATTACK.

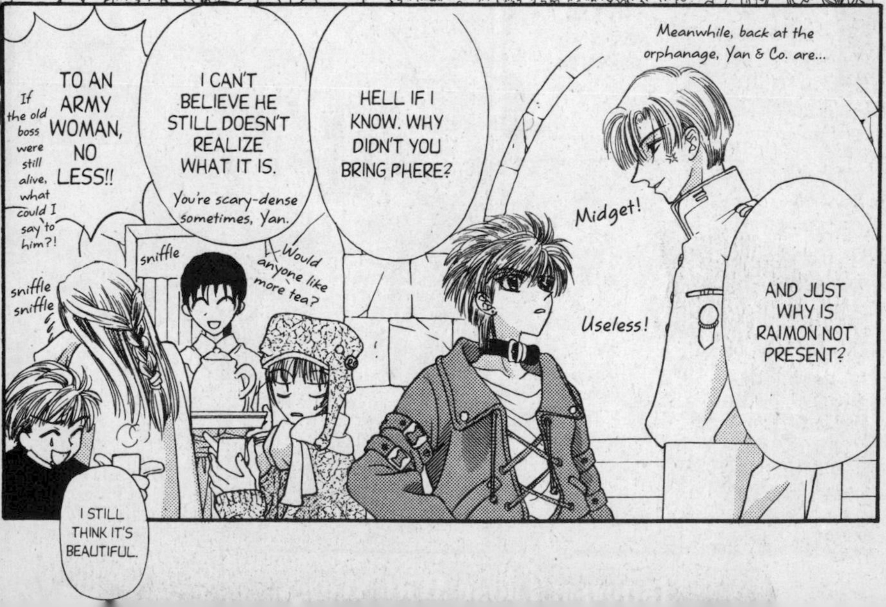
Meanwhile, back at the orphanage, Yan & Co. are...
AND JUST WHY IS RAIMON NOT PRESENT?
Midget!
Useless!
HELL IF I KNOW. WHY DIDN'T YOU BRING PHERE?
I CAN'T BELIEVE HE STILL DOESN'T REALIZE WHAT IT IS.
You're scary-dense sometimes, Yan.
Would anyone like more tea?
TO AN ARMY WOMAN, NO LESS!!
If the old boss were still alive, what could I say to him?!
sniffle
sniffle sniffle
I STILL THINK IT'S BEAUTIFUL.

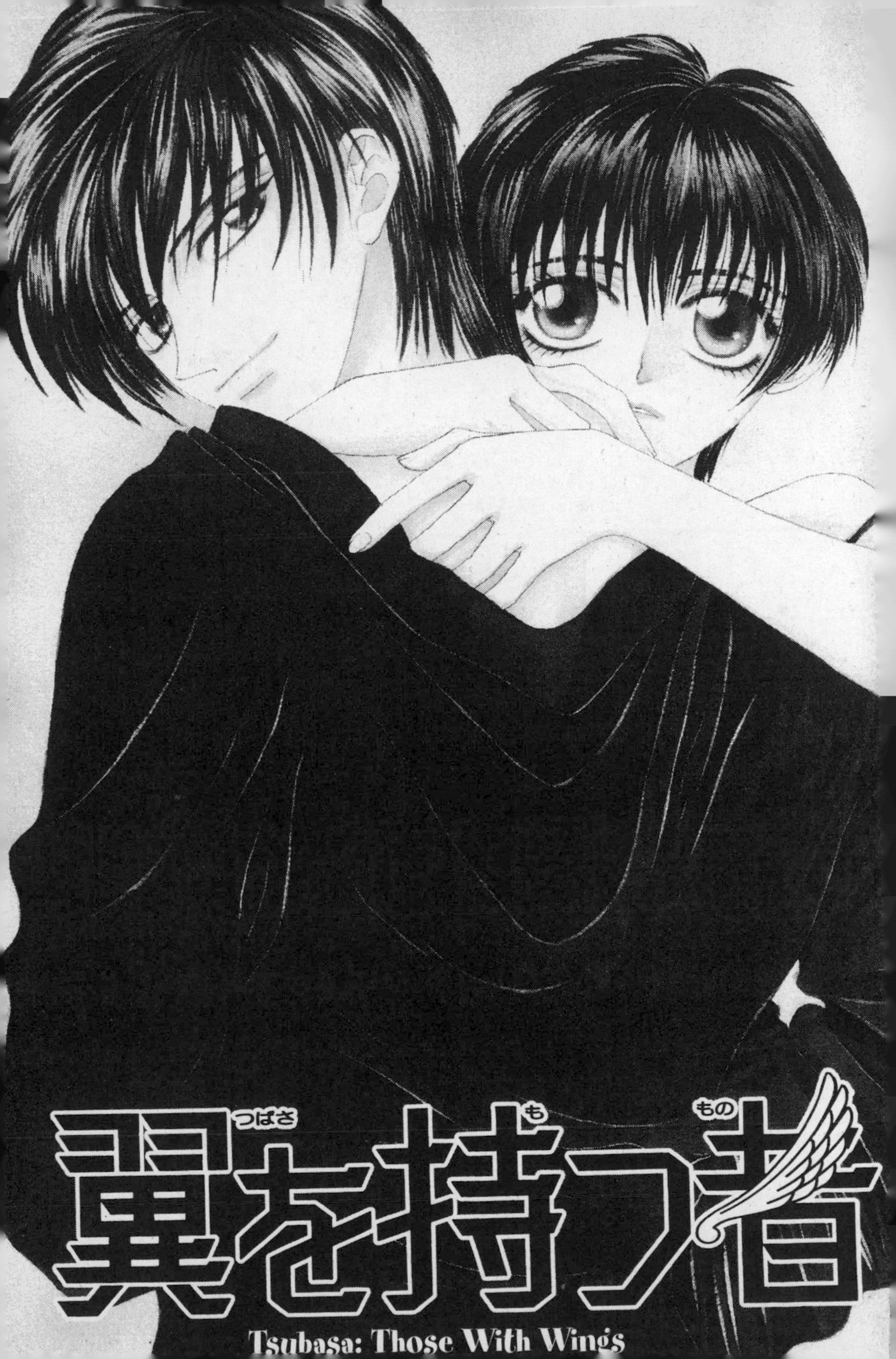
翼を持つ者
つばさ も もの
Tsubasa: Those With Wings

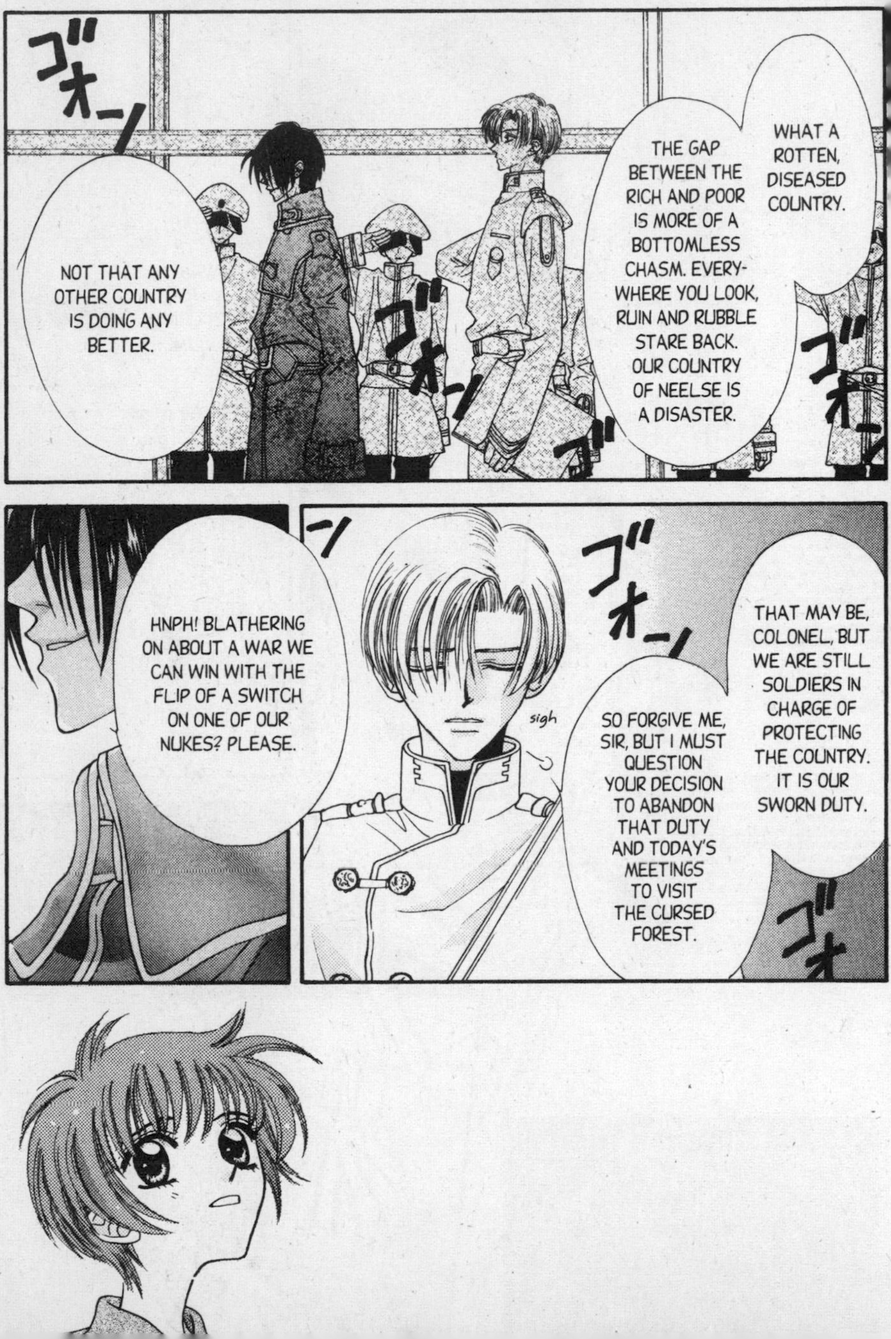
WHAT A ROTTEN, DISEASED COUNTRY.
THE GAP BETWEEN THE RICH AND POOR IS MORE OF A BOTTOMLESS CHASM. EVERY-WHERE YOU LOOK, RUIN AND RUBBLE STARE BACK. OUR COUNTRY OF NEELSE IS A DISASTER.
NOT THAT ANY OTHER COUNTRY IS DOING ANY BETTER.
THAT MAY BE, COLONEL, BUT WE ARE STILL SOLDIERS IN CHARGE OF PROTECTING THE COUNTRY. IT IS OUR SWORN DUTY.
SO FORGIVE ME, SIR, BUT I MUST QUESTION YOUR DECISION TO ABANDON THAT DUTY AND TODAY'S MEETINGS TO VISIT THE CURSED FOREST.
sigh
HNPH! BLATHERING ON ABOUT A WAR WE CAN WIN WITH THE FLIP OF A SWITCH ON ONE OF OUR NUKES? PLEASE.

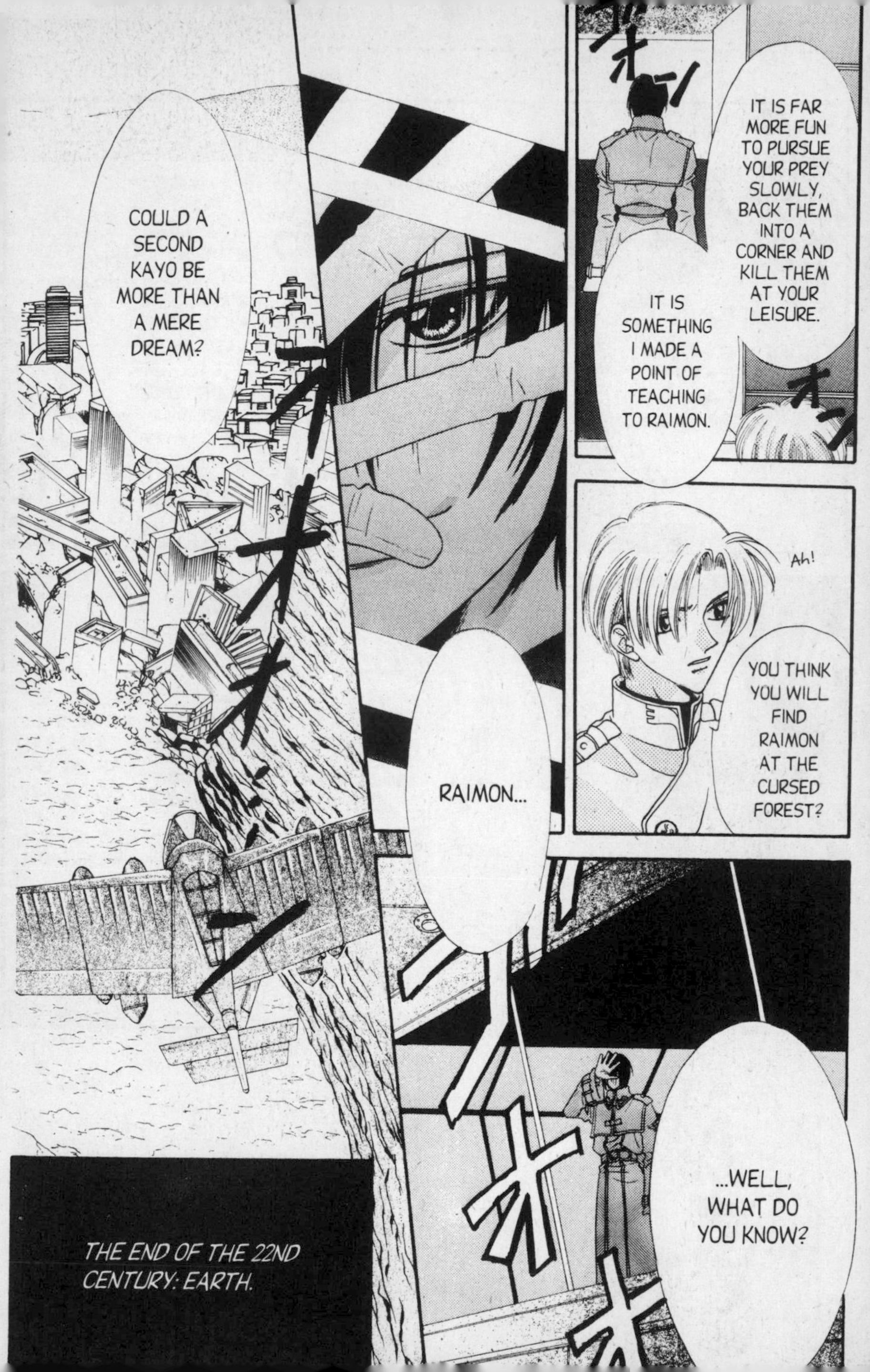
IT IS FAR MORE FUN TO PURSUE YOUR PREY SLOWLY, BACK THEM INTO A CORNER AND KILL THEM AT YOUR LEISURE.
IT IS SOMETHING I MADE A POINT OF TEACHING TO RAIMON.
Ah!
YOU THINK YOU WILL FIND RAIMON AT THE CURSED FOREST?
...WELL, WHAT DO YOU KNOW?
RAIMON...
COULD A SECOND KAYO BE MORE THAN A MERE DREAM?
THE END OF THE 22ND CENTURY: EARTH.

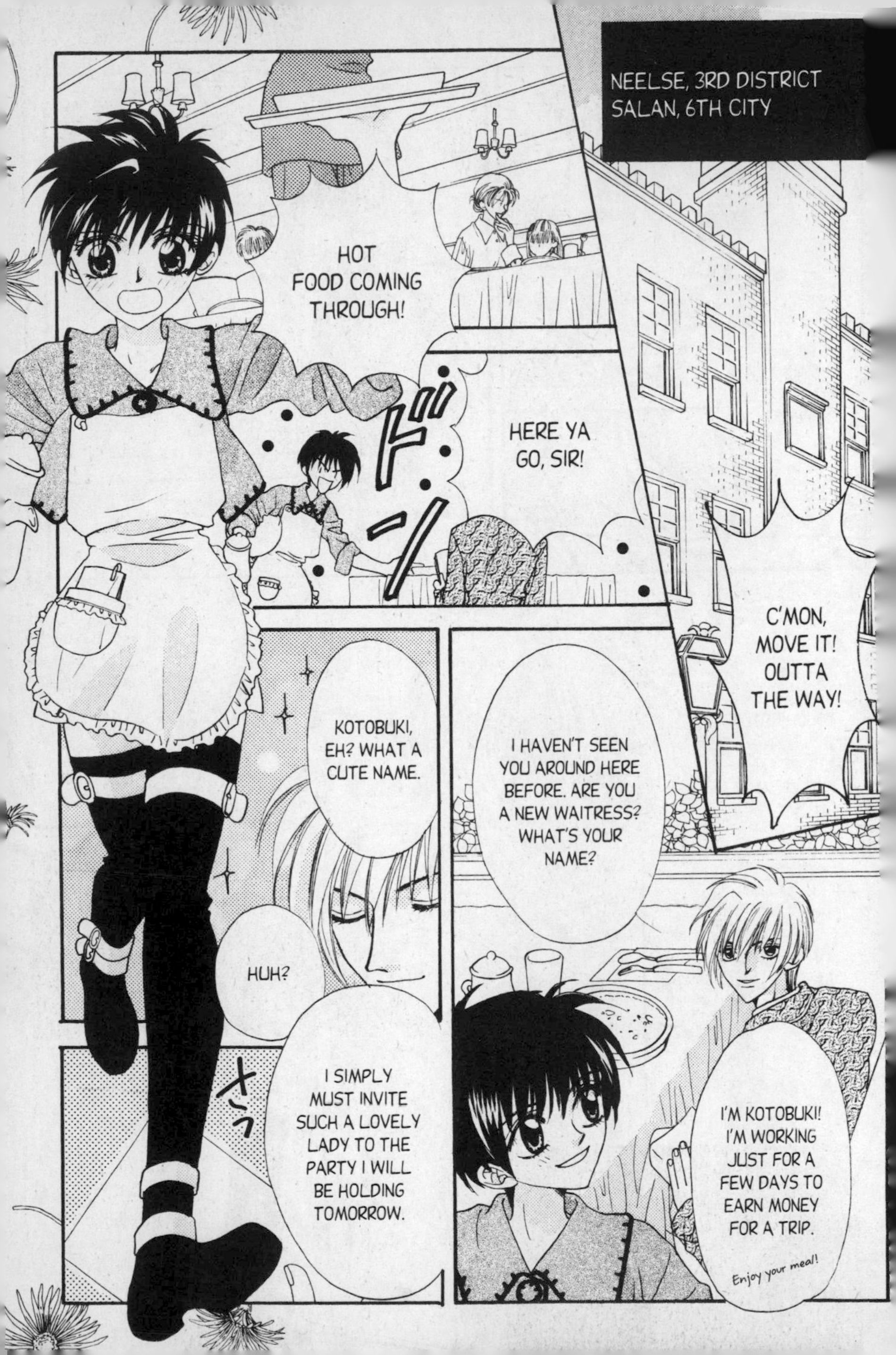
NEELSE, 3RD DISTRICT SALAN, 6TH CITY
C'MON, MOVE IT! OUTTA THE WAY!
HOT FOOD COMING THROUGH!
ドン
HERE YA GO, SIR!
I HAVEN'T SEEN YOU AROUND HERE BEFORE. ARE YOU A NEW WAITRESS? WHAT'S YOUR NAME?
I'M KOTOBUKI! I'M WORKING JUST FOR A FEW DAYS TO EARN MONEY FOR A TRIP.
Enjoy your meal!
KOTOBUKI, EH? WHAT A CUTE NAME.
HUH?
I SIMPLY MUST INVITE SUCH A LOVELY LADY TO THE PARTY I WILL BE HOLDING TOMORROW.

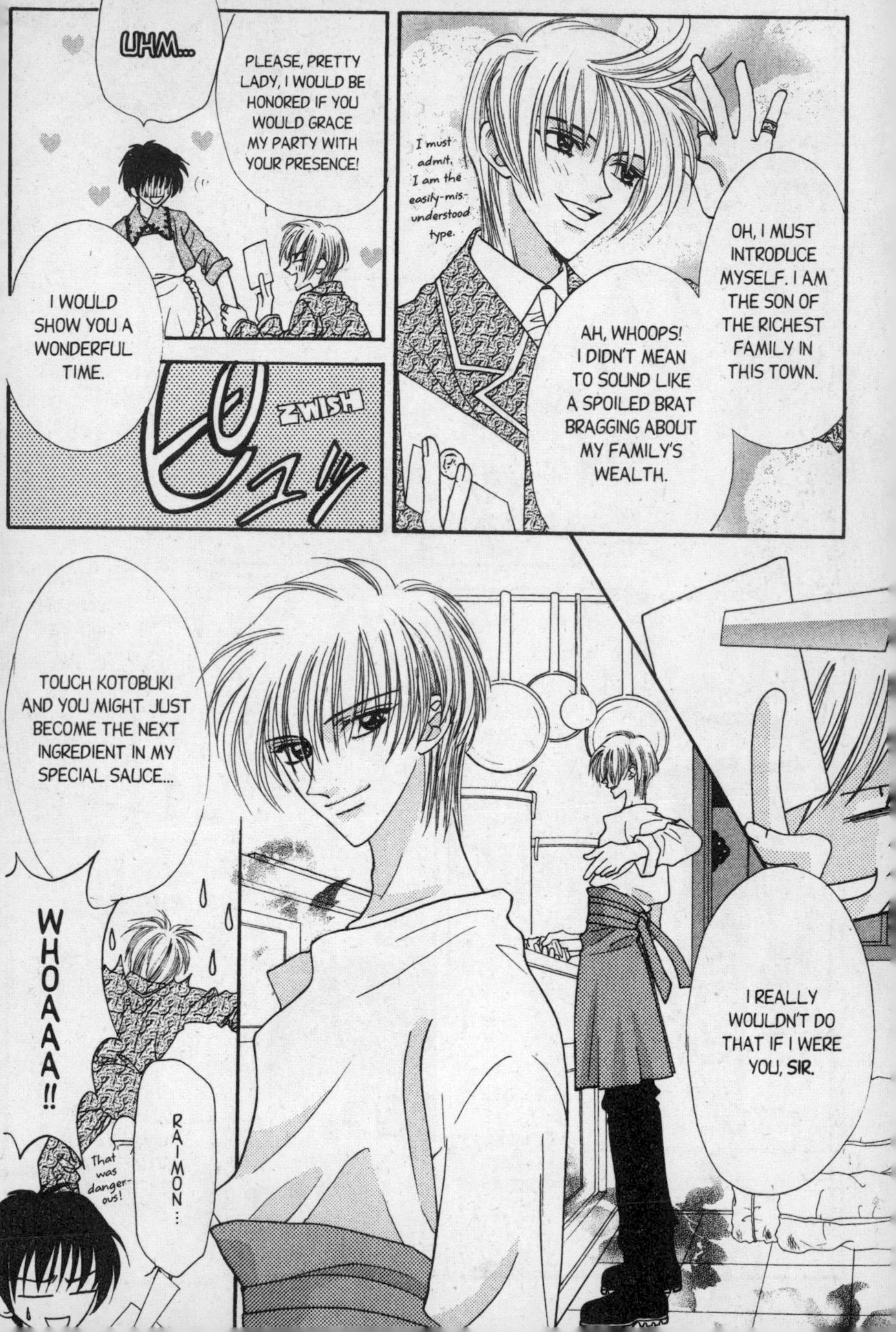

OH, I MUST INTRODUCE MYSELF. I AM THE SON OF THE RICHEST FAMILY IN THIS TOWN.
I must admit, I am the easily-mis-understood type.
AH, WHOOPS! I DIDN'T MEAN TO SOUND LIKE A SPOILED BRAT BRAGGING ABOUT MY FAMILY'S WEALTH.
PLEASE, PRETTY LADY, I WOULD BE HONORED IF YOU WOULD GRACE MY PARTY WITH YOUR PRESENCE!
UHM...
I WOULD SHOW YOU A WONDERFUL TIME.
ZWISH
ヒュッ
I REALLY WOULDN'T DO THAT IF I WERE YOU, SIR.
TOUCH KOTOBUKI AND YOU MIGHT JUST BECOME THE NEXT INGREDIENT IN MY SPECIAL SAUCE...
RAIMON...
WHOAAA!!
That was danger-ous!

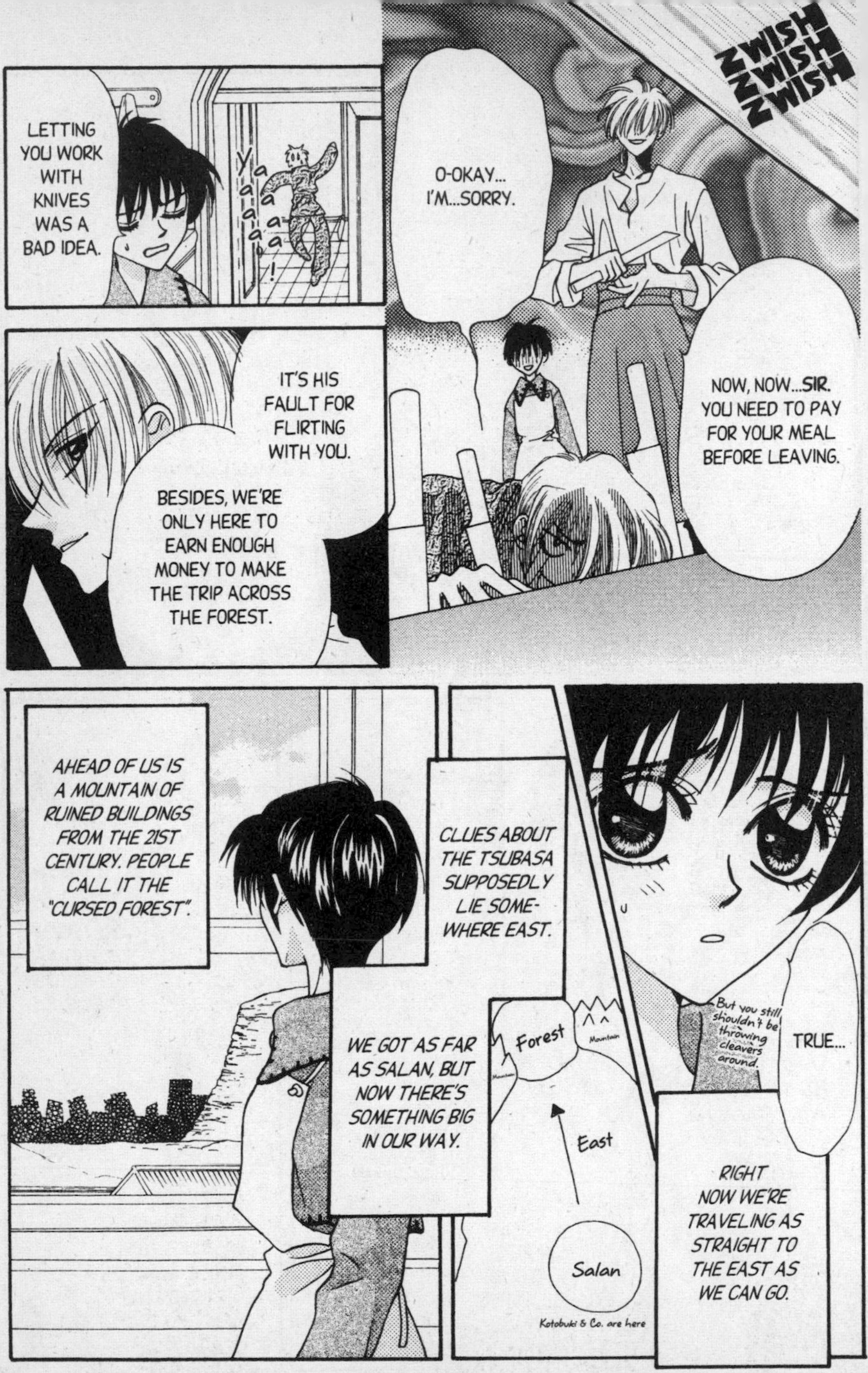
ZWISH ZWISH ZWISH
NOW, NOW...SIR. YOU NEED TO PAY FOR YOUR MEAL BEFORE LEAVING.
O-OKAY... I'M...SORRY.
LETTING YOU WORK WITH KNIVES WAS A BAD IDEA.
Yaaaaaaa!
IT'S HIS FAULT FOR FLIRTING WITH YOU.
BESIDES, WE'RE ONLY HERE TO EARN ENOUGH MONEY TO MAKE THE TRIP ACROSS THE FOREST.
TRUE...
But you still shouldn't be throwing cleavers around.
RIGHT NOW WE'RE TRAVELING AS STRAIGHT TO THE EAST AS WE CAN GO.
CLUES ABOUT THE TSUBASA SUPPOSEDLY LIE SOME-WHERE EAST.
Mountain
Forest
Mountain
East
Salan
Kotobuki & Co. are here
WE GOT AS FAR AS SALAN, BUT NOW THERE'S SOMETHING BIG IN OUR WAY.
AHEAD OF US IS A MOUNTAIN OF RUINED BUILDINGS FROM THE 21ST CENTURY. PEOPLE CALL IT THE "CURSED FOREST".

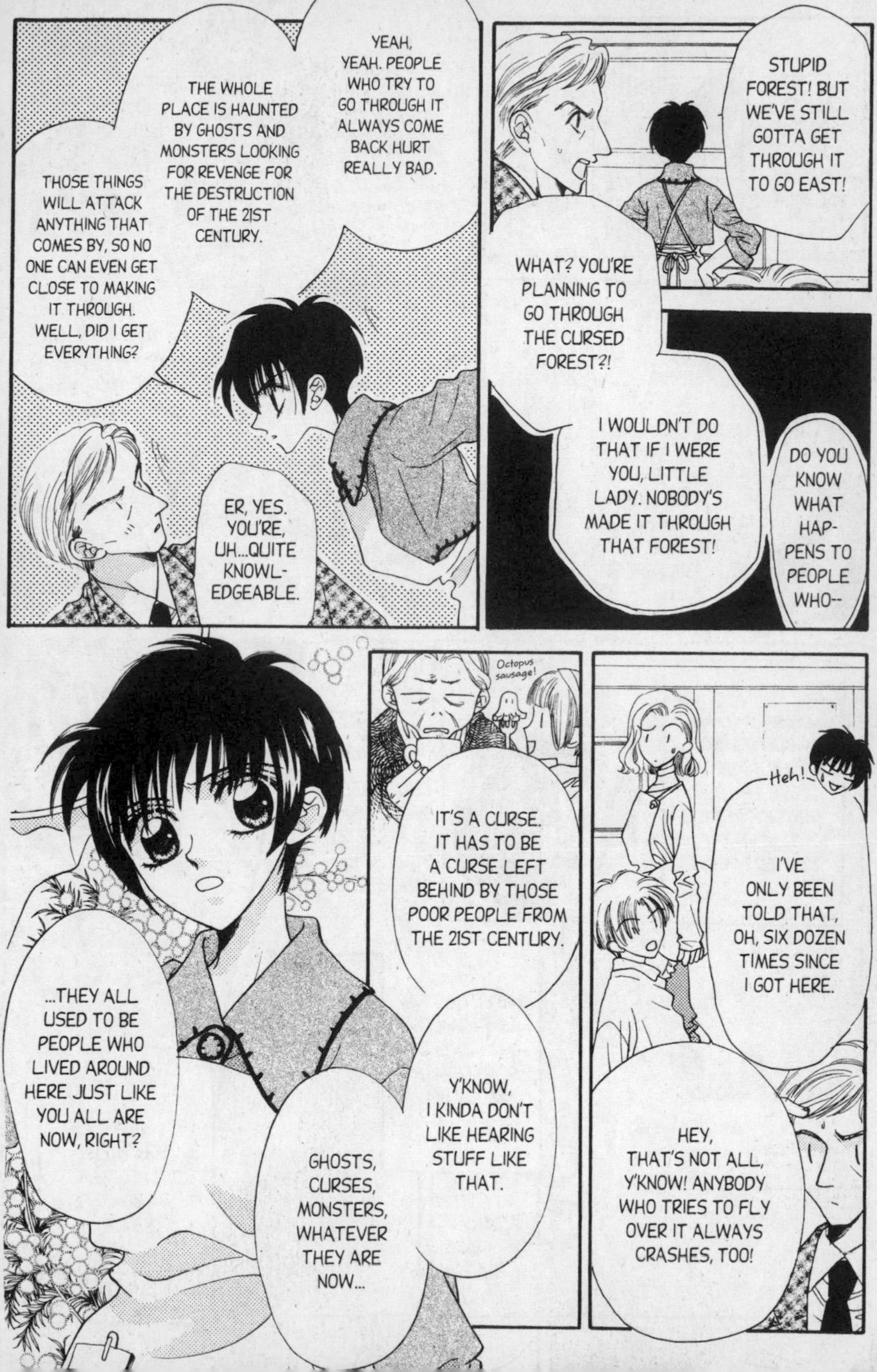

STUPID FOREST! BUT WE'VE STILL GOTTA GET THROUGH IT TO GO EAST!
WHAT? YOU'RE PLANNING TO GO THROUGH THE CURSED FOREST?!
I WOULDN'T DO THAT IF I WERE YOU, LITTLE LADY. NOBODY'S MADE IT THROUGH THAT FOREST!
DO YOU KNOW WHAT HAP-PENS TO PEOPLE WHO--
YEAH, YEAH. PEOPLE WHO TRY TO GO THROUGH IT ALWAYS COME BACK HURT REALLY BAD.
THE WHOLE PLACE IS HAUNTED BY GHOSTS AND MONSTERS LOOKING FOR REVENGE FOR THE DESTRUCTION OF THE 21ST CENTURY.
THOSE THINGS WILL ATTACK ANYTHING THAT COMES BY, SO NO ONE CAN EVEN GET CLOSE TO MAKING IT THROUGH. WELL, DID I GET EVERYTHING?
ER, YES. YOU'RE, UH...QUITE KNOWL-EDGEABLE.
Heh!
I'VE ONLY BEEN TOLD THAT, OH, SIX DOZEN TIMES SINCE I GOT HERE.
HEY, THAT'S NOT ALL, Y'KNOW! ANYBODY WHO TRIES TO FLY OVER IT ALWAYS CRASHES, TOO!
Octopus sausage!
IT'S A CURSE. IT HAS TO BE A CURSE LEFT BEHIND BY THOSE POOR PEOPLE FROM THE 21ST CENTURY.
Y'KNOW, I KINDA DON'T LIKE HEARING STUFF LIKE THAT.
GHOSTS, CURSES, MONSTERS, WHATEVER THEY ARE NOW...
...THEY ALL USED TO BE PEOPLE WHO LIVED AROUND HERE JUST LIKE YOU ALL ARE NOW, RIGHT?

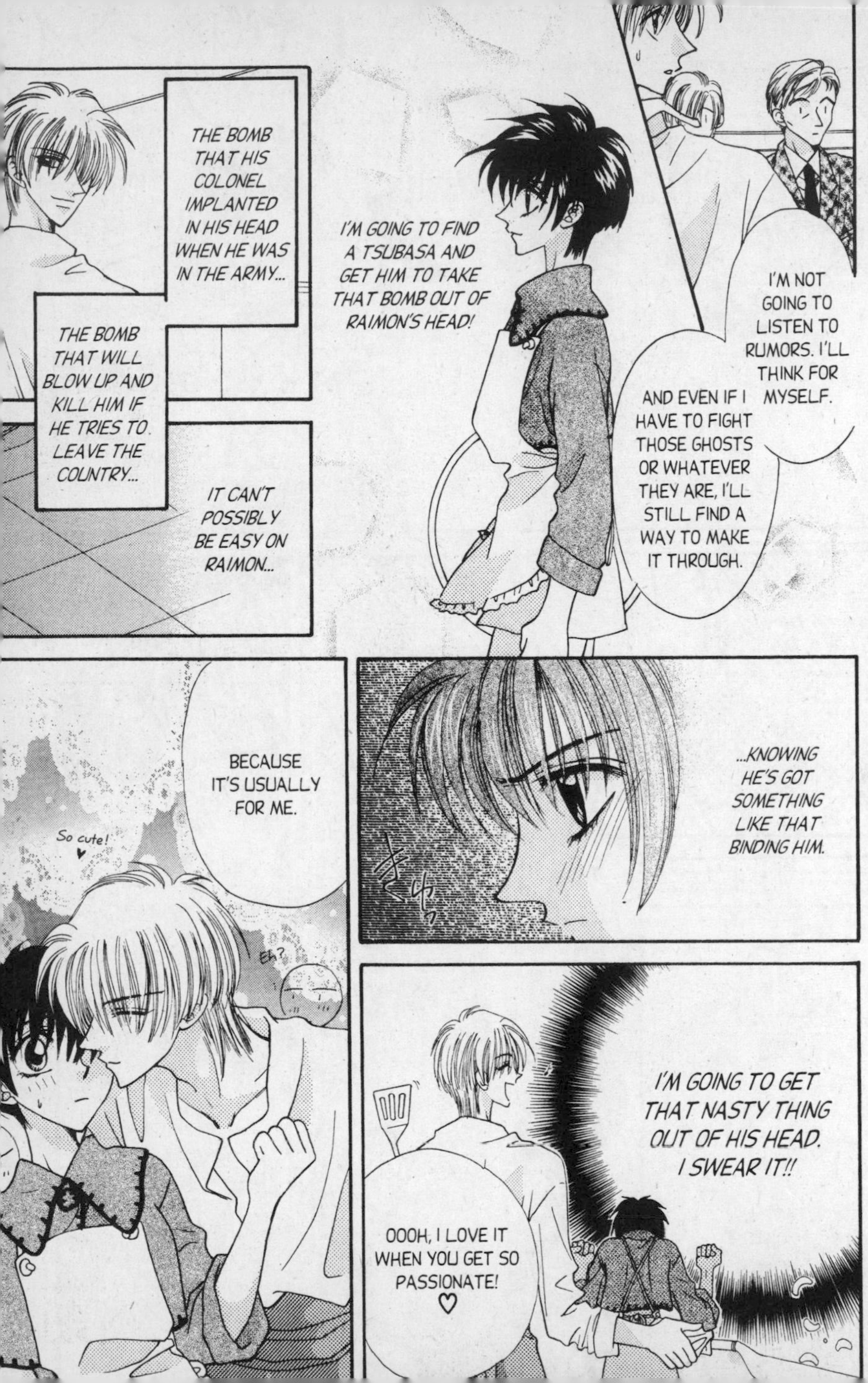
I'M NOT GOING TO LISTEN TO RUMORS. I'LL THINK FOR MYSELF.
AND EVEN IF I HAVE TO FIGHT THOSE GHOSTS OR WHATEVER THEY ARE, I'LL STILL FIND A WAY TO MAKE IT THROUGH.
I'M GOING TO FIND A TSUBASA AND GET HIM TO TAKE THAT BOMB OUT OF RAIMON'S HEAD!
THE BOMB THAT HIS COLONEL IMPLANTED IN HIS HEAD WHEN HE WAS IN THE ARMY...
THE BOMB THAT WILL BLOW UP AND KILL HIM IF HE TRIES TO LEAVE THE COUNTRY...
IT CAN'T POSSIBLY BE EASY ON RAIMON...
...KNOWING HE'S GOT SOMETHING LIKE THAT BINDING HIM.
I'M GOING TO GET THAT NASTY THING OUT OF HIS HEAD. I SWEAR IT!!
OOOH, I LOVE IT WHEN YOU GET SO PASSIONATE! ♡
BECAUSE IT'S USUALLY FOR ME.
So cute! ♥
Eh?

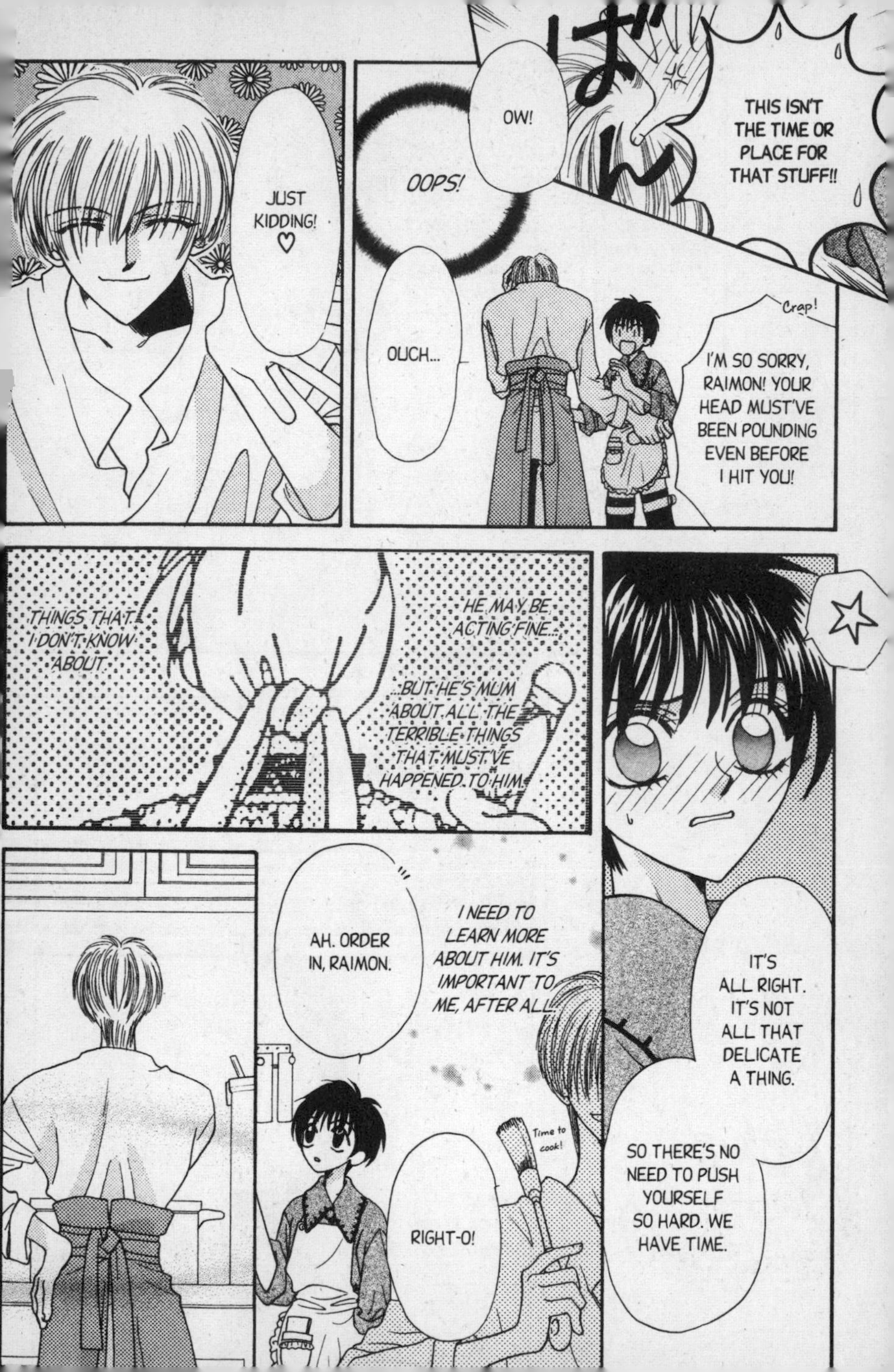
ばん
THIS ISN'T THE TIME OR PLACE FOR THAT STUFF!!
OW!
OOPS!
Crap!
I'M SO SORRY, RAIMON! YOUR HEAD MUST'VE BEEN POUNDING EVEN BEFORE I HIT YOU!
OUCH...
JUST KIDDING! ♡
IT'S ALL RIGHT. IT'S NOT ALL THAT DELICATE A THING.
SO THERE'S NO NEED TO PUSH YOURSELF SO HARD. WE HAVE TIME.
HE MAY BE ACTING FINE...
...BUT HE'S MUM ABOUT ALL THE TERRIBLE THINGS THAT MUST'VE HAPPENED TO HIM.
THINGS THAT I DON'T KNOW ABOUT.
I NEED TO LEARN MORE ABOUT HIM. IT'S IMPORTANT TO ME, AFTER ALL.
AH. ORDER IN, RAIMON.
Time to cook!
RIGHT-O!

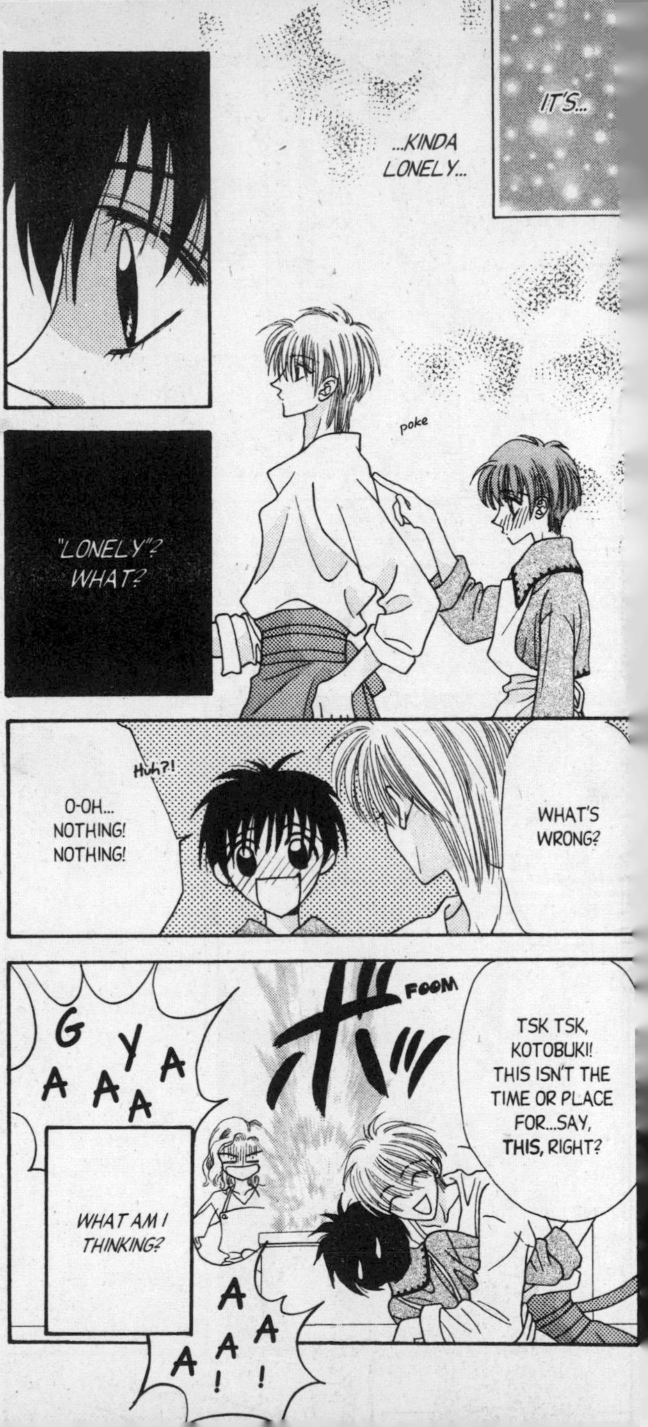
IT'S...
...KINDA LONELY...
poke
"LONELY"? WHAT?
WHAT'S WRONG?
Huh?!
O-OH... NOTHING! NOTHING!
TSK TSK, KOTOBUKI! THIS ISN'T THE TIME OR PLACE FOR...SAY, **THIS**, RIGHT?
FOOM
GYAAAA
WHAT AM I THINKING?
AAAA!!

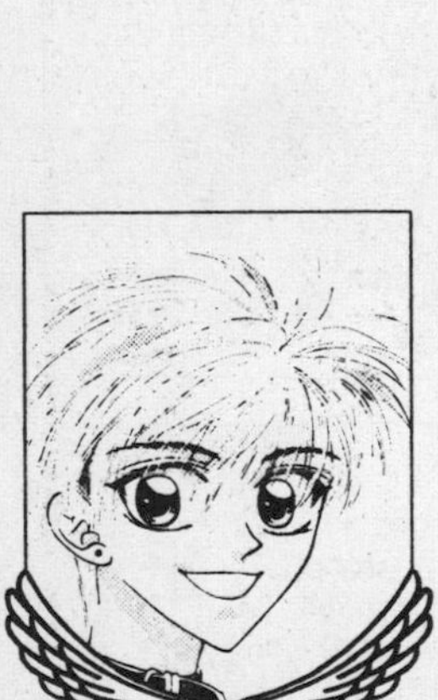

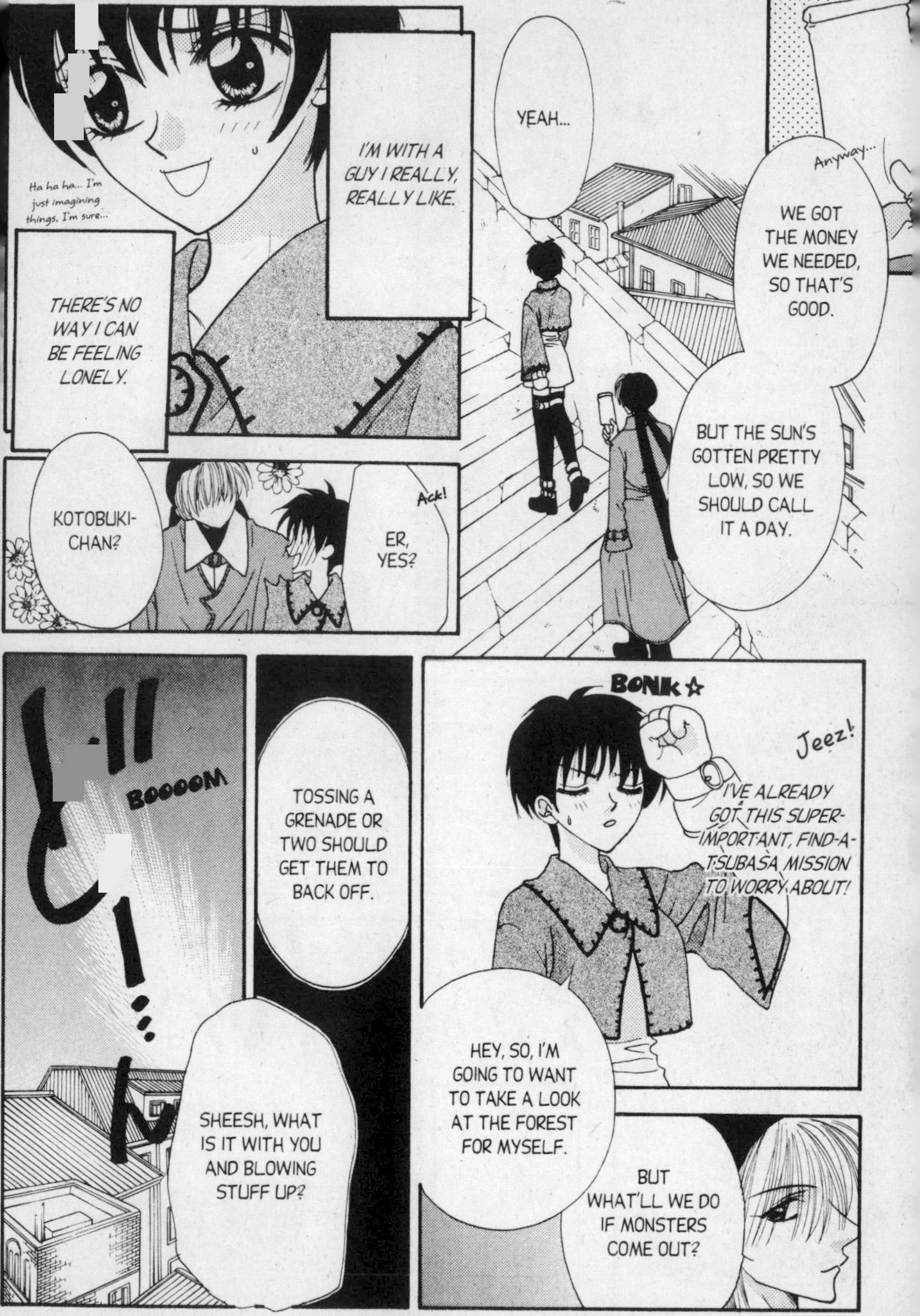

YEAH...
Anyway...
WE GOT THE MONEY WE NEEDED, SO THAT'S GOOD.
BUT THE SUN'S GOTTEN PRETTY LOW, SO WE SHOULD CALL IT A DAY.
I'M WITH A GUY I REALLY, REALLY LIKE.
THERE'S NO WAY I CAN BE FEELING LONELY.
Ha ha ha... I'm just imagining things, I'm sure...
Ack!
ER, YES?
KOTOBUKI-CHAN?
BONK☆
Jeez!
I'VE ALREADY GOT THIS SUPER-IMPORTANT, FIND-A-TSUBASA MISSION TO WORRY ABOUT!
HEY, SO, I'M GOING TO WANT TO TAKE A LOOK AT THE FOREST FOR MYSELF.
BUT WHAT'LL WE DO IF MONSTERS COME OUT?
TOSSING A GRENADE OR TWO SHOULD GET THEM TO BACK OFF.
BOOOOM
SHEESH, WHAT IS IT WITH YOU AND BLOWING STUFF UP?

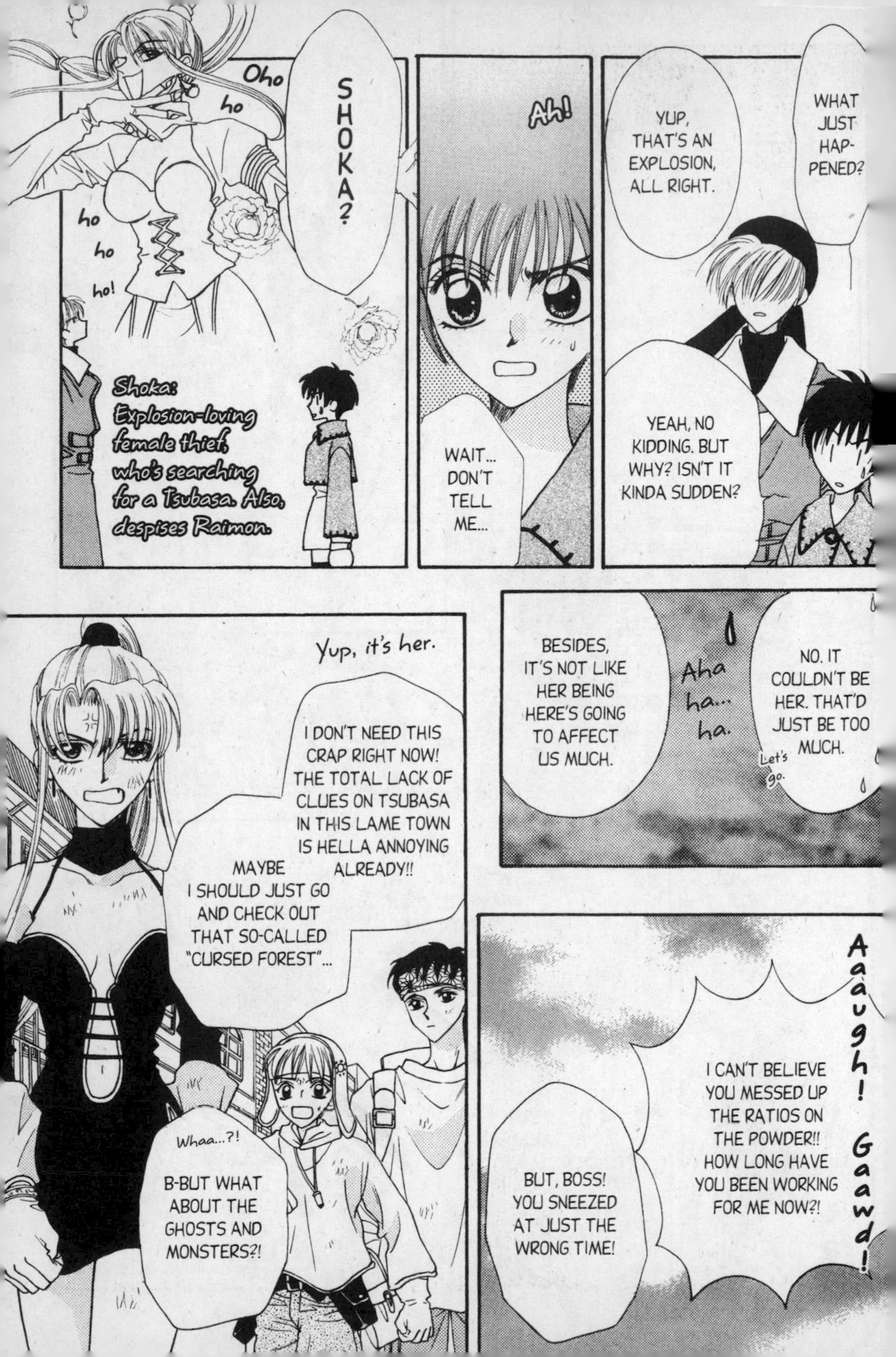
WHAT JUST HAP-PENED?
YUP, THAT'S AN EXPLOSION, ALL RIGHT.
YEAH, NO KIDDING. BUT WHY? ISN'T IT KINDA SUDDEN?
Ah!
WAIT... DON'T TELL ME...
SHOKA?
Oho ho
ho ho ho!
Shoka: Explosion-loving female thief, who's searching for a Tsubasa. Also, despises Raimon.
NO. IT COULDN'T BE HER. THAT'D JUST BE TOO MUCH.
Aha ha... ha.
Let's go.
BESIDES, IT'S NOT LIKE HER BEING HERE'S GOING TO AFFECT US MUCH.
Aaaugh! Gaawd!
I CAN'T BELIEVE YOU MESSED UP THE RATIOS ON THE POWDER!! HOW LONG HAVE YOU BEEN WORKING FOR ME NOW?!
BUT, BOSS! YOU SNEEZED AT JUST THE WRONG TIME!
Yup, it's her.
I DON'T NEED THIS CRAP RIGHT NOW! THE TOTAL LACK OF CLUES ON TSUBASA IN THIS LAME TOWN IS HELLA ANNOYING ALREADY!!
MAYBE I SHOULD JUST GO AND CHECK OUT THAT SO-CALLED "CURSED FOREST"...
Whaa...?!
B-BUT WHAT ABOUT THE GHOSTS AND MONSTERS?!

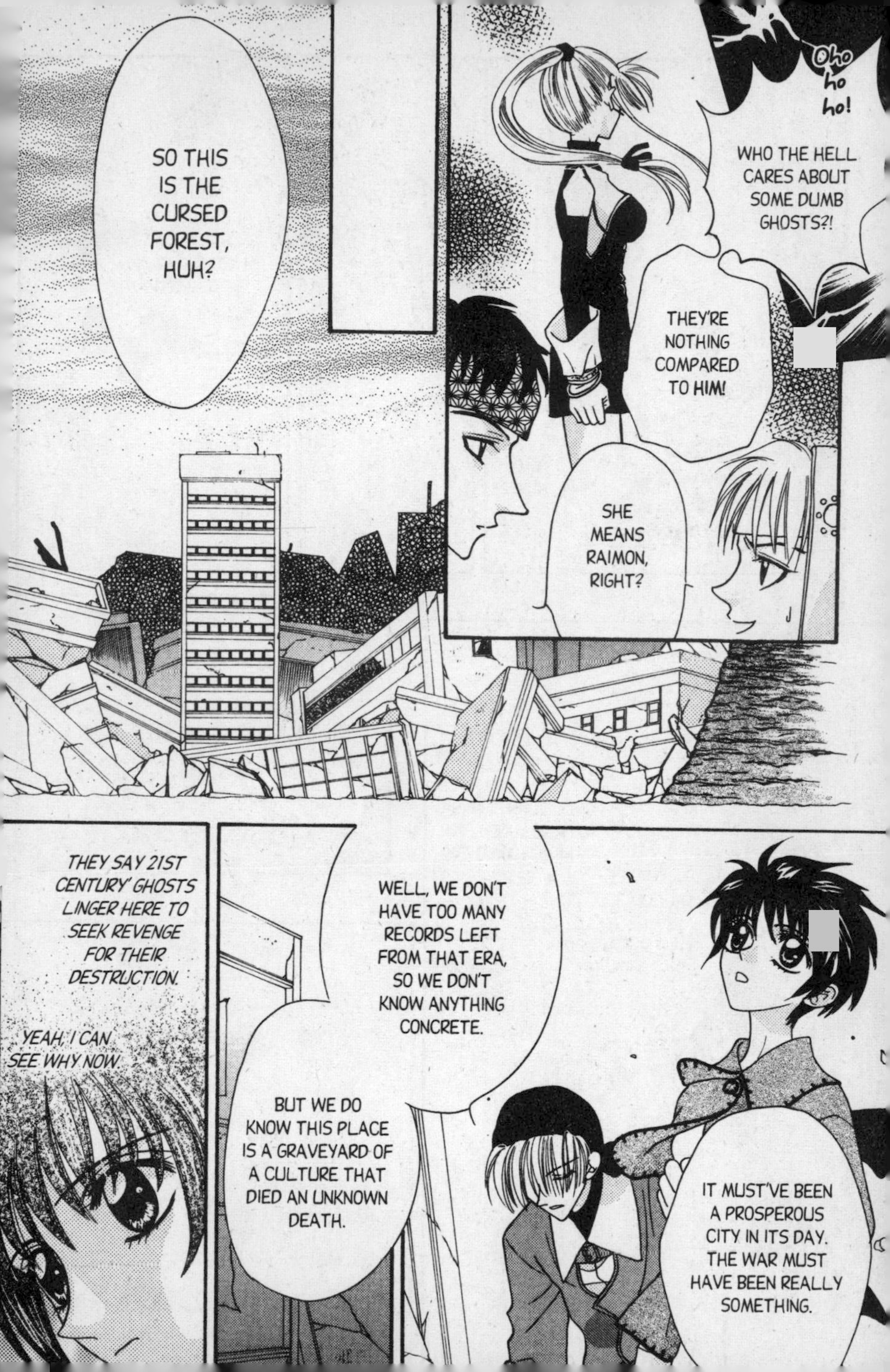
Oho ho ho!
WHO THE HELL CARES ABOUT SOME DUMB GHOSTS?!
THEY'RE NOTHING COMPARED TO HIM!
SHE MEANS RAIMON, RIGHT?
SO THIS IS THE CURSED FOREST, HUH?
IT MUST'VE BEEN A PROSPEROUS CITY IN ITS DAY. THE WAR MUST HAVE BEEN REALLY SOMETHING.
WELL, WE DON'T HAVE TOO MANY RECORDS LEFT FROM THAT ERA, SO WE DON'T KNOW ANYTHING CONCRETE.
BUT WE DO KNOW THIS PLACE IS A GRAVEYARD OF A CULTURE THAT DIED AN UNKNOWN DEATH.
THEY SAY 21ST CENTURY' GHOSTS LINGER HERE TO SEEK REVENGE FOR THEIR DESTRUCTION.
YEAH, I CAN SEE WHY NOW

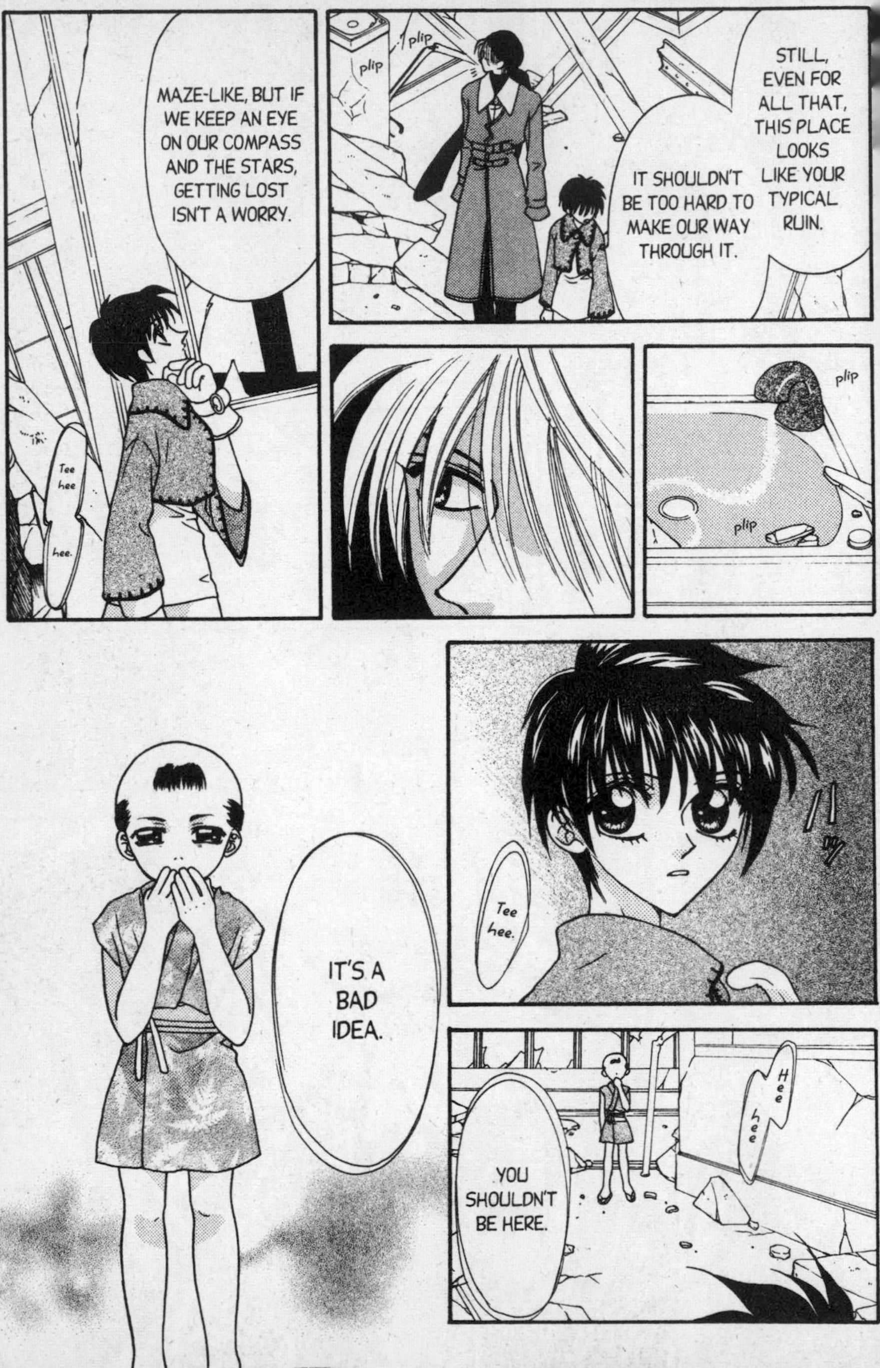
STILL, EVEN FOR ALL THAT, THIS PLACE LOOKS LIKE YOUR TYPICAL RUIN.
IT SHOULDN'T BE TOO HARD TO MAKE OUR WAY THROUGH IT.
plip
plip
MAZE-LIKE, BUT IF WE KEEP AN EYE ON OUR COMPASS AND THE STARS, GETTING LOST ISN'T A WORRY.
Tee hee hee.
plip
plip
Tee hee.
Hee hee
YOU SHOULDN'T BE HERE.
IT'S A BAD IDEA.

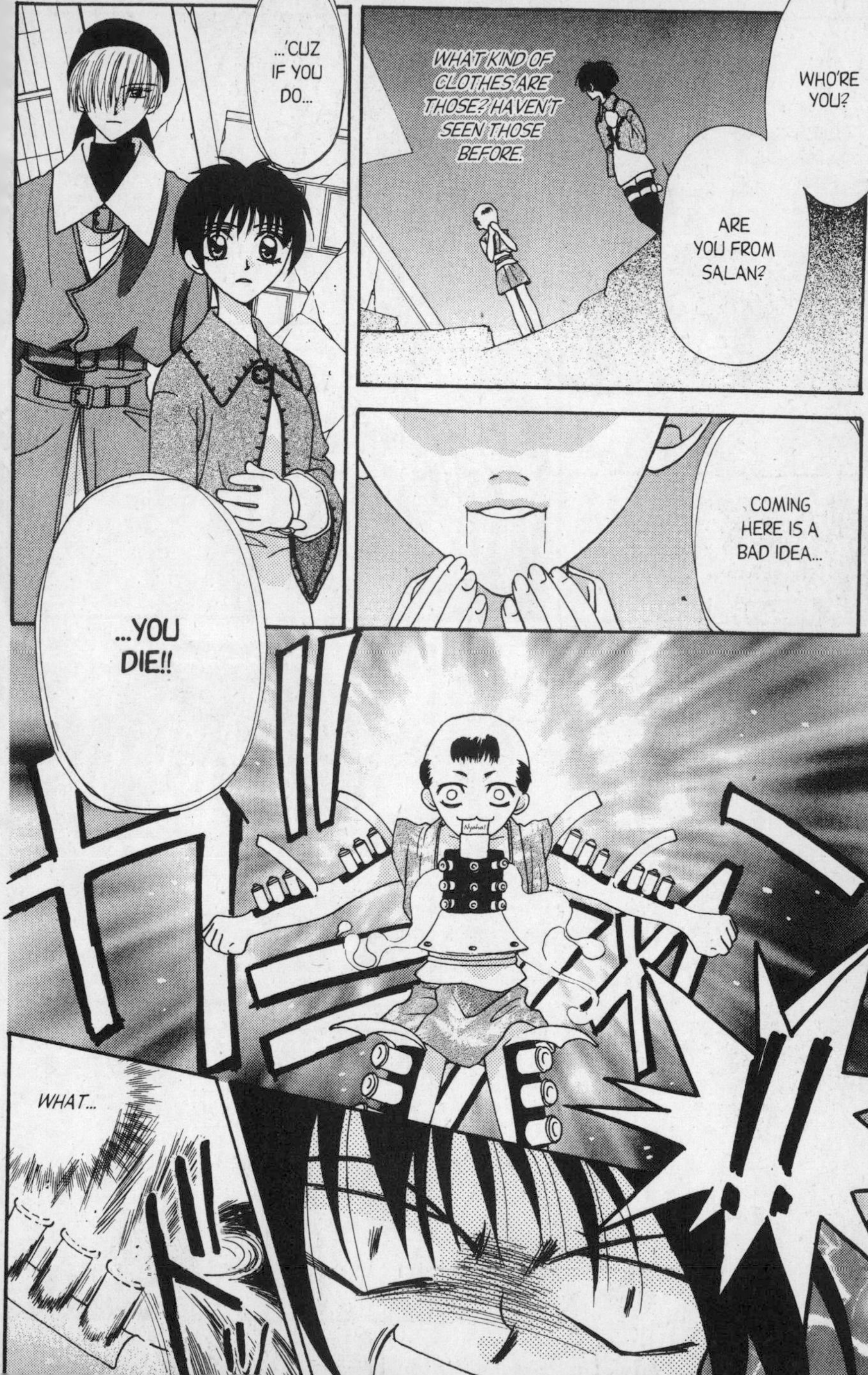
WHO'RE YOU?
ARE YOU FROM SALAN?
WHAT KIND OF CLOTHES ARE THOSE? HAVEN'T SEEN THOSE BEFORE.
COMING HERE IS A BAD IDEA...
...'CUZ IF YOU DO...
...YOU DIE!!
Nyaha!
WHAT...

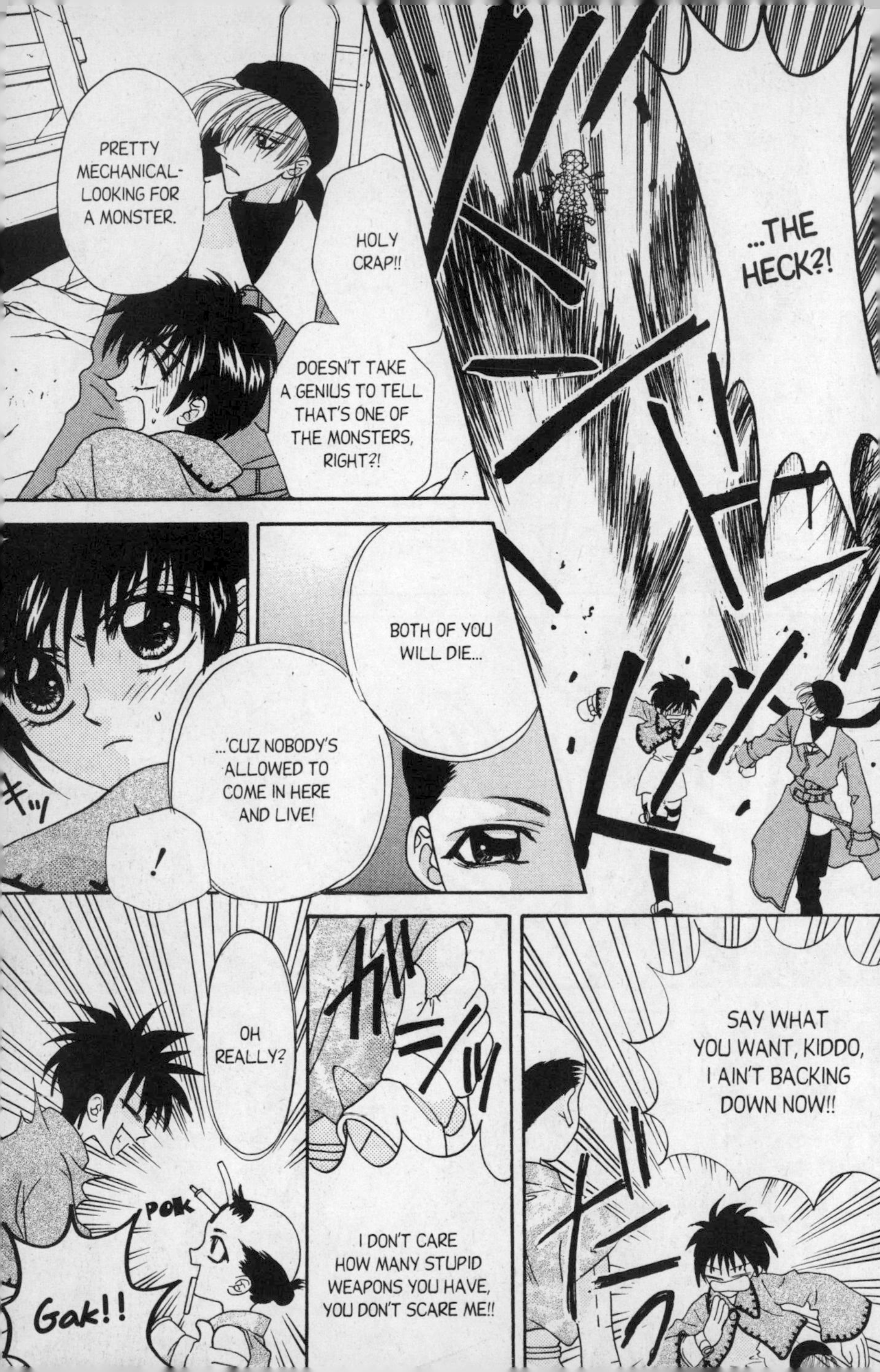
...THE HECK?!
HOLY CRAP!!
PRETTY MECHANICAL-LOOKING FOR A MONSTER.
DOESN'T TAKE A GENIUS TO TELL THAT'S ONE OF THE MONSTERS, RIGHT?!
BOTH OF YOU WILL DIE...
...'CUZ NOBODY'S ALLOWED TO COME IN HERE AND LIVE!
キッ
!
SAY WHAT YOU WANT, KIDDO, I AIN'T BACKING DOWN NOW!!
I DON'T CARE HOW MANY STUPID WEAPONS YOU HAVE, YOU DON'T SCARE ME!!
OH REALLY?
POK
Gak!!

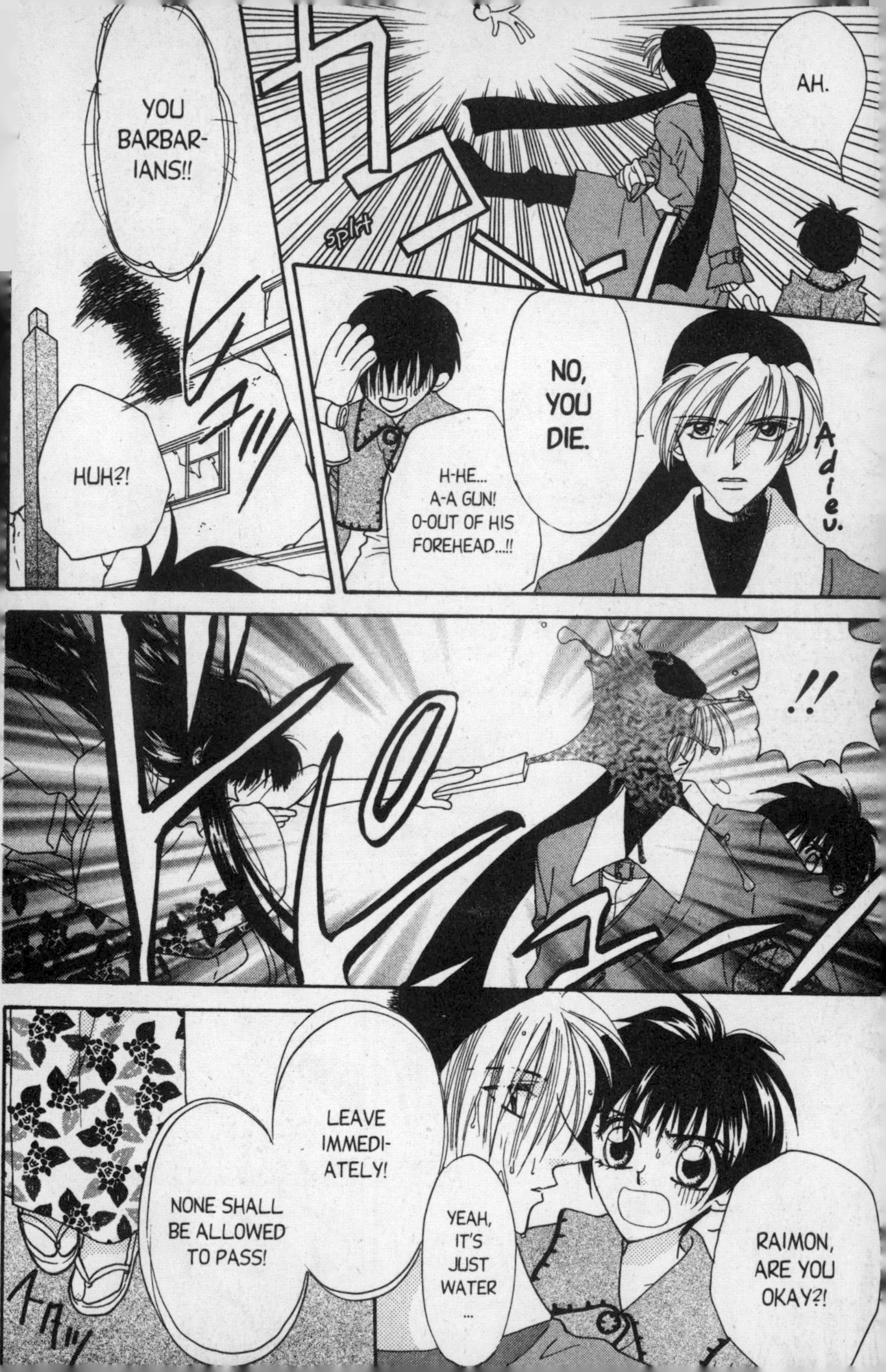
AH.
split
NO, YOU DIE.
Adieu.
H-HE... A-A GUN! O-OUT OF HIS FOREHEAD...!!
YOU BARBARIANS!!
HUH?!
!!
RAIMON, ARE YOU OKAY?!
YEAH, IT'S JUST WATER ...
LEAVE IMMEDIATELY!
NONE SHALL BE ALLOWED TO PASS!

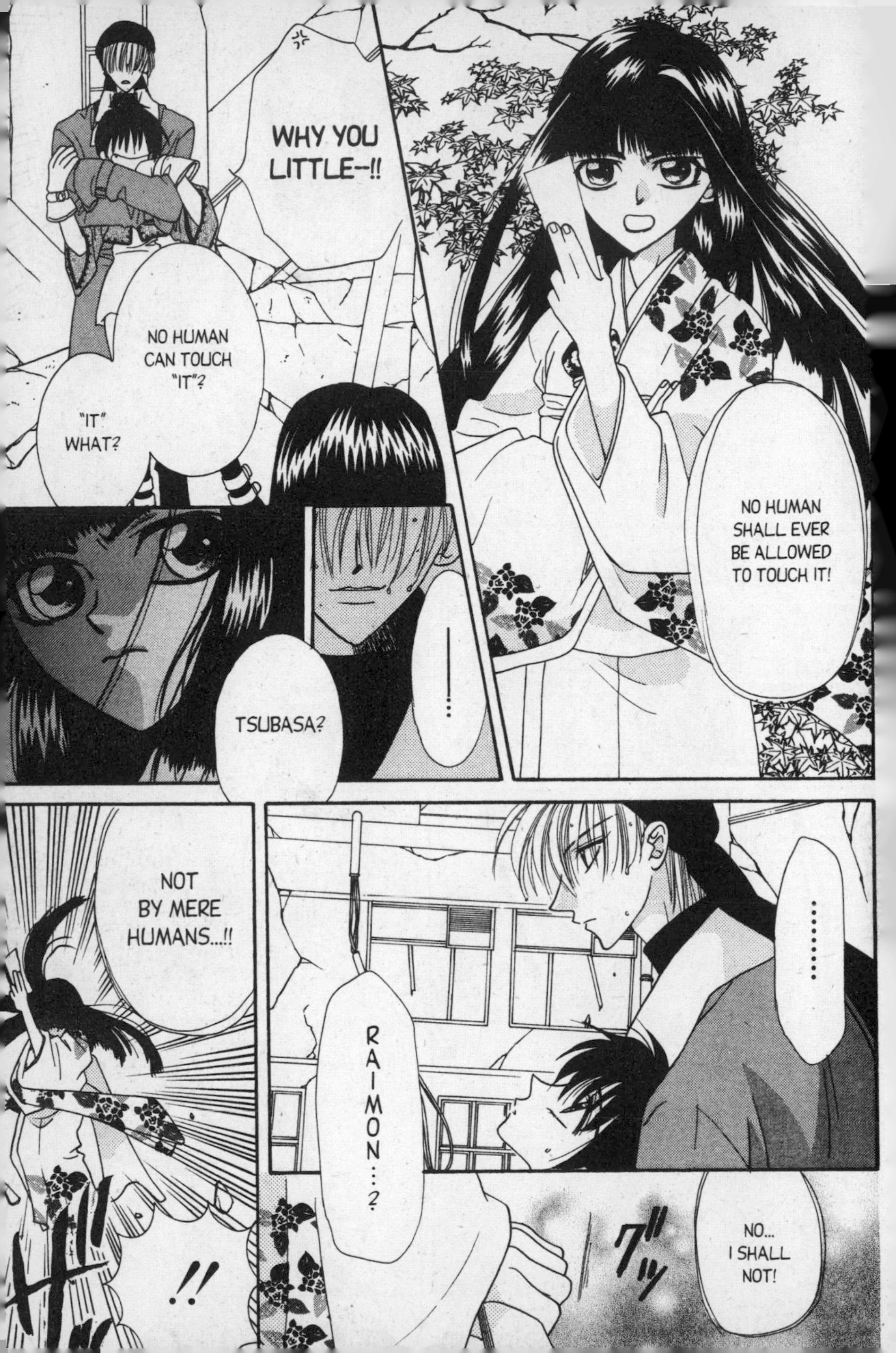
NO HUMAN SHALL EVER BE ALLOWED TO TOUCH IT!
WHY YOU LITTLE--!!
NO HUMAN CAN TOUCH "IT"?
"IT" WHAT?
...
TSUBASA?
......
RAIMON...?
グッ
NO... I SHALL NOT!
NOT BY MERE HUMANS...!!
!!

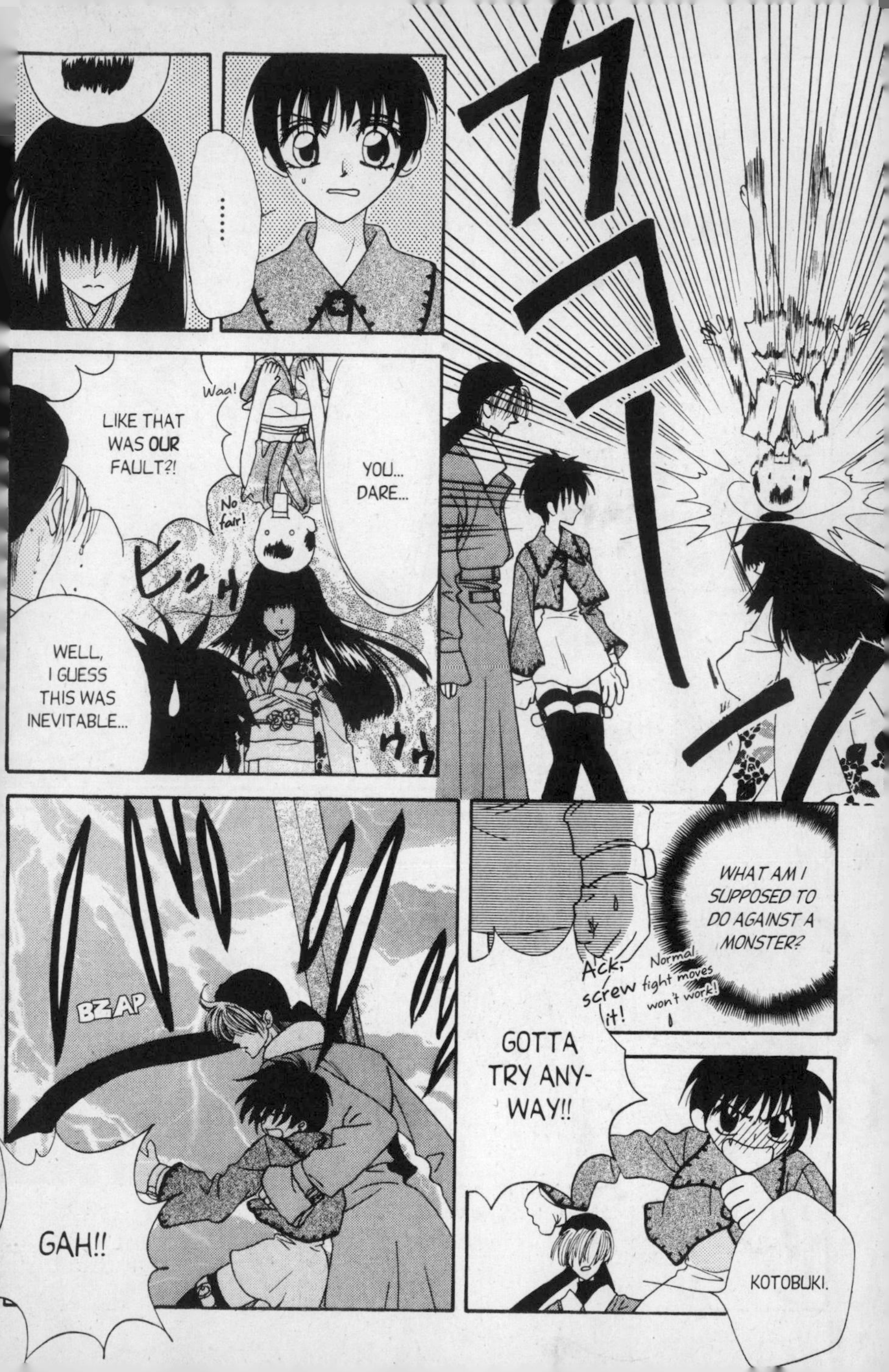

カラーン
......
YOU... DARE...
Waa!
LIKE THAT WAS OUR FAULT?!
No fair!
WELL, I GUESS THIS WAS INEVITABLE...
ウゥ
WHAT AM I SUPPOSED TO DO AGAINST A MONSTER?
Normal fight moves won't work!
Ack, screw it!
GOTTA TRY ANY-WAY!!
KOTOBUKI.
BZAP
GAH!!

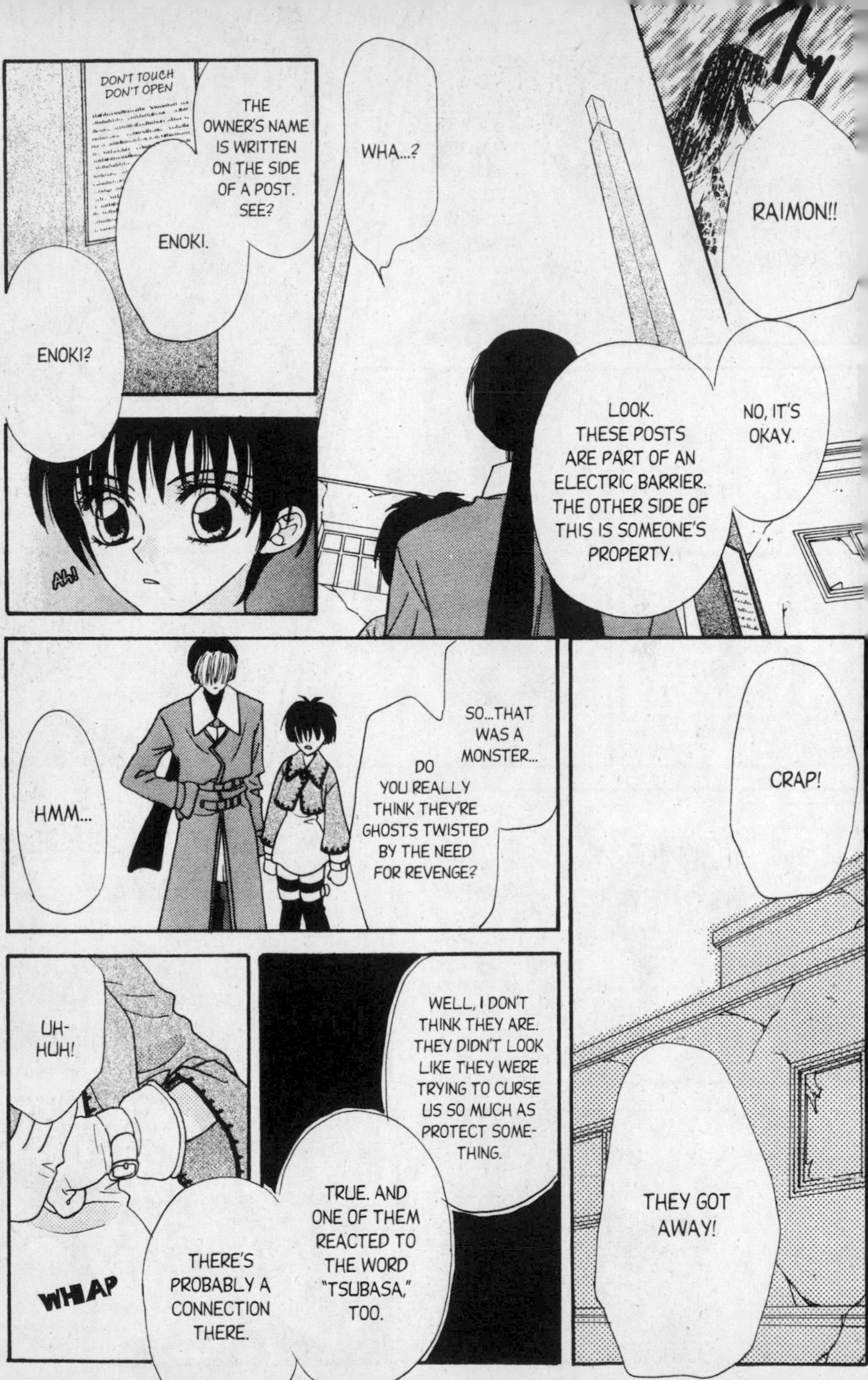
RAIMON!!
NO, IT'S OKAY.
LOOK. THESE POSTS ARE PART OF AN ELECTRIC BARRIER. THE OTHER SIDE OF THIS IS SOMEONE'S PROPERTY.
WHA...?
DON'T TOUCH
DON'T OPEN
THE OWNER'S NAME IS WRITTEN ON THE SIDE OF A POST. SEE?
ENOKI.
ENOKI?
Ah!
CRAP!
THEY GOT AWAY!
SO...THAT WAS A MONSTER...
DO YOU REALLY THINK THEY'RE GHOSTS TWISTED BY THE NEED FOR REVENGE?
HMM...
WELL, I DON'T THINK THEY ARE. THEY DIDN'T LOOK LIKE THEY WERE TRYING TO CURSE US SO MUCH AS PROTECT SOME-THING.
TRUE. AND ONE OF THEM REACTED TO THE WORD "TSUBASA," TOO.
THERE'S PROBABLY A CONNECTION THERE.
UH-HUH!
WHAP

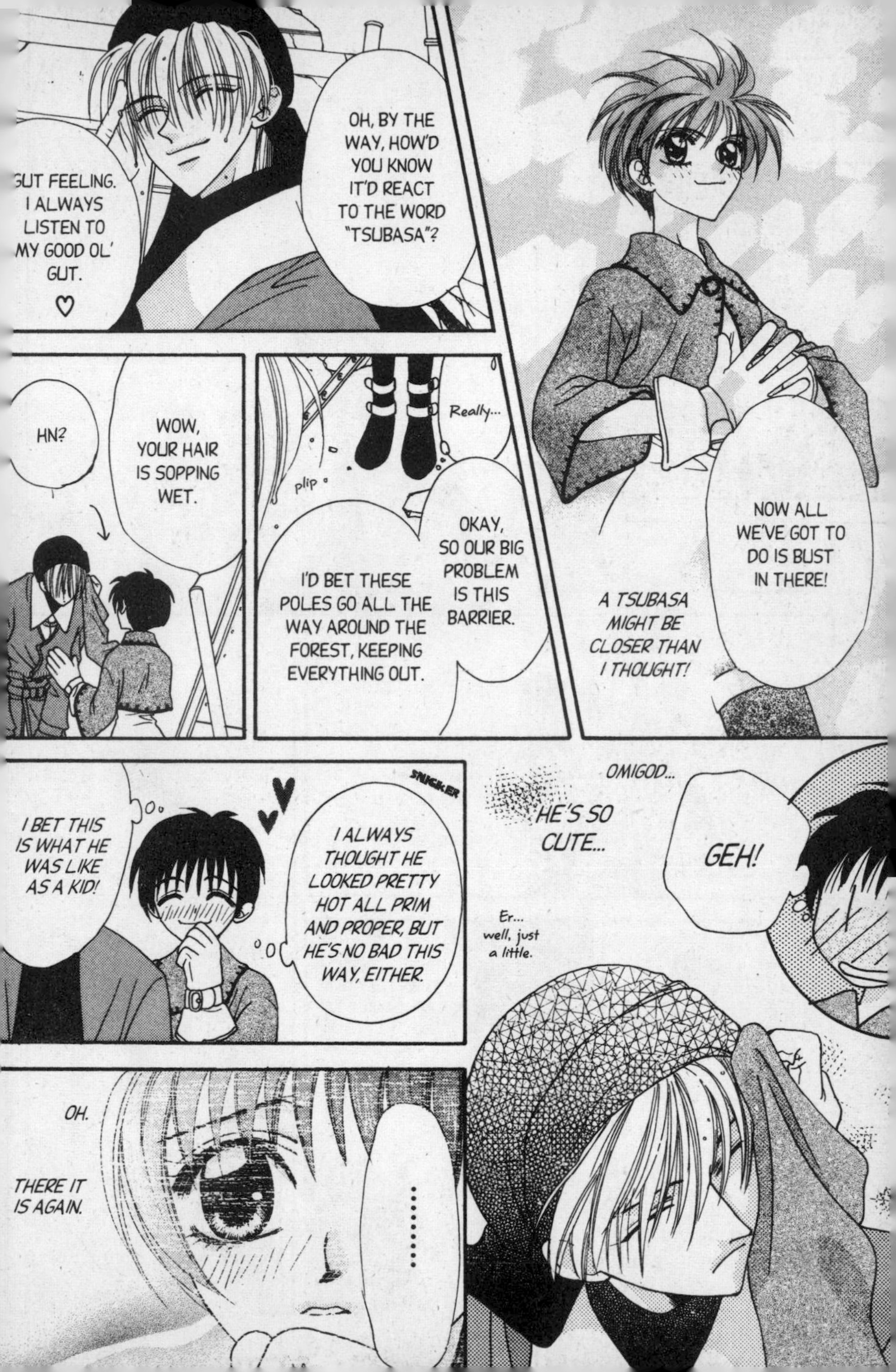

NOW ALL WE'VE GOT TO DO IS BUST IN THERE!
A TSUBASA MIGHT BE CLOSER THAN I THOUGHT!
OH, BY THE WAY, HOW'D YOU KNOW IT'D REACT TO THE WORD "TSUBASA"?
GUT FEELING. I ALWAYS LISTEN TO MY GOOD OL' GUT. ♡
Really...
OKAY, SO OUR BIG PROBLEM IS THIS BARRIER.
plip
I'D BET THESE POLES GO ALL THE WAY AROUND THE FOREST, KEEPING EVERYTHING OUT.
WOW, YOUR HAIR IS SOPPING WET.
HN?
GEH!
OMIGOD...
HE'S SO CUTE...
Er... well, just a little.
SNICKER
I ALWAYS THOUGHT HE LOOKED PRETTY HOT ALL PRIM AND PROPER, BUT HE'S NO BAD THIS WAY, EITHER.
I BET THIS IS WHAT HE WAS LIKE AS A KID!
......
OH.
THERE IT IS AGAIN.

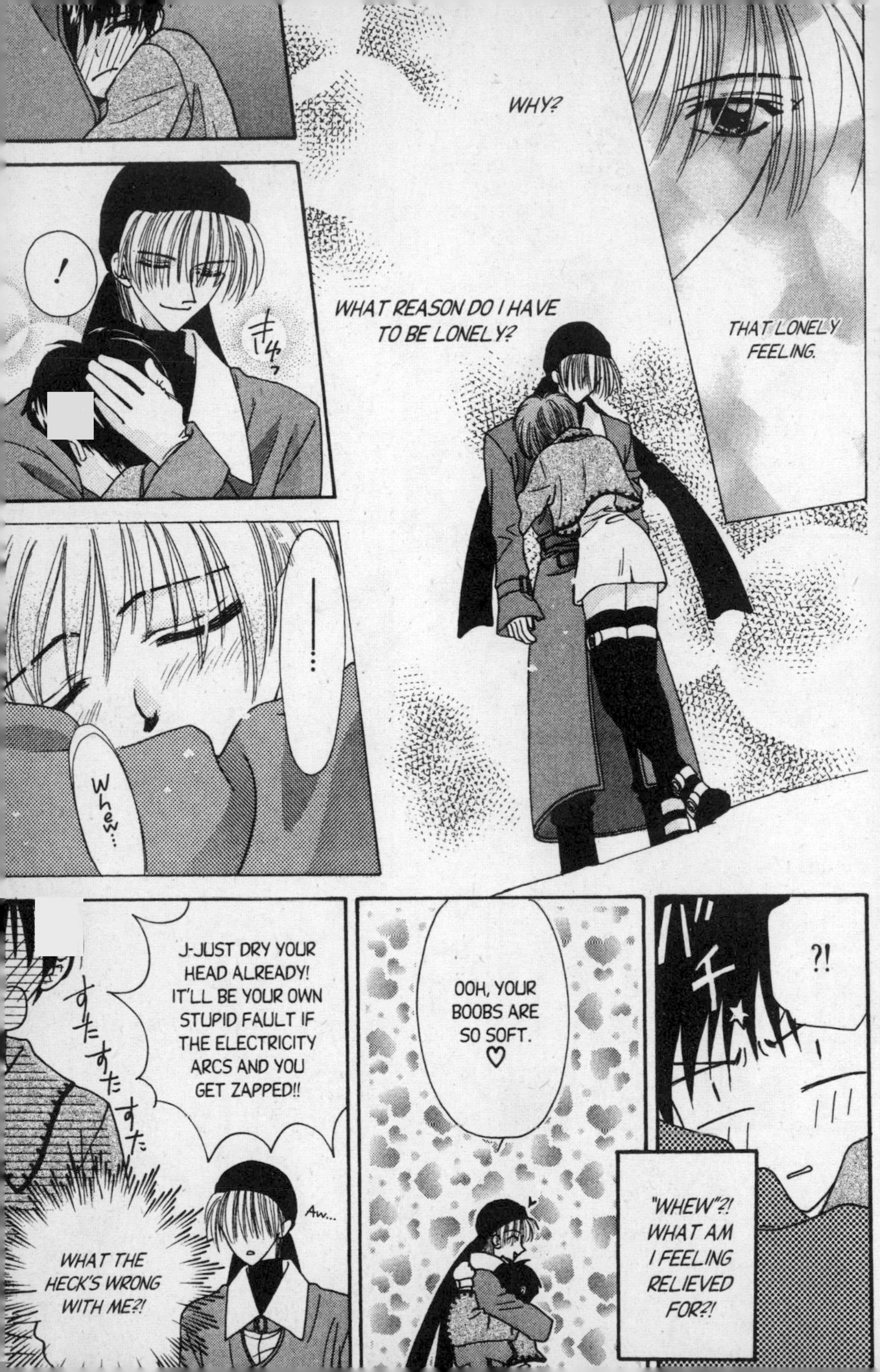

THAT LONELY FEELING.
WHY?
WHAT REASON DO I HAVE TO BE LONELY?
!
......
Whew...
バチ☆
?!
"WHEW"?! WHAT AM I FEELING RELIEVED FOR?!
OOH, YOUR BOOBS ARE SO SOFT. ♡
J-JUST DRY YOUR HEAD ALREADY! IT'LL BE YOUR OWN STUPID FAULT IF THE ELECTRICITY ARCS AND YOU GET ZAPPED!!
すたすたすたすた
Aw...
WHAT THE HECK'S WRONG WITH ME?!

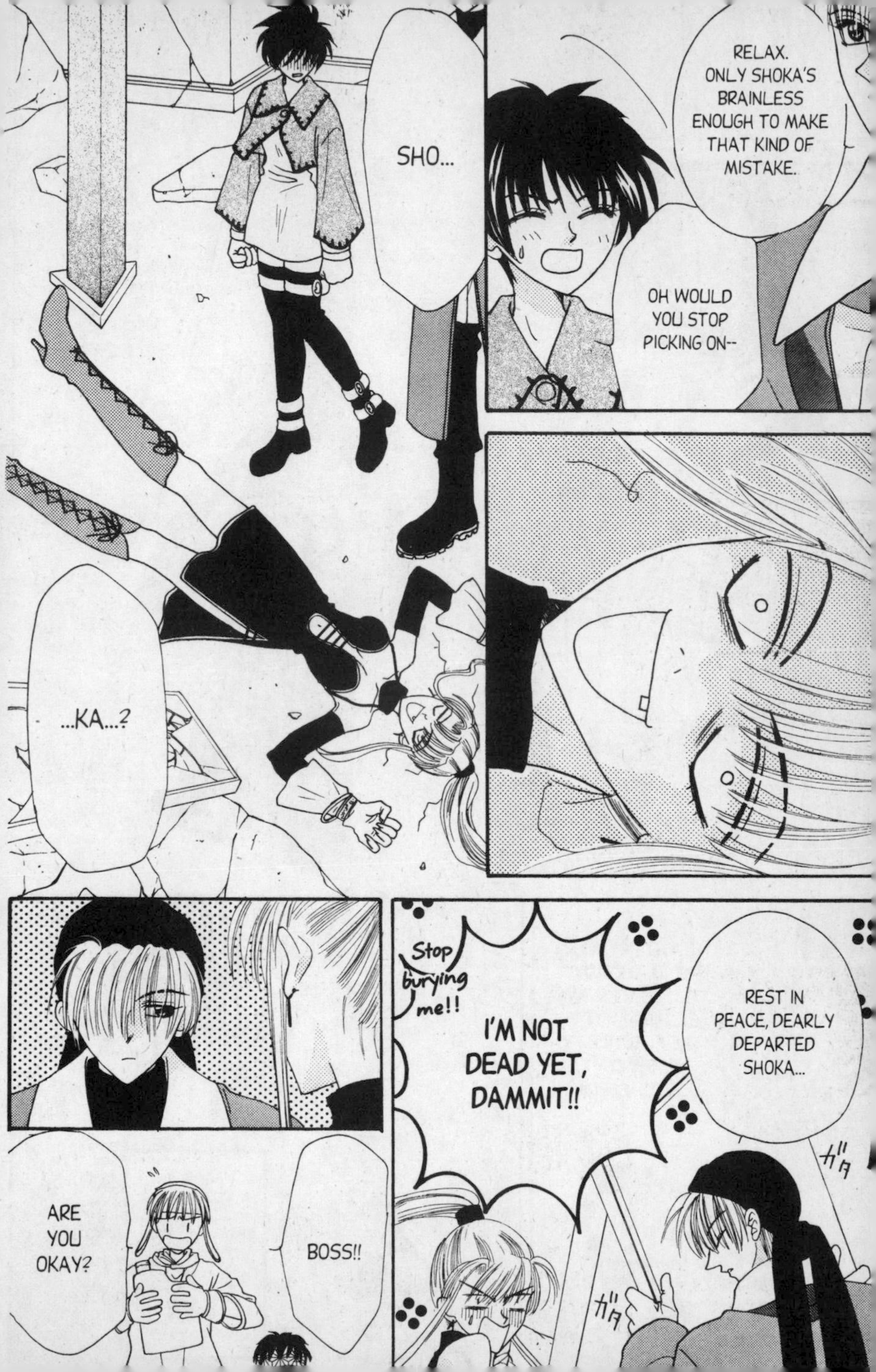
RELAX. ONLY SHOKA'S BRAINLESS ENOUGH TO MAKE THAT KIND OF MISTAKE.
OH WOULD YOU STOP PICKING ON--
SHO...
...KA...?
REST IN PEACE, DEARLY DEPARTED SHOKA...
ガタ
ガタ
I'M NOT DEAD YET, DAMMIT!!
Stop burying me!!
BOSS!!
ARE YOU OKAY?

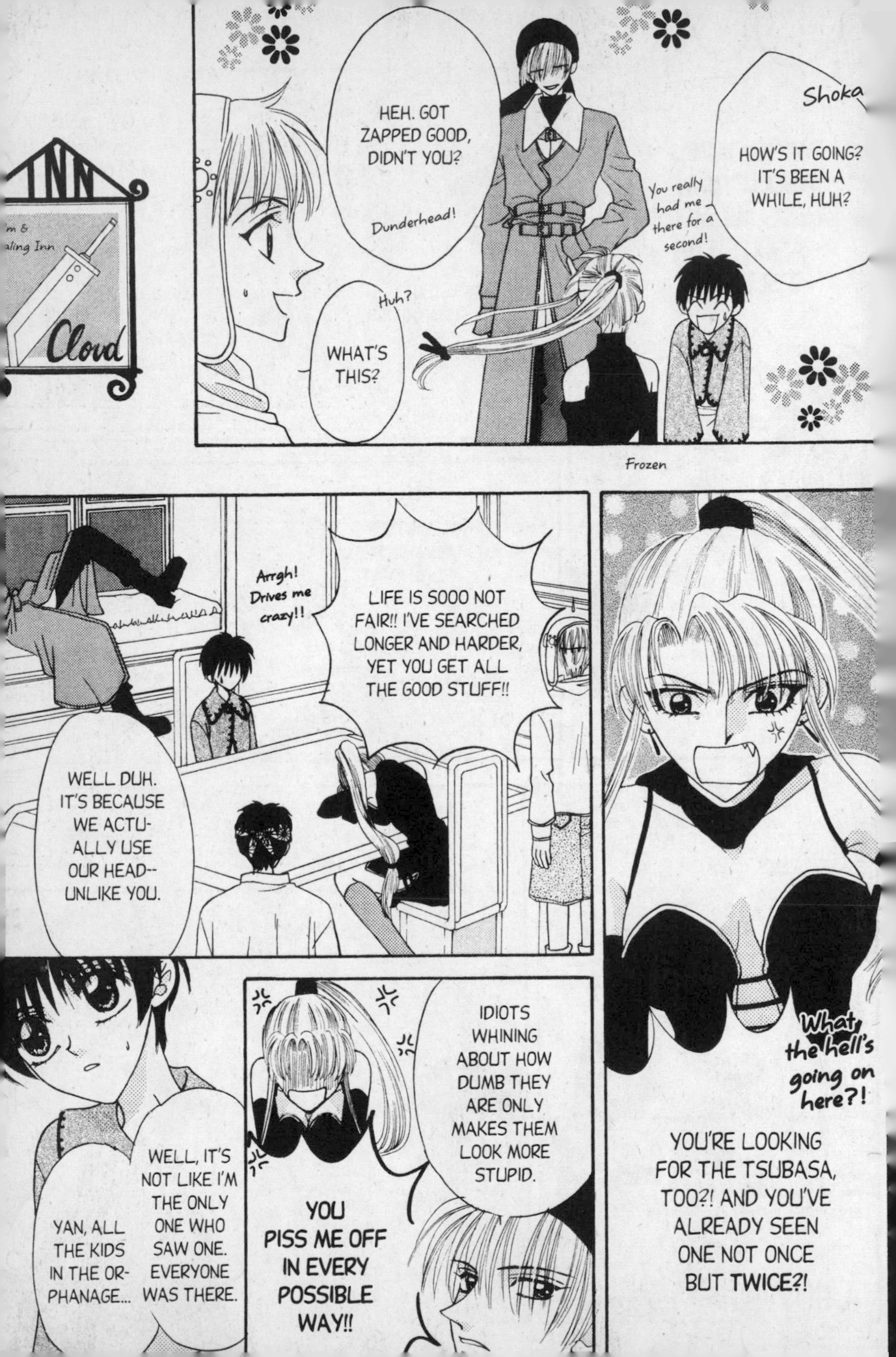

Shoka
HOW'S IT GOING? IT'S BEEN A WHILE, HUH?
You really had me there for a second!
HEH. GOT ZAPPED GOOD, DIDN'T YOU?
Dunderhead!
Huh?
WHAT'S THIS?
INN
Cloud
Frozen
What the hell's going on here?!
YOU'RE LOOKING FOR THE TSUBASA, TOO?! AND YOU'VE ALREADY SEEN ONE NOT ONCE BUT TWICE?!
LIFE IS SOOO NOT FAIR!! I'VE SEARCHED LONGER AND HARDER, YET YOU GET ALL THE GOOD STUFF!!
Arrgh! Drives me crazy!!
WELL DUH. IT'S BECAUSE WE ACTU-ALLY USE OUR HEAD-- UNLIKE YOU.
IDIOTS WHINING ABOUT HOW DUMB THEY ARE ONLY MAKES THEM LOOK MORE STUPID.
YOU PISS ME OFF IN EVERY POSSIBLE WAY!!
WELL, IT'S NOT LIKE I'M THE ONLY ONE WHO SAW ONE. EVERYONE WAS THERE.
YAN, ALL THE KIDS IN THE OR-PHANAGE...

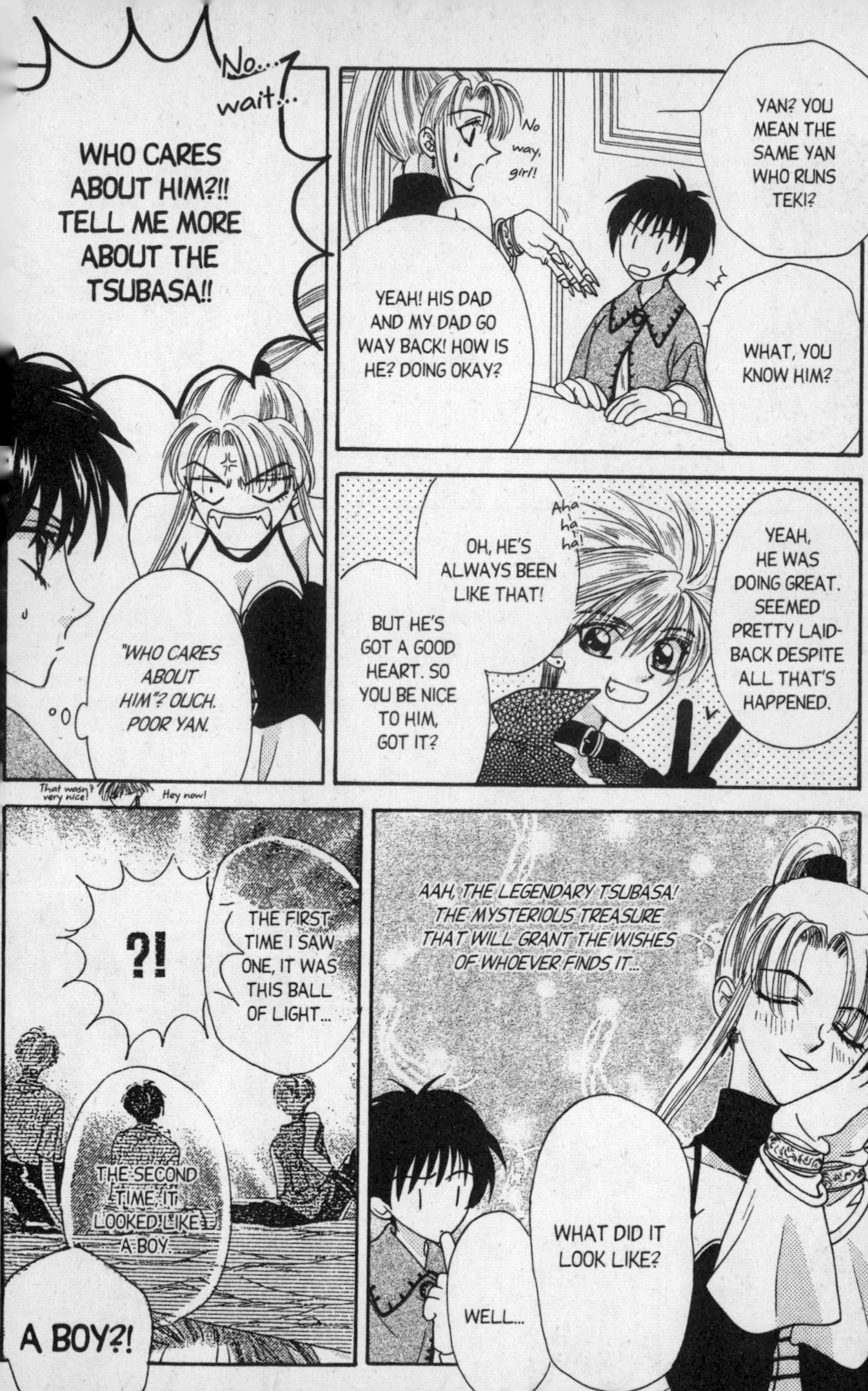
YAN? YOU MEAN THE SAME YAN WHO RUNS TEKI?
WHAT, YOU KNOW HIM?
No way, girl!
YEAH! HIS DAD AND MY DAD GO WAY BACK! HOW IS HE? DOING OKAY?
YEAH, HE WAS DOING GREAT. SEEMED PRETTY LAID-BACK DESPITE ALL THAT'S HAPPENED.
Aha ha ha!
OH, HE'S ALWAYS BEEN LIKE THAT!
BUT HE'S GOT A GOOD HEART. SO YOU BE NICE TO HIM, GOT IT?
No... wait...
WHO CARES ABOUT HIM?!! TELL ME MORE ABOUT THE TSUBASA!!
"WHO CARES ABOUT HIM"? OUCH. POOR YAN.
Hey now!
That wasn't very nice!
AAH, THE LEGENDARY TSUBASA! THE MYSTERIOUS TREASURE THAT WILL GRANT THE WISHES OF WHOEVER FINDS IT...
WHAT DID IT LOOK LIKE?
WELL...
THE FIRST TIME I SAW ONE, IT WAS THIS BALL OF LIGHT...
?!
THE SECOND TIME, IT LOOKED LIKE A BOY.
A BOY?!

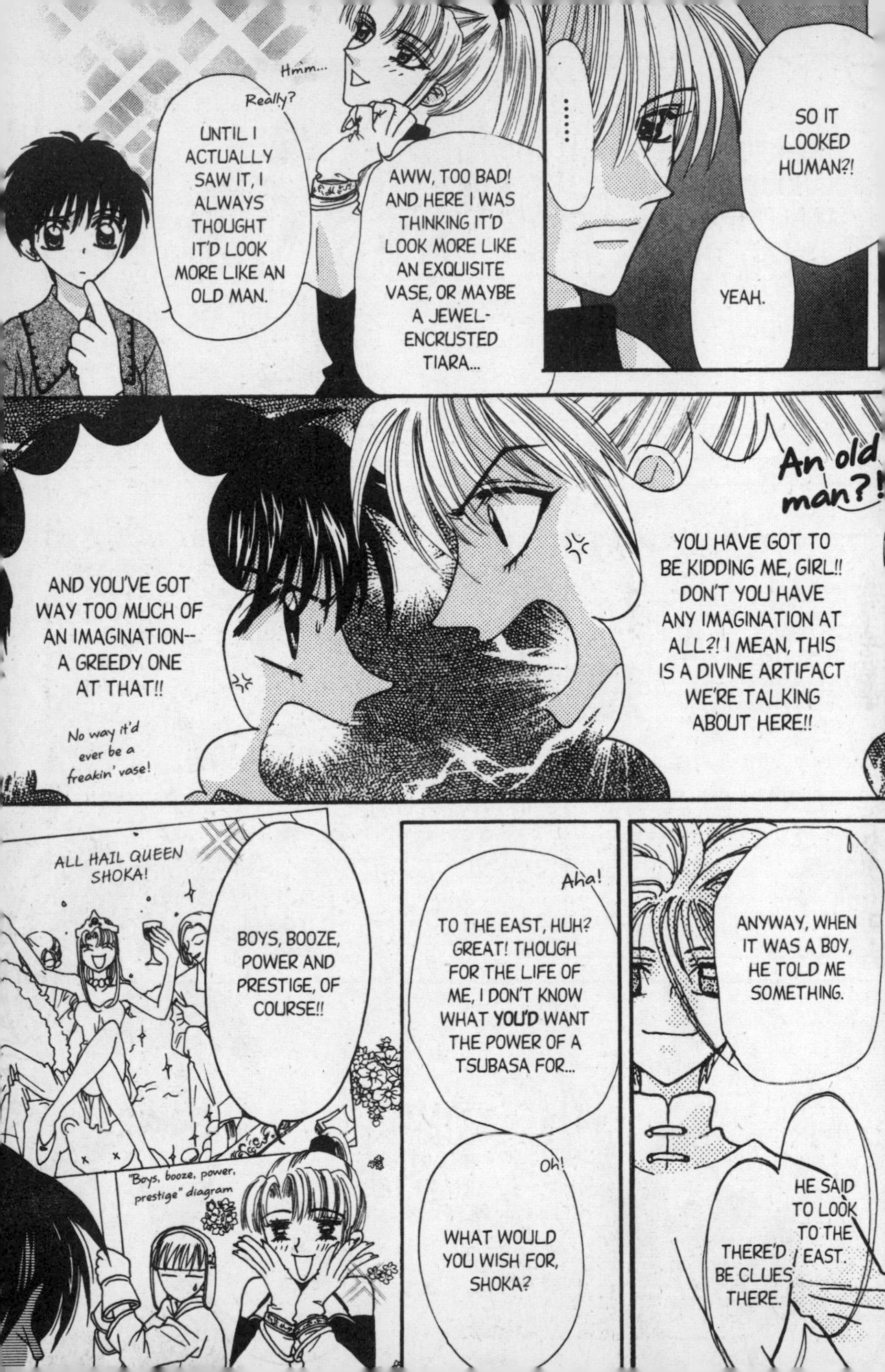

SO IT LOOKED HUMAN?!
......
YEAH.
Hmm...
AWW, TOO BAD! AND HERE I WAS THINKING IT'D LOOK MORE LIKE AN EXQUISITE VASE, OR MAYBE A JEWEL-ENCRUSTED TIARA...
Really?
UNTIL I ACTUALLY SAW IT, I ALWAYS THOUGHT IT'D LOOK MORE LIKE AN OLD MAN.
An old man?!
YOU HAVE GOT TO BE KIDDING ME, GIRL!! DON'T YOU HAVE ANY IMAGINATION AT ALL?! I MEAN, THIS IS A DIVINE ARTIFACT WE'RE TALKING ABOUT HERE!!
AND YOU'VE GOT WAY TOO MUCH OF AN IMAGINATION-- A GREEDY ONE AT THAT!!
No way it'd ever be a freakin' vase!
ANYWAY, WHEN IT WAS A BOY, HE TOLD ME SOMETHING.
HE SAID TO LOOK TO THE EAST.
THERE'D BE CLUES THERE.
Aha!
TO THE EAST, HUH? GREAT! THOUGH FOR THE LIFE OF ME, I DON'T KNOW WHAT YOU'D WANT THE POWER OF A TSUBASA FOR...
Oh!
WHAT WOULD YOU WISH FOR, SHOKA?
BOYS, BOOZE, POWER AND PRESTIGE, OF COURSE!!
ALL HAIL QUEEN SHOKA!
"Boys, booze, power, prestige" diagram

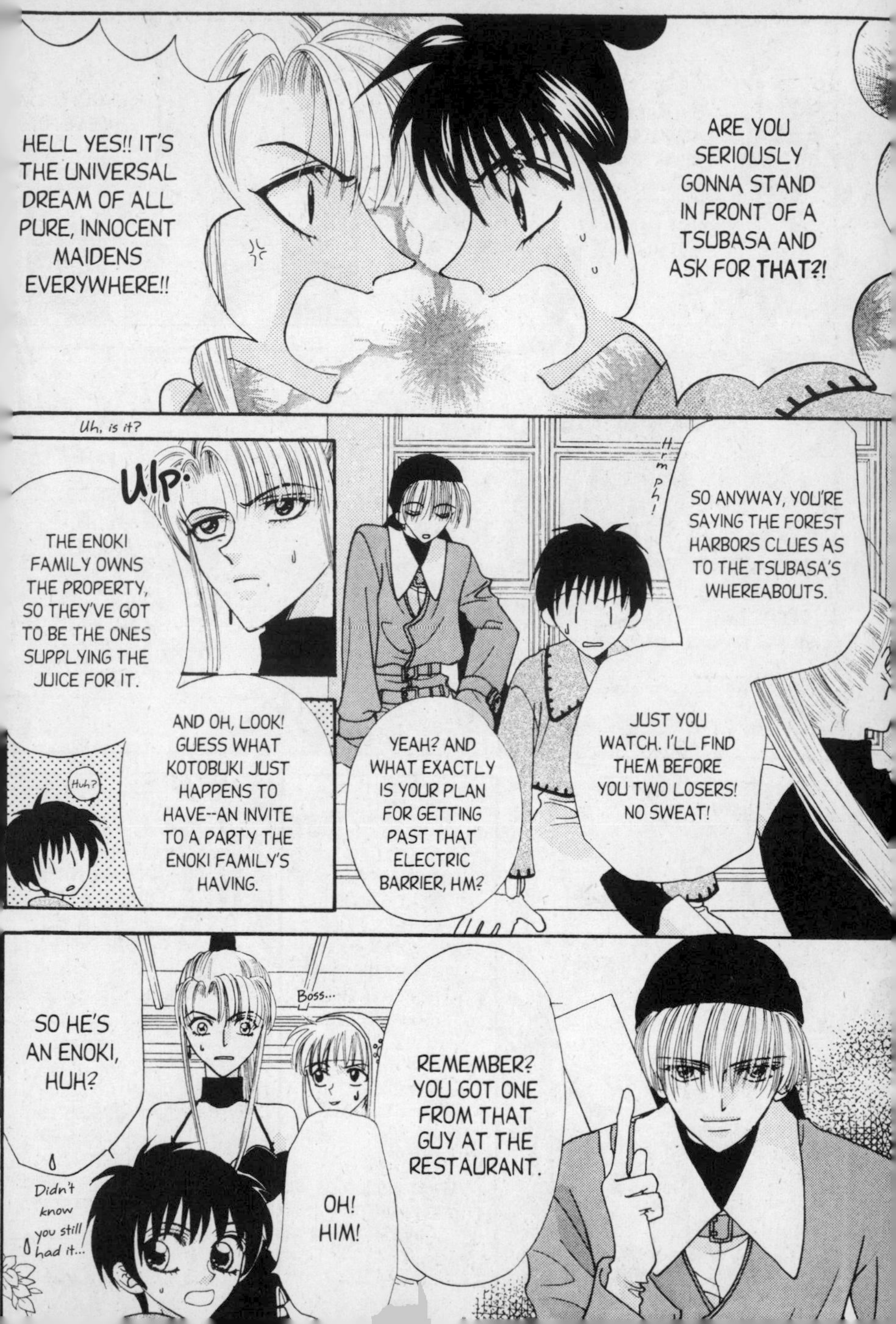
ARE YOU SERIOUSLY GONNA STAND IN FRONT OF A TSUBASA AND ASK FOR THAT?!
HELL YES!! IT'S THE UNIVERSAL DREAM OF ALL PURE, INNOCENT MAIDENS EVERYWHERE!!
Hrmph!
SO ANYWAY, YOU'RE SAYING THE FOREST HARBORS CLUES AS TO THE TSUBASA'S WHEREABOUTS.
JUST YOU WATCH. I'LL FIND THEM BEFORE YOU TWO LOSERS! NO SWEAT!
YEAH? AND WHAT EXACTLY IS YOUR PLAN FOR GETTING PAST THAT ELECTRIC BARRIER, HM?
Uh, is it?
Ulp.
THE ENOKI FAMILY OWNS THE PROPERTY, SO THEY'VE GOT TO BE THE ONES SUPPLYING THE JUICE FOR IT.
AND OH, LOOK! GUESS WHAT KOTOBUKI JUST HAPPENS TO HAVE--AN INVITE TO A PARTY THE ENOKI FAMILY'S HAVING.
Huh?
REMEMBER? YOU GOT ONE FROM THAT GUY AT THE RESTAURANT.
Boss...
SO HE'S AN ENOKI, HUH?
OH! HIM!
Didn't know you still had it...

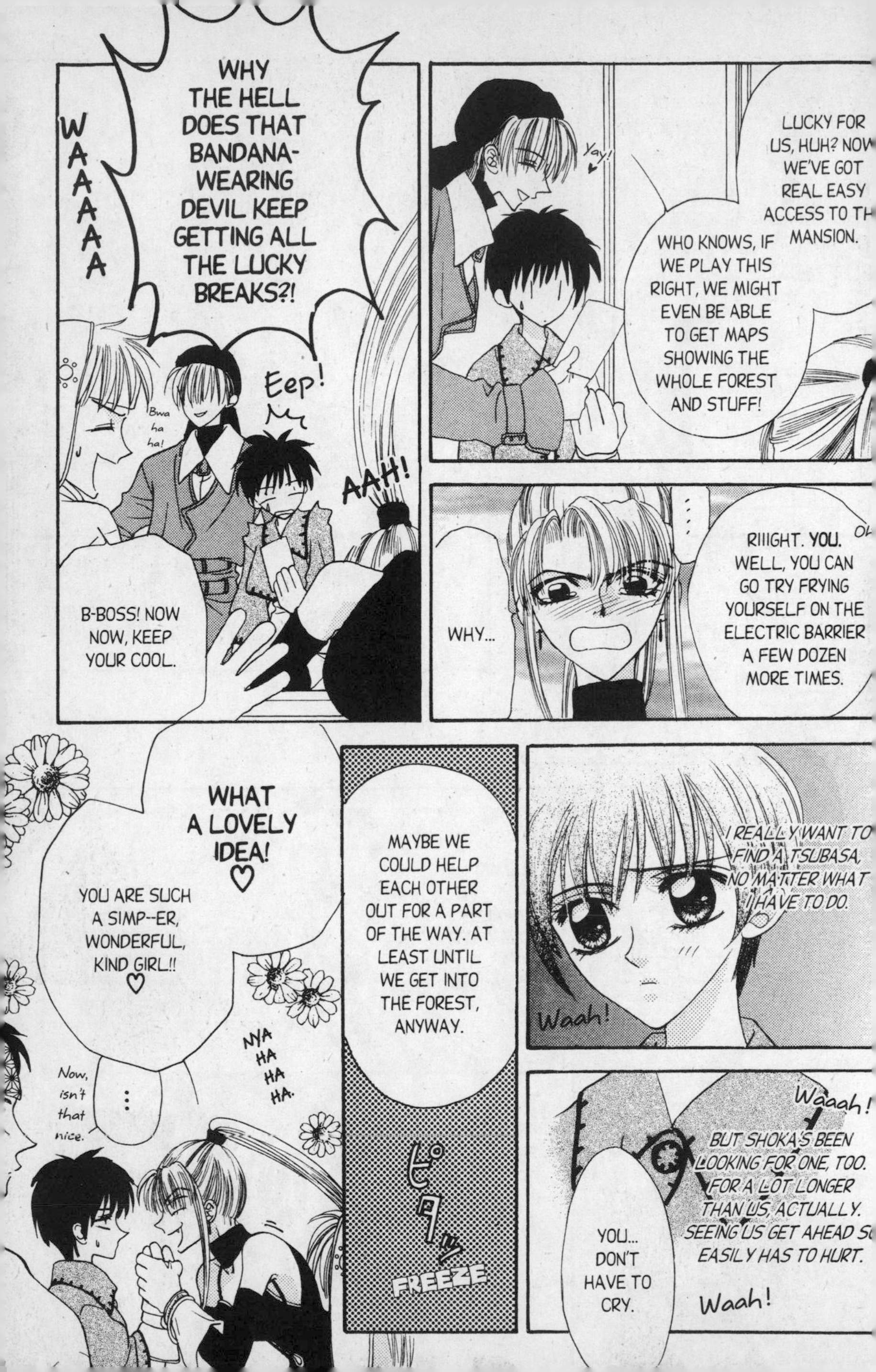
Yay!
LUCKY FOR US, HUH? NOW WE'VE GOT REAL EASY ACCESS TO THE MANSION.
WHO KNOWS, IF WE PLAY THIS RIGHT, WE MIGHT EVEN BE ABLE TO GET MAPS SHOWING THE WHOLE FOREST AND STUFF!
RIIIGHT. YOU. WELL, YOU CAN GO TRY FRYING YOURSELF ON THE ELECTRIC BARRIER A FEW DOZEN MORE TIMES.
....
WHY...
WHY THE HELL DOES THAT BANDANA-WEARING DEVIL KEEP GETTING ALL THE LUCKY BREAKS?!
WAAAAAA
Eep!
Bwa ha ha!
AAH!
B-BOSS! NOW NOW, KEEP YOUR COOL.
I REALLY WANT TO FIND A TSUBASA, NO MATTER WHAT I HAVE TO DO.
Waah!
Waaah!
BUT SHOKA'S BEEN LOOKING FOR ONE, TOO. FOR A LOT LONGER THAN US, ACTUALLY. SEEING US GET AHEAD SO EASILY HAS TO HURT.
YOU... DON'T HAVE TO CRY.
Waah!
MAYBE WE COULD HELP EACH OTHER OUT FOR A PART OF THE WAY. AT LEAST UNTIL WE GET INTO THE FOREST, ANYWAY.
ピタッ
FREEZE
WHAT A LOVELY IDEA! ♡
YOU ARE SUCH A SIMP--ER, WONDERFUL, KIND GIRL!! ♡
NYA HA HA HA.
Now, isn't that nice.
...

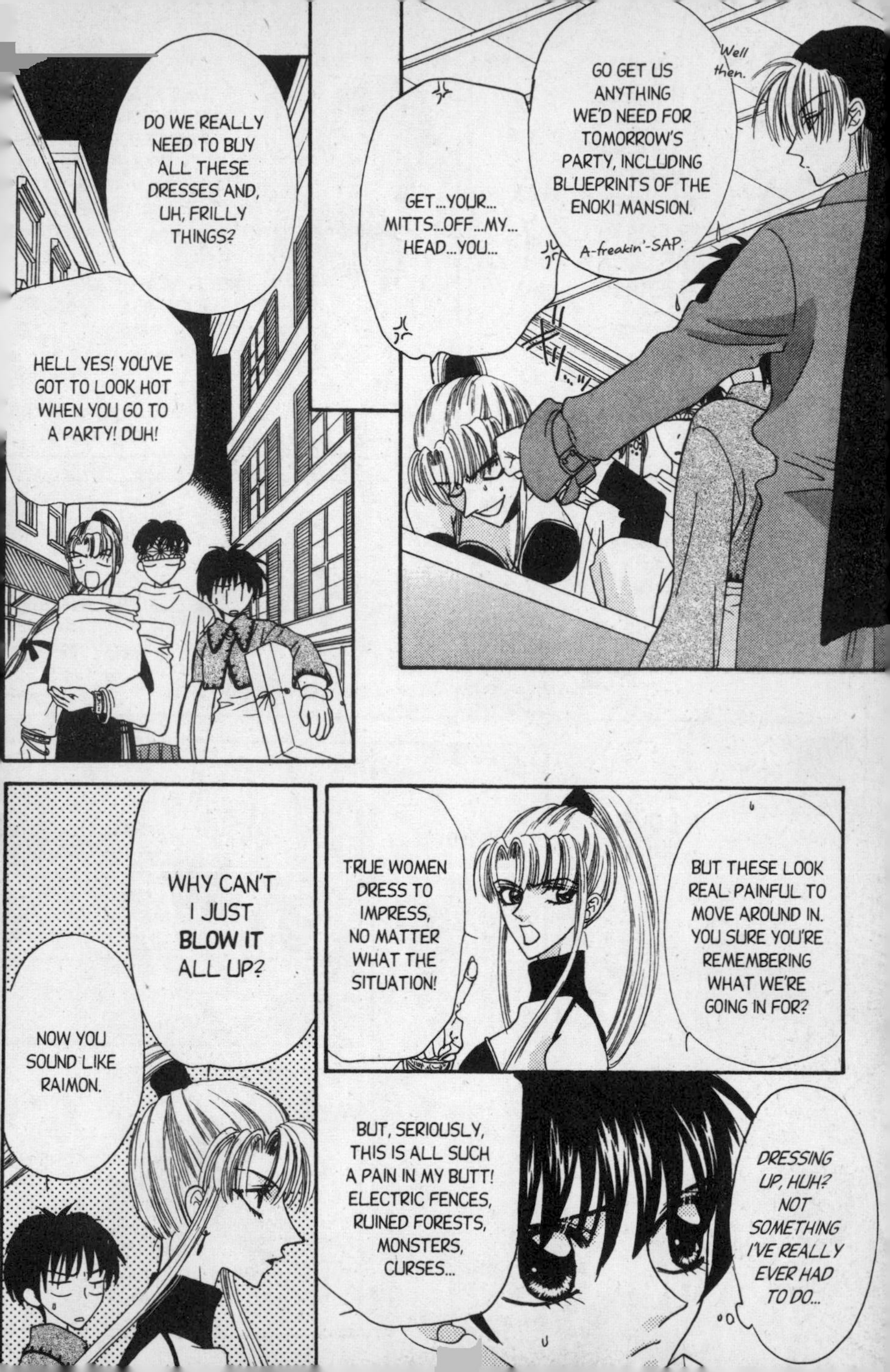
Well then.
GO GET US ANYTHING WE'D NEED FOR TOMORROW'S PARTY, INCLUDING BLUEPRINTS OF THE ENOKI MANSION.
A-freakin'-SAP.
GET...YOUR... MITTS...OFF...MY... HEAD...YOU...
DO WE REALLY NEED TO BUY ALL THESE DRESSES AND, UH, FRILLY THINGS?
HELL YES! YOU'VE GOT TO LOOK HOT WHEN YOU GO TO A PARTY! DUH!
BUT THESE LOOK REAL PAINFUL TO MOVE AROUND IN. YOU SURE YOU'RE REMEMBERING WHAT WE'RE GOING IN FOR?
TRUE WOMEN DRESS TO IMPRESS, NO MATTER WHAT THE SITUATION!
DRESSING UP, HUH? NOT SOMETHING I'VE REALLY EVER HAD TO DO...
BUT, SERIOUSLY, THIS IS ALL SUCH A PAIN IN MY BUTT! ELECTRIC FENCES, RUINED FORESTS, MONSTERS, CURSES...
WHY CAN'T I JUST BLOW IT ALL UP?
NOW YOU SOUND LIKE RAIMON.

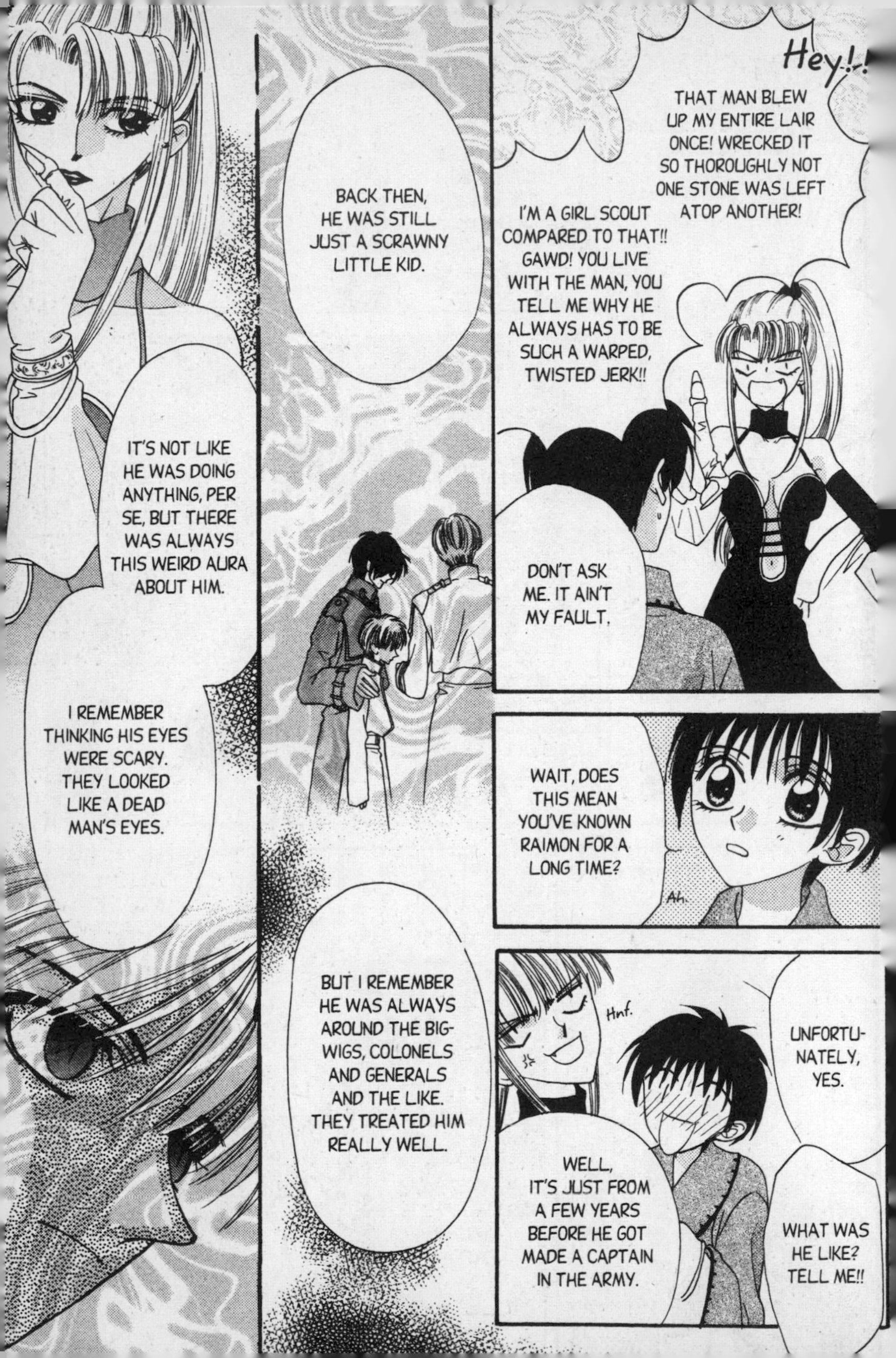
Hey!!
THAT MAN BLEW UP MY ENTIRE LAIR ONCE! WRECKED IT SO THOROUGHLY NOT ONE STONE WAS LEFT ATOP ANOTHER!
I'M A GIRL SCOUT COMPARED TO THAT!! GAWD! YOU LIVE WITH THE MAN, YOU TELL ME WHY HE ALWAYS HAS TO BE SUCH A WARPED, TWISTED JERK!!
DON'T ASK ME. IT AIN'T MY FAULT.
WAIT, DOES THIS MEAN YOU'VE KNOWN RAIMON FOR A LONG TIME?
Ah.
UNFORTU-NATELY, YES.
Hnf.
WHAT WAS HE LIKE? TELL ME!!
WELL, IT'S JUST FROM A FEW YEARS BEFORE HE GOT MADE A CAPTAIN IN THE ARMY.
BACK THEN, HE WAS STILL JUST A SCRAWNY LITTLE KID.
BUT I REMEMBER HE WAS ALWAYS AROUND THE BIG-WIGS, COLONELS AND GENERALS AND THE LIKE. THEY TREATED HIM REALLY WELL.
IT'S NOT LIKE HE WAS DOING ANYTHING, PER SE, BUT THERE WAS ALWAYS THIS WEIRD AURA ABOUT HIM.
I REMEMBER THINKING HIS EYES WERE SCARY. THEY LOOKED LIKE A DEAD MAN'S EYES.

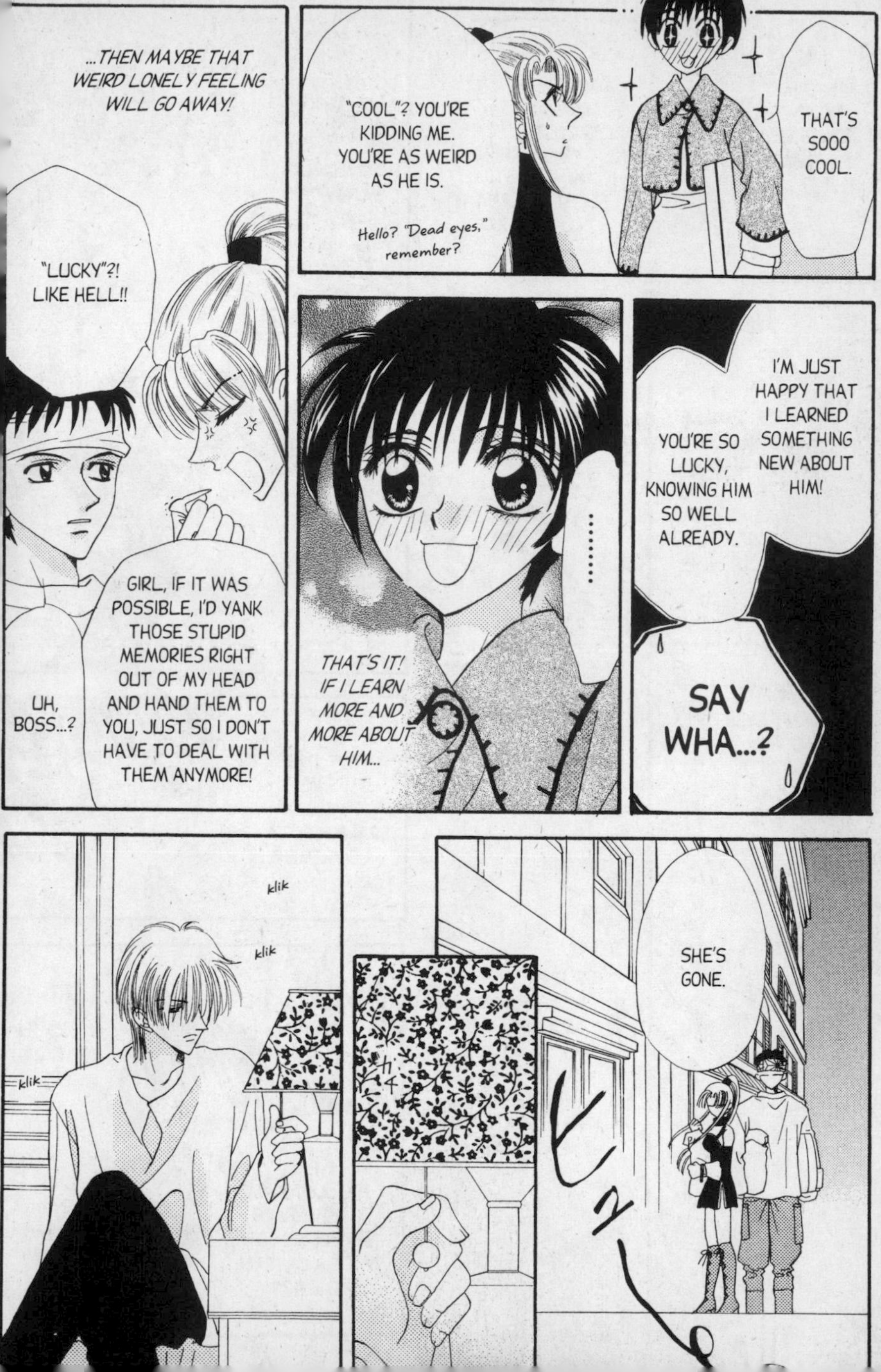
THAT'S SOOO COOL.
"COOL"? YOU'RE KIDDING ME. YOU'RE AS WEIRD AS HE IS.
Hello? "Dead eyes," remember?
I'M JUST HAPPY THAT I LEARNED SOMETHING NEW ABOUT HIM!
YOU'RE SO LUCKY, KNOWING HIM SO WELL ALREADY.
SAY WHA...?
......
THAT'S IT! IF I LEARN MORE AND MORE ABOUT HIM...
...THEN MAYBE THAT WEIRD LONELY FEELING WILL GO AWAY!
"LUCKY"?! LIKE HELL!!
GIRL, IF IT WAS POSSIBLE, I'D YANK THOSE STUPID MEMORIES RIGHT OUT OF MY HEAD AND HAND THEM TO YOU, JUST SO I DON'T HAVE TO DEAL WITH THEM ANYMORE!
UH, BOSS...?
SHE'S GONE.
klik
klik
klik

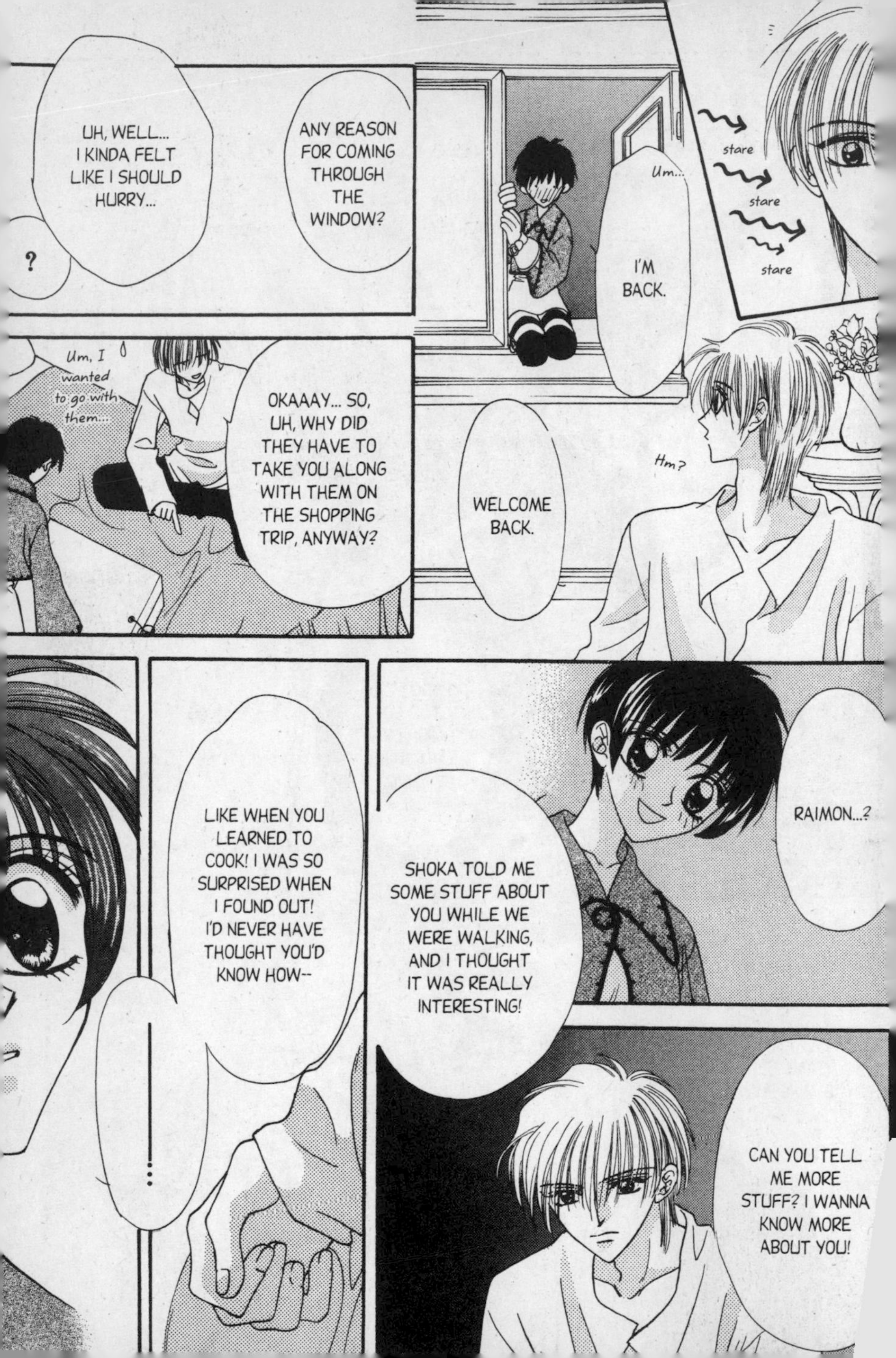
stare
stare
stare
Um...
I'M BACK.
Hm?
WELCOME BACK.
ANY REASON FOR COMING THROUGH THE WINDOW?
UH, WELL... I KINDA FELT LIKE I SHOULD HURRY...
?
OKAAAY... SO, UH, WHY DID THEY HAVE TO TAKE YOU ALONG WITH THEM ON THE SHOPPING TRIP, ANYWAY?
Um, I wanted to go with them...
RAIMON...?
SHOKA TOLD ME SOME STUFF ABOUT YOU WHILE WE WERE WALKING, AND I THOUGHT IT WAS REALLY INTERESTING!
CAN YOU TELL ME MORE STUFF? I WANNA KNOW MORE ABOUT YOU!
LIKE WHEN YOU LEARNED TO COOK! I WAS SO SURPRISED WHEN I FOUND OUT! I'D NEVER HAVE THOUGHT YOU'D KNOW HOW--
......

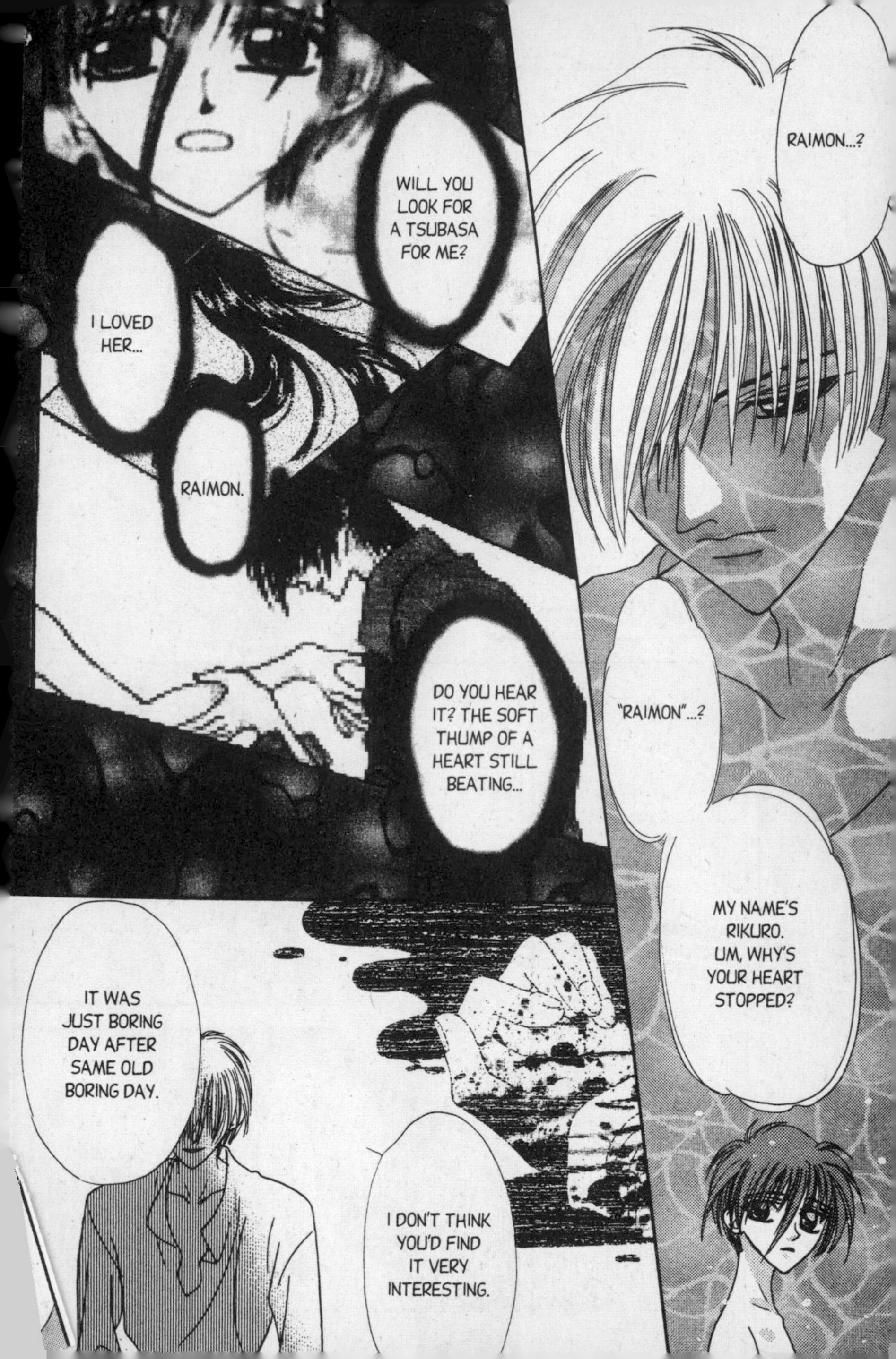
RAIMON...?
"RAIMON"...?
MY NAME'S RIKURO. UM, WHY'S YOUR HEART STOPPED?
WILL YOU LOOK FOR A TSUBASA FOR ME?
I LOVED HER...
RAIMON.
DO YOU HEAR IT? THE SOFT THUMP OF A HEART STILL BEATING...
IT WAS JUST BORING DAY AFTER SAME OLD BORING DAY.
I DON'T THINK YOU'D FIND IT VERY INTERESTING.

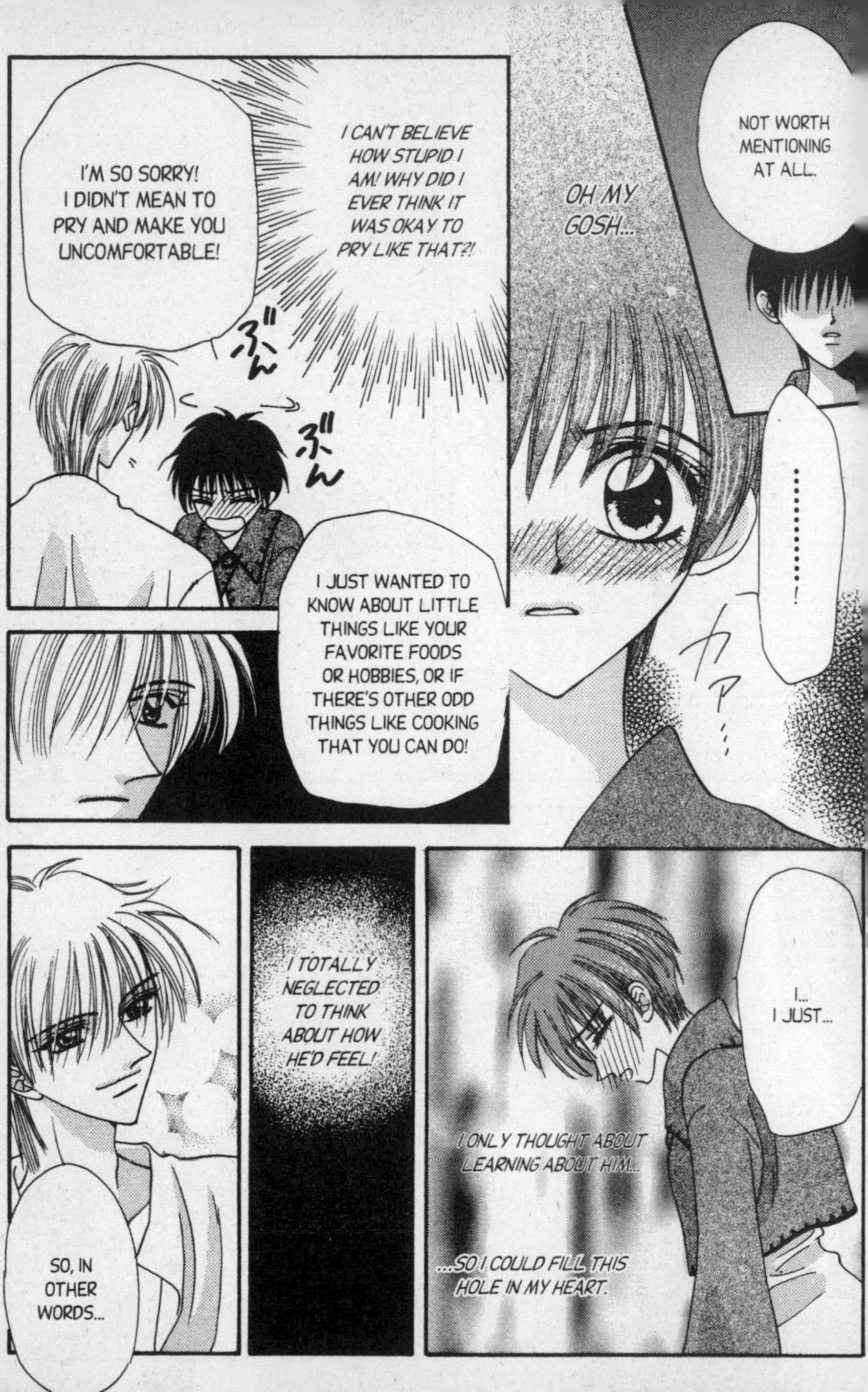
NOT WORTH MENTIONING AT ALL.
OH MY GOSH...
......!
カァ...
I CAN'T BELIEVE HOW STUPID I AM! WHY DID I EVER THINK IT WAS OKAY TO PRY LIKE THAT?!
I'M SO SORRY! I DIDN'T MEAN TO PRY AND MAKE YOU UNCOMFORTABLE!
ぶん
ぶん
I JUST WANTED TO KNOW ABOUT LITTLE THINGS LIKE YOUR FAVORITE FOODS OR HOBBIES, OR IF THERE'S OTHER ODD THINGS LIKE COOKING THAT YOU CAN DO!
I... I JUST...
I ONLY THOUGHT ABOUT LEARNING ABOUT HIM...
...SO I COULD FILL THIS HOLE IN MY HEART.
I TOTALLY NEGLECTED TO THINK ABOUT HOW HE'D FEEL!
SO, IN OTHER WORDS...

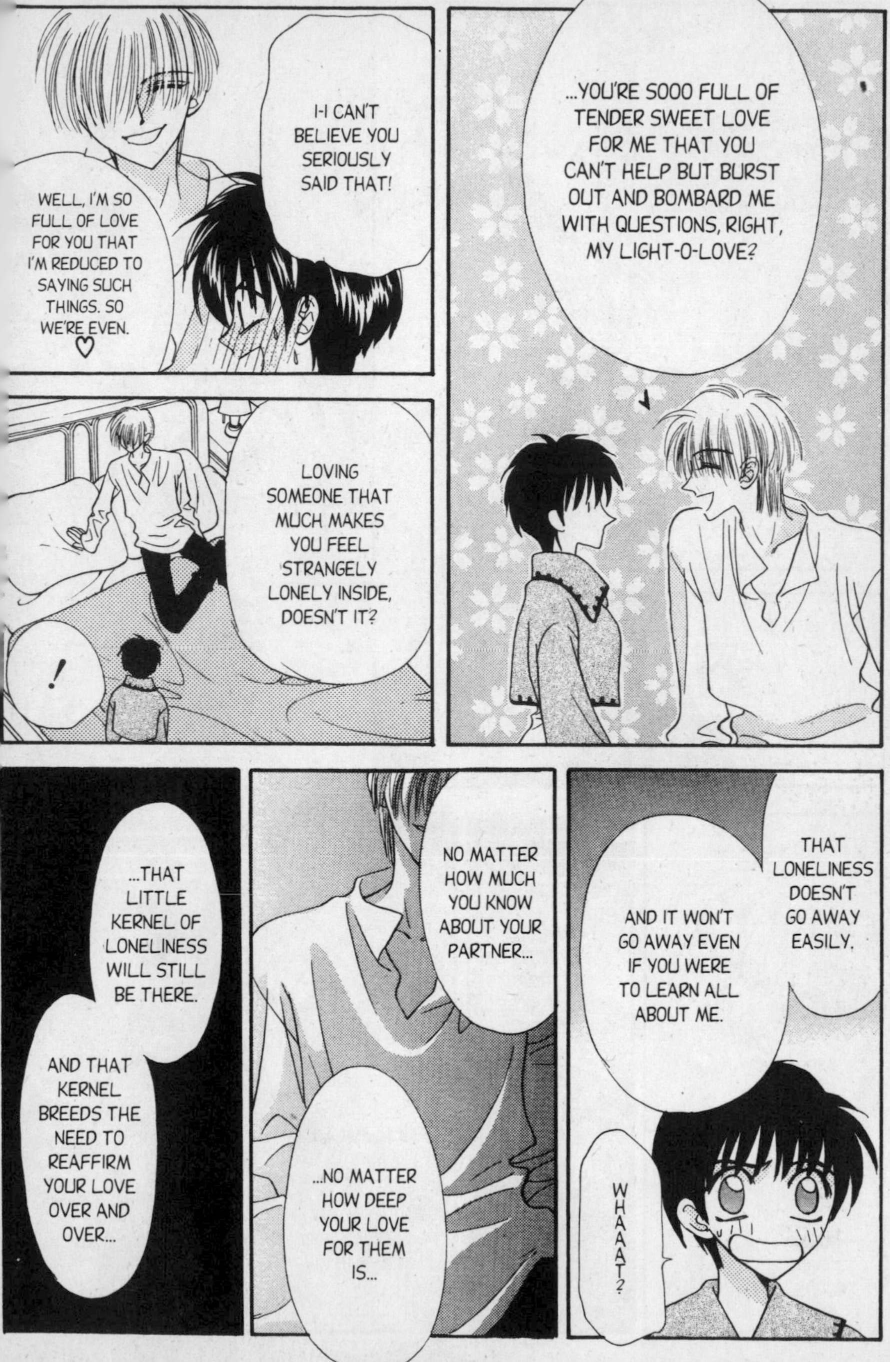
...YOU'RE SOOO FULL OF TENDER SWEET LOVE FOR ME THAT YOU CAN'T HELP BUT BURST OUT AND BOMBARD ME WITH QUESTIONS, RIGHT, MY LIGHT-O-LOVE?
I-I CAN'T BELIEVE YOU SERIOUSLY SAID THAT!
WELL, I'M SO FULL OF LOVE FOR YOU THAT I'M REDUCED TO SAYING SUCH THINGS. SO WE'RE EVEN. ♡
LOVING SOMEONE THAT MUCH MAKES YOU FEEL STRANGELY LONELY INSIDE, DOESN'T IT?
!
THAT LONELINESS DOESN'T GO AWAY EASILY.
AND IT WON'T GO AWAY EVEN IF YOU WERE TO LEARN ALL ABOUT ME.
WHAAAT?
NO MATTER HOW MUCH YOU KNOW ABOUT YOUR PARTNER...
...NO MATTER HOW DEEP YOUR LOVE FOR THEM IS...
...THAT LITTLE KERNEL OF LONELINESS WILL STILL BE THERE.
AND THAT KERNEL BREEDS THE NEED TO REAFFIRM YOUR LOVE OVER AND OVER...

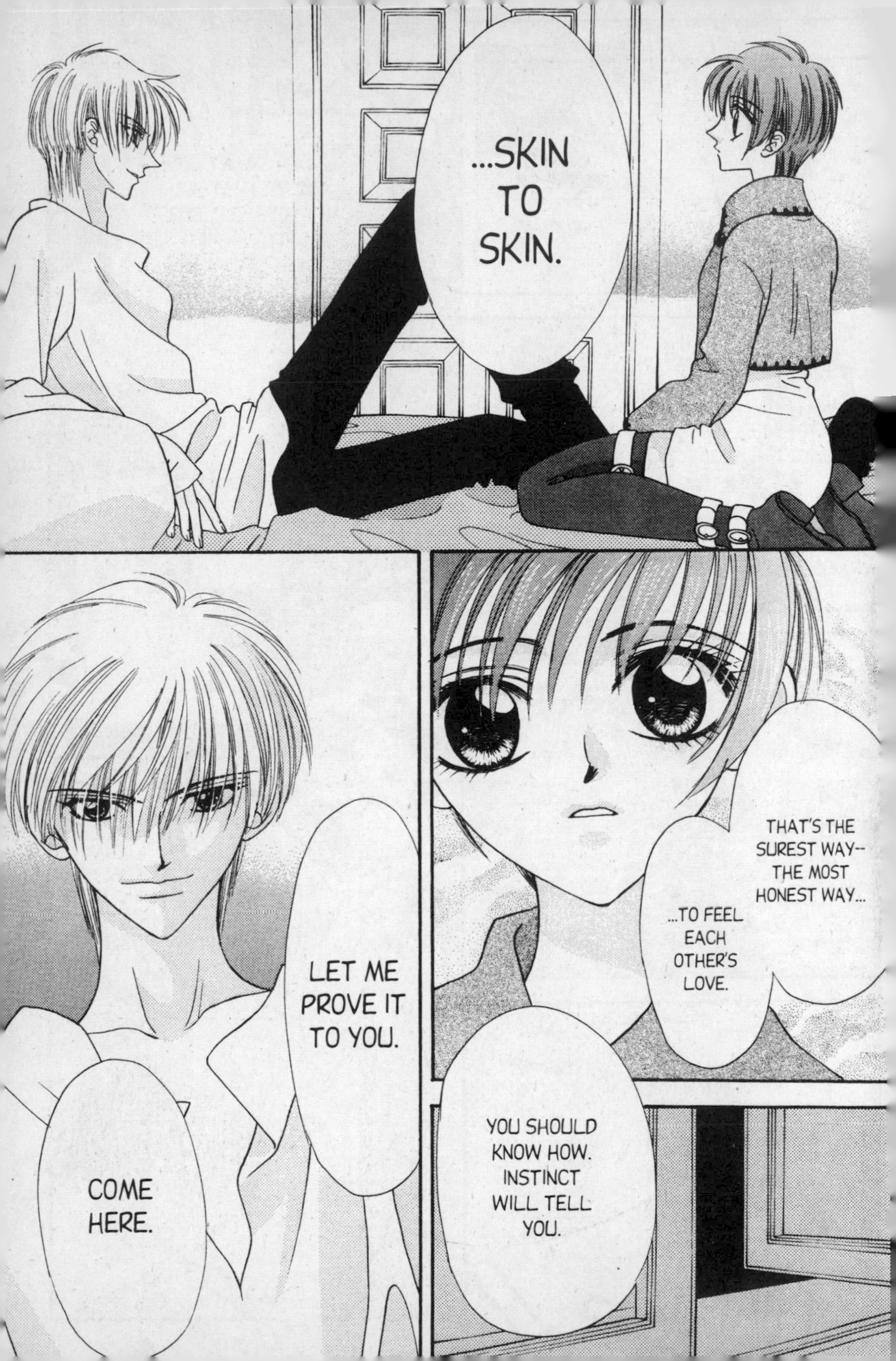
...SKIN TO SKIN.
THAT'S THE SUREST WAY-- THE MOST HONEST WAY...
...TO FEEL EACH OTHER'S LOVE.
YOU SHOULD KNOW HOW. INSTINCT WILL TELL YOU.
LET ME PROVE IT TO YOU.
COME HERE.

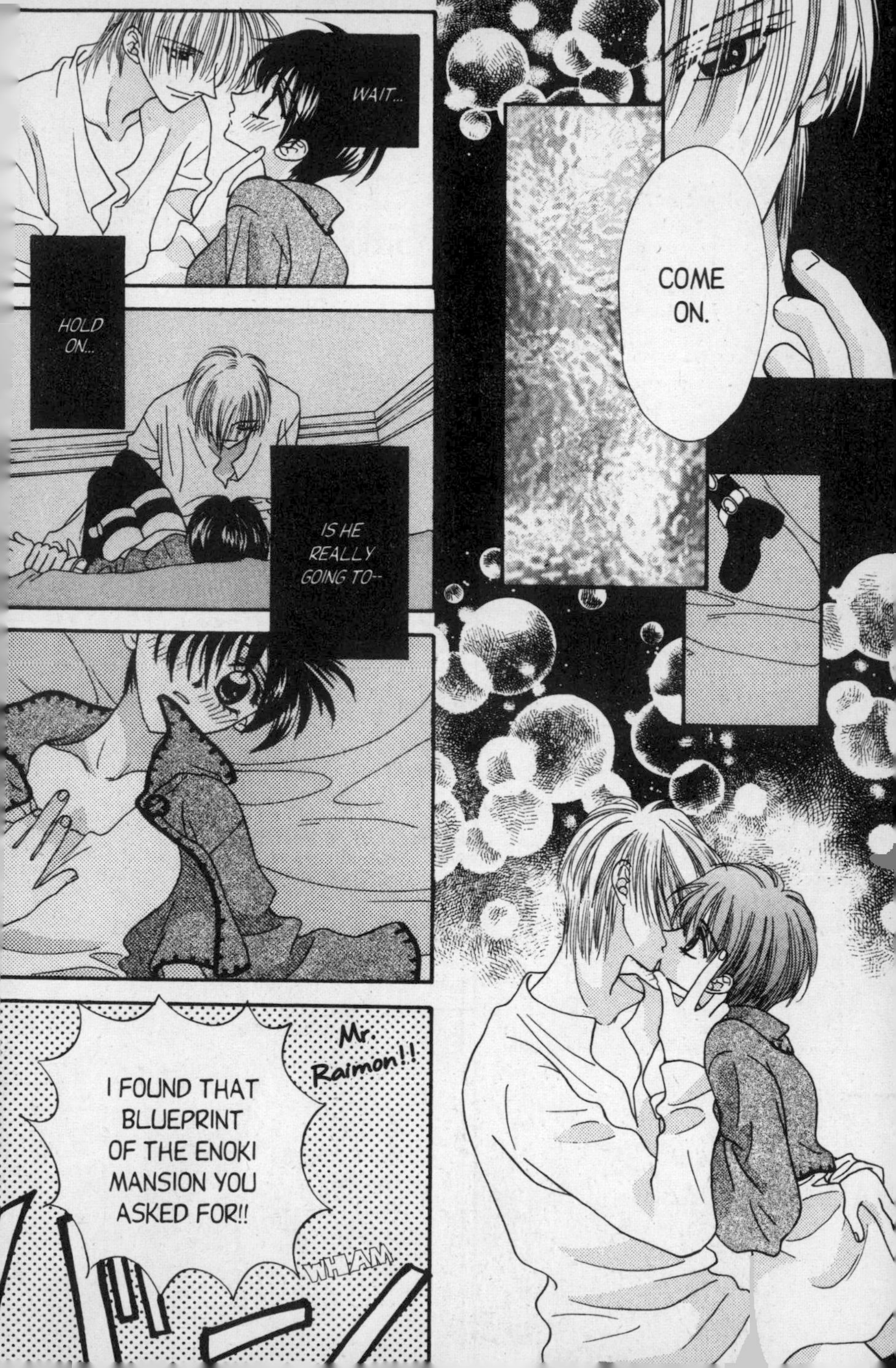
COME ON.
WAIT...
HOLD ON...
IS HE REALLY GOING TO--
Mr. Raimon!!
I FOUND THAT BLUEPRINT OF THE ENOKI MANSION YOU ASKED FOR!!
WHAM

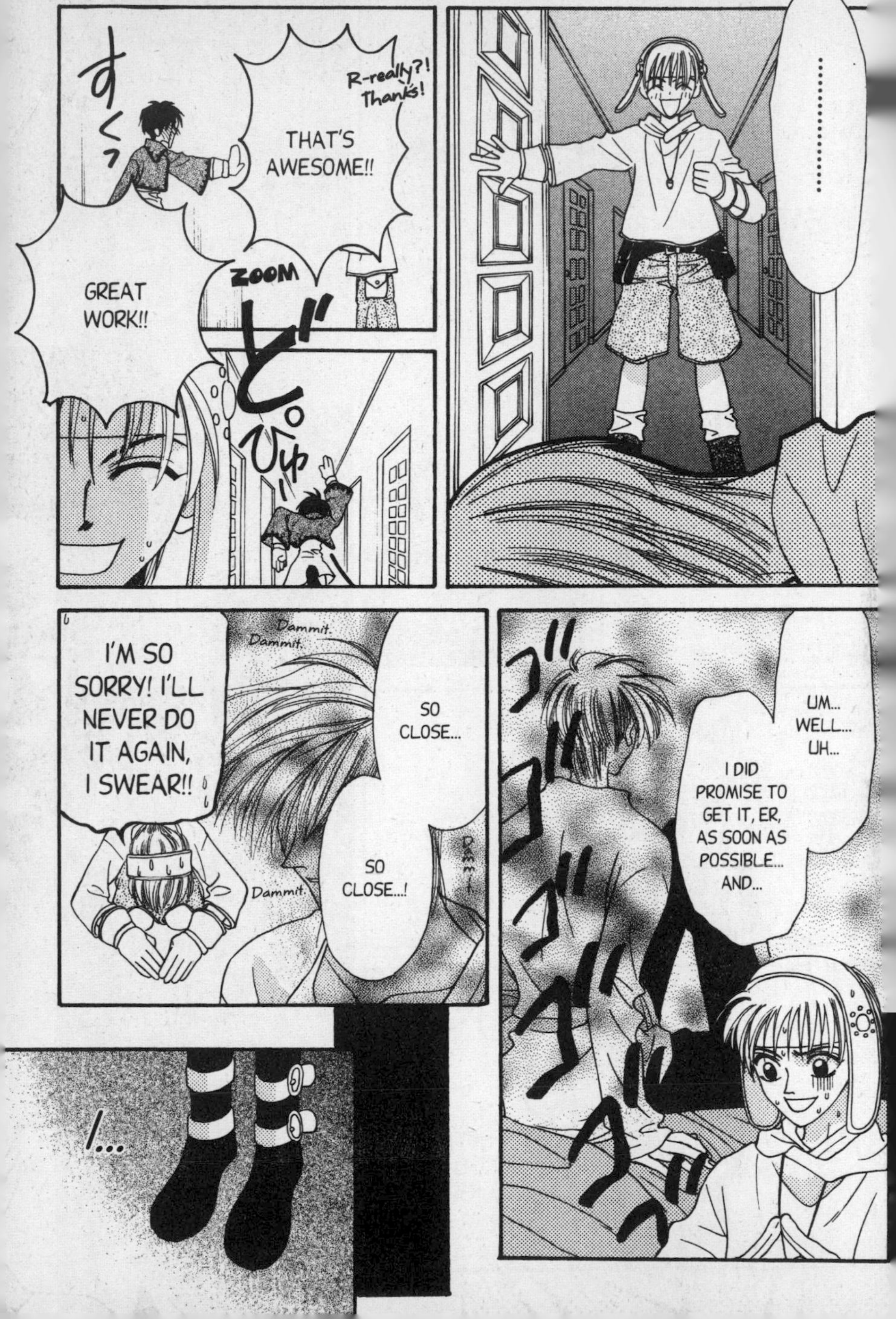

……
R-really?! Thanks!
THAT'S AWESOME!!
GREAT WORK!!
ZOOM
UM... WELL... UH...
I DID PROMISE TO GET IT, ER, AS SOON AS POSSIBLE... AND...
SO CLOSE...
Dammit. Dammit.
SO CLOSE...!
Dammit.
I'M SO SORRY! I'LL NEVER DO IT AGAIN, I SWEAR!!
I...

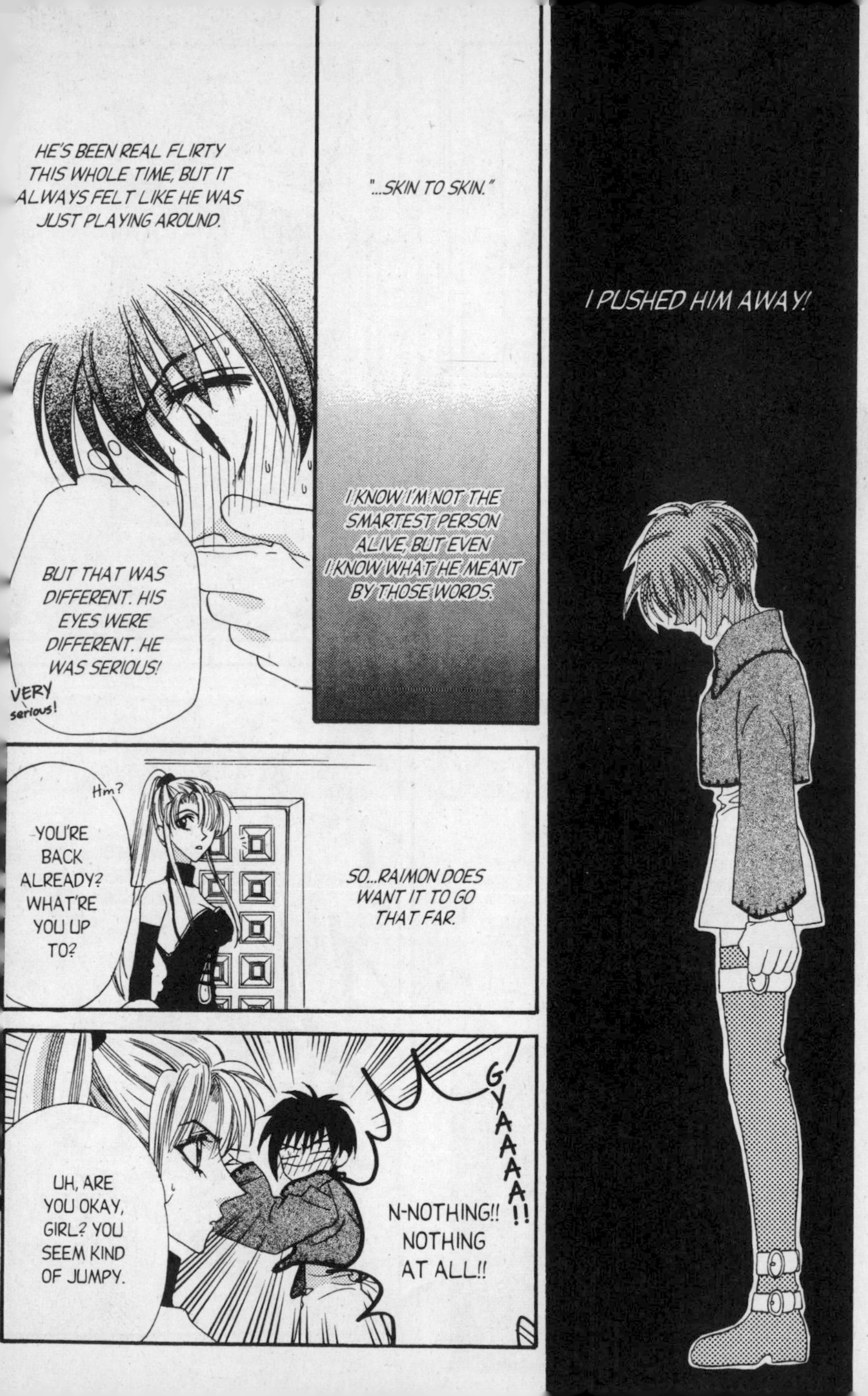
I PUSHED HIM AWAY!
"...SKIN TO SKIN."
I KNOW I'M NOT THE SMARTEST PERSON ALIVE, BUT EVEN I KNOW WHAT HE MEANT BY THOSE WORDS.
HE'S BEEN REAL FLIRTY THIS WHOLE TIME, BUT IT ALWAYS FELT LIKE HE WAS JUST PLAYING AROUND.
BUT THAT WAS DIFFERENT. HIS EYES WERE DIFFERENT. HE WAS SERIOUS!
VERY serious!
SO...RAIMON DOES WANT IT TO GO THAT FAR.
Hm?
YOU'RE BACK ALREADY? WHAT'RE YOU UP TO?
GYAAAAA!!
N-NOTHING!! NOTHING AT ALL!!
UH, ARE YOU OKAY, GIRL? YOU SEEM KIND OF JUMPY.

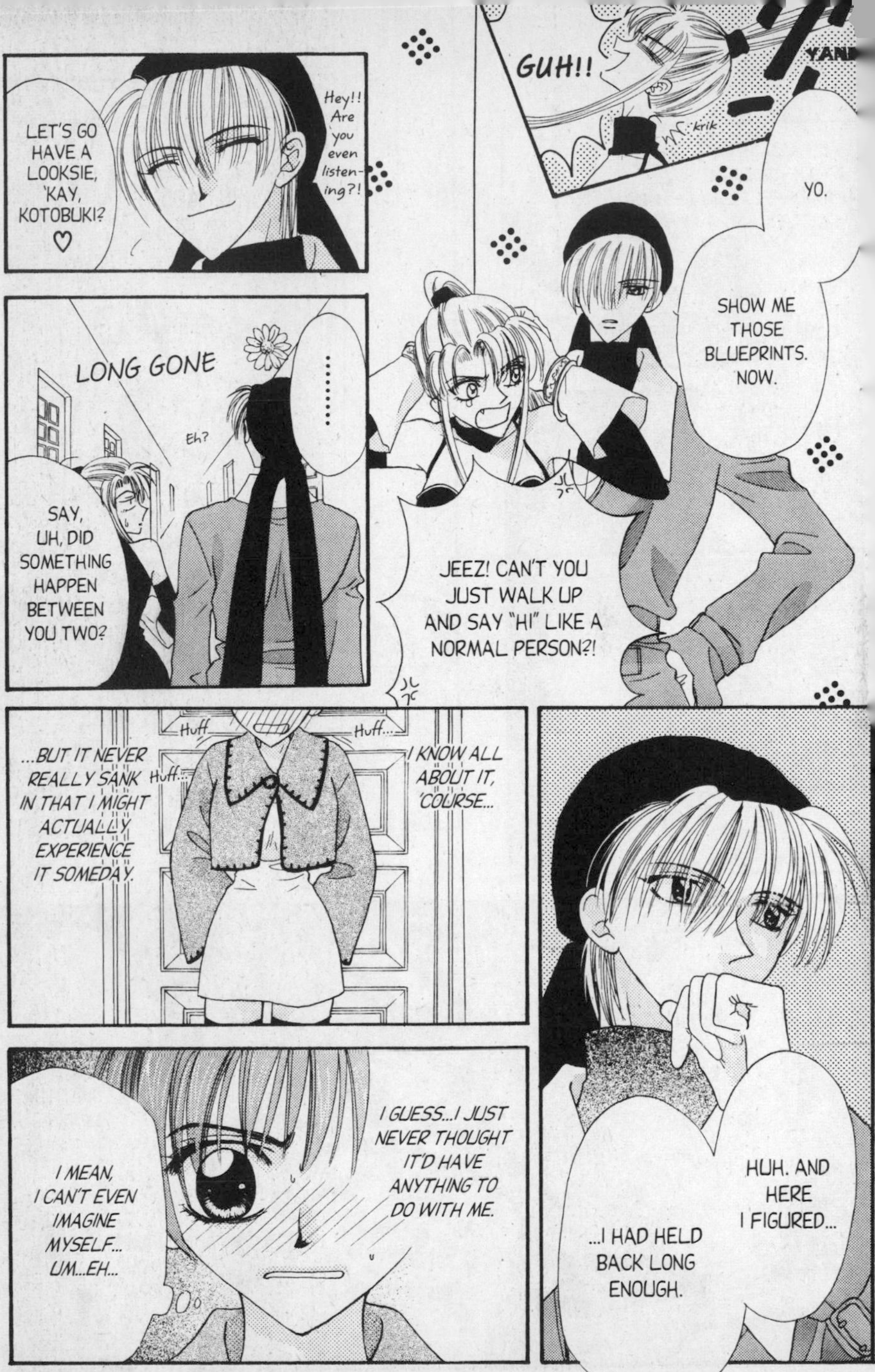
YANK
GUH!!
krik
YO.
SHOW ME THOSE BLUEPRINTS. NOW.
JEEZ! CAN'T YOU JUST WALK UP AND SAY "HI" LIKE A NORMAL PERSON?!
Hey!! Are you even listen-ing?!
LET'S GO HAVE A LOOKSIE, 'KAY, KOTOBUKI? ♡
......
LONG GONE
Eh?
SAY, UH, DID SOMETHING HAPPEN BETWEEN YOU TWO?
HUH. AND HERE I FIGURED...
...I HAD HELD BACK LONG ENOUGH.
Huff...
Huff...
Huff...
I KNOW ALL ABOUT IT, 'COURSE...
...BUT IT NEVER REALLY SANK IN THAT I MIGHT ACTUALLY EXPERIENCE IT SOMEDAY.
I GUESS...I JUST NEVER THOUGHT IT'D HAVE ANYTHING TO DO WITH ME.
I MEAN, I CAN'T EVEN IMAGINE MYSELF... UM...EH...

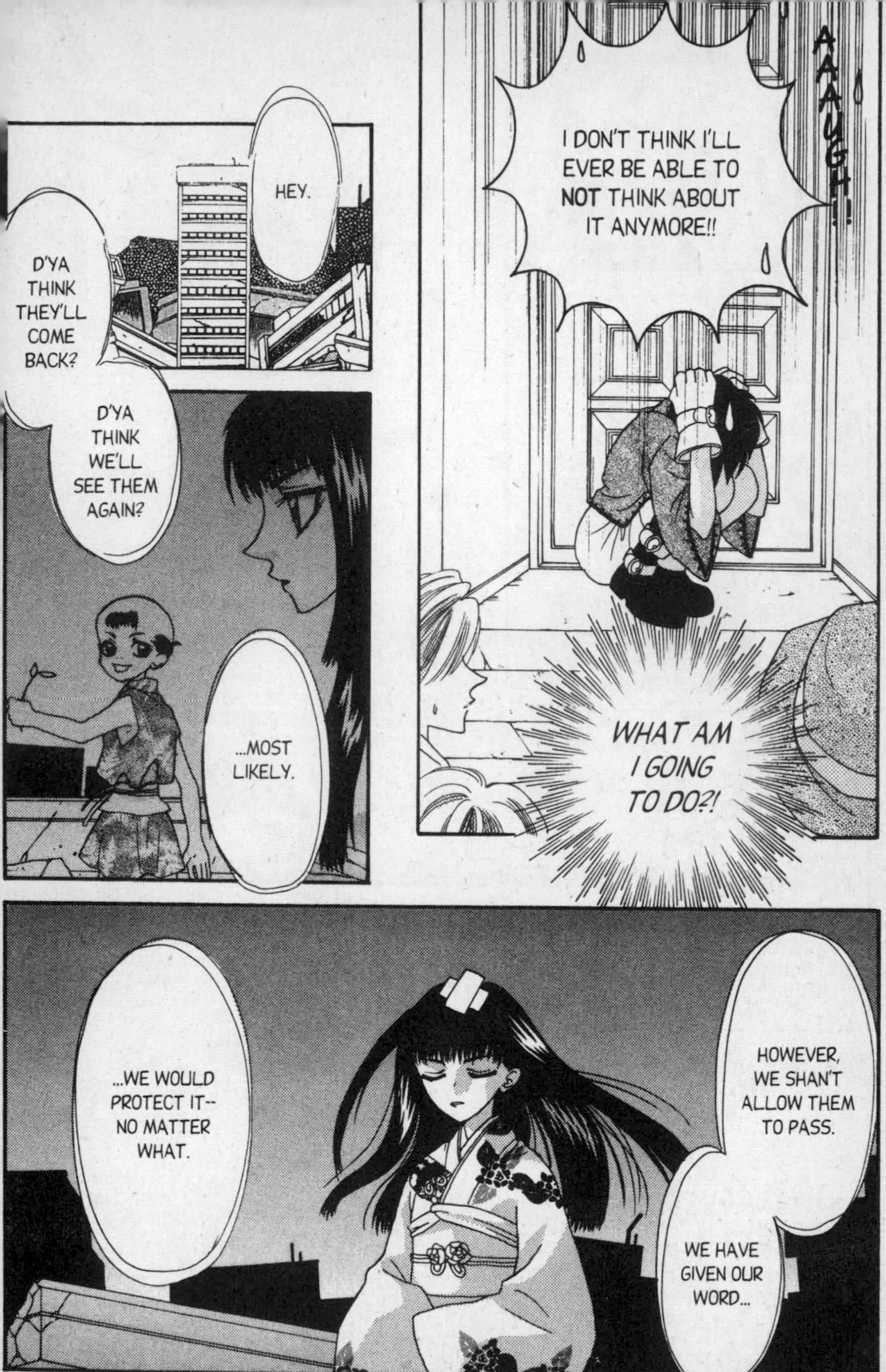
AAAUGH!!
I DON'T THINK I'LL EVER BE ABLE TO NOT THINK ABOUT IT ANYMORE!!
WHAT AM I GOING TO DO?!
HEY.
D'YA THINK THEY'LL COME BACK?
D'YA THINK WE'LL SEE THEM AGAIN?
...MOST LIKELY.
HOWEVER, WE SHAN'T ALLOW THEM TO PASS.
WE HAVE GIVEN OUR WORD...
...WE WOULD PROTECT IT-- NO MATTER WHAT.

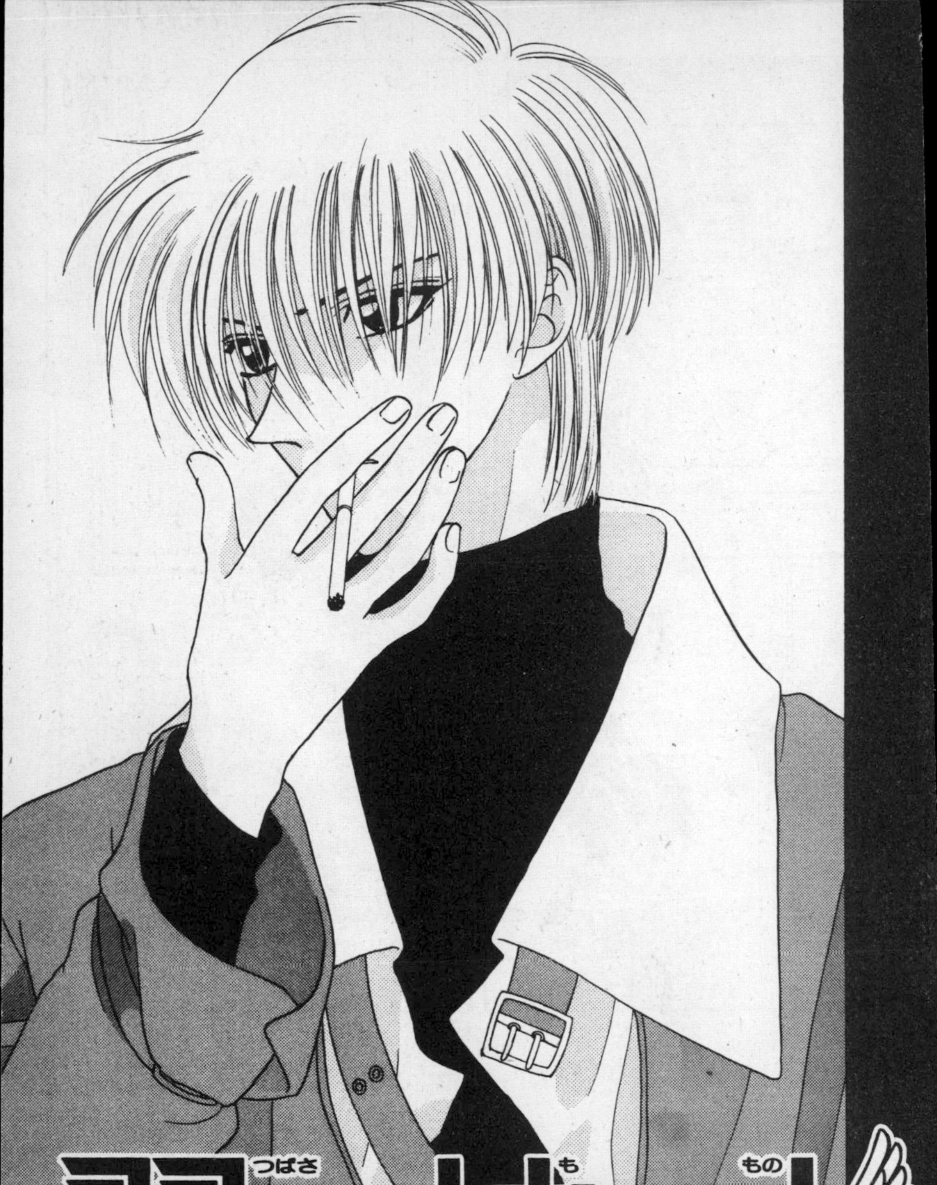

翼(つばさ)を持(も)つ者(もの)

Tsubasa: Those With Wings

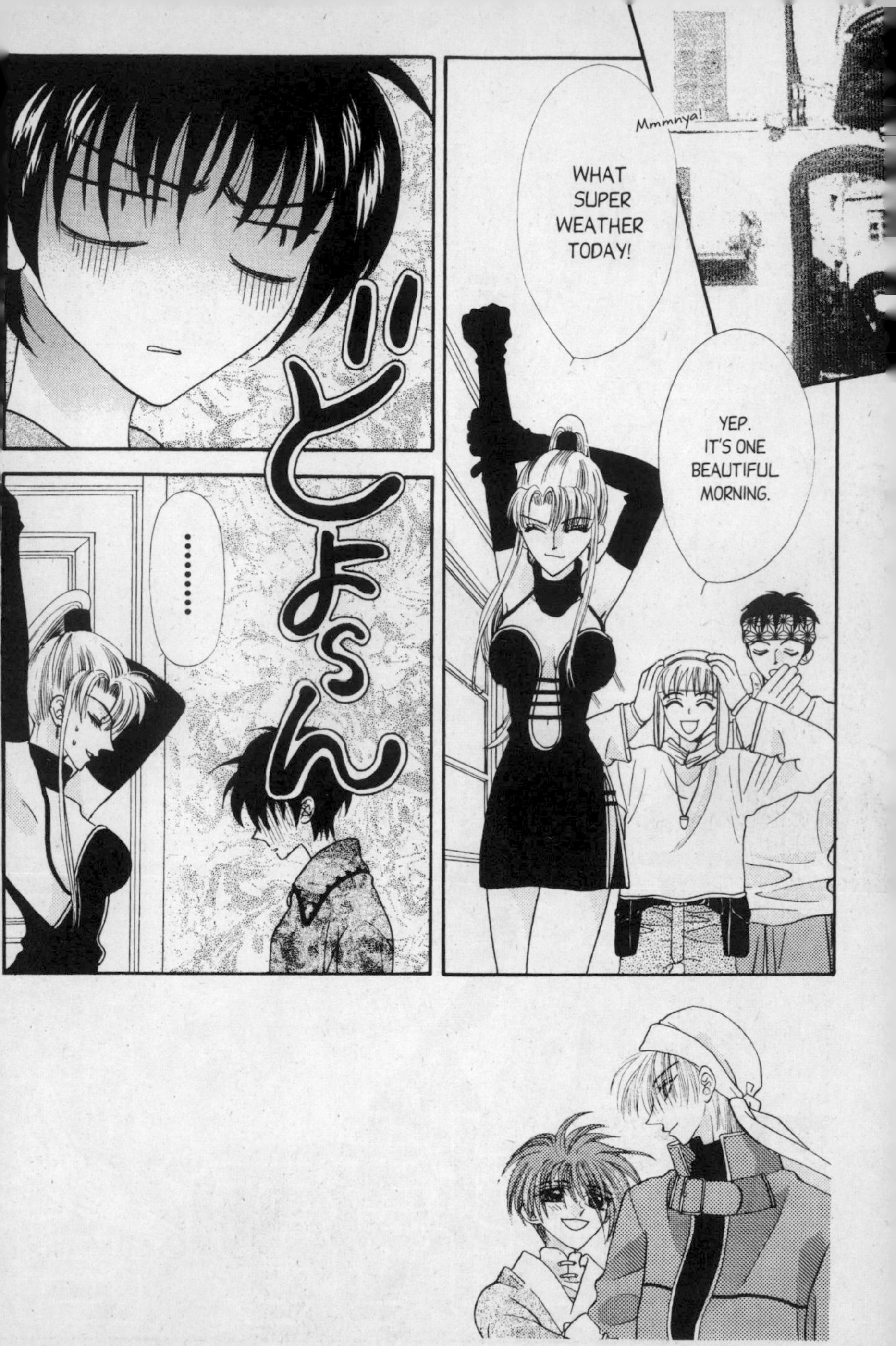
Mmmnya!
WHAT SUPER WEATHER TODAY!
YEP. IT'S ONE BEAUTIFUL MORNING.
どよん
....

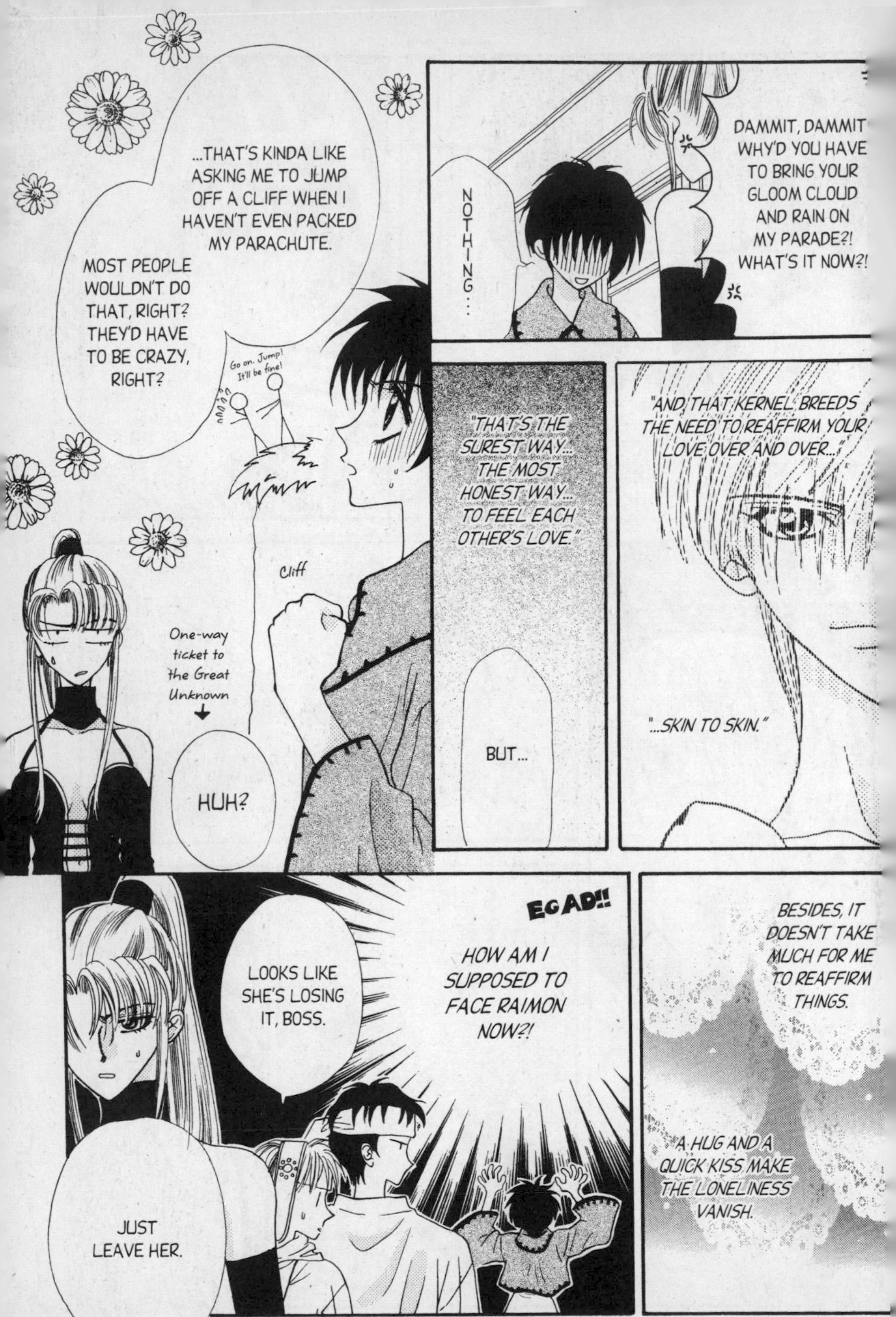

DAMMIT, DAMMIT WHY'D YOU HAVE TO BRING YOUR GLOOM CLOUD AND RAIN ON MY PARADE?! WHAT'S IT NOW?!
NOTHING...
"AND THAT KERNEL BREEDS THE NEED TO REAFFIRM YOUR LOVE OVER AND OVER..."
"...SKIN TO SKIN."
"THAT'S THE SUREST WAY... THE MOST HONEST WAY... TO FEEL EACH OTHER'S LOVE."
BUT...
...THAT'S KINDA LIKE ASKING ME TO JUMP OFF A CLIFF WHEN I HAVEN'T EVEN PACKED MY PARACHUTE.
MOST PEOPLE WOULDN'T DO THAT, RIGHT? THEY'D HAVE TO BE CRAZY, RIGHT?
Go on. Jump! It'll be fine!
Cliff
One-way ticket to the Great Unknown
HUH?
BESIDES, IT DOESN'T TAKE MUCH FOR ME TO REAFFIRM THINGS.
A HUG AND A QUICK KISS MAKE THE LONELINESS VANISH.
EGAD!!
HOW AM I SUPPOSED TO FACE RAIMON NOW?!
LOOKS LIKE SHE'S LOSING IT, BOSS.
JUST LEAVE HER.

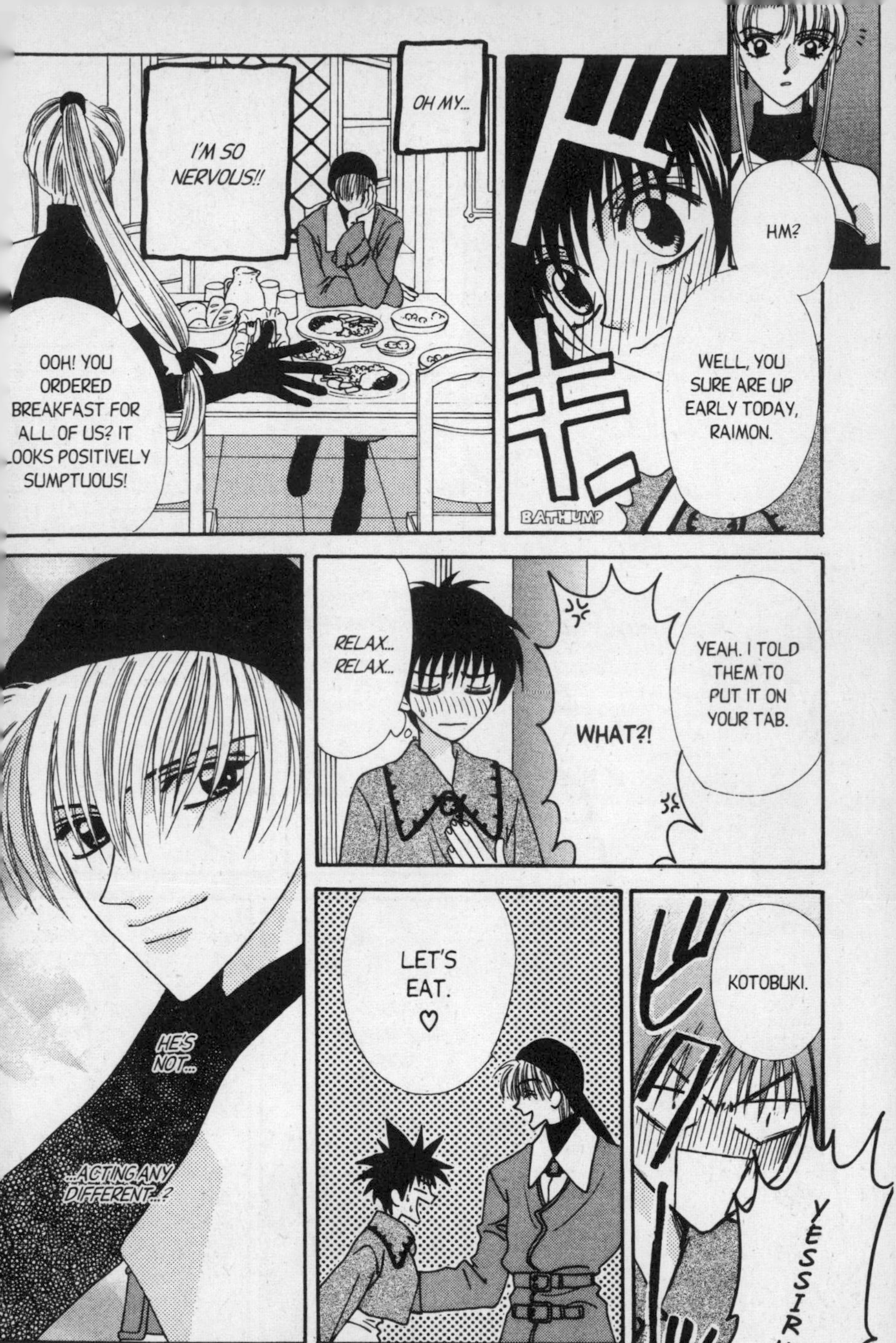
HM?
WELL, YOU SURE ARE UP EARLY TODAY, RAIMON.
BATHUMP
OH MY...
I'M SO NERVOUS!!
OOH! YOU ORDERED BREAKFAST FOR ALL OF US? IT LOOKS POSITIVELY SUMPTUOUS!
YEAH. I TOLD THEM TO PUT IT ON YOUR TAB.
WHAT?!
RELAX... RELAX...
KOTOBUKI.
YESSIR!!!
LET'S EAT. ♥
HE'S NOT...
...ACTING ANY DIFFERENT...?

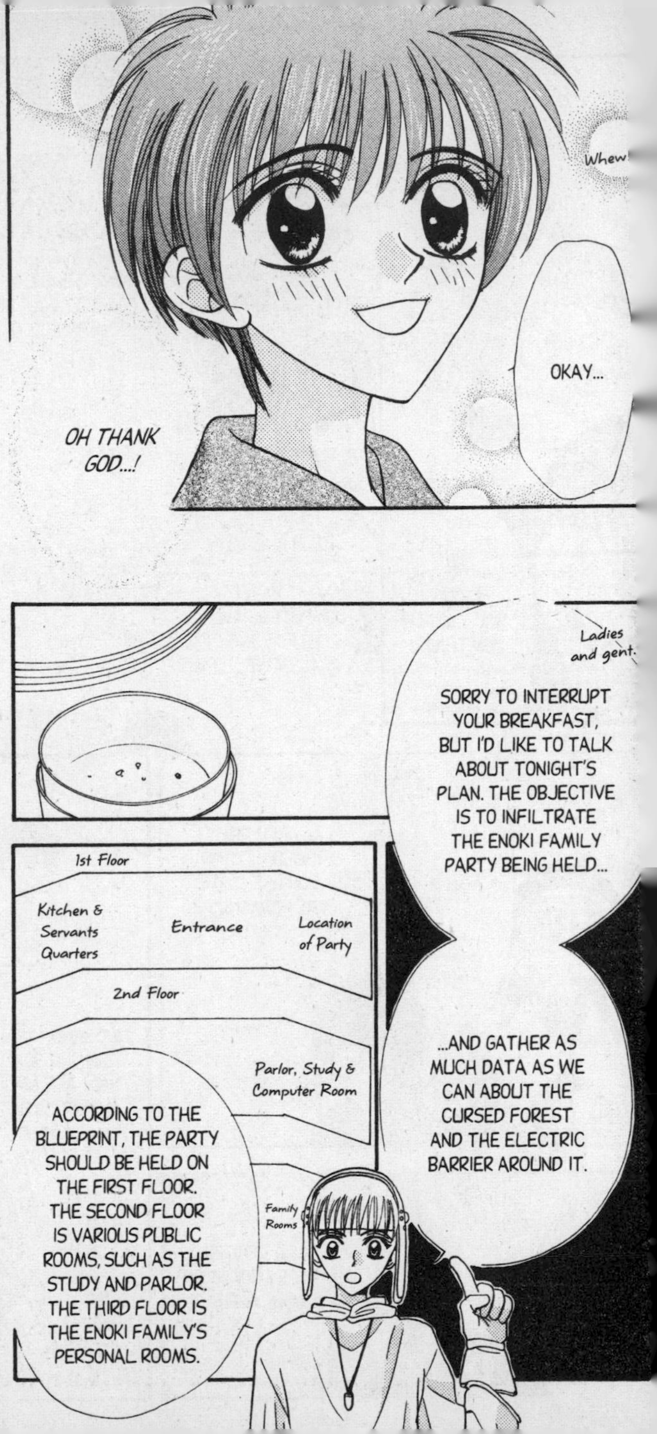
Whew
OKAY...
OH THANK GOD...!
Ladies and gent.
SORRY TO INTERRUPT YOUR BREAKFAST, BUT I'D LIKE TO TALK ABOUT TONIGHT'S PLAN. THE OBJECTIVE IS TO INFILTRATE THE ENOKI FAMILY PARTY BEING HELD...
...AND GATHER AS MUCH DATA AS WE CAN ABOUT THE CURSED FOREST AND THE ELECTRIC BARRIER AROUND IT.
1st Floor
Kitchen & Servants Quarters
Entrance
Location of Party
2nd Floor
Parlor, Study & Computer Room
Family Rooms
ACCORDING TO THE BLUEPRINT, THE PARTY SHOULD BE HELD ON THE FIRST FLOOR. THE SECOND FLOOR IS VARIOUS PUBLIC ROOMS, SUCH AS THE STUDY AND PARLOR. THE THIRD FLOOR IS THE ENOKI FAMILY'S PERSONAL ROOMS.

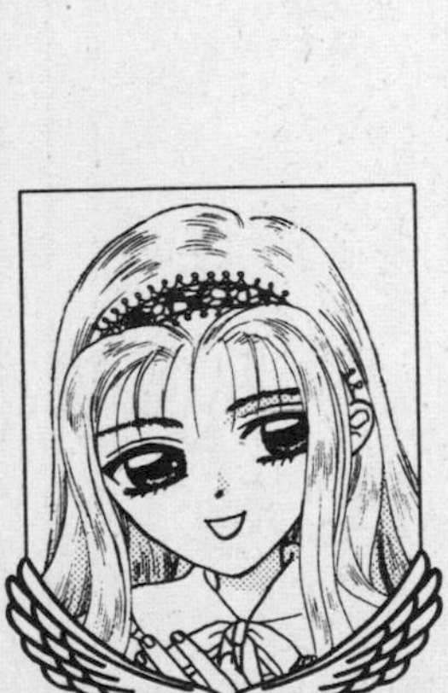

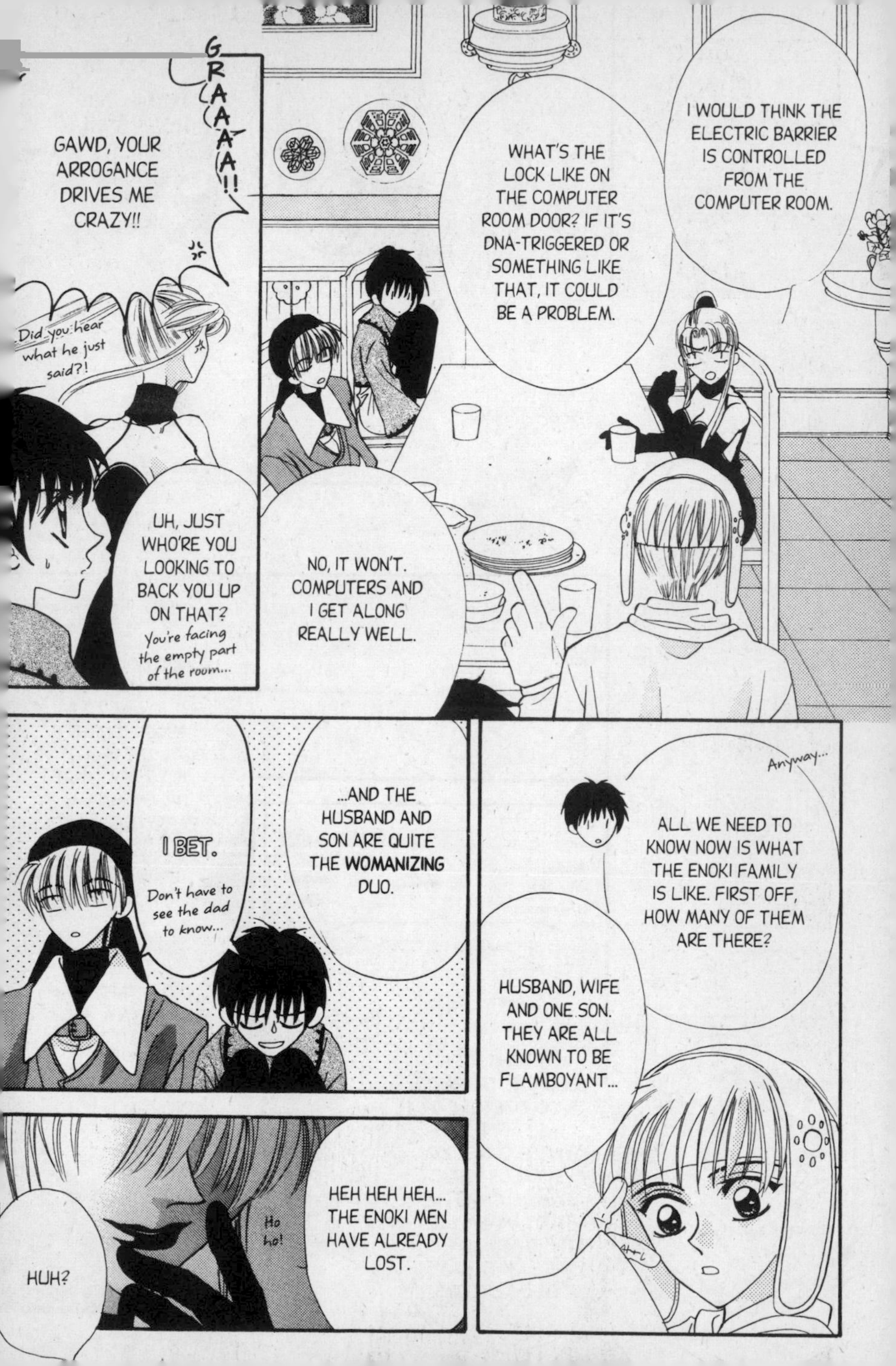
I WOULD THINK THE ELECTRIC BARRIER IS CONTROLLED FROM THE COMPUTER ROOM.
WHAT'S THE LOCK LIKE ON THE COMPUTER ROOM DOOR? IF IT'S DNA-TRIGGERED OR SOMETHING LIKE THAT, IT COULD BE A PROBLEM.
NO, IT WON'T. COMPUTERS AND I GET ALONG REALLY WELL.
GRAAAA!!
GAWD, YOUR ARROGANCE DRIVES ME CRAZY!!
Did you hear what he just said?!
UH, JUST WHO'RE YOU LOOKING TO BACK YOU UP ON THAT?
You're facing the empty part of the room...
Anyway...
ALL WE NEED TO KNOW NOW IS WHAT THE ENOKI FAMILY IS LIKE. FIRST OFF, HOW MANY OF THEM ARE THERE?
HUSBAND, WIFE AND ONE SON. THEY ARE ALL KNOWN TO BE FLAMBOYANT...
...AND THE HUSBAND AND SON ARE QUITE THE WOMANIZING DUO.
I BET.
Don't have to see the dad to know...
HEH HEH HEH... THE ENOKI MEN HAVE ALREADY LOST.
Ho ho!
HUH?

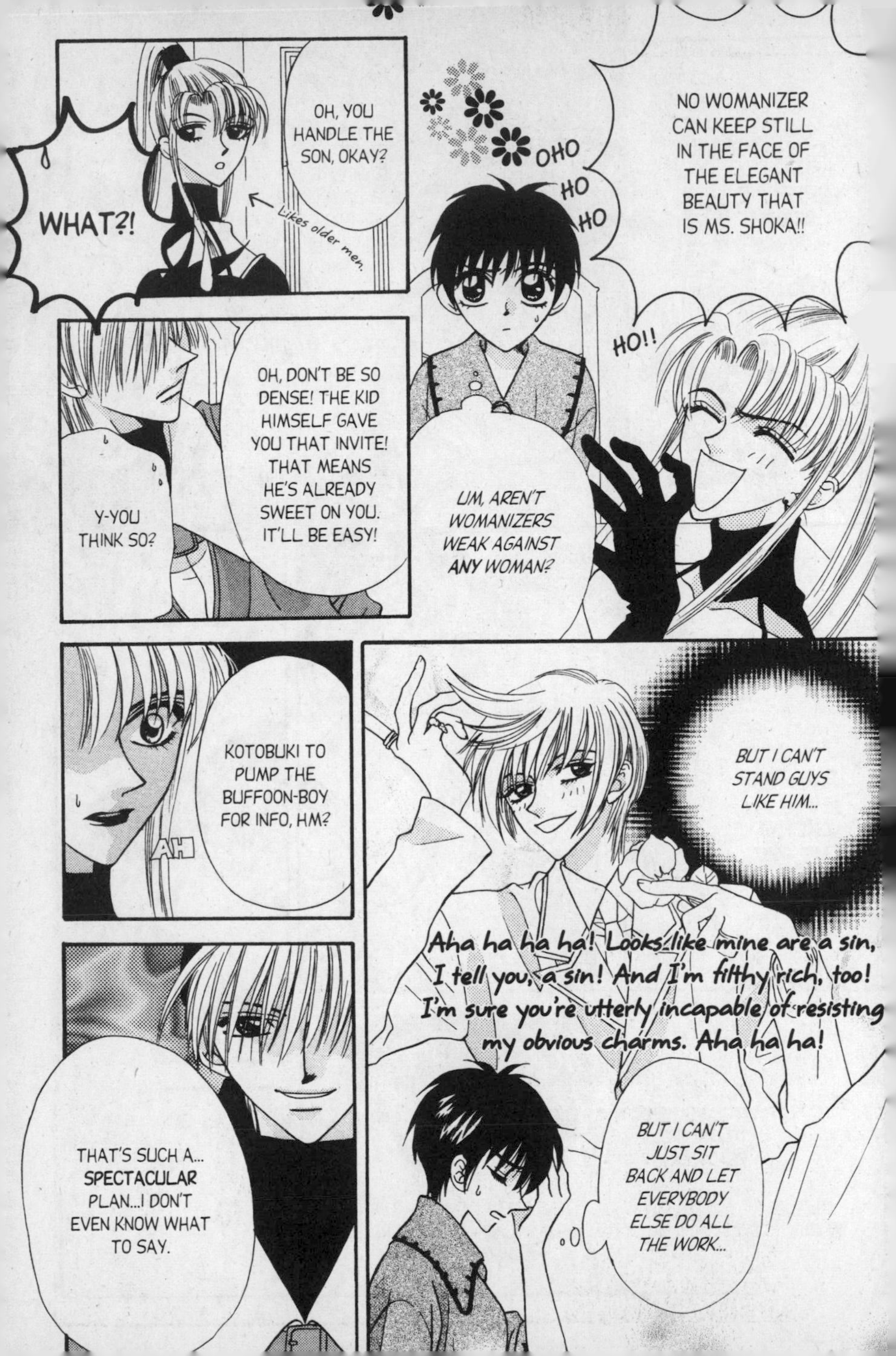
NO WOMANIZER CAN KEEP STILL IN THE FACE OF THE ELEGANT BEAUTY THAT IS MS. SHOKA!!
OHO HO HO
HO!!
UM, AREN'T WOMANIZERS WEAK AGAINST ANY WOMAN?
OH, YOU HANDLE THE SON, OKAY?
Likes older men.
WHAT?!
OH, DON'T BE SO DENSE! THE KID HIMSELF GAVE YOU THAT INVITE! THAT MEANS HE'S ALREADY SWEET ON YOU. IT'LL BE EASY!
Y-YOU THINK SO?
BUT I CAN'T STAND GUYS LIKE HIM...
Aha ha ha ha! Looks like mine are a sin, I tell you, a sin! And I'm filthy rich, too! I'm sure you're utterly incapable of resisting my obvious charms. Aha ha ha!
BUT I CAN'T JUST SIT BACK AND LET EVERYBODY ELSE DO ALL THE WORK...
KOTOBUKI TO PUMP THE BUFFOON-BOY FOR INFO, HM?
AH
THAT'S SUCH A... SPECTACULAR PLAN...I DON'T EVEN KNOW WHAT TO SAY.

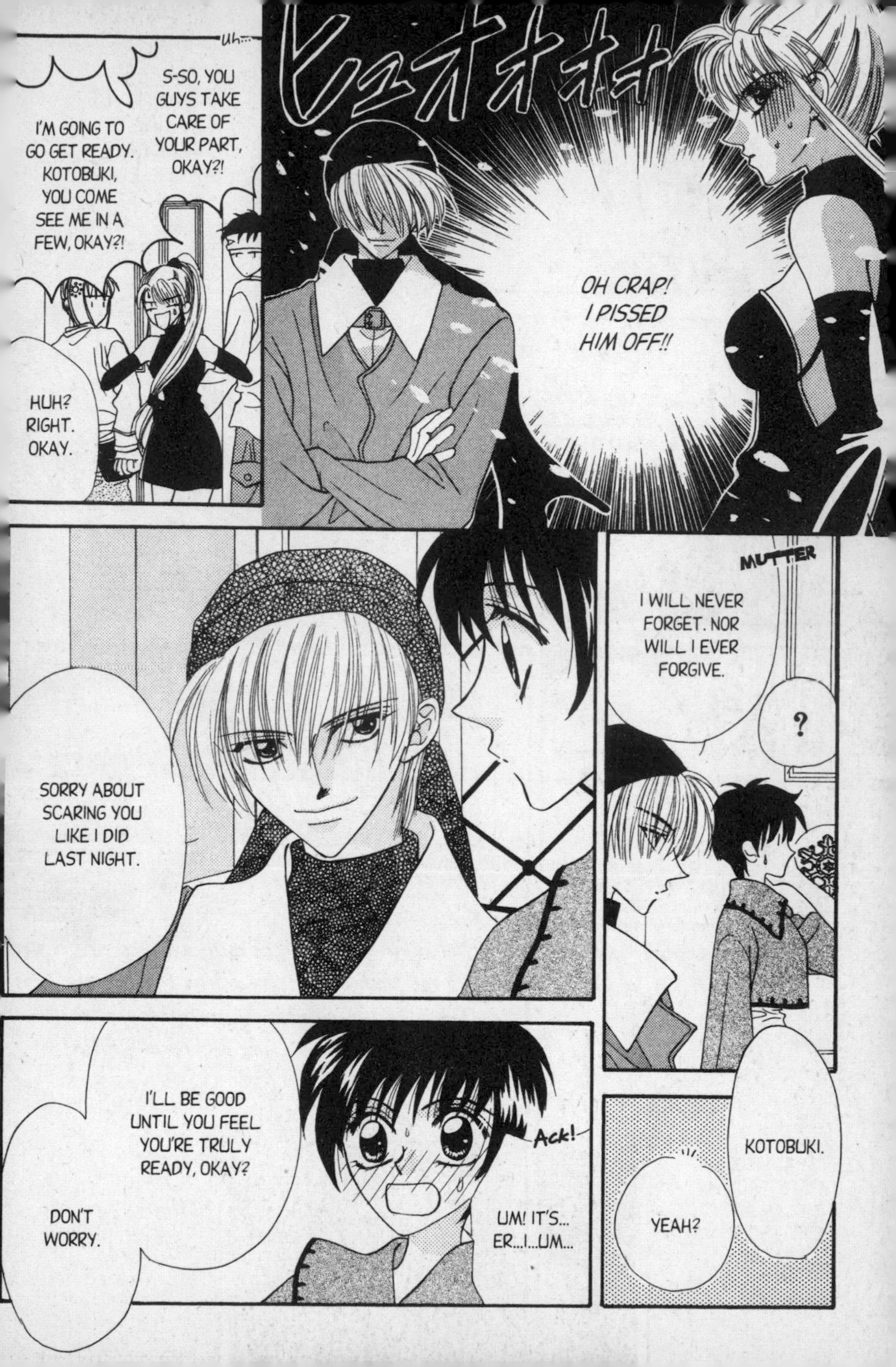

ヒュオオオオ
OH CRAP! I PISSED HIM OFF!!
uh...
S-SO, YOU GUYS TAKE CARE OF YOUR PART, OKAY?!
I'M GOING TO GO GET READY. KOTOBUKI, YOU COME SEE ME IN A FEW, OKAY?!
HUH? RIGHT. OKAY.
MUTTER
I WILL NEVER FORGET. NOR WILL I EVER FORGIVE.
?
SORRY ABOUT SCARING YOU LIKE I DID LAST NIGHT.
KOTOBUKI.
YEAH?
I'LL BE GOOD UNTIL YOU FEEL YOU'RE TRULY READY, OKAY?
Ack!
UM! IT'S... ER...I...UM...
DON'T WORRY.

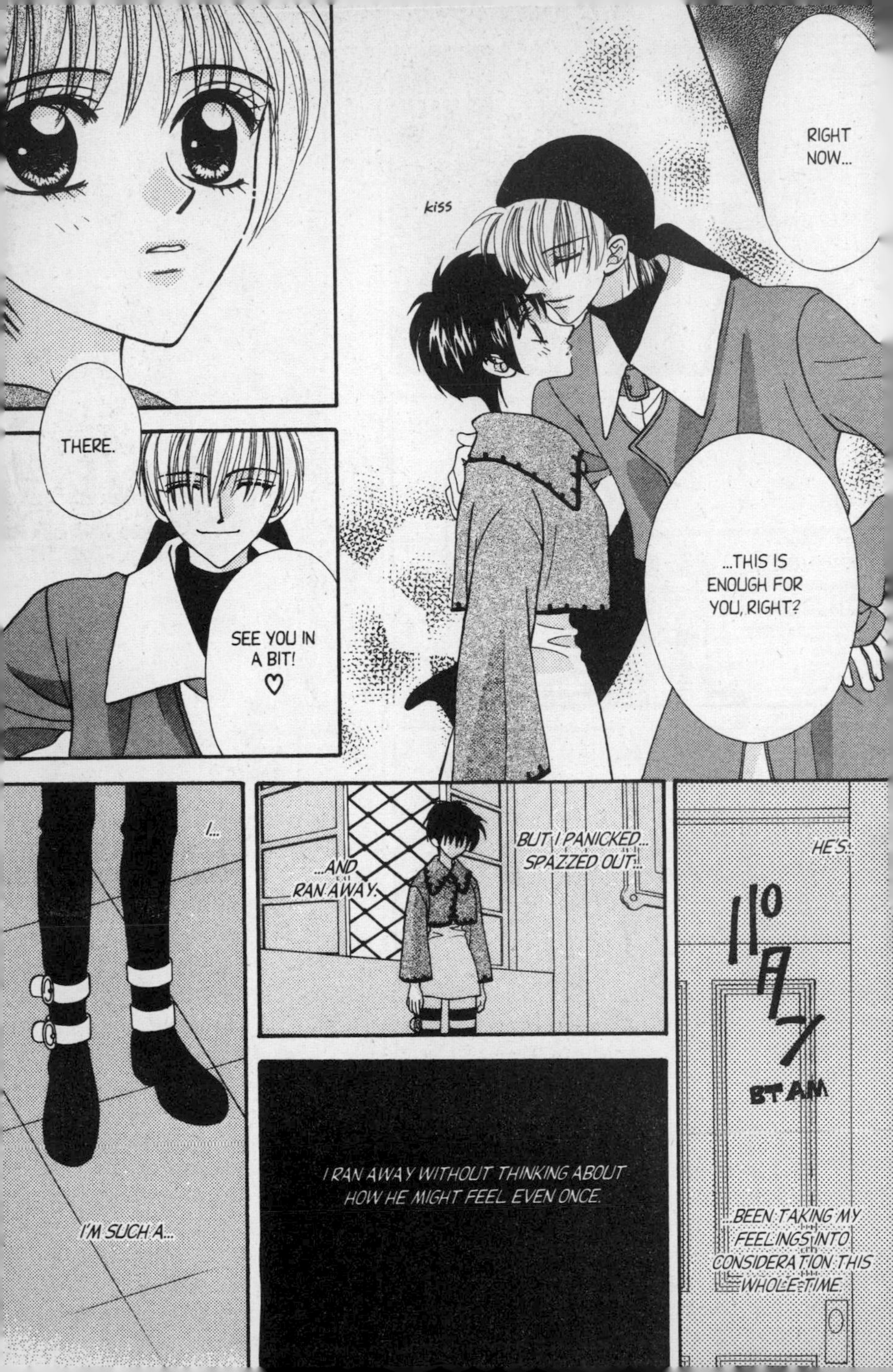

RIGHT NOW...
kiss
...THIS IS ENOUGH FOR YOU, RIGHT?
THERE.
SEE YOU IN A BIT! ♡
HE'S...
パタン
BTAM
...BEEN TAKING MY FEELINGS INTO CONSIDERATION THIS WHOLE TIME.
BUT I PANICKED... SPAZZED OUT...
...AND RAN AWAY.
I RAN AWAY WITHOUT THINKING ABOUT HOW HE MIGHT FEEL EVEN ONCE.
I...
I'M SUCH A...

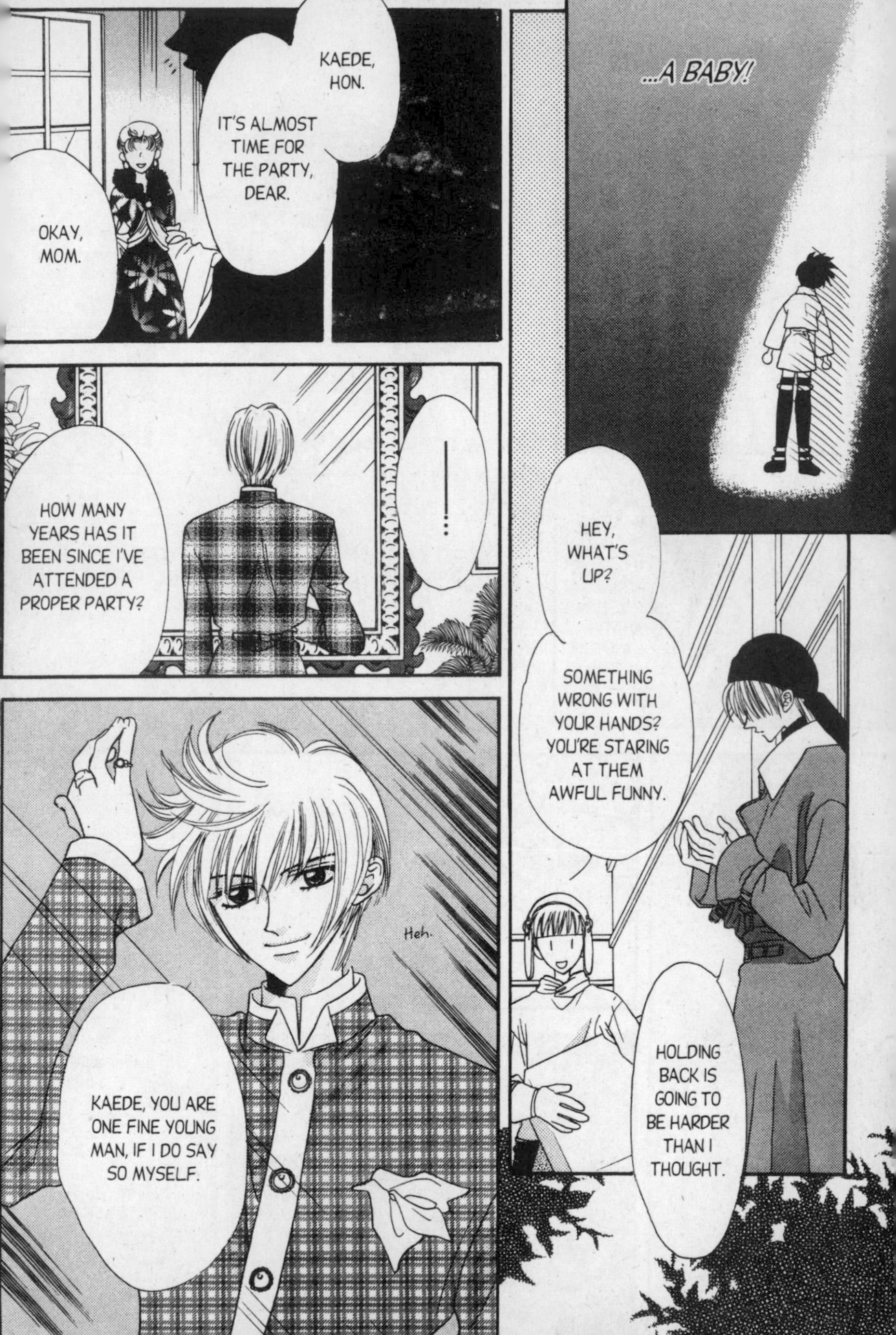

...A BABY!
HEY, WHAT'S UP?
SOMETHING WRONG WITH YOUR HANDS? YOU'RE STARING AT THEM AWFUL FUNNY.
HOLDING BACK IS GOING TO BE HARDER THAN I THOUGHT.
KAEDE, HON.
IT'S ALMOST TIME FOR THE PARTY, DEAR.
OKAY, MOM.
HOW MANY YEARS HAS IT BEEN SINCE I'VE ATTENDED A PROPER PARTY?
Heh.
KAEDE, YOU ARE ONE FINE YOUNG MAN, IF I DO SAY SO MYSELF.

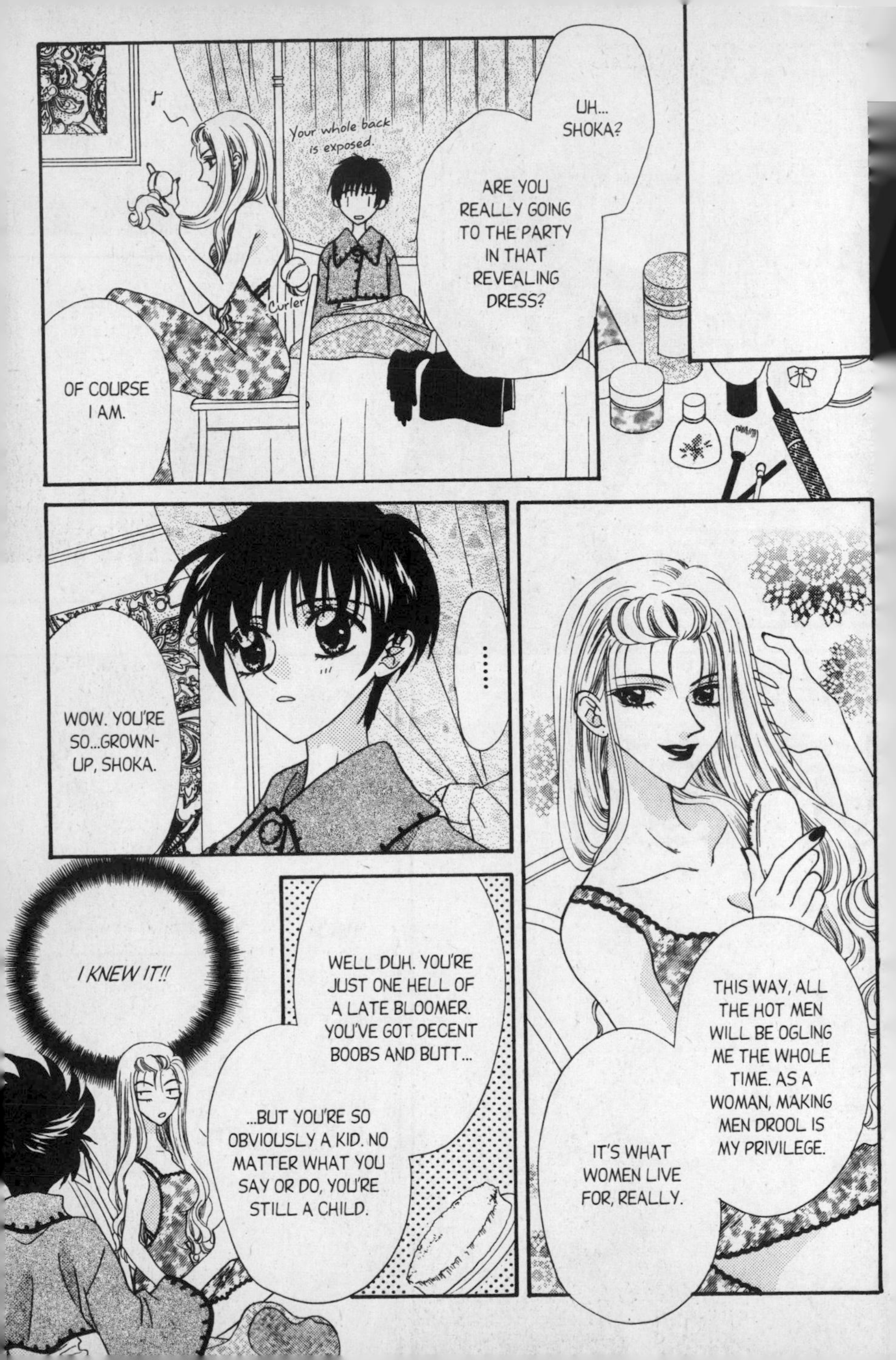
UH... SHOKA?
ARE YOU REALLY GOING TO THE PARTY IN THAT REVEALING DRESS?
Your whole back is exposed.
Curler
OF COURSE I AM.
THIS WAY, ALL THE HOT MEN WILL BE OGLING ME THE WHOLE TIME. AS A WOMAN, MAKING MEN DROOL IS MY PRIVILEGE.
IT'S WHAT WOMEN LIVE FOR, REALLY.
......
WOW. YOU'RE SO...GROWN-UP, SHOKA.
WELL DUH. YOU'RE JUST ONE HELL OF A LATE BLOOMER. YOU'VE GOT DECENT BOOBS AND BUTT...
...BUT YOU'RE SO OBVIOUSLY A KID. NO MATTER WHAT YOU SAY OR DO, YOU'RE STILL A CHILD.
I KNEW IT!!

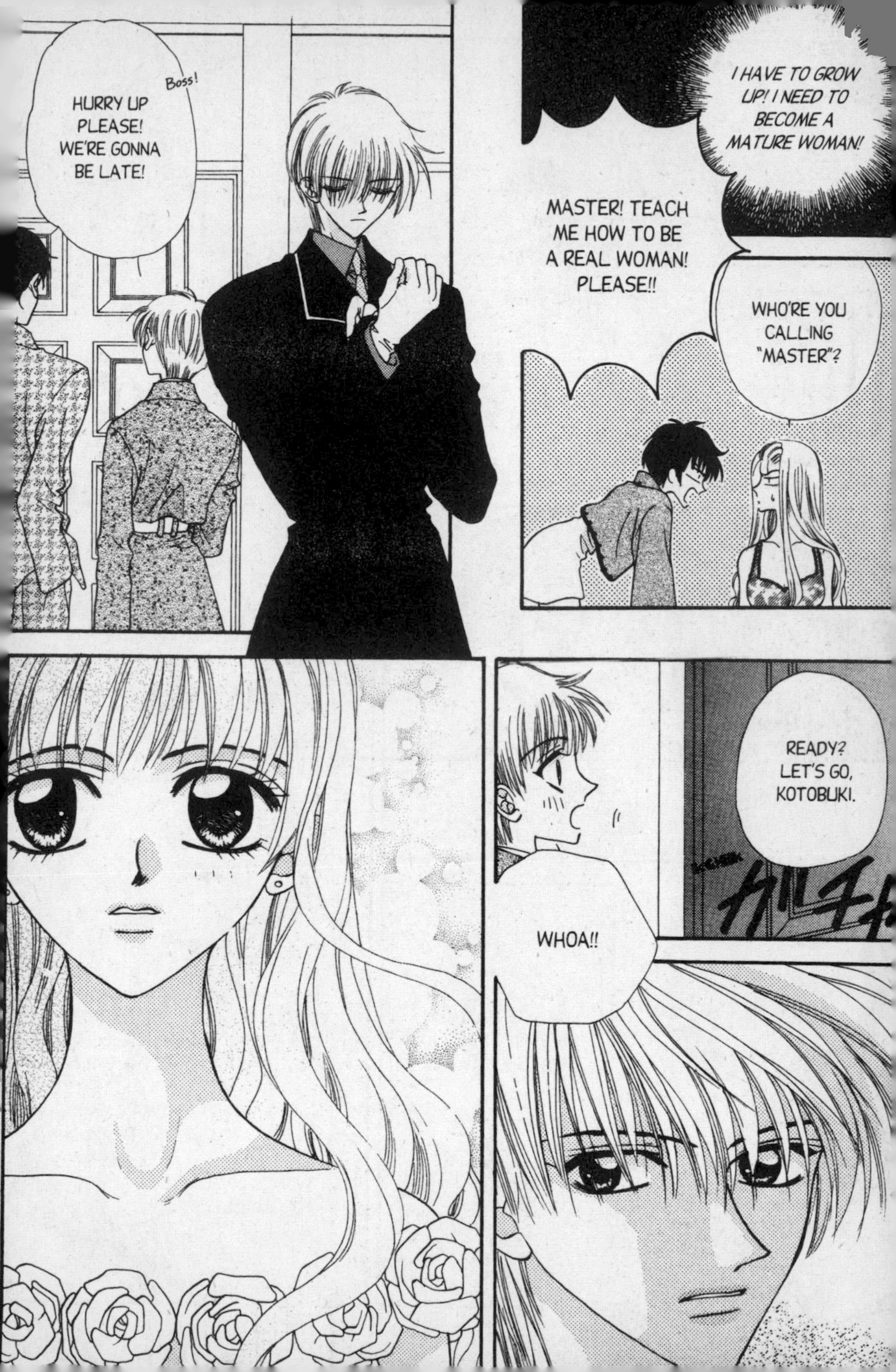
I HAVE TO GROW UP! I NEED TO BECOME A MATURE WOMAN!
MASTER! TEACH ME HOW TO BE A REAL WOMAN! PLEASE!!
WHO'RE YOU CALLING "MASTER"?
Boss!
HURRY UP PLEASE! WE'RE GONNA BE LATE!
READY? LET'S GO, KOTOBUKI.
WHOA!!

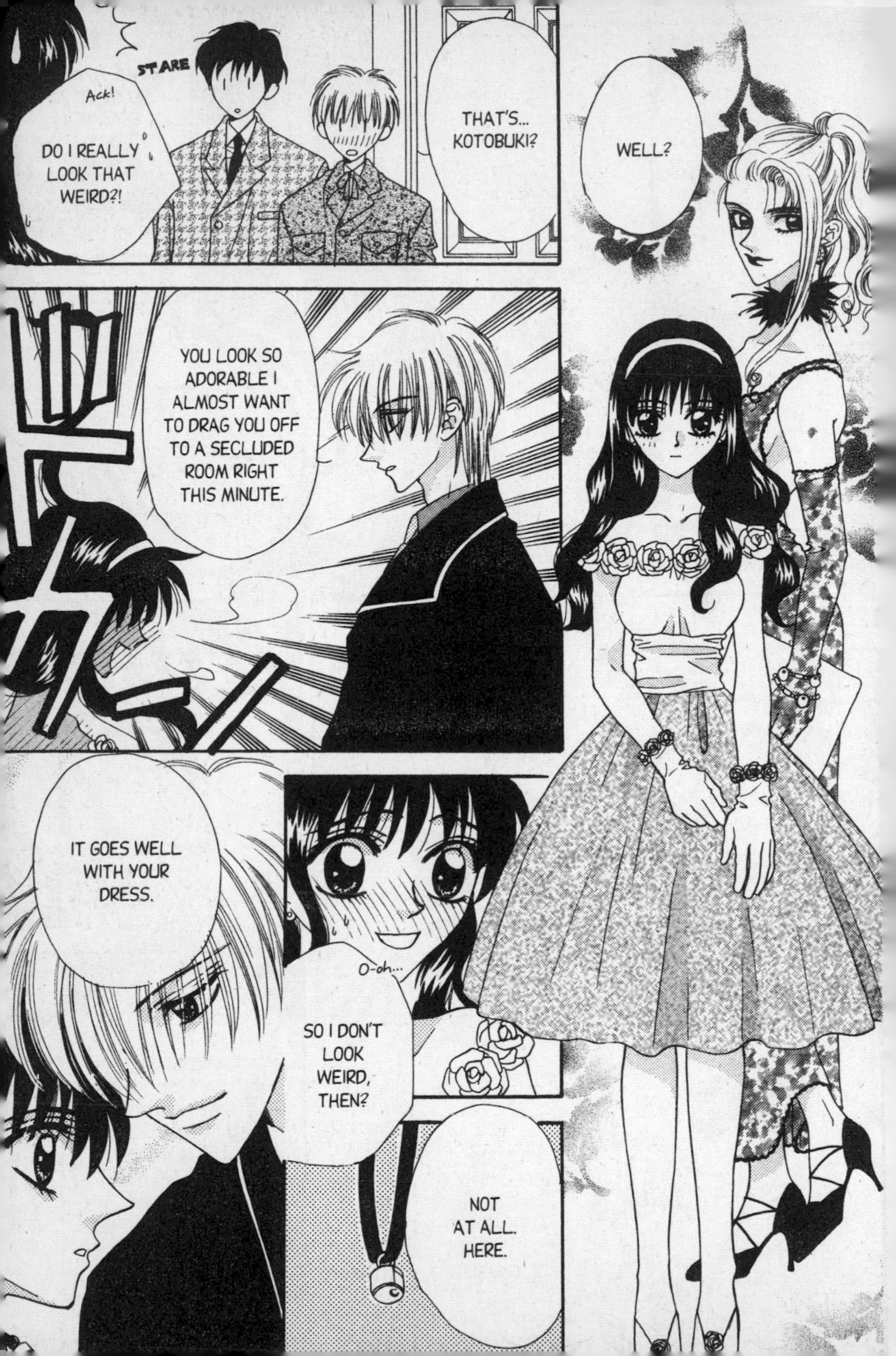
WELL?
THAT'S... KOTOBUKI?
STARE
Ack!
DO I REALLY LOOK THAT WEIRD?!
YOU LOOK SO ADORABLE I ALMOST WANT TO DRAG YOU OFF TO A SECLUDED ROOM RIGHT THIS MINUTE.
O-oh...
SO I DON'T LOOK WEIRD, THEN?
NOT AT ALL. HERE.
IT GOES WELL WITH YOUR DRESS.

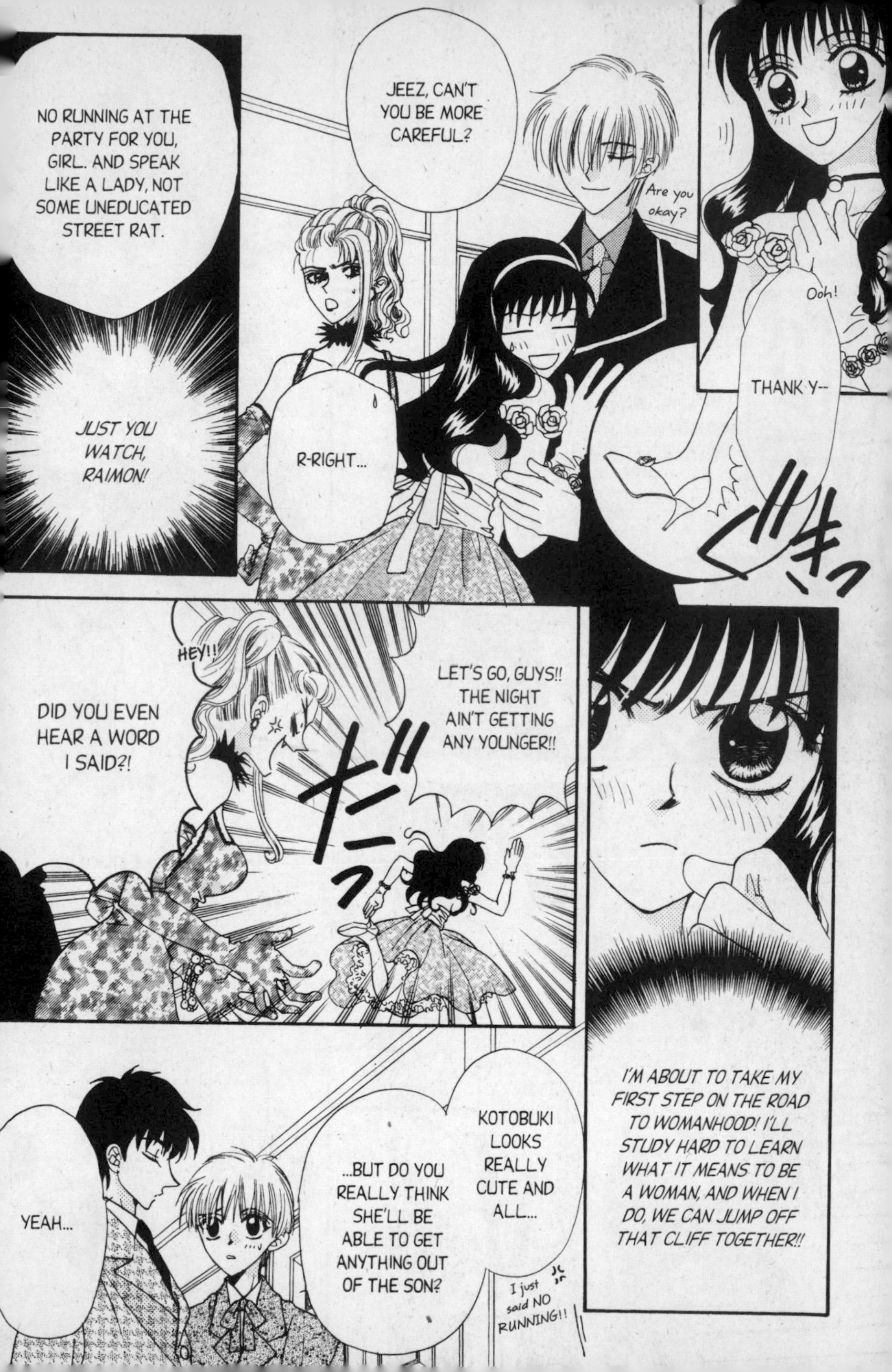
Ooh!
THANK Y--
Are you okay?
JEEZ, CAN'T YOU BE MORE CAREFUL?
R-RIGHT...
NO RUNNING AT THE PARTY FOR YOU, GIRL. AND SPEAK LIKE A LADY, NOT SOME UNEDUCATED STREET RAT.
JUST YOU WATCH, RAIMON!
I'M ABOUT TO TAKE MY FIRST STEP ON THE ROAD TO WOMANHOOD! I'LL STUDY HARD TO LEARN WHAT IT MEANS TO BE A WOMAN, AND WHEN I DO, WE CAN JUMP OFF THAT CLIFF TOGETHER!!
LET'S GO, GUYS!! THE NIGHT AIN'T GETTING ANY YOUNGER!!
HEY!!
DID YOU EVEN HEAR A WORD I SAID?!
KOTOBUKI LOOKS REALLY CUTE AND ALL...
...BUT DO YOU REALLY THINK SHE'LL BE ABLE TO GET ANYTHING OUT OF THE SON?
YEAH...
I just said NO RUNNING!!

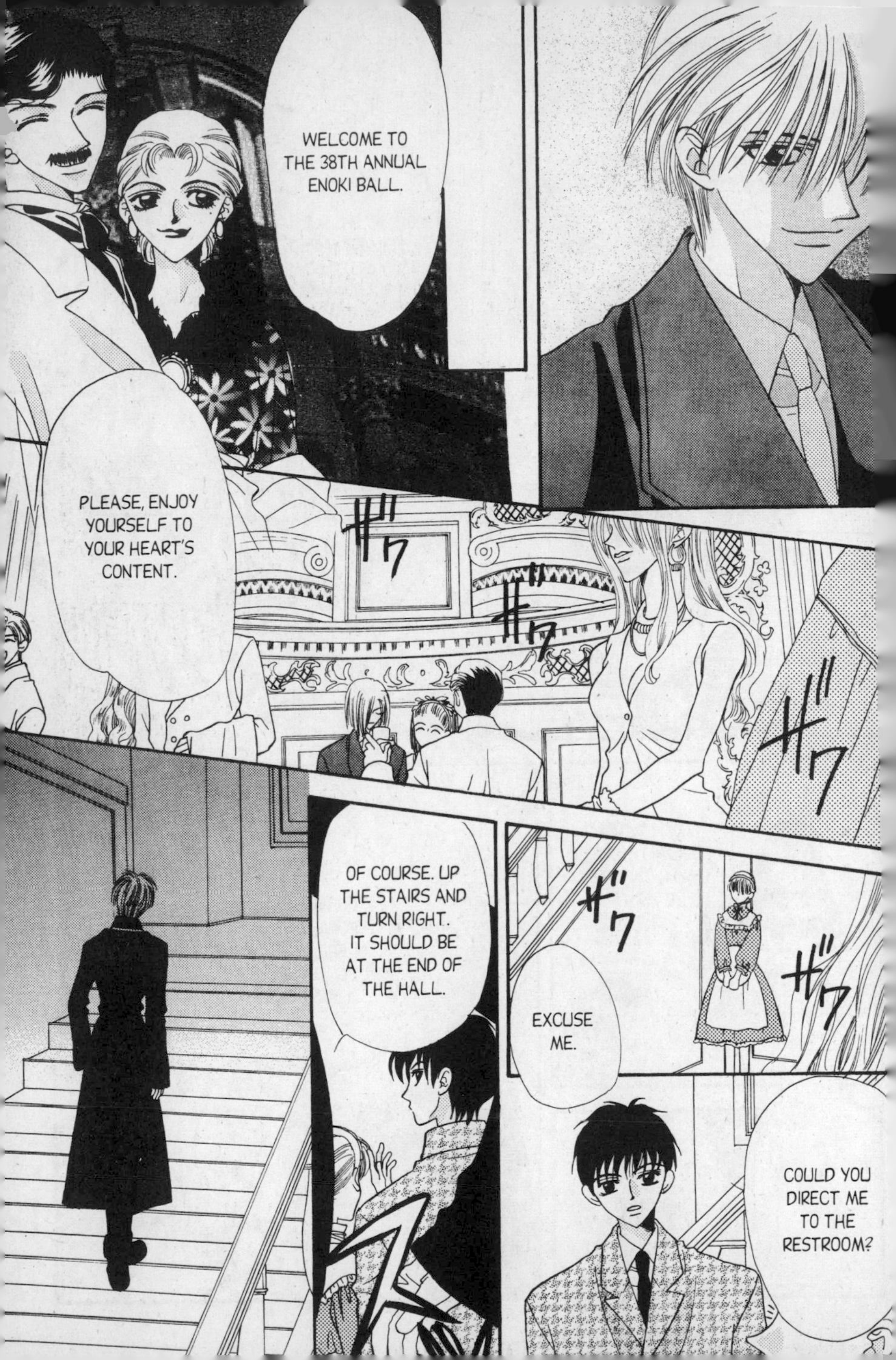
WELCOME TO THE 38TH ANNUAL ENOKI BALL.
PLEASE, ENJOY YOURSELF TO YOUR HEART'S CONTENT.
ザワ
ザワ
ザワ
ザワ
ザワ
EXCUSE ME.
COULD YOU DIRECT ME TO THE RESTROOM?
OF COURSE. UP THE STAIRS AND TURN RIGHT. IT SHOULD BE AT THE END OF THE HALL.

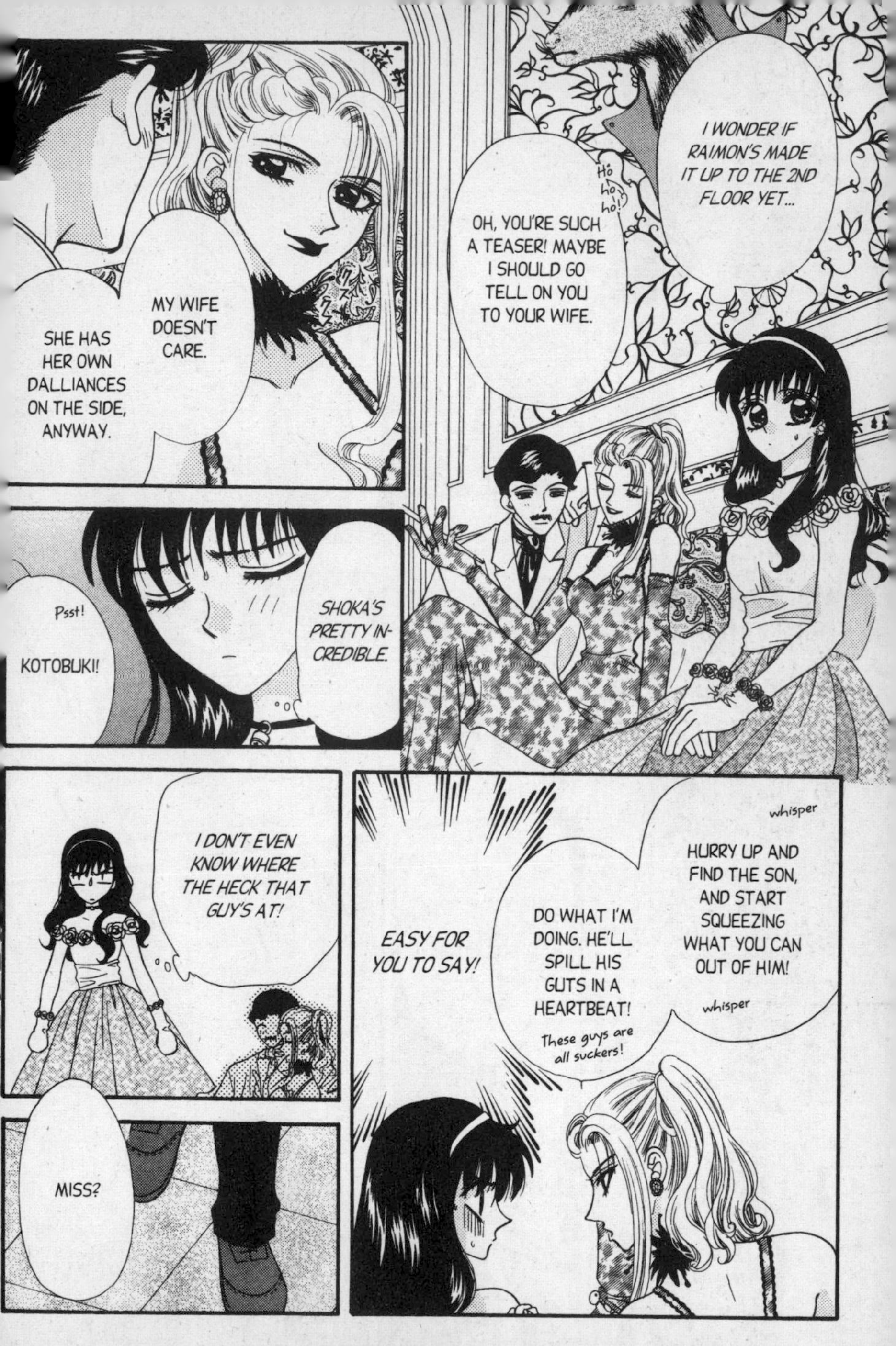
I WONDER IF RAIMON'S MADE IT UP TO THE 2ND FLOOR YET...
Ho ho ho!
OH, YOU'RE SUCH A TEASER! MAYBE I SHOULD GO TELL ON YOU TO YOUR WIFE.
MY WIFE DOESN'T CARE.
SHE HAS HER OWN DALLIANCES ON THE SIDE, ANYWAY.
SHOKA'S PRETTY IN-CREDIBLE.
Psst!
KOTOBUKI!
whisper
HURRY UP AND FIND THE SON, AND START SQUEEZING WHAT YOU CAN OUT OF HIM!
whisper
DO WHAT I'M DOING. HE'LL SPILL HIS GUTS IN A HEARTBEAT!
These guys are all suckers!
EASY FOR YOU TO SAY!
I DON'T EVEN KNOW WHERE THE HECK THAT GUY'S AT!
MISS?

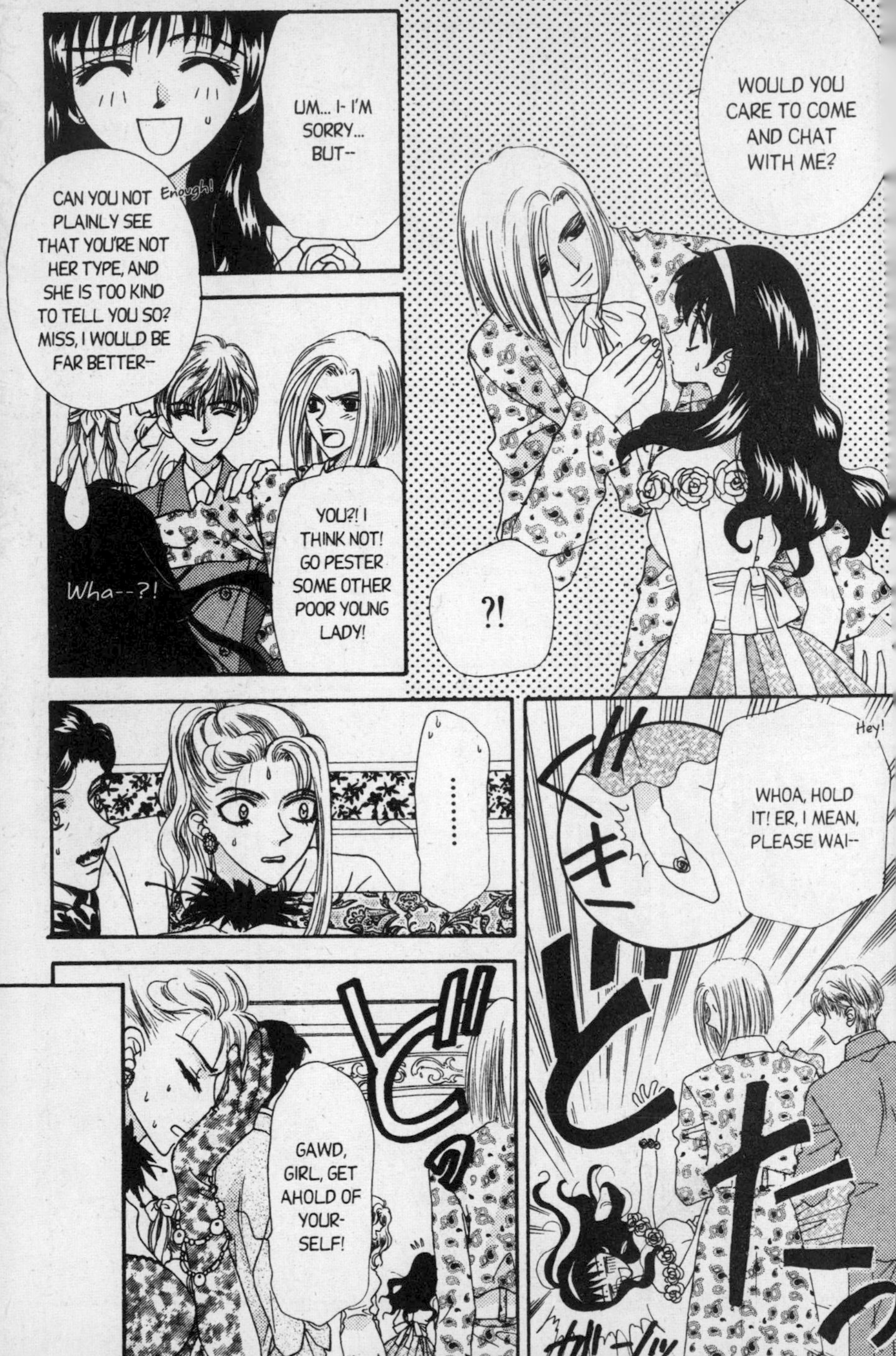
WOULD YOU CARE TO COME AND CHAT WITH ME?
?!
UM... I- I'M SORRY... BUT--
Enough!
CAN YOU NOT PLAINLY SEE THAT YOU'RE NOT HER TYPE, AND SHE IS TOO KIND TO TELL YOU SO? MISS, I WOULD BE FAR BETTER--
YOU?! I THINK NOT! GO PESTER SOME OTHER POOR YOUNG LADY!
Wha--?!
Hey!
WHOA, HOLD IT! ER, I MEAN, PLEASE WAI--
......
GAWD, GIRL, GET AHOLD OF YOURSELF!

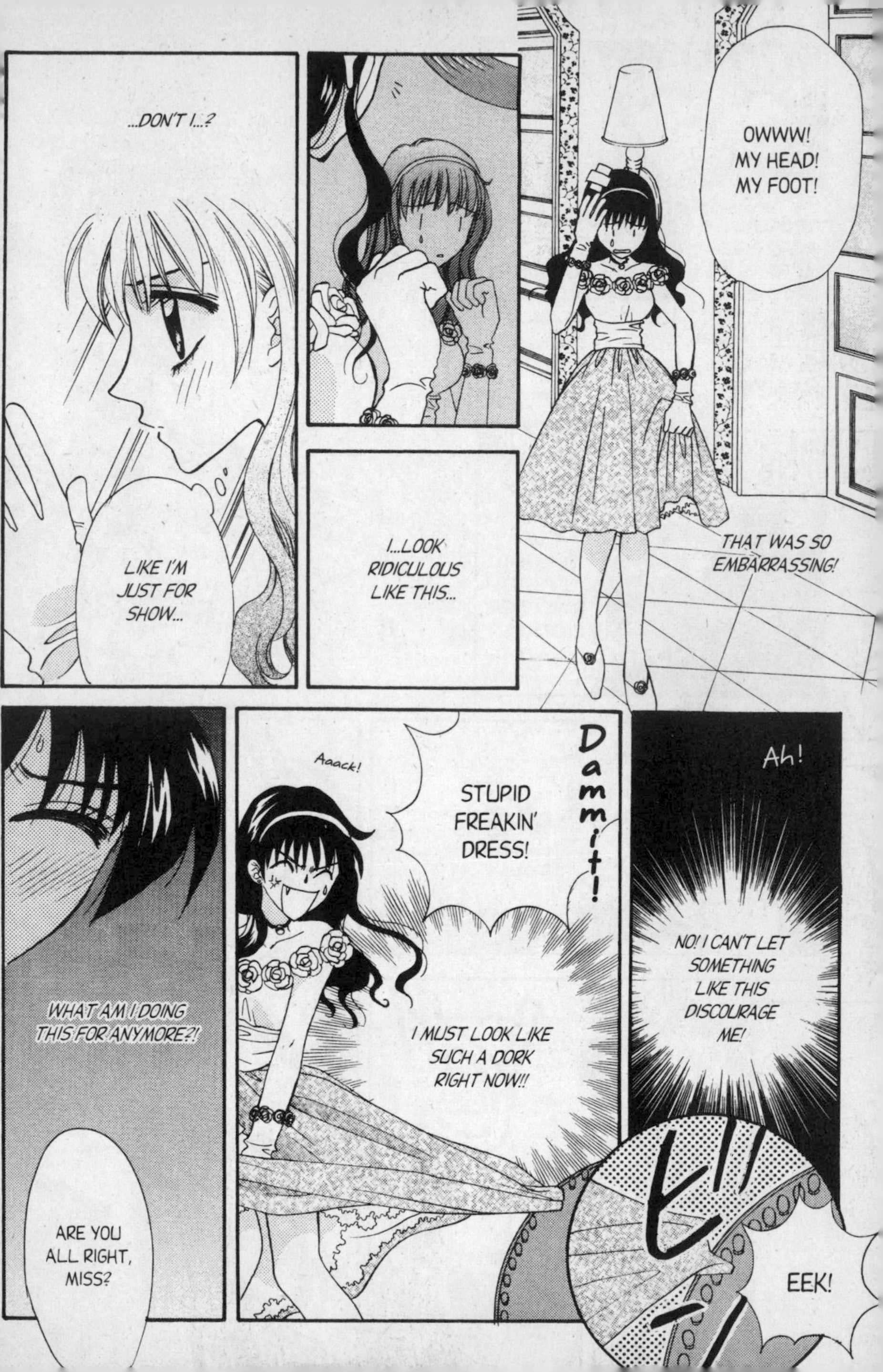
OWWW! MY HEAD! MY FOOT!
THAT WAS SO EMBARRASSING!
I...LOOK RIDICULOUS LIKE THIS...
...DON'T I...?
LIKE I'M JUST FOR SHOW...
Ah!
NO! I CAN'T LET SOMETHING LIKE THIS DISCOURAGE ME!
EEK!
Dammit!
STUPID FREAKIN' DRESS!
Aaack!
I MUST LOOK LIKE SUCH A DORK RIGHT NOW!!
WHAT AM I DOING THIS FOR ANYMORE?!
ARE YOU ALL RIGHT, MISS?

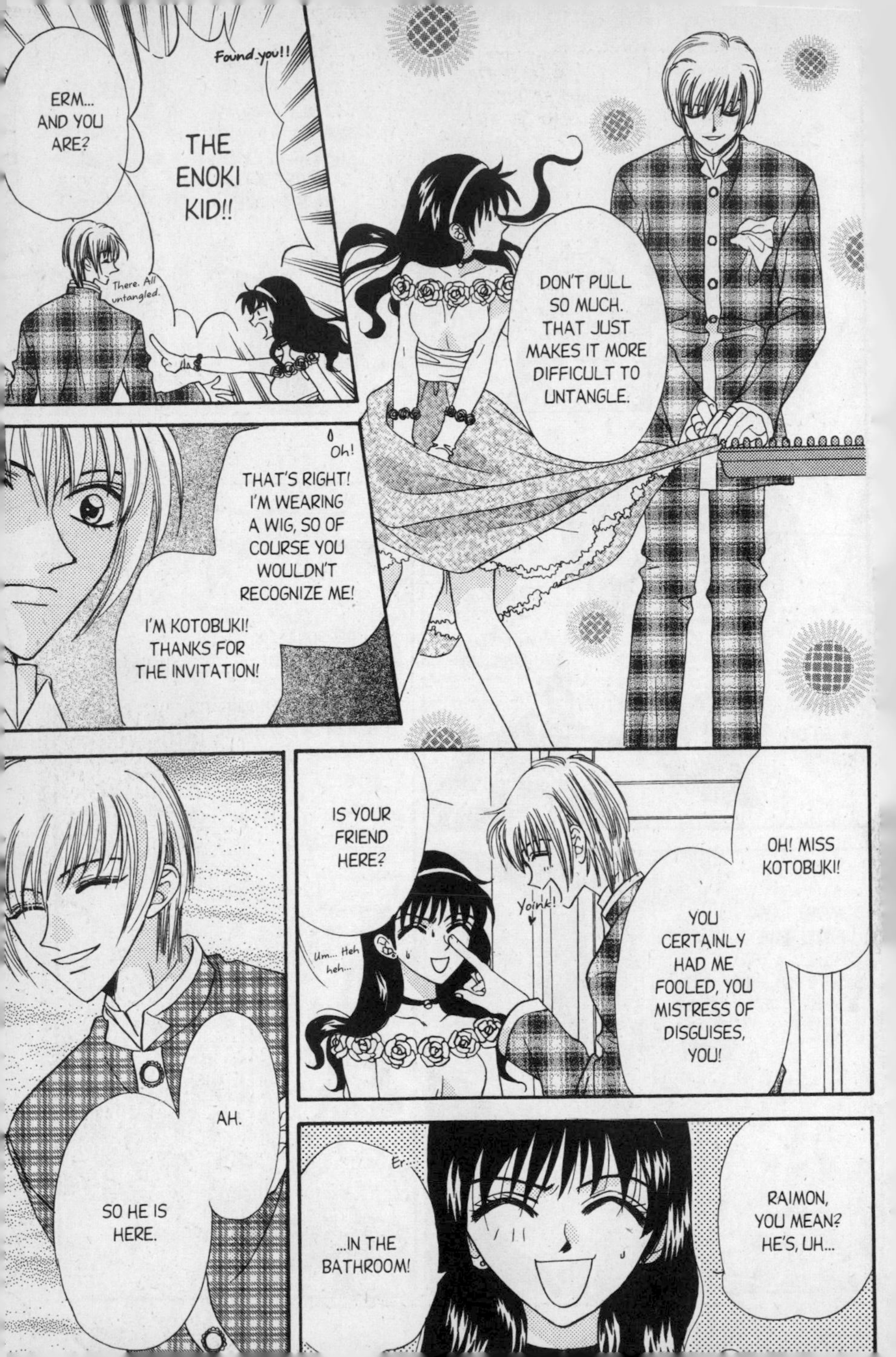
DON'T PULL SO MUCH. THAT JUST MAKES IT MORE DIFFICULT TO UNTANGLE.
Found you!!
THE ENOKI KID!!
ERM... AND YOU ARE?
There. All untangled.
Oh!
THAT'S RIGHT! I'M WEARING A WIG, SO OF COURSE YOU WOULDN'T RECOGNIZE ME!
I'M KOTOBUKI! THANKS FOR THE INVITATION!
OH! MISS KOTOBUKI!
YOU CERTAINLY HAD ME FOOLED, YOU MISTRESS OF DISGUISES, YOU!
IS YOUR FRIEND HERE?
Yoink!
Um... Heh heh...
RAIMON, YOU MEAN? HE'S, UH...
Er...
...IN THE BATHROOM!
AH.
SO HE IS HERE.

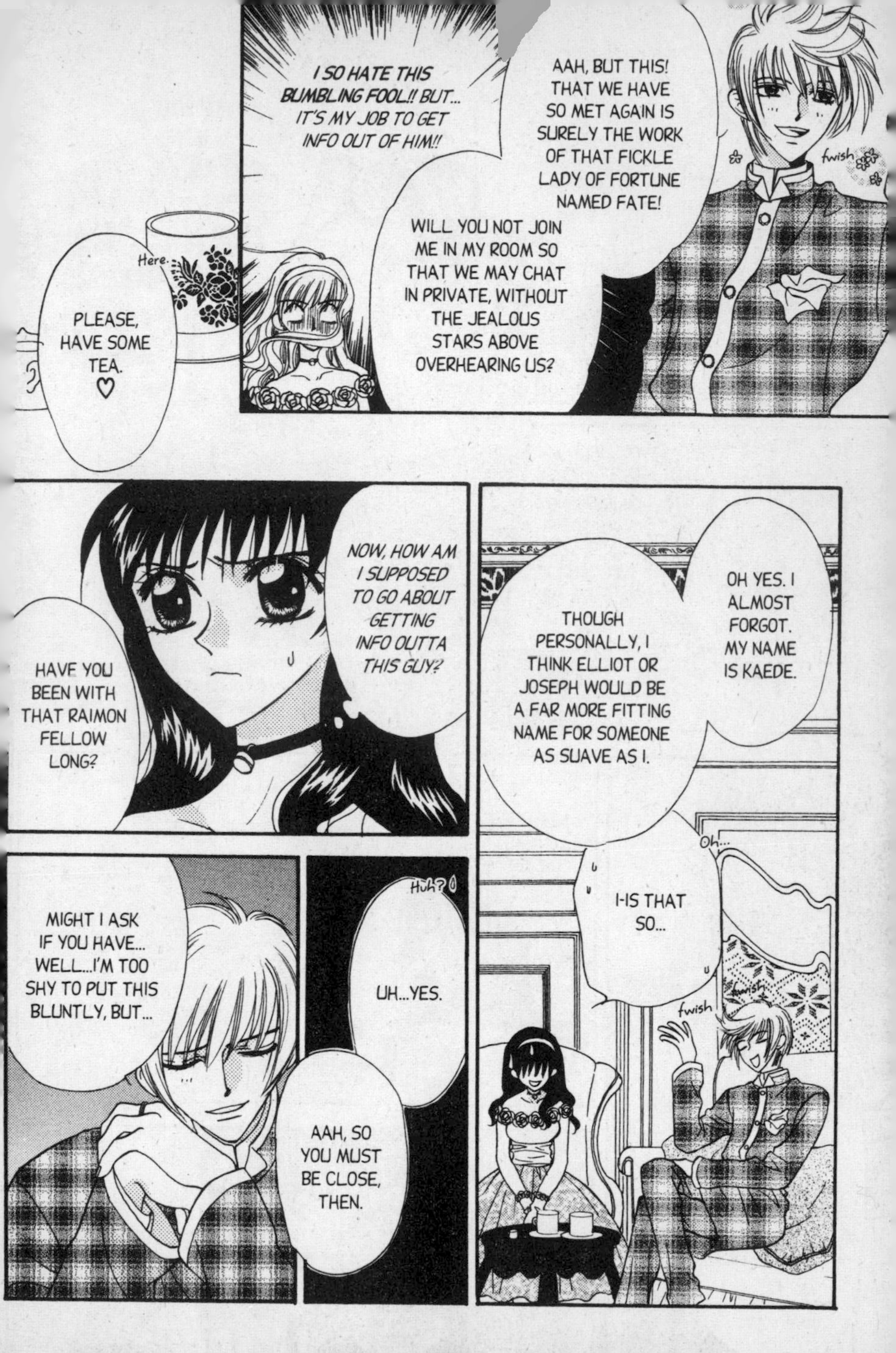
fwish
AAH, BUT THIS! THAT WE HAVE SO MET AGAIN IS SURELY THE WORK OF THAT FICKLE LADY OF FORTUNE NAMED FATE!
WILL YOU NOT JOIN ME IN MY ROOM SO THAT WE MAY CHAT IN PRIVATE, WITHOUT THE JEALOUS STARS ABOVE OVERHEARING US?
I SO HATE THIS BUMBLING FOOL!! BUT... IT'S MY JOB TO GET INFO OUT OF HIM!!
Here.
PLEASE, HAVE SOME TEA. ♡
OH YES. I ALMOST FORGOT. MY NAME IS KAEDE.
THOUGH PERSONALLY, I THINK ELLIOT OR JOSEPH WOULD BE A FAR MORE FITTING NAME FOR SOMEONE AS SUAVE AS I.
Oh...
I-IS THAT SO...
fwish
fwish
NOW, HOW AM I SUPPOSED TO GO ABOUT GETTING INFO OUTTA THIS GUY?
HAVE YOU BEEN WITH THAT RAIMON FELLOW LONG?
Huh?
UH...YES.
AAH, SO YOU MUST BE CLOSE, THEN.
MIGHT I ASK IF YOU HAVE... WELL...I'M TOO SHY TO PUT THIS BLUNTLY, BUT...

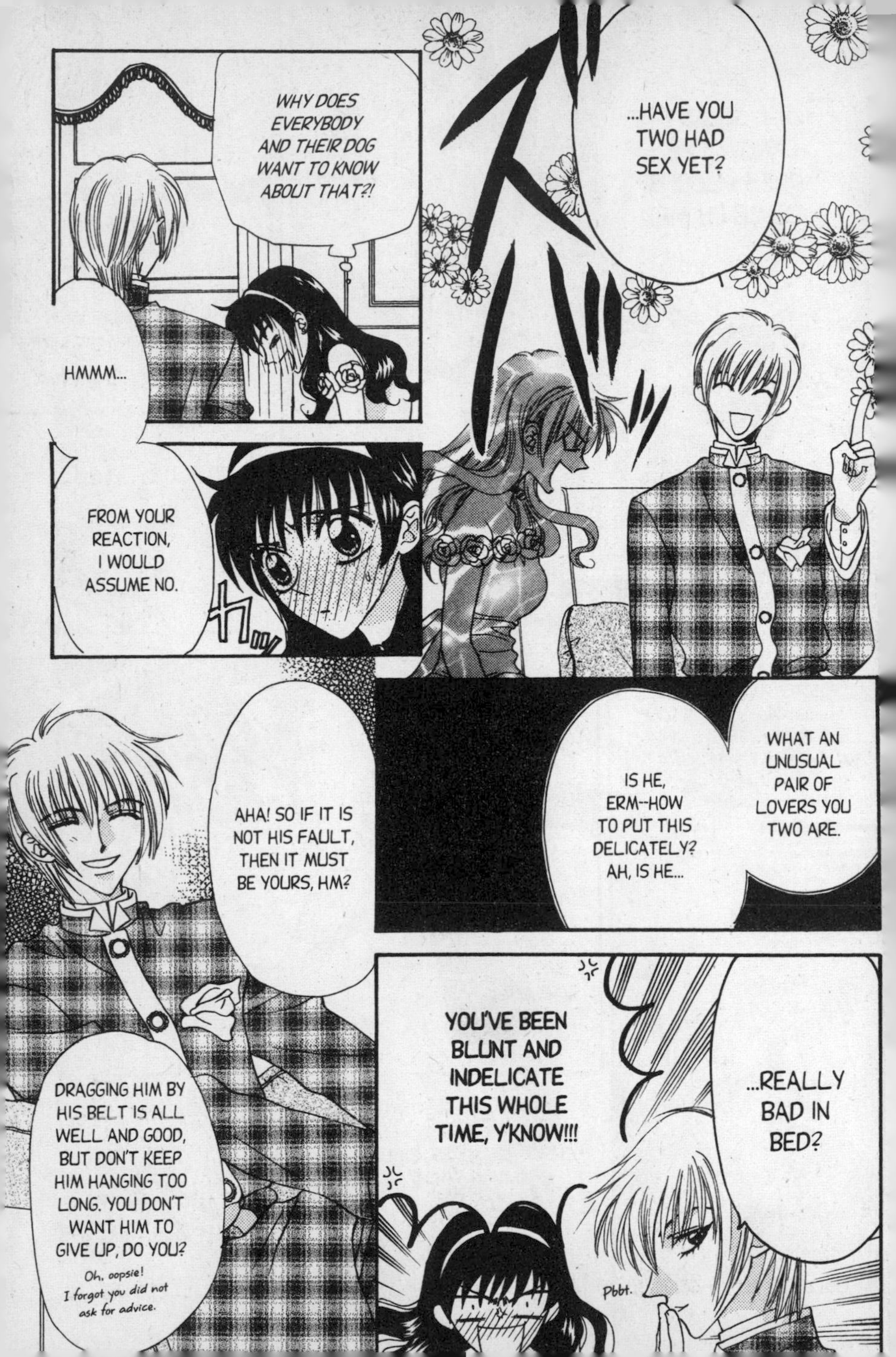
...HAVE YOU TWO HAD SEX YET?
WHY DOES EVERYBODY AND THEIR DOG WANT TO KNOW ABOUT THAT?!
HMMM...
FROM YOUR REACTION, I WOULD ASSUME NO.
WHAT AN UNUSUAL PAIR OF LOVERS YOU TWO ARE.
IS HE, ERM--HOW TO PUT THIS DELICATELY? AH, IS HE...
...REALLY BAD IN BED?
YOU'VE BEEN BLUNT AND INDELICATE THIS WHOLE TIME, Y'KNOW!!!
Pbbt.
AHA! SO IF IT IS NOT HIS FAULT, THEN IT MUST BE YOURS, HM?
DRAGGING HIM BY HIS BELT IS ALL WELL AND GOOD, BUT DON'T KEEP HIM HANGING TOO LONG. YOU DON'T WANT HIM TO GIVE UP, DO YOU?
Oh, oopsie! I forgot you did not ask for advice.

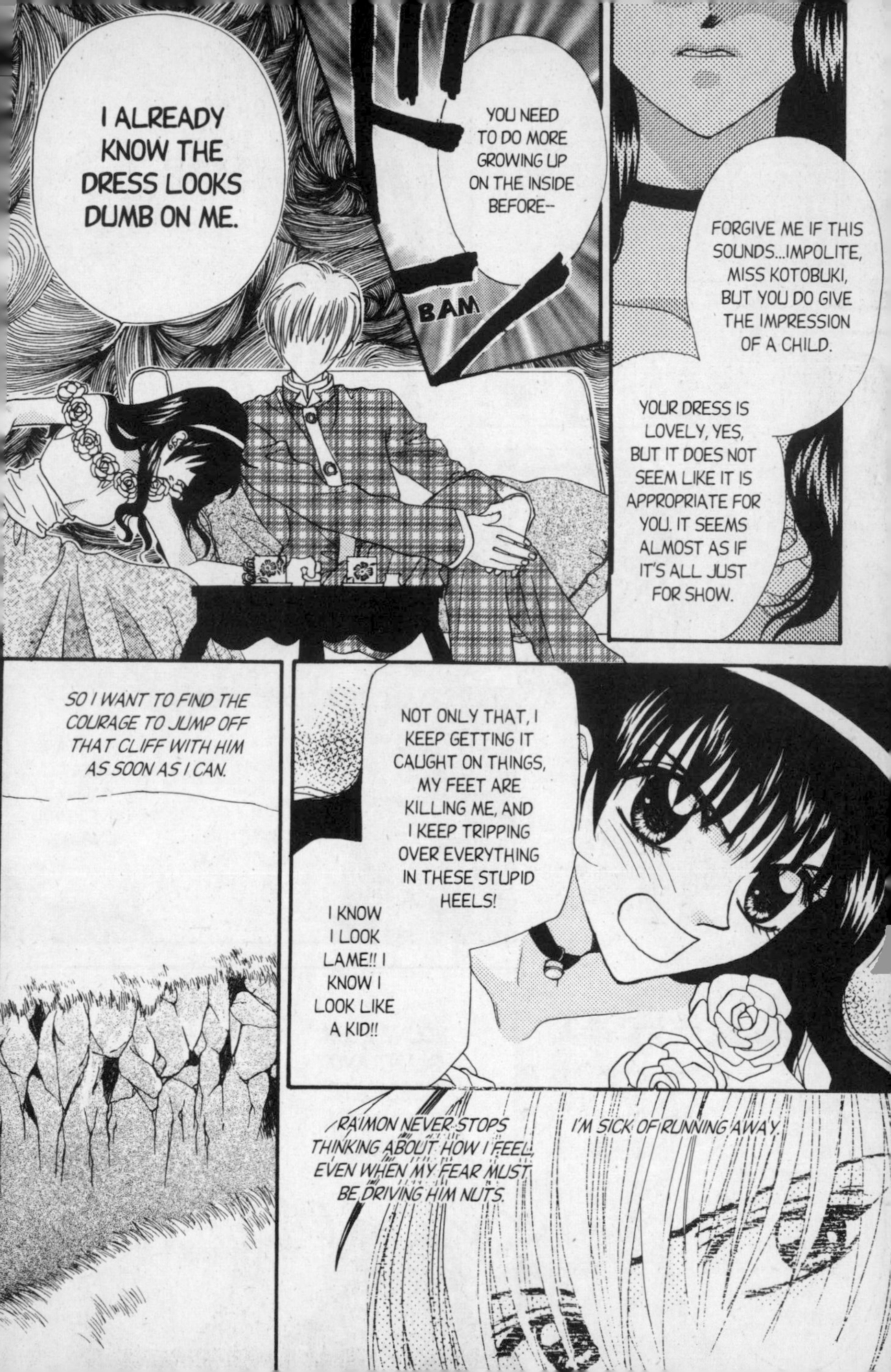
FORGIVE ME IF THIS SOUNDS...IMPOLITE, MISS KOTOBUKI, BUT YOU DO GIVE THE IMPRESSION OF A CHILD.
YOUR DRESS IS LOVELY, YES, BUT IT DOES NOT SEEM LIKE IT IS APPROPRIATE FOR YOU. IT SEEMS ALMOST AS IF IT'S ALL JUST FOR SHOW.
YOU NEED TO DO MORE GROWING UP ON THE INSIDE BEFORE--
BAM
I ALREADY KNOW THE DRESS LOOKS DUMB ON ME.
NOT ONLY THAT, I KEEP GETTING IT CAUGHT ON THINGS, MY FEET ARE KILLING ME, AND I KEEP TRIPPING OVER EVERYTHING IN THESE STUPID HEELS!
I KNOW I LOOK LAME!! I KNOW I LOOK LIKE A KID!!
I'M SICK OF RUNNING AWAY.
RAIMON NEVER STOPS THINKING ABOUT HOW I FEEL, EVEN WHEN MY FEAR MUST BE DRIVING HIM NUTS.
SO I WANT TO FIND THE COURAGE TO JUMP OFF THAT CLIFF WITH HIM AS SOON AS I CAN.

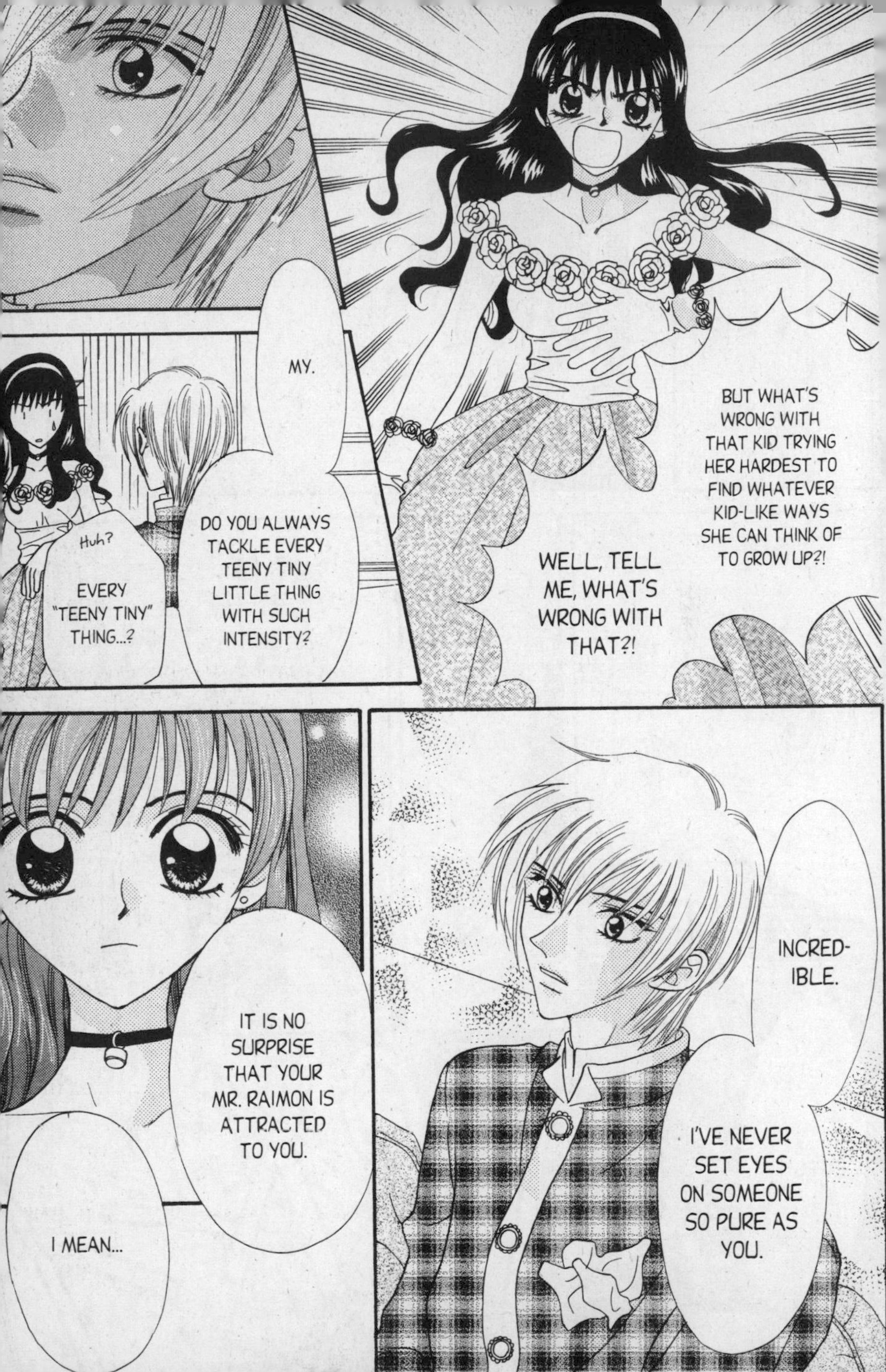
BUT WHAT'S WRONG WITH THAT KID TRYING HER HARDEST TO FIND WHATEVER KID-LIKE WAYS SHE CAN THINK OF TO GROW UP?!
WELL, TELL ME, WHAT'S WRONG WITH THAT?!
MY.
DO YOU ALWAYS TACKLE EVERY TEENY TINY LITTLE THING WITH SUCH INTENSITY?
Huh?
EVERY "TEENY TINY" THING...?
INCRED-IBLE.
I'VE NEVER SET EYES ON SOMEONE SO PURE AS YOU.
IT IS NO SURPRISE THAT YOUR MR. RAIMON IS ATTRACTED TO YOU.
I MEAN...

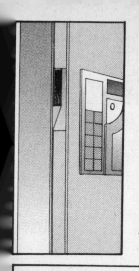

THE HECK?!

...EVEN I FIND MYSELF WANTING YOU.

AS EXPECTED.

BWAAAN

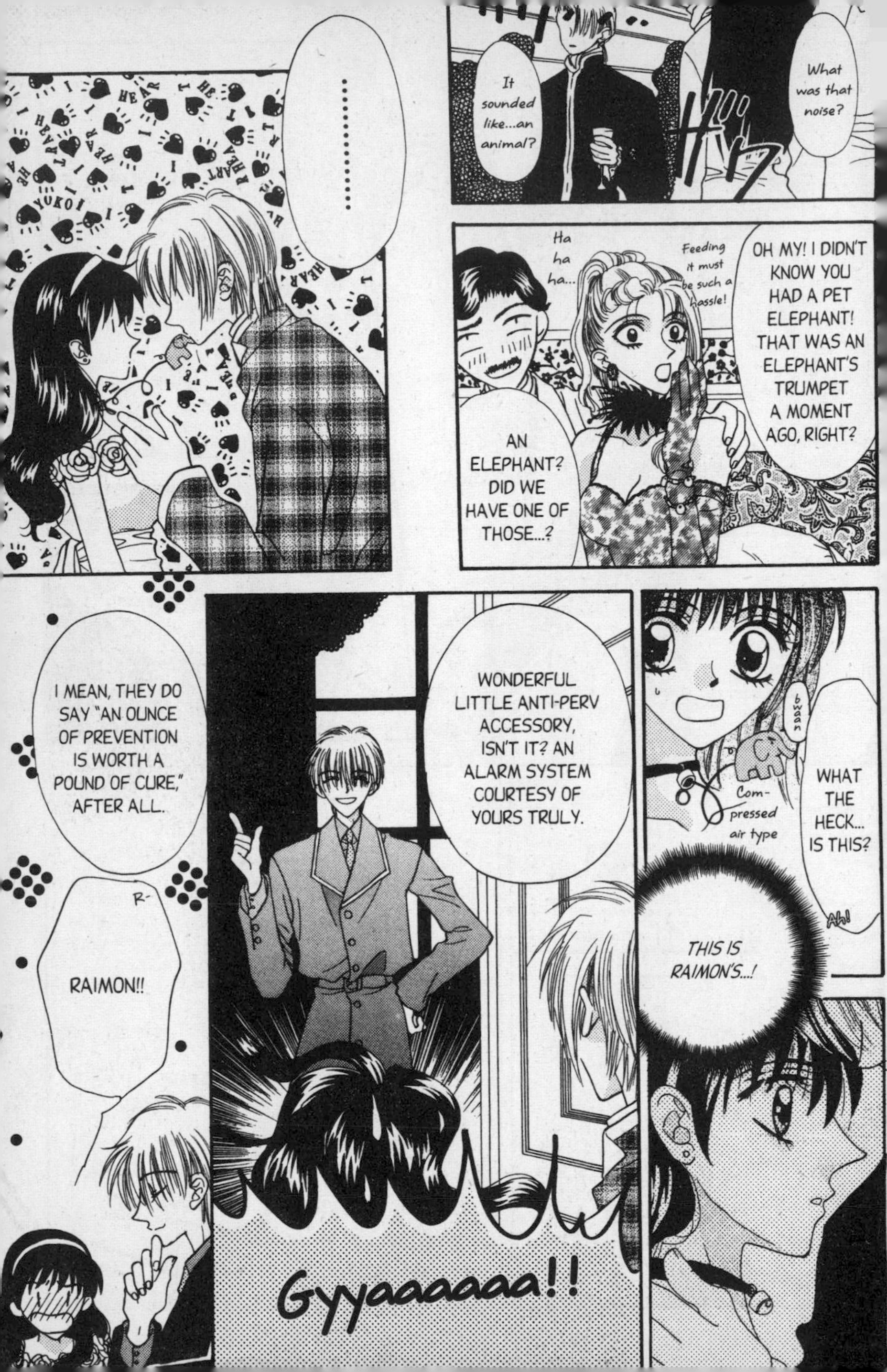

What was that noise?
It sounded like...an animal?
OH MY! I DIDN'T KNOW YOU HAD A PET ELEPHANT! THAT WAS AN ELEPHANT'S TRUMPET A MOMENT AGO, RIGHT?
Feeding it must be such a hassle!
Ha ha ha...
AN ELEPHANT? DID WE HAVE ONE OF THOSE...?
....
bwaan
WHAT THE HECK... IS THIS?
Com-pressed air type
Ah!
THIS IS RAIMON'S...!
WONDERFUL LITTLE ANTI-PERV ACCESSORY, ISN'T IT? AN ALARM SYSTEM COURTESY OF YOURS TRULY.
I MEAN, THEY DO SAY "AN OUNCE OF PREVENTION IS WORTH A POUND OF CURE," AFTER ALL.
R- RAIMON!!
Gyyaaaaaaa!!

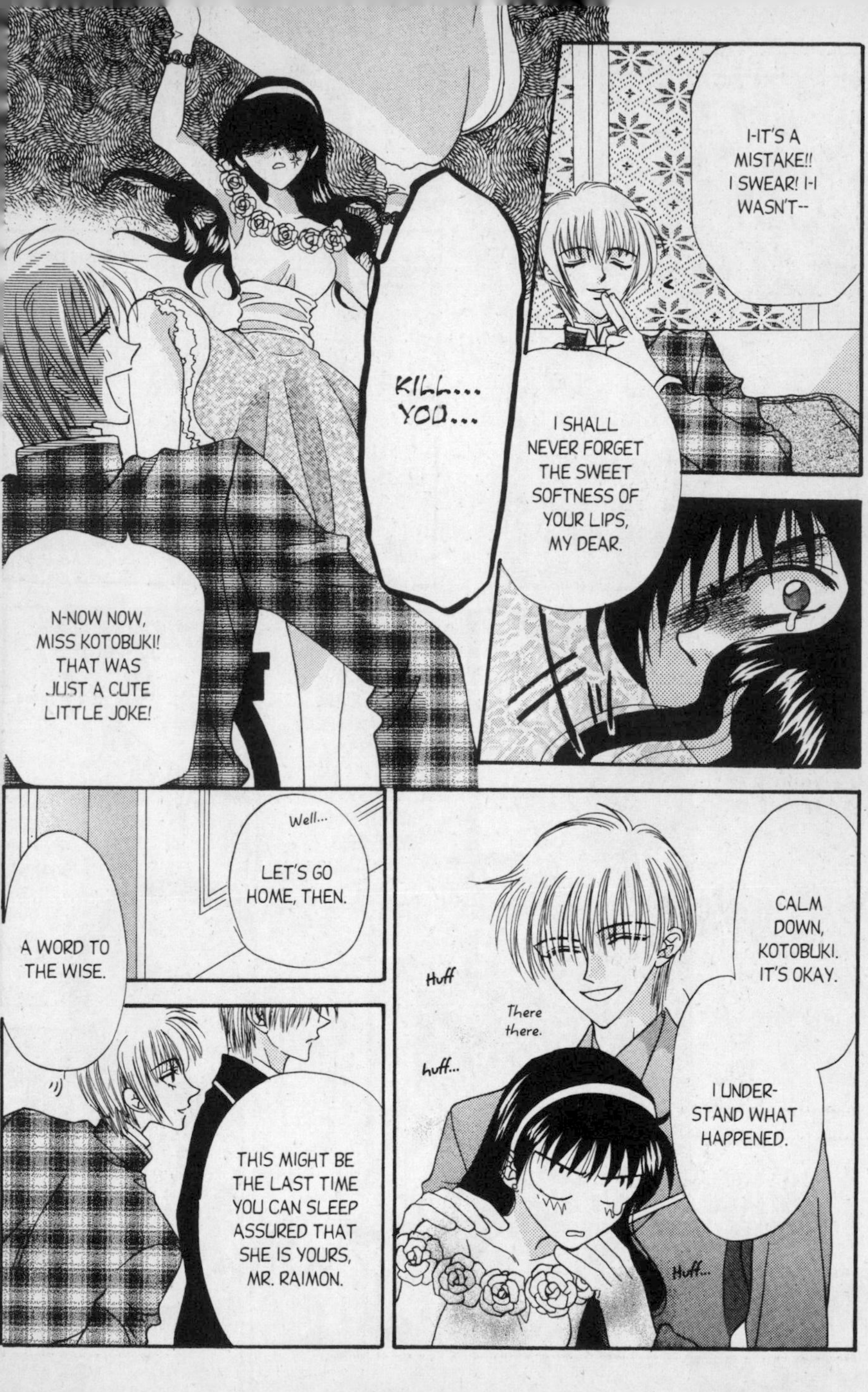
I-IT'S A MISTAKE!! I SWEAR! I-I WASN'T--
I SHALL NEVER FORGET THE SWEET SOFTNESS OF YOUR LIPS, MY DEAR.
KILL... YOU...
N-NOW NOW, MISS KOTOBUKI! THAT WAS JUST A CUTE LITTLE JOKE!
CALM DOWN, KOTOBUKI. IT'S OKAY.
I UNDER-STAND WHAT HAPPENED.
Huff
There there.
huff...
Huff...
Well...
LET'S GO HOME, THEN.
A WORD TO THE WISE.
THIS MIGHT BE THE LAST TIME YOU CAN SLEEP ASSURED THAT SHE IS YOURS, MR. RAIMON.

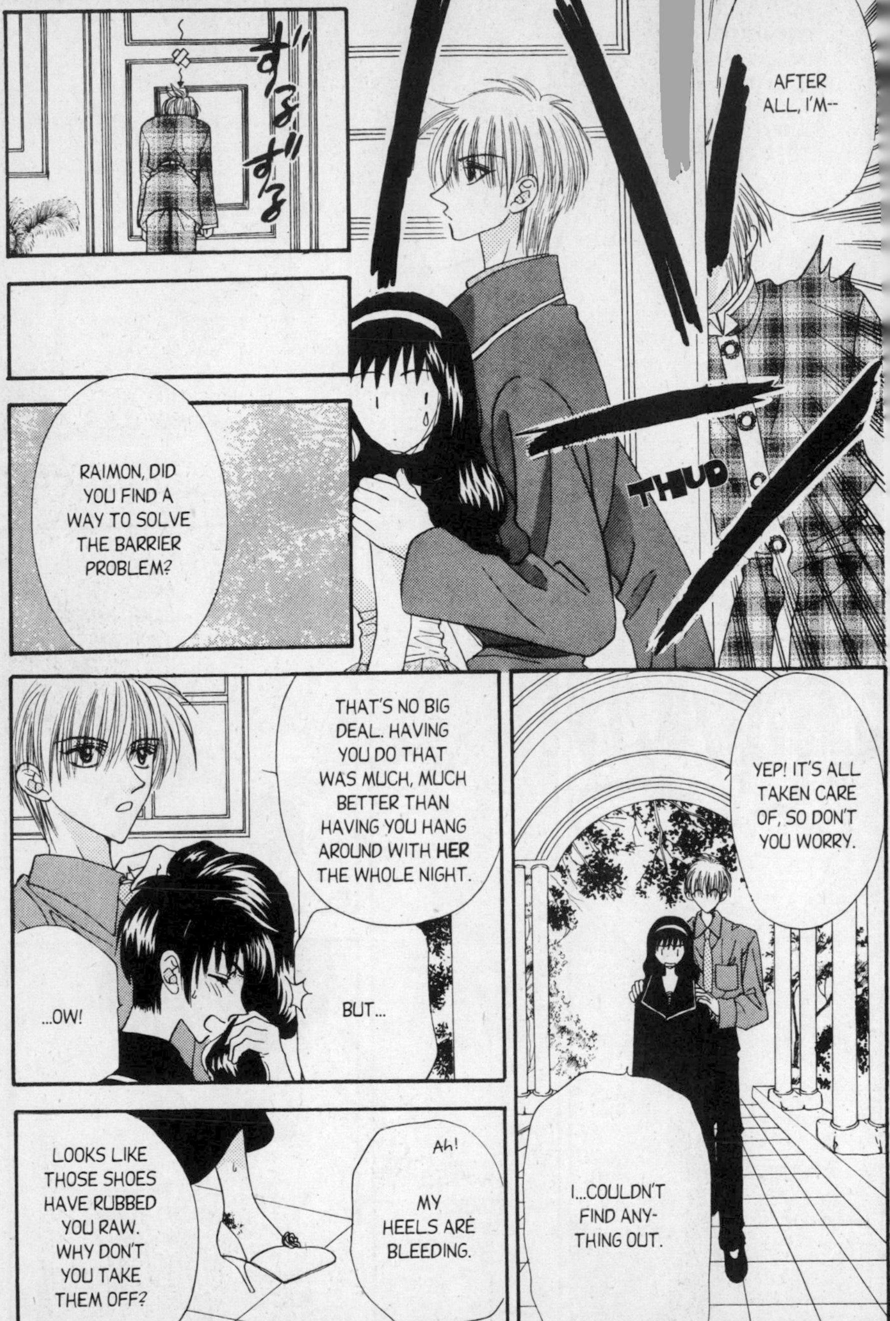
AFTER ALL, I'M--
THUD
ずるずる
RAIMON, DID YOU FIND A WAY TO SOLVE THE BARRIER PROBLEM?
YEP! IT'S ALL TAKEN CARE OF, SO DON'T YOU WORRY.
I...COULDN'T FIND ANY-THING OUT.
THAT'S NO BIG DEAL. HAVING YOU DO THAT WAS MUCH, MUCH BETTER THAN HAVING YOU HANG AROUND WITH HER THE WHOLE NIGHT.
BUT...
...OW!
Ah!
MY HEELS ARE BLEEDING.
LOOKS LIKE THOSE SHOES HAVE RUBBED YOU RAW. WHY DON'T YOU TAKE THEM OFF?

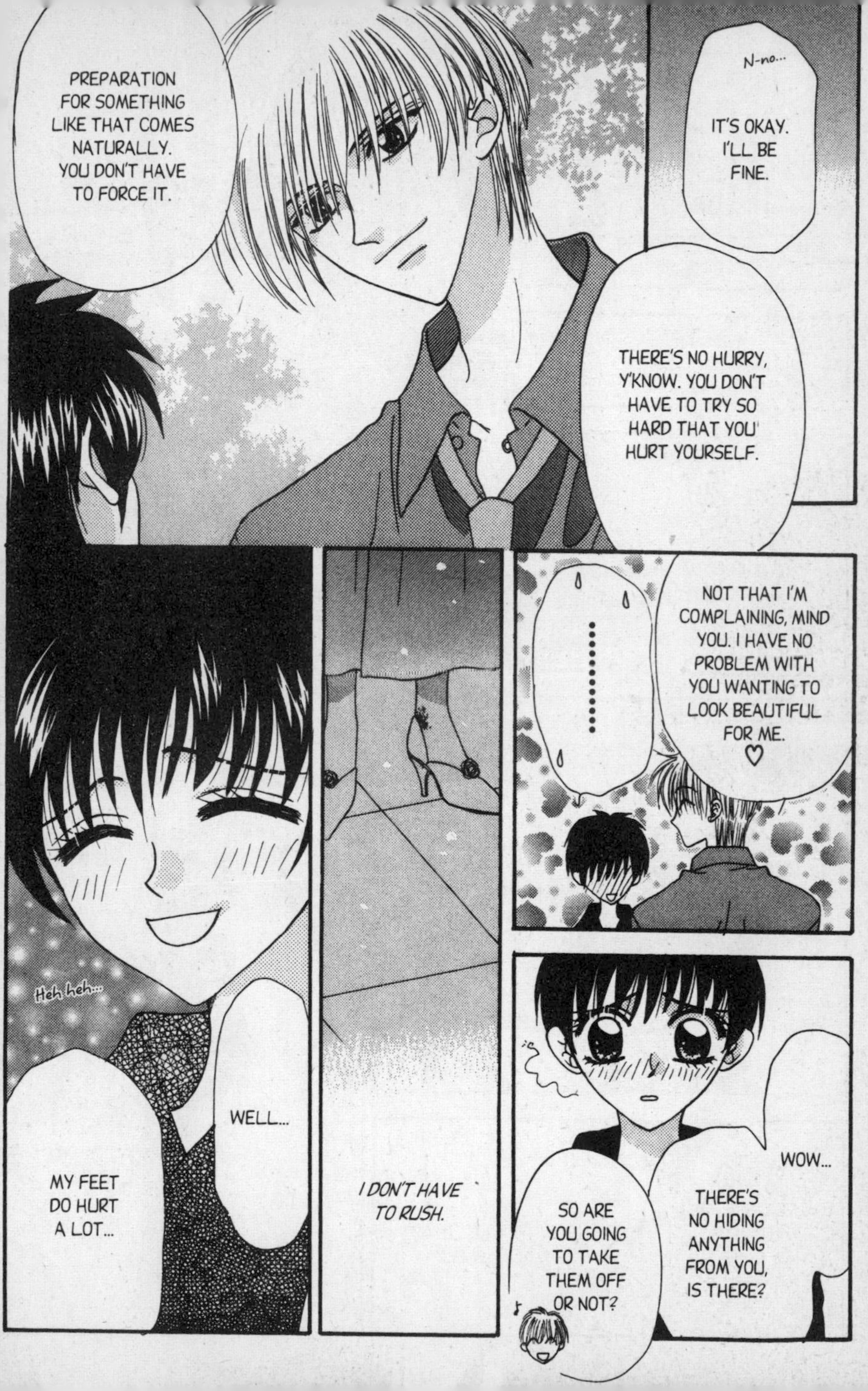

N-no...
IT'S OKAY. I'LL BE FINE.
THERE'S NO HURRY, Y'KNOW. YOU DON'T HAVE TO TRY SO HARD THAT YOU HURT YOURSELF.
PREPARATION FOR SOMETHING LIKE THAT COMES NATURALLY. YOU DON'T HAVE TO FORCE IT.
NOT THAT I'M COMPLAINING, MIND YOU. I HAVE NO PROBLEM WITH YOU WANTING TO LOOK BEAUTIFUL FOR ME. ♡
....
WOW...
THERE'S NO HIDING ANYTHING FROM YOU, IS THERE?
SO ARE YOU GOING TO TAKE THEM OFF OR NOT?
I DON'T HAVE TO RUSH.
Heh heh...
WELL...
MY FEET DO HURT A LOT...

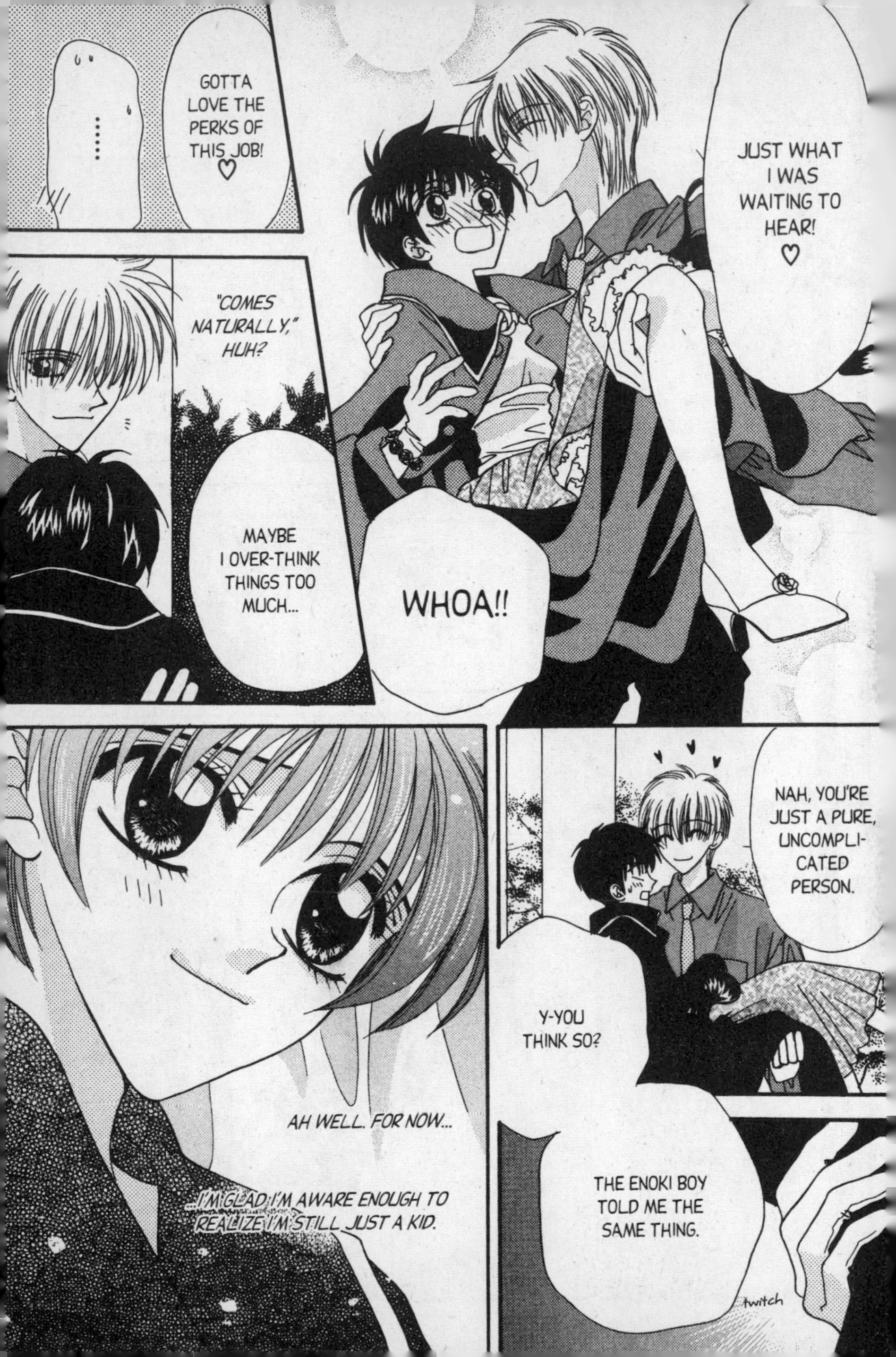

JUST WHAT I WAS WAITING TO HEAR! ♡
WHOA!!
GOTTA LOVE THE PERKS OF THIS JOB! ♡
......
"COMES NATURALLY," HUH?
MAYBE I OVER-THINK THINGS TOO MUCH...
NAH, YOU'RE JUST A PURE, UNCOMPLI-CATED PERSON.
Y-YOU THINK SO?
THE ENOKI BOY TOLD ME THE SAME THING.
twitch
AH WELL. FOR NOW...
...I'M GLAD I'M AWARE ENOUGH TO REALIZE I'M STILL JUST A KID.

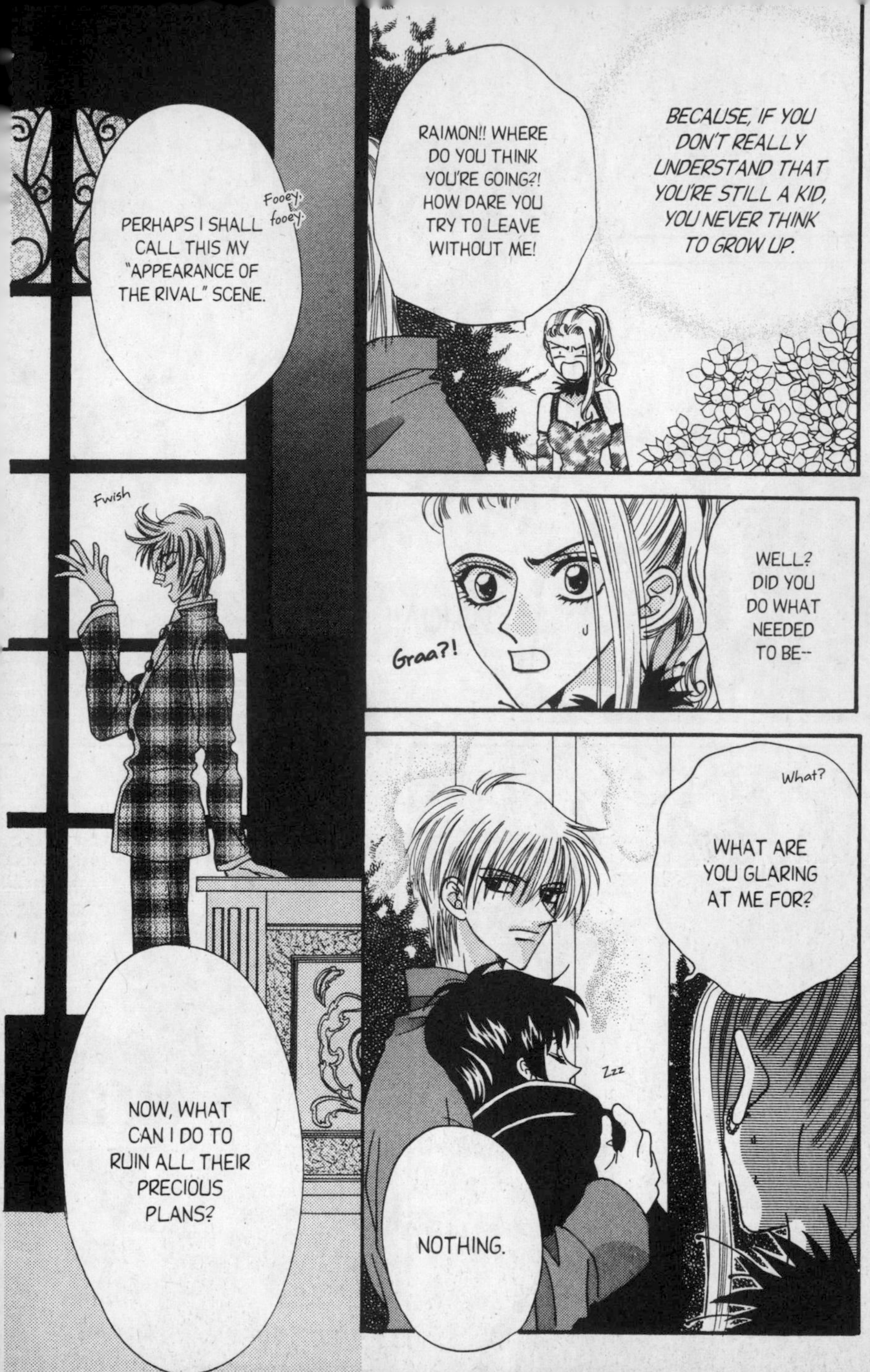
BECAUSE, IF YOU DON'T REALLY UNDERSTAND THAT YOU'RE STILL A KID, YOU NEVER THINK TO GROW UP.
RAIMON!! WHERE DO YOU THINK YOU'RE GOING?! HOW DARE YOU TRY TO LEAVE WITHOUT ME!
WELL? DID YOU DO WHAT NEEDED TO BE--
Graa?!
What?
WHAT ARE YOU GLARING AT ME FOR?
Zzz
NOTHING.
Fooey, fooey.
PERHAPS I SHALL CALL THIS MY "APPEARANCE OF THE RIVAL" SCENE.
Fwish
NOW, WHAT CAN I DO TO RUIN ALL THEIR PRECIOUS PLANS?

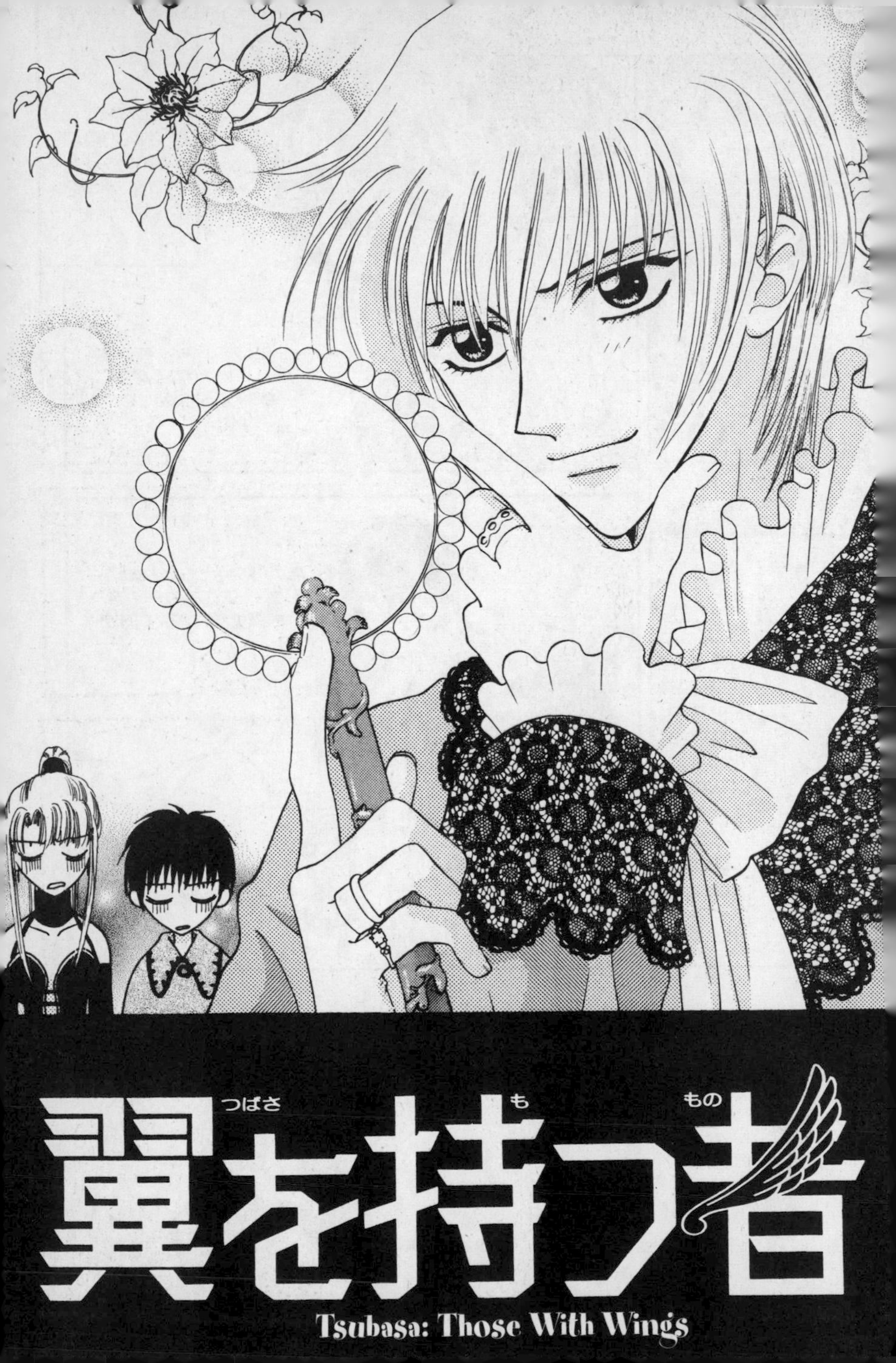

翼を持つ者

Tsubasa: Those With Wings

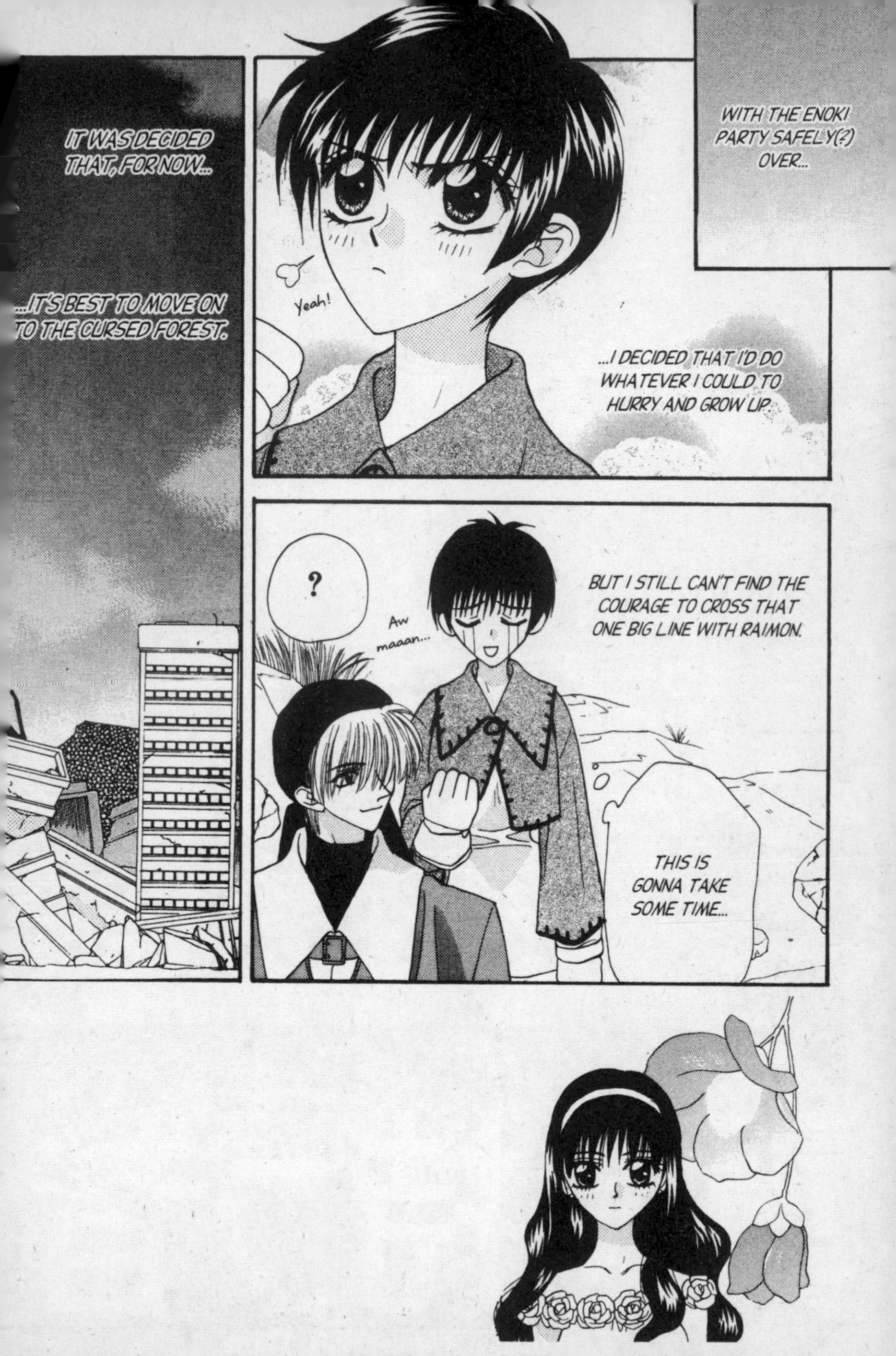
WITH THE ENOKI PARTY SAFELY(?) OVER...
Yeah!
...I DECIDED THAT I'D DO WHATEVER I COULD TO HURRY AND GROW UP.
?
Aw maaan...
BUT I STILL CAN'T FIND THE COURAGE TO CROSS THAT ONE BIG LINE WITH RAIMON.
THIS IS GONNA TAKE SOME TIME...
IT WAS DECIDED THAT, FOR NOW...
...IT'S BEST TO MOVE ON TO THE CURSED FOREST.

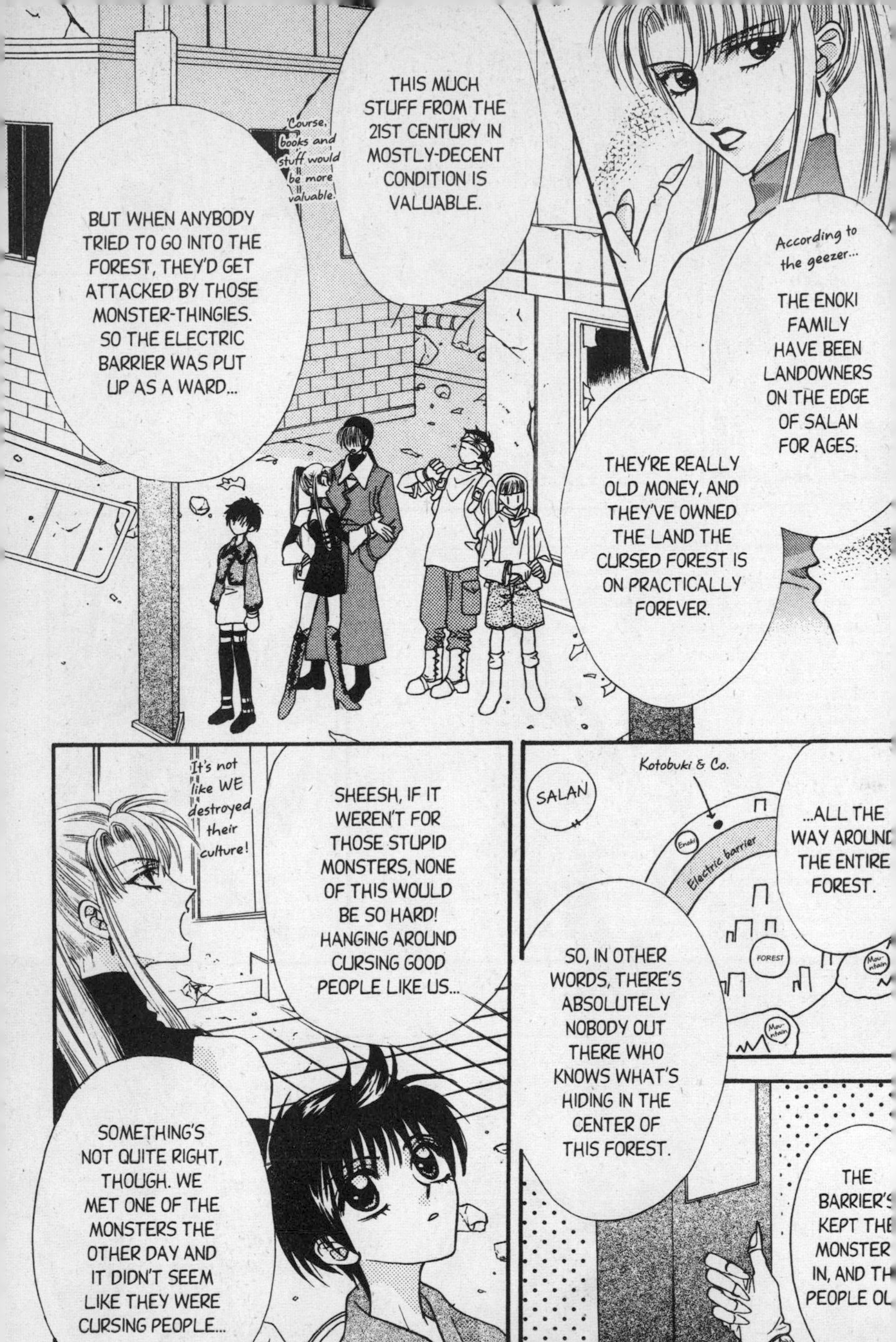
According to the geezer...
THE ENOKI FAMILY HAVE BEEN LANDOWNERS ON THE EDGE OF SALAN FOR AGES.
THEY'RE REALLY OLD MONEY, AND THEY'VE OWNED THE LAND THE CURSED FOREST IS ON PRACTICALLY FOREVER.
THIS MUCH STUFF FROM THE 21ST CENTURY IN MOSTLY-DECENT CONDITION IS VALUABLE.
'Course, books and stuff would be more valuable.
BUT WHEN ANYBODY TRIED TO GO INTO THE FOREST, THEY'D GET ATTACKED BY THOSE MONSTER-THINGIES. SO THE ELECTRIC BARRIER WAS PUT UP AS A WARD...
...ALL THE WAY AROUND THE ENTIRE FOREST.
Kotobuki & Co.
SALAN
Enoki
Electric barrier
FOREST
Mountain
Mountain
SO, IN OTHER WORDS, THERE'S ABSOLUTELY NOBODY OUT THERE WHO KNOWS WHAT'S HIDING IN THE CENTER OF THIS FOREST.
THE BARRIER'S KEPT THE MONSTER IN, AND TH PEOPLE OL
SHEESH, IF IT WEREN'T FOR THOSE STUPID MONSTERS, NONE OF THIS WOULD BE SO HARD! HANGING AROUND CURSING GOOD PEOPLE LIKE US...
It's not like WE destroyed their culture!
SOMETHING'S NOT QUITE RIGHT, THOUGH. WE MET ONE OF THE MONSTERS THE OTHER DAY AND IT DIDN'T SEEM LIKE THEY WERE CURSING PEOPLE...

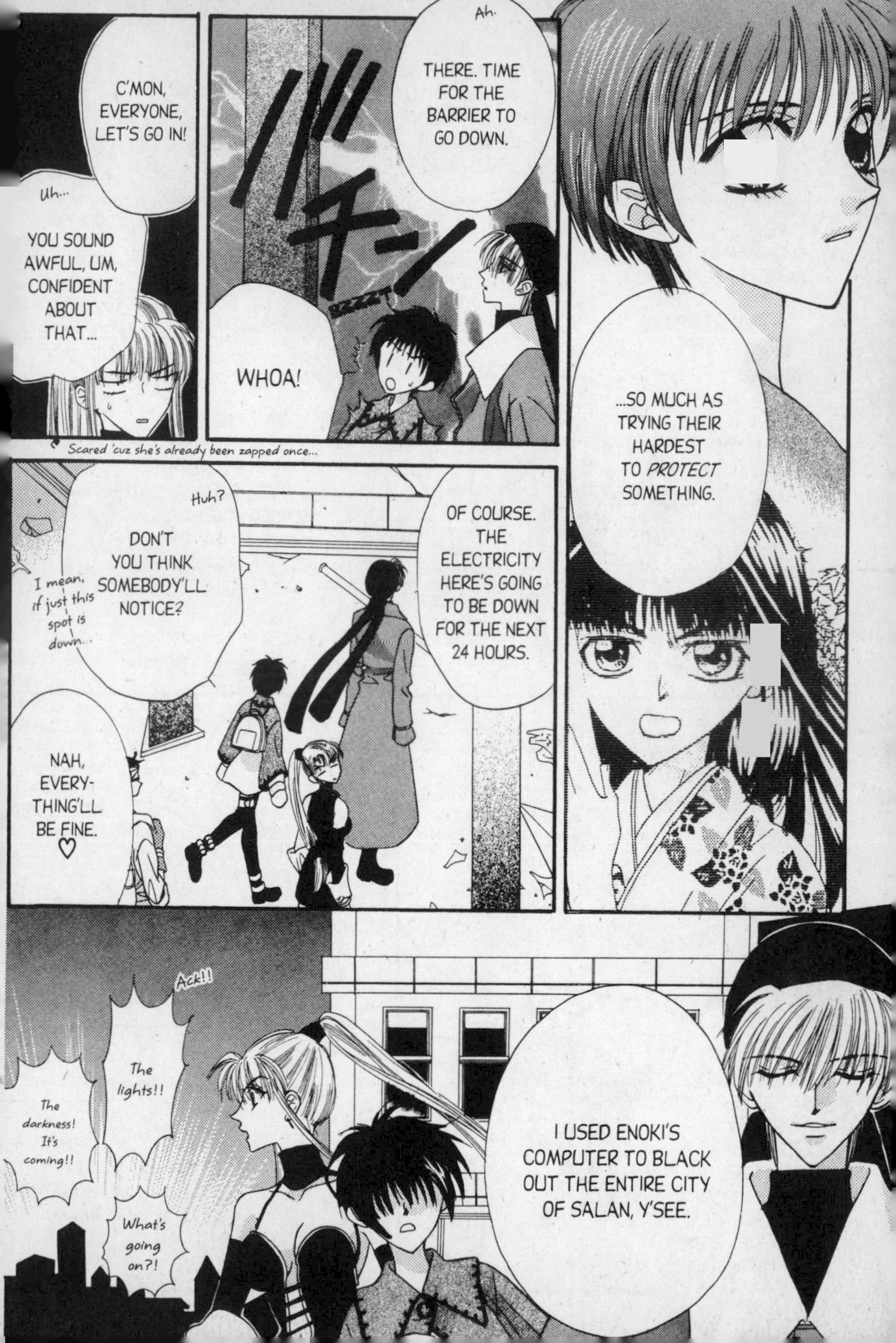
...SO MUCH AS TRYING THEIR HARDEST TO *PROTECT* SOMETHING.
Ah.
THERE. TIME FOR THE BARRIER TO GO DOWN.
WHOA!
C'MON, EVERYONE, LET'S GO IN!
Uh...
YOU SOUND AWFUL, UM, CONFIDENT ABOUT THAT...
Scared 'cuz she's already been zapped once...
OF COURSE. THE ELECTRICITY HERE'S GOING TO BE DOWN FOR THE NEXT 24 HOURS.
Huh?
DON'T YOU THINK SOMEBODY'LL NOTICE?
I mean, if just this spot is down...
NAH, EVERYTHING'LL BE FINE. ♡
I USED ENOKI'S COMPUTER TO BLACK OUT THE ENTIRE CITY OF SALAN, Y'SEE.
Ack!!
The lights!!
The darkness! It's coming!!
What's going on?!

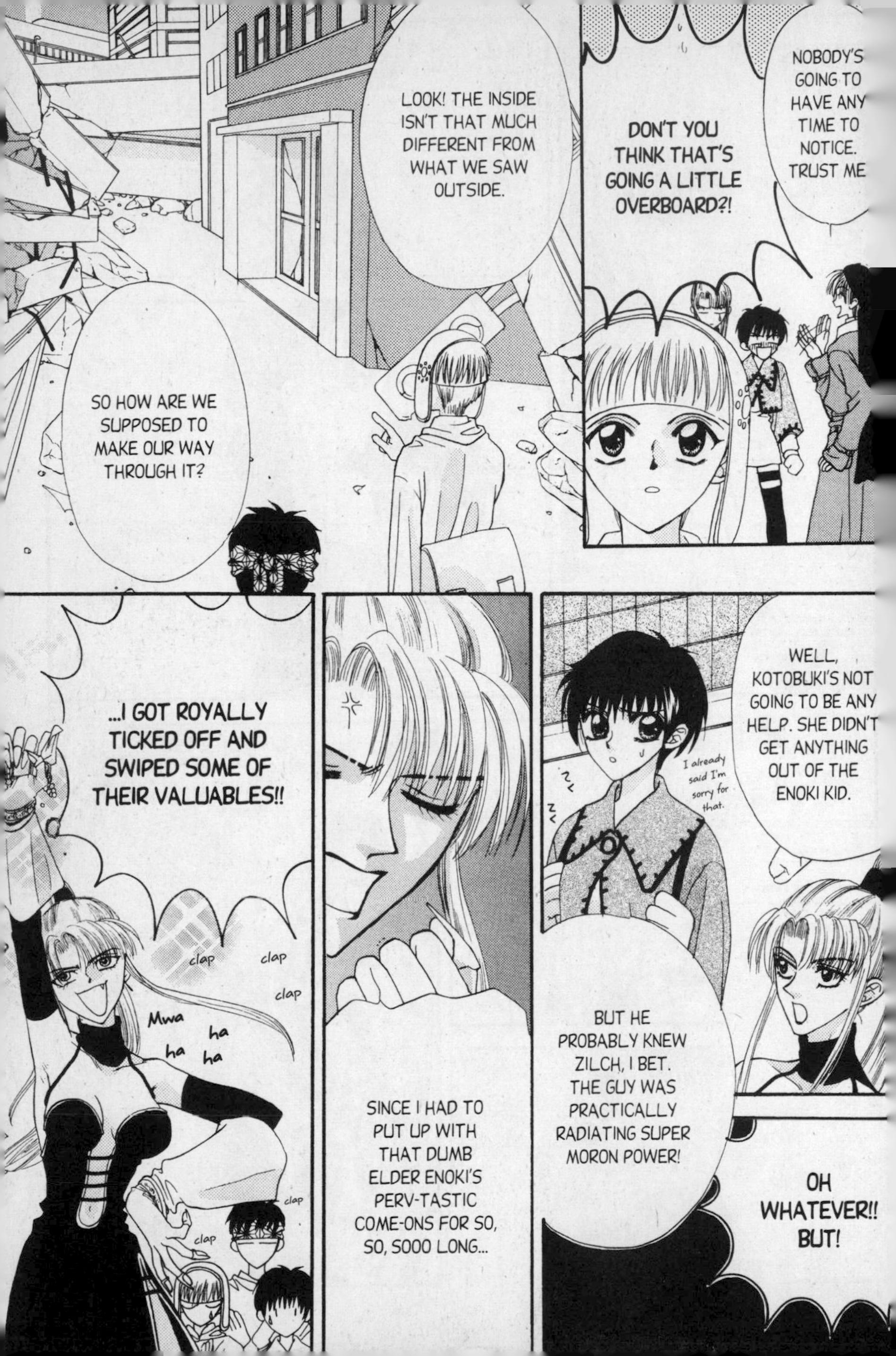
NOBODY'S GOING TO HAVE ANY TIME TO NOTICE. TRUST ME.
DON'T YOU THINK THAT'S GOING A LITTLE OVERBOARD?!
LOOK! THE INSIDE ISN'T THAT MUCH DIFFERENT FROM WHAT WE SAW OUTSIDE.
SO HOW ARE WE SUPPOSED TO MAKE OUR WAY THROUGH IT?
WELL, KOTOBUKI'S NOT GOING TO BE ANY HELP. SHE DIDN'T GET ANYTHING OUT OF THE ENOKI KID.
I already said I'm sorry for that.
BUT HE PROBABLY KNEW ZILCH, I BET. THE GUY WAS PRACTICALLY RADIATING SUPER MORON POWER!
OH WHATEVER!! BUT!
SINCE I HAD TO PUT UP WITH THAT DUMB ELDER ENOKI'S PERV-TASTIC COME-ONS FOR SO, SO, SOOO LONG...
...I GOT ROYALLY TICKED OFF AND SWIPED SOME OF THEIR VALUABLES!!
clap clap clap
Mwa ha ha ha
clap
clap

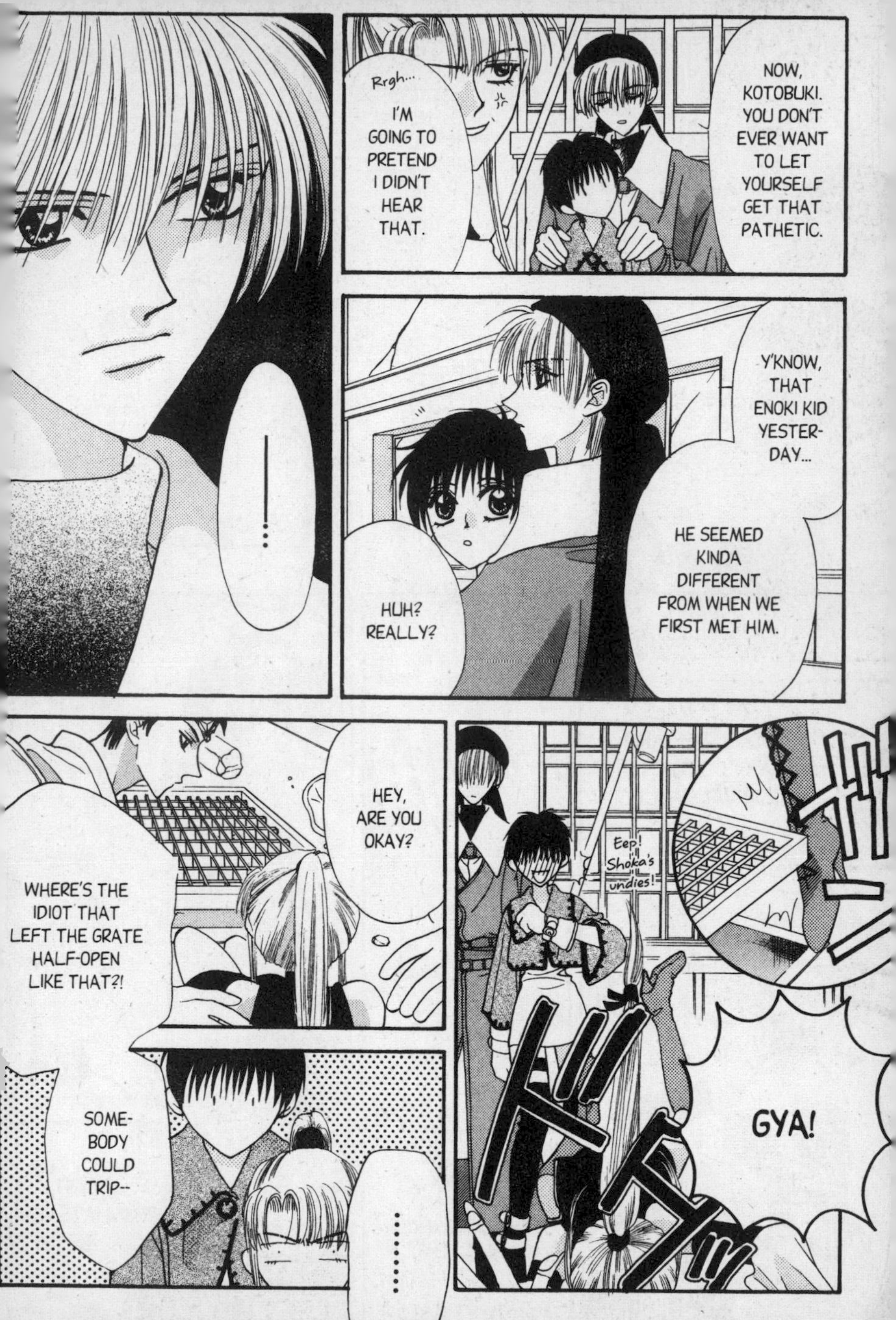
NOW, KOTOBUKI. YOU DON'T EVER WANT TO LET YOURSELF GET THAT PATHETIC.
Rrgh...
I'M GOING TO PRETEND I DIDN'T HEAR THAT.
Y'KNOW, THAT ENOKI KID YESTER-DAY...
HE SEEMED KINDA DIFFERENT FROM WHEN WE FIRST MET HIM.
HUH? REALLY?
......
GYA!
Eep! Shoka's undies!
HEY, ARE YOU OKAY?
WHERE'S THE IDIOT THAT LEFT THE GRATE HALF-OPEN LIKE THAT?!
SOME-BODY COULD TRIP--
......

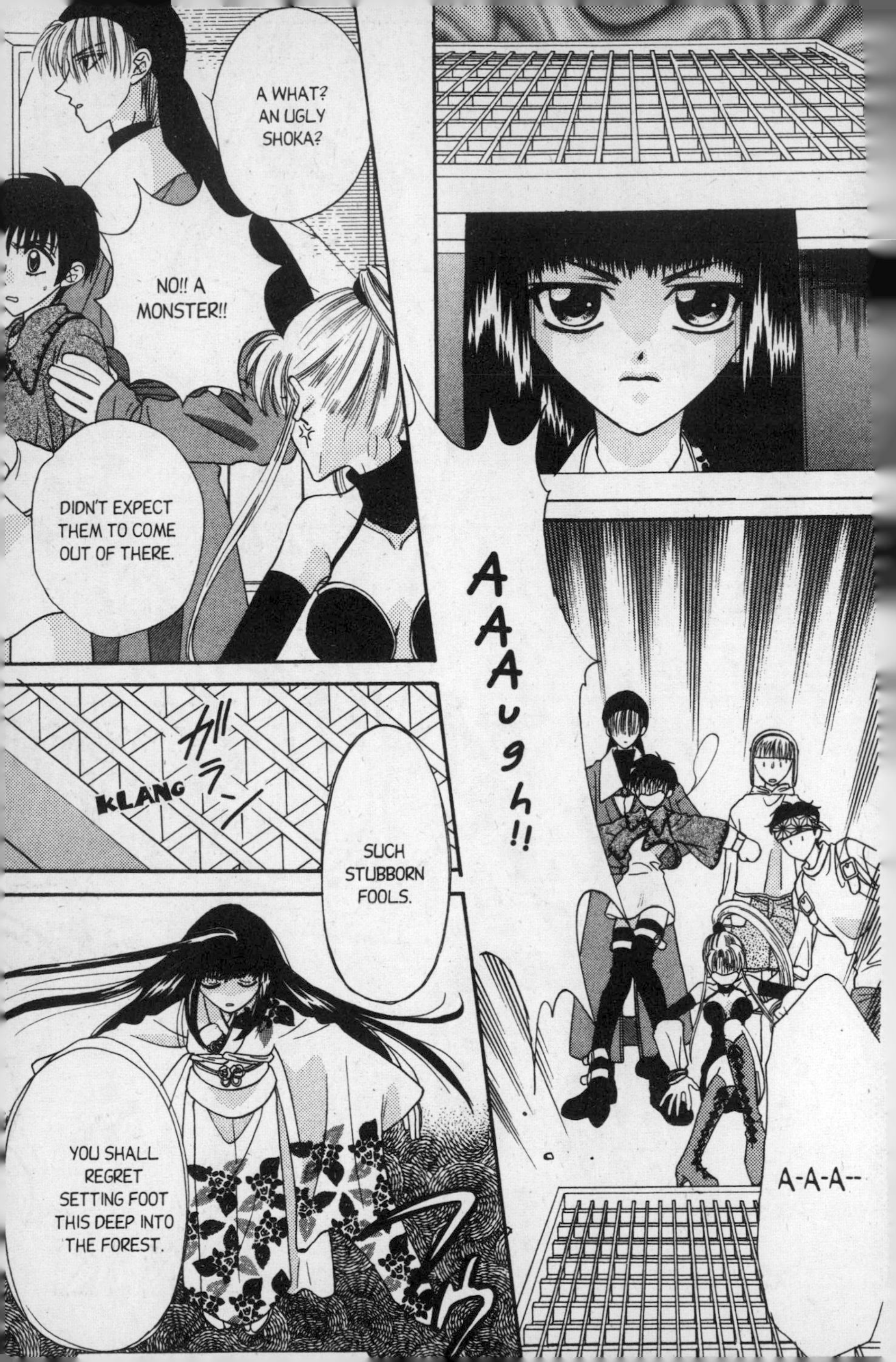
A WHAT? AN UGLY SHOKA?
NO!! A MONSTER!!
DIDN'T EXPECT THEM TO COME OUT OF THERE.
KLANG
SUCH STUBBORN FOOLS.
YOU SHALL REGRET SETTING FOOT THIS DEEP INTO THE FOREST.
AAAugh!!
A-A-A--

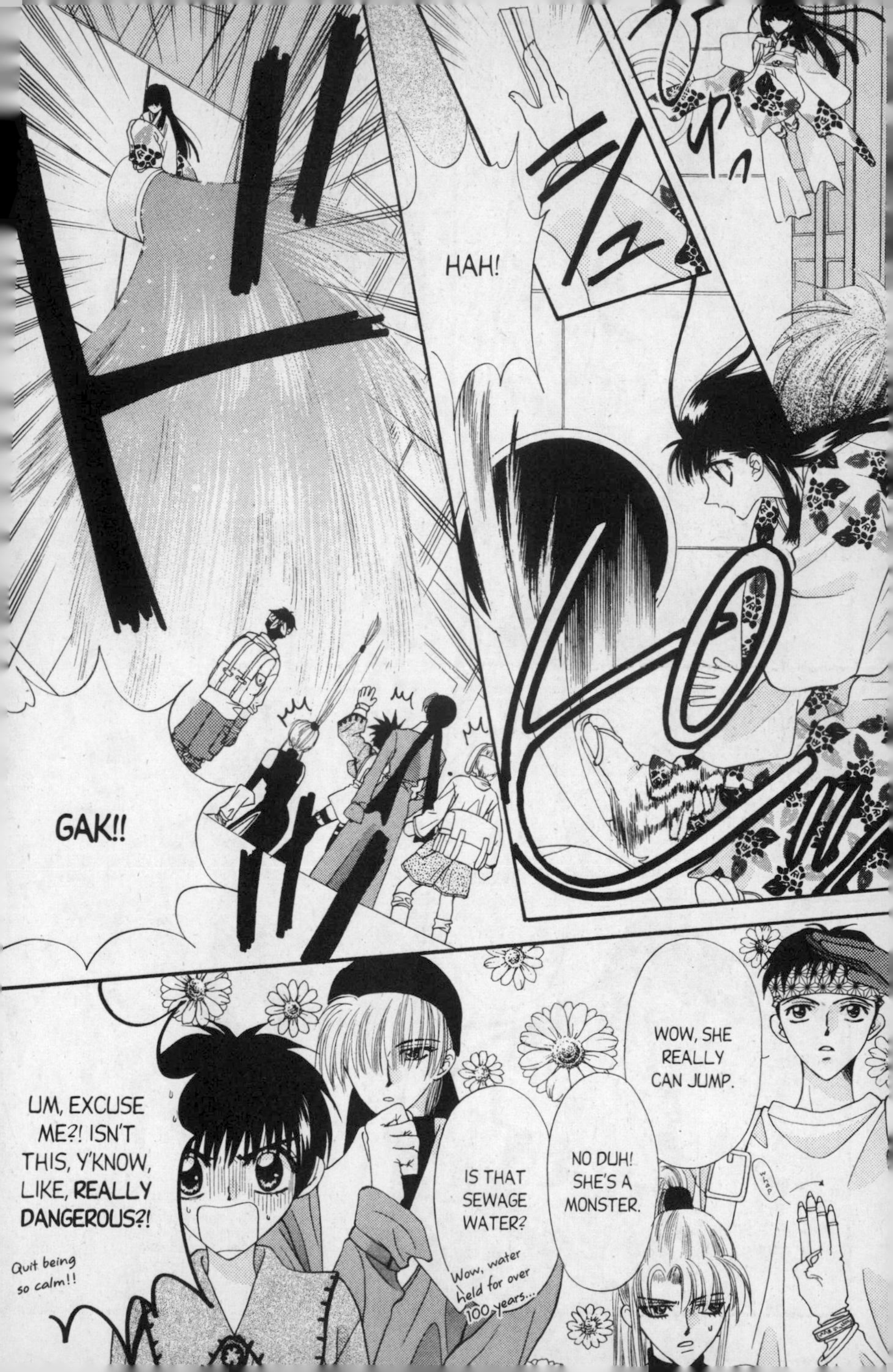
HAH!
GAK!!
WOW, SHE REALLY CAN JUMP.
NO DUH! SHE'S A MONSTER.
IS THAT SEWAGE WATER?
Wow, water held for over 100 years...
UM, EXCUSE ME?! ISN'T THIS, Y'KNOW, LIKE, REALLY DANGEROUS?!
Quit being so calm!!

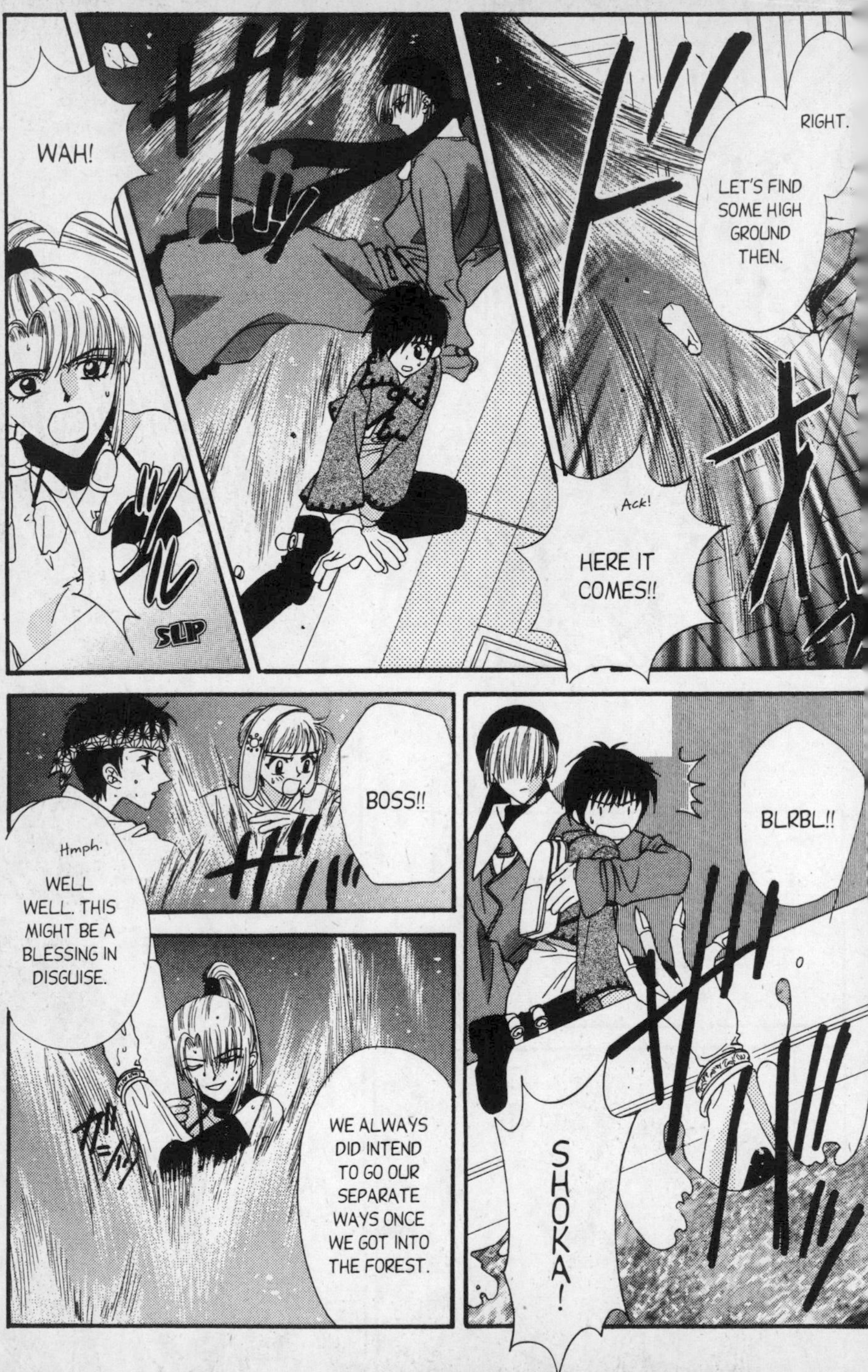
RIGHT.
LET'S FIND SOME HIGH GROUND THEN.
Ack!
HERE IT COMES!!
WAH!
SLIP
BLRBL!!
SHOKA!
BOSS!!
Hmph.
WELL WELL. THIS MIGHT BE A BLESSING IN DISGUISE.
WE ALWAYS DID INTEND TO GO OUR SEPARATE WAYS ONCE WE GOT INTO THE FOREST.

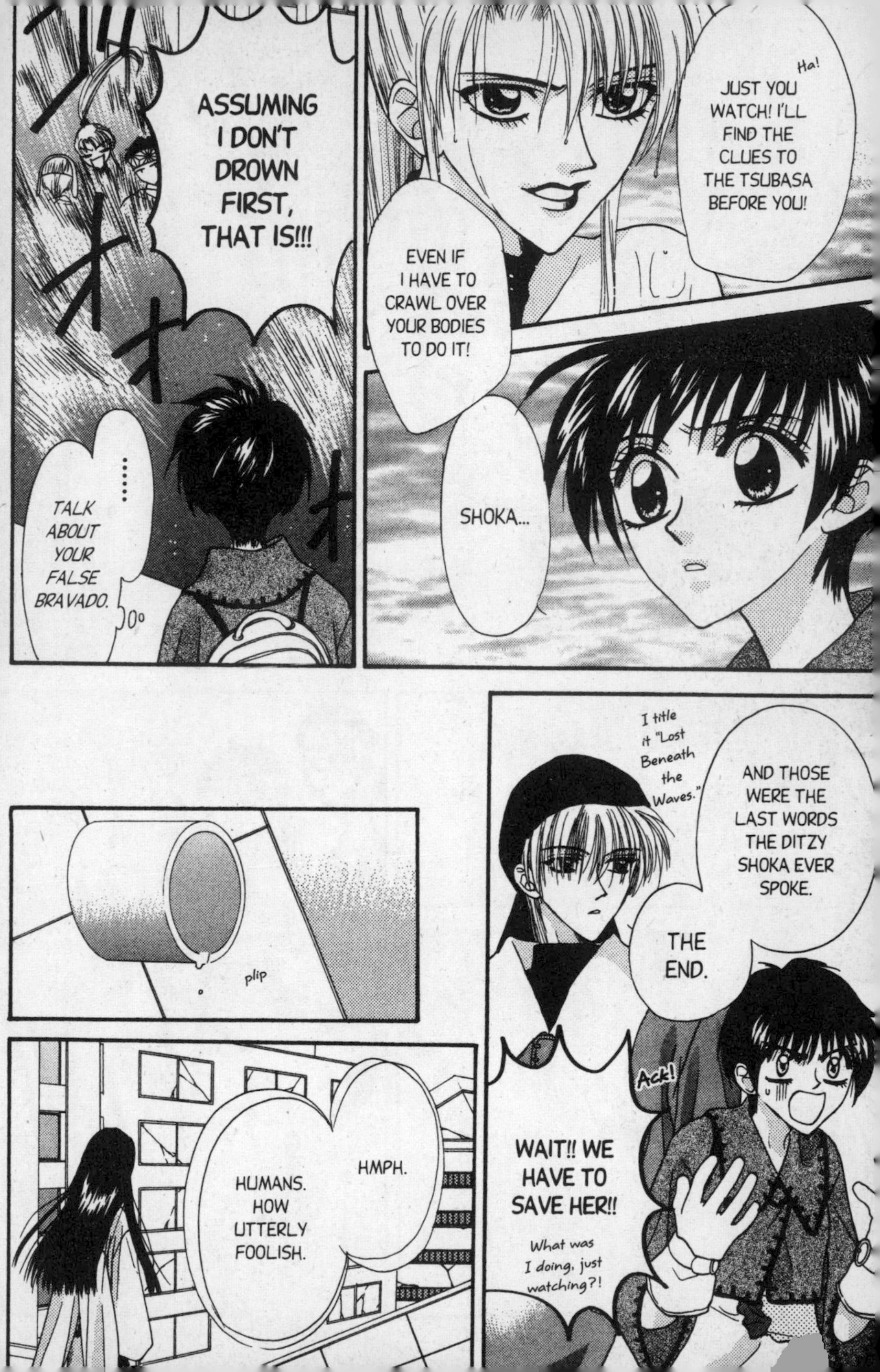

Ha!
JUST YOU WATCH! I'LL FIND THE CLUES TO THE TSUBASA BEFORE YOU!
EVEN IF I HAVE TO CRAWL OVER YOUR BODIES TO DO IT!
SHOKA...
ASSUMING I DON'T DROWN FIRST, THAT IS!!!
......
TALK ABOUT YOUR FALSE BRAVADO.
I title it "Lost Beneath the Waves."
AND THOSE WERE THE LAST WORDS THE DITZY SHOKA EVER SPOKE.
THE END.
Ack!
WAIT!! WE HAVE TO SAVE HER!!
What was I doing, just watching?!
plip
HMPH.
HUMANS. HOW UTTERLY FOOLISH.

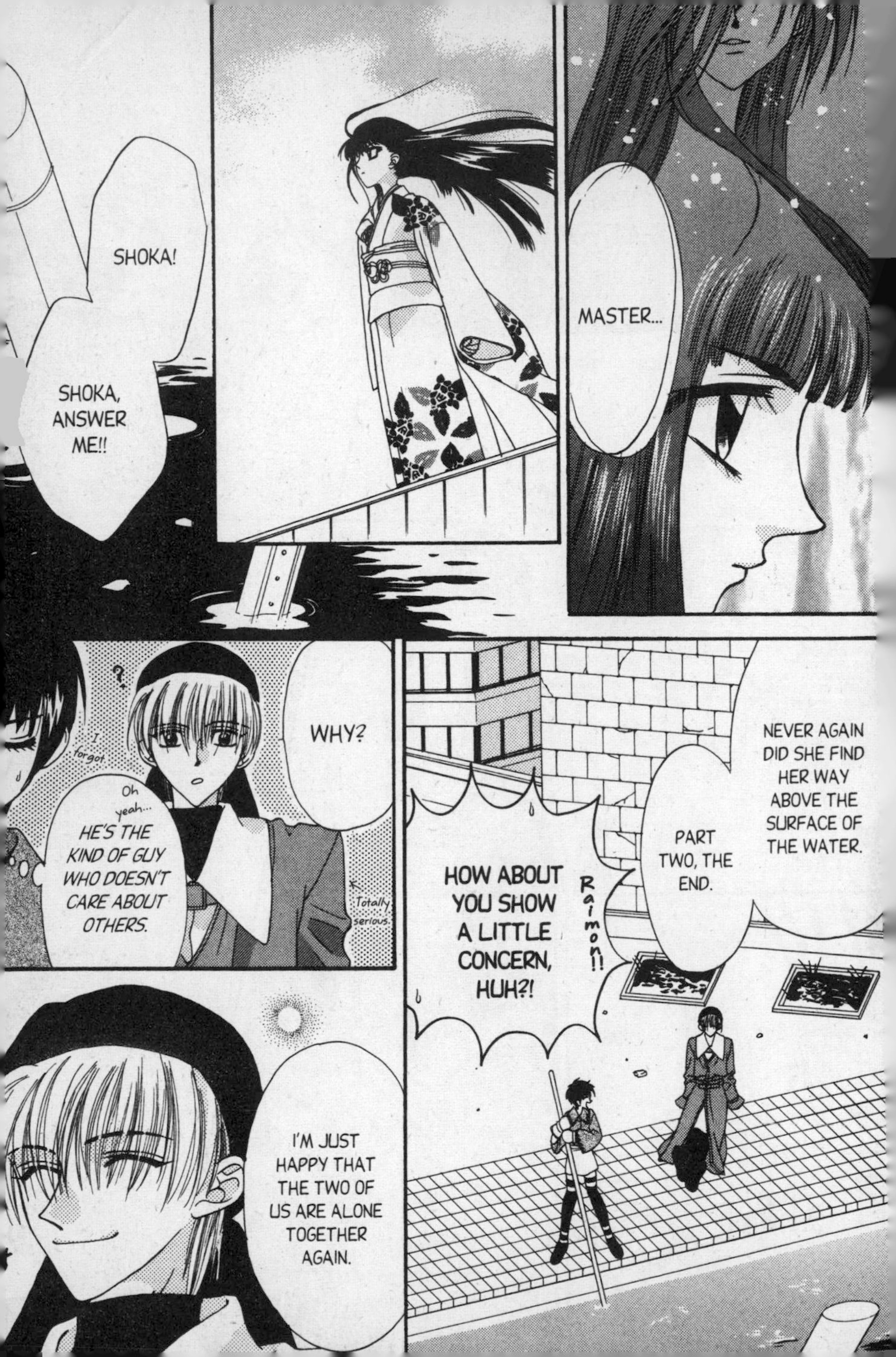
MASTER...
SHOKA!
SHOKA, ANSWER ME!!
NEVER AGAIN DID SHE FIND HER WAY ABOVE THE SURFACE OF THE WATER.
PART TWO, THE END.
HOW ABOUT YOU SHOW A LITTLE CONCERN, HUH?!
Raimon!!
WHY?
I forgot
Oh yeah... HE'S THE KIND OF GUY WHO DOESN'T CARE ABOUT OTHERS.
Totally serious.
I'M JUST HAPPY THAT THE TWO OF US ARE ALONE TOGETHER AGAIN.

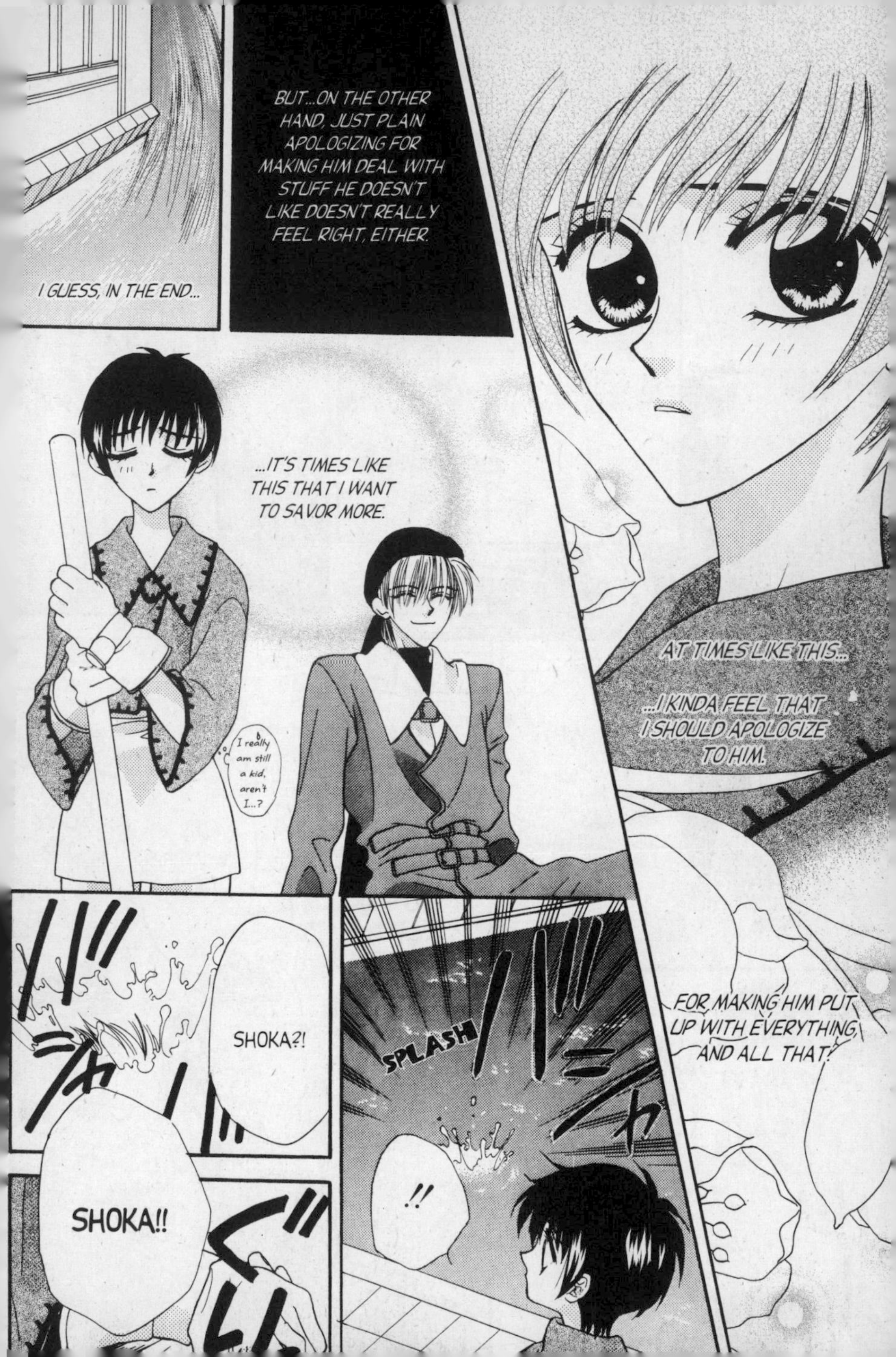

AT TIMES LIKE THIS...
...I KINDA FEEL THAT I SHOULD APOLOGIZE TO HIM.
FOR MAKING HIM PUT UP WITH EVERYTHING, AND ALL THAT!
BUT...ON THE OTHER HAND, JUST PLAIN APOLOGIZING FOR MAKING HIM DEAL WITH STUFF HE DOESN'T LIKE DOESN'T REALLY FEEL RIGHT, EITHER.
I GUESS, IN THE END...
...IT'S TIMES LIKE THIS THAT I WANT TO SAVOR MORE.
I really am still a kid, aren't I...?
SPLASH
!!
SHOKA?!
SHOKA!!

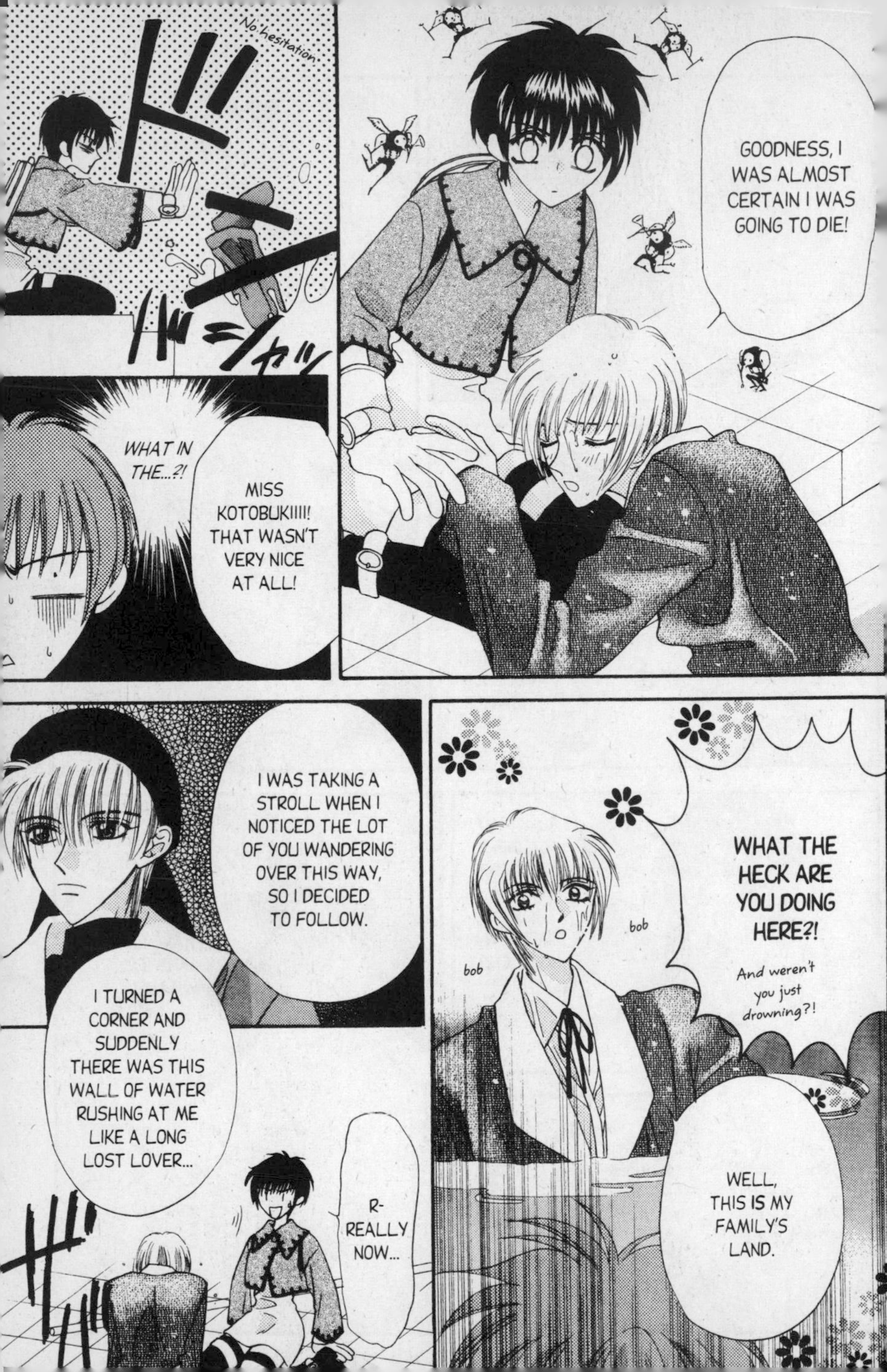
GOODNESS, I WAS ALMOST CERTAIN I WAS GOING TO DIE!
No hesitation.
MISS KOTOBUKIIII! THAT WASN'T VERY NICE AT ALL!
WHAT IN THE...?!
WHAT THE HECK ARE YOU DOING HERE?!
And weren't you just drowning?!
bob
bob
WELL, THIS IS MY FAMILY'S LAND.
I WAS TAKING A STROLL WHEN I NOTICED THE LOT OF YOU WANDERING OVER THIS WAY, SO I DECIDED TO FOLLOW.
I TURNED A CORNER AND SUDDENLY THERE WAS THIS WALL OF WATER RUSHING AT ME LIKE A LONG LOST LOVER...
R-REALLY NOW...

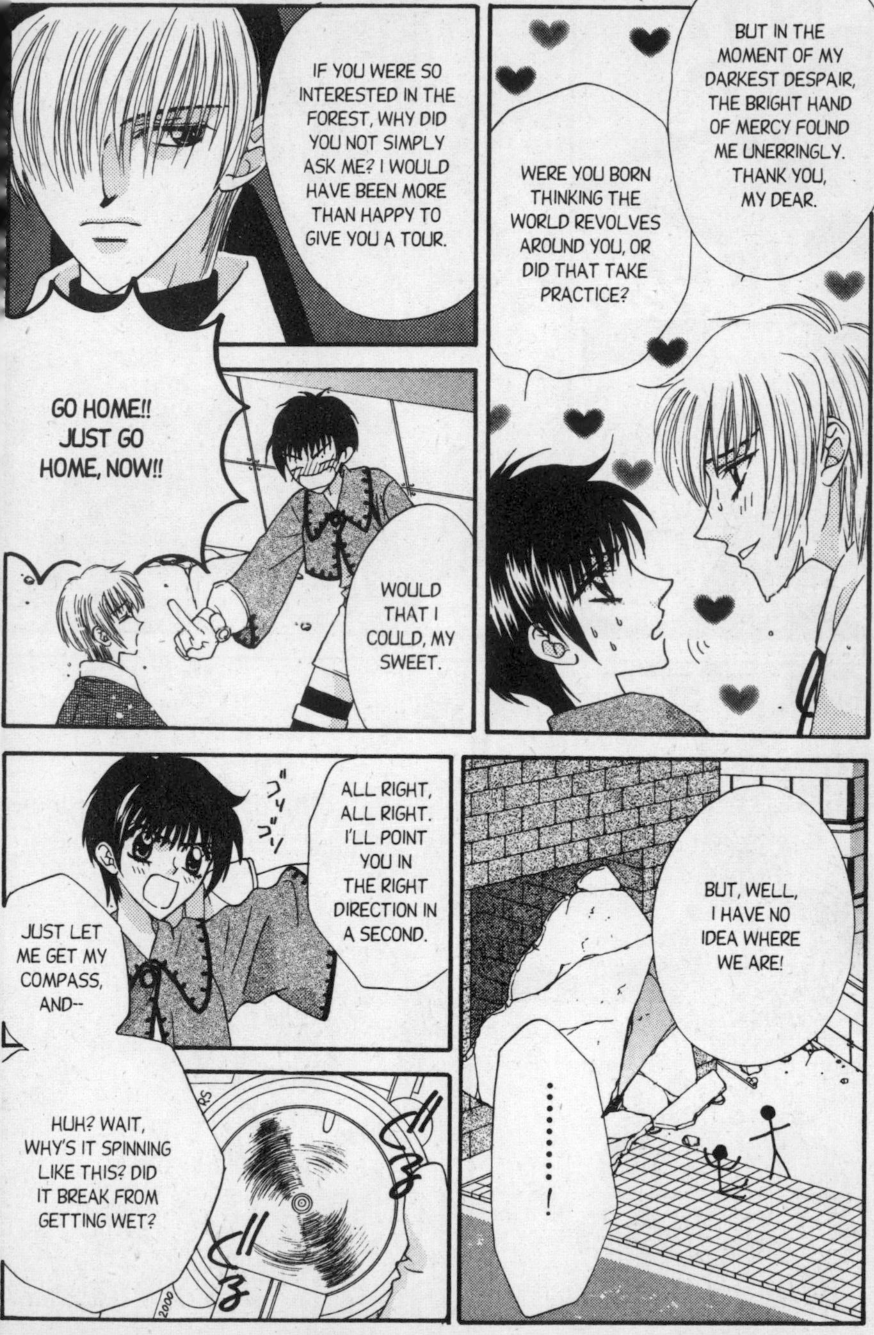
IF YOU WERE SO INTERESTED IN THE FOREST, WHY DID YOU NOT SIMPLY ASK ME? I WOULD HAVE BEEN MORE THAN HAPPY TO GIVE YOU A TOUR.
GO HOME!! JUST GO HOME, NOW!!
WOULD THAT I COULD, MY SWEET.
BUT IN THE MOMENT OF MY DARKEST DESPAIR, THE BRIGHT HAND OF MERCY FOUND ME UNERRINGLY. THANK YOU, MY DEAR.
WERE YOU BORN THINKING THE WORLD REVOLVES AROUND YOU, OR DID THAT TAKE PRACTICE?
ALL RIGHT, ALL RIGHT. I'LL POINT YOU IN THE RIGHT DIRECTION IN A SECOND.
JUST LET ME GET MY COMPASS, AND--
HUH? WAIT, WHY'S IT SPINNING LIKE THIS? DID IT BREAK FROM GETTING WET?
BUT, WELL, I HAVE NO IDEA WHERE WE ARE!
......!

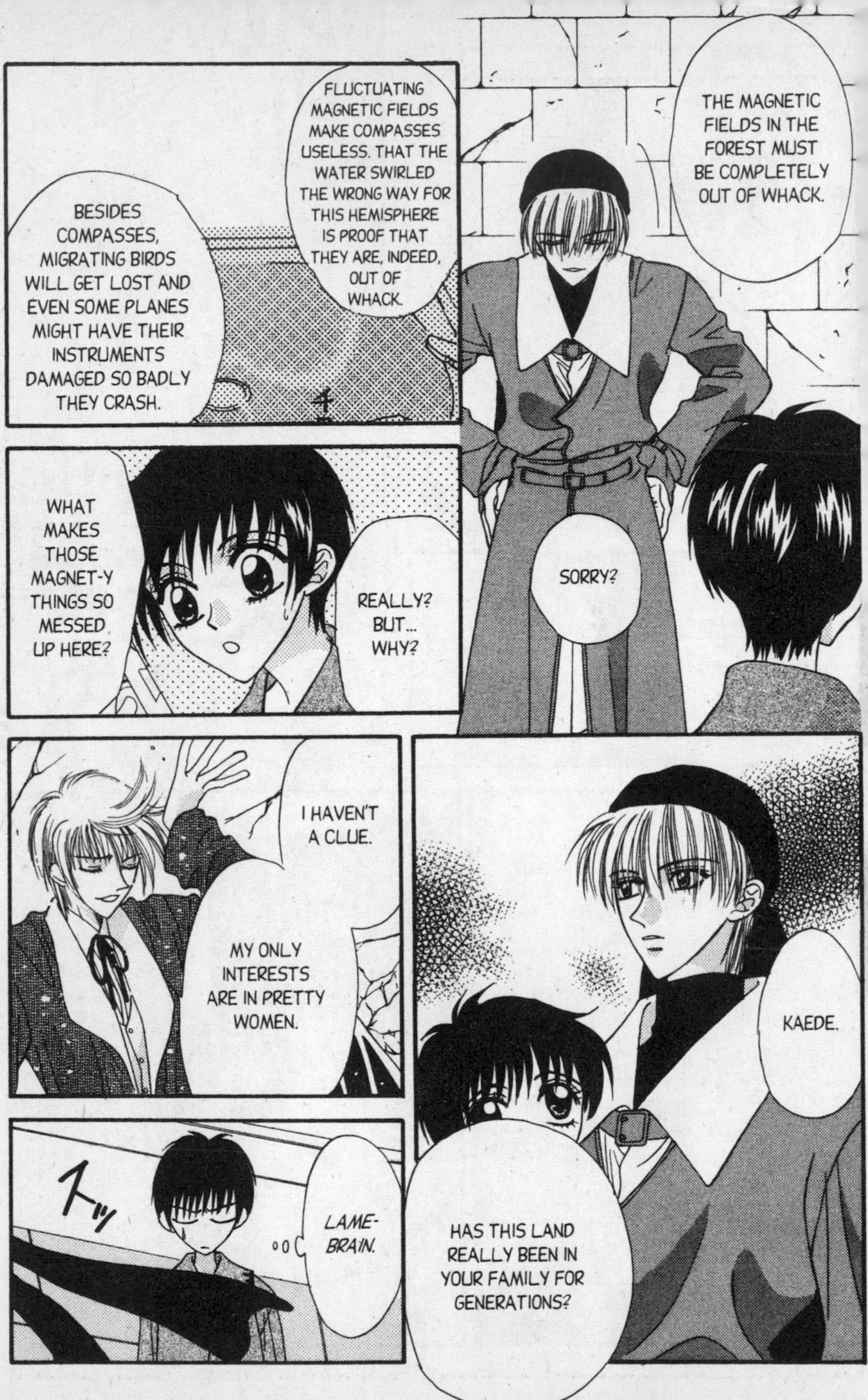
THE MAGNETIC FIELDS IN THE FOREST MUST BE COMPLETELY OUT OF WHACK.
SORRY?
FLUCTUATING MAGNETIC FIELDS MAKE COMPASSES USELESS. THAT THE WATER SWIRLED THE WRONG WAY FOR THIS HEMISPHERE IS PROOF THAT THEY ARE, INDEED, OUT OF WHACK.
BESIDES COMPASSES, MIGRATING BIRDS WILL GET LOST AND EVEN SOME PLANES MIGHT HAVE THEIR INSTRUMENTS DAMAGED SO BADLY THEY CRASH.
REALLY? BUT... WHY?
WHAT MAKES THOSE MAGNET-Y THINGS SO MESSED UP HERE?
KAEDE.
HAS THIS LAND REALLY BEEN IN YOUR FAMILY FOR GENERATIONS?
I HAVEN'T A CLUE.
MY ONLY INTERESTS ARE IN PRETTY WOMEN.
LAME-BRAIN.
トッ

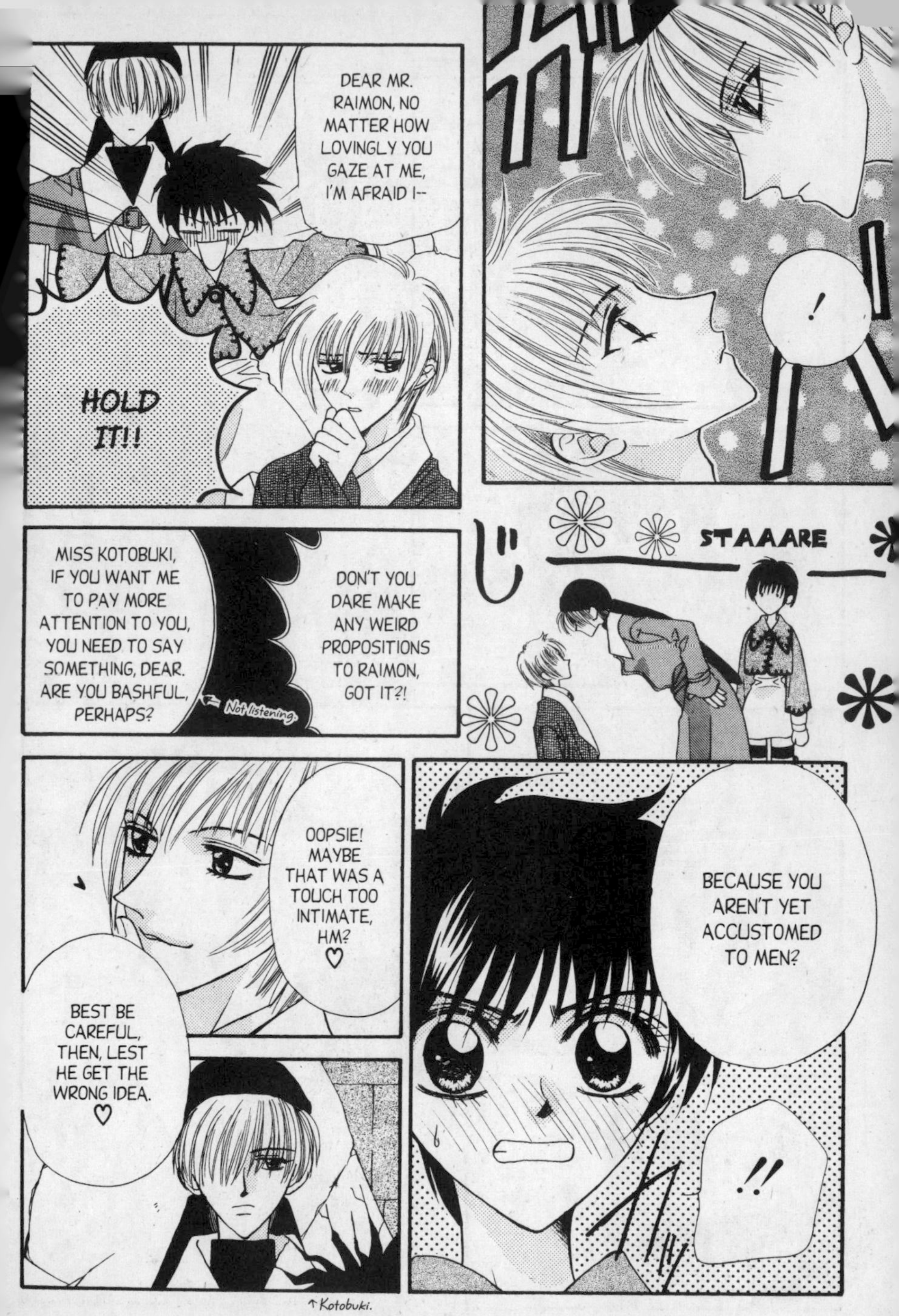
!
DEAR MR. RAIMON, NO MATTER HOW LOVINGLY YOU GAZE AT ME, I'M AFRAID I--
HOLD IT!!
STAAARE
DON'T YOU DARE MAKE ANY WEIRD PROPOSITIONS TO RAIMON, GOT IT?!
MISS KOTOBUKI, IF YOU WANT ME TO PAY MORE ATTENTION TO YOU, YOU NEED TO SAY SOMETHING, DEAR. ARE YOU BASHFUL, PERHAPS?
Not listening.
BECAUSE YOU AREN'T YET ACCUSTOMED TO MEN?
!!
OOPSIE! MAYBE THAT WAS A TOUCH TOO INTIMATE, HM? ♡
BEST BE CAREFUL, THEN, LEST HE GET THE WRONG IDEA. ♡
↑Kotobuki.

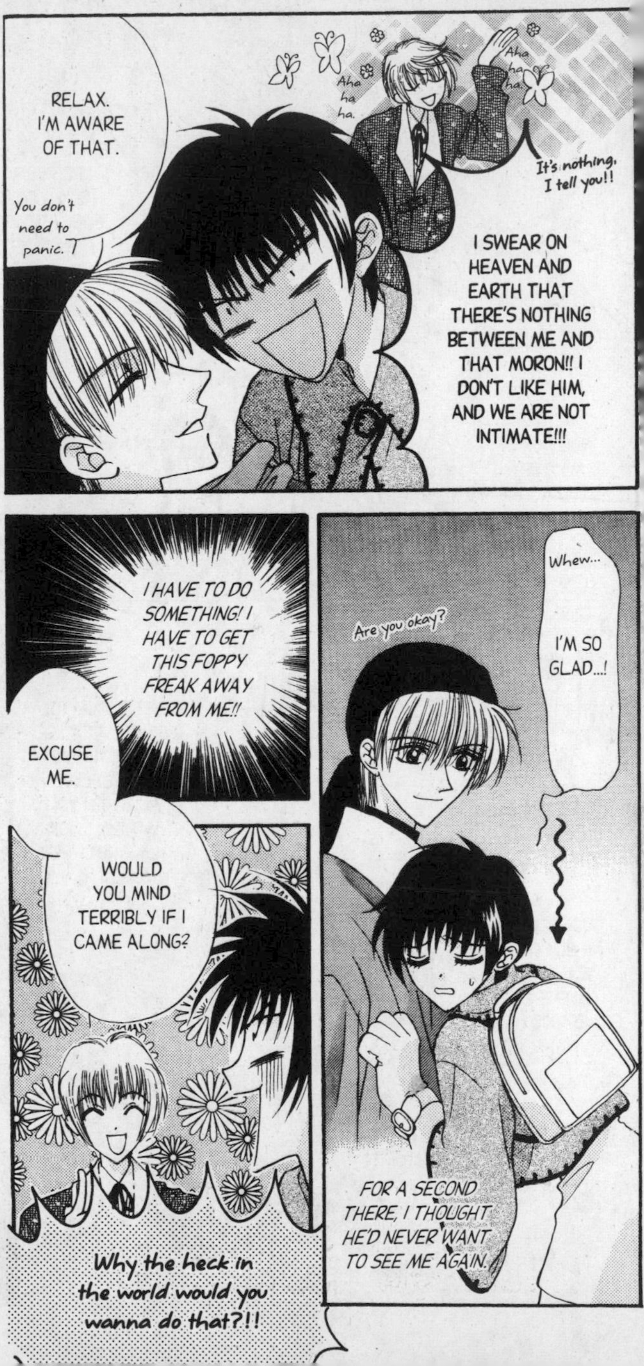
Aha ha ha.
It's nothing, I tell you!!
I SWEAR ON HEAVEN AND EARTH THAT THERE'S NOTHING BETWEEN ME AND THAT MORON!! I DON'T LIKE HIM, AND WE ARE NOT INTIMATE!!!
Aha ha ha.
RELAX. I'M AWARE OF THAT.
You don't need to panic.
Whew...
I'M SO GLAD...!
Are you okay?
FOR A SECOND THERE, I THOUGHT HE'D NEVER WANT TO SEE ME AGAIN.
I HAVE TO DO SOMETHING! I HAVE TO GET THIS FOPPY FREAK AWAY FROM ME!!
EXCUSE ME.
WOULD YOU MIND TERRIBLY IF I CAME ALONG?
Why the heck in the world would you wanna do that?!!
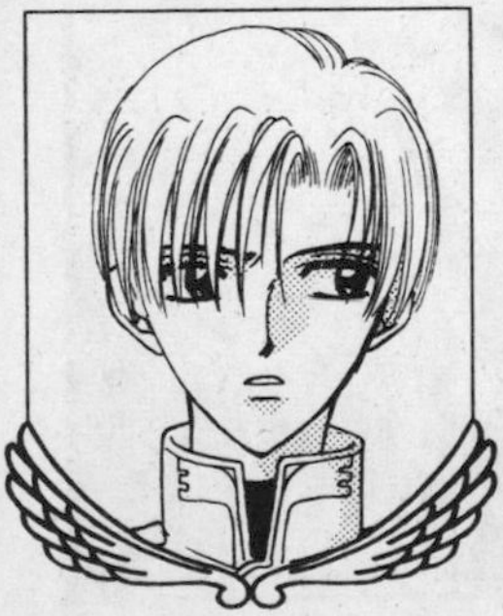

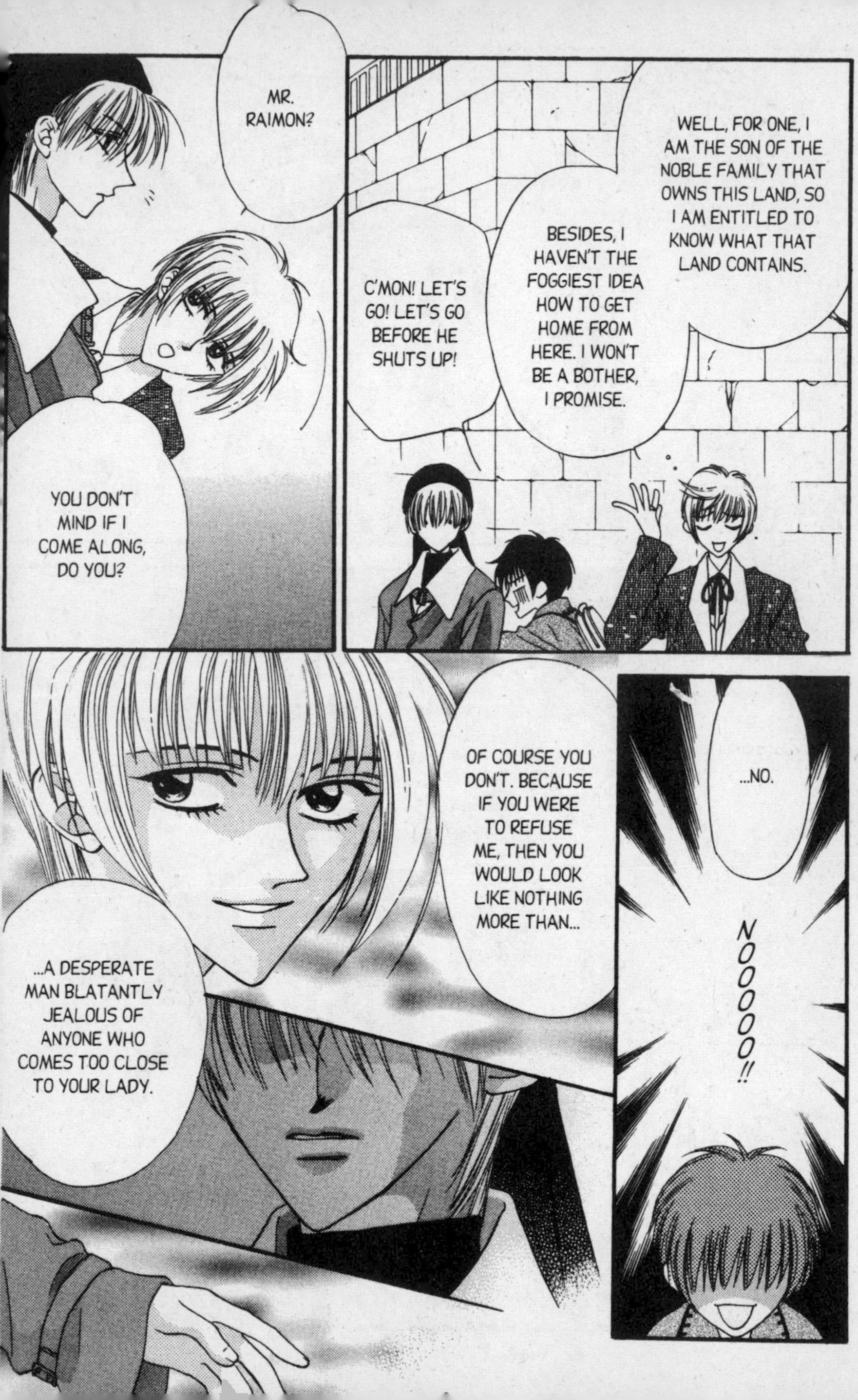
WELL, FOR ONE, I AM THE SON OF THE NOBLE FAMILY THAT OWNS THIS LAND, SO I AM ENTITLED TO KNOW WHAT THAT LAND CONTAINS.
BESIDES, I HAVEN'T THE FOGGIEST IDEA HOW TO GET HOME FROM HERE. I WON'T BE A BOTHER, I PROMISE.
C'MON! LET'S GO! LET'S GO BEFORE HE SHUTS UP!
MR. RAIMON?
YOU DON'T MIND IF I COME ALONG, DO YOU?
...NO.
NOOOOOO!!
OF COURSE YOU DON'T. BECAUSE IF YOU WERE TO REFUSE ME, THEN YOU WOULD LOOK LIKE NOTHING MORE THAN...
...A DESPERATE MAN BLATANTLY JEALOUS OF ANYONE WHO COMES TOO CLOSE TO YOUR LADY.

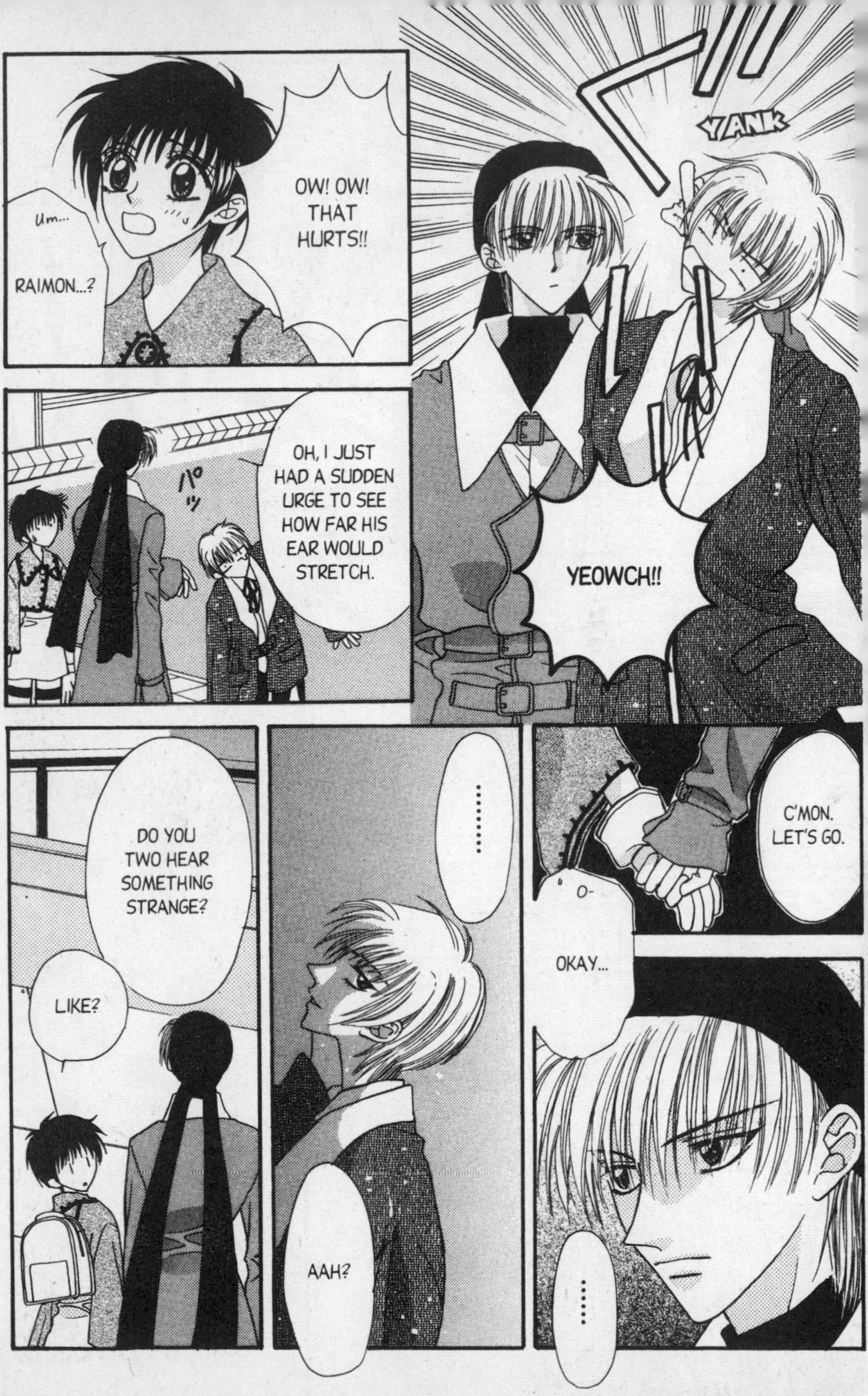
YANK
YEOWCH!!
OW! OW! THAT HURTS!!
Um...
RAIMON...?
OH, I JUST HAD A SUDDEN URGE TO SEE HOW FAR HIS EAR WOULD STRETCH.
パッ
C'MON. LET'S GO.
O- OKAY...
......
......
AAH?
DO YOU TWO HEAR SOMETHING STRANGE?
LIKE?

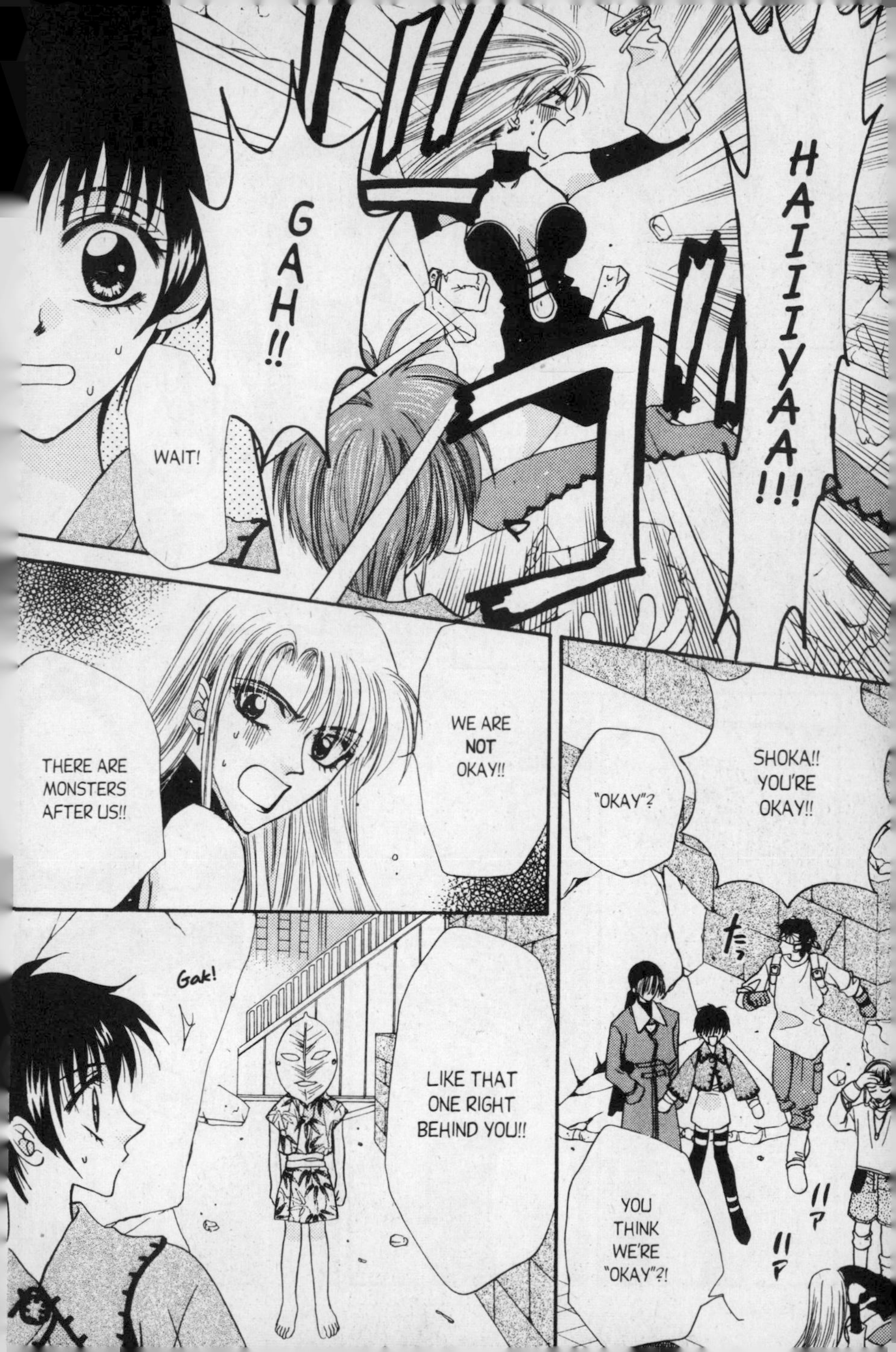
HAIIIYAA!!!
GAH!!
WAIT!
SHOKA!! YOU'RE OKAY!!
"OKAY"?
YOU THINK WE'RE "OKAY"?!
WE ARE NOT OKAY!!
THERE ARE MONSTERS AFTER US!!
LIKE THAT ONE RIGHT BEHIND YOU!!
Gak!

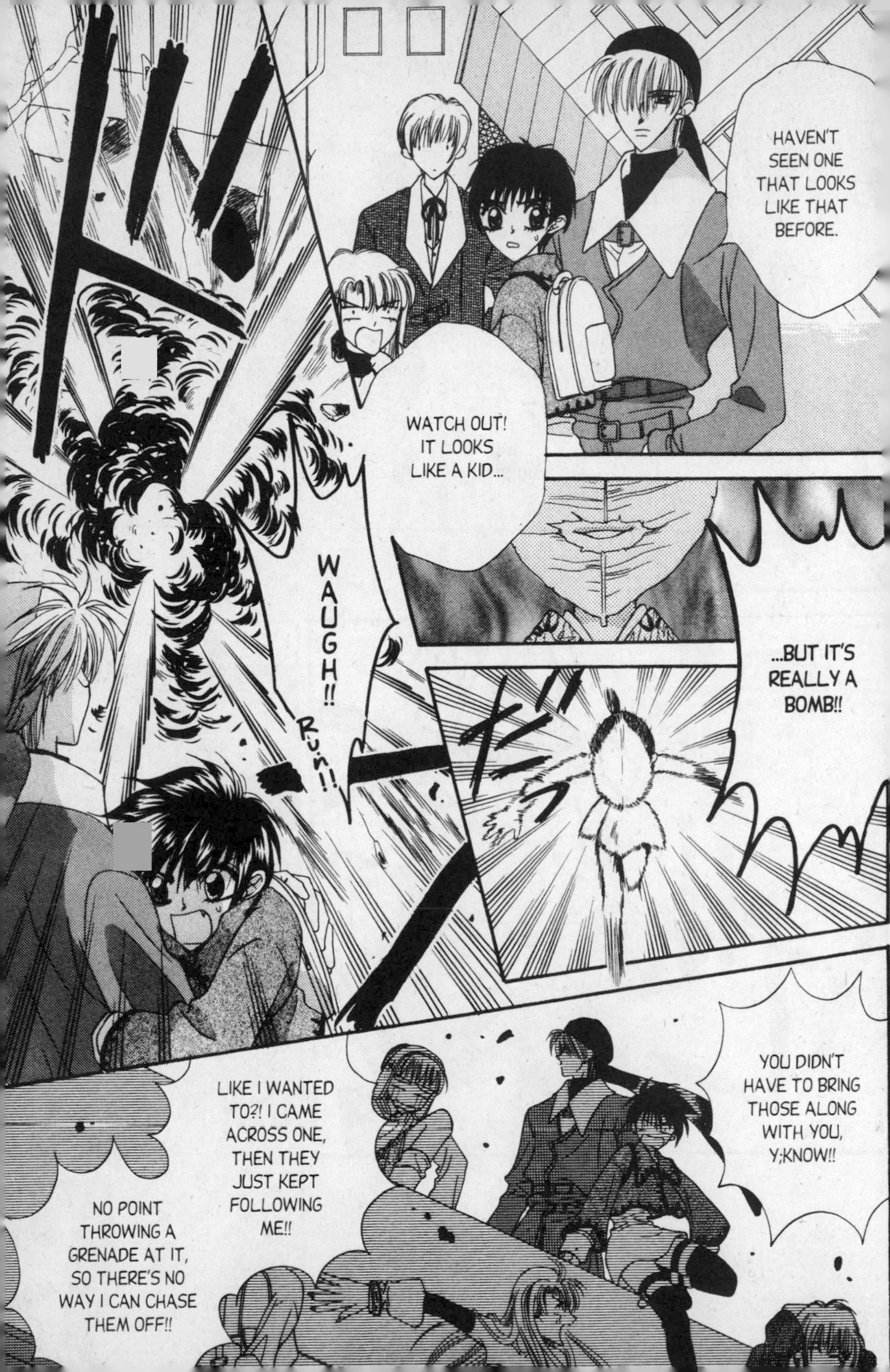
HAVEN'T SEEN ONE THAT LOOKS LIKE THAT BEFORE.
WATCH OUT! IT LOOKS LIKE A KID...
...BUT IT'S REALLY A BOMB!!
WAUGH!!
Run!!
YOU DIDN'T HAVE TO BRING THOSE ALONG WITH YOU, Y;KNOW!!
LIKE I WANTED TO?! I CAME ACROSS ONE, THEN THEY JUST KEPT FOLLOWING ME!!
NO POINT THROWING A GRENADE AT IT, SO THERE'S NO WAY I CAN CHASE THEM OFF!!

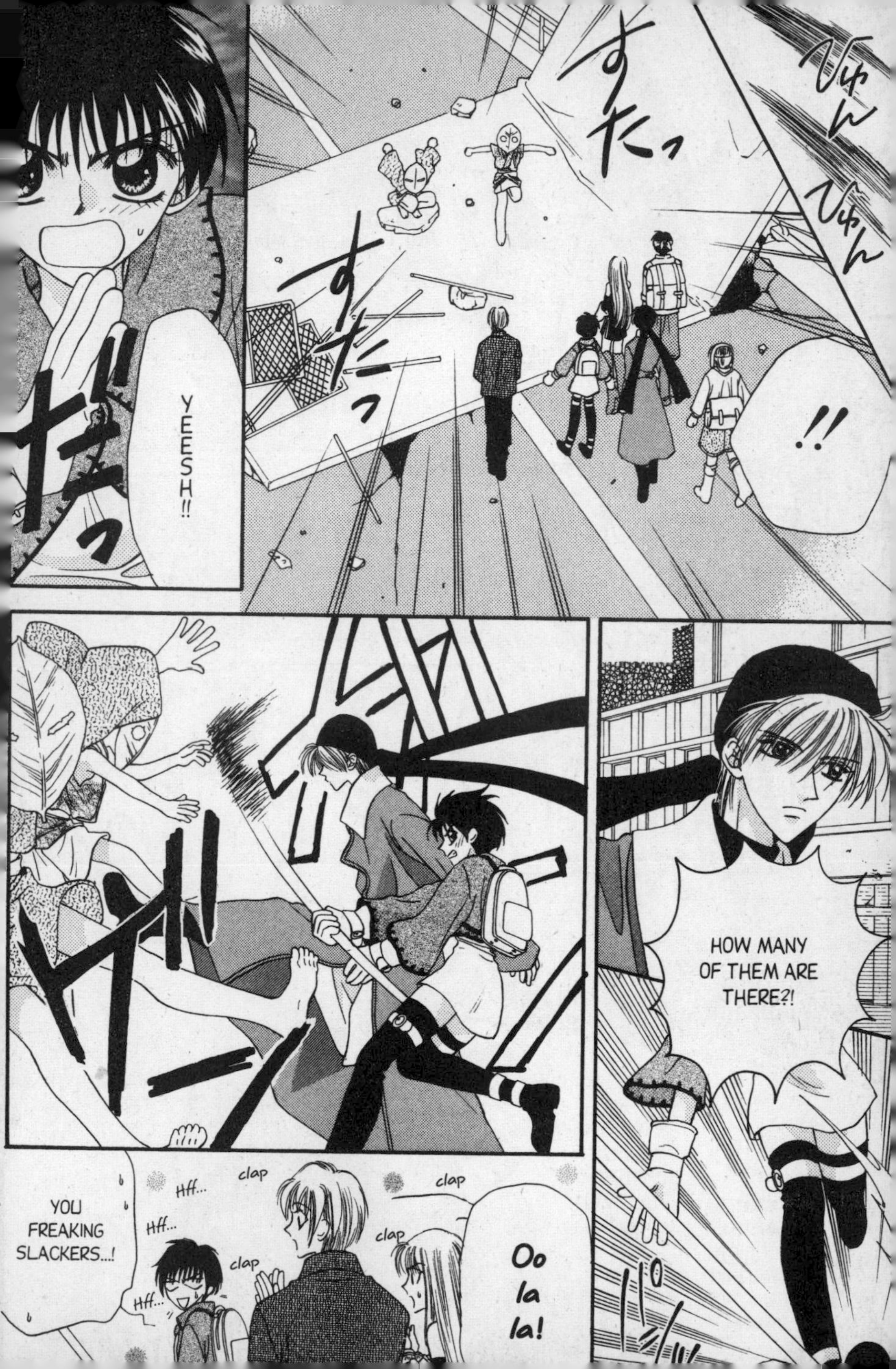

ひゅん
ひゅん
ひゅん
すたっ
!!
すたたっ
YEEESH!!
HOW MANY OF THEM ARE THERE?!
clap
Oo la la!
clap
clap
clap
Hff...
Hff...
Hff...
YOU FREAKING SLACKERS...!

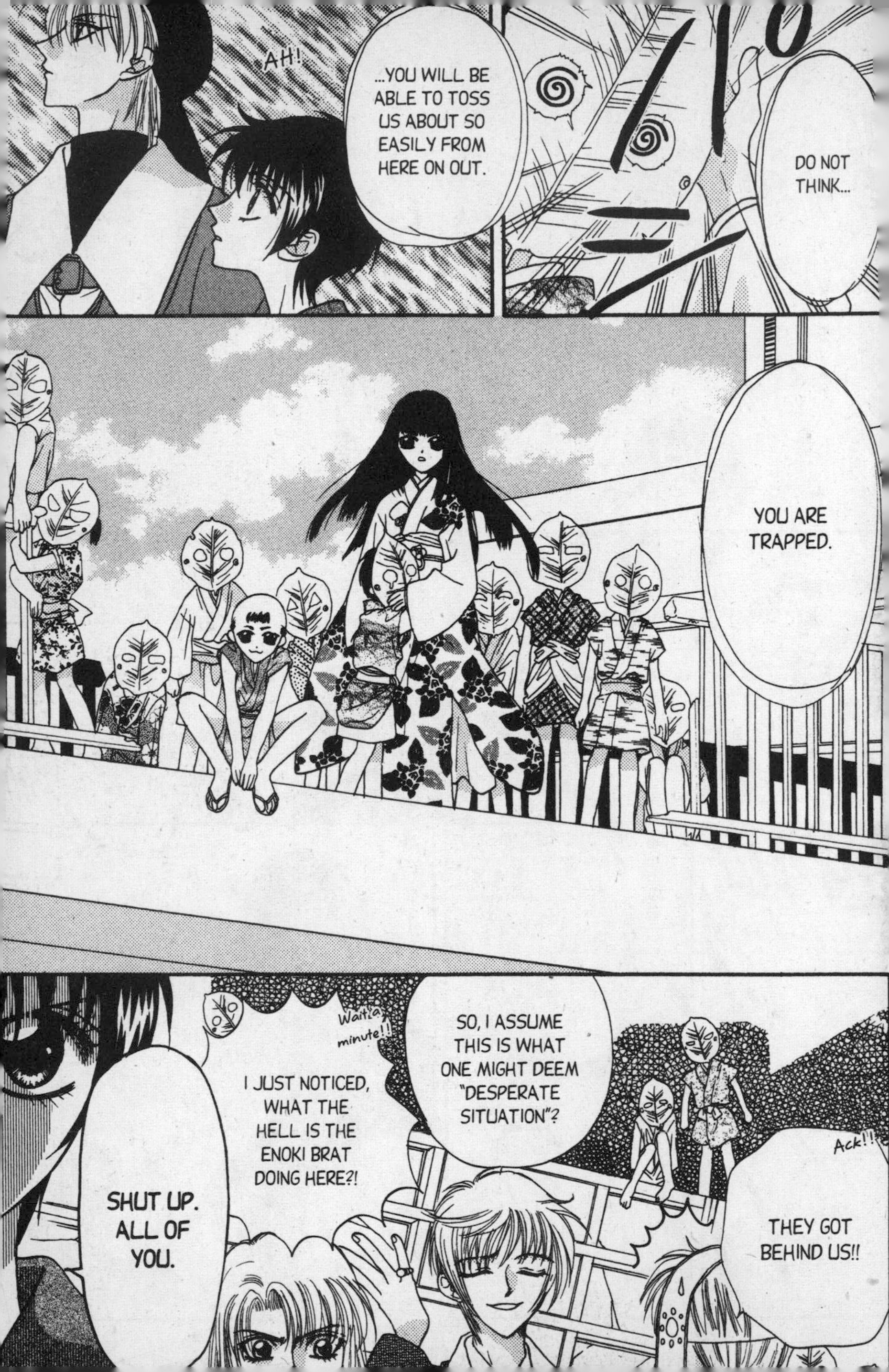
DO NOT THINK...
...YOU WILL BE ABLE TO TOSS US ABOUT SO EASILY FROM HERE ON OUT.
AH!
YOU ARE TRAPPED.
Ack!!
THEY GOT BEHIND US!!
SO, I ASSUME THIS IS WHAT ONE MIGHT DEEM "DESPERATE SITUATION"?
Wait a minute!!
I JUST NOTICED, WHAT THE HELL IS THE ENOKI BRAT DOING HERE?!
SHUT UP. ALL OF YOU.

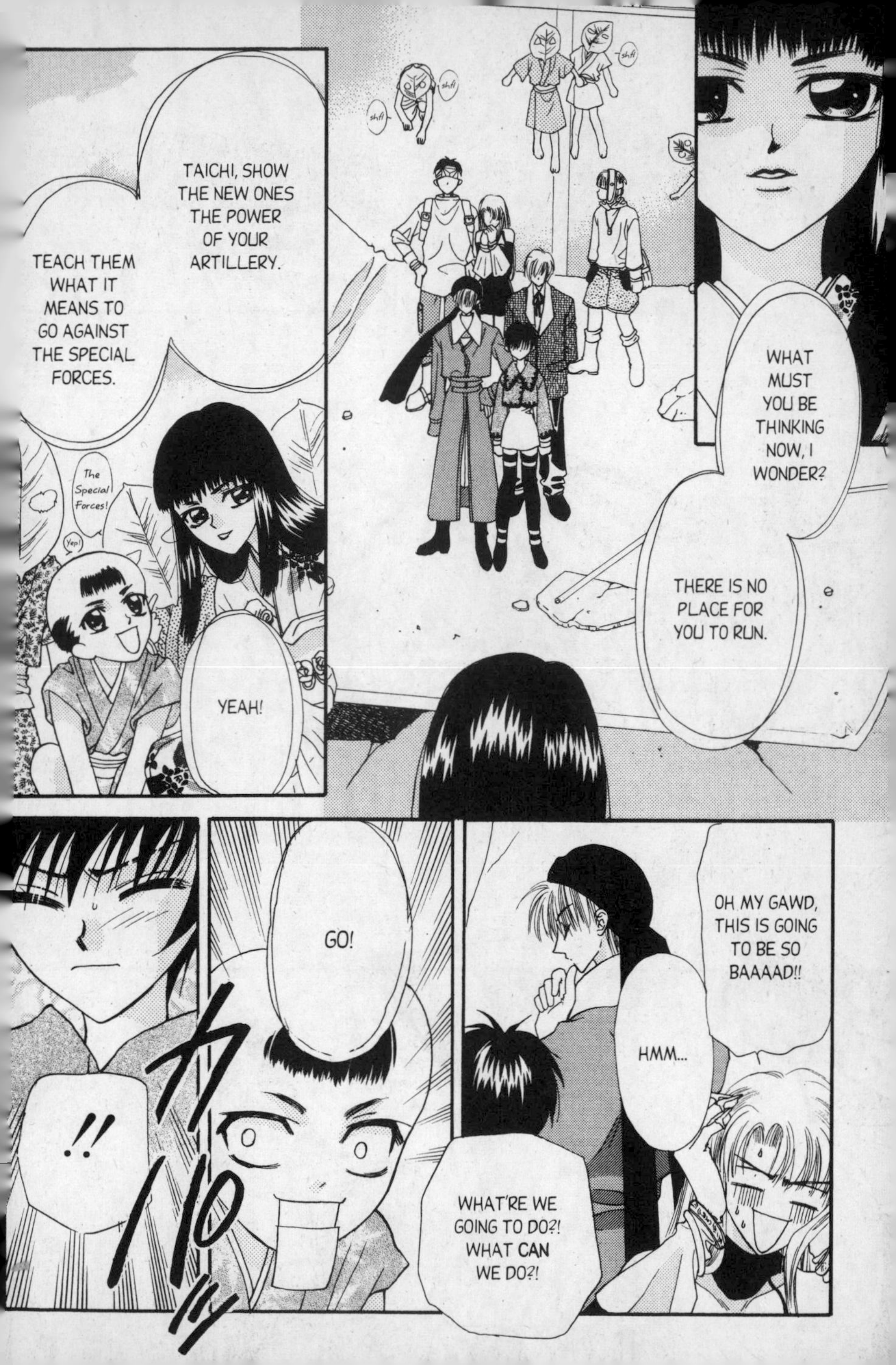
shfi
shfi
shfi
WHAT MUST YOU BE THINKING NOW, I WONDER?
THERE IS NO PLACE FOR YOU TO RUN.
TAICHI, SHOW THE NEW ONES THE POWER OF YOUR ARTILLERY.
TEACH THEM WHAT IT MEANS TO GO AGAINST THE SPECIAL FORCES.
The Special Forces!
Yep!
YEAH!
OH MY GAWD, THIS IS GOING TO BE SO BAAAAD!!
HMM...
WHAT'RE WE GOING TO DO?! WHAT CAN WE DO?!
GO!
!!

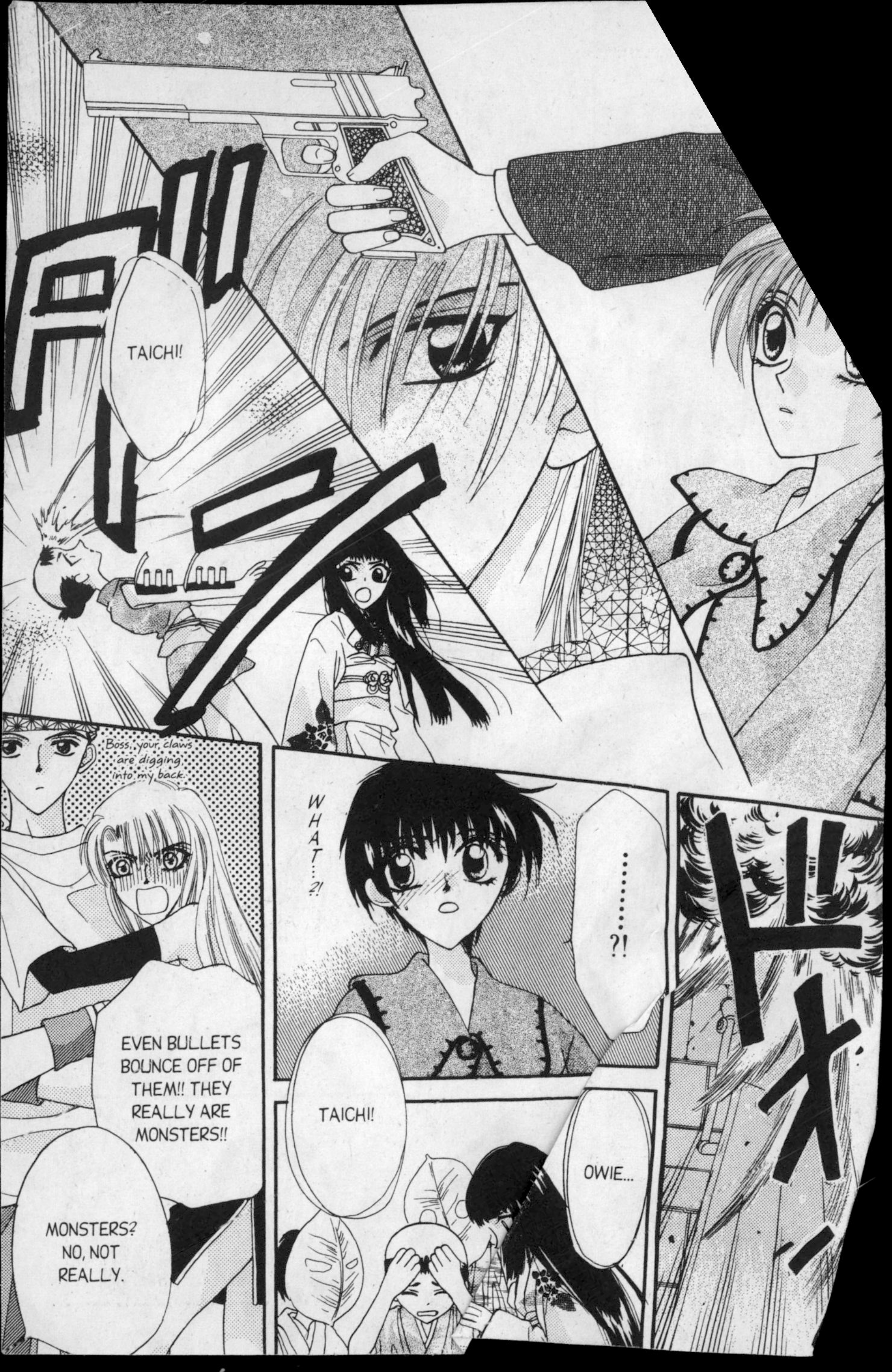
TAICHI!
......?!
WHAT...?!
OWIE...
TAICHI!
Boss, your claws are digging into my back.
EVEN BULLETS BOUNCE OFF OF THEM!! THEY REALLY ARE MONSTERS!!
MONSTERS? NO, NOT REALLY.

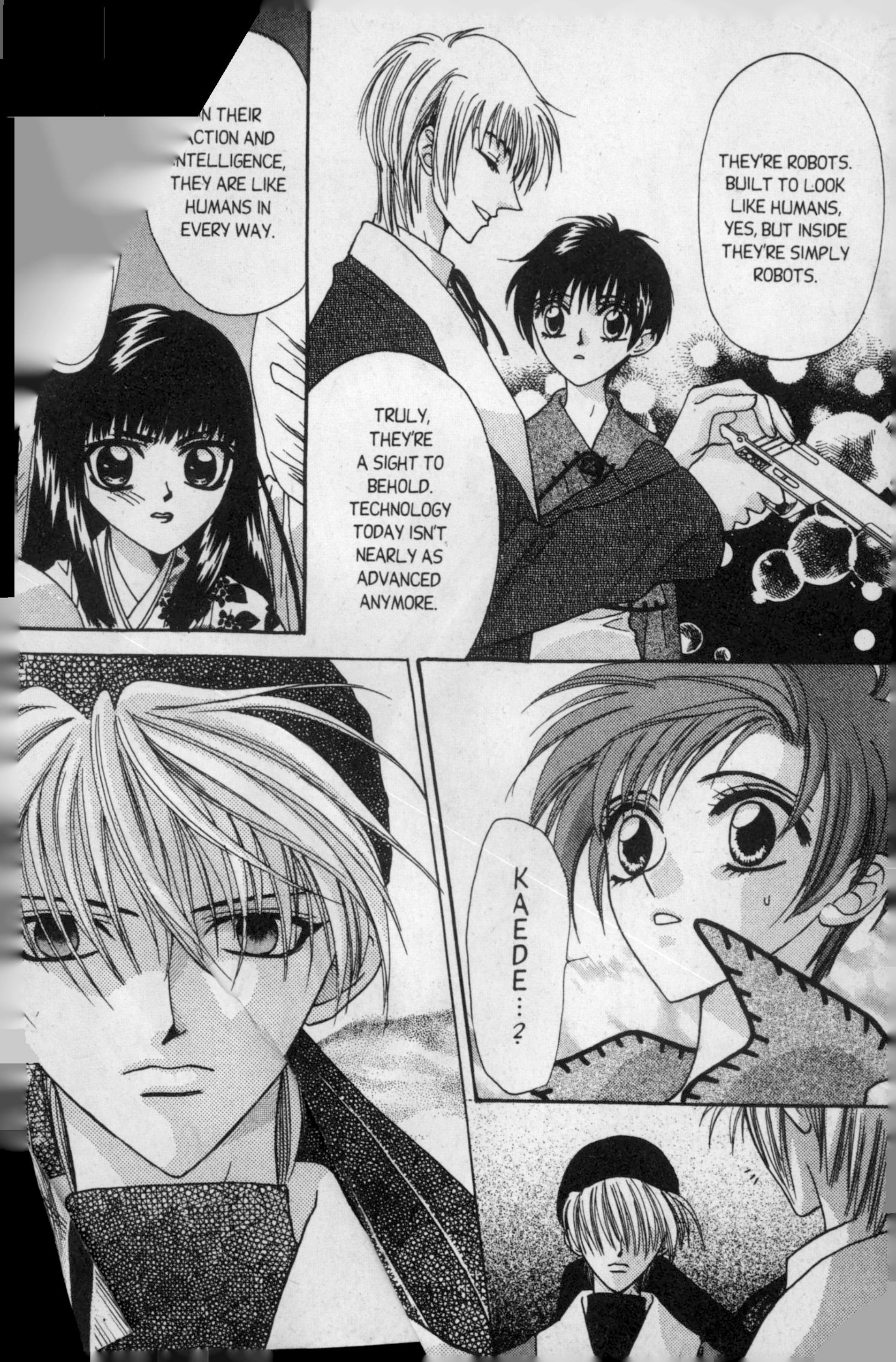

THEY'RE ROBOTS. BUILT TO LOOK LIKE HUMANS, YES, BUT INSIDE THEY'RE SIMPLY ROBOTS.
TRULY, THEY'RE A SIGHT TO BEHOLD. TECHNOLOGY TODAY ISN'T NEARLY AS ADVANCED ANYMORE.
N THEIR ACTION AND NTELLIGENCE, THEY ARE LIKE HUMANS IN EVERY WAY.
KAEDE...?

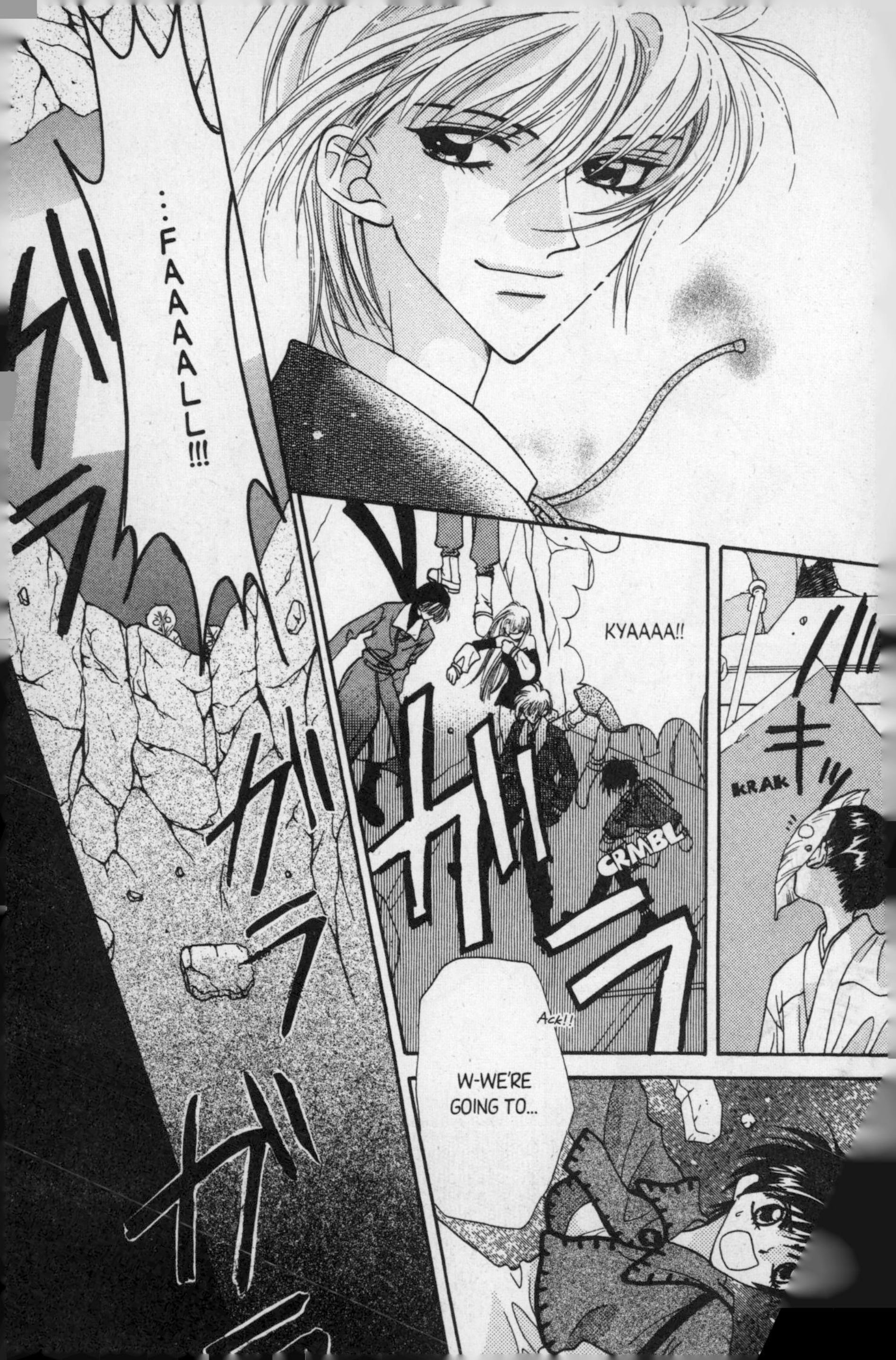
...FAAAAALL!!!
KRAK
KYAAAA!!
CRMBL
Ack!!
W-WE'RE GOING TO...

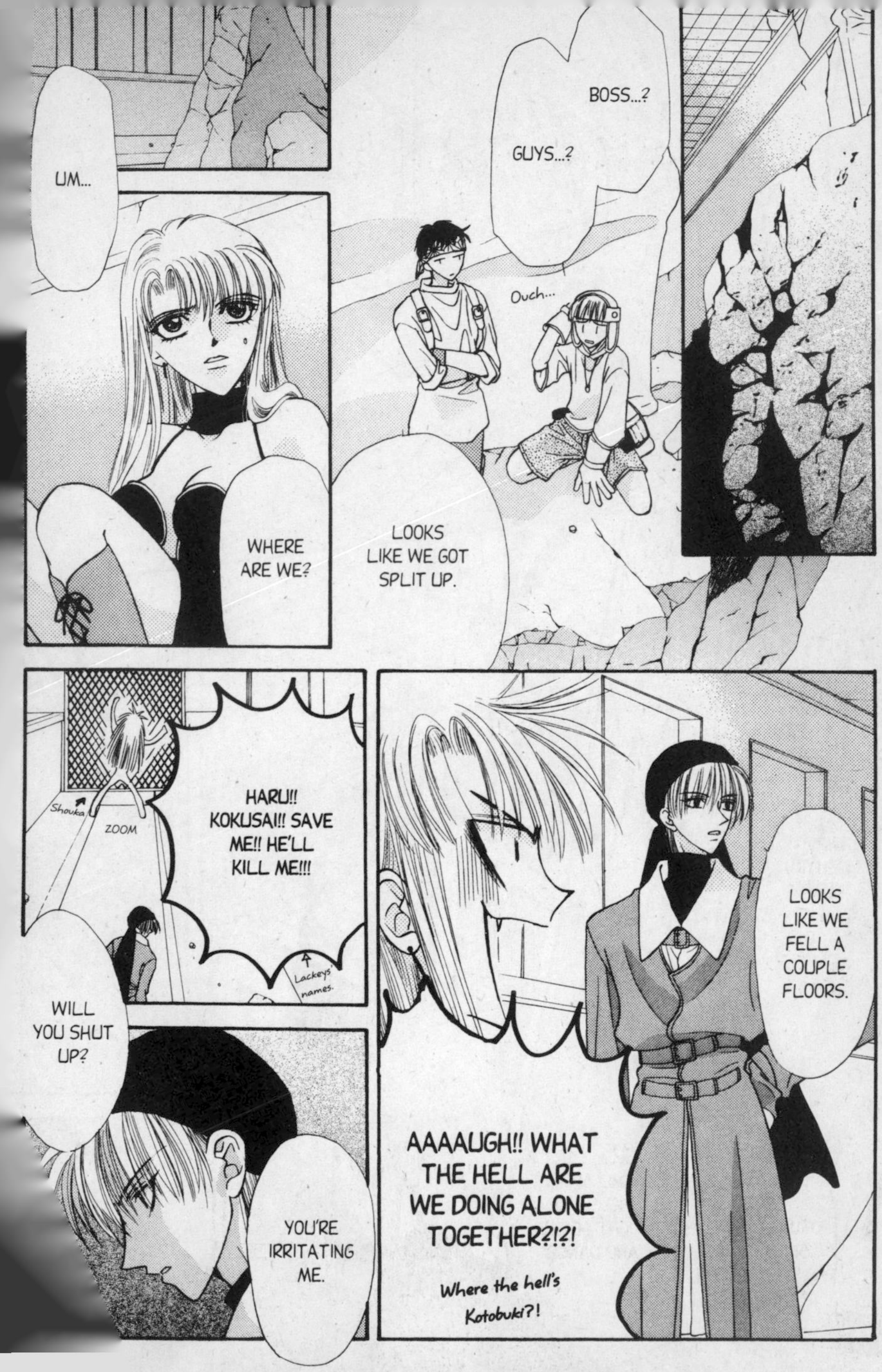
BOSS...?
GUYS...?
Ouch...
LOOKS LIKE WE GOT SPLIT UP.
UM...
WHERE ARE WE?
LOOKS LIKE WE FELL A COUPLE FLOORS.
AAAAUGH!! WHAT THE HELL ARE WE DOING ALONE TOGETHER?!?!
Where the hell's Kotobuki?!
HARU!! KOKUSAI!! SAVE ME!! HE'LL KILL ME!!!
Shouka
ZOOM
Lackeys' names.
WILL YOU SHUT UP?
YOU'RE IRRITATING ME.

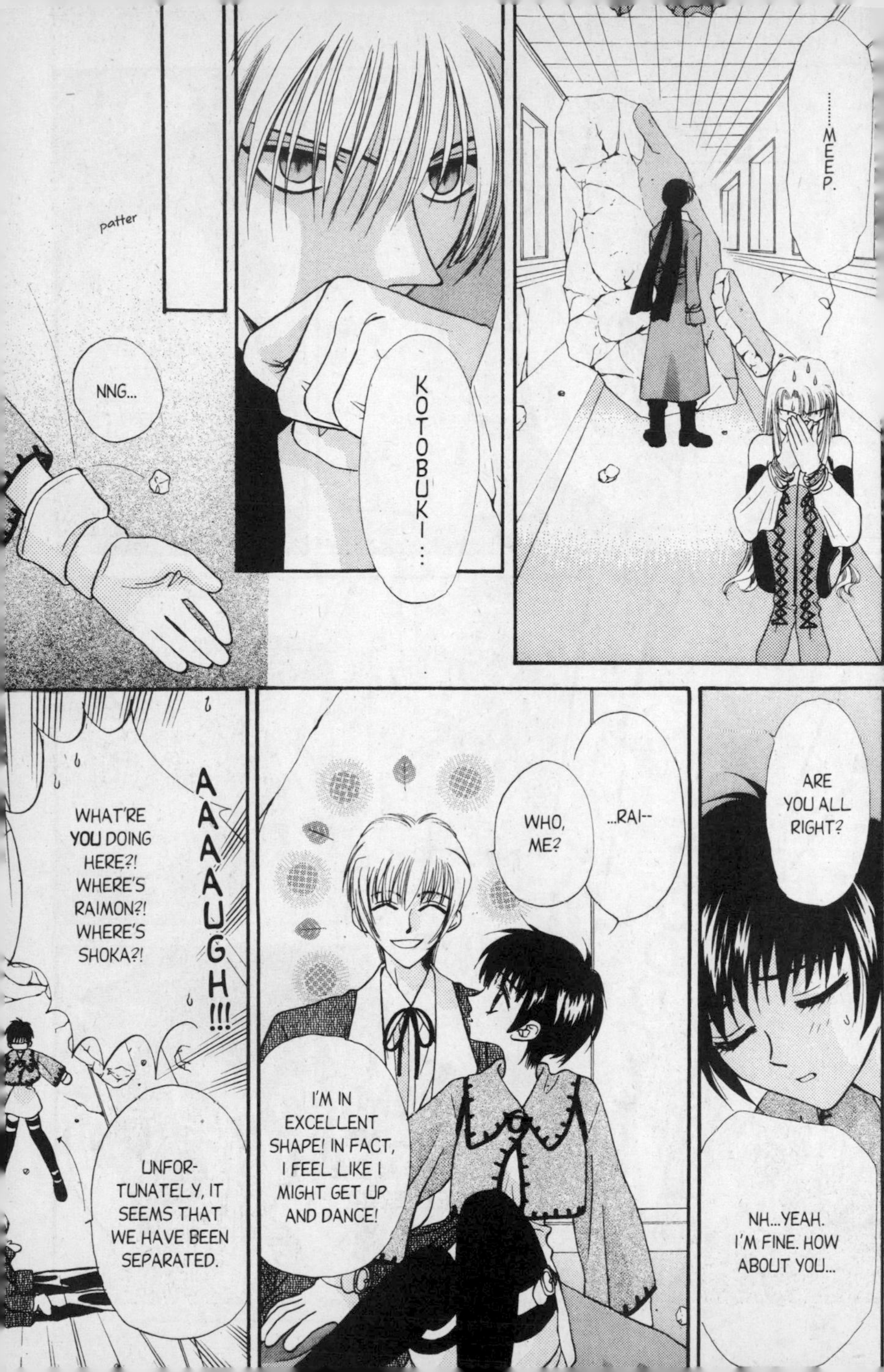
......MEEP.
KOTOBUKI...
patter
NNG...
ARE YOU ALL RIGHT?
NH...YEAH. I'M FINE. HOW ABOUT YOU...
...RAI--
WHO, ME?
I'M IN EXCELLENT SHAPE! IN FACT, I FEEL LIKE I MIGHT GET UP AND DANCE!
AAAAAUGH!!!
WHAT'RE YOU DOING HERE?! WHERE'S RAIMON?! WHERE'S SHOKA?!
UNFOR-TUNATELY, IT SEEMS THAT WE HAVE BEEN SEPARATED.

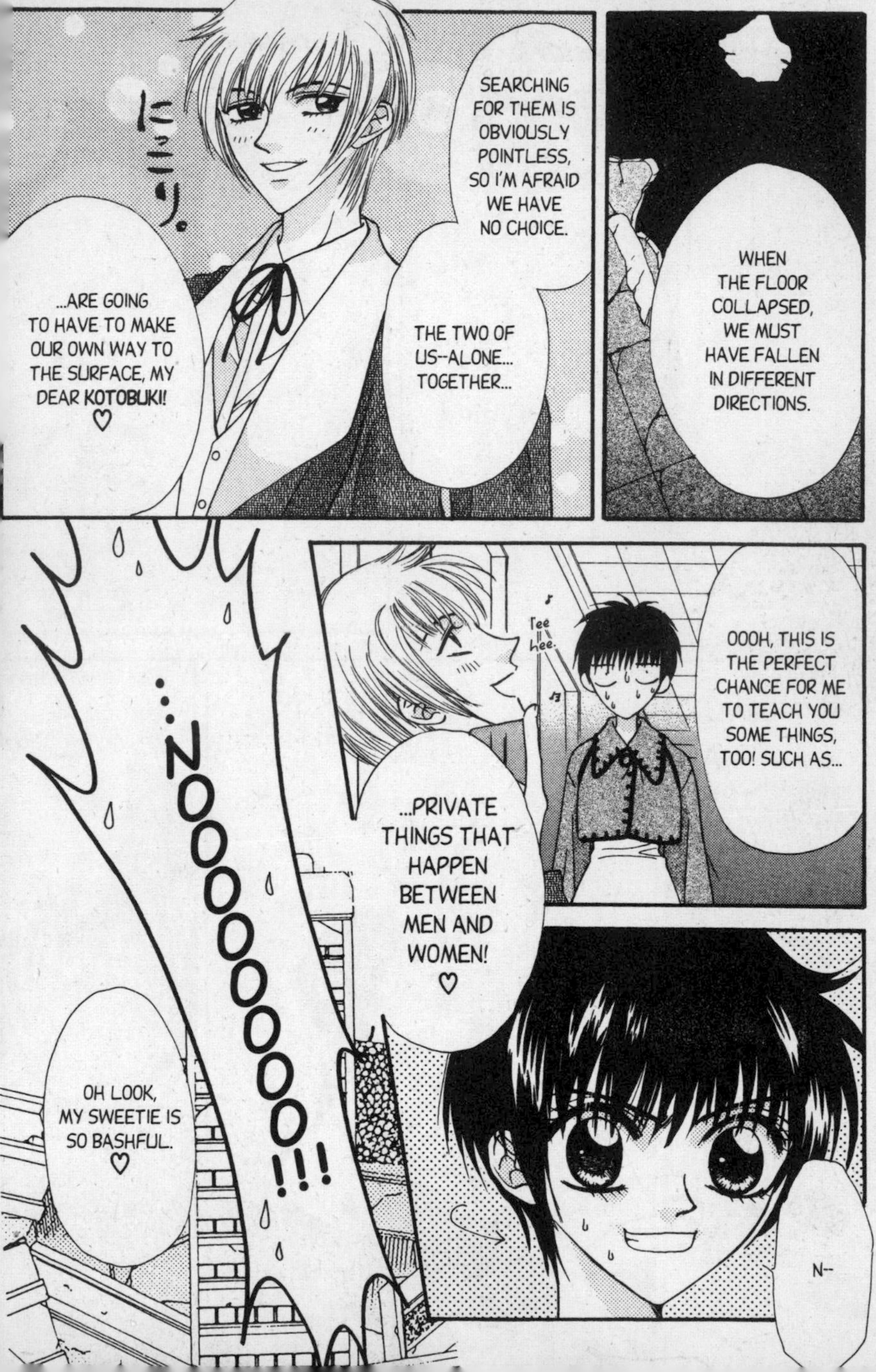
WHEN THE FLOOR COLLAPSED, WE MUST HAVE FALLEN IN DIFFERENT DIRECTIONS.
SEARCHING FOR THEM IS OBVIOUSLY POINTLESS, SO I'M AFRAID WE HAVE NO CHOICE.
にこり。
THE TWO OF US--ALONE... TOGETHER...
...ARE GOING TO HAVE TO MAKE OUR OWN WAY TO THE SURFACE, MY DEAR KOTOBUKI! ♡
OOOH, THIS IS THE PERFECT CHANCE FOR ME TO TEACH YOU SOME THINGS, TOO! SUCH AS...
Tee hee.
...PRIVATE THINGS THAT HAPPEN BETWEEN MEN AND WOMEN! ♡
N--
...NOOOOOOOO!!!
OH LOOK, MY SWEETIE IS SO BASHFUL. ♡

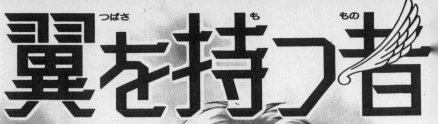

翼を持つ者

Tsubasa: Those With Wings

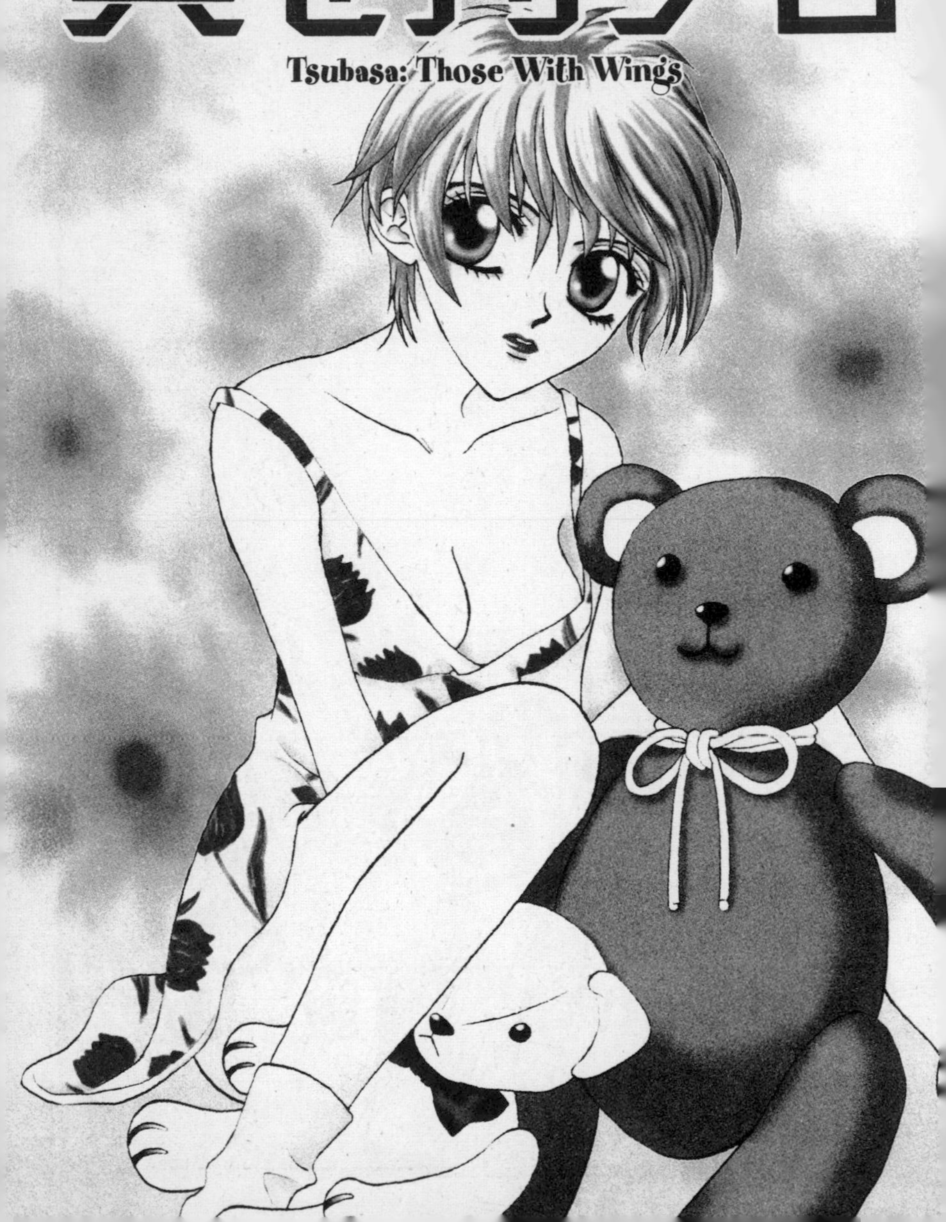

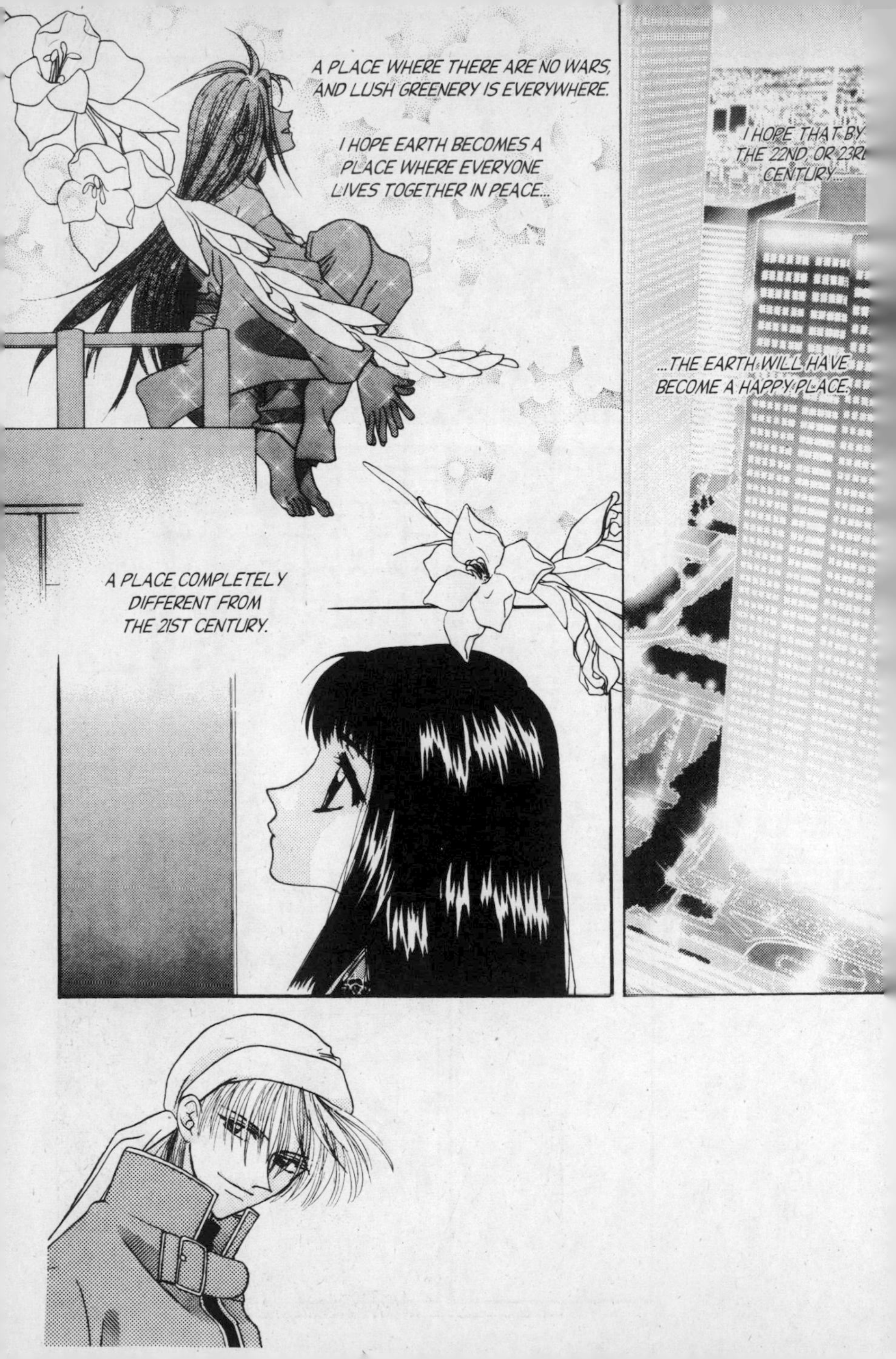
I HOPE THAT BY THE 22ND, OR 23R CENTURY...
...THE EARTH WILL HAVE BECOME A HAPPY PLACE.
A PLACE WHERE THERE ARE NO WARS, AND LUSH GREENERY IS EVERYWHERE.
I HOPE EARTH BECOMES A PLACE WHERE EVERYONE LIVES TOGETHER IN PEACE...
A PLACE COMPLETELY DIFFERENT FROM THE 21ST CENTURY.

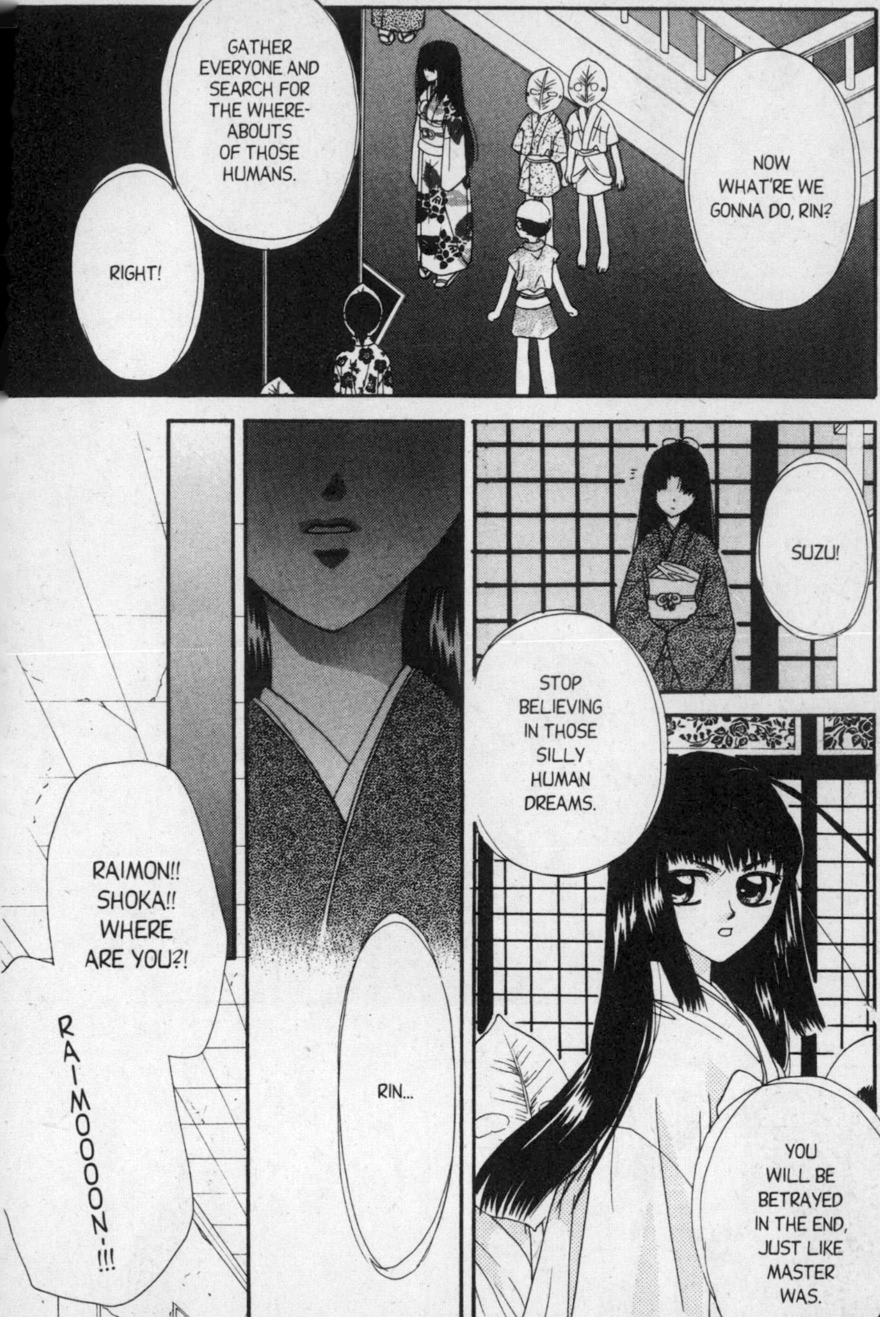
NOW WHAT'RE WE GONNA DO, RIN?
GATHER EVERYONE AND SEARCH FOR THE WHEREABOUTS OF THOSE HUMANS.
RIGHT!
SUZU!
STOP BELIEVING IN THOSE SILLY HUMAN DREAMS.
YOU WILL BE BETRAYED IN THE END, JUST LIKE MASTER WAS.
RIN...
RAIMON!! SHOKA!! WHERE ARE YOU?!
RAIMOOOOON-!!!

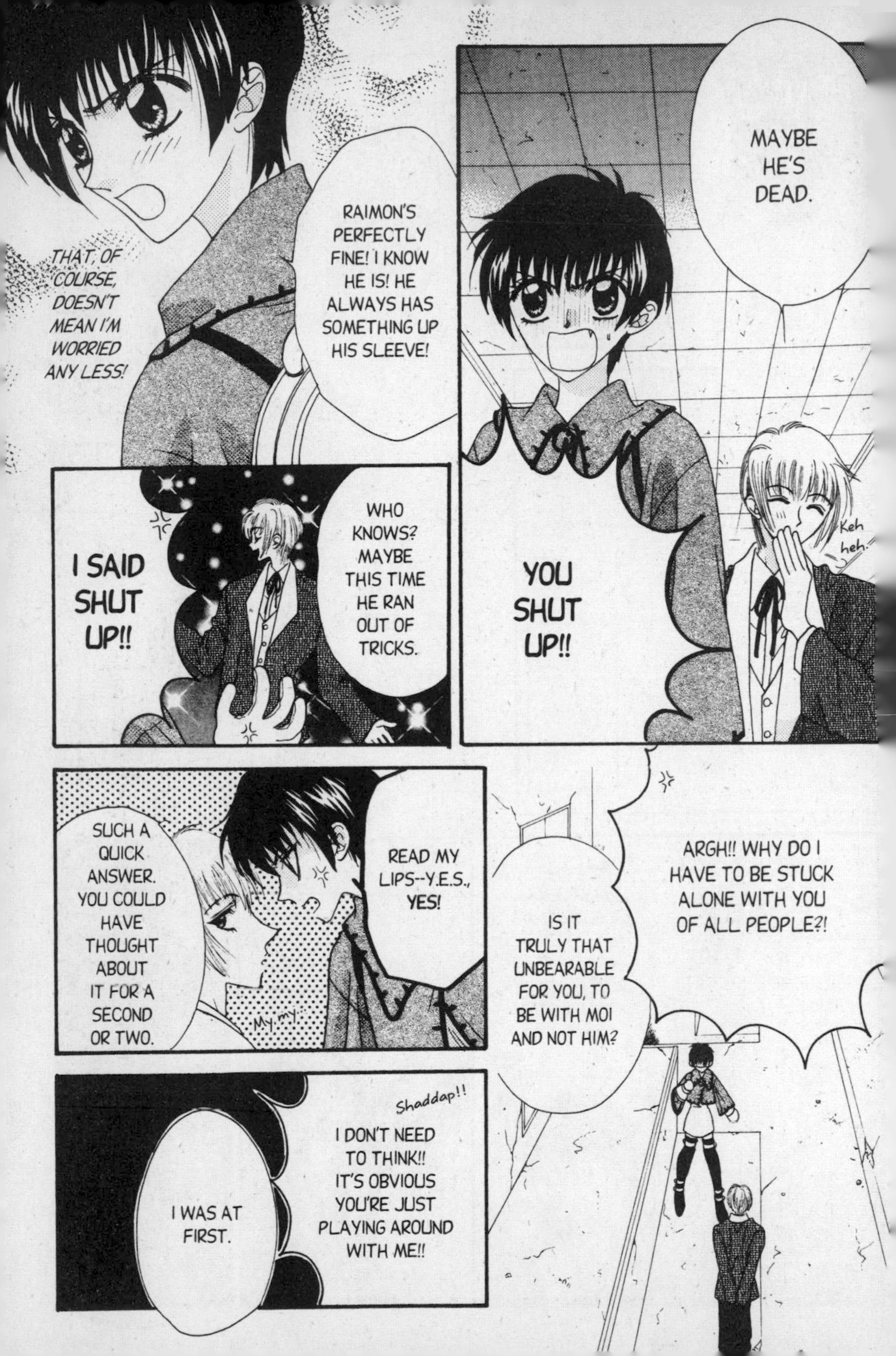
MAYBE HE'S DEAD.
YOU SHUT UP!!
Keh heh.
RAIMON'S PERFECTLY FINE! I KNOW HE IS! HE ALWAYS HAS SOMETHING UP HIS SLEEVE!
THAT, OF COURSE, DOESN'T MEAN I'M WORRIED ANY LESS!
WHO KNOWS? MAYBE THIS TIME HE RAN OUT OF TRICKS.
I SAID SHUT UP!!
ARGH!! WHY DO I HAVE TO BE STUCK ALONE WITH YOU OF ALL PEOPLE?!
IS IT TRULY THAT UNBEARABLE FOR YOU, TO BE WITH MOI AND NOT HIM?
READ MY LIPS--Y.E.S., YES!
SUCH A QUICK ANSWER. YOU COULD HAVE THOUGHT ABOUT IT FOR A SECOND OR TWO.
My my.
Shaddap!!
I DON'T NEED TO THINK!! IT'S OBVIOUS YOU'RE JUST PLAYING AROUND WITH ME!!
I WAS AT FIRST.

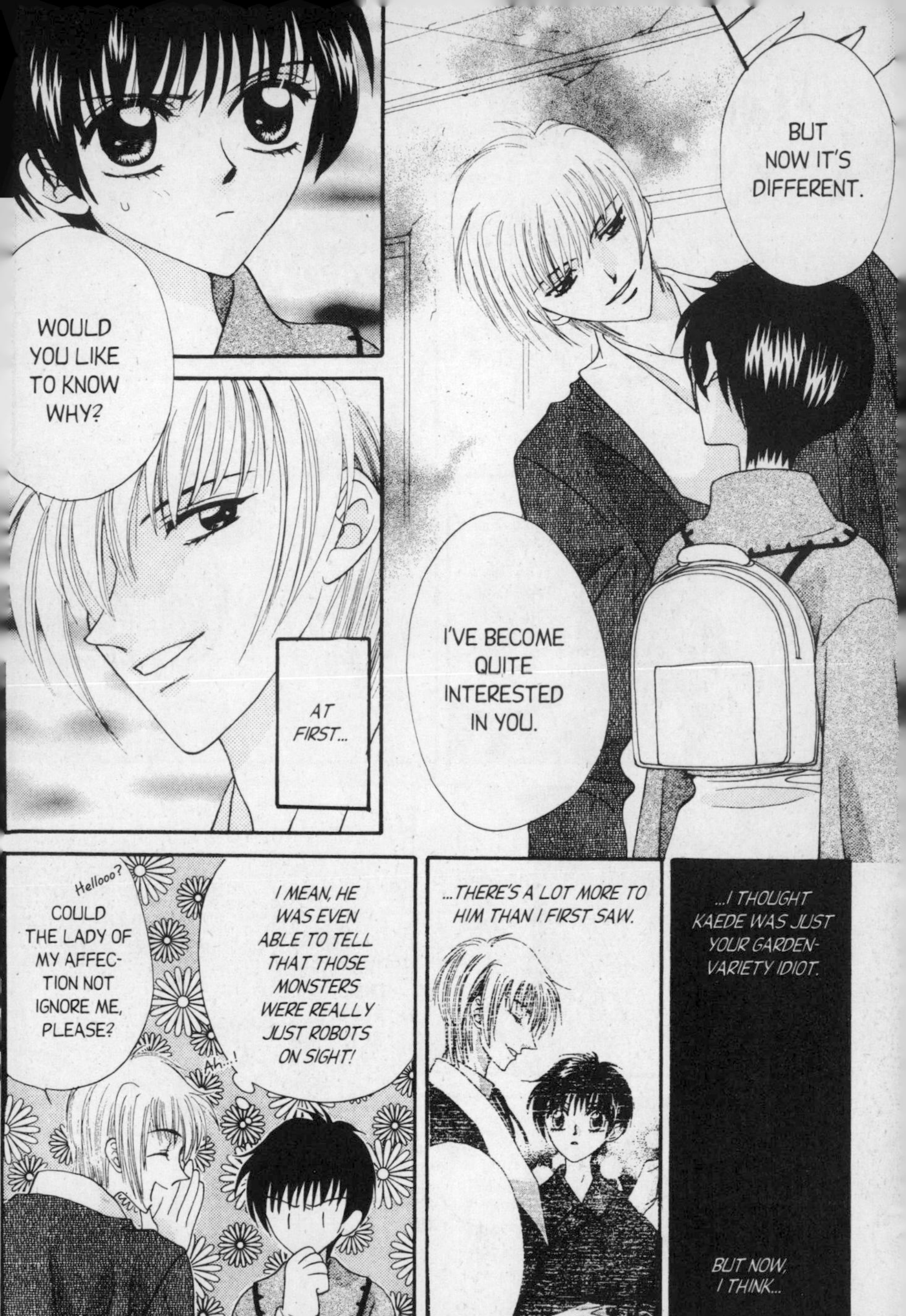
BUT NOW IT'S DIFFERENT.
I'VE BECOME QUITE INTERESTED IN YOU.
WOULD YOU LIKE TO KNOW WHY?
AT FIRST...
...I THOUGHT KAEDE WAS JUST YOUR GARDEN-VARIETY IDIOT.
BUT NOW, I THINK...
...THERE'S A LOT MORE TO HIM THAN I FIRST SAW.
I MEAN, HE WAS EVEN ABLE TO TELL THAT THOSE MONSTERS WERE REALLY JUST ROBOTS ON SIGHT!
Hellooo?
COULD THE LADY OF MY AFFEC-TION NOT IGNORE ME, PLEASE?
Ah...!

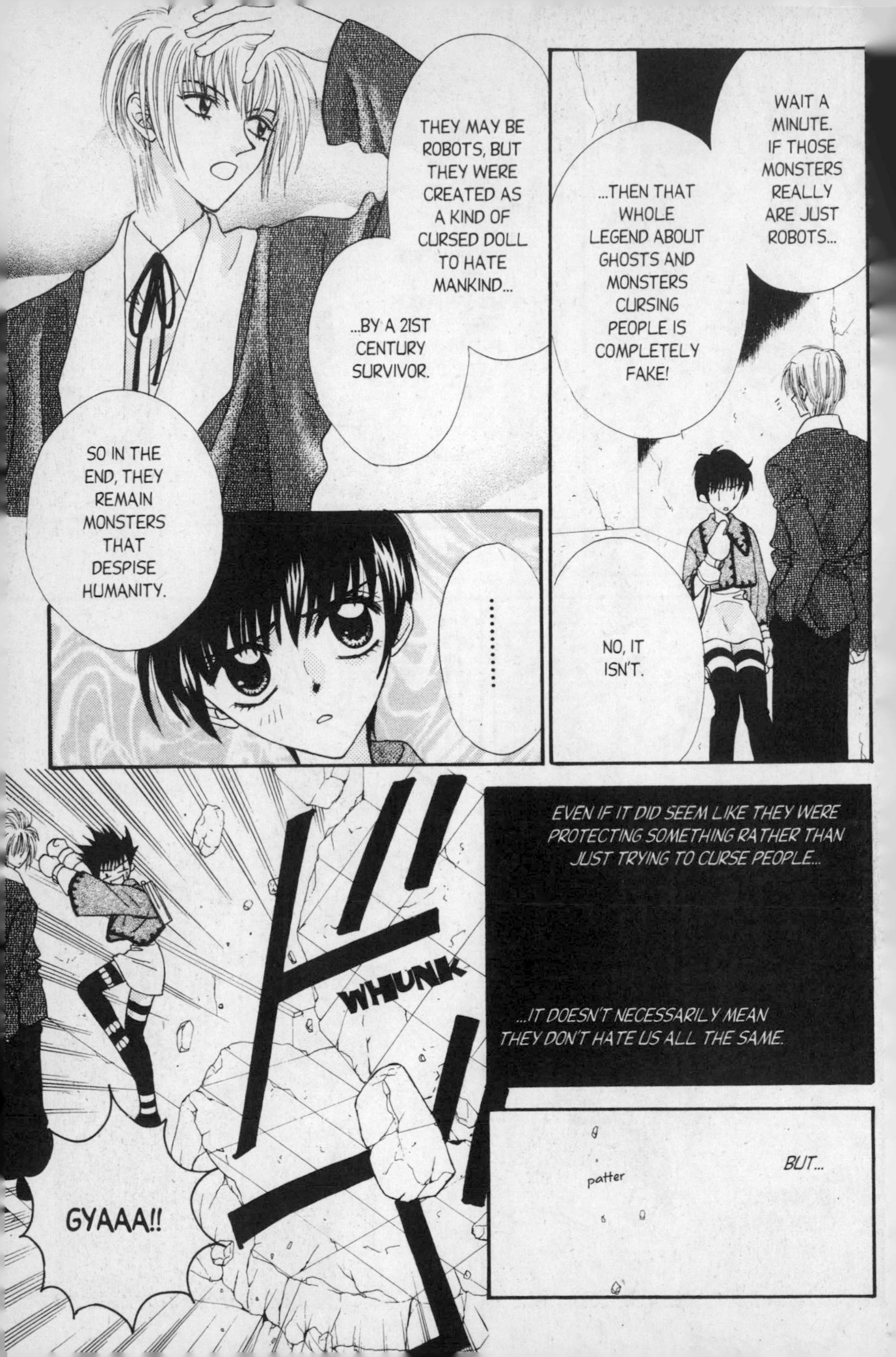
WAIT A MINUTE. IF THOSE MONSTERS REALLY ARE JUST ROBOTS...
...THEN THAT WHOLE LEGEND ABOUT GHOSTS AND MONSTERS CURSING PEOPLE IS COMPLETELY FAKE!
NO, IT ISN'T.
THEY MAY BE ROBOTS, BUT THEY WERE CREATED AS A KIND OF CURSED DOLL TO HATE MANKIND...
...BY A 21ST CENTURY SURVIVOR.
SO IN THE END, THEY REMAIN MONSTERS THAT DESPISE HUMANITY.
......
EVEN IF IT DID SEEM LIKE THEY WERE PROTECTING SOMETHING RATHER THAN JUST TRYING TO CURSE PEOPLE...
...IT DOESN'T NECESSARILY MEAN THEY DON'T HATE US ALL THE SAME.
BUT...
patter
WHUNK
GYAAA!!

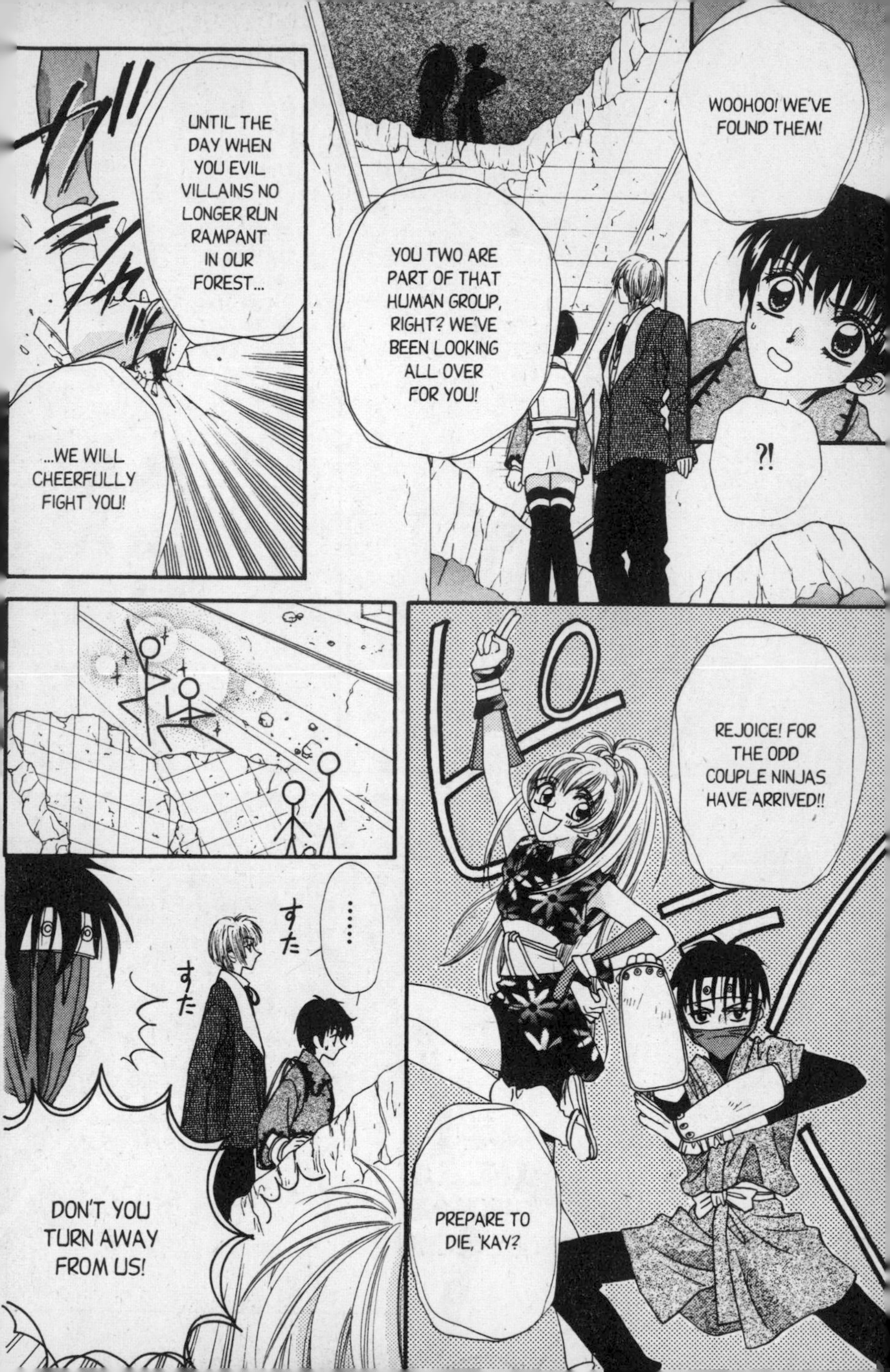
WOOHOO! WE'VE FOUND THEM!
?!
YOU TWO ARE PART OF THAT HUMAN GROUP, RIGHT? WE'VE BEEN LOOKING ALL OVER FOR YOU!
UNTIL THE DAY WHEN YOU EVIL VILLAINS NO LONGER RUN RAMPANT IN OUR FOREST...
...WE WILL CHEERFULLY FIGHT YOU!
REJOICE! FOR THE ODD COUPLE NINJAS HAVE ARRIVED!!
PREPARE TO DIE, 'KAY?
......
すた
すた
DON'T YOU TURN AWAY FROM US!

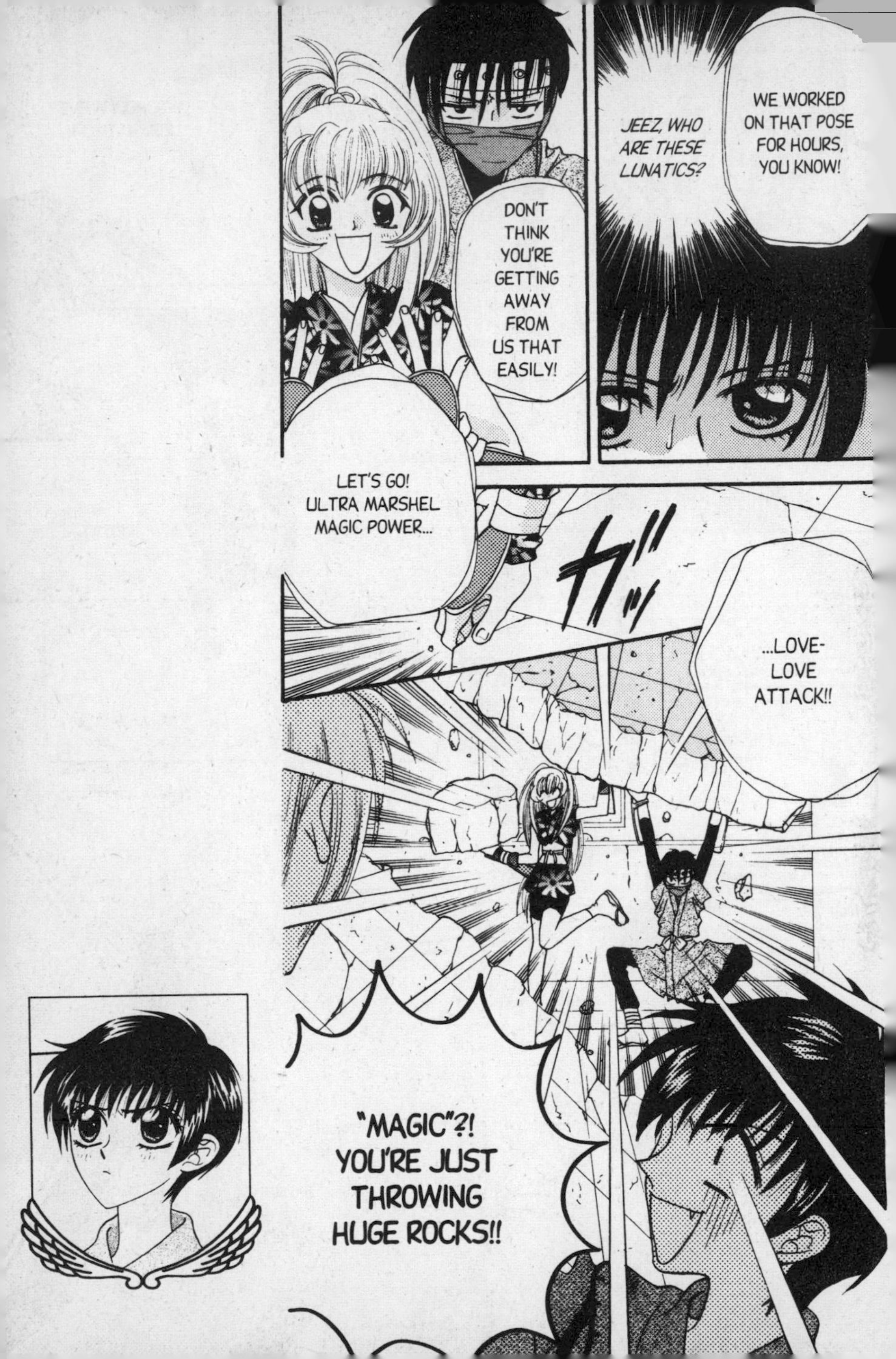
WE WORKED ON THAT POSE FOR HOURS, YOU KNOW!
JEEZ, WHO ARE THESE LUNATICS?
DON'T THINK YOU'RE GETTING AWAY FROM US THAT EASILY!
LET'S GO! ULTRA MARSHEL MAGIC POWER...
...LOVE-LOVE ATTACK!!
ガッ
"MAGIC"?! YOU'RE JUST THROWING HUGE ROCKS!!

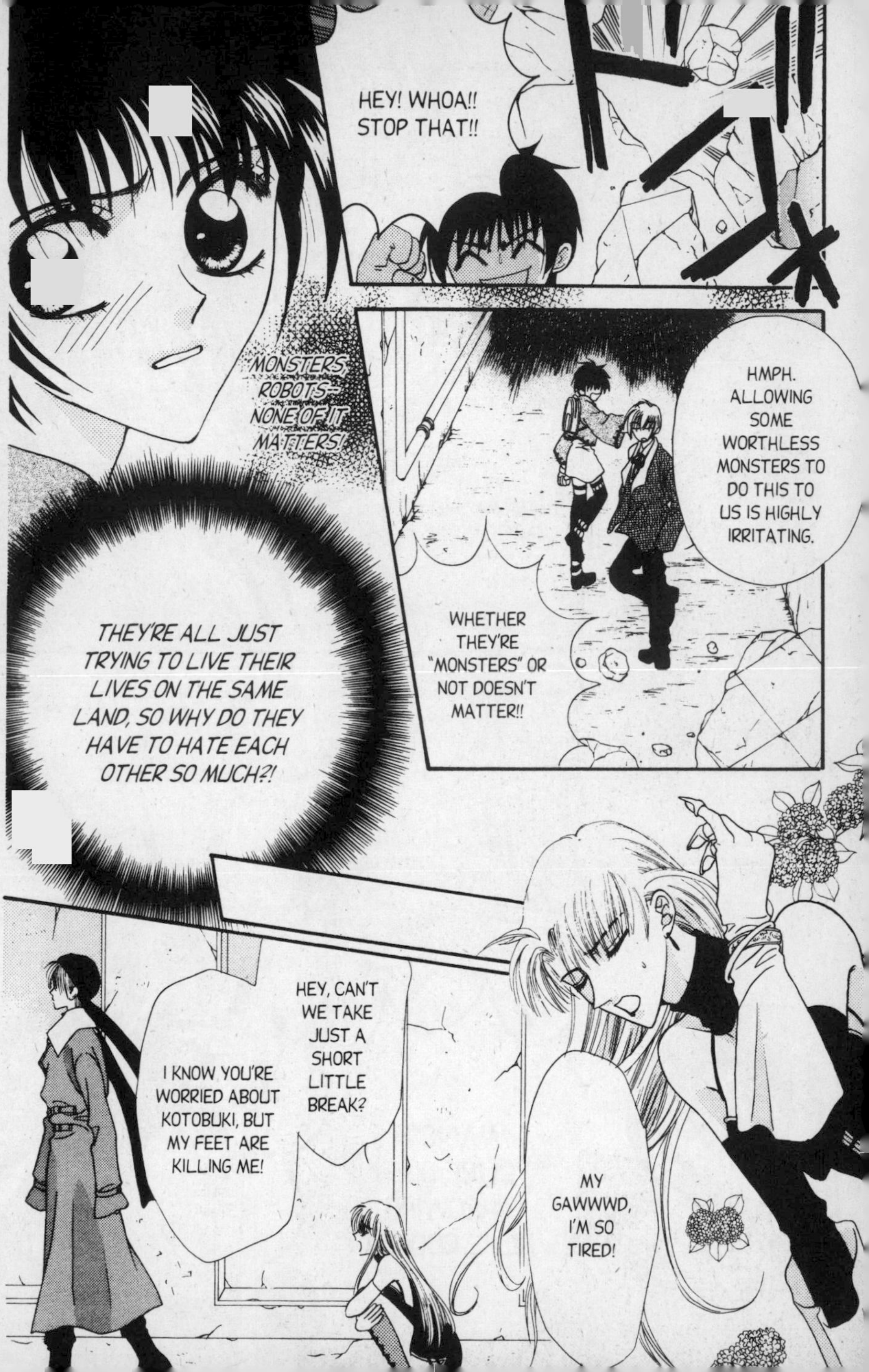
HEY! WHOA!! STOP THAT!!
HMPH. ALLOWING SOME WORTHLESS MONSTERS TO DO THIS TO US IS HIGHLY IRRITATING.
WHETHER THEY'RE "MONSTERS" OR NOT DOESN'T MATTER!!
MONSTERS, ROBOTS— NONE OF IT MATTERS!
THEY'RE ALL JUST TRYING TO LIVE THEIR LIVES ON THE SAME LAND, SO WHY DO THEY HAVE TO HATE EACH OTHER SO MUCH?!
MY GAWWWD, I'M SO TIRED!
HEY, CAN'T WE TAKE JUST A SHORT LITTLE BREAK?
I KNOW YOU'RE WORRIED ABOUT KOTOBUKI, BUT MY FEET ARE KILLING ME!

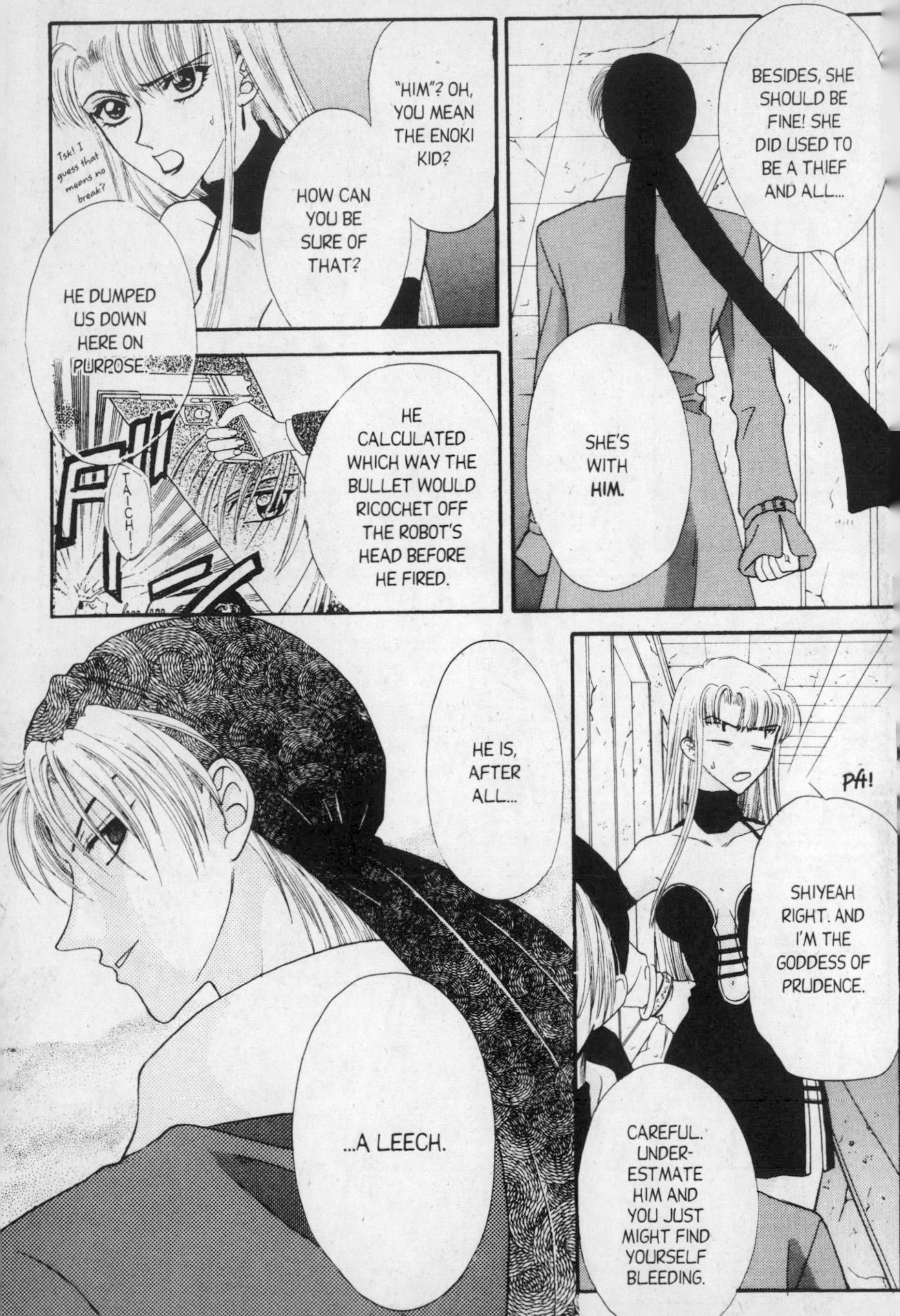
BESIDES, SHE SHOULD BE FINE! SHE DID USED TO BE A THIEF AND ALL...
SHE'S WITH **HIM.**
"HIM"? OH, YOU MEAN THE ENOKI KID?
Tsk! I guess that means no break?
HOW CAN YOU BE SURE OF THAT?
HE DUMPED US DOWN HERE ON PURPOSE.
TAICHI!
HE CALCULATED WHICH WAY THE BULLET WOULD RICOCHET OFF THE ROBOT'S HEAD BEFORE HE FIRED.
Pft!
SHIYEAH RIGHT. AND I'M THE GODDESS OF PRUDENCE.
CAREFUL. UNDER-ESTMATE HIM AND YOU JUST MIGHT FIND YOURSELF BLEEDING.
HE IS, AFTER ALL...
...A LEECH.

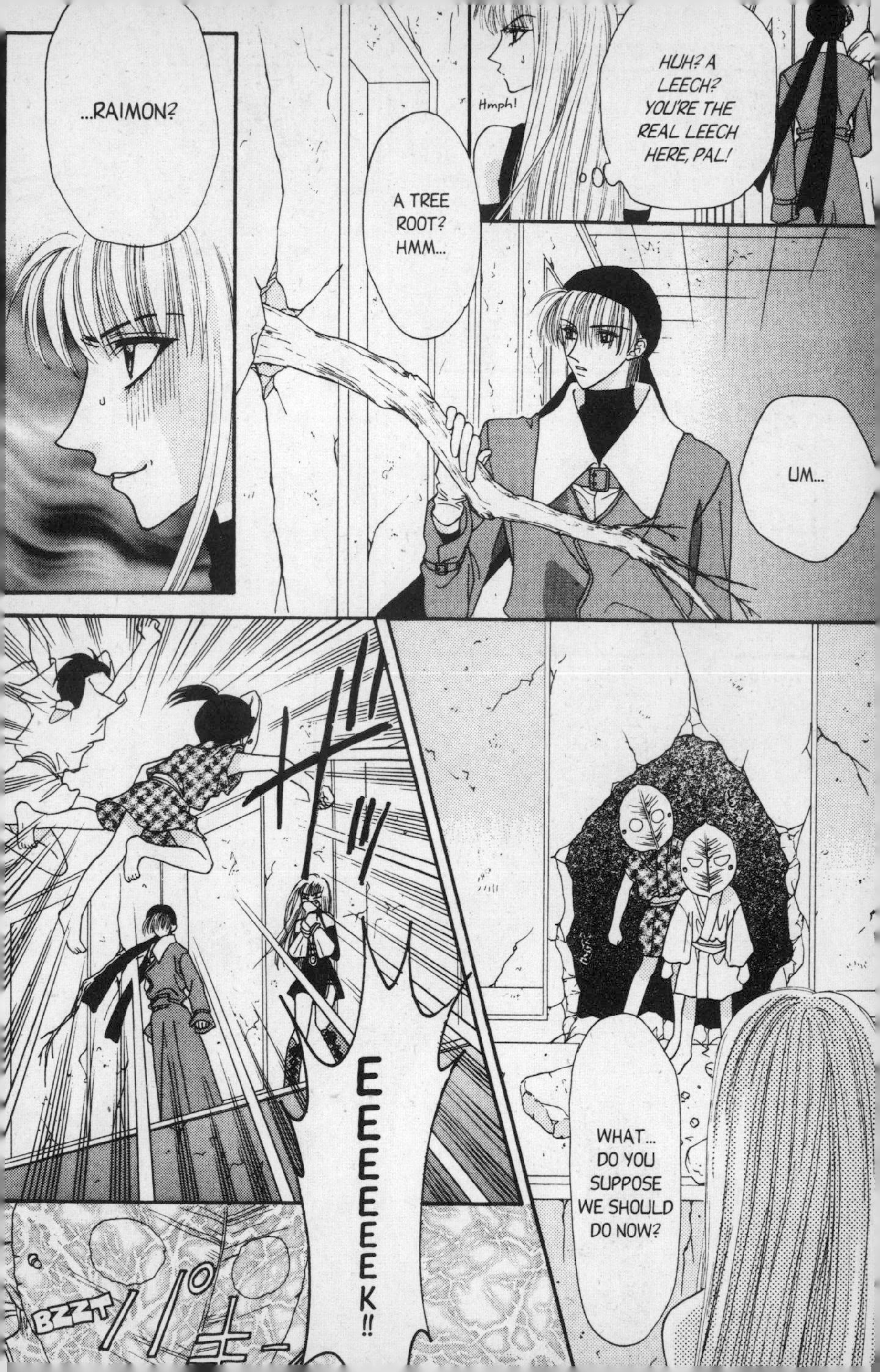
Hmph!
HUH? A LEECH? YOU'RE THE REAL LEECH HERE, PAL!
A TREE ROOT? HMM...
UM...
...RAIMON?
WHAT... DO YOU SUPPOSE WE SHOULD DO NOW?
EEEEEEK!!
BZZT

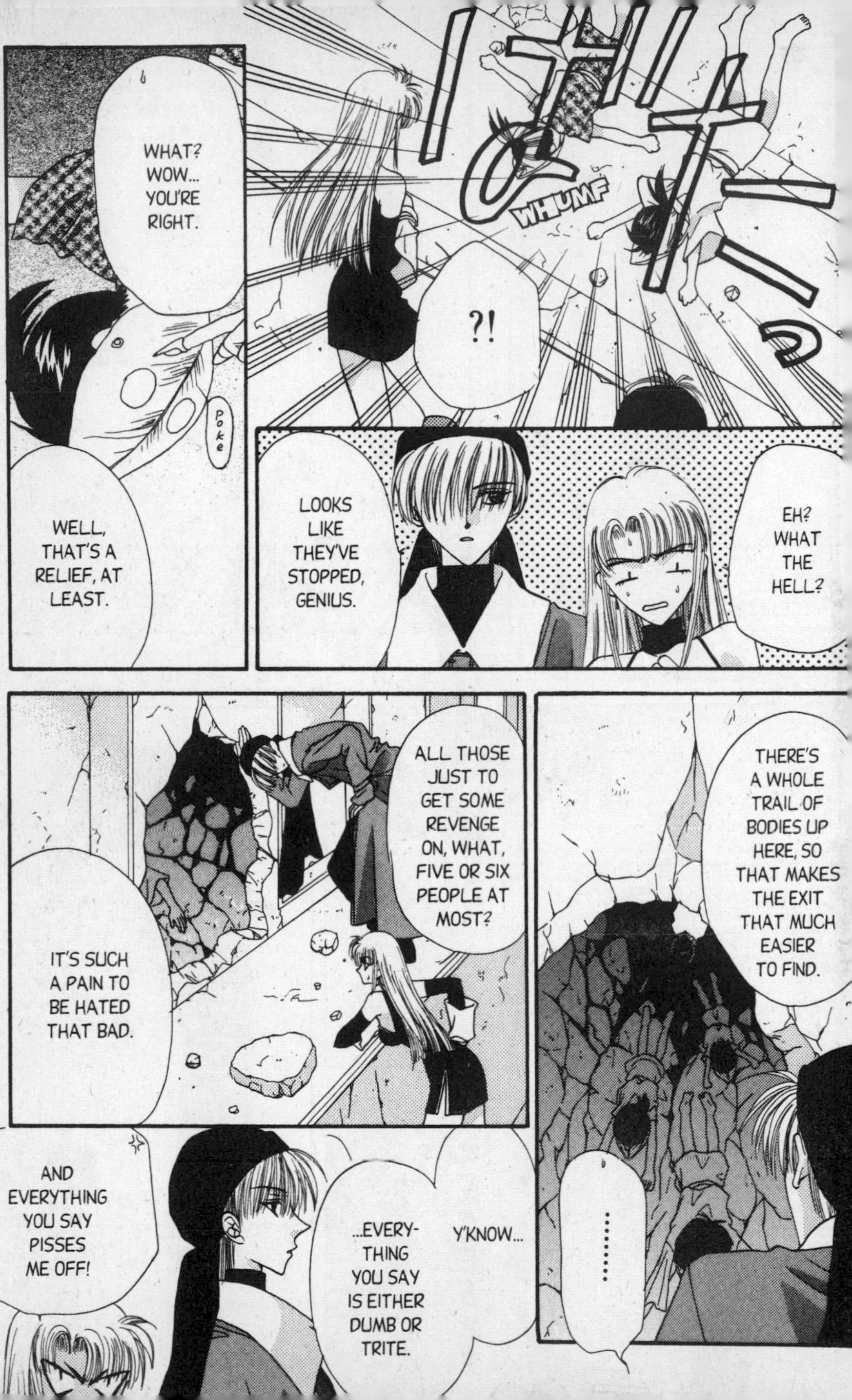
WHUMF
?!
EH? WHAT THE HELL?
LOOKS LIKE THEY'VE STOPPED, GENIUS.
WHAT? WOW... YOU'RE RIGHT.
Poke
WELL, THAT'S A RELIEF, AT LEAST.
THERE'S A WHOLE TRAIL OF BODIES UP HERE, SO THAT MAKES THE EXIT THAT MUCH EASIER TO FIND.
......
ALL THOSE JUST TO GET SOME REVENGE ON, WHAT, FIVE OR SIX PEOPLE AT MOST?
IT'S SUCH A PAIN TO BE HATED THAT BAD.
Y'KNOW...
...EVERY-THING YOU SAY IS EITHER DUMB OR TRITE.
AND EVERYTHING YOU SAY PISSES ME OFF!

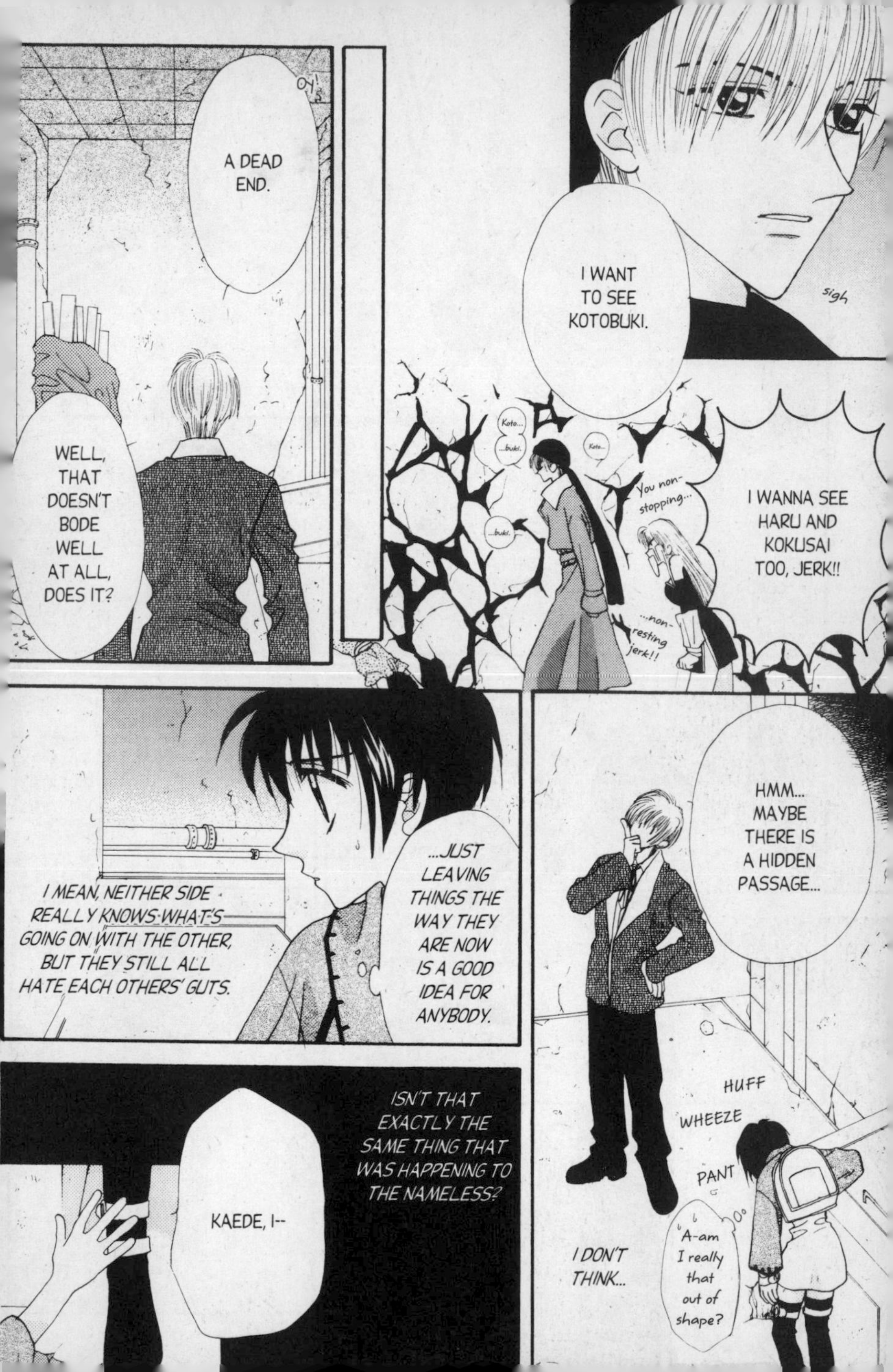
I WANT TO SEE KOTOBUKI.
sigh
I WANNA SEE HARU AND KOKUSAI TOO, JERK!!
Koto...
...buki.
Koto...
...buki.
You non-stopping...
...non-resting jerk!!
OY!
A DEAD END.
WELL, THAT DOESN'T BODE WELL AT ALL, DOES IT?
HMM... MAYBE THERE IS A HIDDEN PASSAGE...
HUFF
WHEEZE
PANT
A-am I really that out of shape?
I DON'T THINK...
...JUST LEAVING THINGS THE WAY THEY ARE NOW IS A GOOD IDEA FOR ANYBODY.
I MEAN, NEITHER SIDE REALLY KNOWS WHAT'S GOING ON WITH THE OTHER, BUT THEY STILL ALL HATE EACH OTHERS' GUTS.
ISN'T THAT EXACTLY THE SAME THING THAT WAS HAPPENING TO THE NAMELESS?
KAEDE, I--

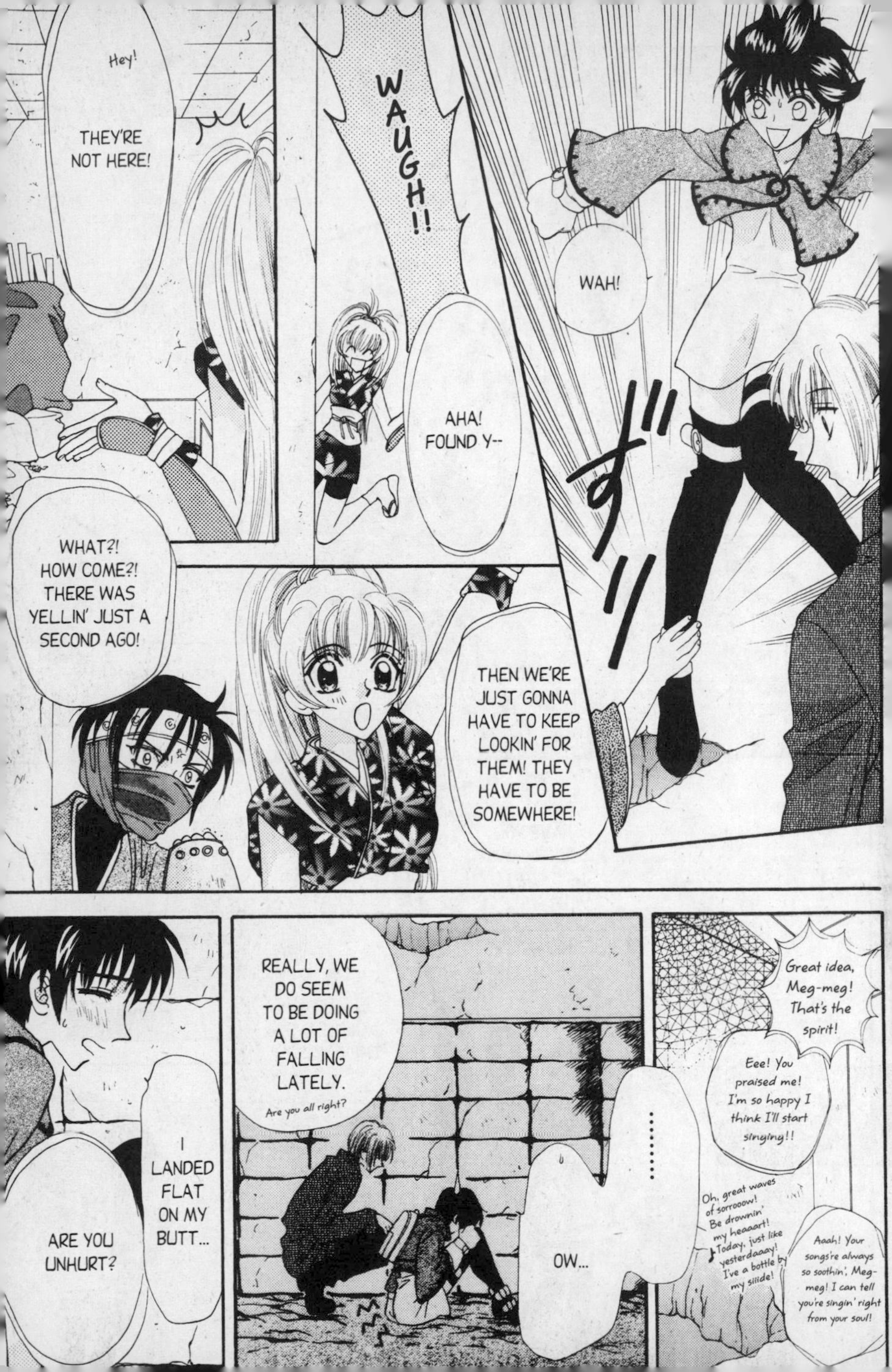
WAH!
ず
WAUGH!!
AHA! FOUND Y--
Hey!
THEY'RE NOT HERE!
WHAT?! HOW COME?! THERE WAS YELLIN' JUST A SECOND AGO!
THEN WE'RE JUST GONNA HAVE TO KEEP LOOKIN' FOR THEM! THEY HAVE TO BE SOMEWHERE!
Great idea, Meg-meg! That's the spirit!
Eee! You praised me! I'm so happy I think I'll start singing!!
Oh, great waves of sorrooow! Be drownin' my heaaart! Today, just like yesterdaaay! I've a bottle by my siiide!
Aaah! Your songs're always so soothin', Meg-meg! I can tell you're singin' right from your soul!
REALLY, WE DO SEEM TO BE DOING A LOT OF FALLING LATELY.
Are you all right?
......
OW...
I LANDED FLAT ON MY BUTT...
ARE YOU UNHURT?

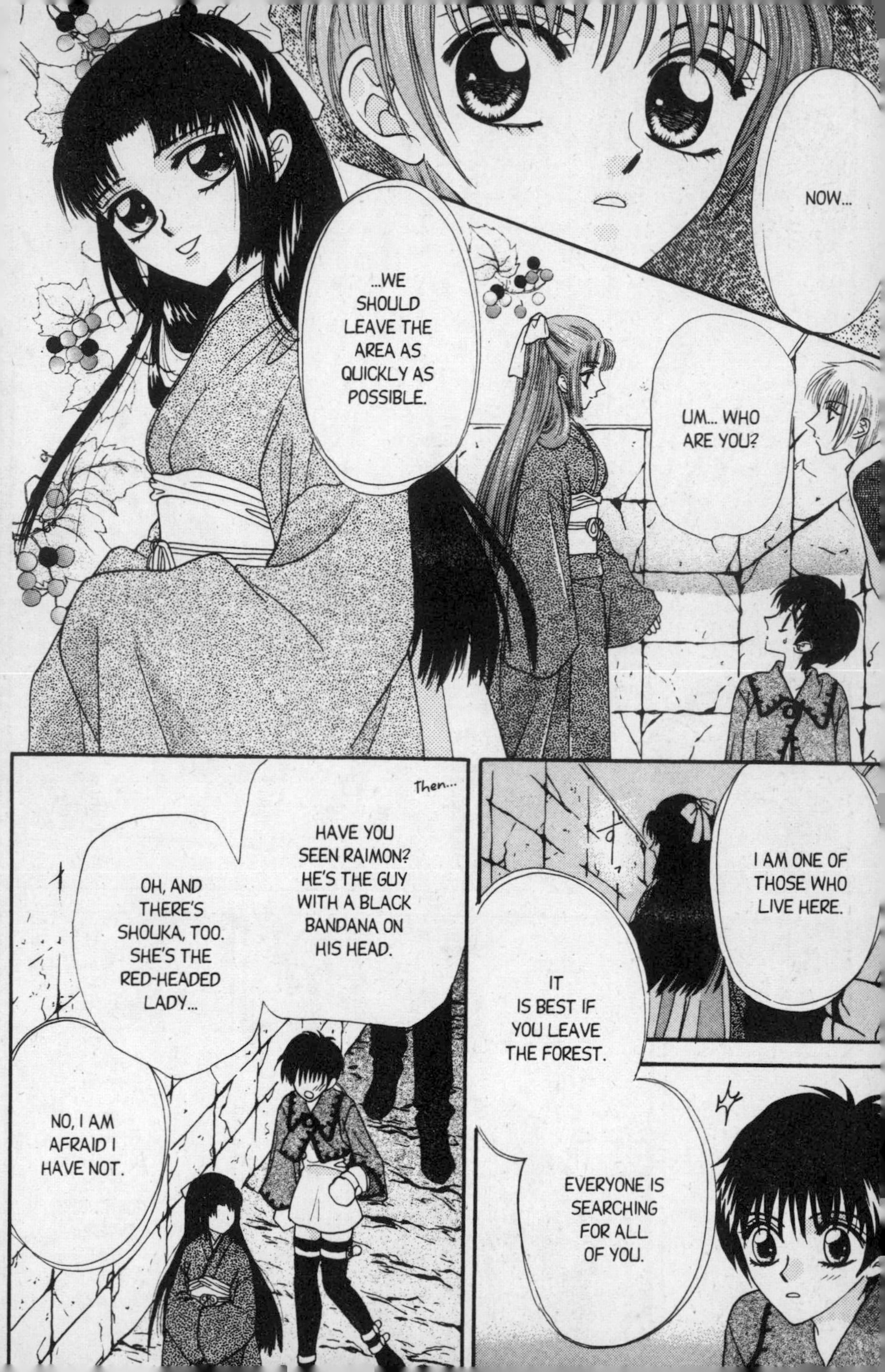
NOW...
...WE SHOULD LEAVE THE AREA AS QUICKLY AS POSSIBLE.
UM... WHO ARE YOU?
I AM ONE OF THOSE WHO LIVE HERE.
IT IS BEST IF YOU LEAVE THE FOREST.
EVERYONE IS SEARCHING FOR ALL OF YOU.
Then...
HAVE YOU SEEN RAIMON? HE'S THE GUY WITH A BLACK BANDANA ON HIS HEAD.
OH, AND THERE'S SHOUKA, TOO. SHE'S THE RED-HEADED LADY...
NO, I AM AFRAID I HAVE NOT.

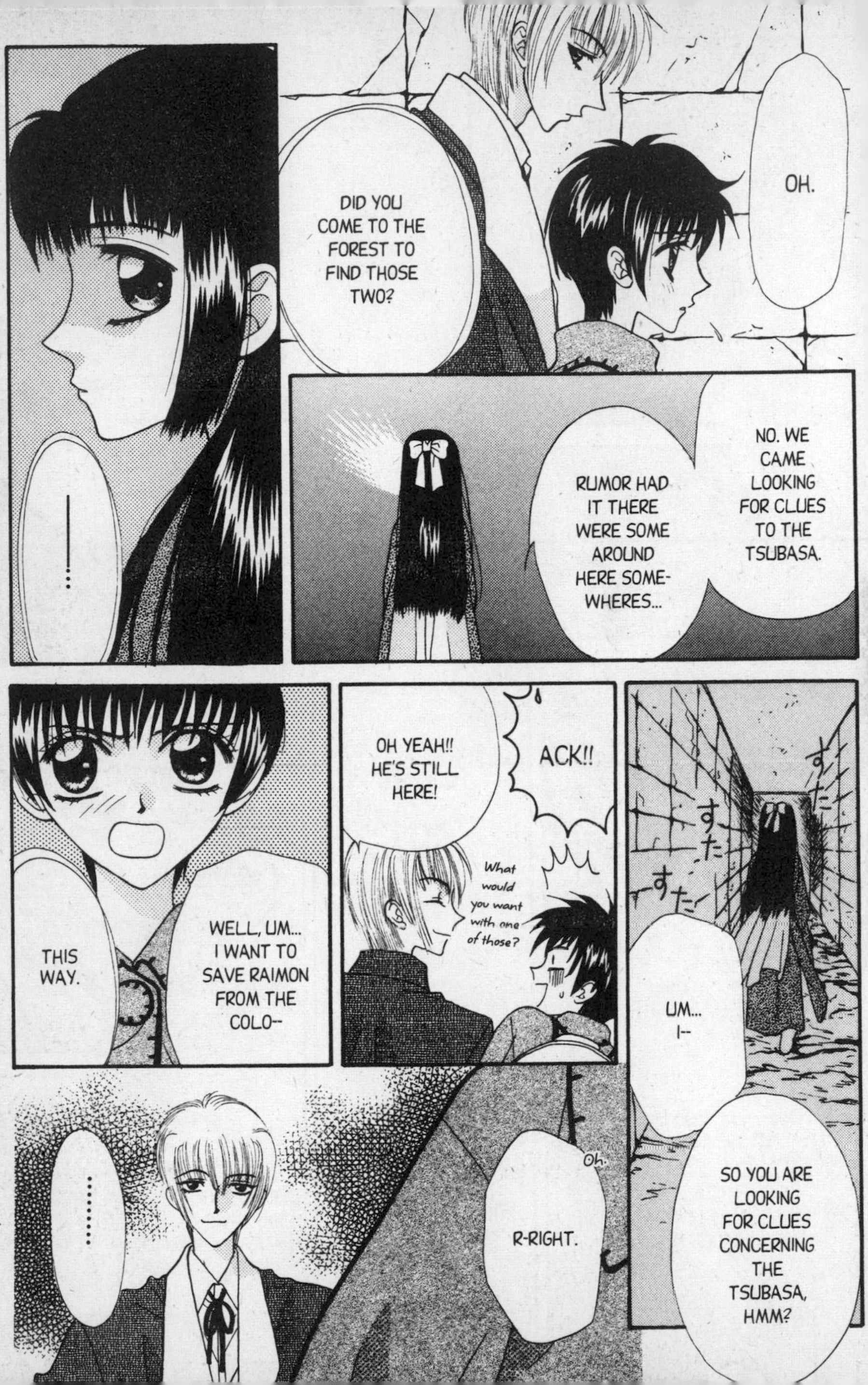
OH.
DID YOU COME TO THE FOREST TO FIND THOSE TWO?
NO. WE CAME LOOKING FOR CLUES TO THE TSUBASA.
RUMOR HAD IT THERE WERE SOME AROUND HERE SOME-WHERES...
......
すた
すた
すた
UM... I--
SO YOU ARE LOOKING FOR CLUES CONCERNING THE TSUBASA, HMM?
ACK!!
OH YEAH!! HE'S STILL HERE!
What would you want with one of those?
WELL, UM... I WANT TO SAVE RAIMON FROM THE COLO--
THIS WAY.
Oh.
R-RIGHT.
......

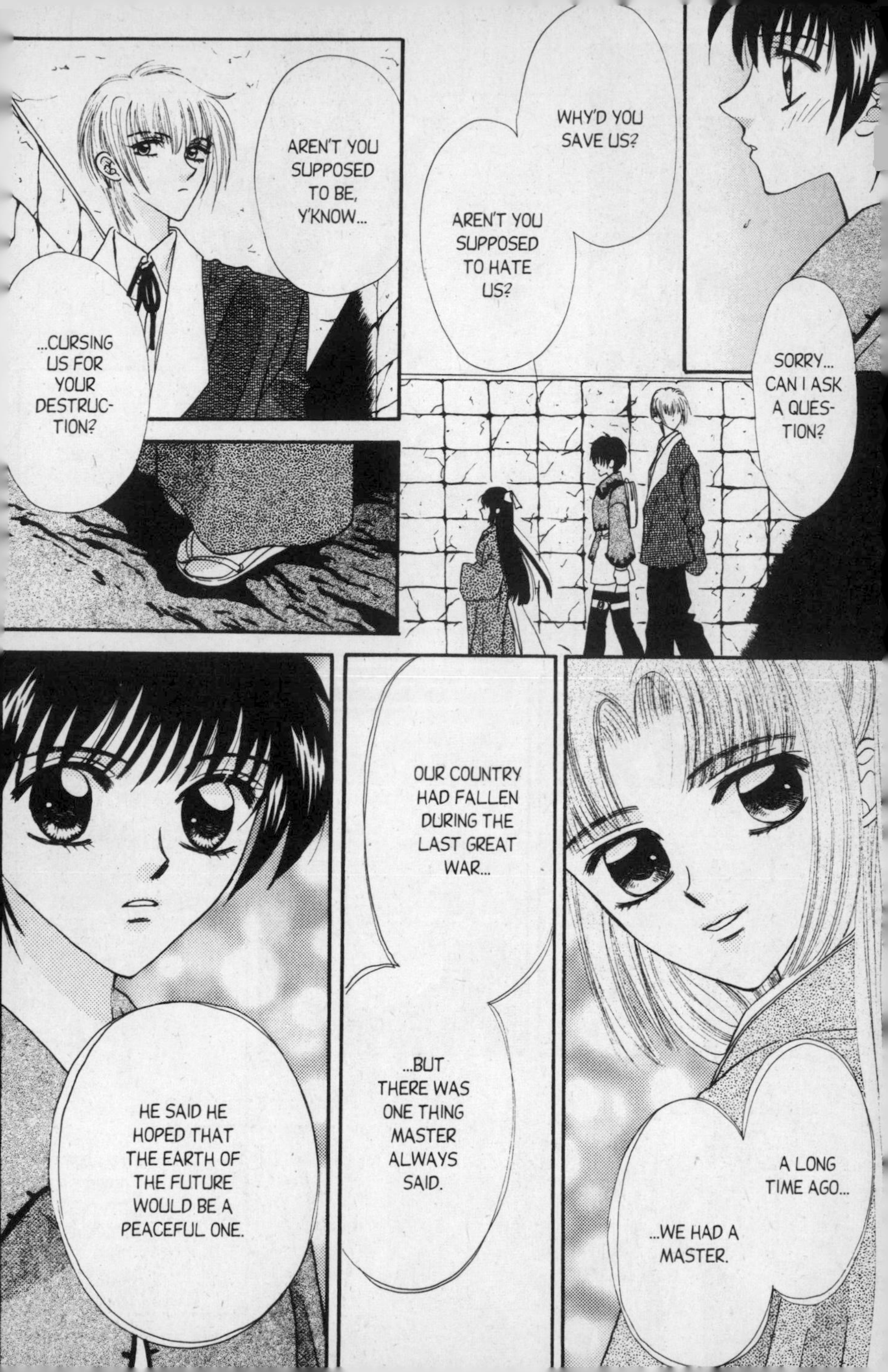
SORRY... CAN I ASK A QUESTION?
WHY'D YOU SAVE US?
AREN'T YOU SUPPOSED TO HATE US?
AREN'T YOU SUPPOSED TO BE, Y'KNOW...
...CURSING US FOR YOUR DESTRUCTION?
A LONG TIME AGO...
...WE HAD A MASTER.
OUR COUNTRY HAD FALLEN DURING THE LAST GREAT WAR...
...BUT THERE WAS ONE THING MASTER ALWAYS SAID.
HE SAID HE HOPED THAT THE EARTH OF THE FUTURE WOULD BE A PEACEFUL ONE.

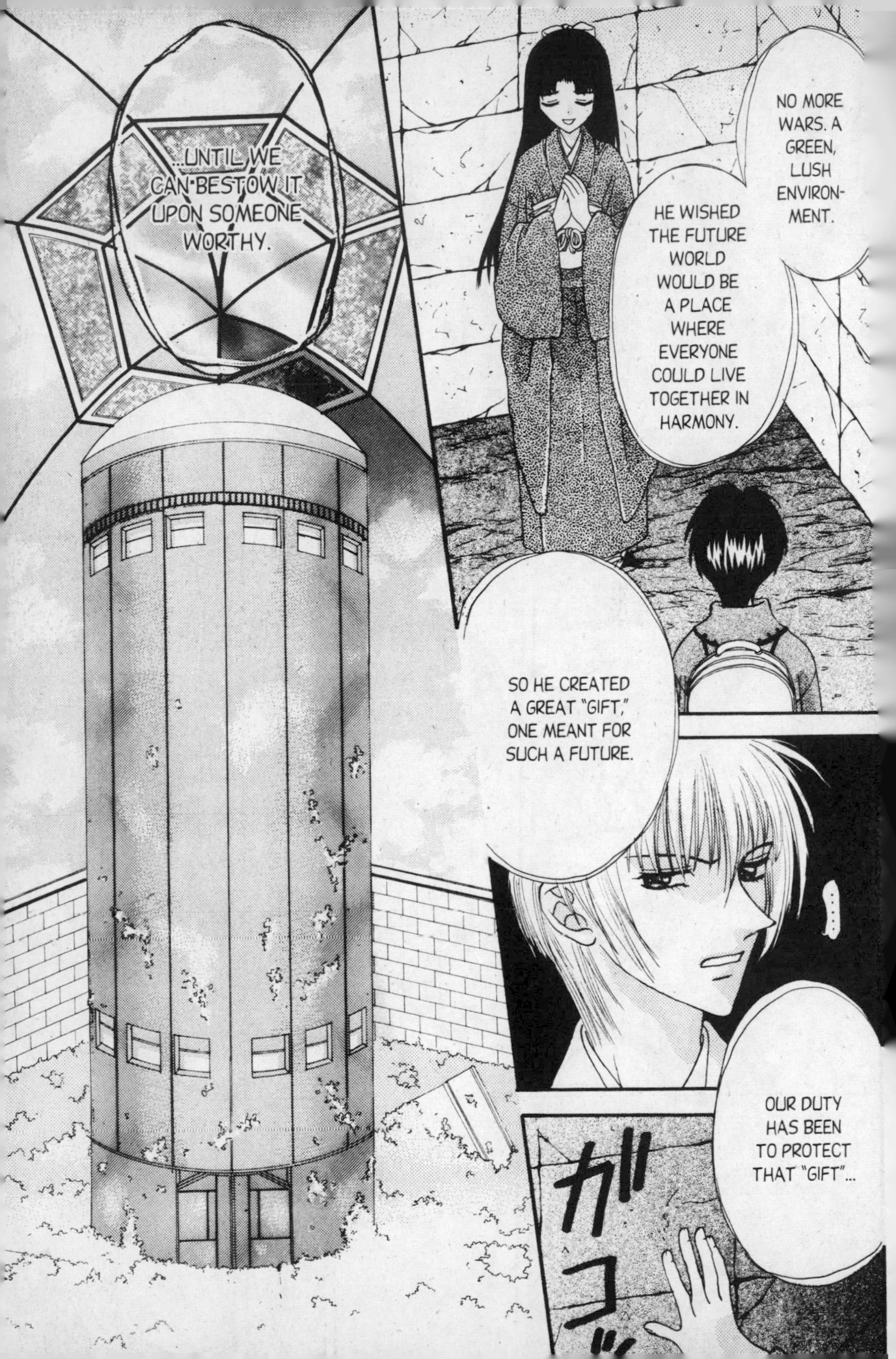
NO MORE WARS. A GREEN, LUSH ENVIRON-MENT.
HE WISHED THE FUTURE WORLD WOULD BE A PLACE WHERE EVERYONE COULD LIVE TOGETHER IN HARMONY.
SO HE CREATED A GREAT "GIFT," ONE MEANT FOR SUCH A FUTURE.
...
OUR DUTY HAS BEEN TO PROTECT THAT "GIFT"...
ガゴ
...UNTIL WE CAN BESTOW IT UPON SOMEONE WORTHY.

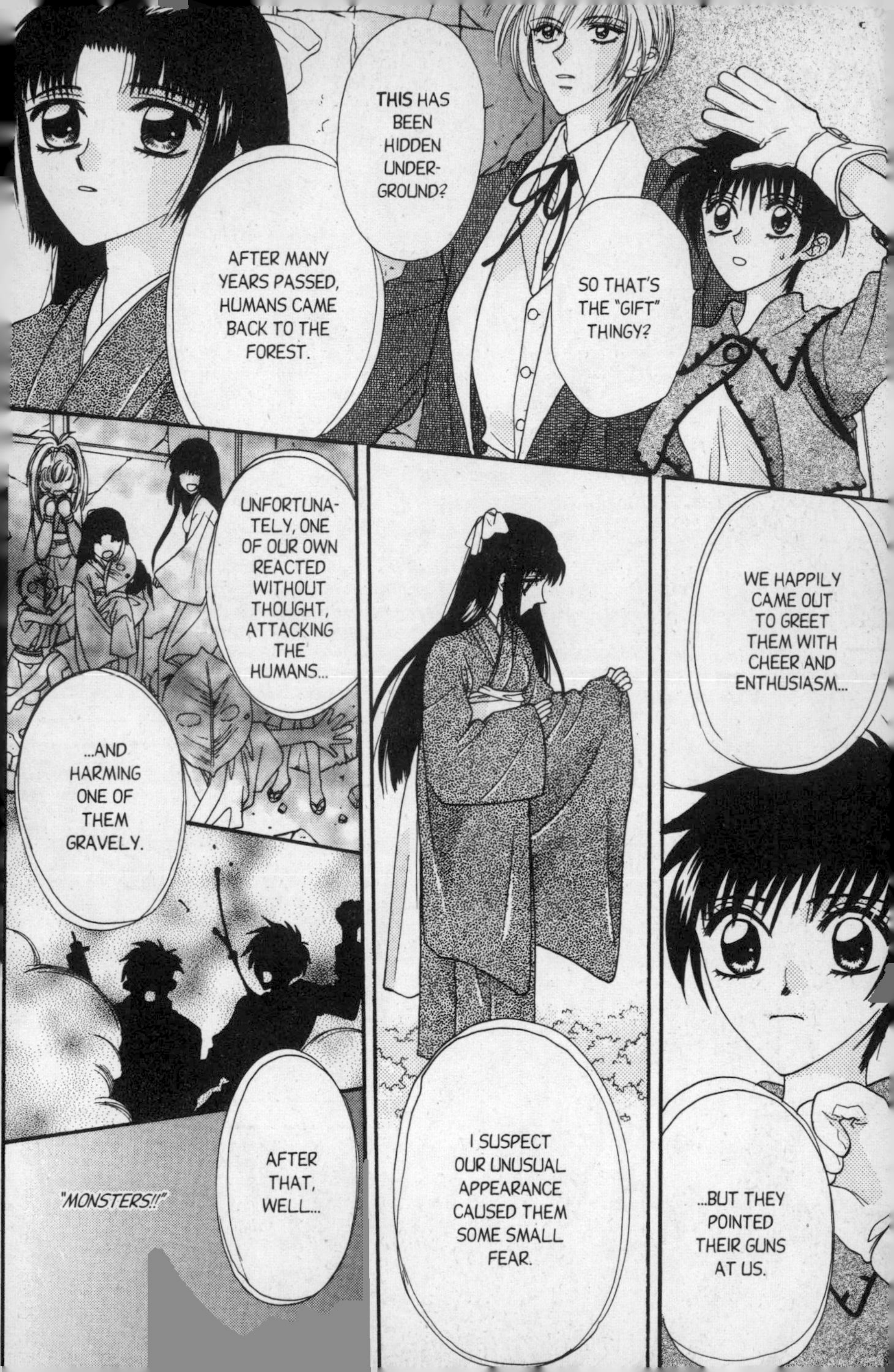
SO THAT'S THE "GIFT" THINGY?
THIS HAS BEEN HIDDEN UNDERGROUND?
AFTER MANY YEARS PASSED, HUMANS CAME BACK TO THE FOREST.
WE HAPPILY CAME OUT TO GREET THEM WITH CHEER AND ENTHUSIASM...
...BUT THEY POINTED THEIR GUNS AT US.
I SUSPECT OUR UNUSUAL APPEARANCE CAUSED THEM SOME SMALL FEAR.
UNFORTUNATELY, ONE OF OUR OWN REACTED WITHOUT THOUGHT, ATTACKING THE HUMANS...
...AND HARMING ONE OF THEM GRAVELY.
AFTER THAT, WELL...
"MONSTERS!!"

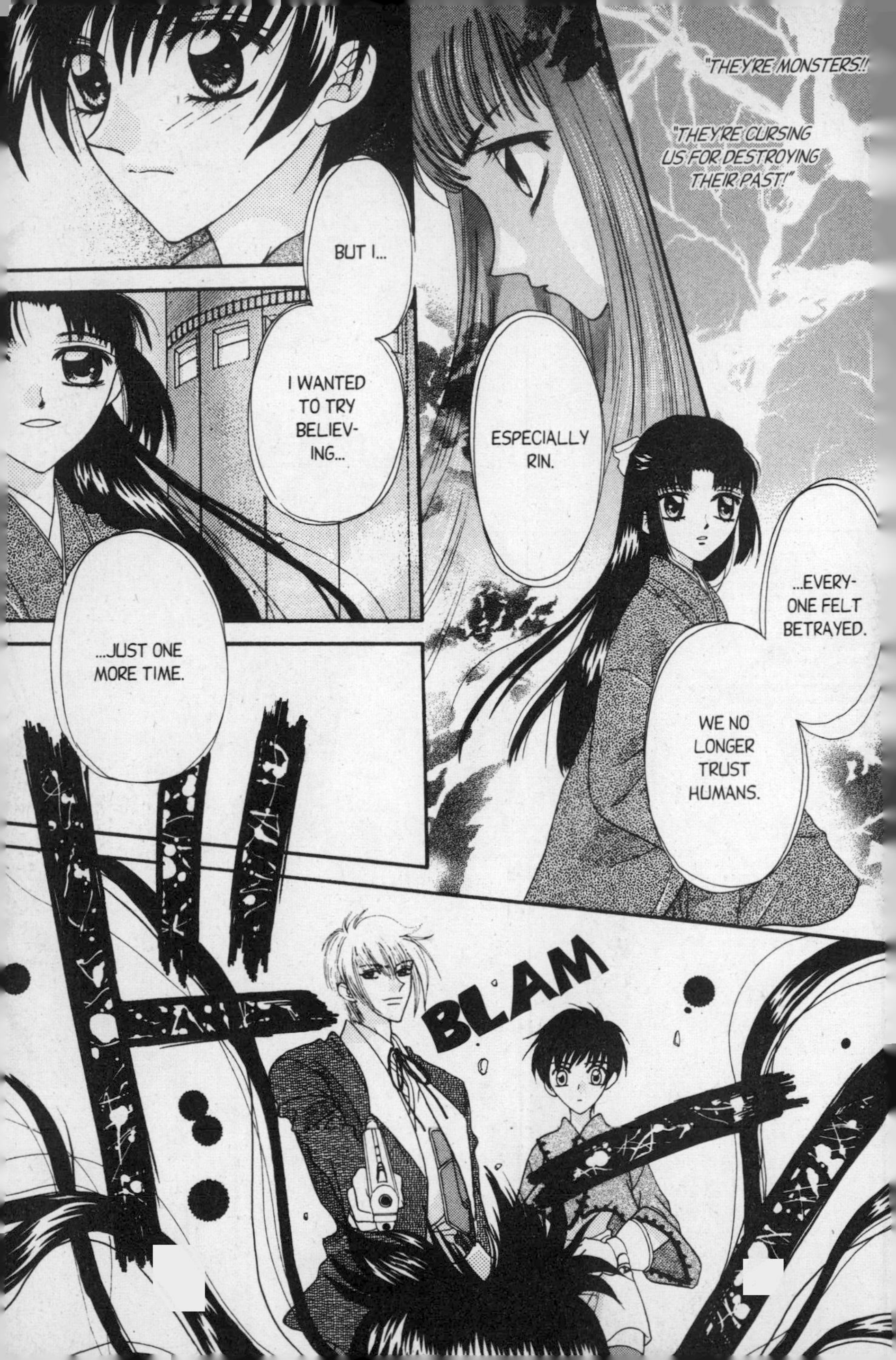
"THEY'RE MONSTERS!!
"THEY'RE CURSING US FOR DESTROYING THEIR PAST!"
ESPECIALLY RIN.
...EVERY-ONE FELT BETRAYED.
WE NO LONGER TRUST HUMANS.
BUT I...
I WANTED TO TRY BELIEV-ING...
...JUST ONE MORE TIME.
BLAM

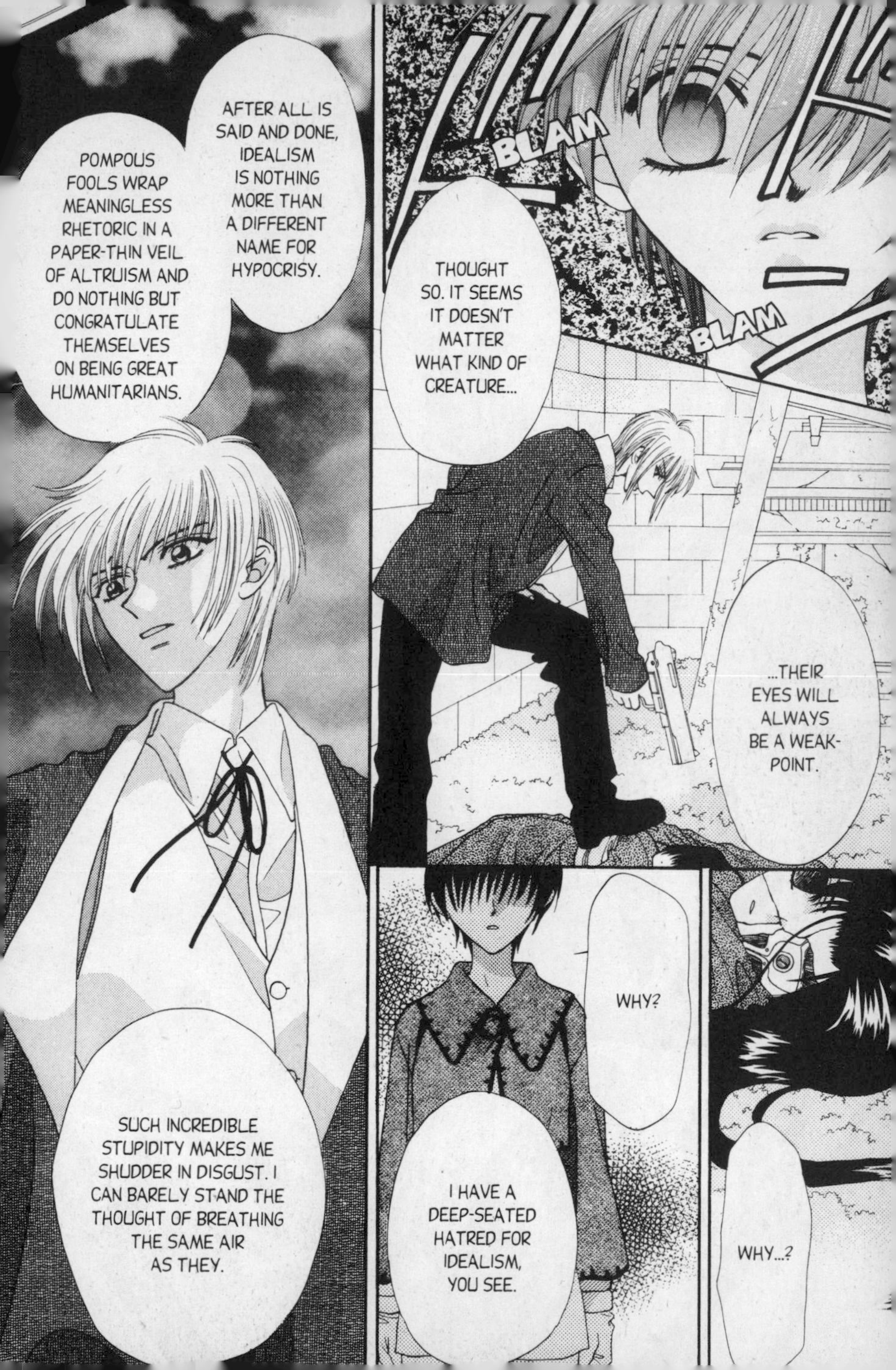
BLAM
BLAM
THOUGHT SO. IT SEEMS IT DOESN'T MATTER WHAT KIND OF CREATURE...
...THEIR EYES WILL ALWAYS BE A WEAK-POINT.
WHY...?
WHY?
I HAVE A DEEP-SEATED HATRED FOR IDEALISM, YOU SEE.
AFTER ALL IS SAID AND DONE, IDEALISM IS NOTHING MORE THAN A DIFFERENT NAME FOR HYPOCRISY.
POMPOUS FOOLS WRAP MEANINGLESS RHETORIC IN A PAPER-THIN VEIL OF ALTRUISM AND DO NOTHING BUT CONGRATULATE THEMSELVES ON BEING GREAT HUMANITARIANS.
SUCH INCREDIBLE STUPIDITY MAKES ME SHUDDER IN DISGUST. I CAN BARELY STAND THE THOUGHT OF BREATHING THE SAME AIR AS THEY.

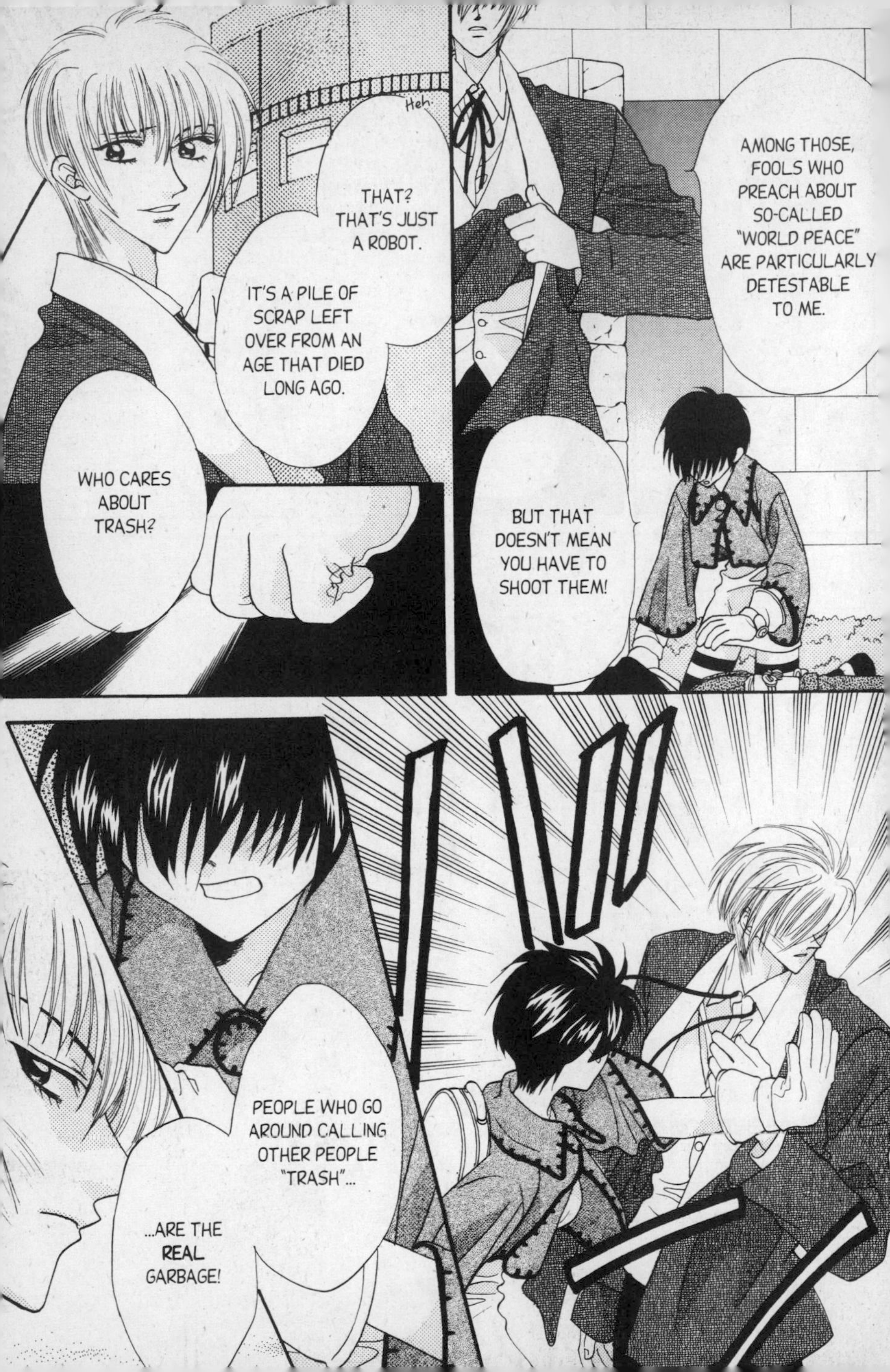
AMONG THOSE, FOOLS WHO PREACH ABOUT SO-CALLED "WORLD PEACE" ARE PARTICULARLY DETESTABLE TO ME.
BUT THAT DOESN'T MEAN YOU HAVE TO SHOOT THEM!
Heh.
THAT? THAT'S JUST A ROBOT.
IT'S A PILE OF SCRAP LEFT OVER FROM AN AGE THAT DIED LONG AGO.
WHO CARES ABOUT TRASH?
PEOPLE WHO GO AROUND CALLING OTHER PEOPLE "TRASH"...
...ARE THE **REAL** GARBAGE!

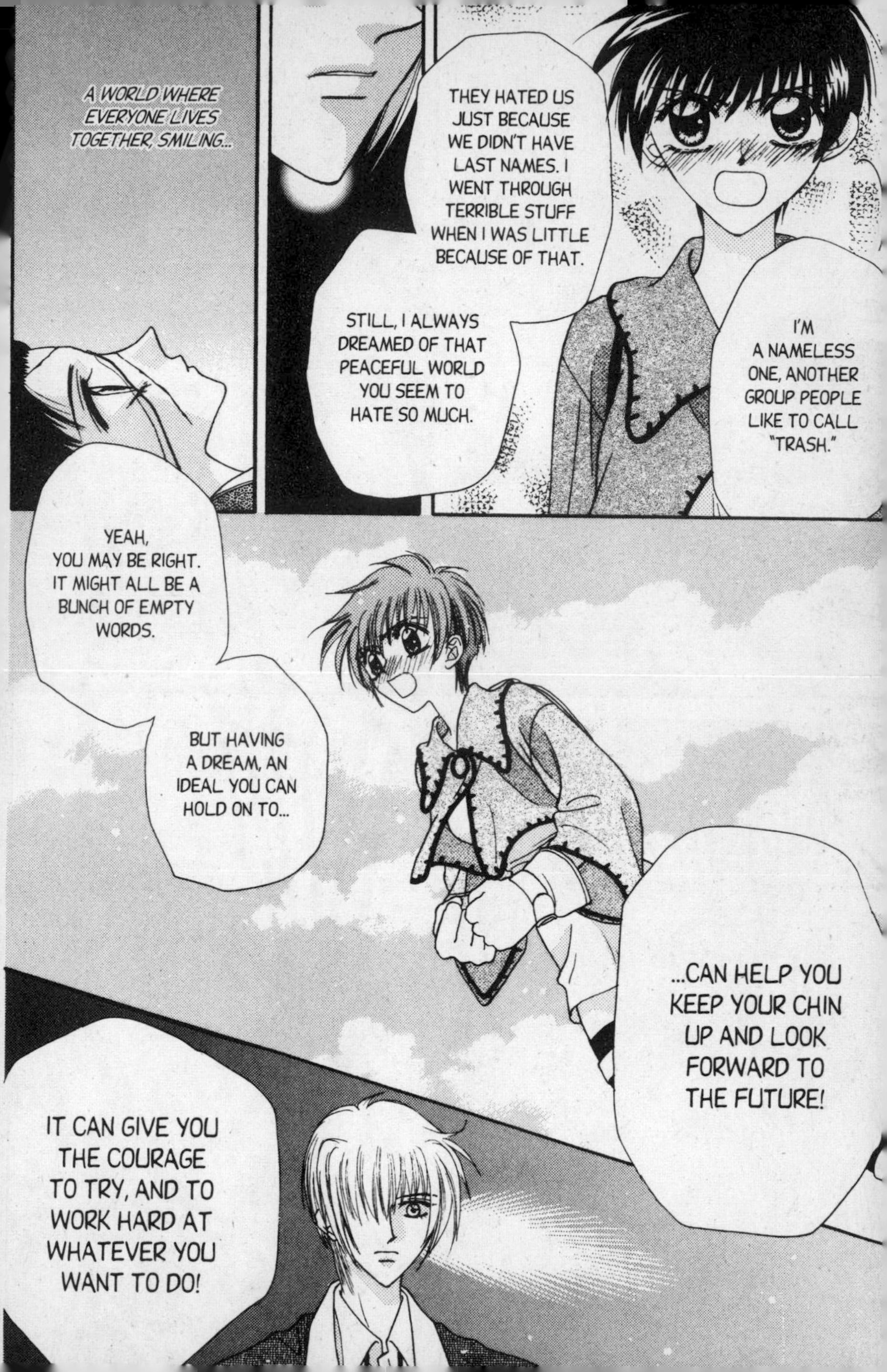
I'M A NAMELESS ONE, ANOTHER GROUP PEOPLE LIKE TO CALL "TRASH."
THEY HATED US JUST BECAUSE WE DIDN'T HAVE LAST NAMES. I WENT THROUGH TERRIBLE STUFF WHEN I WAS LITTLE BECAUSE OF THAT.
STILL, I ALWAYS DREAMED OF THAT PEACEFUL WORLD YOU SEEM TO HATE SO MUCH.
A WORLD WHERE EVERYONE LIVES TOGETHER, SMILING...
YEAH, YOU MAY BE RIGHT. IT MIGHT ALL BE A BUNCH OF EMPTY WORDS.
BUT HAVING A DREAM, AN IDEAL YOU CAN HOLD ON TO...
...CAN HELP YOU KEEP YOUR CHIN UP AND LOOK FORWARD TO THE FUTURE!
IT CAN GIVE YOU THE COURAGE TO TRY, AND TO WORK HARD AT WHATEVER YOU WANT TO DO!

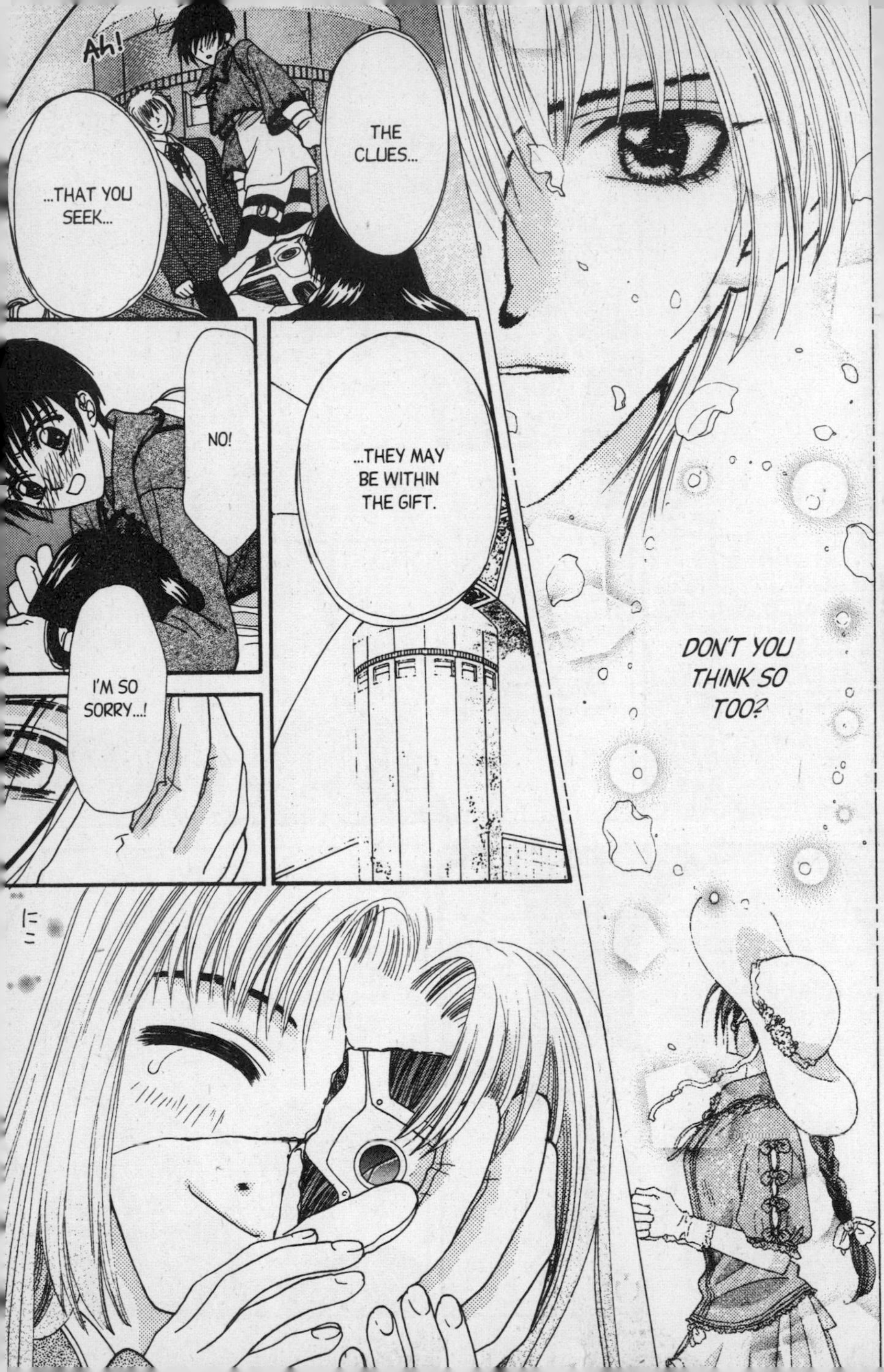
DON'T YOU THINK SO TOO?
Ah!
THE CLUES...
...THAT YOU SEEK...
...THEY MAY BE WITHIN THE GIFT.
NO!
I'M SO SORRY...!

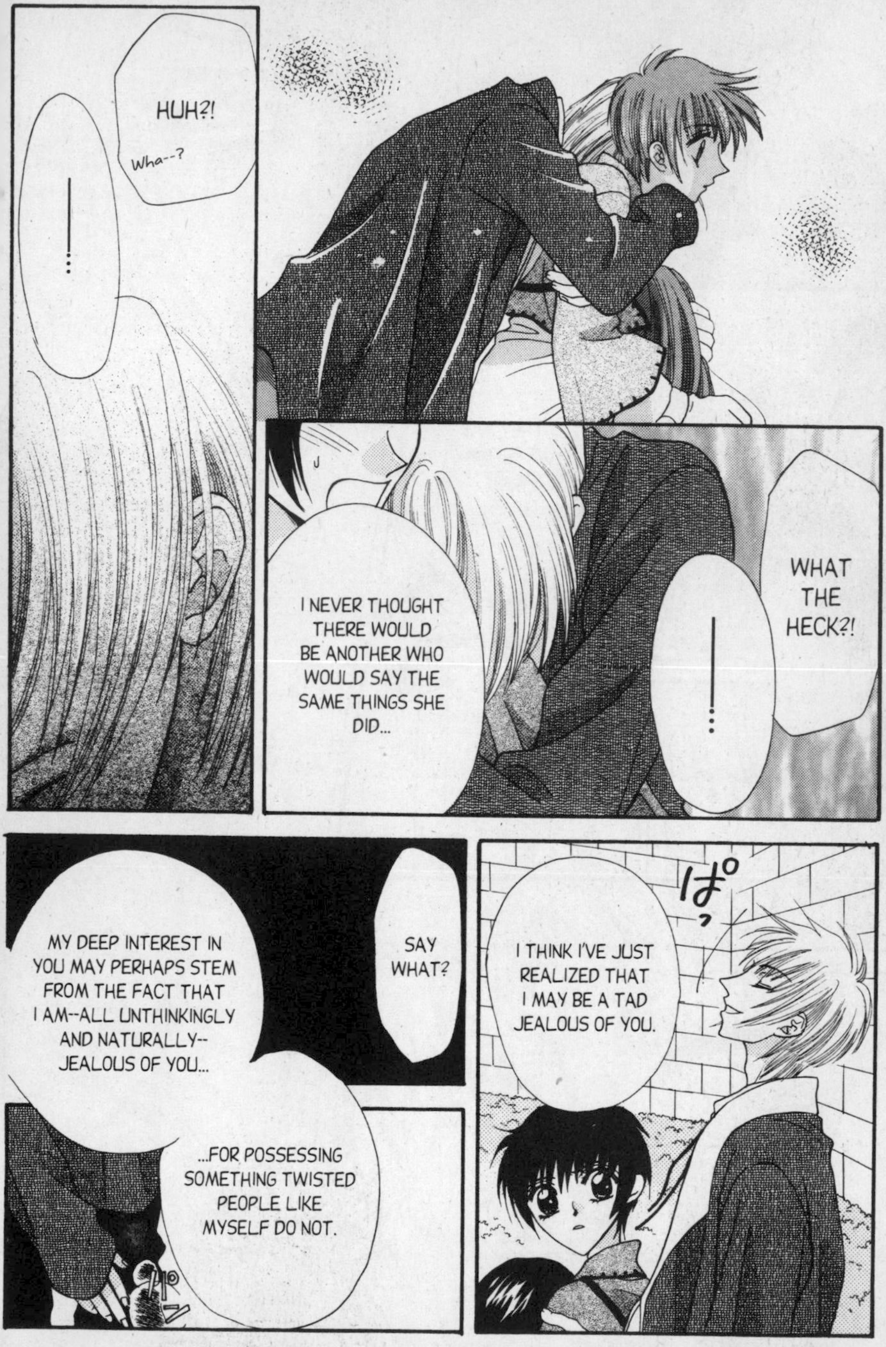
WHAT THE HECK?!
—…
I NEVER THOUGHT THERE WOULD BE ANOTHER WHO WOULD SAY THE SAME THINGS SHE DID...
HUH?!
Wha--?
—…
ぱっ
I THINK I'VE JUST REALIZED THAT I MAY BE A TAD JEALOUS OF YOU.
SAY WHAT?
MY DEEP INTEREST IN YOU MAY PERHAPS STEM FROM THE FACT THAT I AM--ALL UNTHINKINGLY AND NATURALLY-- JEALOUS OF YOU...
...FOR POSSESSING SOMETHING TWISTED PEOPLE LIKE MYSELF DO NOT.

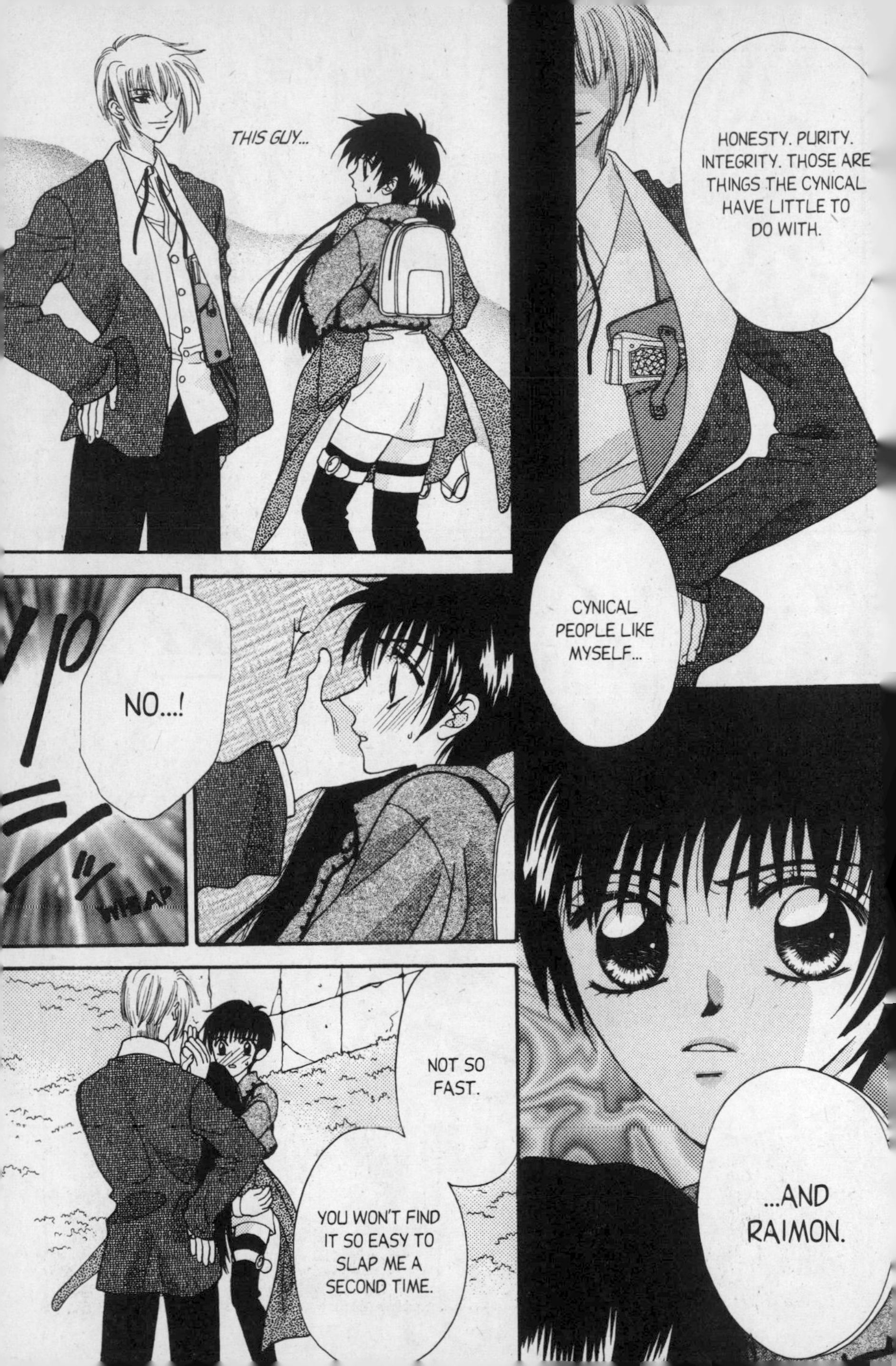

HONESTY. PURITY. INTEGRITY. THOSE ARE THINGS THE CYNICAL HAVE LITTLE TO DO WITH.
CYNICAL PEOPLE LIKE MYSELF...
...AND RAIMON.
THIS GUY...
NO...!
WHAP
NOT SO FAST.
YOU WON'T FIND IT SO EASY TO SLAP ME A SECOND TIME.

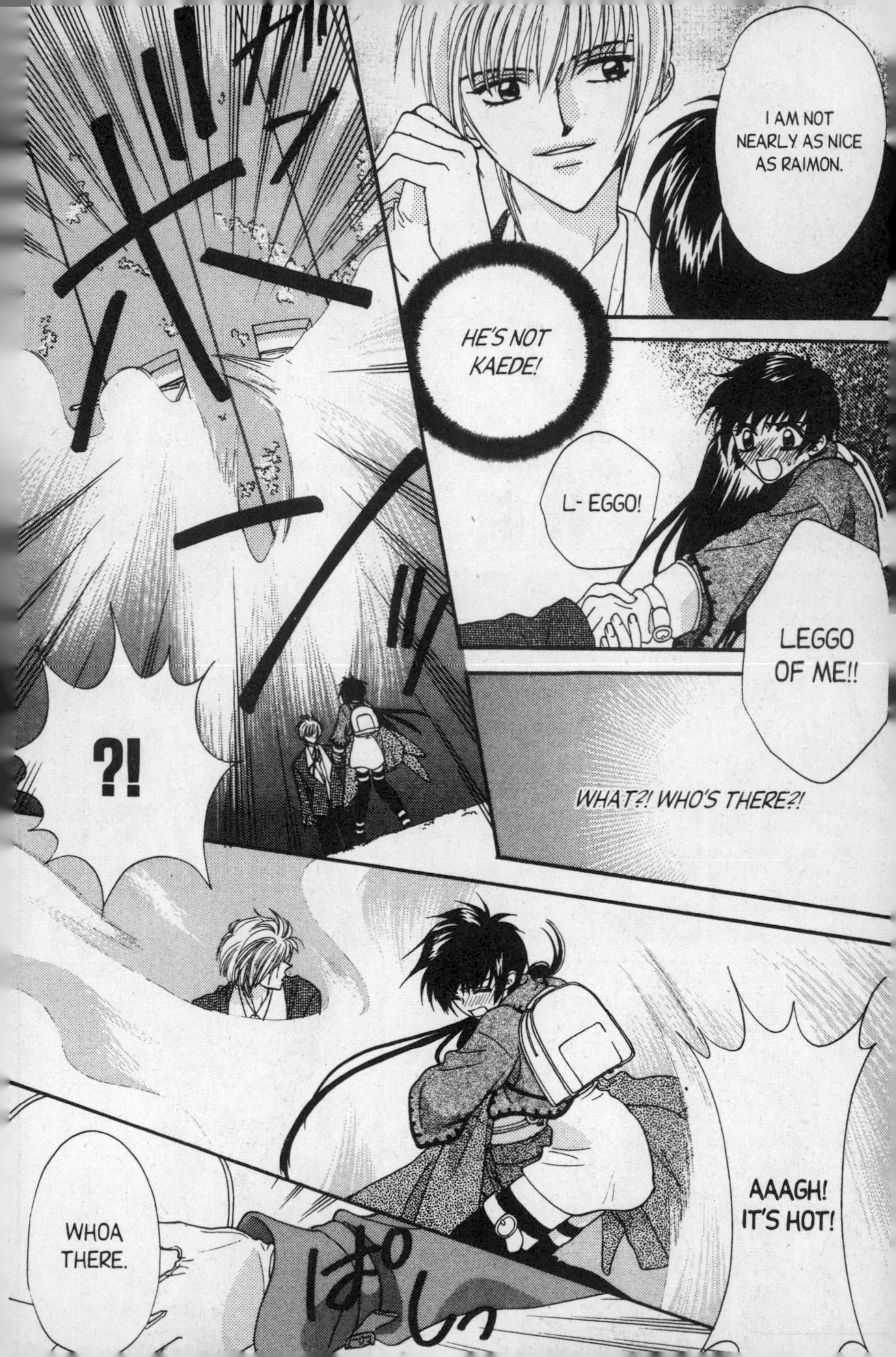
I AM NOT NEARLY AS NICE AS RAIMON.
HE'S NOT KAEDE!
L- EGGO!
LEGGO OF ME!!
WHAT?! WHO'S THERE?!
?!
AAAGH! IT'S HOT!
WHOA THERE.
ぱしっ

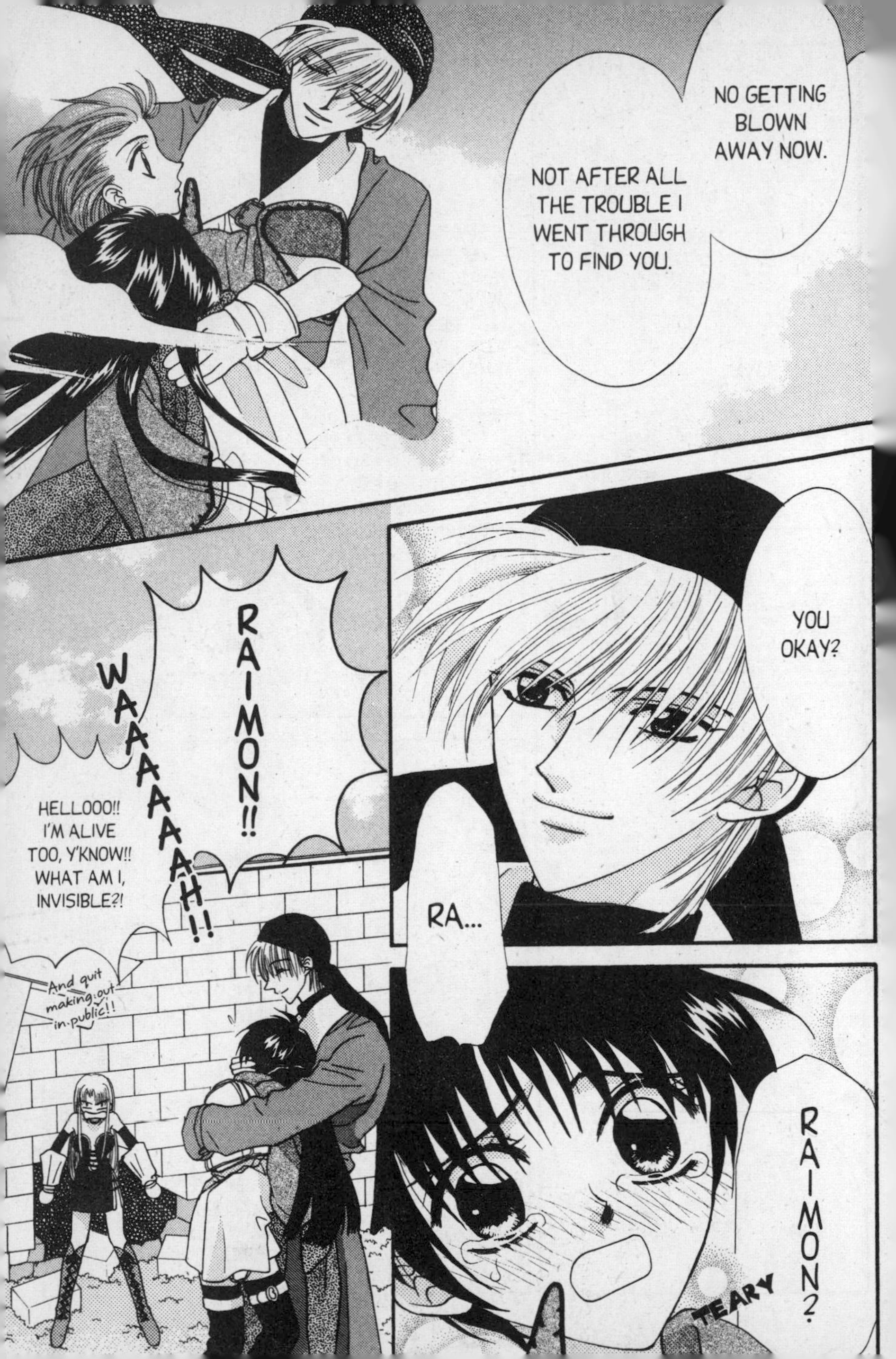
NO GETTING BLOWN AWAY NOW.
NOT AFTER ALL THE TROUBLE I WENT THROUGH TO FIND YOU.
YOU OKAY?
RA...
RAIMON?
TEARY
RAIMON!!
WAAAAAAAH!!
HELLOOO!! I'M ALIVE TOO, Y'KNOW!! WHAT AM I, INVISIBLE?!
And quit making out in public!!

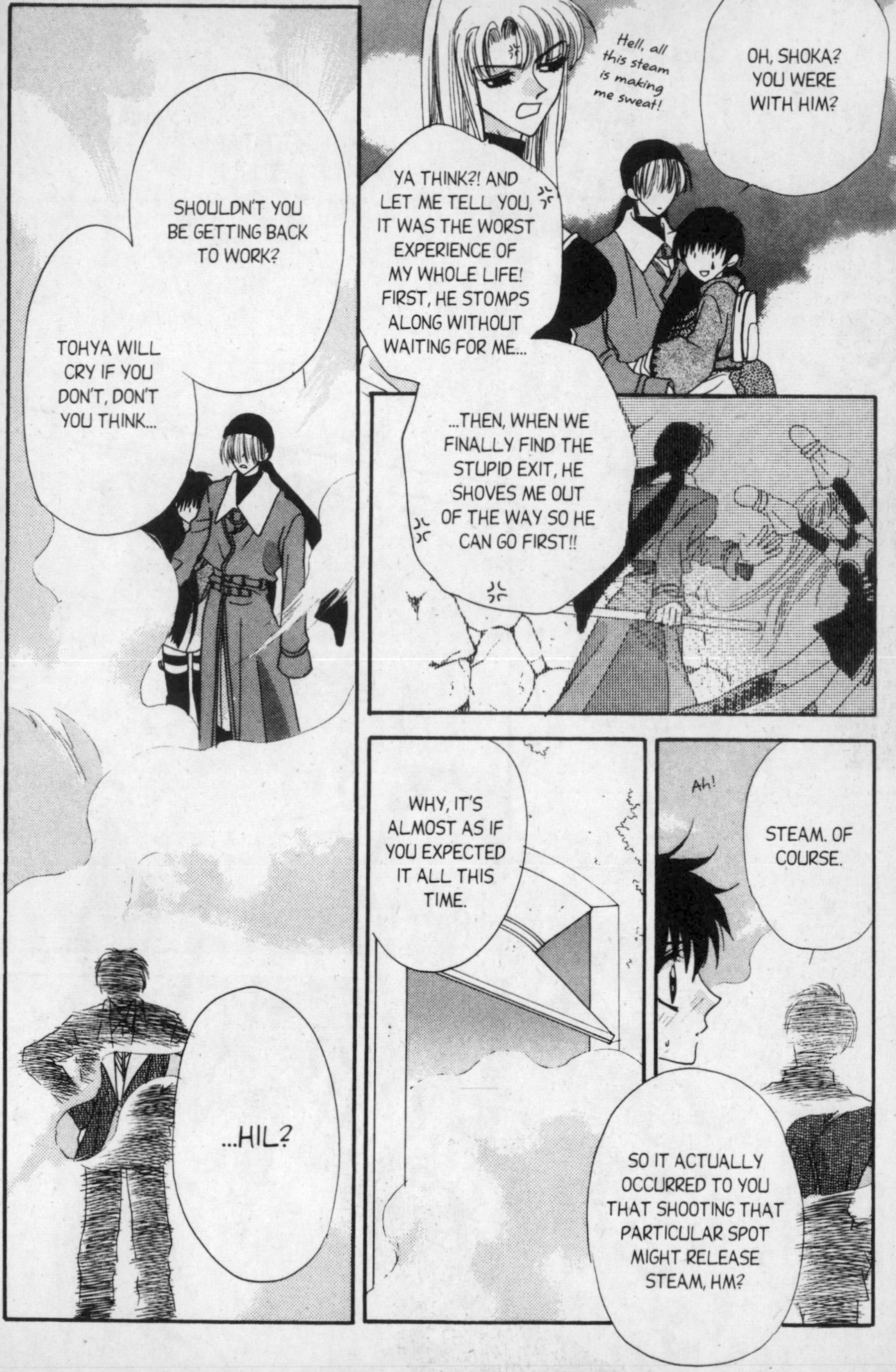
OH, SHOKA? YOU WERE WITH HIM?
Hell, all this steam is making me sweat!
YA THINK?! AND LET ME TELL YOU, IT WAS THE WORST EXPERIENCE OF MY WHOLE LIFE! FIRST, HE STOMPS ALONG WITHOUT WAITING FOR ME...
...THEN, WHEN WE FINALLY FIND THE STUPID EXIT, HE SHOVES ME OUT OF THE WAY SO HE CAN GO FIRST!!
Ah!
STEAM. OF COURSE.
SO IT ACTUALLY OCCURRED TO YOU THAT SHOOTING THAT PARTICULAR SPOT MIGHT RELEASE STEAM, HM?
WHY, IT'S ALMOST AS IF YOU EXPECTED IT ALL THIS TIME.
SHOULDN'T YOU BE GETTING BACK TO WORK?
TOHYA WILL CRY IF YOU DON'T, DON'T YOU THINK...
...HIL?

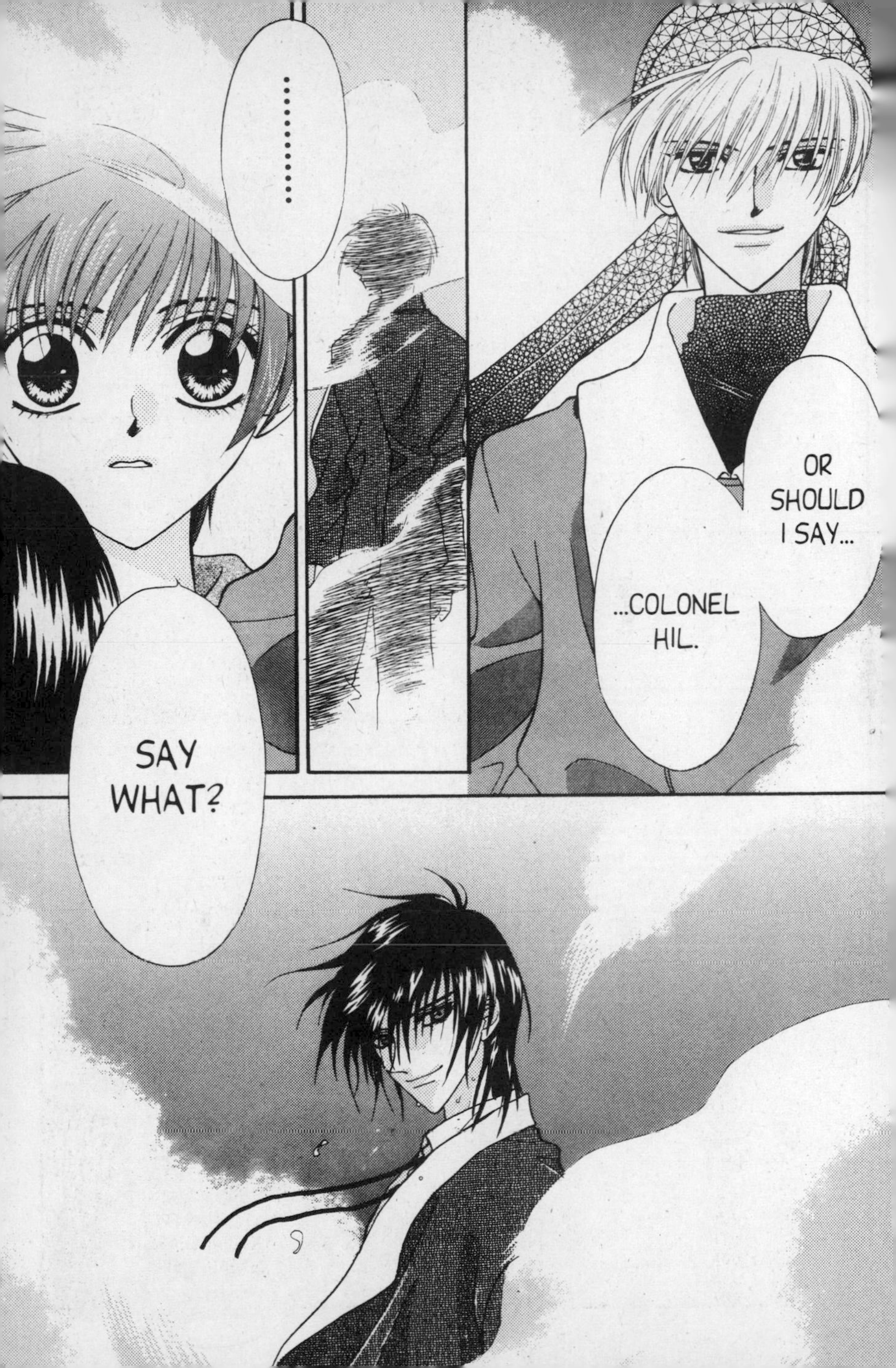
OR SHOULD I SAY...
...COLONEL HIL.
....
SAY WHAT?

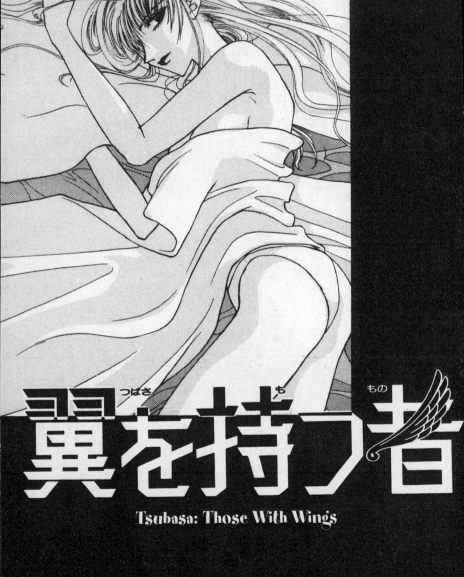

翼を持つ者

Tsubasa: Those With Wings

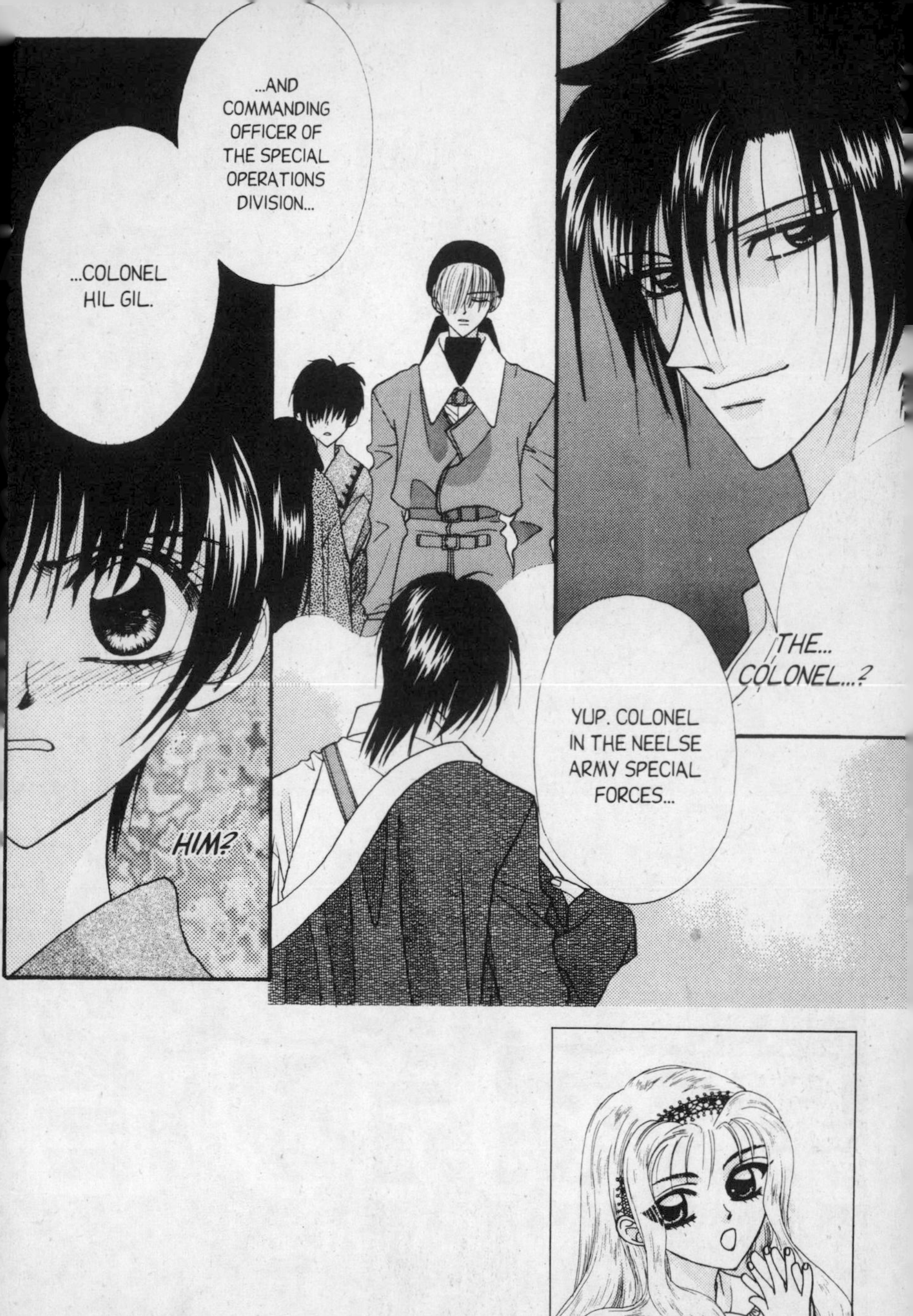
THE... COLONEL...?
YUP. COLONEL IN THE NEELSE ARMY SPECIAL FORCES...
...AND COMMANDING OFFICER OF THE SPECIAL OPERATIONS DIVISION...
...COLONEL HIL GIL.
HIM?

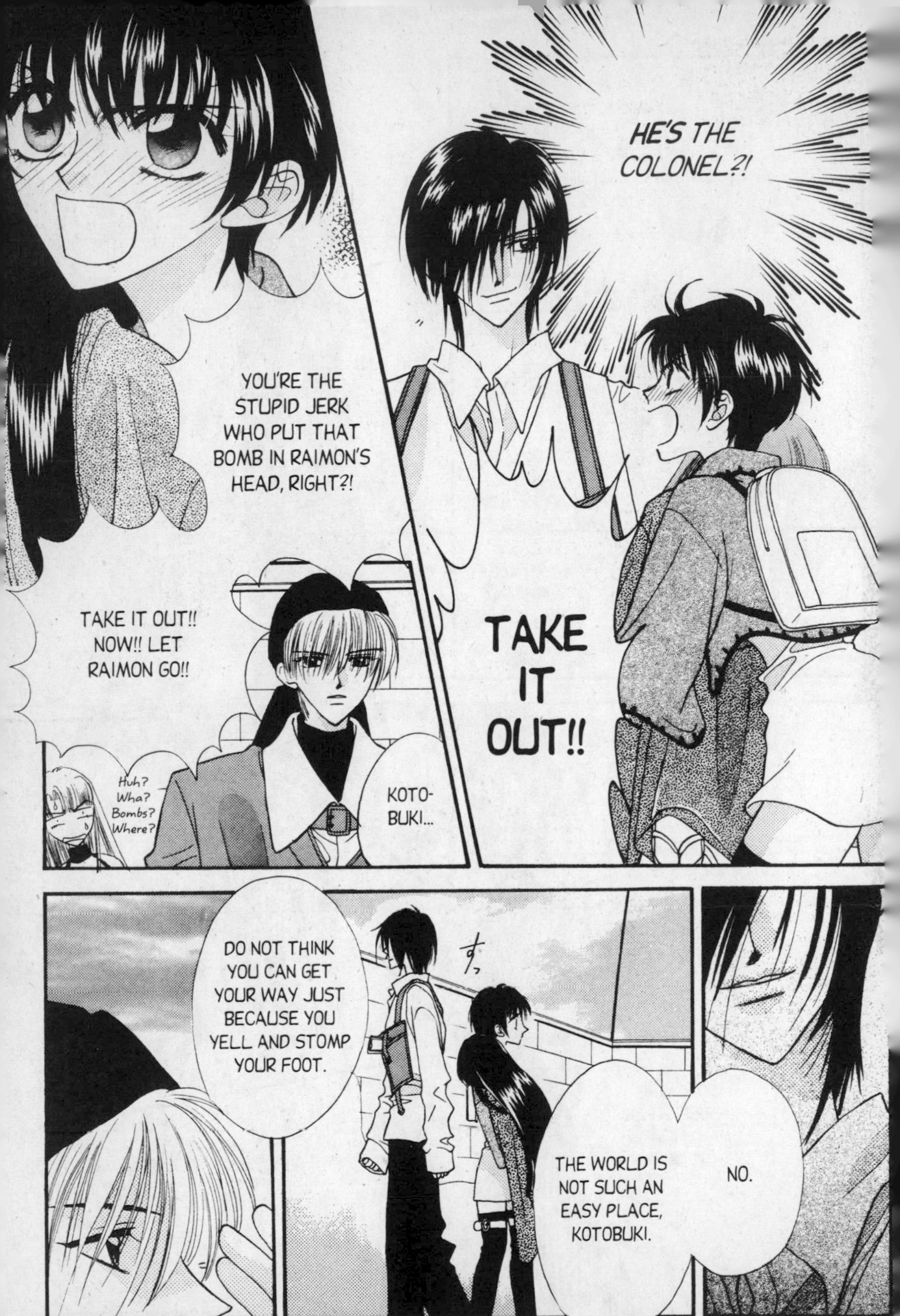
HE'S THE COLONEL?!
TAKE IT OUT!!
YOU'RE THE STUPID JERK WHO PUT THAT BOMB IN RAIMON'S HEAD, RIGHT?!
TAKE IT OUT!! NOW!! LET RAIMON GO!!
KOTO-BUKI...
Huh? Wha? Bombs? Where?
NO.
THE WORLD IS NOT SUCH AN EASY PLACE, KOTOBUKI.
すっ
DO NOT THINK YOU CAN GET YOUR WAY JUST BECAUSE YOU YELL AND STOMP YOUR FOOT.

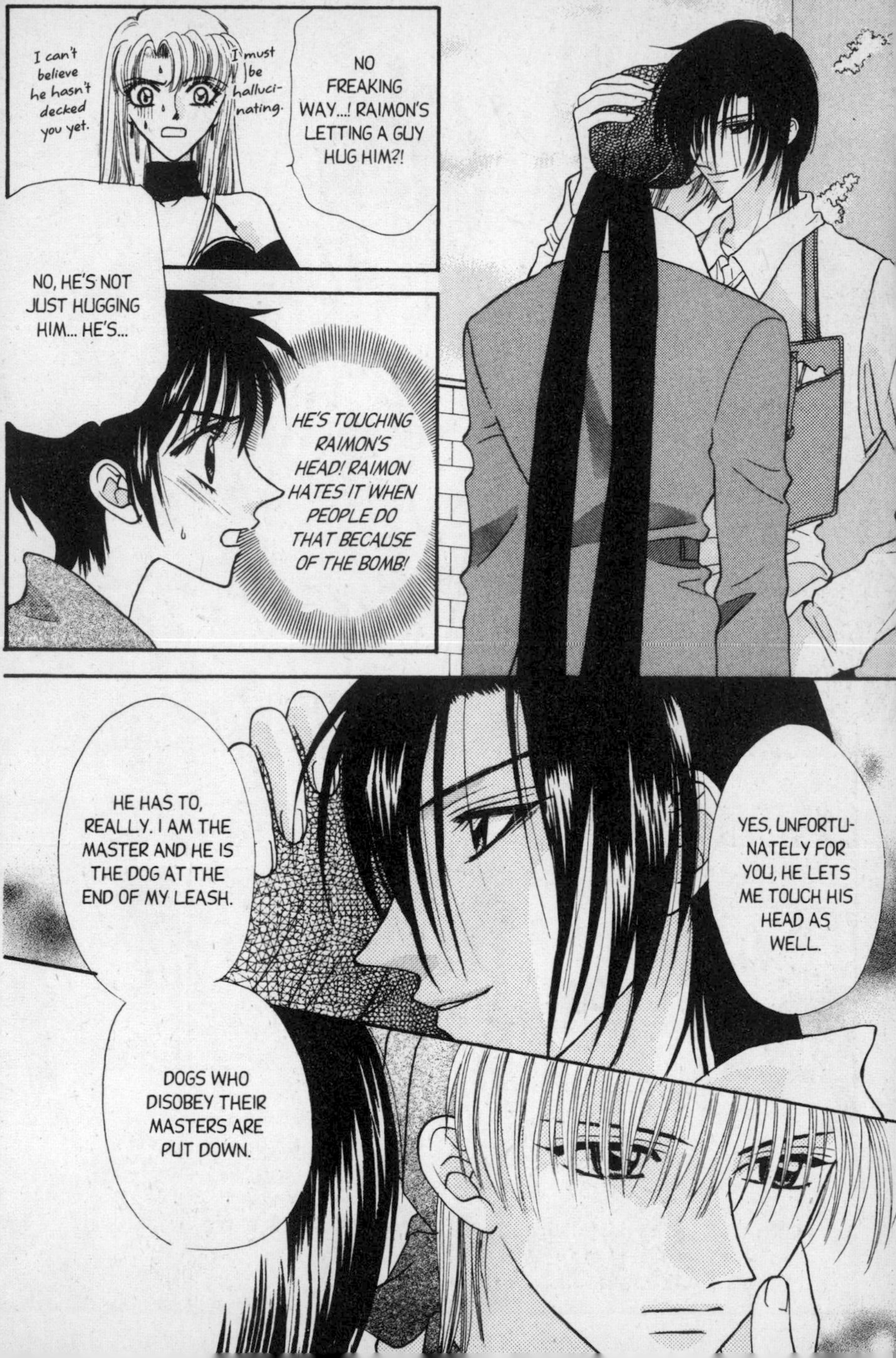
NO FREAKING WAY...! RAIMON'S LETTING A GUY HUG HIM?!
I must be halluci-nating.
I can't believe he hasn't decked you yet.
NO, HE'S NOT JUST HUGGING HIM... HE'S...
HE'S TOUCHING RAIMON'S HEAD! RAIMON HATES IT WHEN PEOPLE DO THAT BECAUSE OF THE BOMB!
YES, UNFORTU-NATELY FOR YOU, HE LETS ME TOUCH HIS HEAD AS WELL.
HE HAS TO, REALLY. I AM THE MASTER AND HE IS THE DOG AT THE END OF MY LEASH.
DOGS WHO DISOBEY THEIR MASTERS ARE PUT DOWN.

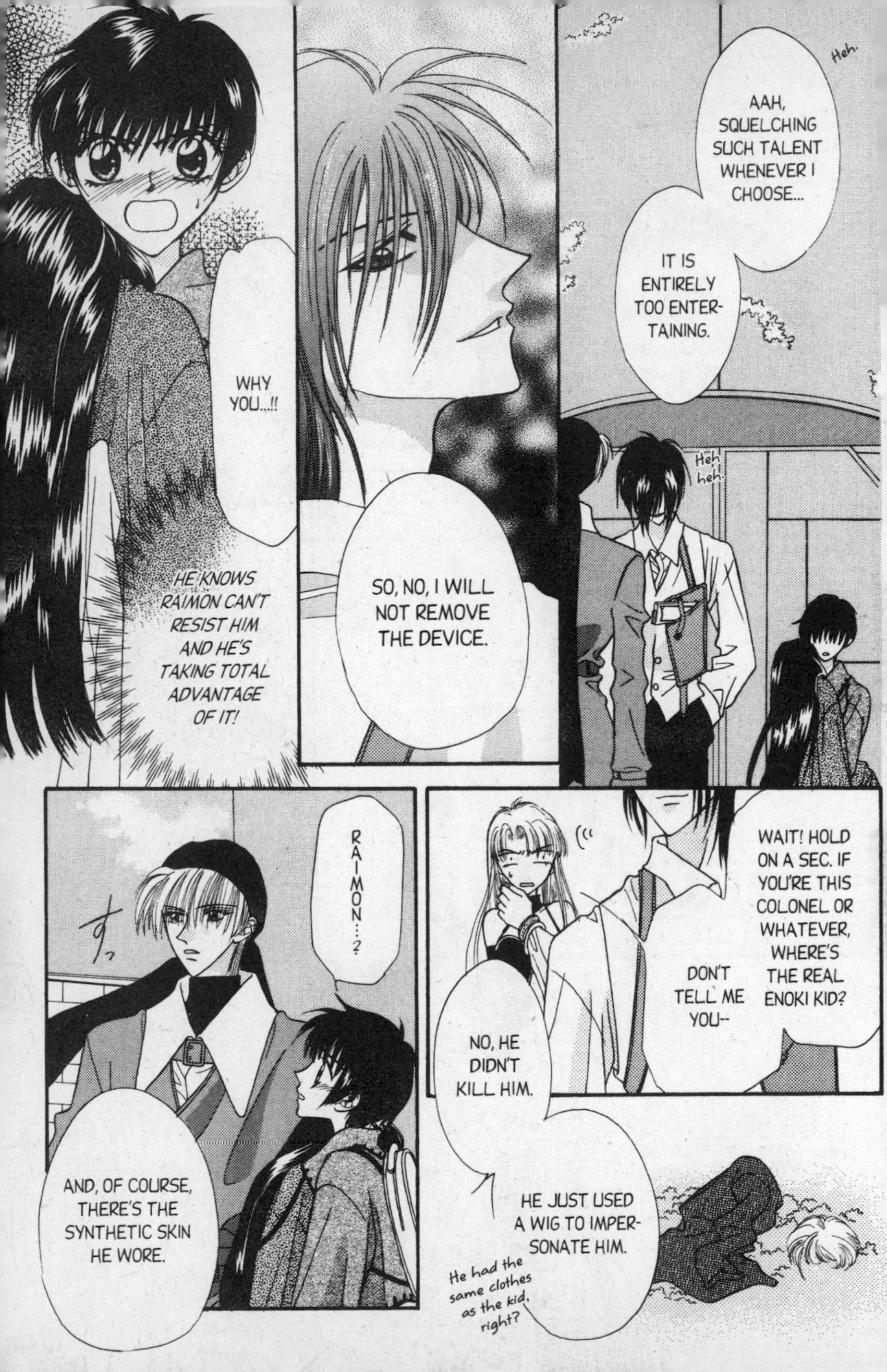
Heh.
AAH, SQUELCHING SUCH TALENT WHENEVER I CHOOSE...
IT IS ENTIRELY TOO ENTERTAINING.
Heh heh.
SO, NO, I WILL NOT REMOVE THE DEVICE.
WHY YOU...!!
HE KNOWS RAIMON CAN'T RESIST HIM AND HE'S TAKING TOTAL ADVANTAGE OF IT!
WAIT! HOLD ON A SEC. IF YOU'RE THIS COLONEL OR WHATEVER, WHERE'S THE REAL ENOKI KID?
DON'T TELL ME YOU--
NO, HE DIDN'T KILL HIM.
HE JUST USED A WIG TO IMPERSONATE HIM.
He had the same clothes as the kid, right?
RAIMON...?
すっ
AND, OF COURSE, THERE'S THE SYNTHETIC SKIN HE WORE.

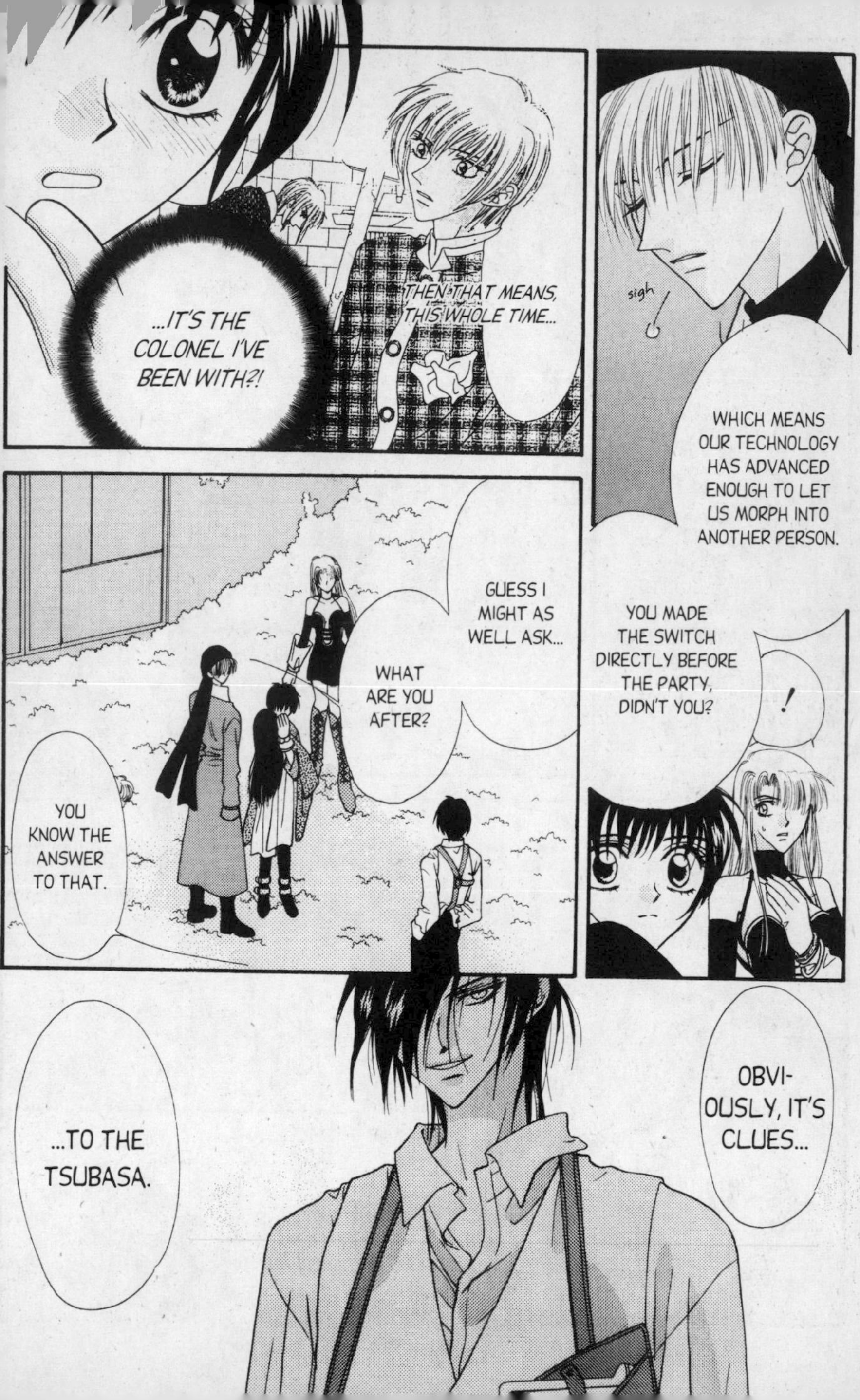
sigh
WHICH MEANS OUR TECHNOLOGY HAS ADVANCED ENOUGH TO LET US MORPH INTO ANOTHER PERSON.
THEN THAT MEANS, THIS WHOLE TIME...
...IT'S THE COLONEL I'VE BEEN WITH?!
YOU MADE THE SWITCH DIRECTLY BEFORE THE PARTY, DIDN'T YOU?
!
GUESS I MIGHT AS WELL ASK...
WHAT ARE YOU AFTER?
YOU KNOW THE ANSWER TO THAT.
OBVI-OUSLY, IT'S CLUES...
...TO THE TSUBASA.

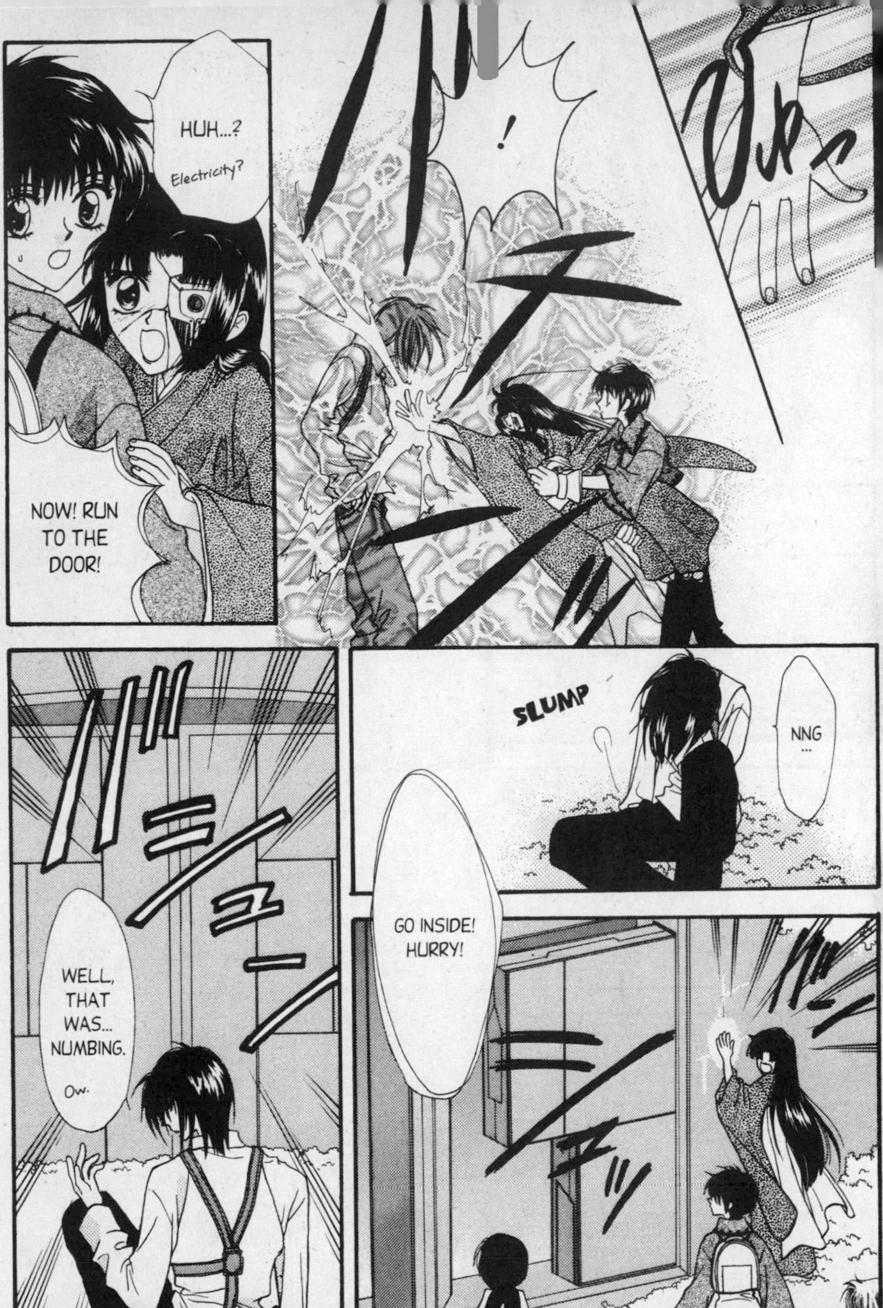
!
HUH...?
Electricity?
NOW! RUN TO THE DOOR!
SLUMP
NNG ...
GO INSIDE! HURRY!
WELL, THAT WAS... NUMBING.
Ow.

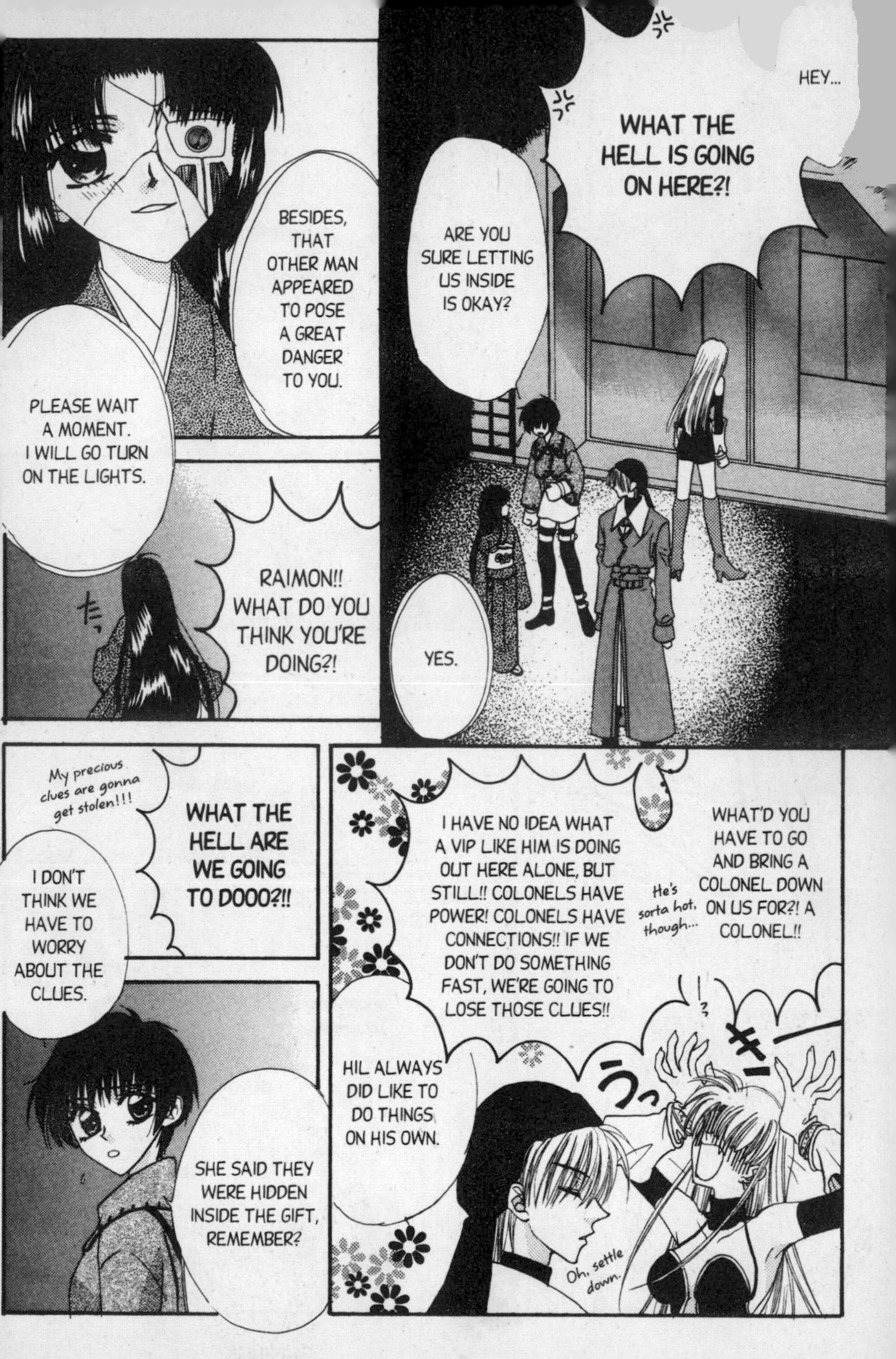
HEY...
WHAT THE HELL IS GOING ON HERE?!
ARE YOU SURE LETTING US INSIDE IS OKAY?
YES.
BESIDES, THAT OTHER MAN APPEARED TO POSE A GREAT DANGER TO YOU.
PLEASE WAIT A MOMENT. I WILL GO TURN ON THE LIGHTS.
RAIMON!! WHAT DO YOU THINK YOU'RE DOING?!
WHAT'D YOU HAVE TO GO AND BRING A COLONEL DOWN ON US FOR?! A COLONEL!!
He's sorta hot, though...
I HAVE NO IDEA WHAT A VIP LIKE HIM IS DOING OUT HERE ALONE, BUT STILL!! COLONELS HAVE POWER! COLONELS HAVE CONNECTIONS!! IF WE DON'T DO SOMETHING FAST, WE'RE GOING TO LOSE THOSE CLUES!!
HIL ALWAYS DID LIKE TO DO THINGS ON HIS OWN.
Oh, settle down.
WHAT THE HELL ARE WE GOING TO DOOO?!!
My precious clues are gonna get stolen!!!
I DON'T THINK WE HAVE TO WORRY ABOUT THE CLUES.
SHE SAID THEY WERE HIDDEN INSIDE THE GIFT, REMEMBER?

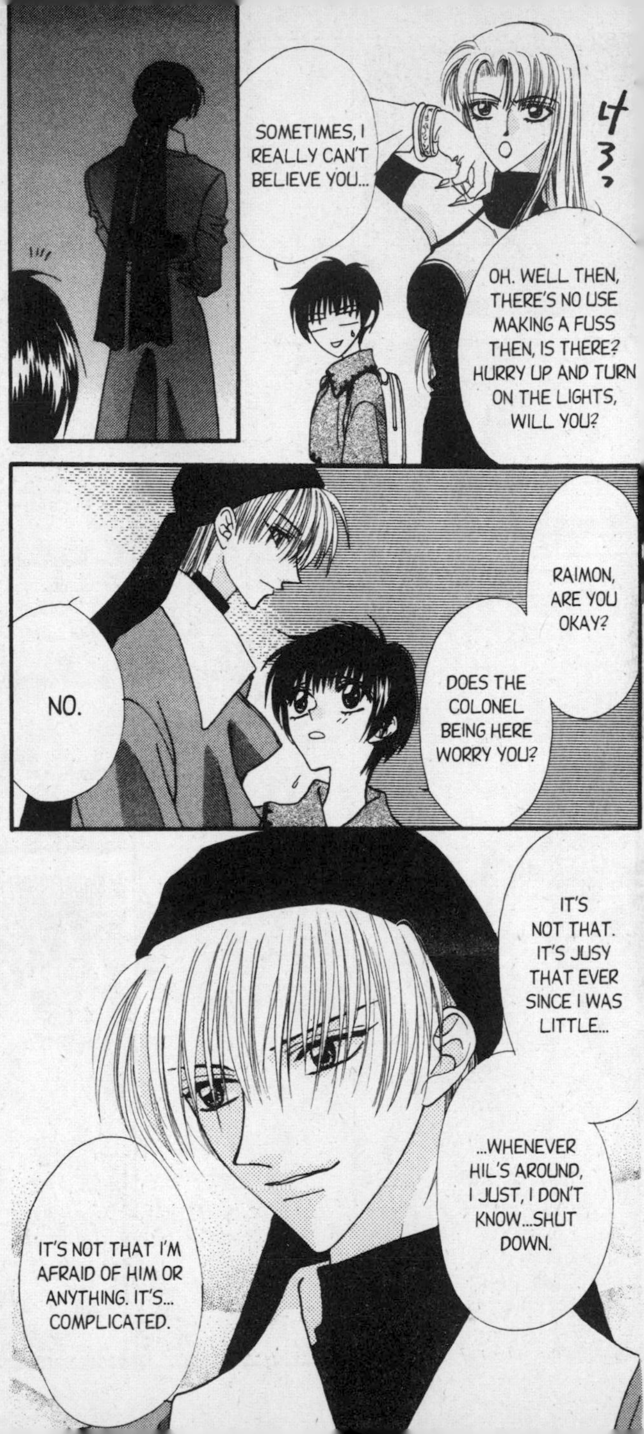
けろっ
SOMETIMES, I REALLY CAN'T BELIEVE YOU...
OH. WELL THEN, THERE'S NO USE MAKING A FUSS THEN, IS THERE? HURRY UP AND TURN ON THE LIGHTS, WILL YOU?
RAIMON, ARE YOU OKAY?
DOES THE COLONEL BEING HERE WORRY YOU?
NO.
IT'S NOT THAT. IT'S JUSY THAT EVER SINCE I WAS LITTLE...
...WHENEVER HIL'S AROUND, I JUST, I DON'T KNOW...SHUT DOWN.
IT'S NOT THAT I'M AFRAID OF HIM OR ANYTHING. IT'S... COMPLICATED.

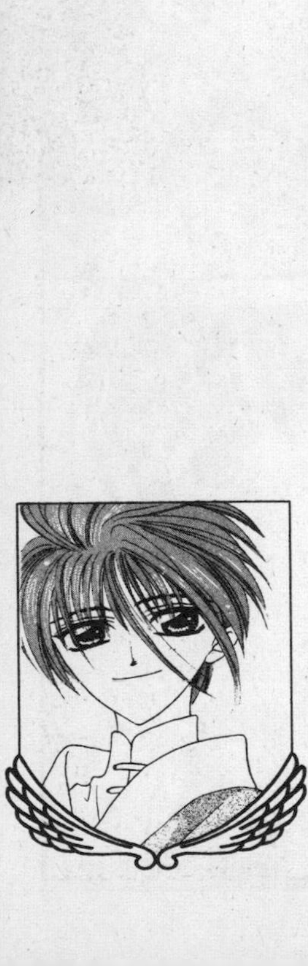

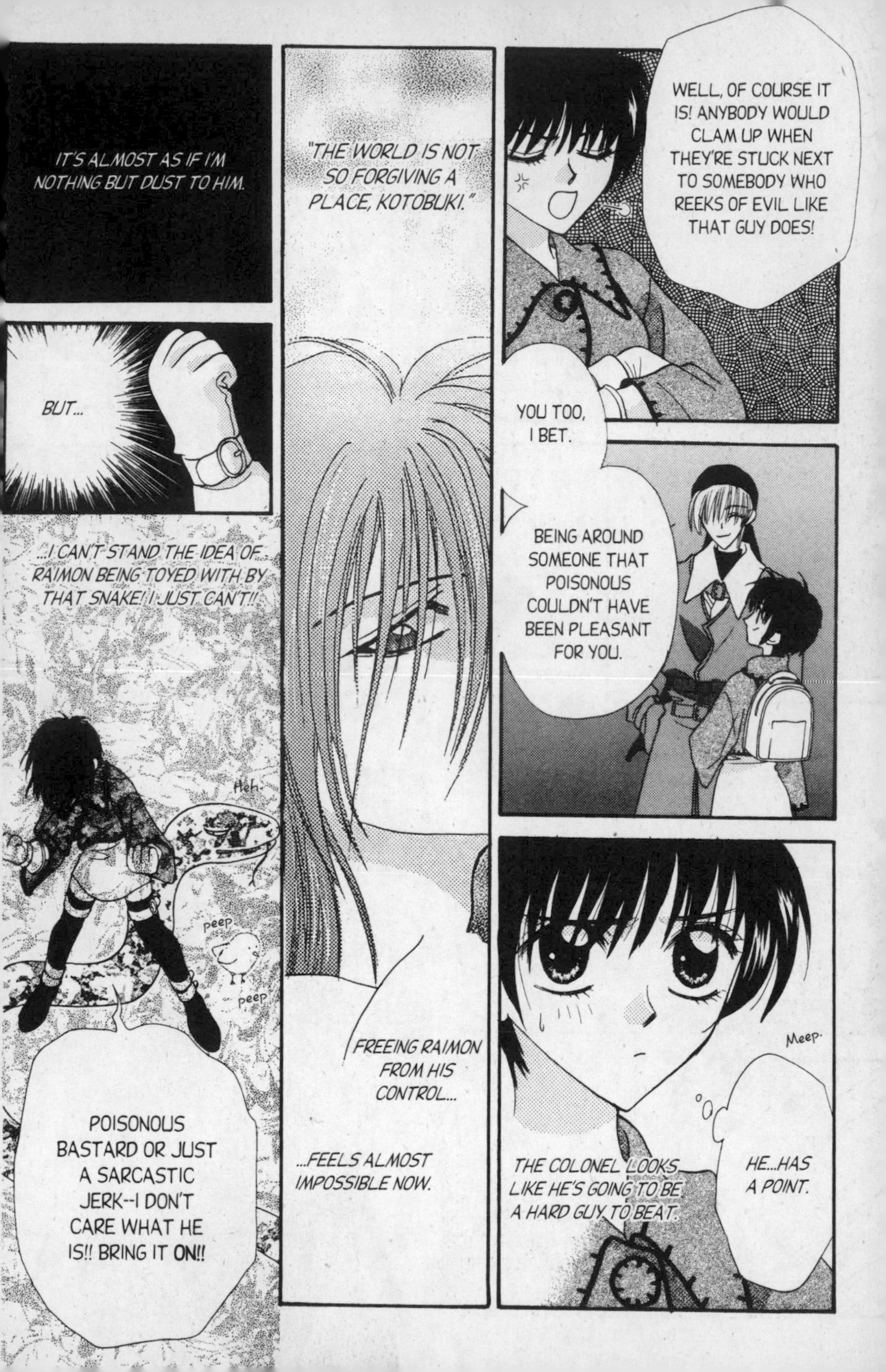
WELL, OF COURSE IT IS! ANYBODY WOULD CLAM UP WHEN THEY'RE STUCK NEXT TO SOMEBODY WHO REEKS OF EVIL LIKE THAT GUY DOES!
YOU TOO, I BET.
BEING AROUND SOMEONE THAT POISONOUS COULDN'T HAVE BEEN PLEASANT FOR YOU.
Meep.
HE...HAS A POINT.
THE COLONEL LOOKS LIKE HE'S GOING TO BE A HARD GUY TO BEAT.
"THE WORLD IS NOT SO FORGIVING A PLACE, KOTOBUKI."
FREEING RAIMON FROM HIS CONTROL...
...FEELS ALMOST IMPOSSIBLE NOW.
IT'S ALMOST AS IF I'M NOTHING BUT DUST TO HIM.
BUT...
...I CAN'T STAND THE IDEA OF RAIMON BEING TOYED WITH BY THAT SNAKE! I JUST CAN'T!!
Heh-
peep
peep
POISONOUS BASTARD OR JUST A SARCASTIC JERK--I DON'T CARE WHAT HE IS!! BRING IT ON!!

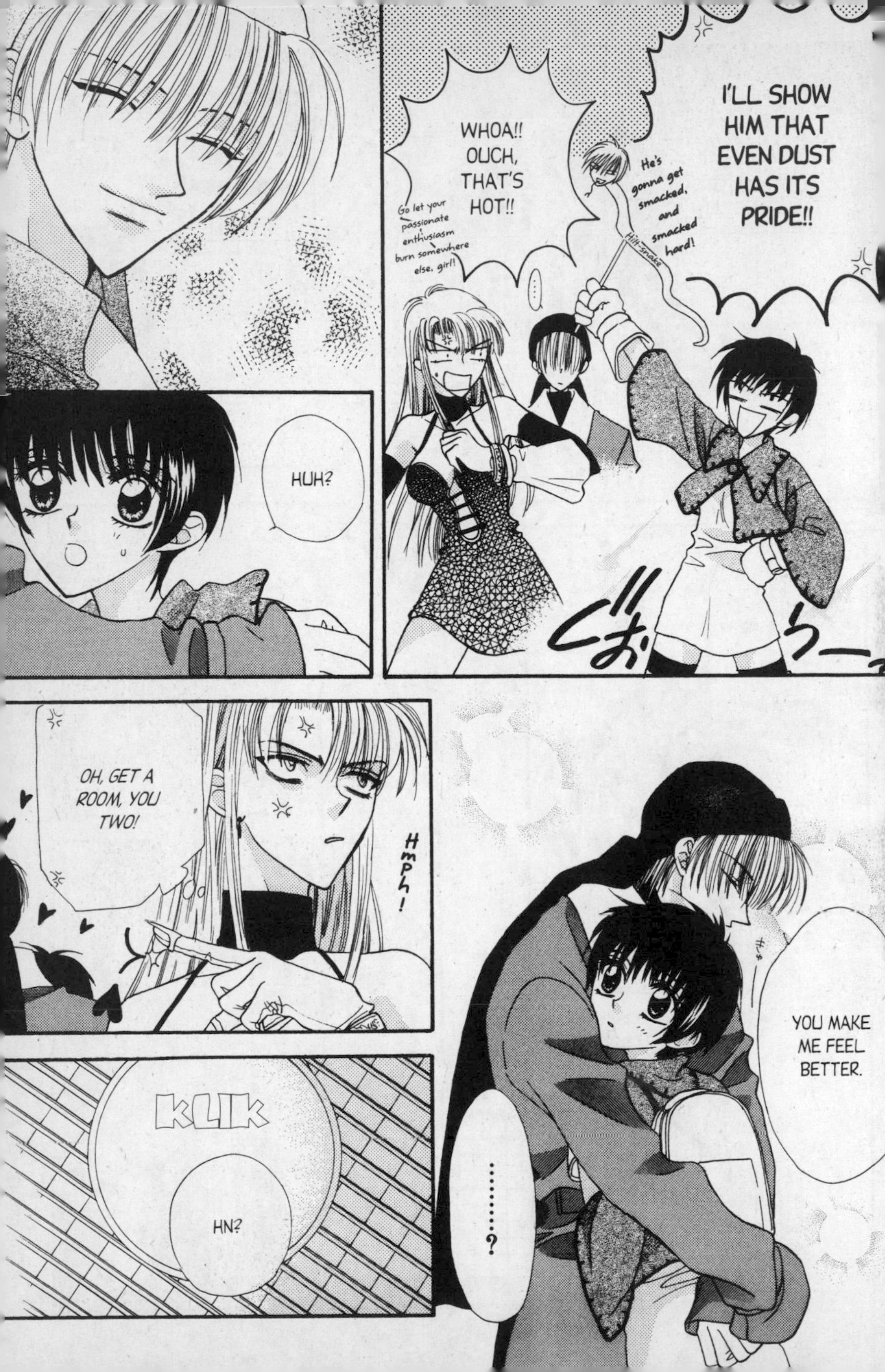
I'LL SHOW HIM THAT EVEN DUST HAS ITS PRIDE!!
He's gonna get smacked, and smacked hard!
Hilt-snake
WHOA!! OUCH, THAT'S HOT!!
Go let your passionate enthusiasm burn somewhere else, girl!
...
HUH?
YOU MAKE ME FEEL BETTER.
......?
OH, GET A ROOM, YOU TWO!
Hmph!
KLIK
HN?

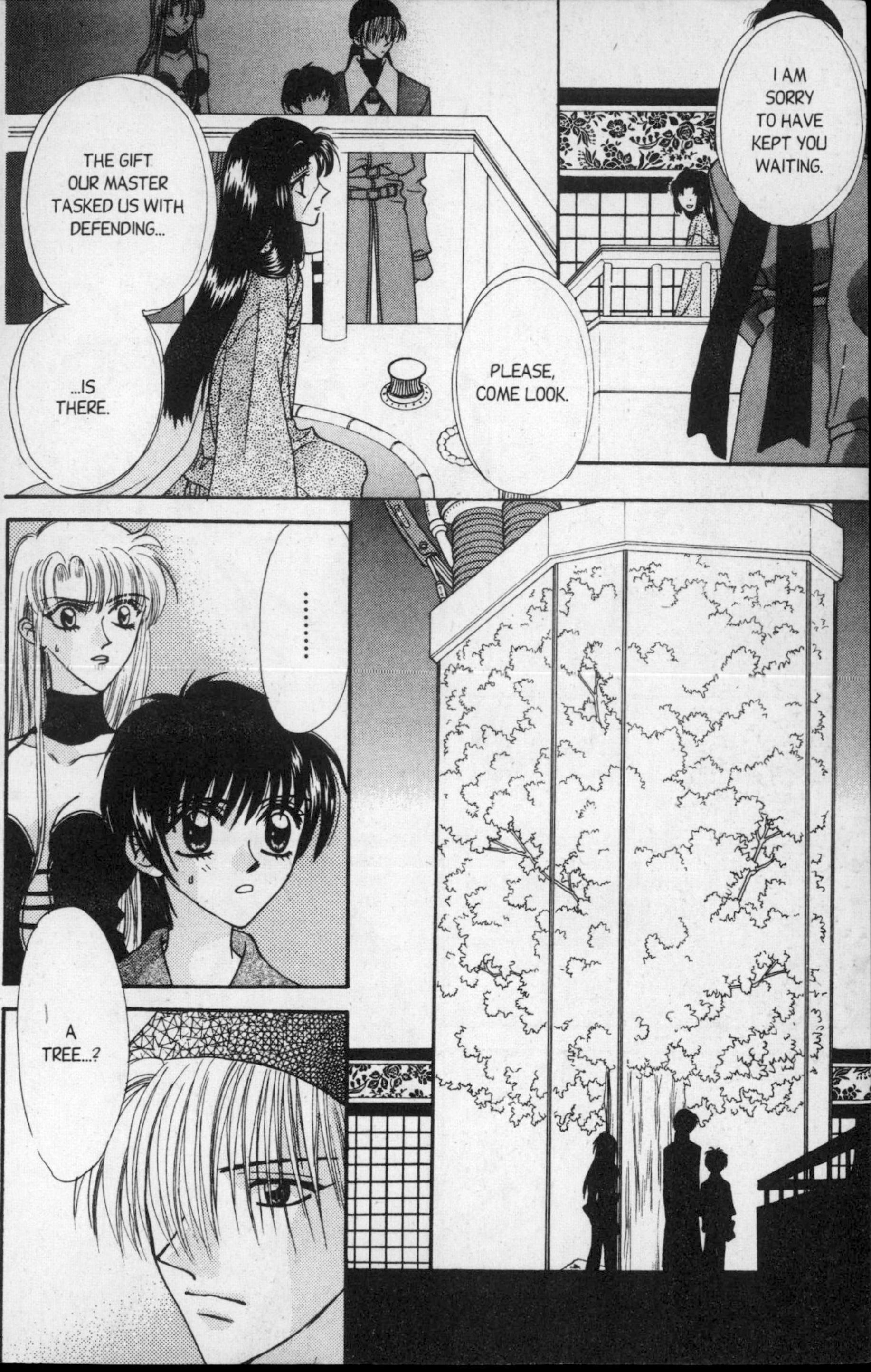
I AM SORRY TO HAVE KEPT YOU WAITING.
PLEASE, COME LOOK.
THE GIFT OUR MASTER TASKED US WITH DEFENDING...
...IS THERE.
......
A TREE...?

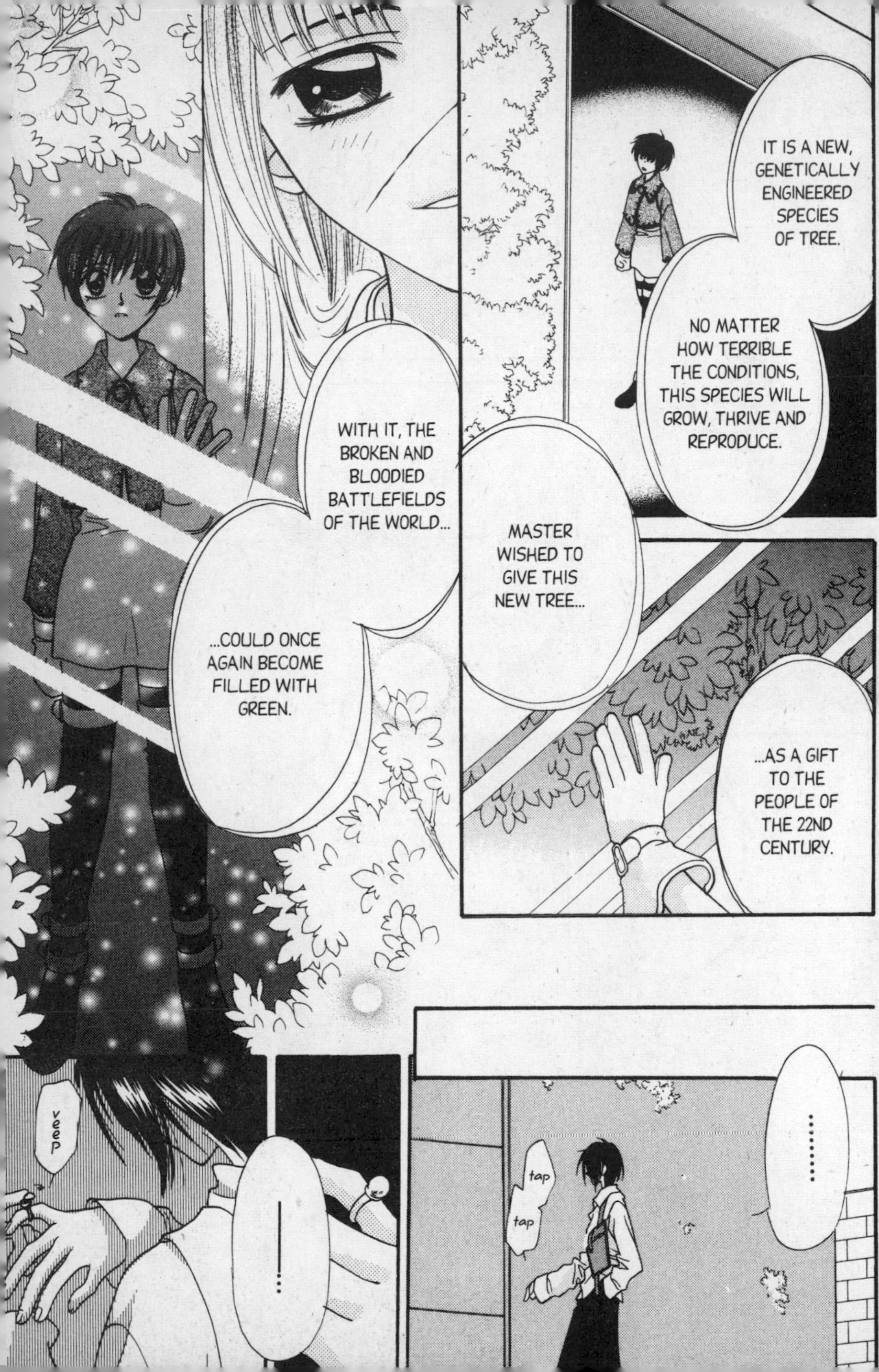
IT IS A NEW, GENETICALLY ENGINEERED SPECIES OF TREE.
NO MATTER HOW TERRIBLE THE CONDITIONS, THIS SPECIES WILL GROW, THRIVE AND REPRODUCE.
MASTER WISHED TO GIVE THIS NEW TREE...
...AS A GIFT TO THE PEOPLE OF THE 22ND CENTURY.
WITH IT, THE BROKEN AND BLOODIED BATTLEFIELDS OF THE WORLD...
...COULD ONCE AGAIN BECOME FILLED WITH GREEN.
....
tap
tap
veep
......

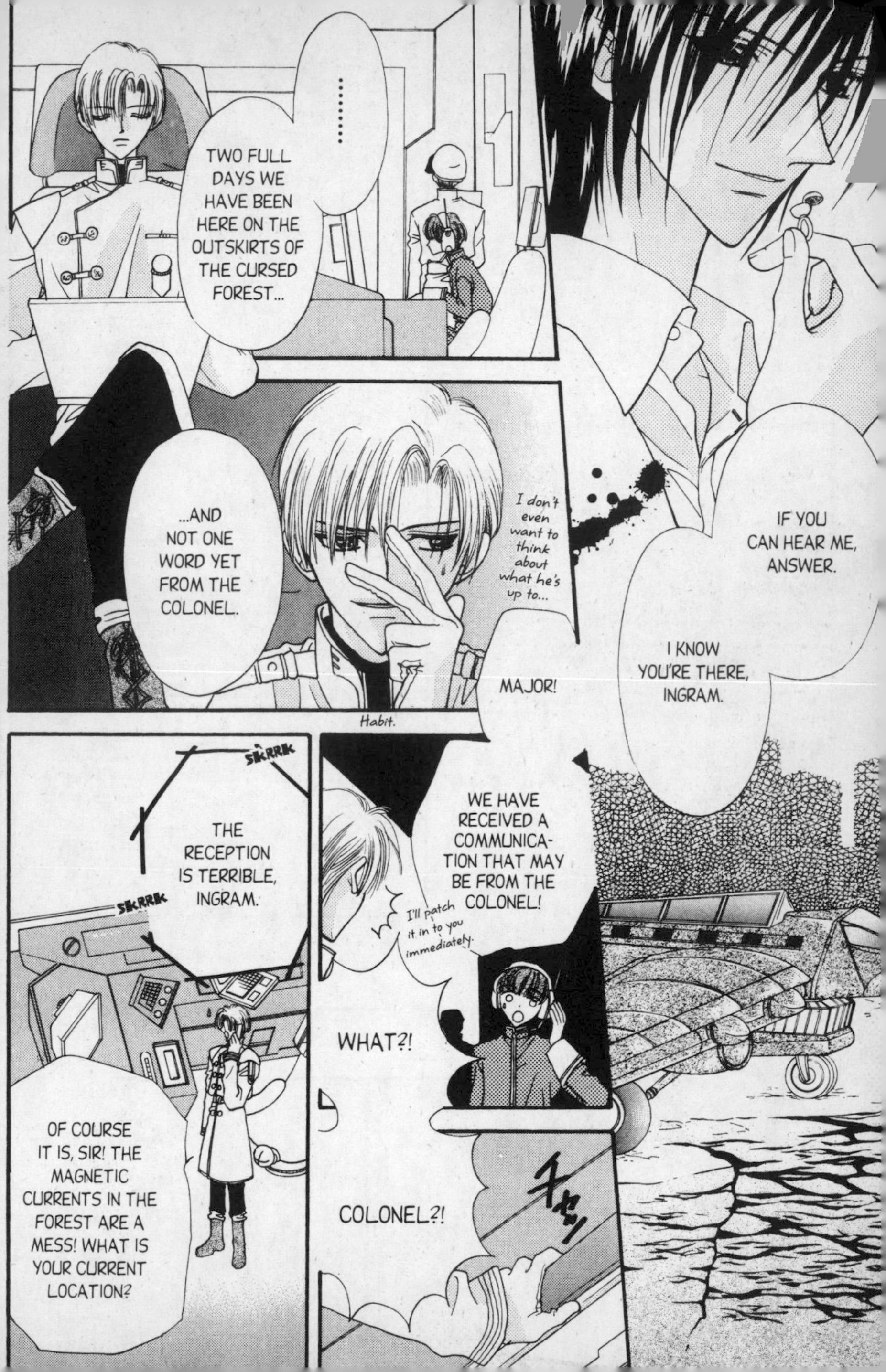
IF YOU CAN HEAR ME, ANSWER.
I KNOW YOU'RE THERE, INGRAM.
......
TWO FULL DAYS WE HAVE BEEN HERE ON THE OUTSKIRTS OF THE CURSED FOREST...
...AND NOT ONE WORD YET FROM THE COLONEL.
I don't even want to think about what he's up to...
Habit.
MAJOR!
WE HAVE RECEIVED A COMMUNICATION THAT MAY BE FROM THE COLONEL!
I'll patch it in to you immediately.
WHAT?!
COLONEL?!
SKRRK
THE RECEPTION IS TERRIBLE, INGRAM.
SKRRK
OF COURSE IT IS, SIR! THE MAGNETIC CURRENTS IN THE FOREST ARE A MESS! WHAT IS YOUR CURRENT LOCATION?

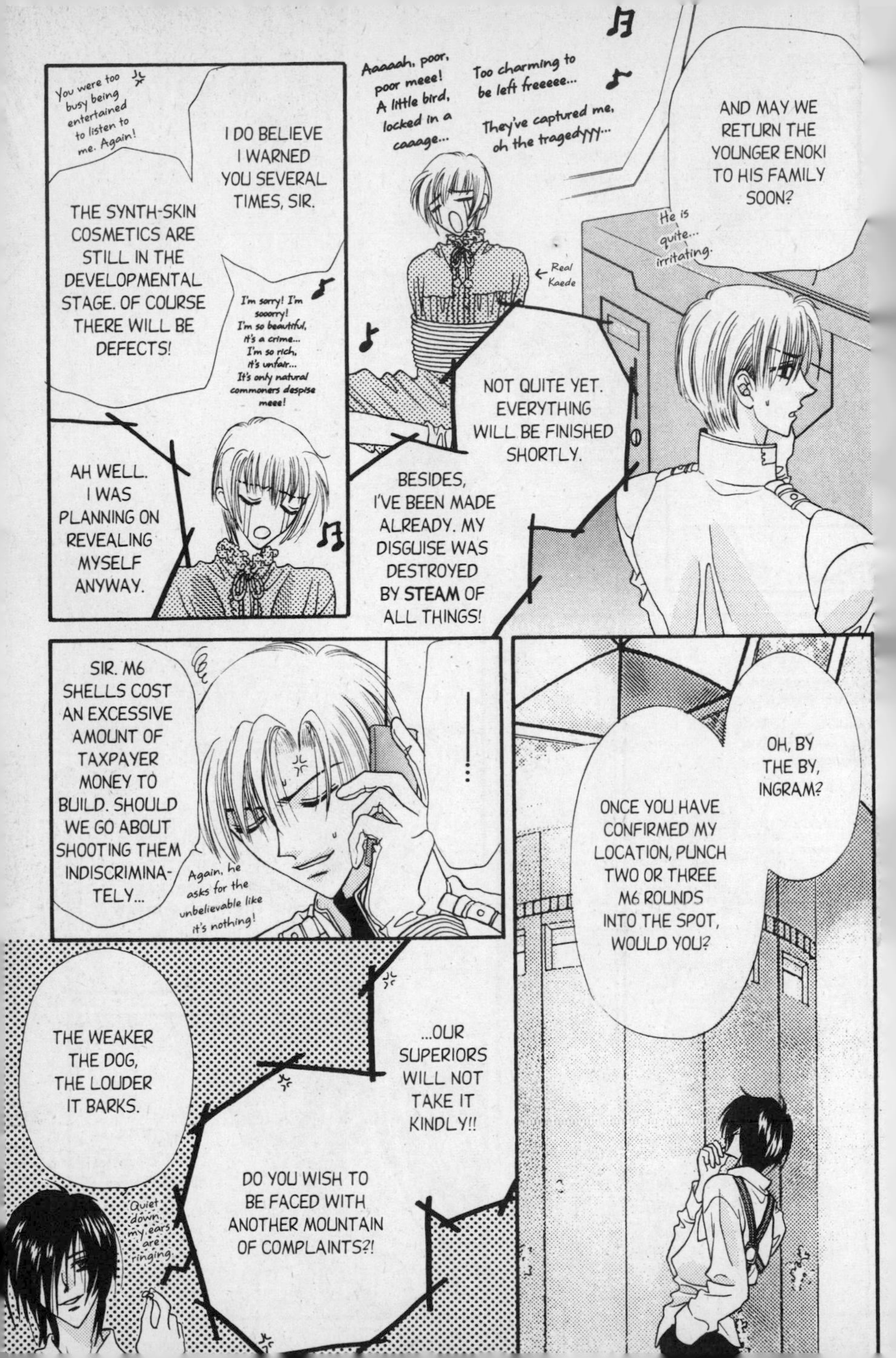

AND MAY WE RETURN THE YOUNGER ENOKI TO HIS FAMILY SOON?
He is quite... irritating.
NOT QUITE YET. EVERYTHING WILL BE FINISHED SHORTLY.
BESIDES, I'VE BEEN MADE ALREADY. MY DISGUISE WAS DESTROYED BY STEAM OF ALL THINGS!
Too charming to be left freeeee... They've captured me, oh the tragedyyy...
Aaaaah, poor, poor meee! A little bird, locked in a caaage...
Real Kaede
I DO BELIEVE I WARNED YOU SEVERAL TIMES, SIR.
You were too busy being entertained to listen to me. Again!
THE SYNTH-SKIN COSMETICS ARE STILL IN THE DEVELOPMENTAL STAGE. OF COURSE THERE WILL BE DEFECTS!
I'm sorry! I'm sooorry! I'm so beautiful, it's a crime... I'm so rich, it's unfair... It's only natural commoners despise meee!
AH WELL. I WAS PLANNING ON REVEALING MYSELF ANYWAY.
OH, BY THE BY, INGRAM?
ONCE YOU HAVE CONFIRMED MY LOCATION, PUNCH TWO OR THREE M6 ROUNDS INTO THE SPOT, WOULD YOU?
......
SIR. M6 SHELLS COST AN EXCESSIVE AMOUNT OF TAXPAYER MONEY TO BUILD. SHOULD WE GO ABOUT SHOOTING THEM INDISCRIMINATELY...
Again, he asks for the unbelievable like it's nothing!
...OUR SUPERIORS WILL NOT TAKE IT KINDLY!!
DO YOU WISH TO BE FACED WITH ANOTHER MOUNTAIN OF COMPLAINTS?!
THE WEAKER THE DOG, THE LOUDER IT BARKS.
Quiet down, my ears are ringing.

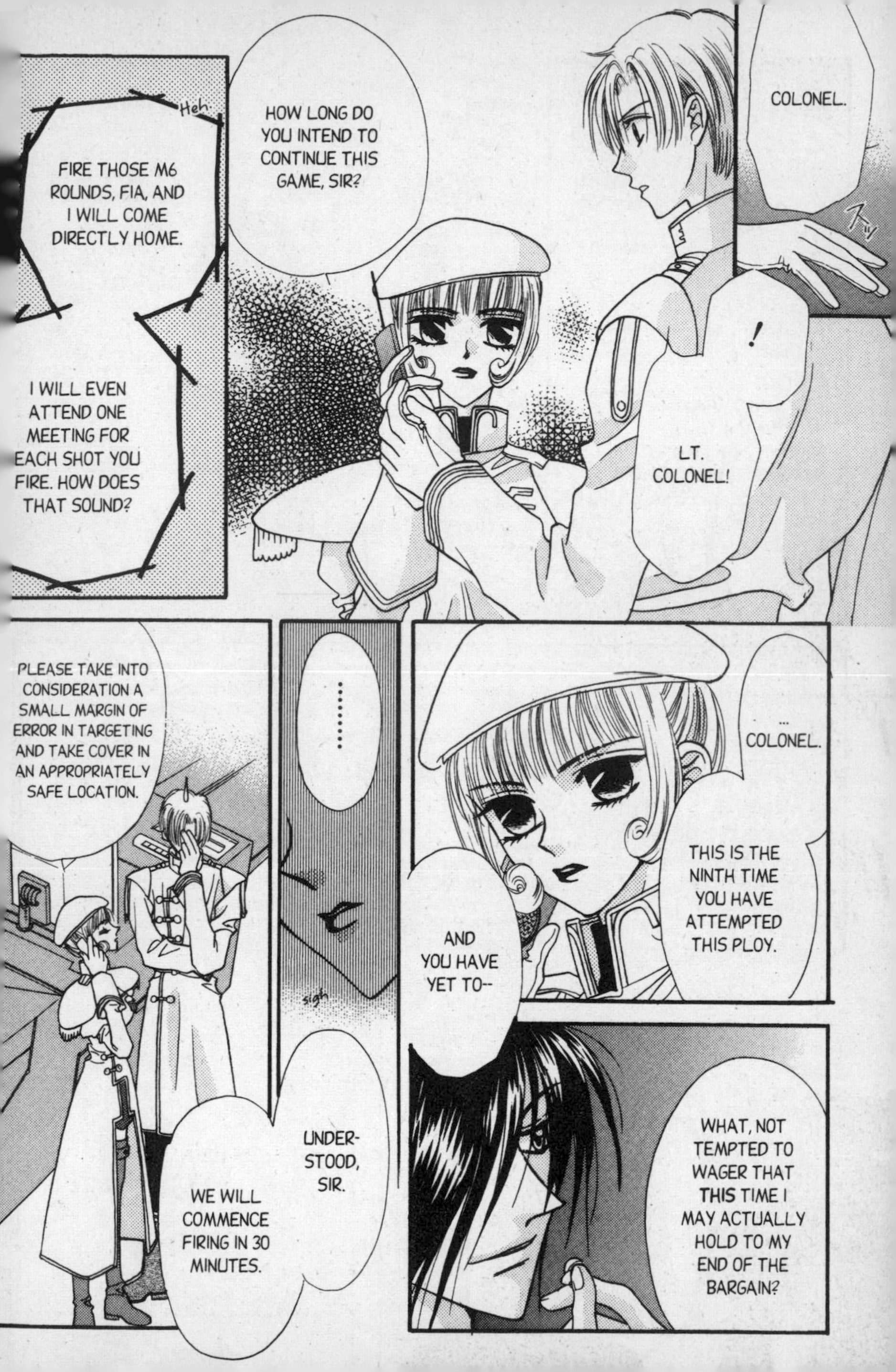
COLONEL.
スッ
HOW LONG DO YOU INTEND TO CONTINUE THIS GAME, SIR?
!
LT. COLONEL!
Heh
FIRE THOSE M6 ROUNDS, FIA, AND I WILL COME DIRECTLY HOME.
I WILL EVEN ATTEND ONE MEETING FOR EACH SHOT YOU FIRE. HOW DOES THAT SOUND?
... COLONEL.
THIS IS THE NINTH TIME YOU HAVE ATTEMPTED THIS PLOY.
AND YOU HAVE YET TO--
WHAT, NOT TEMPTED TO WAGER THAT THIS TIME I MAY ACTUALLY HOLD TO MY END OF THE BARGAIN?
......
sigh
PLEASE TAKE INTO CONSIDERATION A SMALL MARGIN OF ERROR IN TARGETING AND TAKE COVER IN AN APPROPRIATELY SAFE LOCATION.
UNDER-STOOD, SIR.
WE WILL COMMENCE FIRING IN 30 MINUTES.

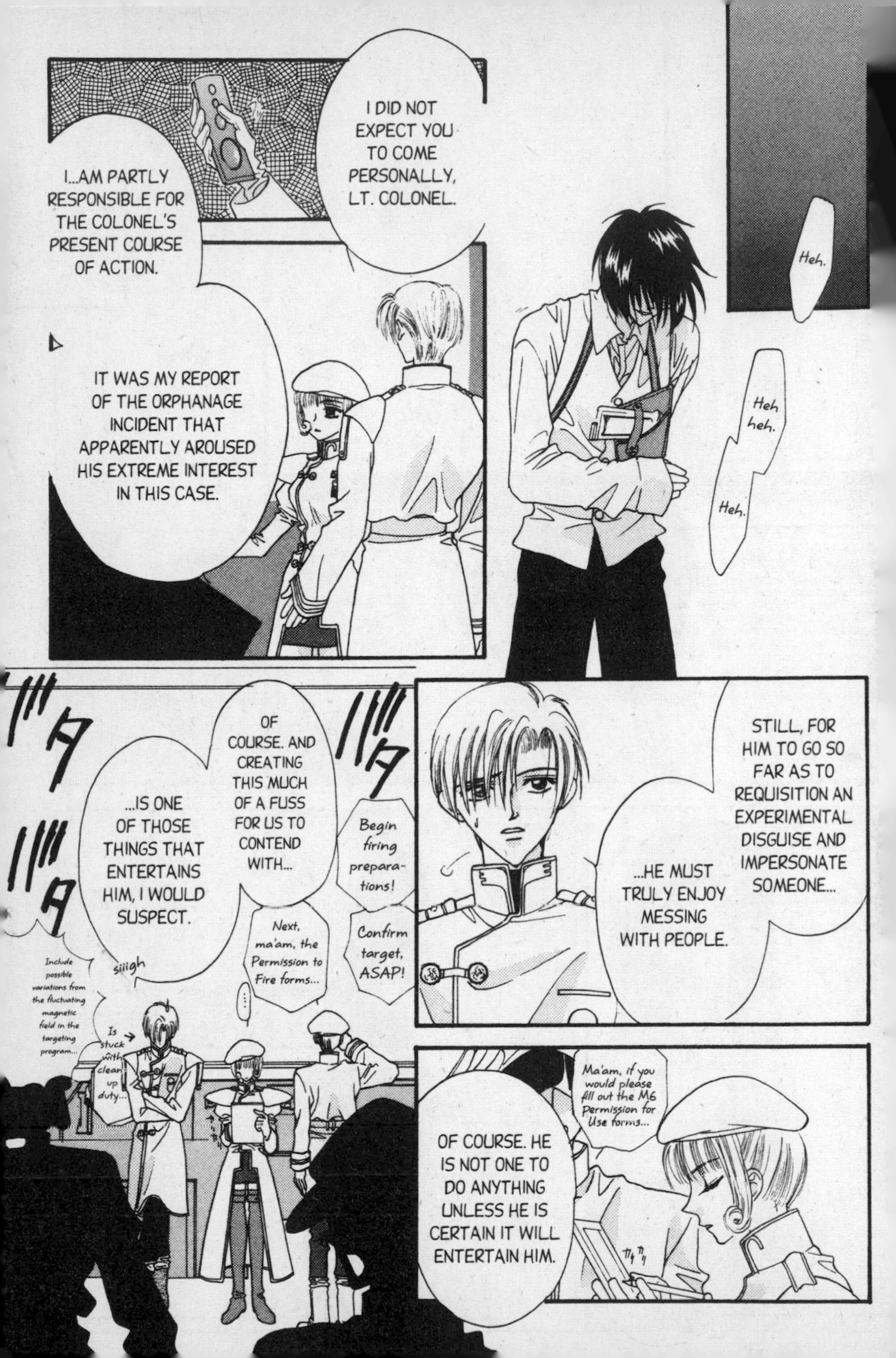
Heh.
Heh heh.
Heh.
I DID NOT EXPECT YOU TO COME PERSONALLY, LT. COLONEL.
I...AM PARTLY RESPONSIBLE FOR THE COLONEL'S PRESENT COURSE OF ACTION.
IT WAS MY REPORT OF THE ORPHANAGE INCIDENT THAT APPARENTLY AROUSED HIS EXTREME INTEREST IN THIS CASE.
STILL, FOR HIM TO GO SO FAR AS TO REQUISITION AN EXPERIMENTAL DISGUISE AND IMPERSONATE SOMEONE...
...HE MUST TRULY ENJOY MESSING WITH PEOPLE.
Ma'am, if you would please fill out the M6 Permission for Use forms...
OF COURSE. HE IS NOT ONE TO DO ANYTHING UNLESS HE IS CERTAIN IT WILL ENTERTAIN HIM.
ダ
OF COURSE. AND CREATING THIS MUCH OF A FUSS FOR US TO CONTEND WITH...
Begin firing preparations!
ダ
...IS ONE OF THOSE THINGS THAT ENTERTAINS HIM, I WOULD SUSPECT.
ダ
Confirm target, ASAP!
Next, ma'am, the Permission to Fire forms...
...
siiigh
Include possible variations from the fluctuating magnetic field in the targeting program...
Is stuck with clean-up duty...

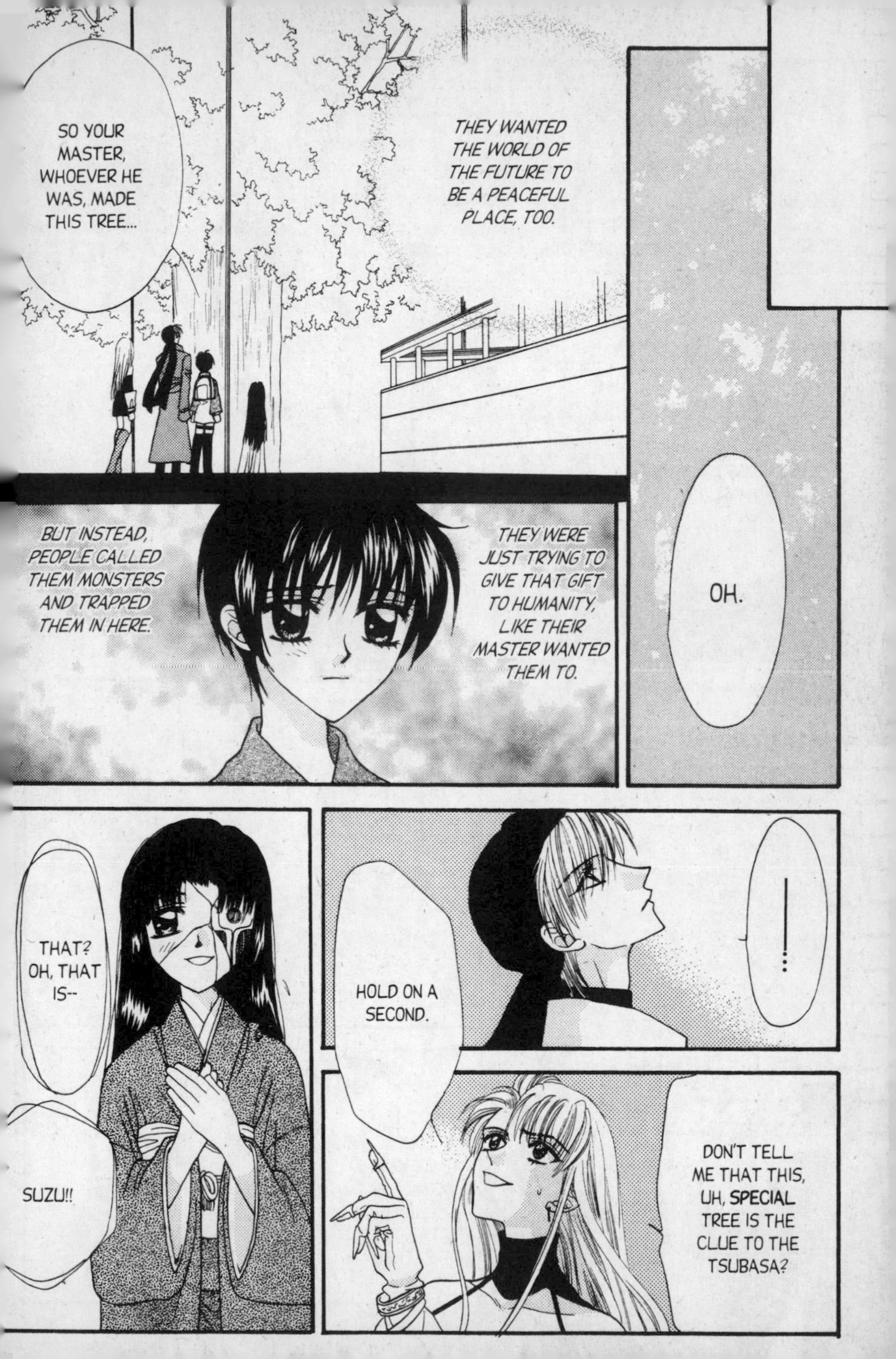
SO YOUR MASTER, WHOEVER HE WAS, MADE THIS TREE...
THEY WANTED THE WORLD OF THE FUTURE TO BE A PEACEFUL PLACE, TOO.
THEY WERE JUST TRYING TO GIVE THAT GIFT TO HUMANITY, LIKE THEIR MASTER WANTED THEM TO.
BUT INSTEAD, PEOPLE CALLED THEM MONSTERS AND TRAPPED THEM IN HERE.
OH.
!
HOLD ON A SECOND.
DON'T TELL ME THAT THIS, UH, SPECIAL TREE IS THE CLUE TO THE TSUBASA?
THAT? OH, THAT IS--
SUZU!!

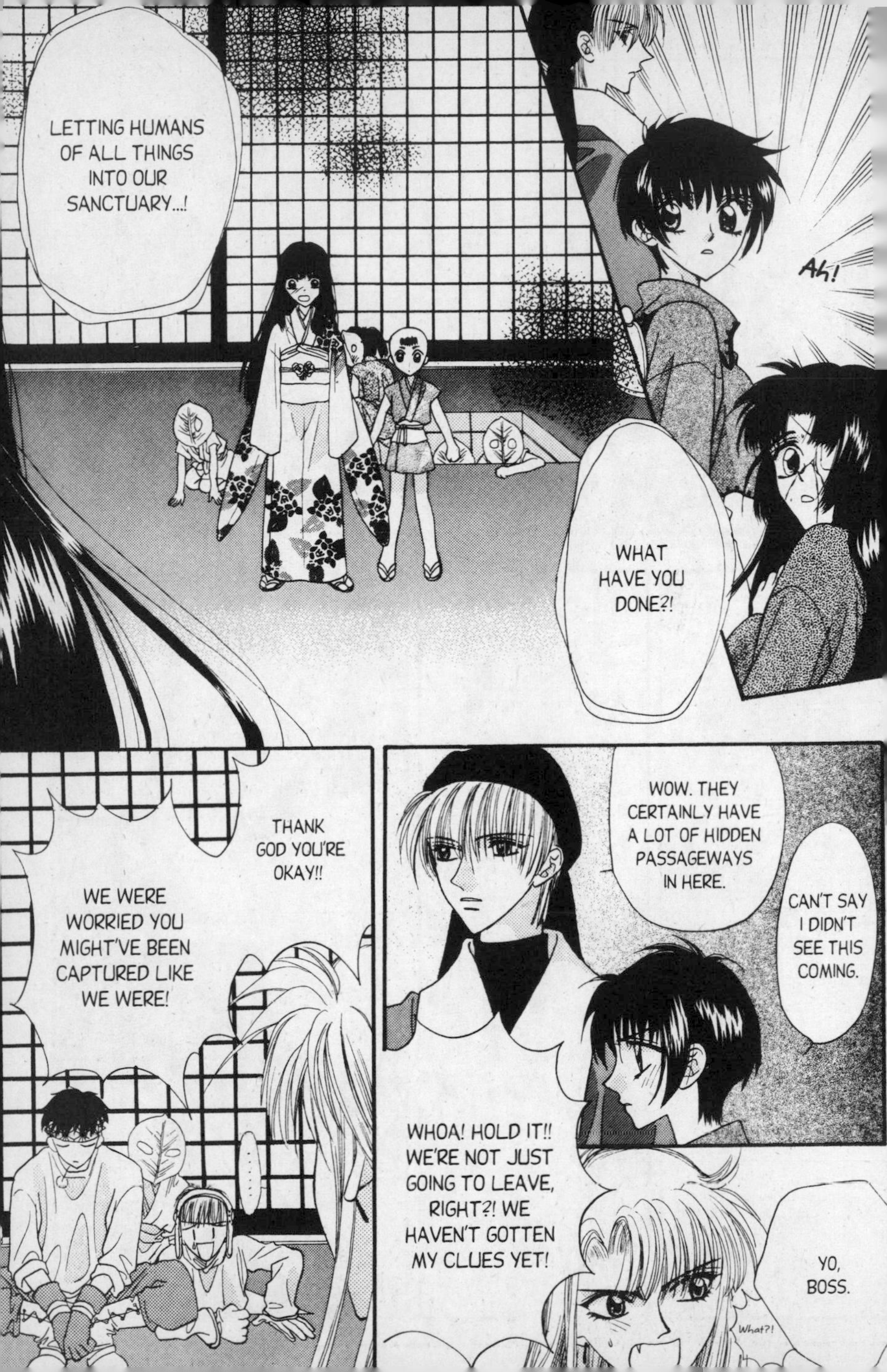

Ah!
WHAT HAVE YOU DONE?!
LETTING HUMANS OF ALL THINGS INTO OUR SANCTUARY...!
WOW. THEY CERTAINLY HAVE A LOT OF HIDDEN PASSAGEWAYS IN HERE.
CAN'T SAY I DIDN'T SEE THIS COMING.
YO, BOSS.
What?!
WHOA! HOLD IT!! WE'RE NOT JUST GOING TO LEAVE, RIGHT?! WE HAVEN'T GOTTEN MY CLUES YET!
THANK GOD YOU'RE OKAY!!
WE WERE WORRIED YOU MIGHT'VE BEEN CAPTURED LIKE WE WERE!
...

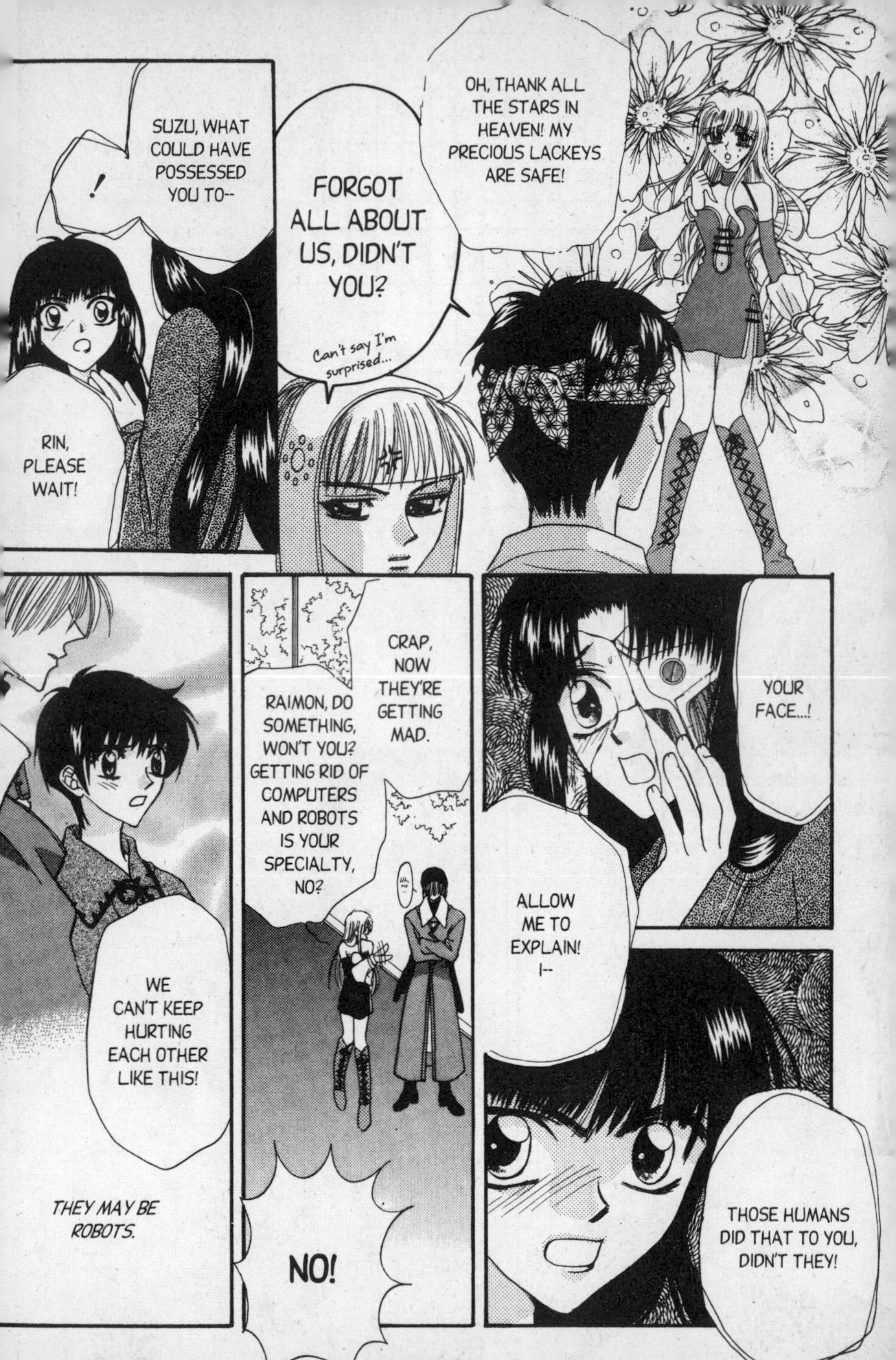
OH, THANK ALL THE STARS IN HEAVEN! MY PRECIOUS LACKEYS ARE SAFE!
FORGOT ALL ABOUT US, DIDN'T YOU?
Can't say I'm surprised...
SUZU, WHAT COULD HAVE POSSESSED YOU TO--
!
RIN, PLEASE WAIT!
YOUR FACE...!
ALLOW ME TO EXPLAIN! I--
THOSE HUMANS DID THAT TO YOU, DIDN'T THEY!
CRAP, NOW THEY'RE GETTING MAD.
RAIMON, DO SOMETHING, WON'T YOU? GETTING RID OF COMPUTERS AND ROBOTS IS YOUR SPECIALTY, NO?
NO!
WE CAN'T KEEP HURTING EACH OTHER LIKE THIS!
THEY MAY BE ROBOTS.

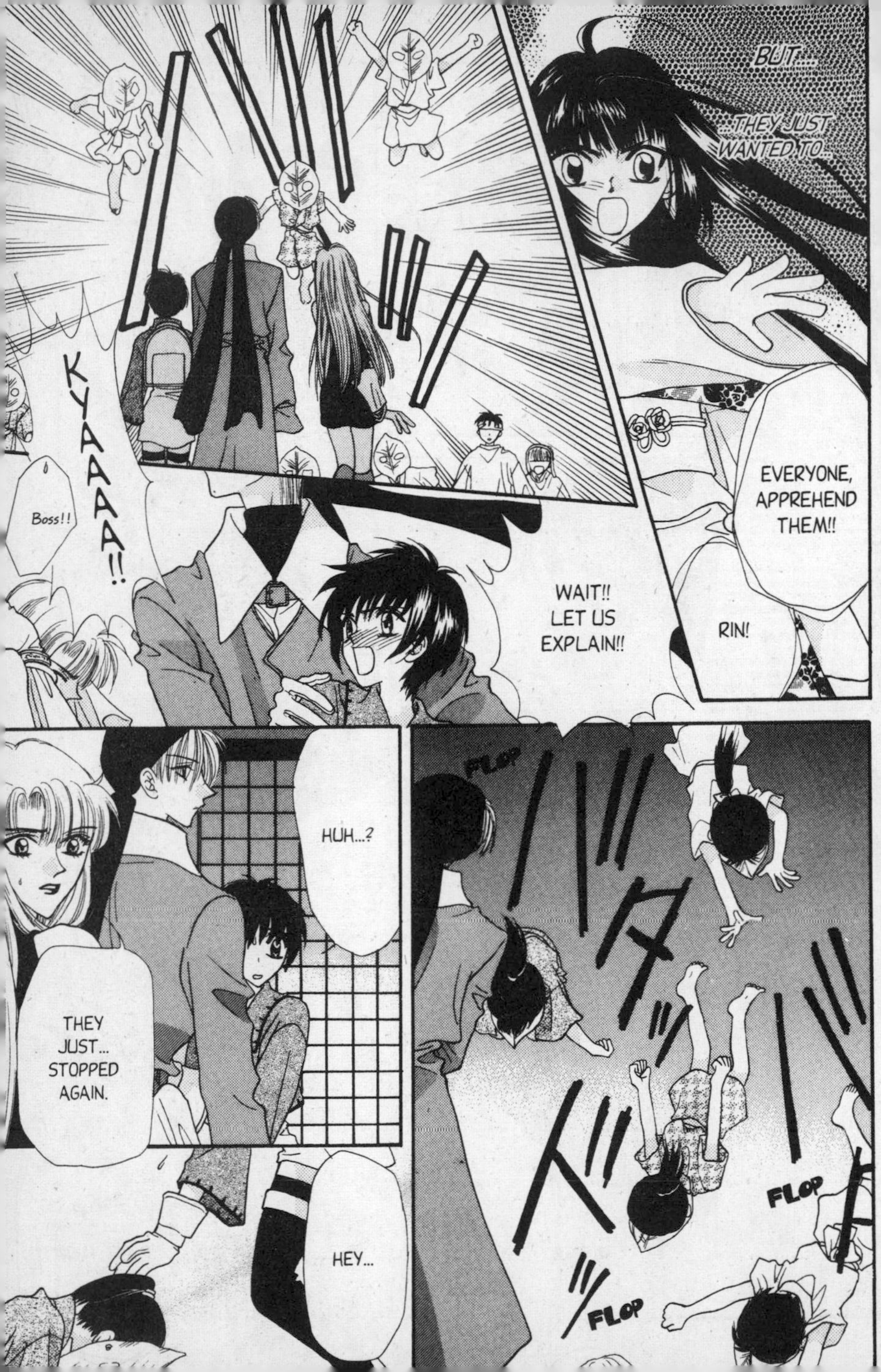
BUT...
...THEY JUST WANTED TO...
EVERYONE, APPREHEND THEM!!
RIN!
WAIT!! LET US EXPLAIN!!
KYAAAA!!
Boss!!
FLOP
FLOP
FLOP
HUH...?
THEY JUST... STOPPED AGAIN.
HEY...

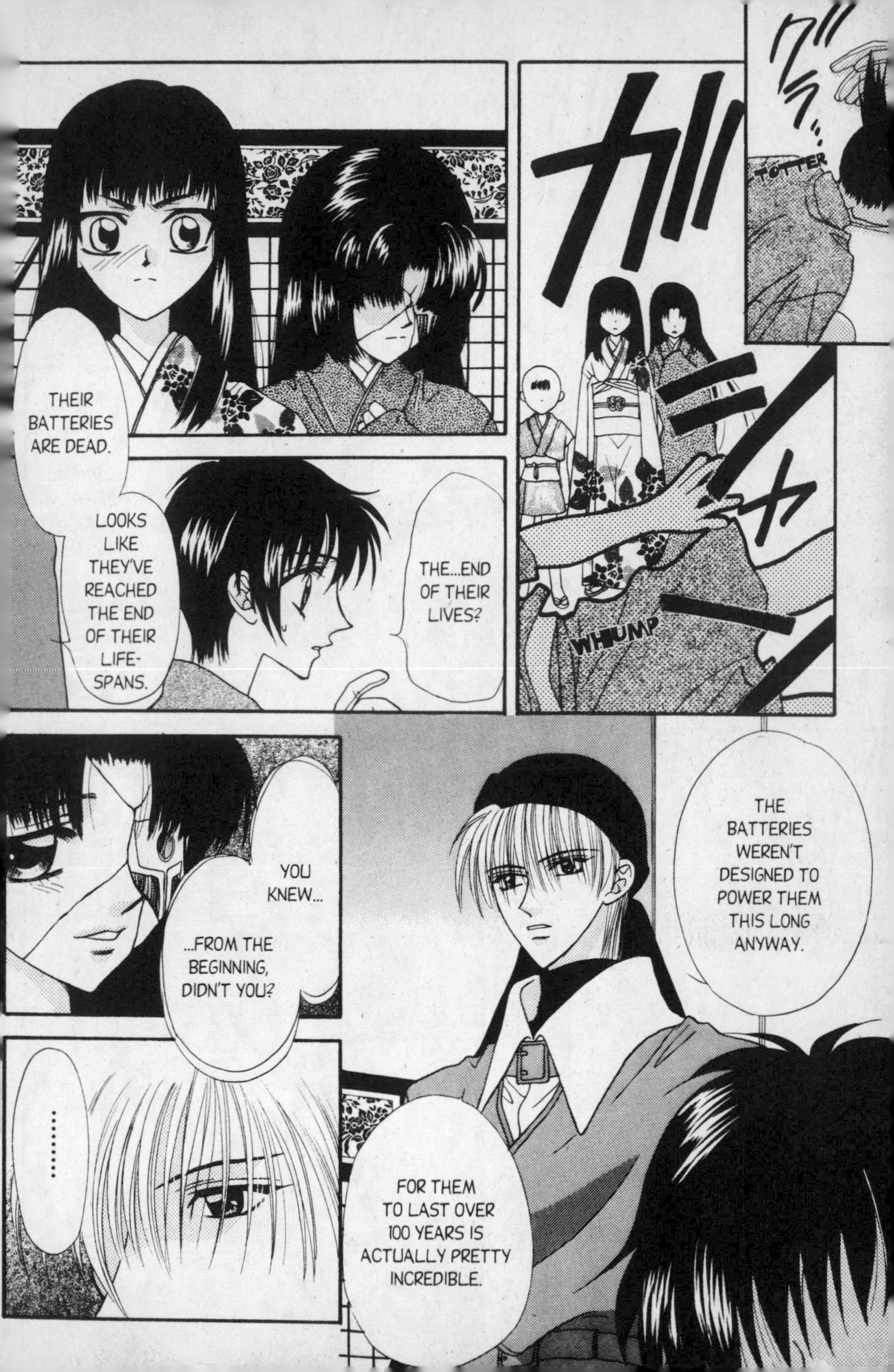
TOTTER
WHUMP
THEIR BATTERIES ARE DEAD.
LOOKS LIKE THEY'VE REACHED THE END OF THEIR LIFE-SPANS.
THE...END OF THEIR LIVES?
THE BATTERIES WEREN'T DESIGNED TO POWER THEM THIS LONG ANYWAY.
FOR THEM TO LAST OVER 100 YEARS IS ACTUALLY PRETTY INCREDIBLE.
YOU KNEW...
...FROM THE BEGINNING, DIDN'T YOU?
......

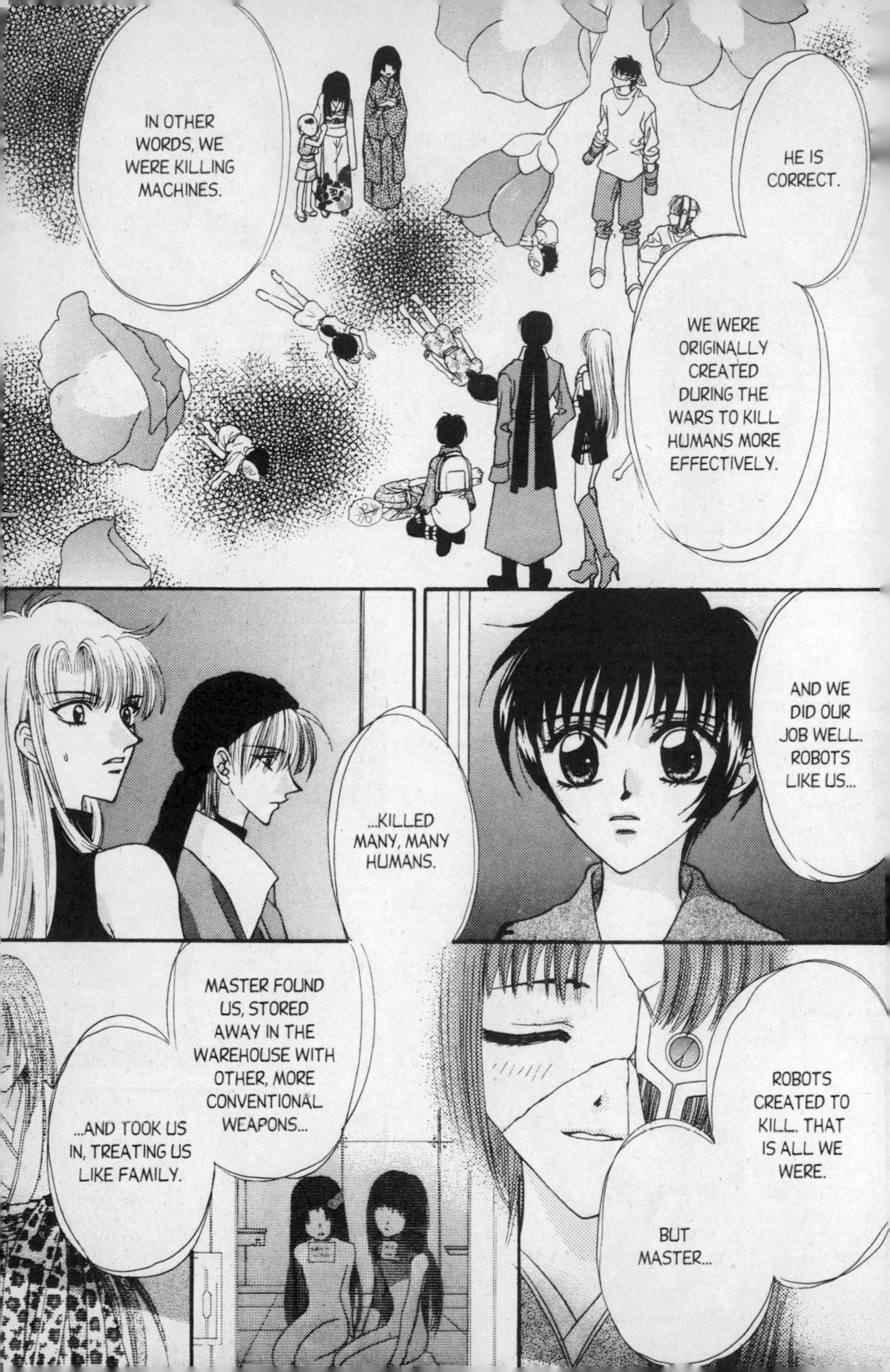
HE IS CORRECT.
WE WERE ORIGINALLY CREATED DURING THE WARS TO KILL HUMANS MORE EFFECTIVELY.
IN OTHER WORDS, WE WERE KILLING MACHINES.
AND WE DID OUR JOB WELL. ROBOTS LIKE US...
...KILLED MANY, MANY HUMANS.
ROBOTS CREATED TO KILL. THAT IS ALL WE WERE.
BUT MASTER...
MASTER FOUND US, STORED AWAY IN THE WAREHOUSE WITH OTHER, MORE CONVENTIONAL WEAPONS...
...AND TOOK US IN, TREATING US LIKE FAMILY.

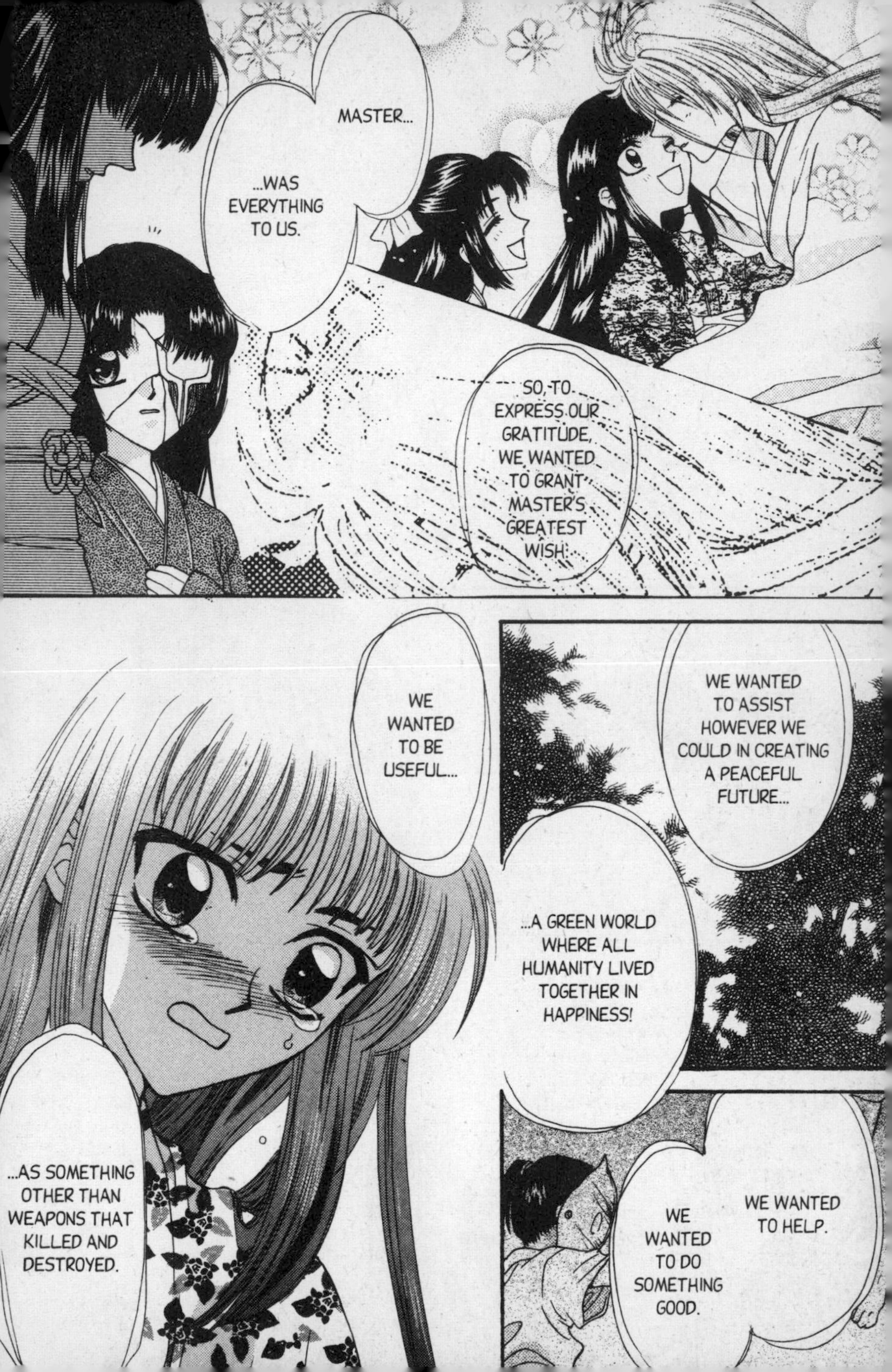
MASTER... ...WAS EVERYTHING TO US.
SO, TO EXPRESS OUR GRATITUDE, WE WANTED TO GRANT MASTER'S GREATEST WISH.
WE WANTED TO ASSIST HOWEVER WE COULD IN CREATING A PEACEFUL FUTURE...
...A GREEN WORLD WHERE ALL HUMANITY LIVED TOGETHER IN HAPPINESS!
WE WANTED TO HELP.
WE WANTED TO DO SOMETHING GOOD.
WE WANTED TO BE USEFUL...
...AS SOMETHING OTHER THAN WEAPONS THAT KILLED AND DESTROYED.

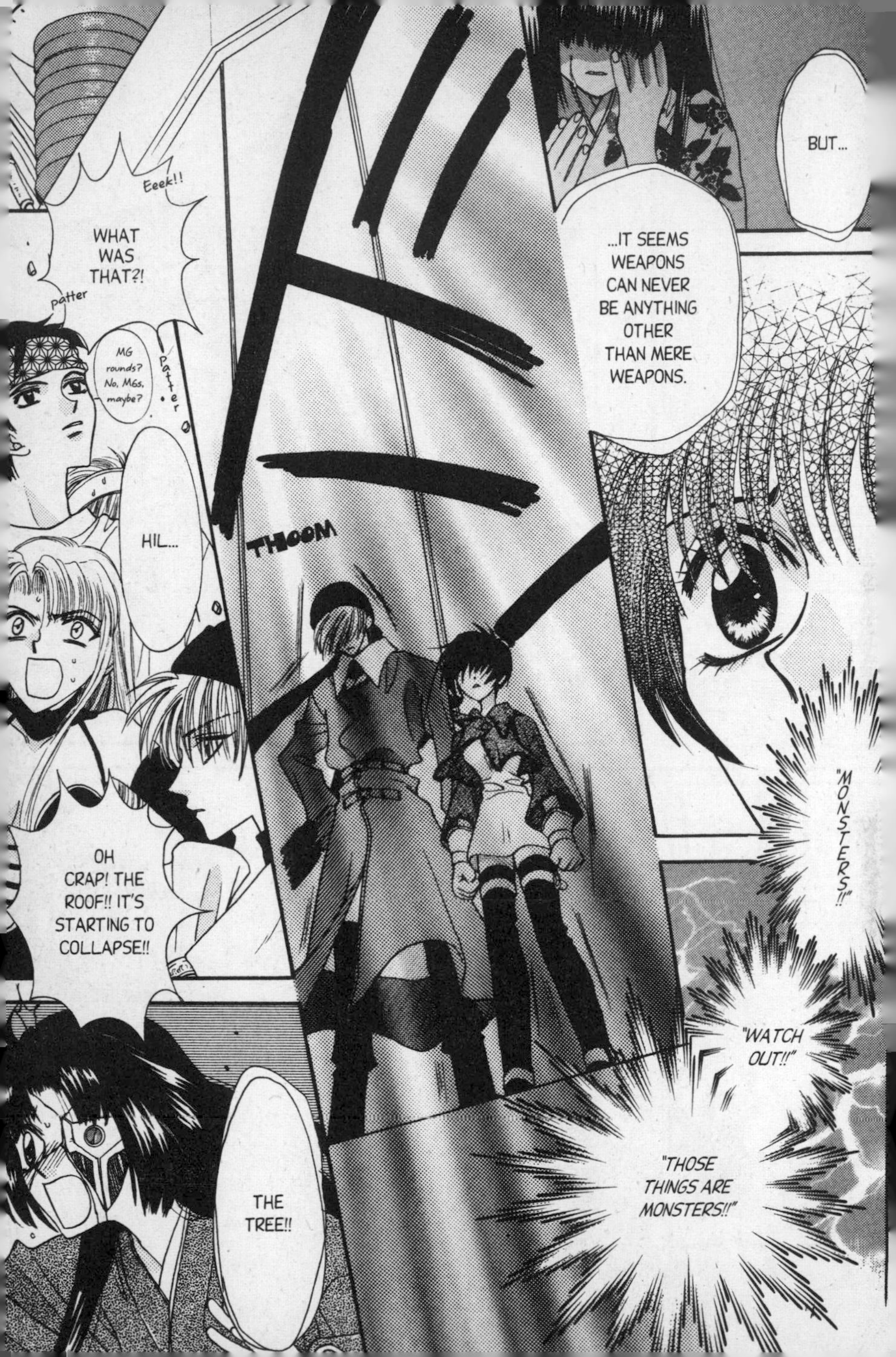
BUT...
...IT SEEMS WEAPONS CAN NEVER BE ANYTHING OTHER THAN MERE WEAPONS.
"MONSTERS!!"
"WATCH OUT!!"
"THOSE THINGS ARE MONSTERS!!"
THOOM
Eeek!!
WHAT WAS THAT?!
patter
Patter
MG rounds? No, M6s, maybe?
HIL...
OH CRAP! THE ROOF!! IT'S STARTING TO COLLAPSE!!
THE TREE!!

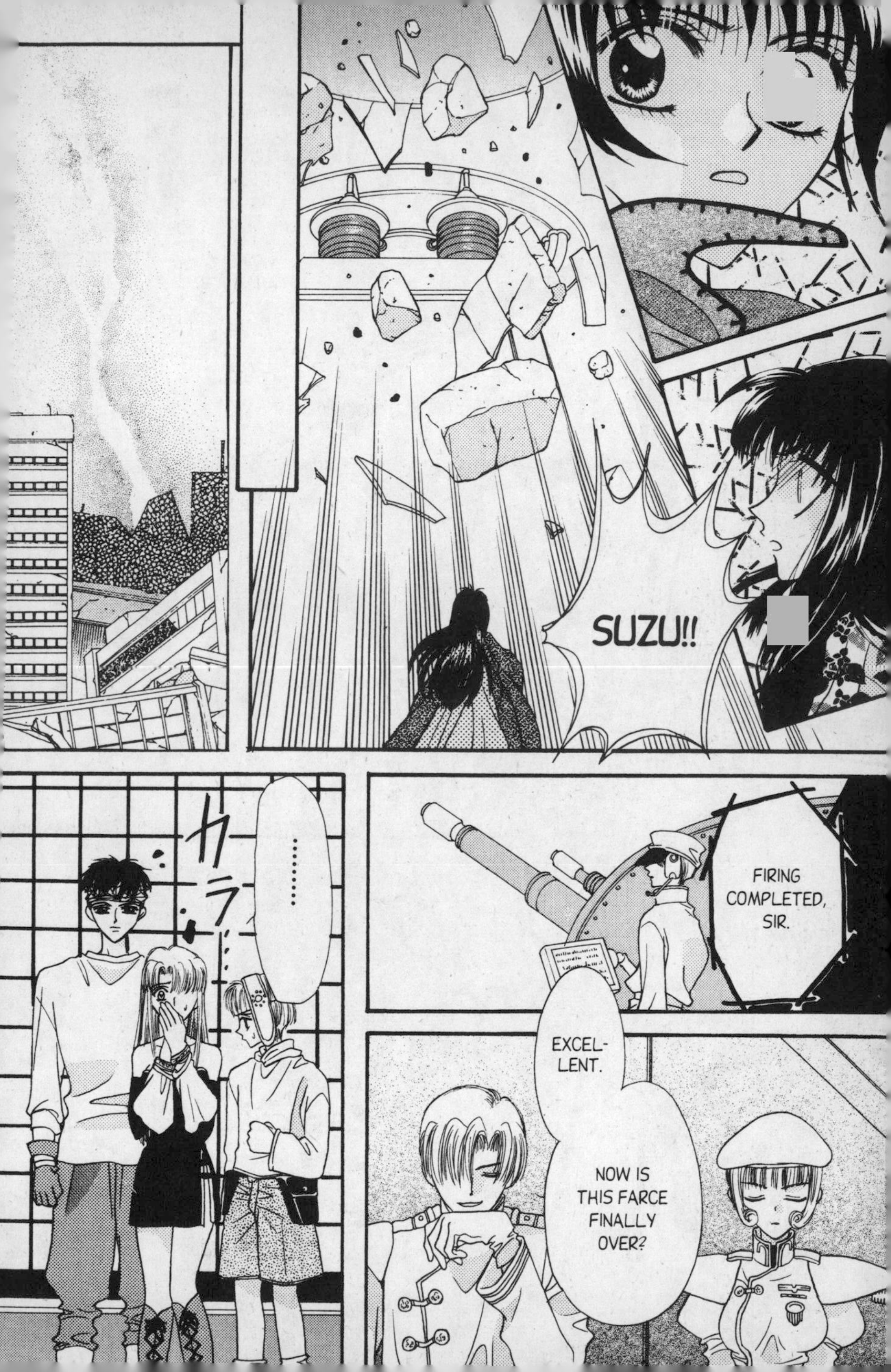
SUZU!!
FIRING COMPLETED, SIR.
EXCEL-LENT.
NOW IS THIS FARCE FINALLY OVER?
......
カラ

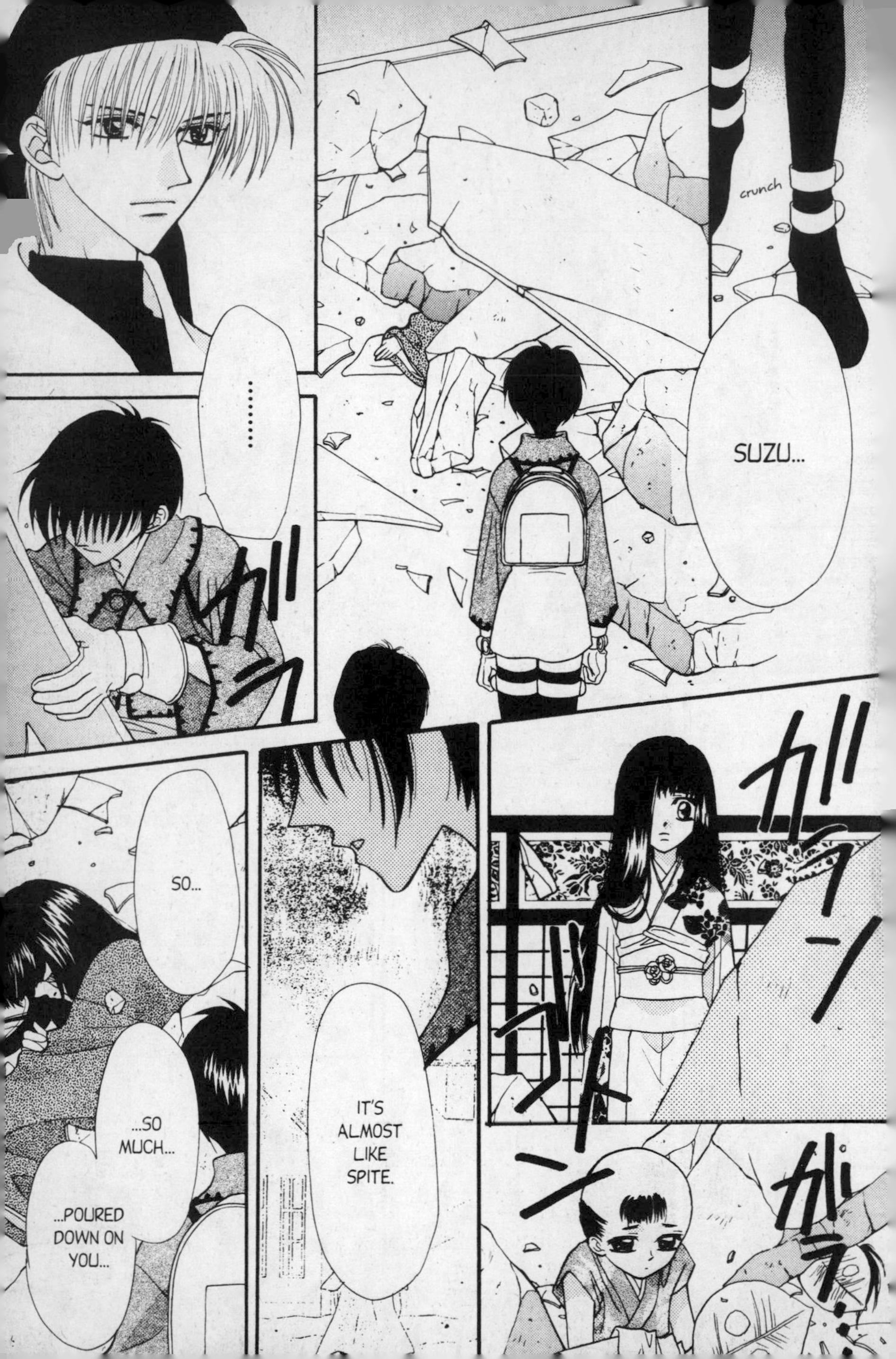
crunch
SUZU...
......
IT'S ALMOST LIKE SPITE.
SO...
...SO MUCH...
...POURED DOWN ON YOU...

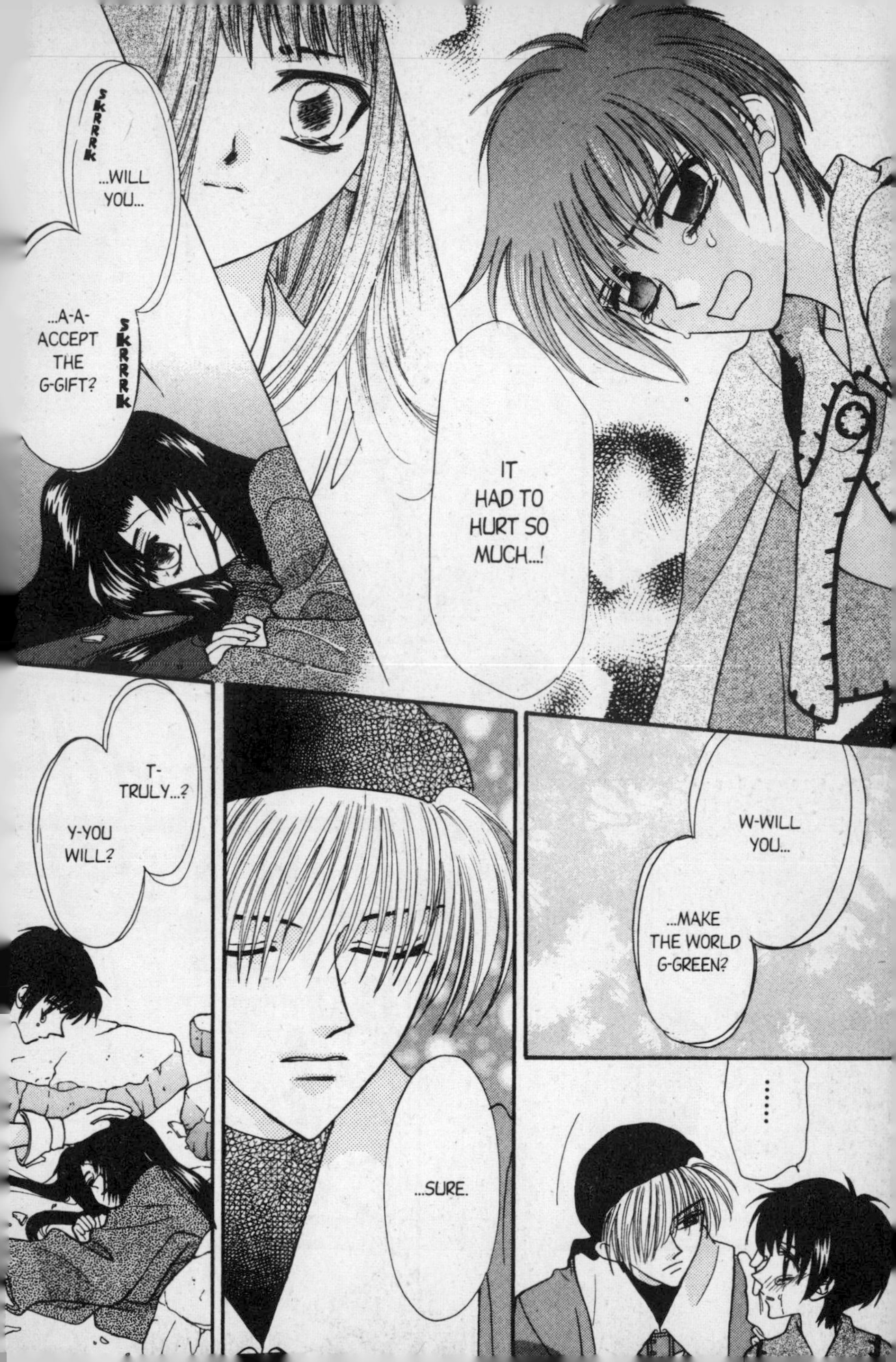

IT HAD TO HURT SO MUCH...!
SKRRRK
...WILL YOU...
...A-A-ACCEPT THE G-GIFT?
SKRRRK
W-WILL YOU...
...MAKE THE WORLD G-GREEN?
......
...SURE.
T-TRULY...?
Y-YOU WILL?

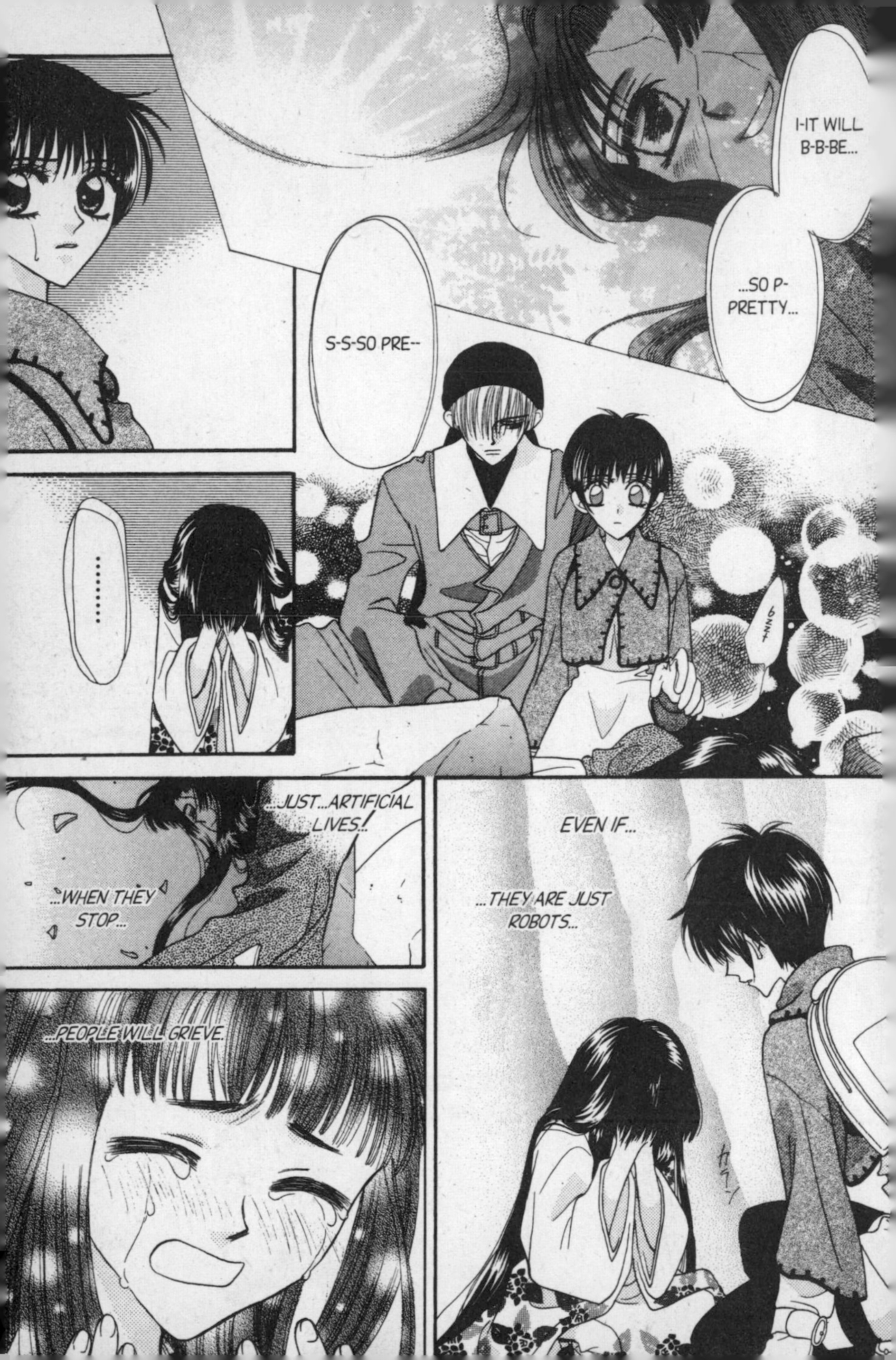

I-IT WILL B-B-BE...
...SO P-PRETTY...
S-S-SO PRE--
bzzt
......
EVEN IF...
...THEY ARE JUST ROBOTS...
...JUST...ARTIFICIAL LIVES!
...WHEN THEY STOP...
...PEOPLE WILL GRIEVE.

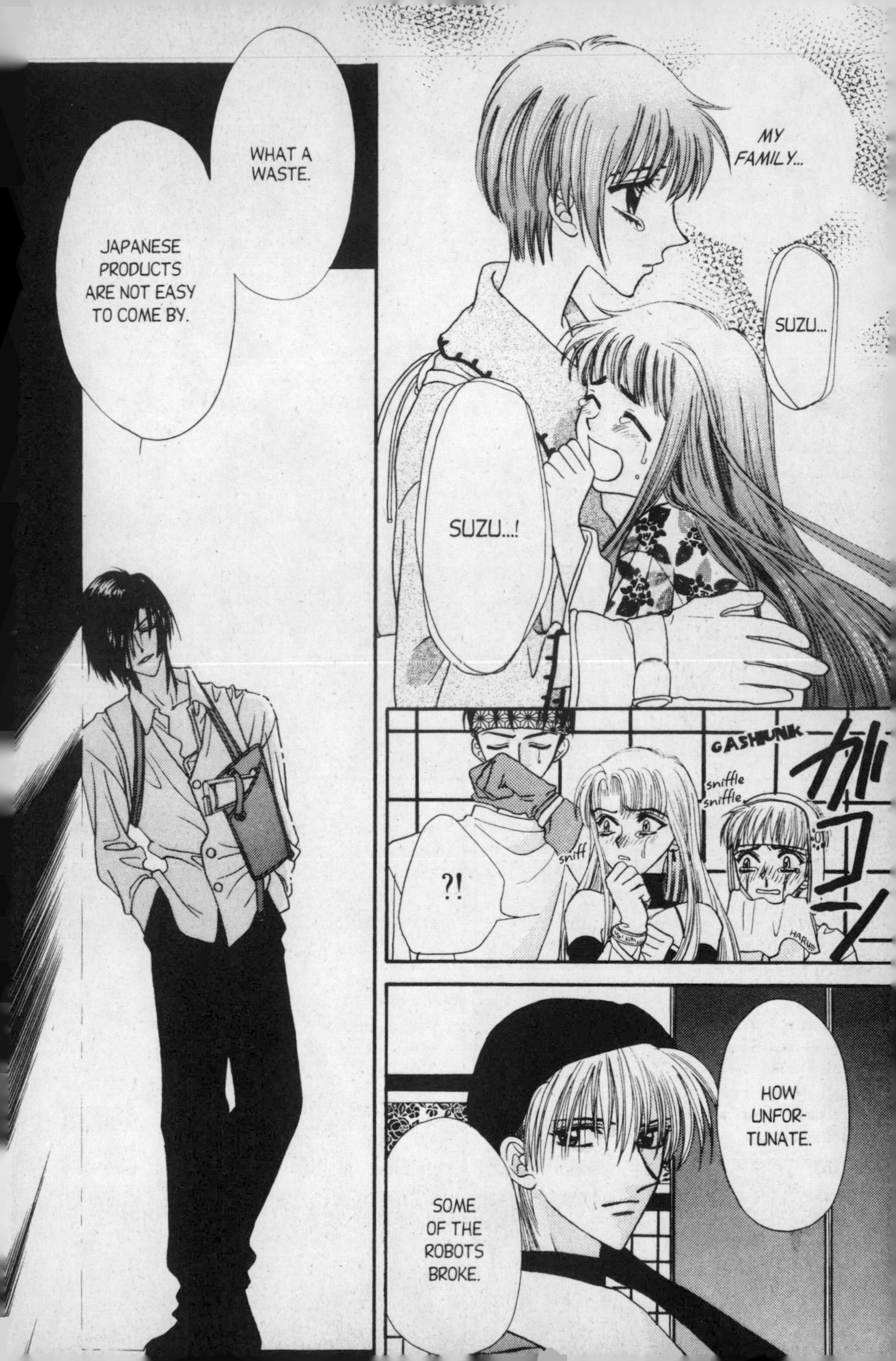
MY FAMILY...
SUZU...
SUZU...!
ガコーン
GASHUNK
sniffle sniffle
sniff
?!
HOW UNFOR-TUNATE.
SOME OF THE ROBOTS BROKE.
WHAT A WASTE.
JAPANESE PRODUCTS ARE NOT EASY TO COME BY.

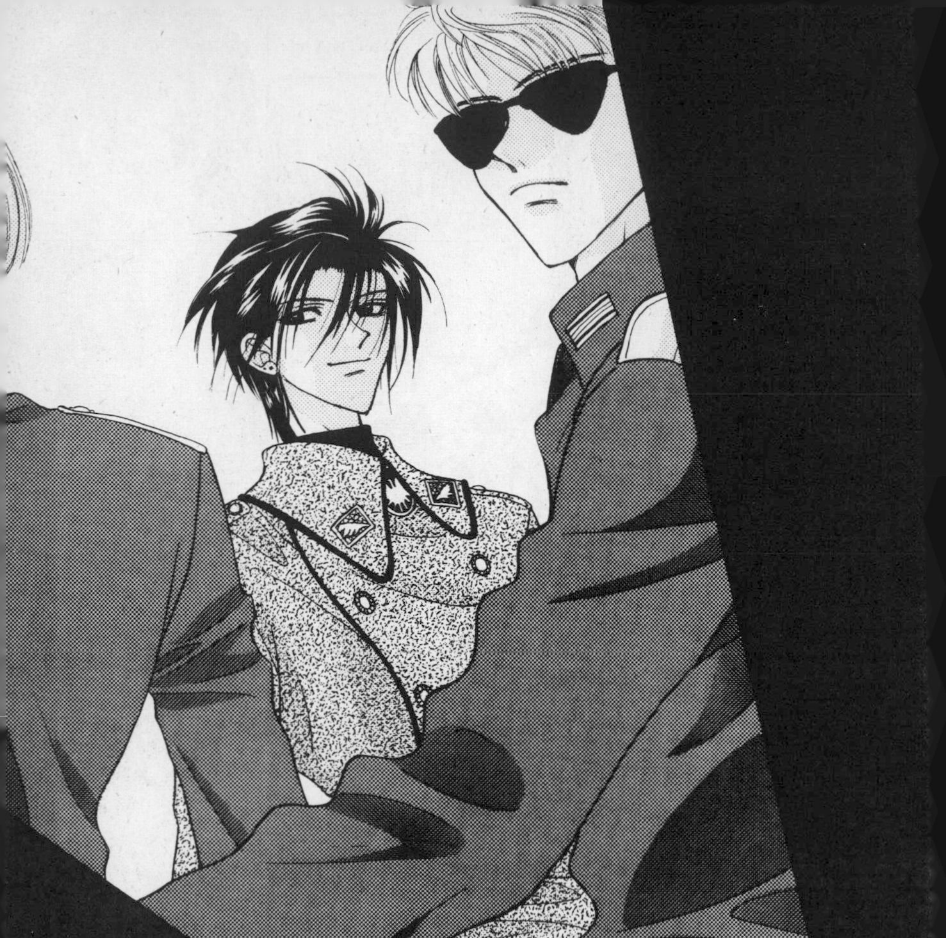

翼(つばさ)を持(も)つ者(もの)

Tsubasa: Those With Wings

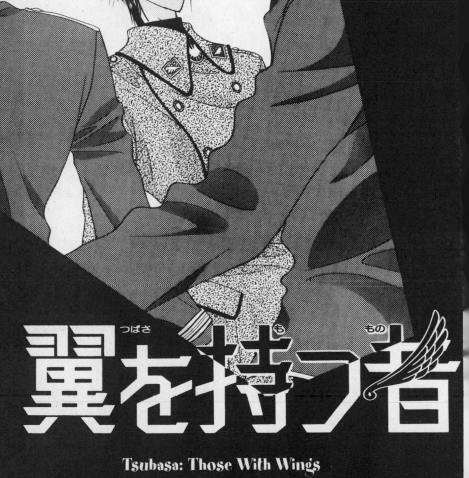

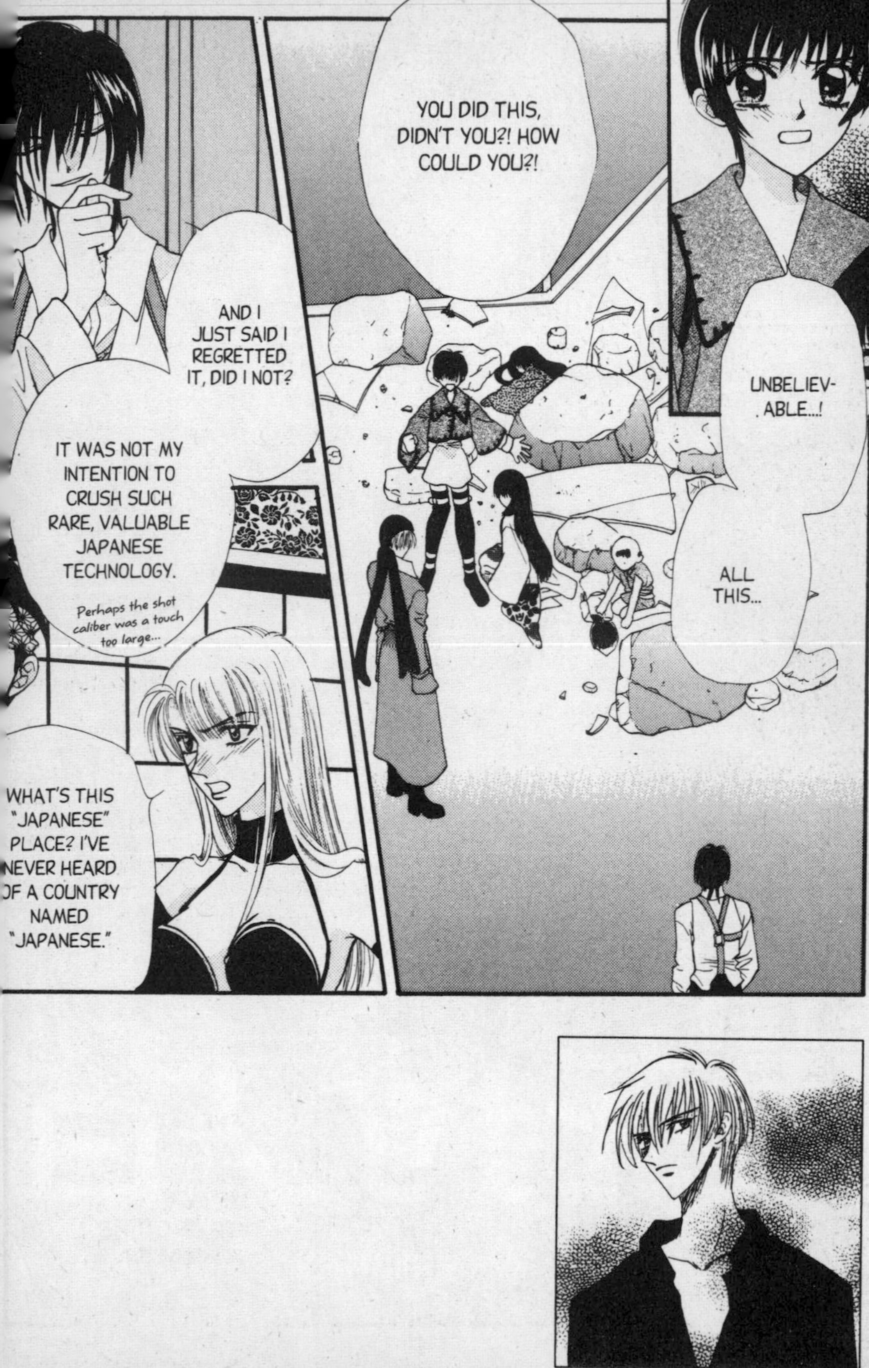
UNBELIEV-ABLE...!
ALL THIS...
YOU DID THIS, DIDN'T YOU?! HOW COULD YOU?!
AND I JUST SAID I REGRETTED IT, DID I NOT?
IT WAS NOT MY INTENTION TO CRUSH SUCH RARE, VALUABLE JAPANESE TECHNOLOGY.
Perhaps the shot caliber was a touch too large...
WHAT'S THIS "JAPANESE" PLACE? I'VE NEVER HEARD OF A COUNTRY NAMED "JAPANESE."

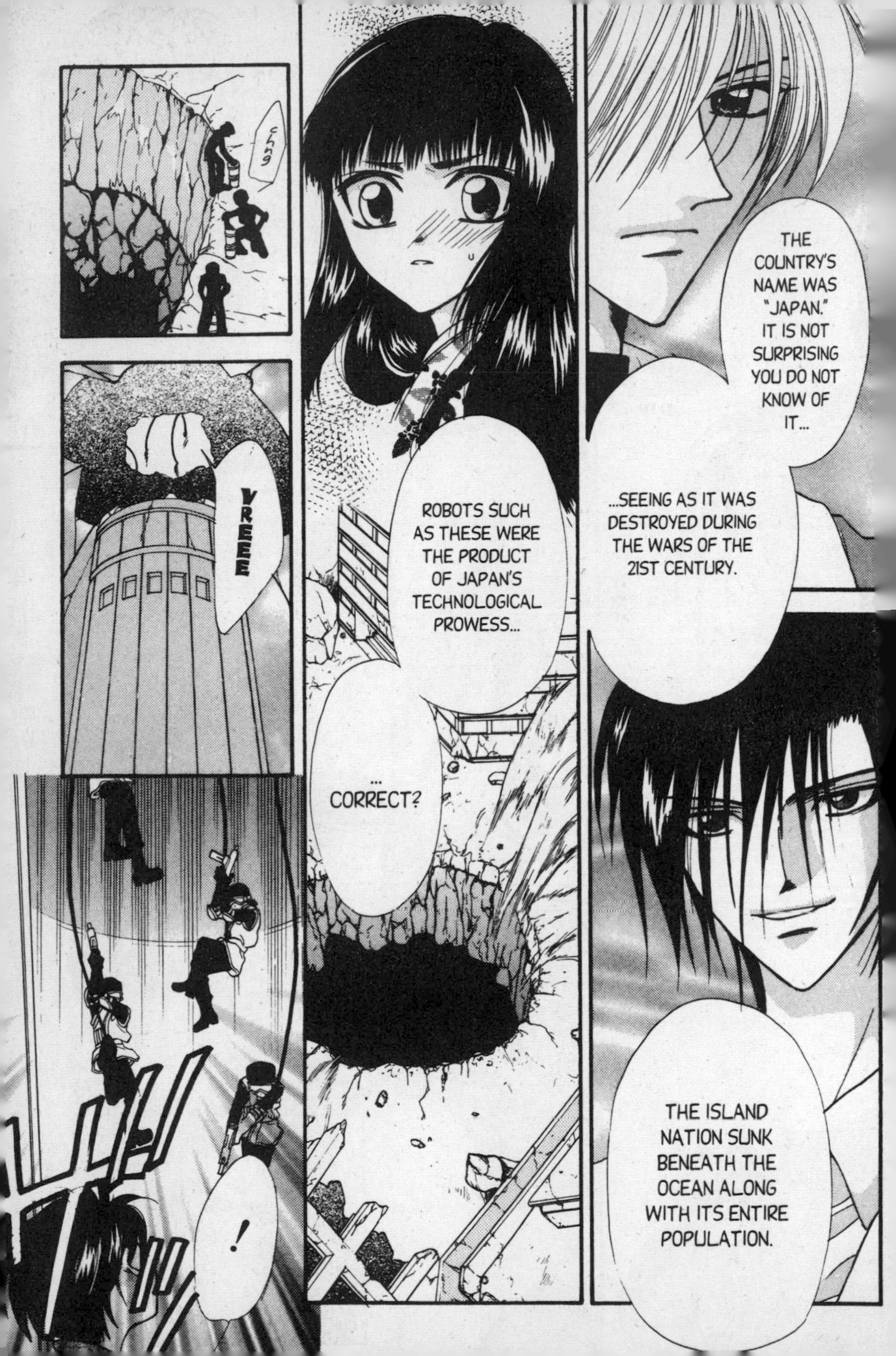

THE COUNTRY'S NAME WAS "JAPAN." IT IS NOT SURPRISING YOU DO NOT KNOW OF IT...
...SEEING AS IT WAS DESTROYED DURING THE WARS OF THE 21ST CENTURY.
THE ISLAND NATION SUNK BENEATH THE OCEAN ALONG WITH ITS ENTIRE POPULATION.
ROBOTS SUCH AS THESE WERE THE PRODUCT OF JAPAN'S TECHNOLOGICAL PROWESS...
... CORRECT?
chng
VREEE
!

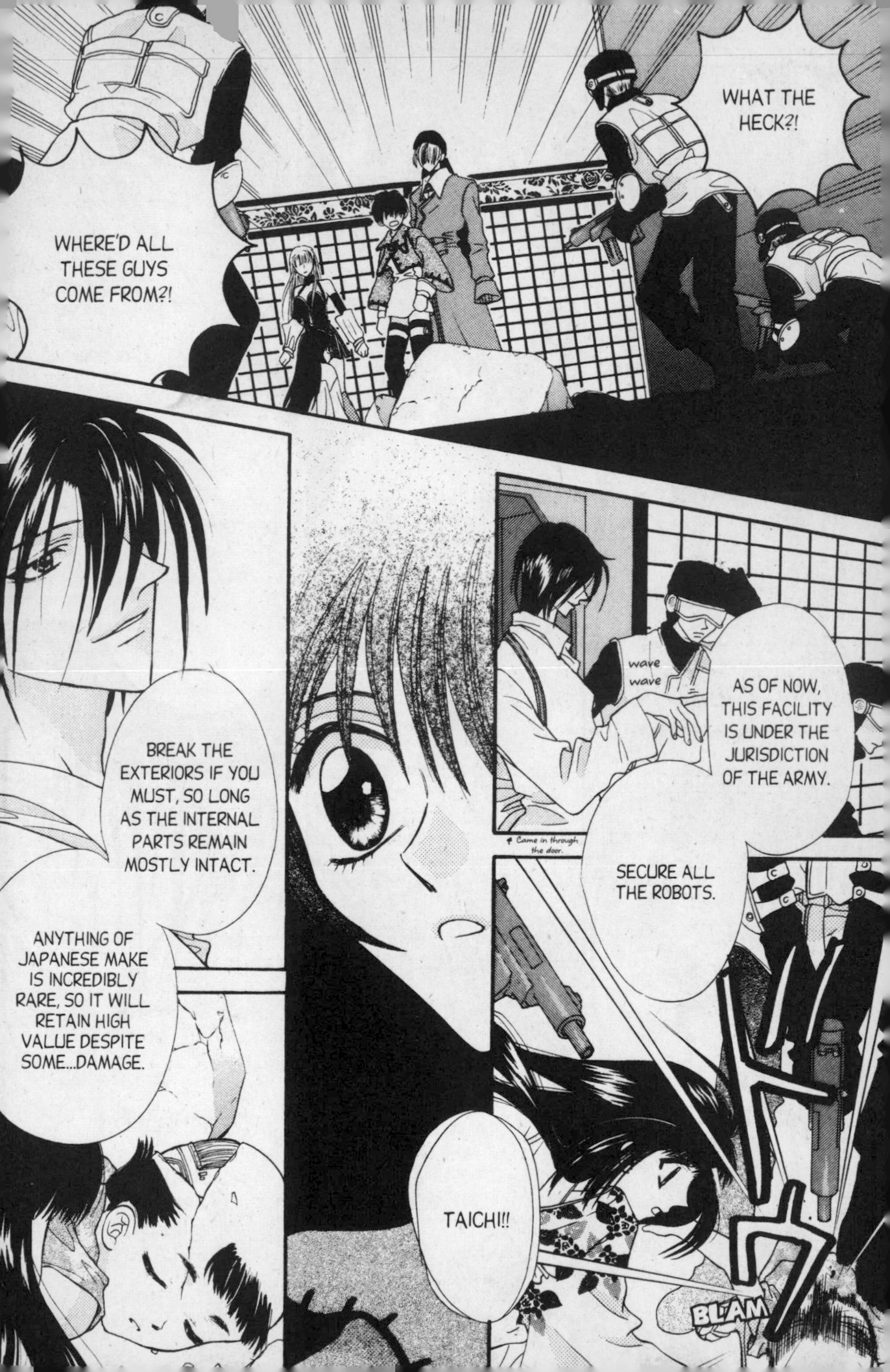
WHAT THE HECK?!
WHERE'D ALL THESE GUYS COME FROM?!
wave wave
AS OF NOW, THIS FACILITY IS UNDER THE JURISDICTION OF THE ARMY.
Came in through the door.
SECURE ALL THE ROBOTS.
BREAK THE EXTERIORS IF YOU MUST, SO LONG AS THE INTERNAL PARTS REMAIN MOSTLY INTACT.
ANYTHING OF JAPANESE MAKE IS INCREDIBLY RARE, SO IT WILL RETAIN HIGH VALUE DESPITE SOME...DAMAGE.
TAICHI!!
BLAM

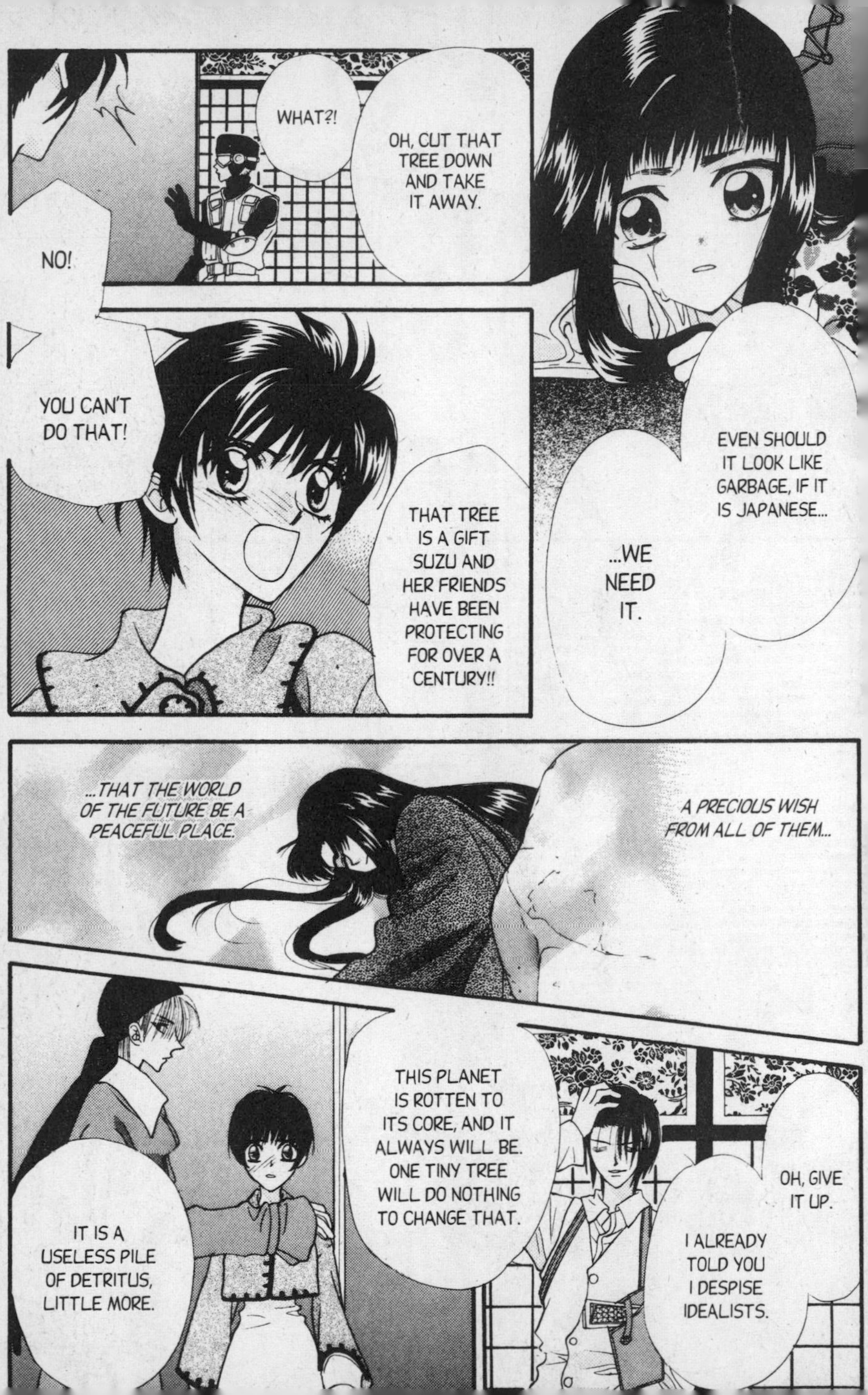
EVEN SHOULD IT LOOK LIKE GARBAGE, IF IT IS JAPANESE...
...WE NEED IT.
WHAT?!
OH, CUT THAT TREE DOWN AND TAKE IT AWAY.
NO!
YOU CAN'T DO THAT!
THAT TREE IS A GIFT SUZU AND HER FRIENDS HAVE BEEN PROTECTING FOR OVER A CENTURY!!
A PRECIOUS WISH FROM ALL OF THEM...
...THAT THE WORLD OF THE FUTURE BE A PEACEFUL PLACE.
OH, GIVE IT UP.
I ALREADY TOLD YOU I DESPISE IDEALISTS.
THIS PLANET IS ROTTEN TO ITS CORE, AND IT ALWAYS WILL BE. ONE TINY TREE WILL DO NOTHING TO CHANGE THAT.
IT IS A USELESS PILE OF DETRITUS, LITTLE MORE.

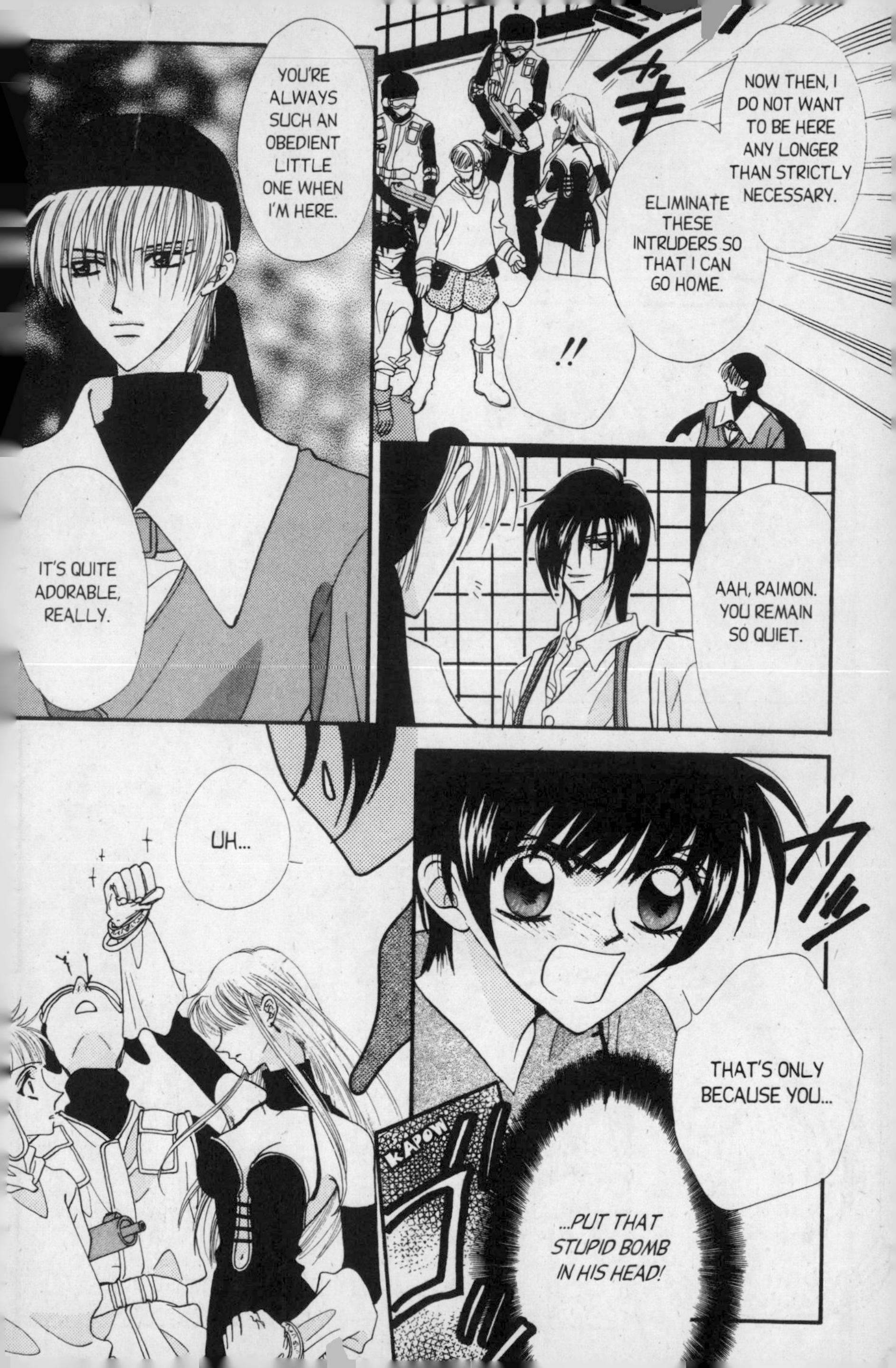
NOW THEN, I DO NOT WANT TO BE HERE ANY LONGER THAN STRICTLY NECESSARY.
ELIMINATE THESE INTRUDERS SO THAT I CAN GO HOME.
!!
AAH, RAIMON. YOU REMAIN SO QUIET.
YOU'RE ALWAYS SUCH AN OBEDIENT LITTLE ONE WHEN I'M HERE.
IT'S QUITE ADORABLE, REALLY.
THAT'S ONLY BECAUSE YOU...
...PUT THAT STUPID BOMB IN HIS HEAD!
KAPON
UH...

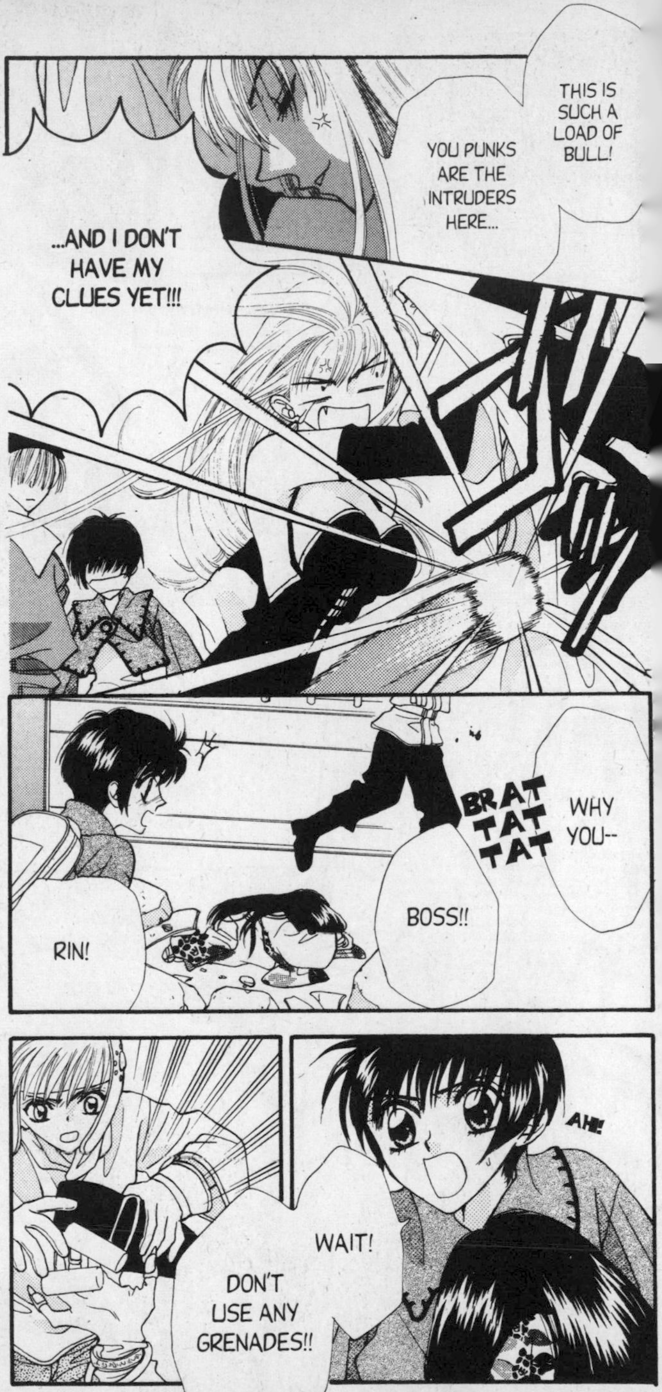
THIS IS SUCH A LOAD OF BULL!
YOU PUNKS ARE THE INTRUDERS HERE...
...AND I DON'T HAVE MY CLUES YET!!!
WHY YOU--
BRAT TAT TAT
BOSS!!
RIN!
AH!
WAIT!
DON'T USE ANY GRENADES!!

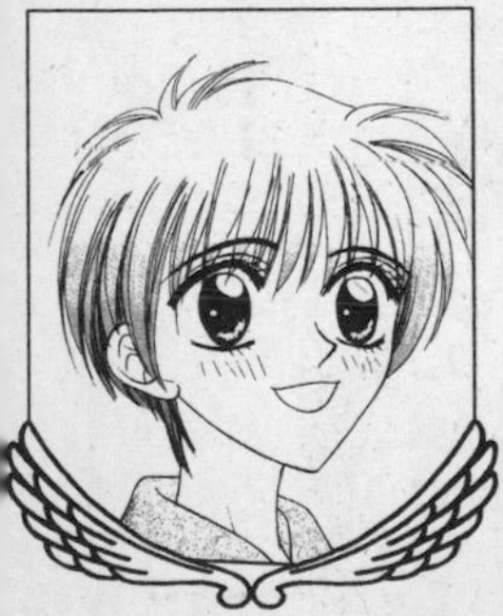

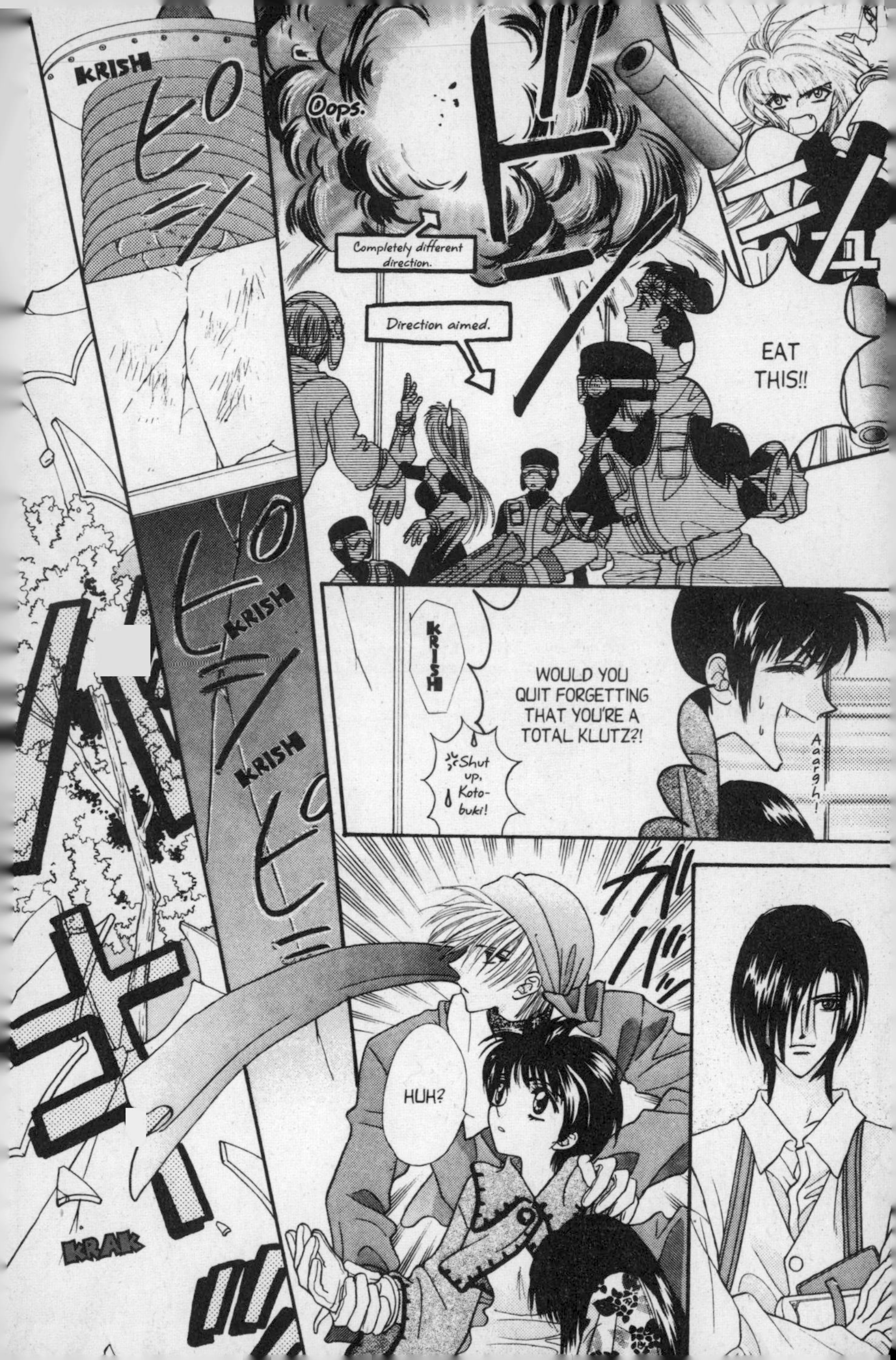
EAT THIS!!
Oops.
Completely different direction.
Direction aimed.
WOULD YOU QUIT FORGETTING THAT YOU'RE A TOTAL KLUTZ?!
Aaargh!
KRISH
Shut up, Kotobuki!
HUH?
KRISH
KRISH
KRISH
KRAK

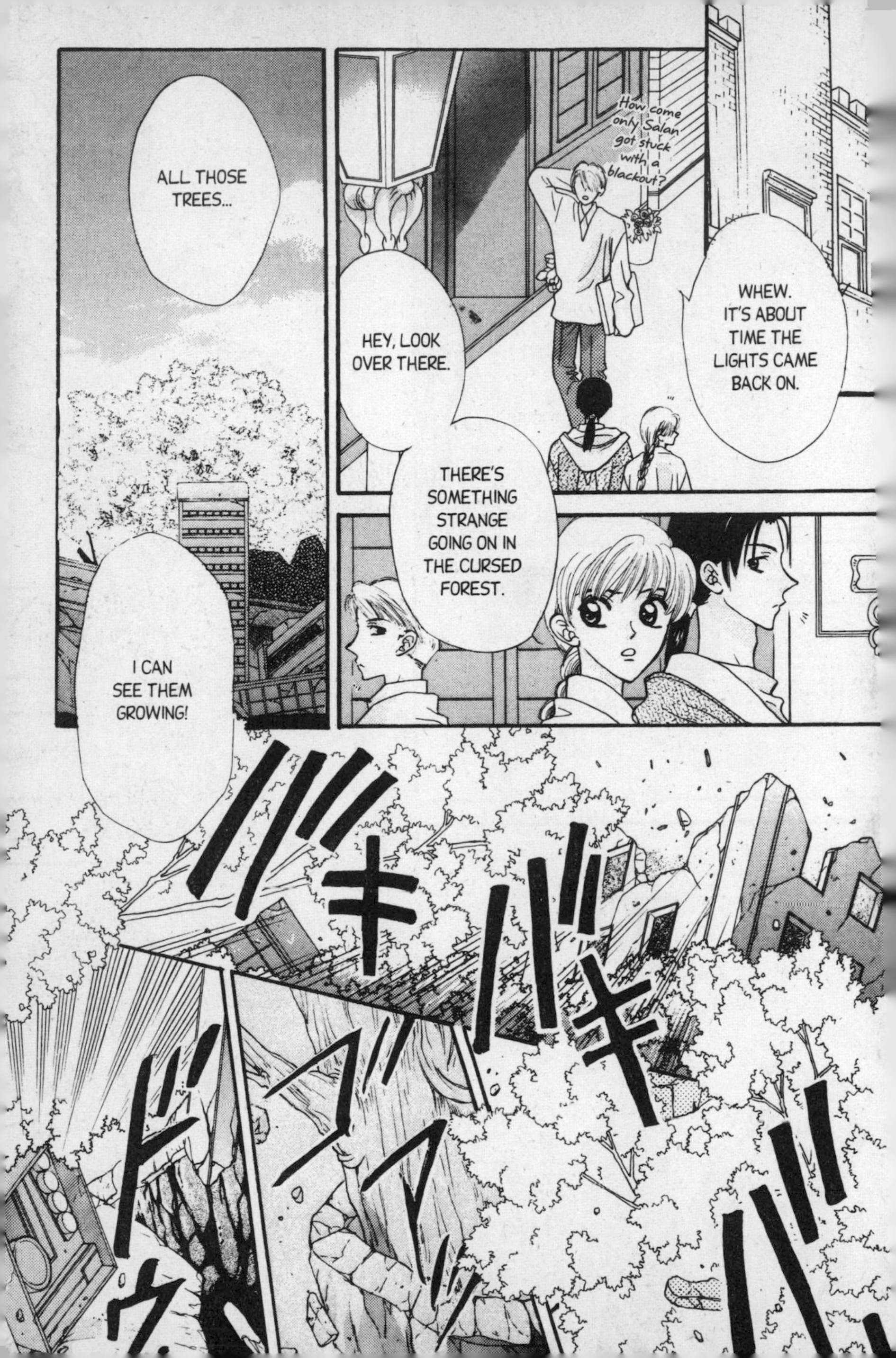
WHEW. IT'S ABOUT TIME THE LIGHTS CAME BACK ON.
How come only Salan got stuck with a blackout?
HEY, LOOK OVER THERE.
THERE'S SOMETHING STRANGE GOING ON IN THE CURSED FOREST.
ALL THOSE TREES...
I CAN SEE THEM GROWING!

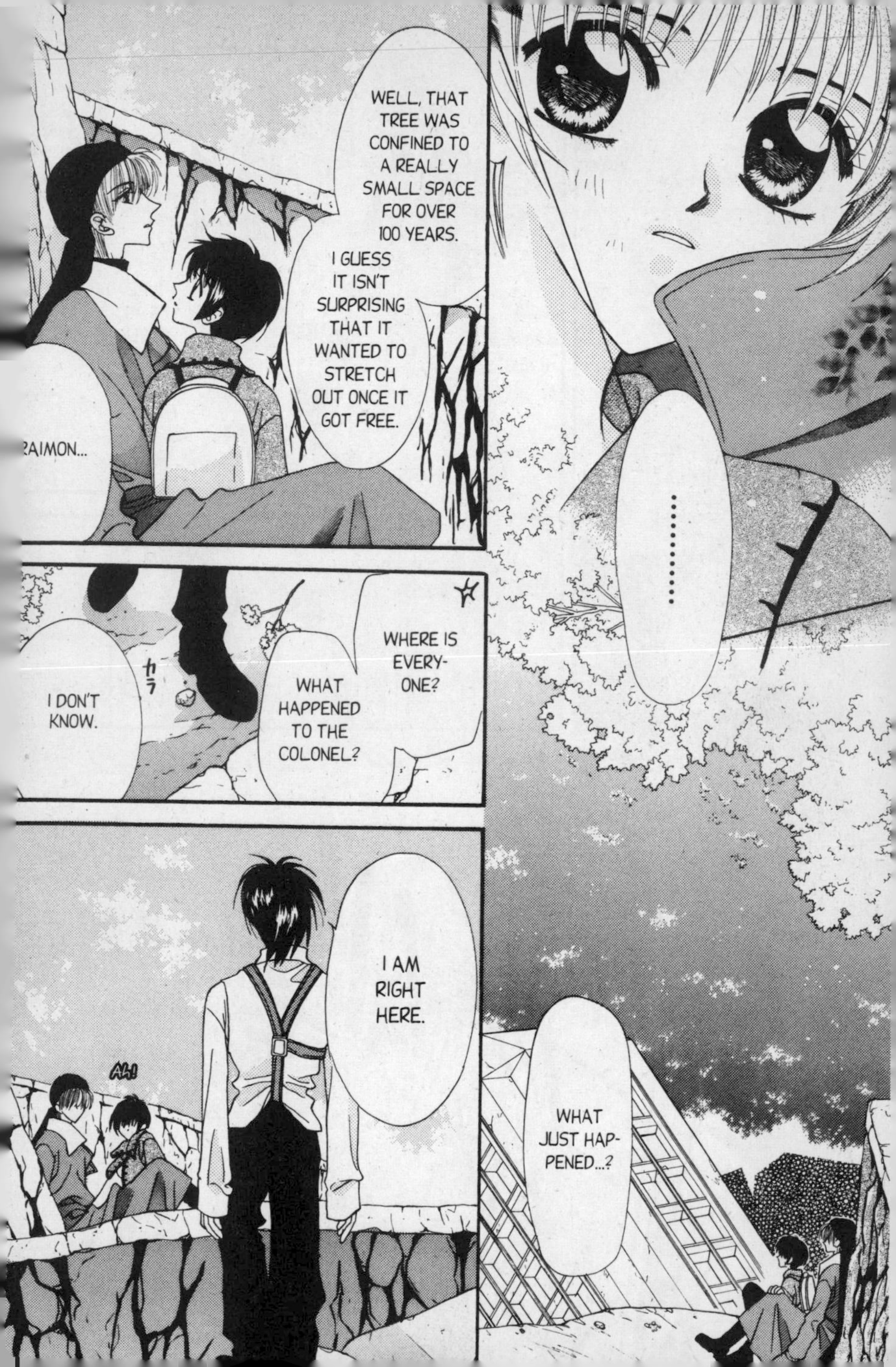

......
WHAT JUST HAPPENED...?
WELL, THAT TREE WAS CONFINED TO A REALLY SMALL SPACE FOR OVER 100 YEARS.
I GUESS IT ISN'T SURPRISING THAT IT WANTED TO STRETCH OUT ONCE IT GOT FREE.
RAIMON...
WHERE IS EVERYONE?
WHAT HAPPENED TO THE COLONEL?
カラ
I DON'T KNOW.
I AM RIGHT HERE.
AH!

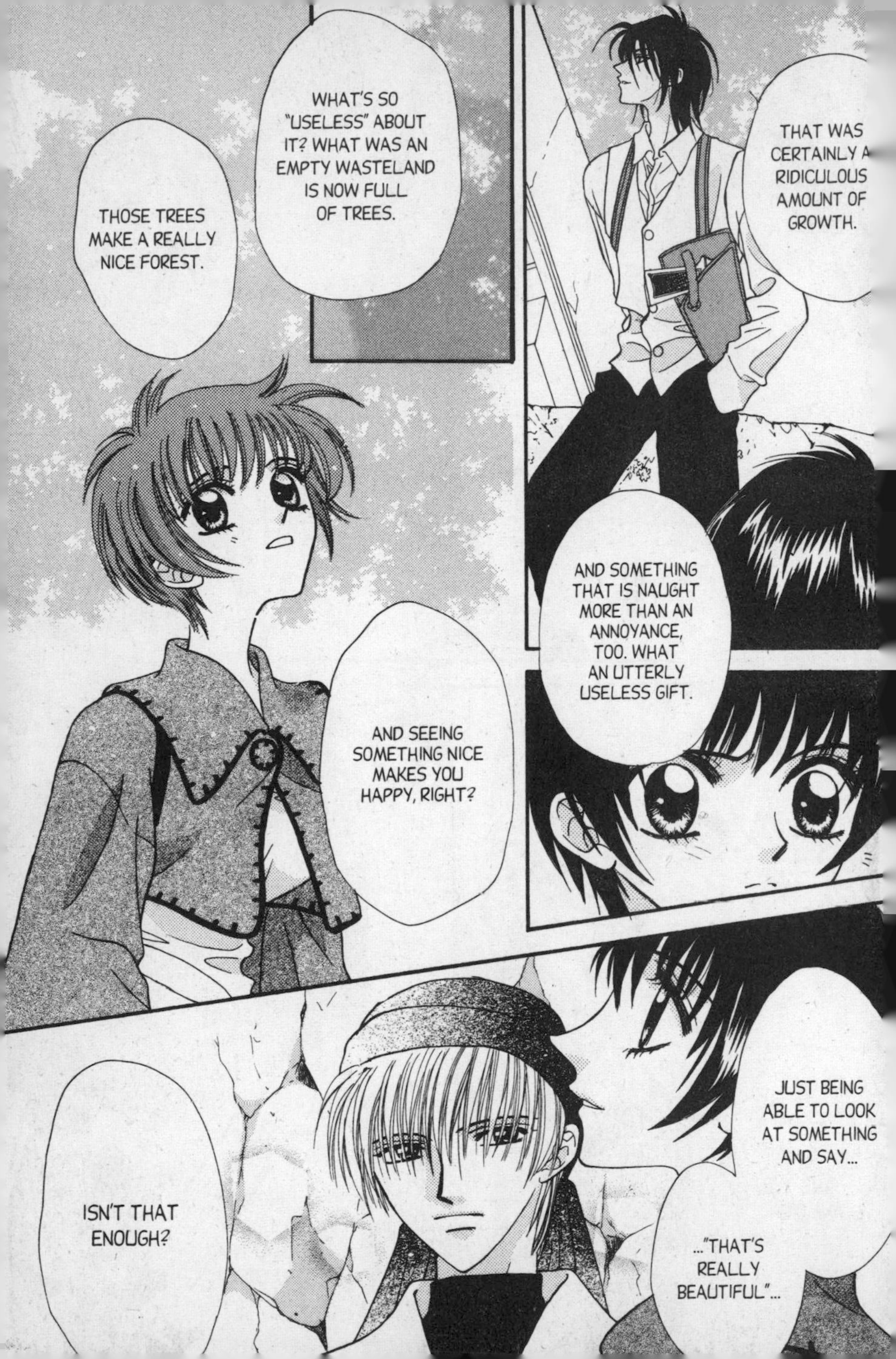
THAT WAS CERTAINLY A RIDICULOUS AMOUNT OF GROWTH.
AND SOMETHING THAT IS NAUGHT MORE THAN AN ANNOYANCE, TOO. WHAT AN UTTERLY USELESS GIFT.
WHAT'S SO "USELESS" ABOUT IT? WHAT WAS AN EMPTY WASTELAND IS NOW FULL OF TREES.
THOSE TREES MAKE A REALLY NICE FOREST.
AND SEEING SOMETHING NICE MAKES YOU HAPPY, RIGHT?
JUST BEING ABLE TO LOOK AT SOMETHING AND SAY...
..."THAT'S REALLY BEAUTIFUL"...
ISN'T THAT ENOUGH?

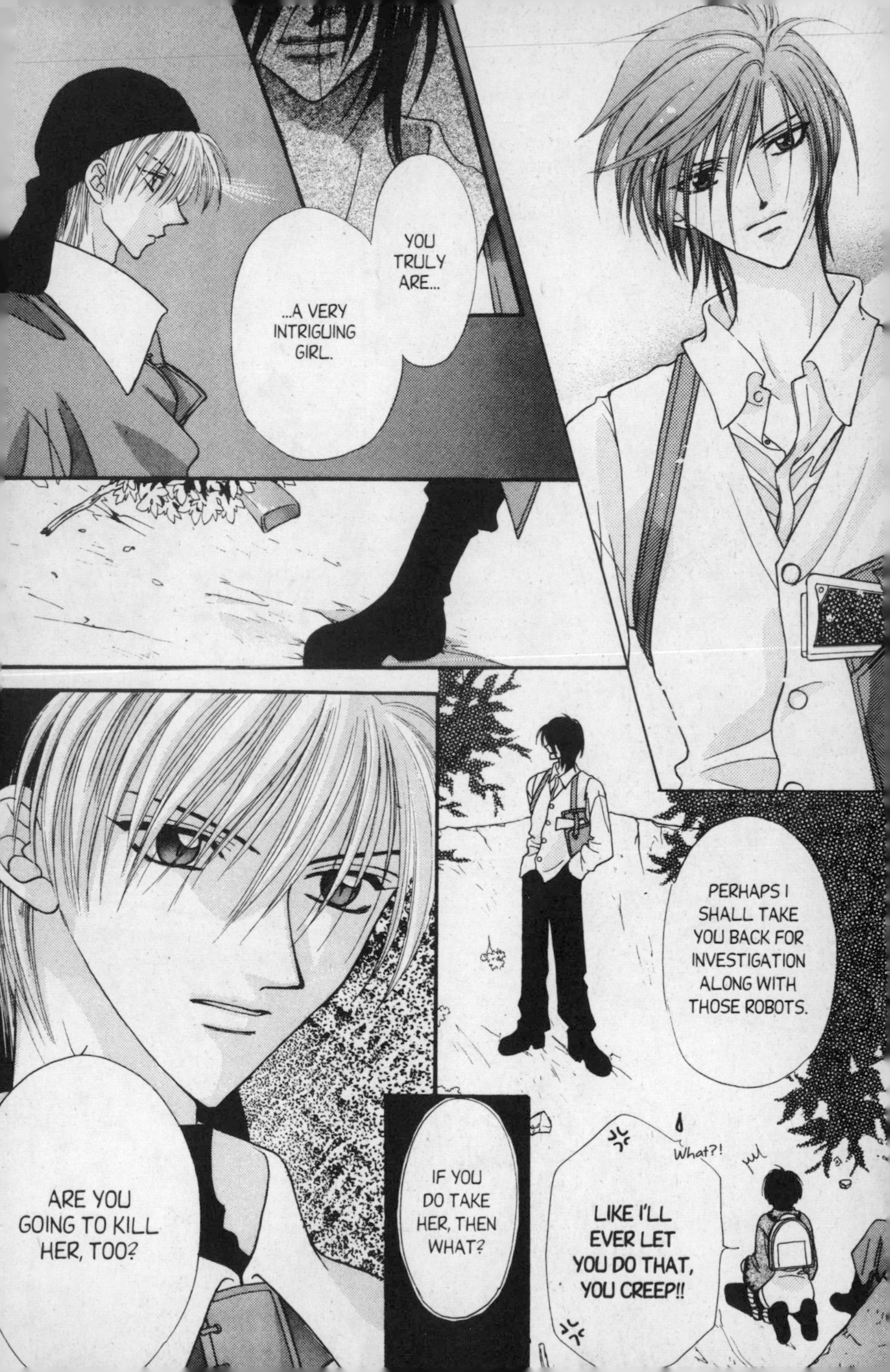
YOU TRULY ARE...
...A VERY INTRIGUING GIRL.
PERHAPS I SHALL TAKE YOU BACK FOR INVESTIGATION ALONG WITH THOSE ROBOTS.
What?!
LIKE I'LL EVER LET YOU DO THAT, YOU CREEP!!
IF YOU DO TAKE HER, THEN WHAT?
ARE YOU GOING TO KILL HER, TOO?

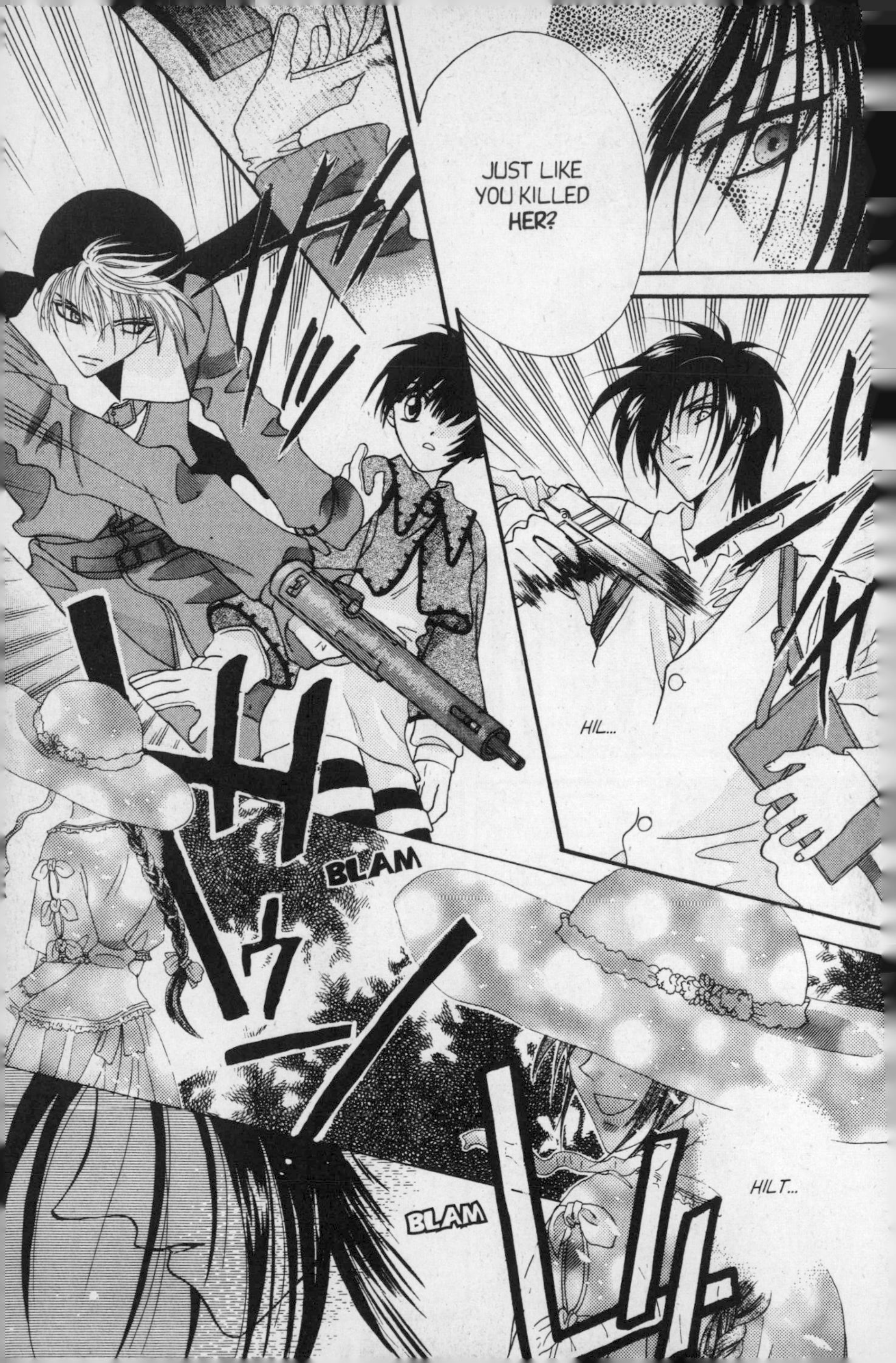
JUST LIKE YOU KILLED HER?
HIL...
BLAM
HILT...
BLAM

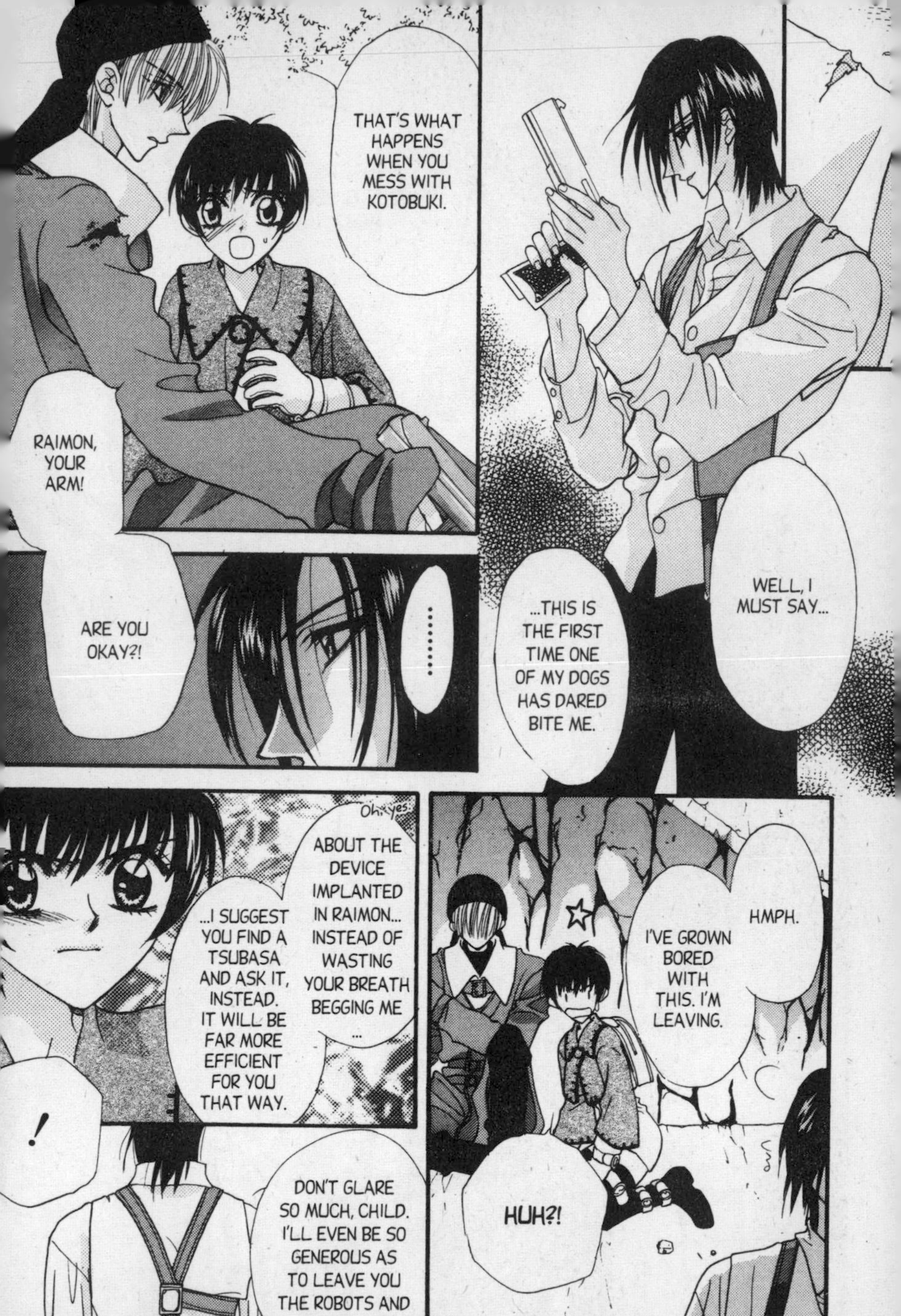
WELL, I MUST SAY...
...THIS IS THE FIRST TIME ONE OF MY DOGS HAS DARED BITE ME.
THAT'S WHAT HAPPENS WHEN YOU MESS WITH KOTOBUKI.
RAIMON, YOUR ARM!
....
ARE YOU OKAY?!
HMPH.
I'VE GROWN BORED WITH THIS. I'M LEAVING.
HUH?!
Oh, yes.
ABOUT THE DEVICE IMPLANTED IN RAIMON... INSTEAD OF WASTING YOUR BREATH BEGGING ME ...
...I SUGGEST YOU FIND A TSUBASA AND ASK IT, INSTEAD. IT WILL BE FAR MORE EFFICIENT FOR YOU THAT WAY.
!
DON'T GLARE SO MUCH, CHILD. I'LL EVEN BE SO GENEROUS AS TO LEAVE YOU THE ROBOTS AND THE TREES.

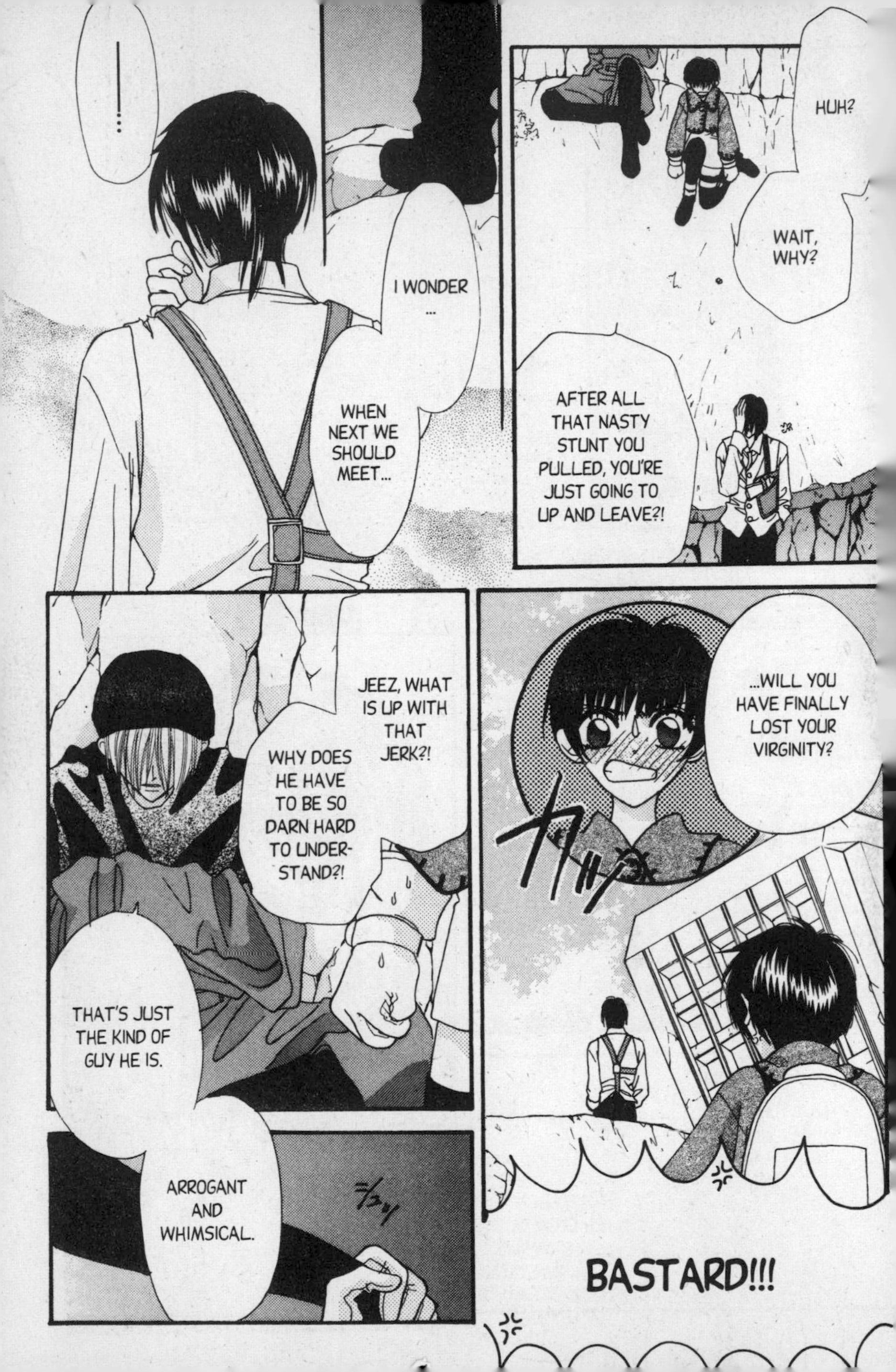
HUH?
WAIT, WHY?
AFTER ALL THAT NASTY STUNT YOU PULLED, YOU'RE JUST GOING TO UP AND LEAVE?!
—...
I WONDER ...
WHEN NEXT WE SHOULD MEET...
...WILL YOU HAVE FINALLY LOST YOUR VIRGINITY?
BASTARD!!!
JEEZ, WHAT IS UP WITH THAT JERK?!
WHY DOES HE HAVE TO BE SO DARN HARD TO UNDER-STAND?!
THAT'S JUST THE KIND OF GUY HE IS.
ARROGANT AND WHIMSICAL.

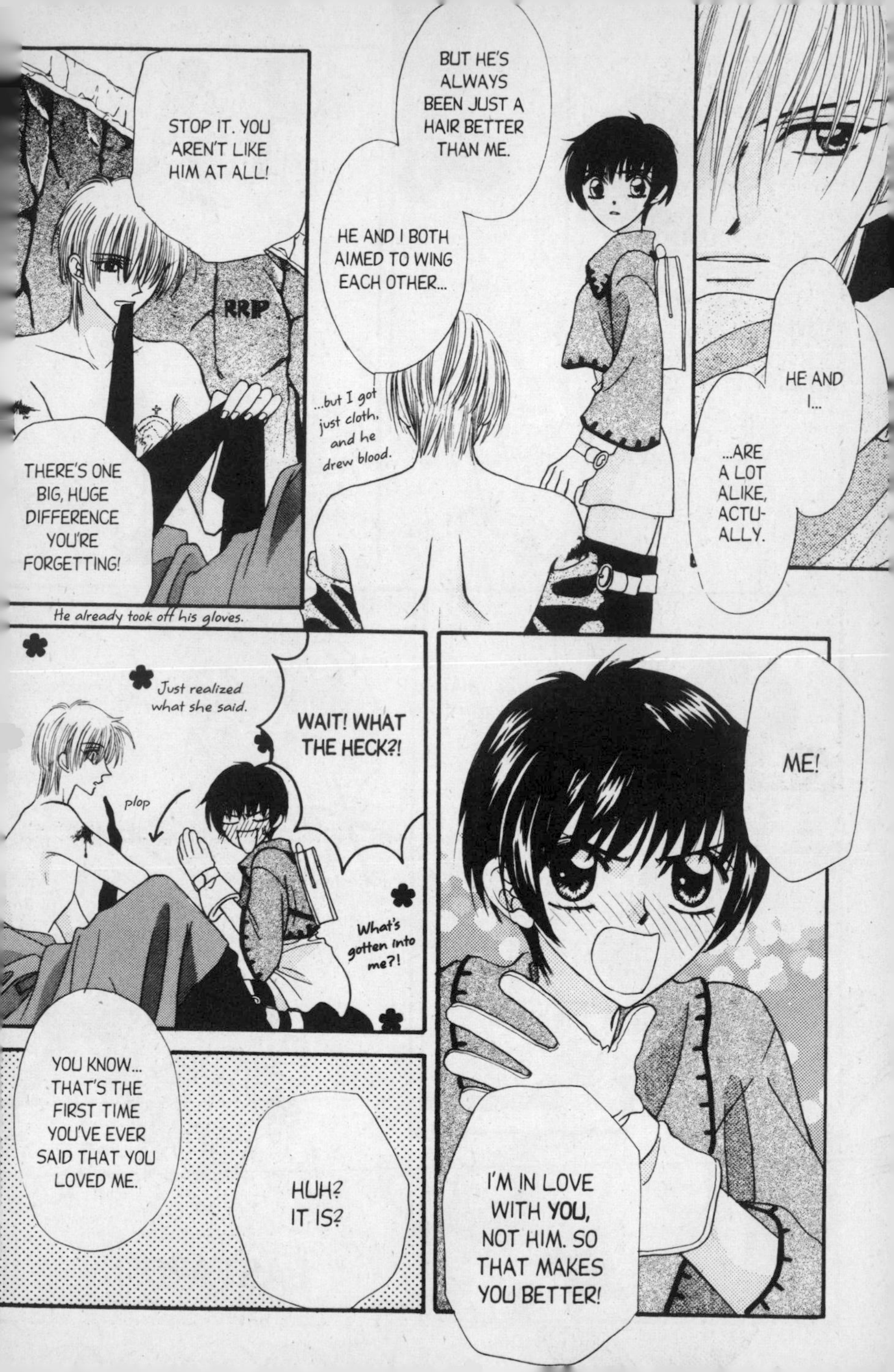
HE AND I...
...ARE A LOT ALIKE, ACTUALLY.
BUT HE'S ALWAYS BEEN JUST A HAIR BETTER THAN ME.
HE AND I BOTH AIMED TO WING EACH OTHER...
...but I got just cloth, and he drew blood.
STOP IT. YOU AREN'T LIKE HIM AT ALL!
RRIP
THERE'S ONE BIG, HUGE DIFFERENCE YOU'RE FORGETTING!
He already took off his gloves.
ME!
I'M IN LOVE WITH YOU, NOT HIM. SO THAT MAKES YOU BETTER!
WAIT! WHAT THE HECK?!
Just realized what she said.
plop
What's gotten into me?!
YOU KNOW... THAT'S THE FIRST TIME YOU'VE EVER SAID THAT YOU LOVED ME.
HUH? IT IS?

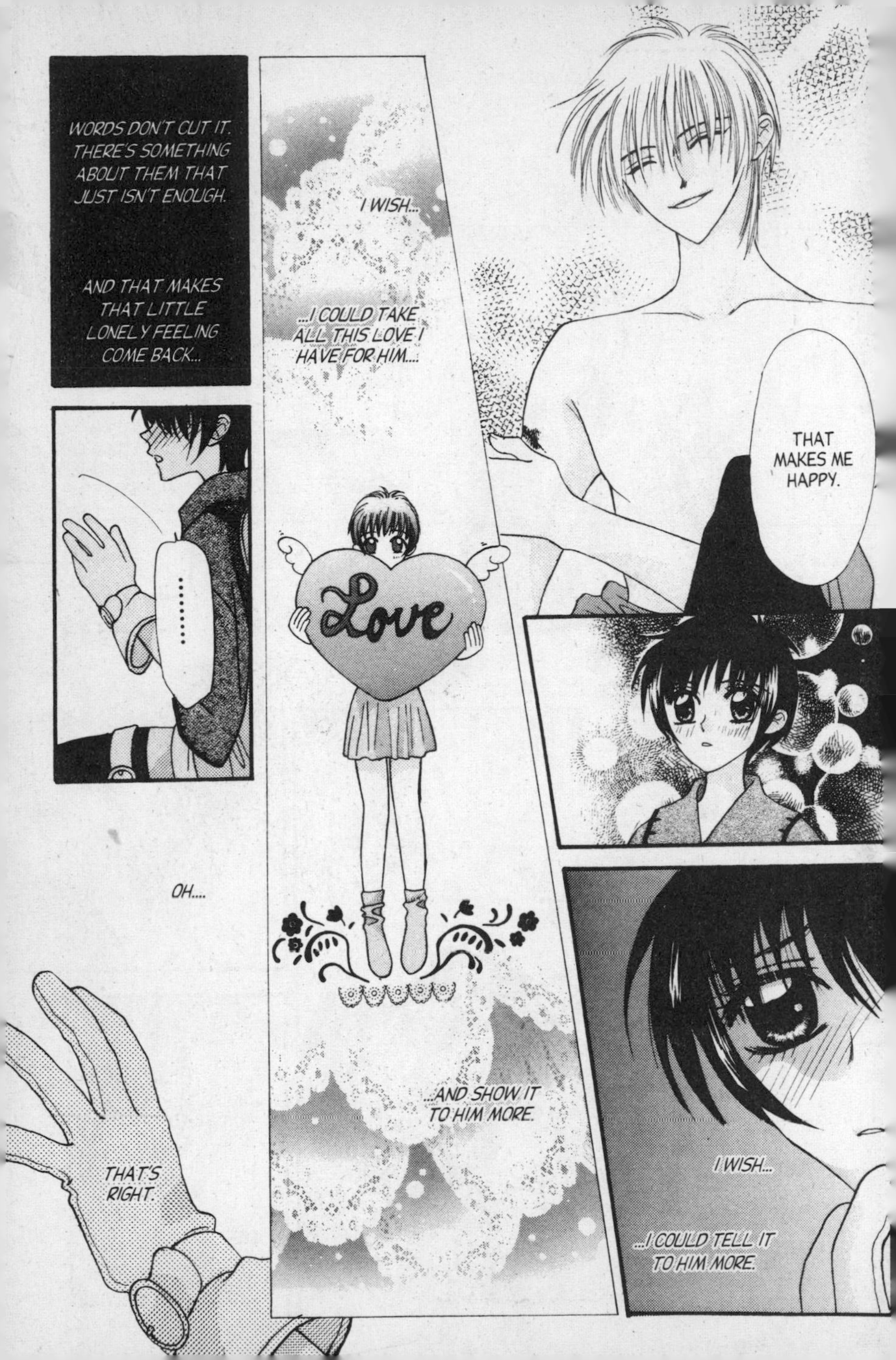
THAT MAKES ME HAPPY.
I WISH...
...I COULD TELL IT TO HIM MORE.
I WISH...
...I COULD TAKE ALL THIS LOVE I HAVE FOR HIM....
Love
...AND SHOW IT TO HIM MORE.
WORDS DON'T CUT IT. THERE'S SOMETHING ABOUT THEM THAT JUST ISN'T ENOUGH.
AND THAT MAKES THAT LITTLE LONELY FEELING COME BACK...
......
OH....
THAT'S RIGHT.

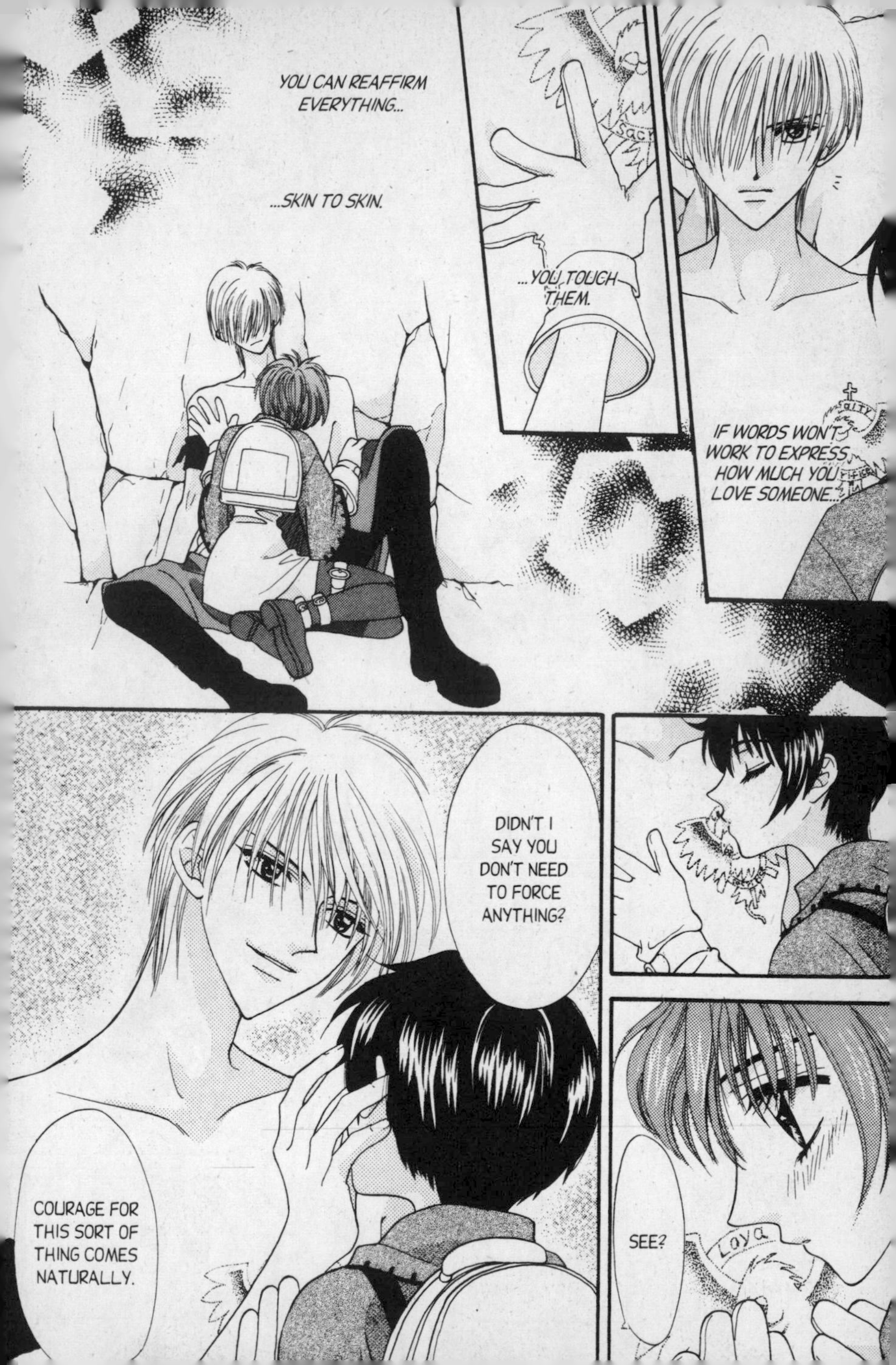
IF WORDS WON'T WORK TO EXPRESS HOW MUCH YOU LOVE SOMEONE...
...YOU TOUCH THEM.
YOU CAN REAFFIRM EVERYTHING...
...SKIN TO SKIN.
SEE?
DIDN'T I SAY YOU DON'T NEED TO FORCE ANYTHING?
COURAGE FOR THIS SORT OF THING COMES NATURALLY.

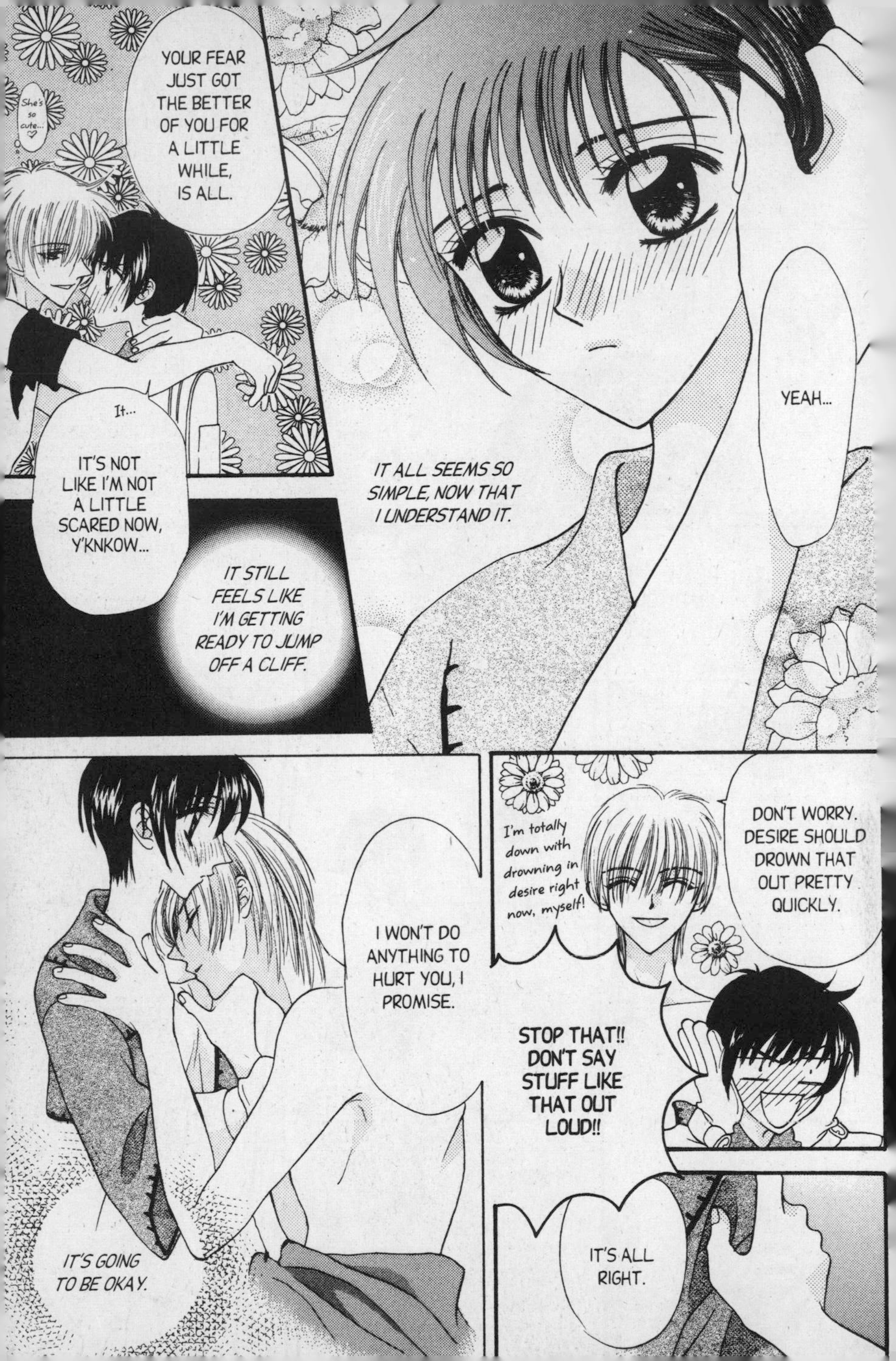
YEAH...
IT ALL SEEMS SO SIMPLE, NOW THAT I UNDERSTAND IT.
YOUR FEAR JUST GOT THE BETTER OF YOU FOR A LITTLE WHILE, IS ALL.
She's so cute...♡
It...
IT'S NOT LIKE I'M NOT A LITTLE SCARED NOW, Y'KNKOW...
IT STILL FEELS LIKE I'M GETTING READY TO JUMP OFF A CLIFF.
DON'T WORRY. DESIRE SHOULD DROWN THAT OUT PRETTY QUICKLY.
I'm totally down with drowning in desire right now, myself!
STOP THAT!! DON'T SAY STUFF LIKE THAT OUT LOUD!!
IT'S ALL RIGHT.
I WON'T DO ANYTHING TO HURT YOU, I PROMISE.
IT'S GOING TO BE OKAY.

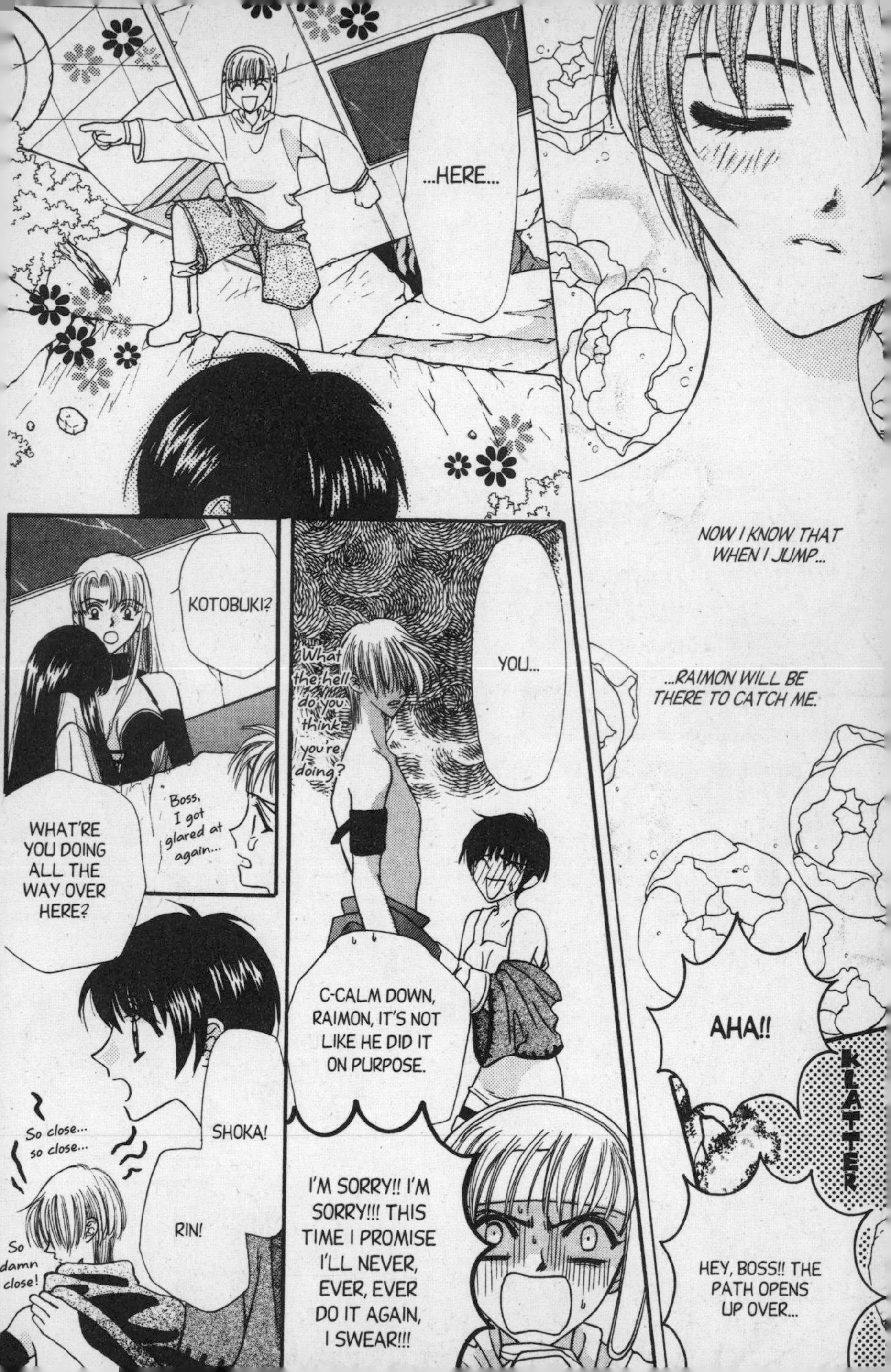
NOW I KNOW THAT WHEN I JUMP...
...RAIMON WILL BE THERE TO CATCH ME.
AHA!!
KLATTER
HEY, BOSS!! THE PATH OPENS UP OVER...
...HERE...
YOU...
What the hell do you think you're doing?
KOTOBUKI!?
Boss, I got glared at again...
C-CALM DOWN, RAIMON, IT'S NOT LIKE HE DID IT ON PURPOSE.
I'M SORRY!! I'M SORRY!!! THIS TIME I PROMISE I'LL NEVER, EVER, EVER DO IT AGAIN, I SWEAR!!!
WHAT'RE YOU DOING ALL THE WAY OVER HERE?
SHOKA!
RIN!
So close... so close...
So damn close!

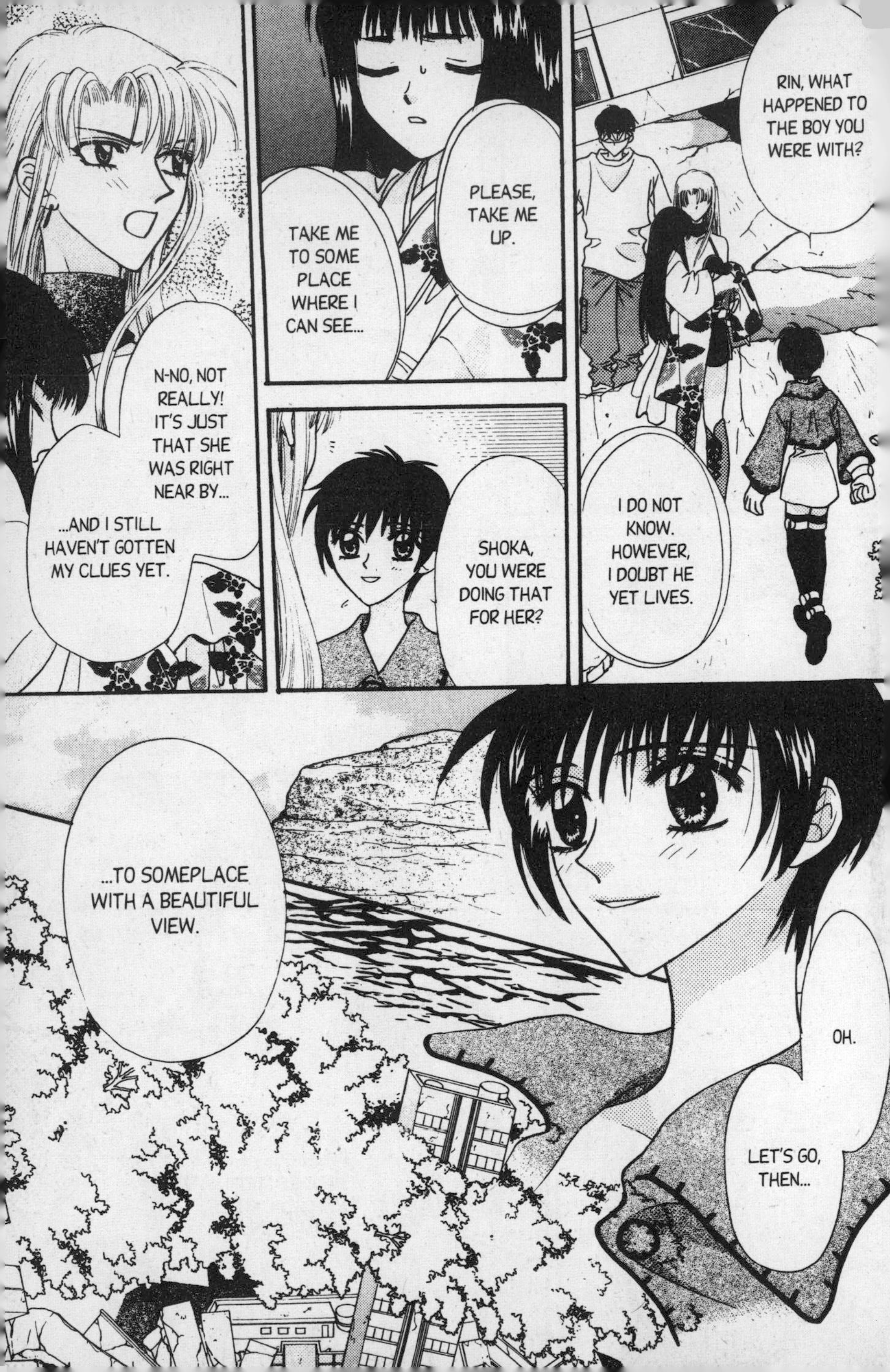
RIN, WHAT HAPPENED TO THE BOY YOU WERE WITH?
I DO NOT KNOW. HOWEVER, I DOUBT HE YET LIVES.
PLEASE, TAKE ME UP.
TAKE ME TO SOME PLACE WHERE I CAN SEE...
SHOKA, YOU WERE DOING THAT FOR HER?
N-NO, NOT REALLY! IT'S JUST THAT SHE WAS RIGHT NEAR BY...
...AND I STILL HAVEN'T GOTTEN MY CLUES YET.
OH.
LET'S GO, THEN...
...TO SOMEPLACE WITH A BEAUTIFUL VIEW.

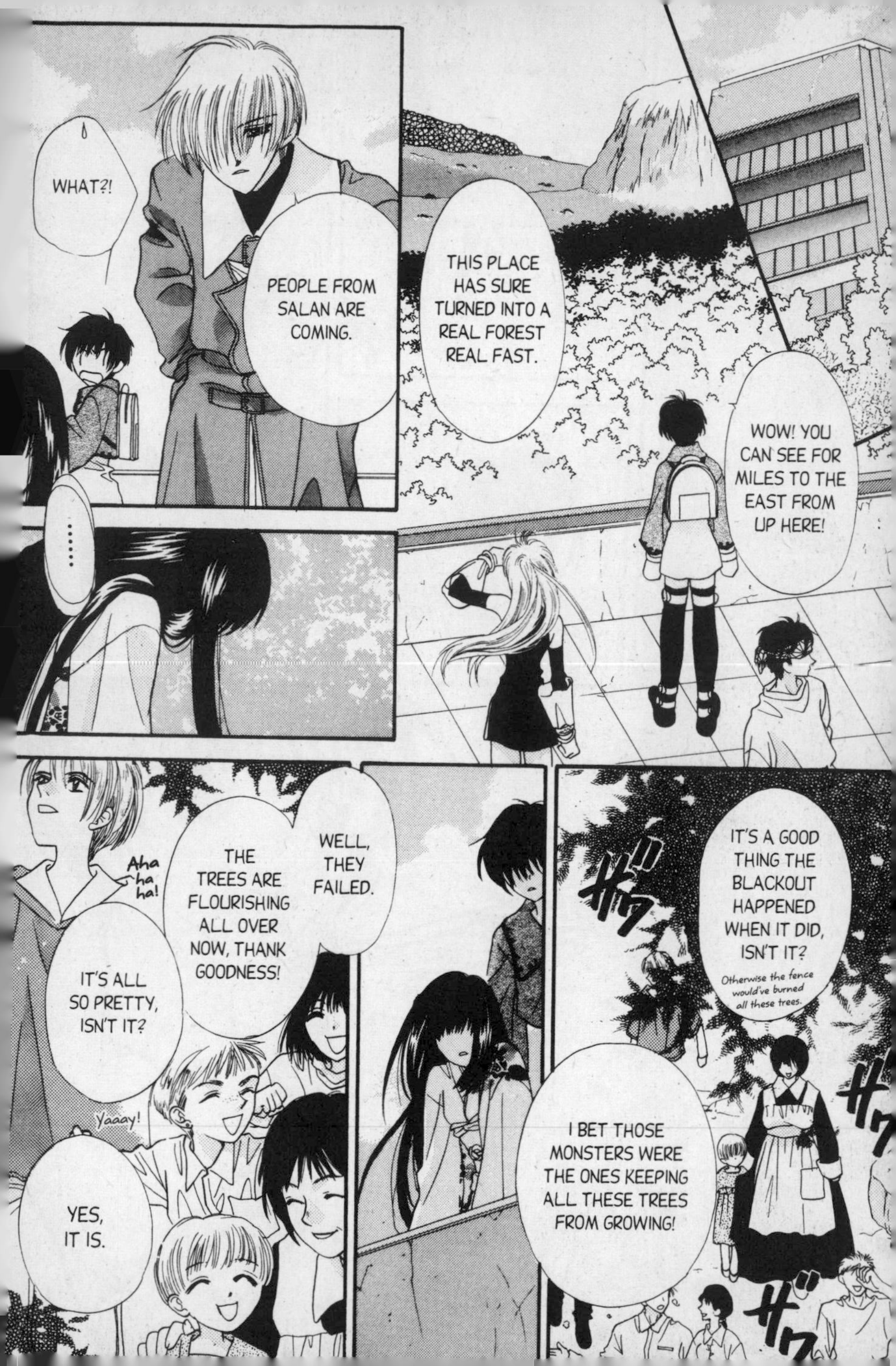
WOW! YOU CAN SEE FOR MILES TO THE EAST FROM UP HERE!
THIS PLACE HAS SURE TURNED INTO A REAL FOREST REAL FAST.
PEOPLE FROM SALAN ARE COMING.
WHAT?!
......
ザワ
IT'S A GOOD THING THE BLACKOUT HAPPENED WHEN IT DID, ISN'T IT?
Otherwise the fence would've burned all these trees.
ザワ
I BET THOSE MONSTERS WERE THE ONES KEEPING ALL THESE TREES FROM GROWING!
ザワ
WELL, THEY FAILED.
THE TREES ARE FLOURISHING ALL OVER NOW, THANK GOODNESS!
Aha ha ha!
IT'S ALL SO PRETTY, ISN'T IT?
Yaaay!
YES, IT IS.

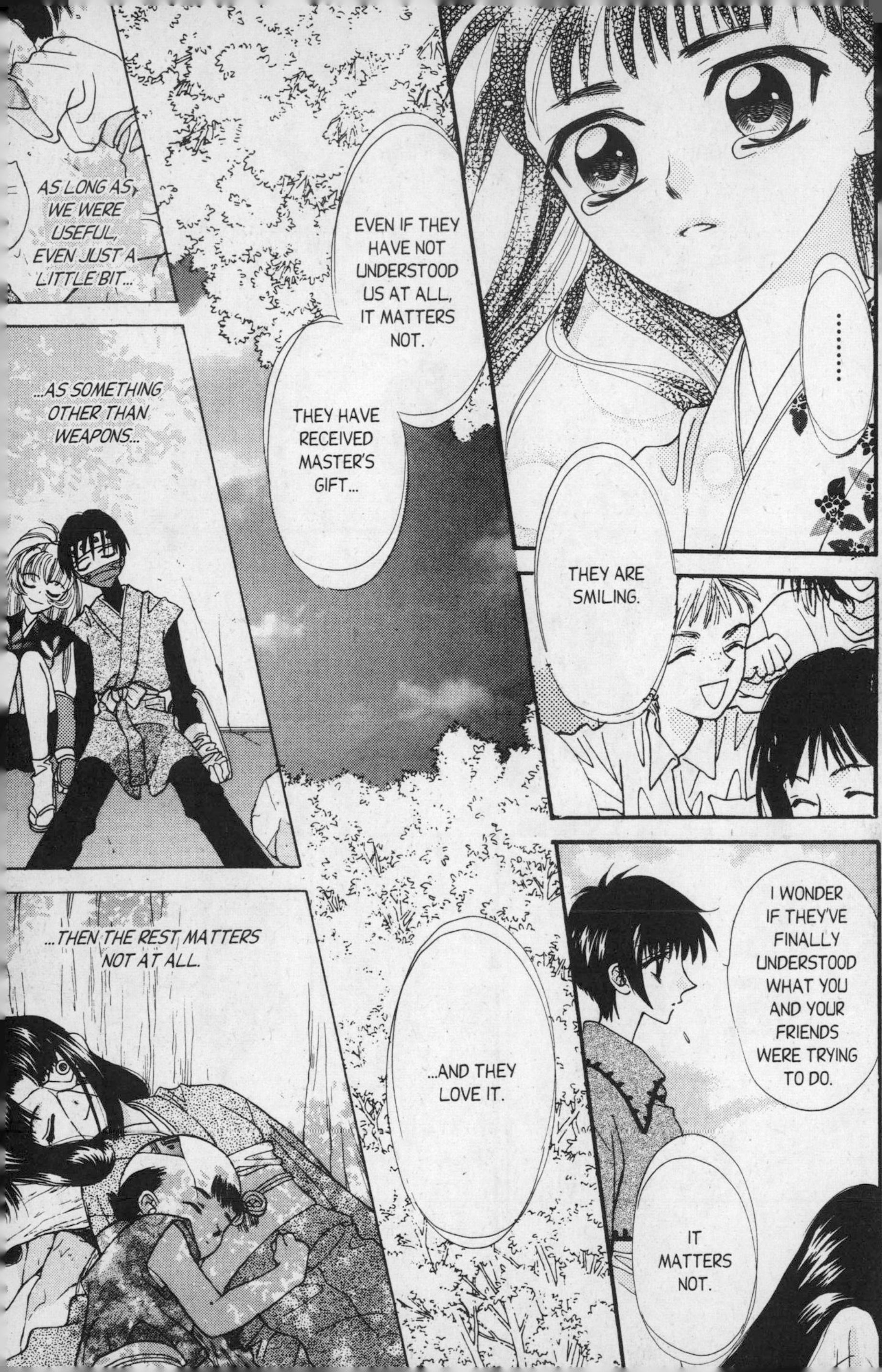
I WONDER IF THEY'VE FINALLY UNDERSTOOD WHAT YOU AND YOUR FRIENDS WERE TRYING TO DO.
......
IT MATTERS NOT.
EVEN IF THEY HAVE NOT UNDERSTOOD US AT ALL, IT MATTERS NOT.
THEY HAVE RECEIVED MASTER'S GIFT...
THEY ARE SMILING.
...AND THEY LOVE IT.
AS LONG AS WE WERE USEFUL, EVEN JUST A LITTLE BIT...
...AS SOMETHING OTHER THAN WEAPONS...
...THEN THE REST MATTERS NOT AT ALL.

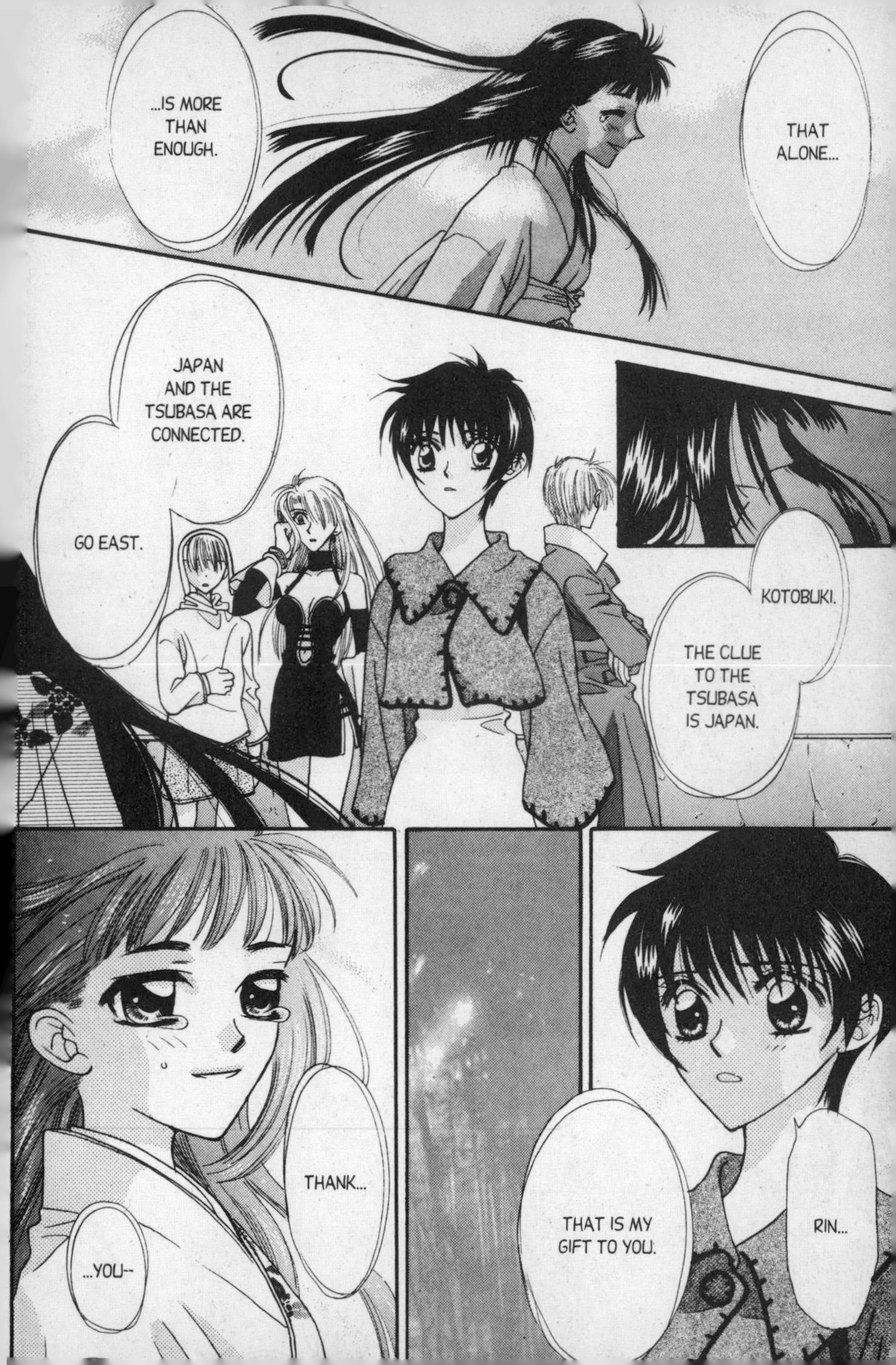
THAT ALONE...
...IS MORE THAN ENOUGH.
KOTOBUKI.
THE CLUE TO THE TSUBASA IS JAPAN.
JAPAN AND THE TSUBASA ARE CONNECTED.
GO EAST.
RIN...
THAT IS MY GIFT TO YOU.
THANK...
...YOU--

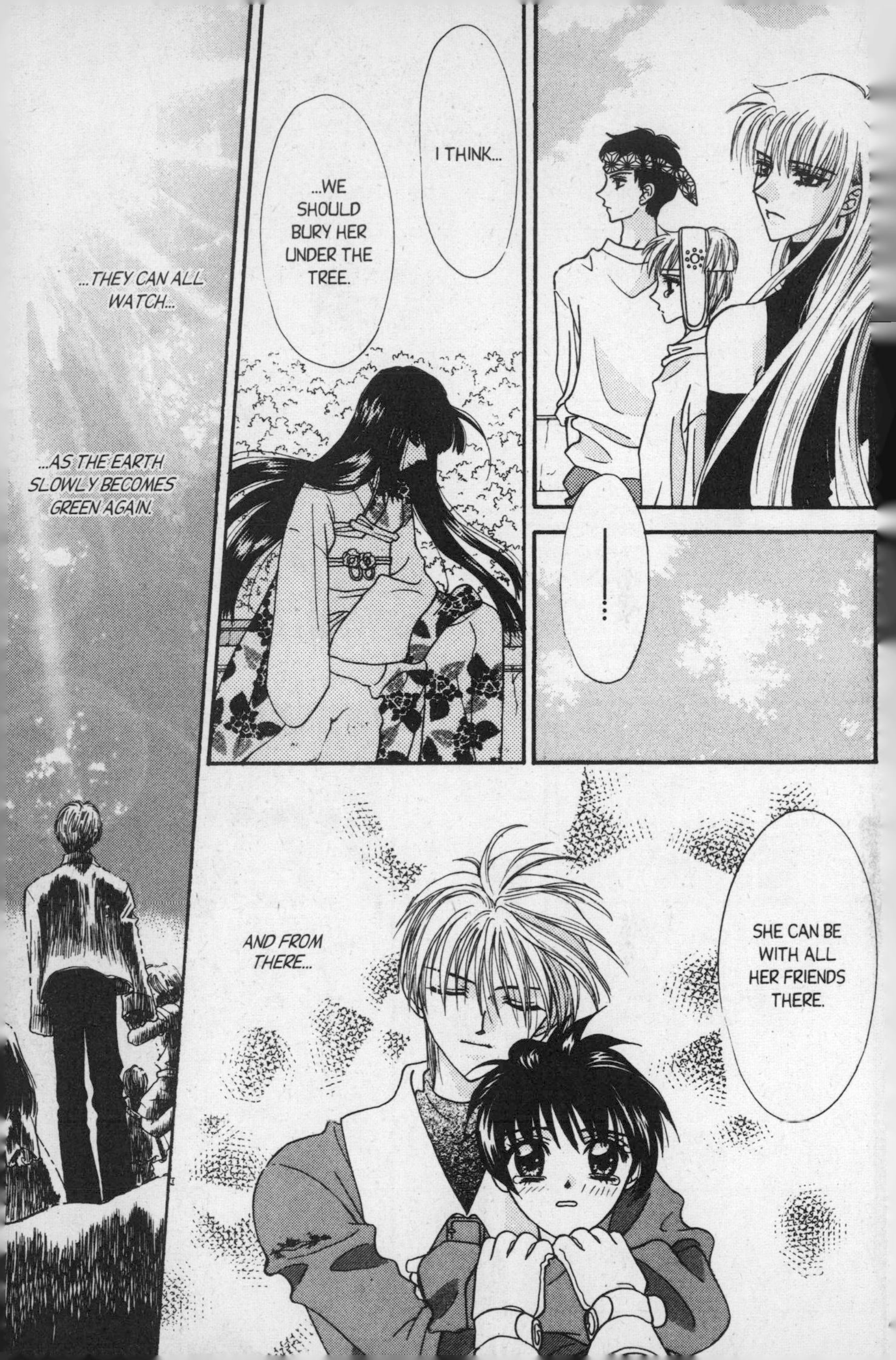
—...!
I THINK...
...WE SHOULD BURY HER UNDER THE TREE.
SHE CAN BE WITH ALL HER FRIENDS THERE.
AND FROM THERE...
...THEY CAN ALL WATCH...
...AS THE EARTH SLOWLY BECOMES GREEN AGAIN.

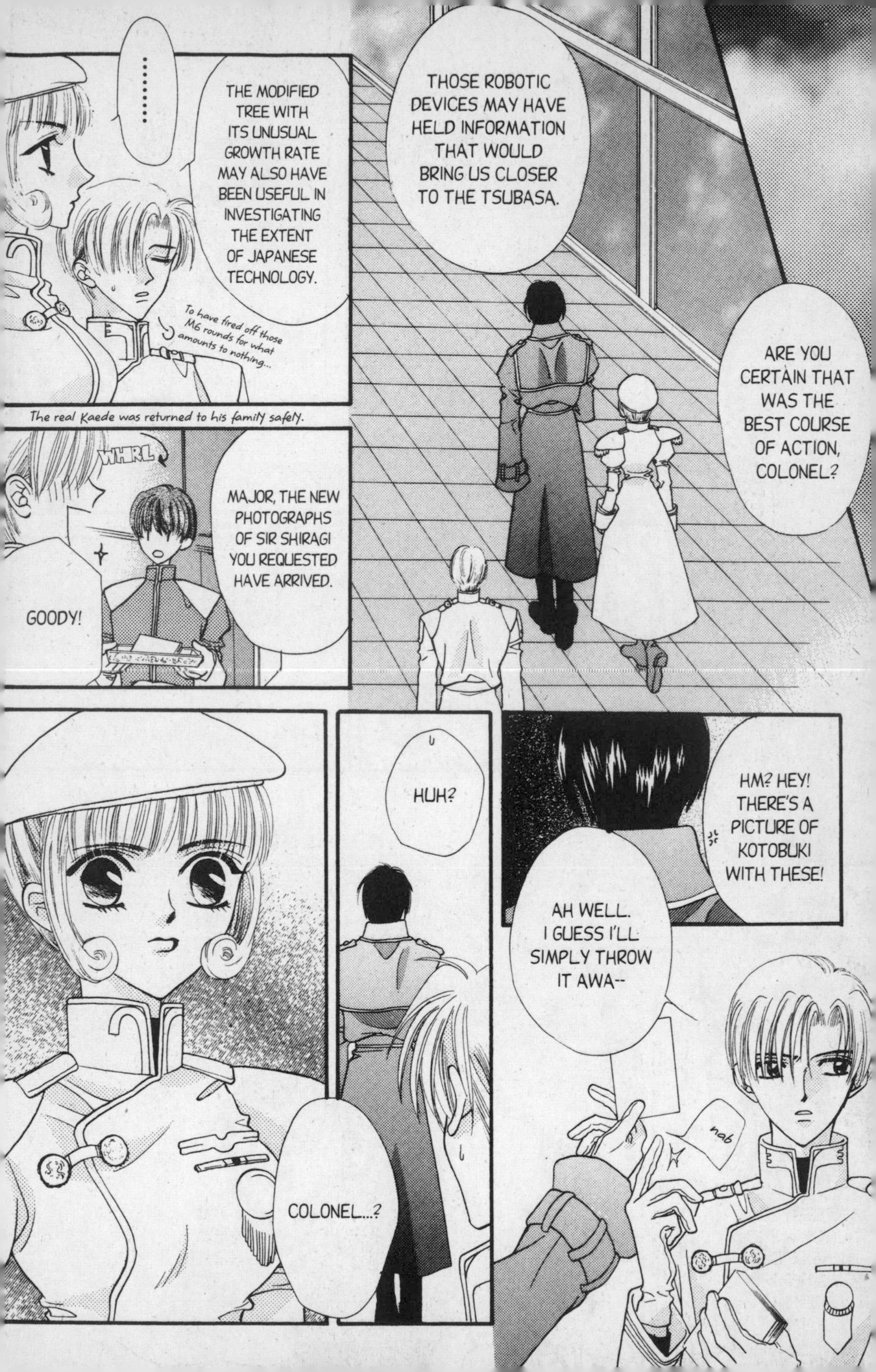
THOSE ROBOTIC DEVICES MAY HAVE HELD INFORMATION THAT WOULD BRING US CLOSER TO THE TSUBASA.
ARE YOU CERTAIN THAT WAS THE BEST COURSE OF ACTION, COLONEL?
THE MODIFIED TREE WITH ITS UNUSUAL GROWTH RATE MAY ALSO HAVE BEEN USEFUL IN INVESTIGATING THE EXTENT OF JAPANESE TECHNOLOGY.
....
To have fired off those M6 rounds for what amounts to nothing...
The real Kaede was returned to his family safely.
MAJOR, THE NEW PHOTOGRAPHS OF SIR SHIRAGI YOU REQUESTED HAVE ARRIVED.
WHRL
GOODY!
HM? HEY! THERE'S A PICTURE OF KOTOBUKI WITH THESE!
AH WELL. I GUESS I'LL SIMPLY THROW IT AWA--
nab
HUH?
COLONEL...?

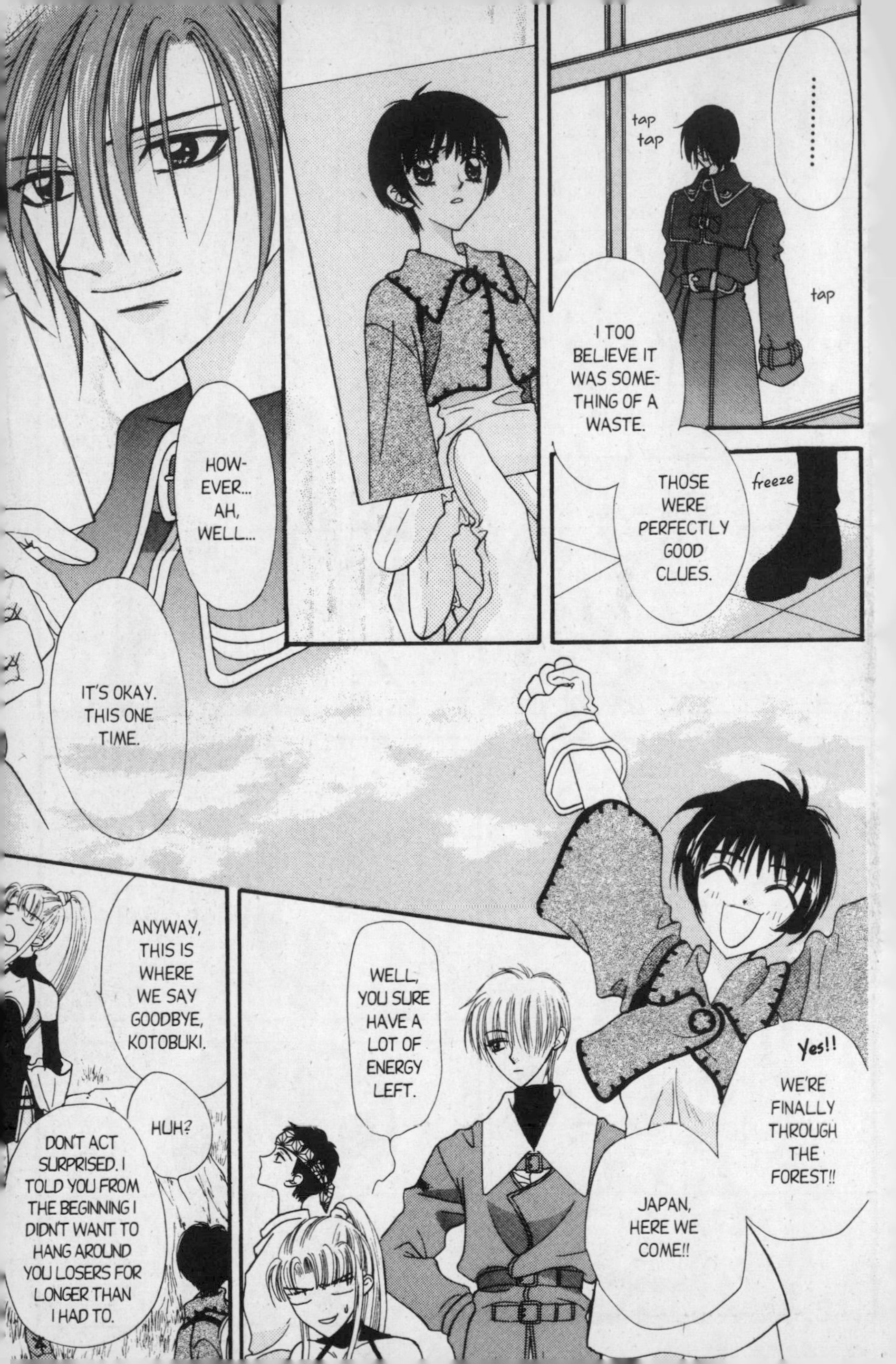
......
tap tap
tap
I TOO BELIEVE IT WAS SOMETHING OF A WASTE.
THOSE WERE PERFECTLY GOOD CLUES.
freeze
HOW-EVER... AH, WELL...
IT'S OKAY. THIS ONE TIME.
Yes!!
WE'RE FINALLY THROUGH THE FOREST!!
JAPAN, HERE WE COME!!
WELL, YOU SURE HAVE A LOT OF ENERGY LEFT.
ANYWAY, THIS IS WHERE WE SAY GOODBYE, KOTOBUKI.
HUH?
DON'T ACT SURPRISED. I TOLD YOU FROM THE BEGINNING I DIDN'T WANT TO HANG AROUND YOU LOSERS FOR LONGER THAN I HAD TO.

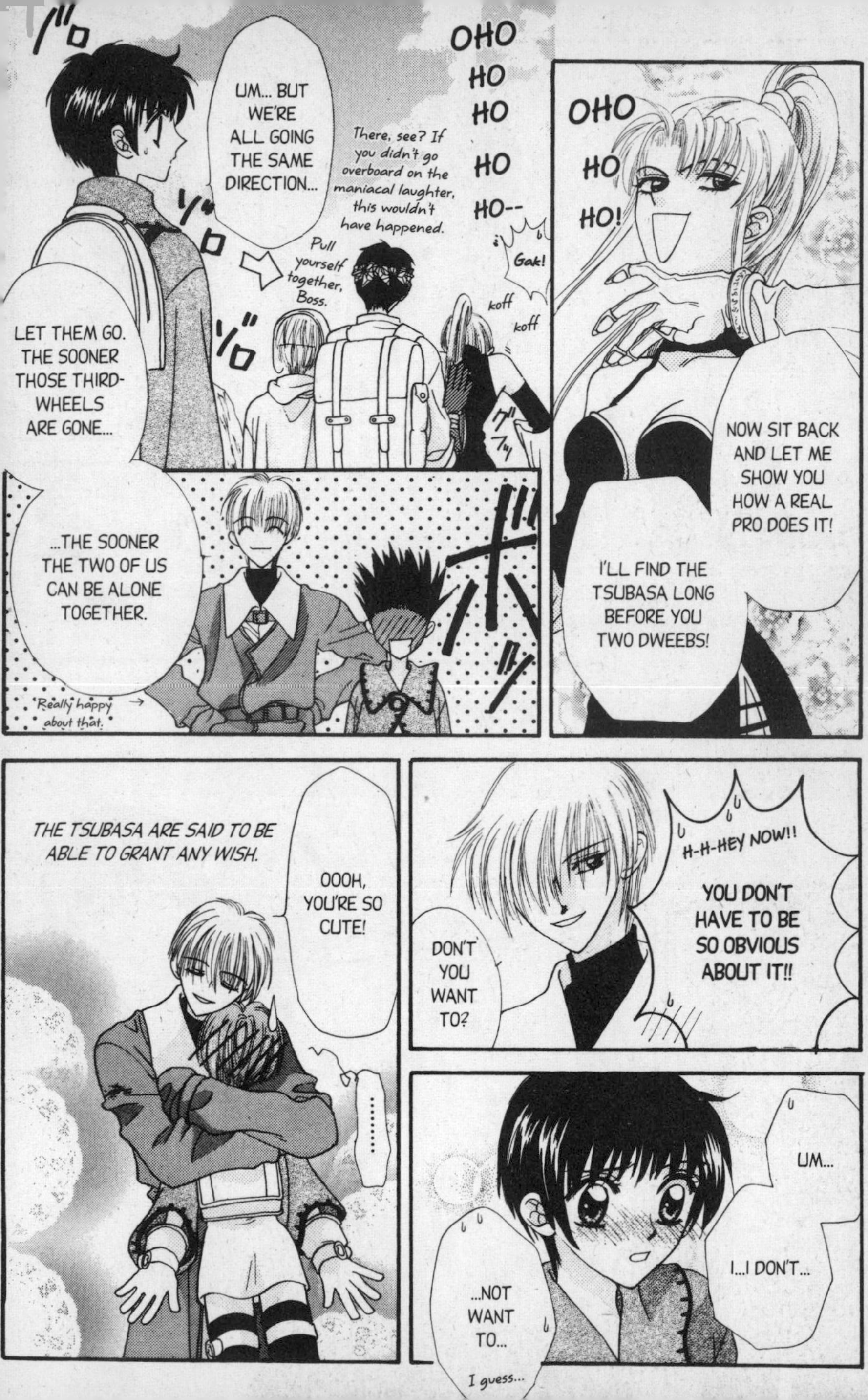
OHO
HO
HO!
NOW SIT BACK AND LET ME SHOW YOU HOW A REAL PRO DOES IT!
I'LL FIND THE TSUBASA LONG BEFORE YOU TWO DWEEBS!
OHO HO HO HO HO--
Gak!
koff koff
UM... BUT WE'RE ALL GOING THE SAME DIRECTION...
There, see? If you didn't go overboard on the maniacal laughter, this wouldn't have happened.
Pull yourself together, Boss.
LET THEM GO. THE SOONER THOSE THIRD-WHEELS ARE GONE...
...THE SOONER THE TWO OF US CAN BE ALONE TOGETHER.
Really happy about that.
H-H-HEY NOW!!
YOU DON'T HAVE TO BE SO OBVIOUS ABOUT IT!!
DON'T YOU WANT TO?
UM...
I...I DON'T...
...NOT WANT TO...
I guess...
THE TSUBASA ARE SAID TO BE ABLE TO GRANT ANY WISH.
OOOH, YOU'RE SO CUTE!
....

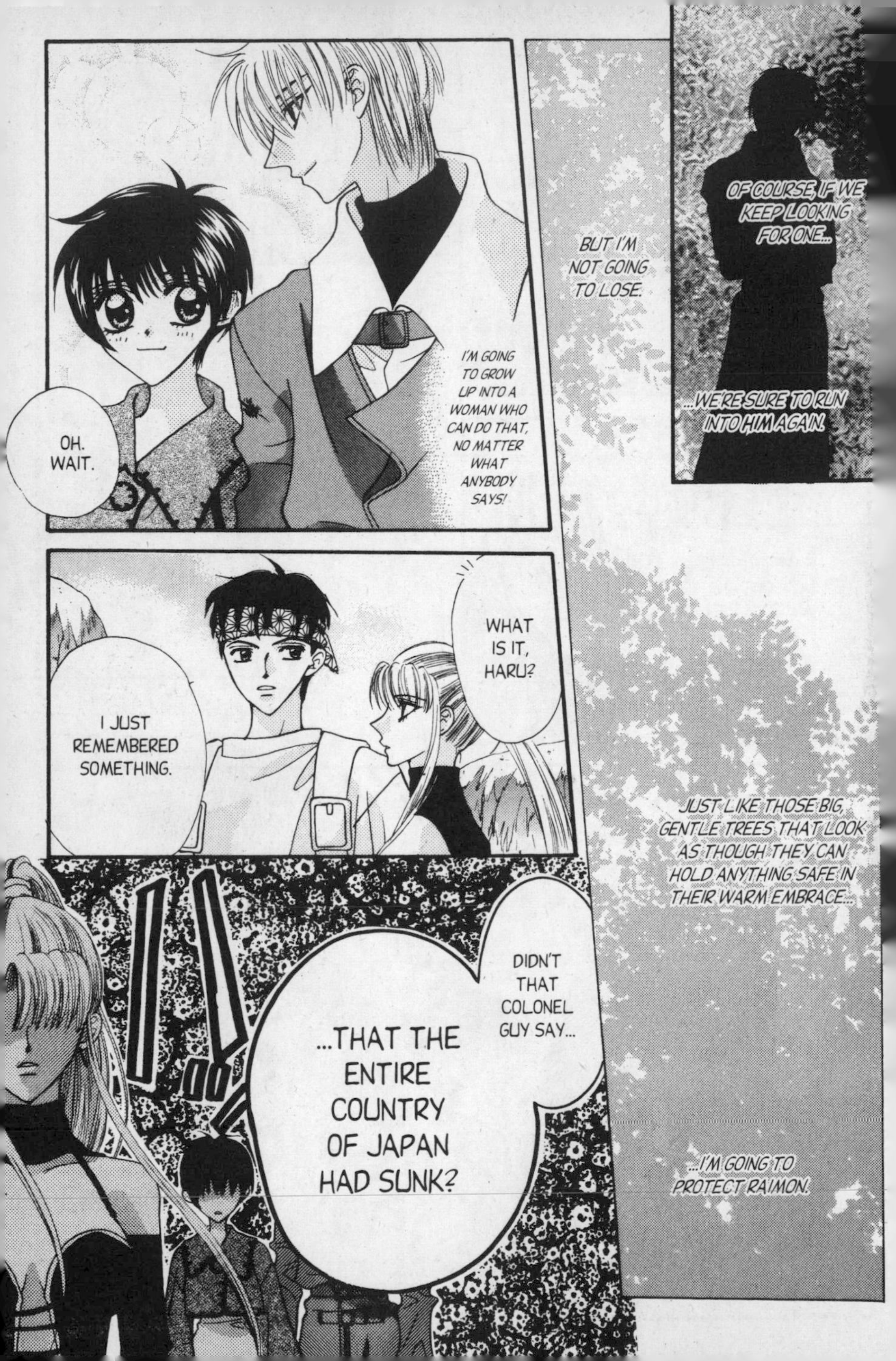

OF COURSE, IF WE KEEP LOOKING FOR ONE...
...WE'RE SURE TO RUN INTO HIM AGAIN.
BUT I'M NOT GOING TO LOSE.
JUST LIKE THOSE BIG, GENTLE TREES THAT LOOK AS THOUGH THEY CAN HOLD ANYTHING SAFE IN THEIR WARM EMBRACE...
...I'M GOING TO PROTECT RAIMON.
I'M GOING TO GROW UP INTO A WOMAN WHO CAN DO THAT, NO MATTER WHAT ANYBODY SAYS!
OH. WAIT.
WHAT IS IT, HARU?
I JUST REMEMBERED SOMETHING.
DIDN'T THAT COLONEL GUY SAY...
...THAT THE ENTIRE COUNTRY OF JAPAN HAD SUNK?

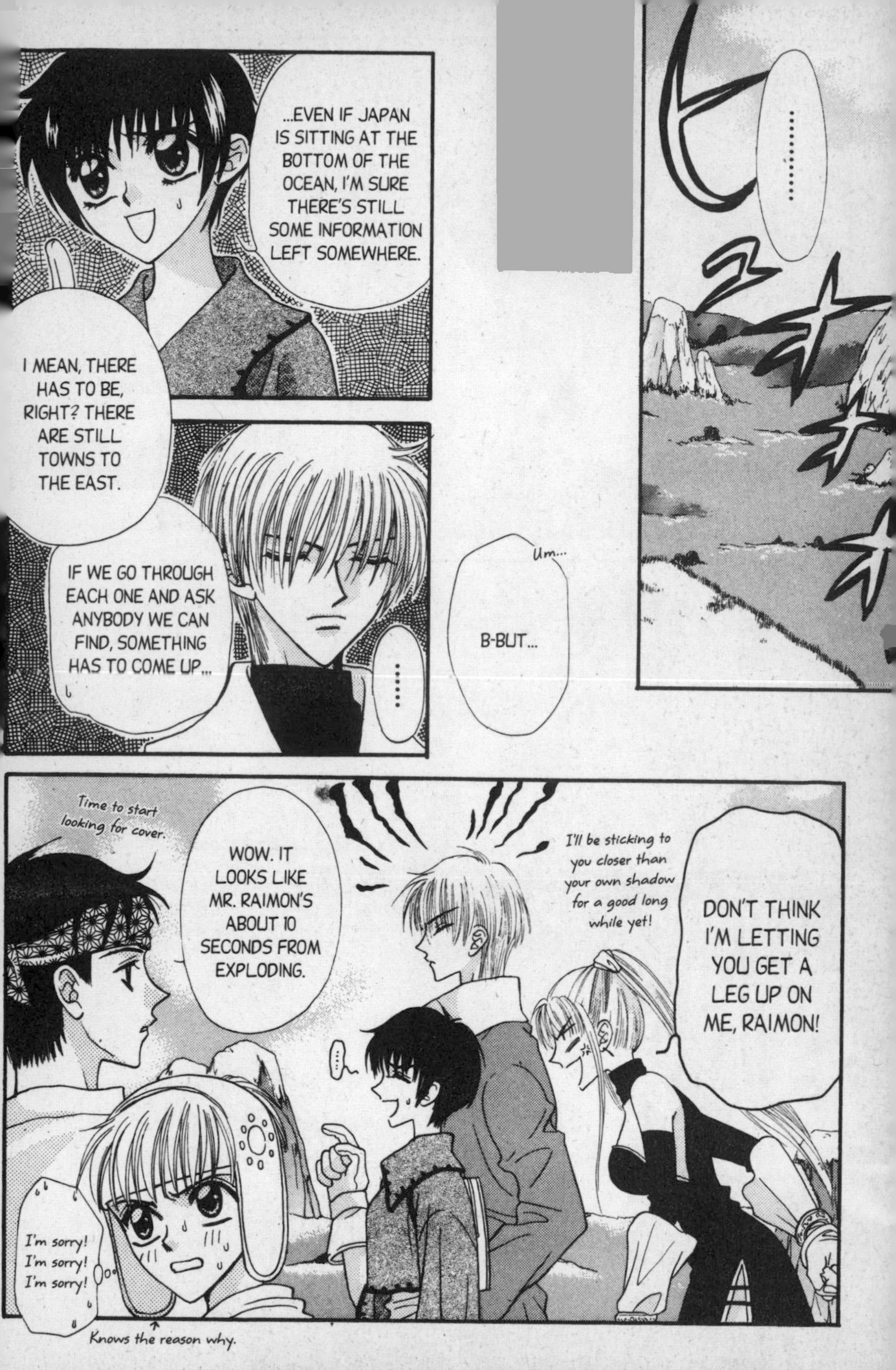
......
...EVEN IF JAPAN IS SITTING AT THE BOTTOM OF THE OCEAN, I'M SURE THERE'S STILL SOME INFORMATION LEFT SOMEWHERE.
I MEAN, THERE HAS TO BE, RIGHT? THERE ARE STILL TOWNS TO THE EAST.
IF WE GO THROUGH EACH ONE AND ASK ANYBODY WE CAN FIND, SOMETHING HAS TO COME UP...
......
Um...
B-BUT...
DON'T THINK I'M LETTING YOU GET A LEG UP ON ME, RAIMON!
I'll be sticking to you closer than your own shadow for a good long while yet!
WOW. IT LOOKS LIKE MR. RAIMON'S ABOUT 10 SECONDS FROM EXPLODING.
Time to start looking for cover.
...
I'm sorry! I'm sorry! I'm sorry!
Knows the reason why.

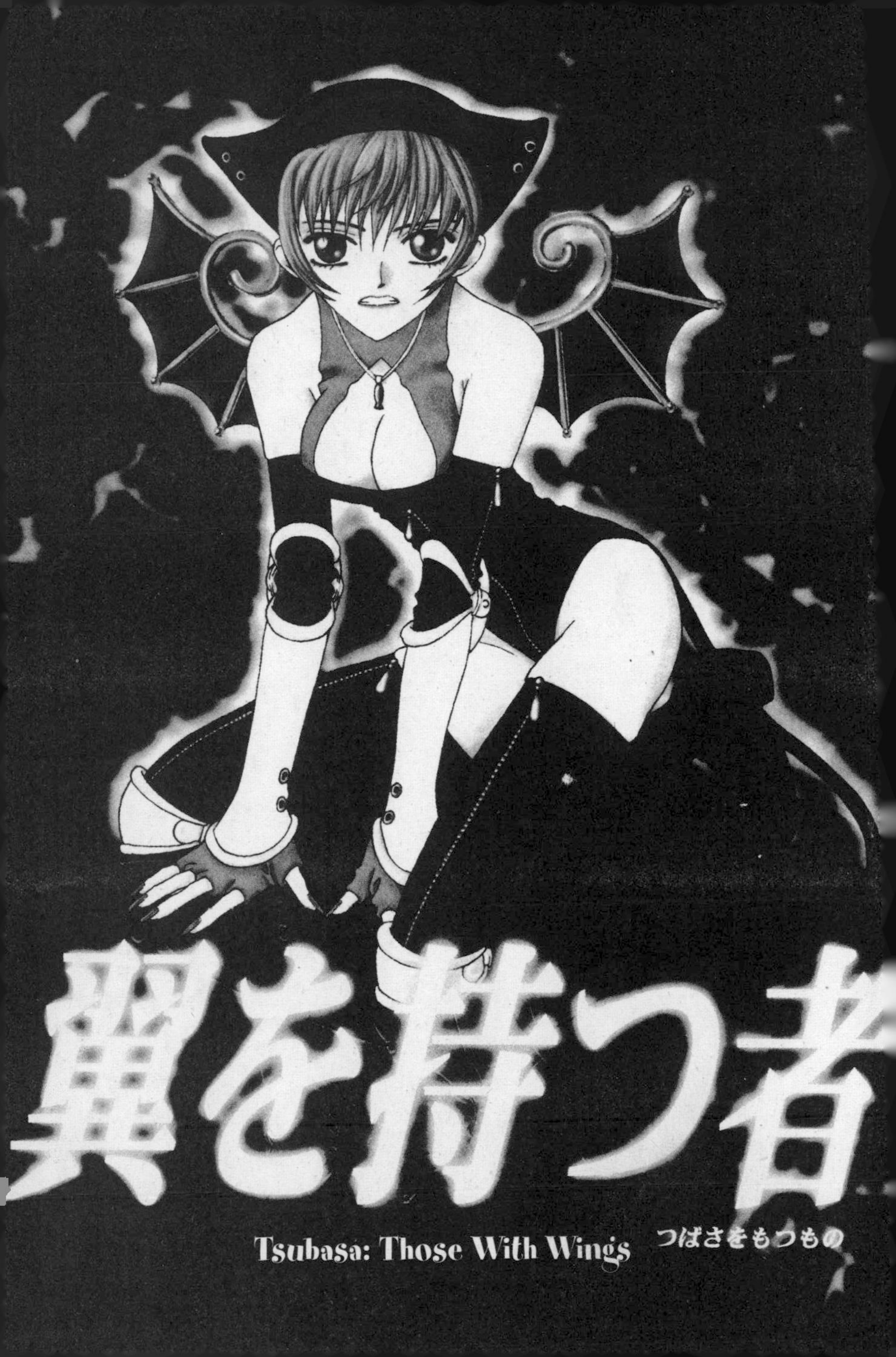
翼を持つ者
Tsubasa: Those With Wings
つばさをもつもの

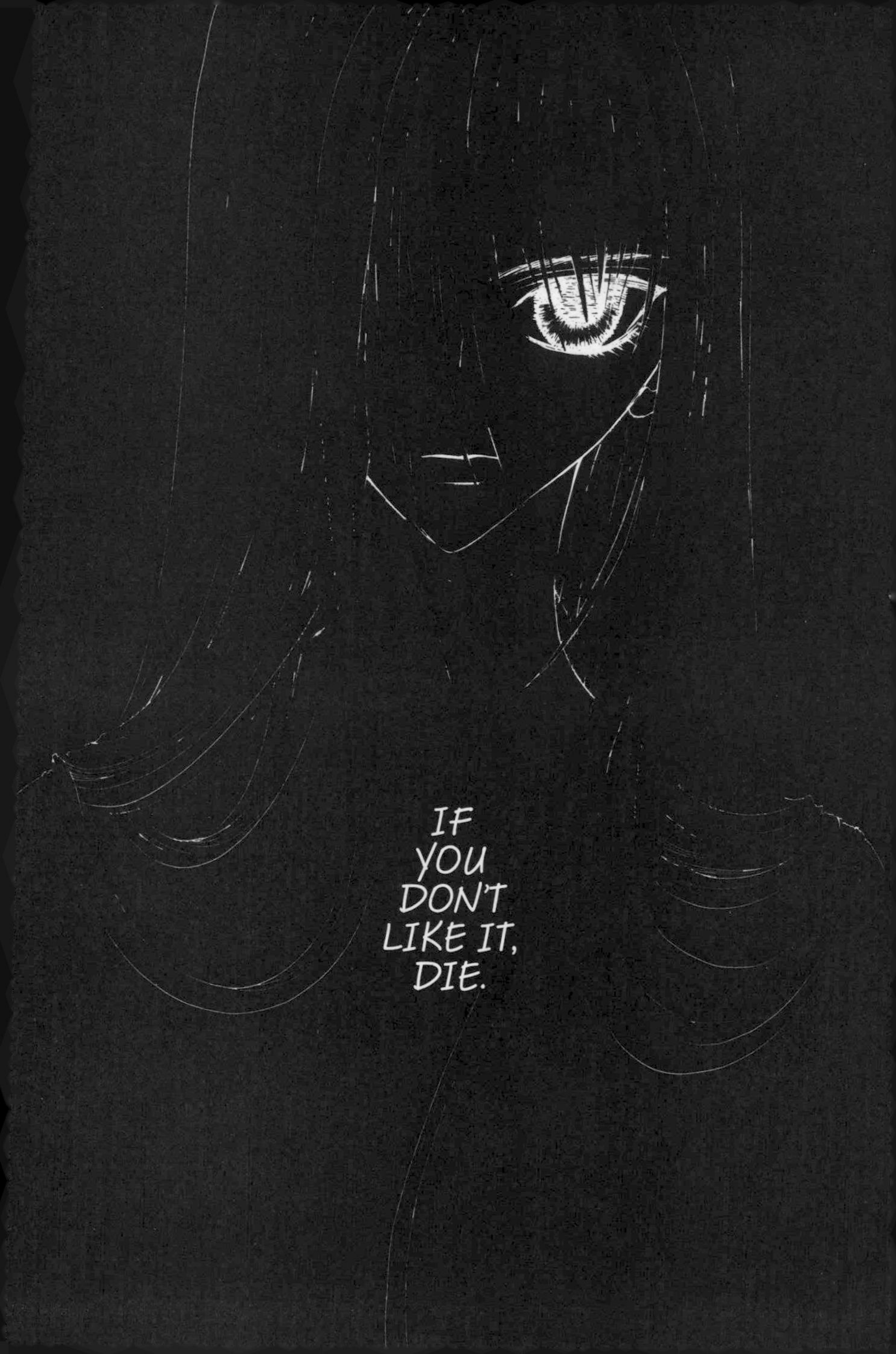
IF YOU DON'T LIKE IT, DIE.

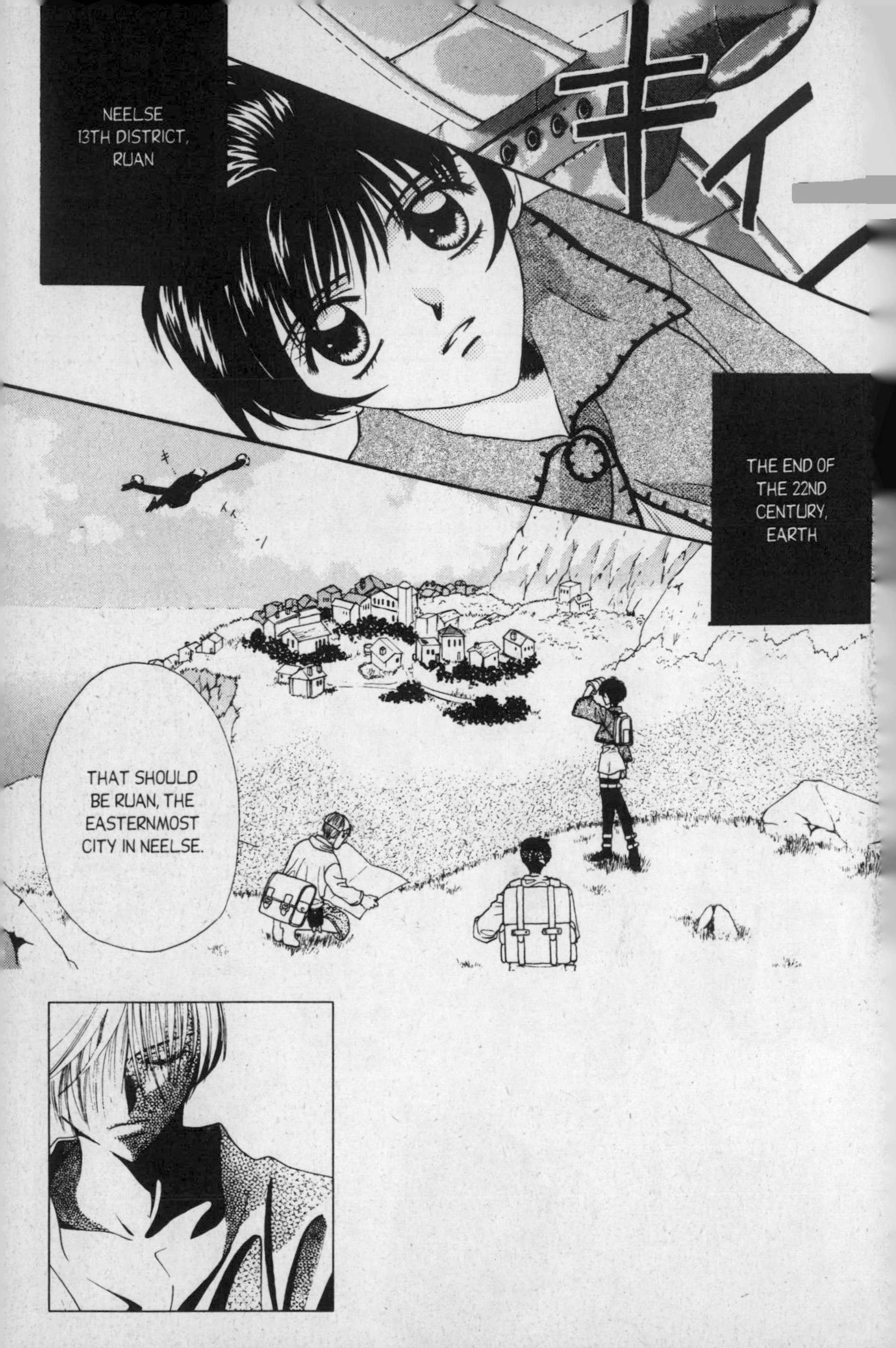
キイ
NEELSE 13TH DISTRICT, RUAN
THE END OF THE 22ND CENTURY, EARTH
THAT SHOULD BE RUAN, THE EASTERNMOST CITY IN NEELSE.

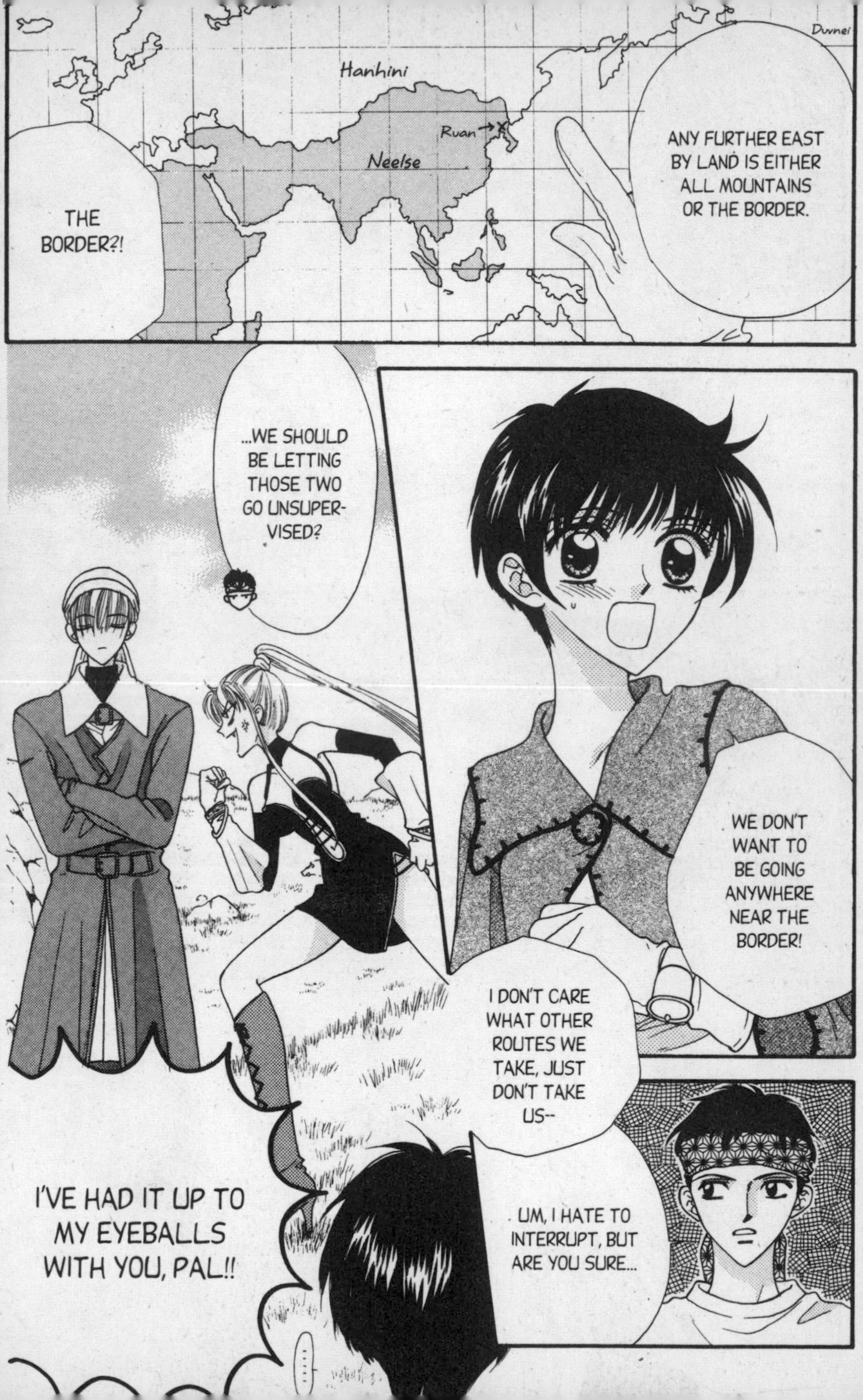
Duvnei
Hanhini
Ruan
Neelse
ANY FURTHER EAST BY LAND IS EITHER ALL MOUNTAINS OR THE BORDER.
THE BORDER?!
WE DON'T WANT TO BE GOING ANYWHERE NEAR THE BORDER!
I DON'T CARE WHAT OTHER ROUTES WE TAKE, JUST DON'T TAKE US--
UM, I HATE TO INTERRUPT, BUT ARE YOU SURE...
...WE SHOULD BE LETTING THOSE TWO GO UNSUPERVISED?
I'VE HAD IT UP TO MY EYEBALLS WITH YOU, PAL!!
...

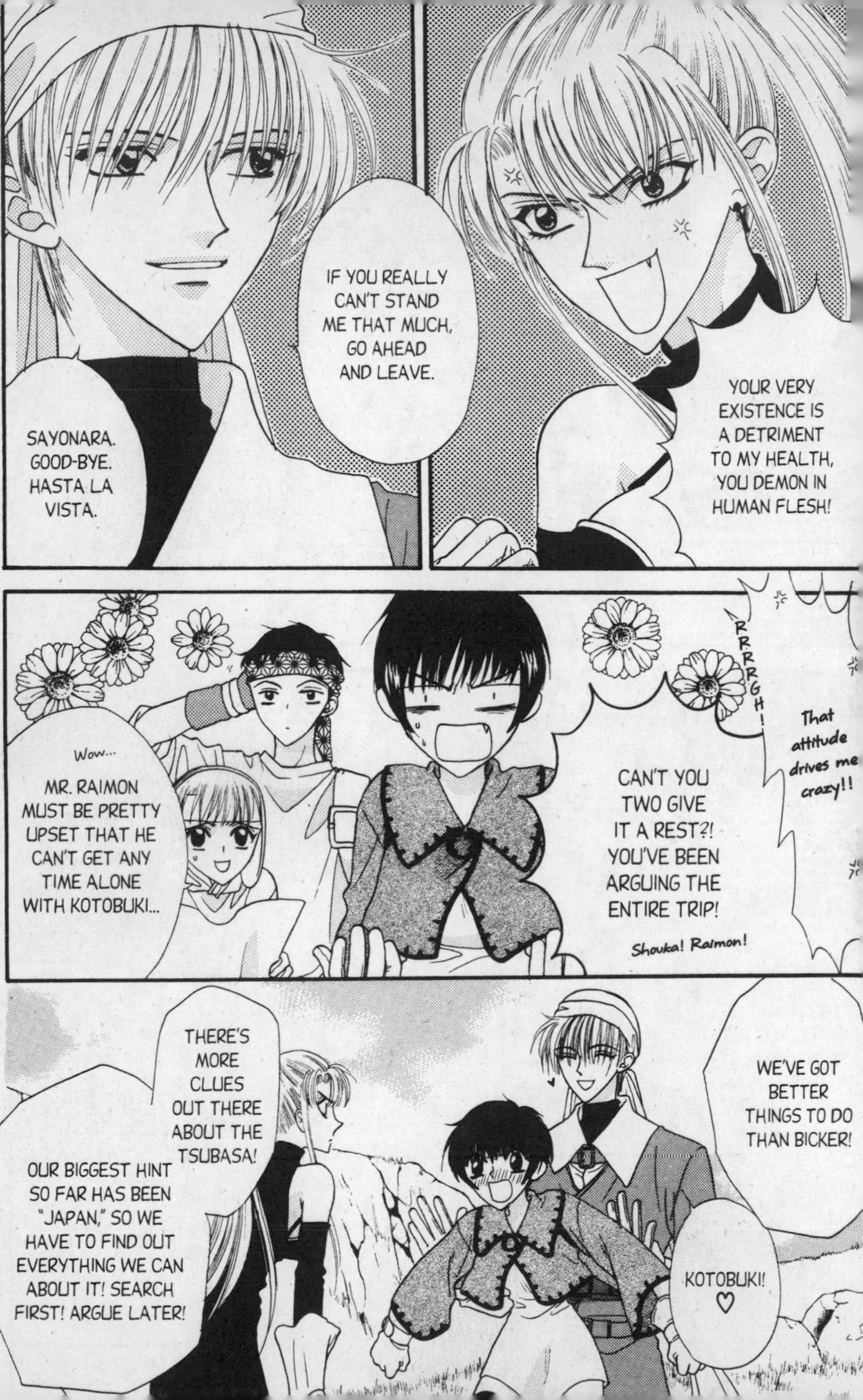
YOUR VERY EXISTENCE IS A DETRIMENT TO MY HEALTH, YOU DEMON IN HUMAN FLESH!
IF YOU REALLY CAN'T STAND ME THAT MUCH, GO AHEAD AND LEAVE.
SAYONARA. GOOD-BYE. HASTA LA VISTA.
RRRRGH!
That attitude drives me crazy!!
CAN'T YOU TWO GIVE IT A REST?! YOU'VE BEEN ARGUING THE ENTIRE TRIP!
Shouka! Raimon!
Wow...
MR. RAIMON MUST BE PRETTY UPSET THAT HE CAN'T GET ANY TIME ALONE WITH KOTOBUKI...
WE'VE GOT BETTER THINGS TO DO THAN BICKER!
THERE'S MORE CLUES OUT THERE ABOUT THE TSUBASA!
OUR BIGGEST HINT SO FAR HAS BEEN "JAPAN," SO WE HAVE TO FIND OUT EVERYTHING WE CAN ABOUT IT! SEARCH FIRST! ARGUE LATER!
KOTOBUKI! ♡

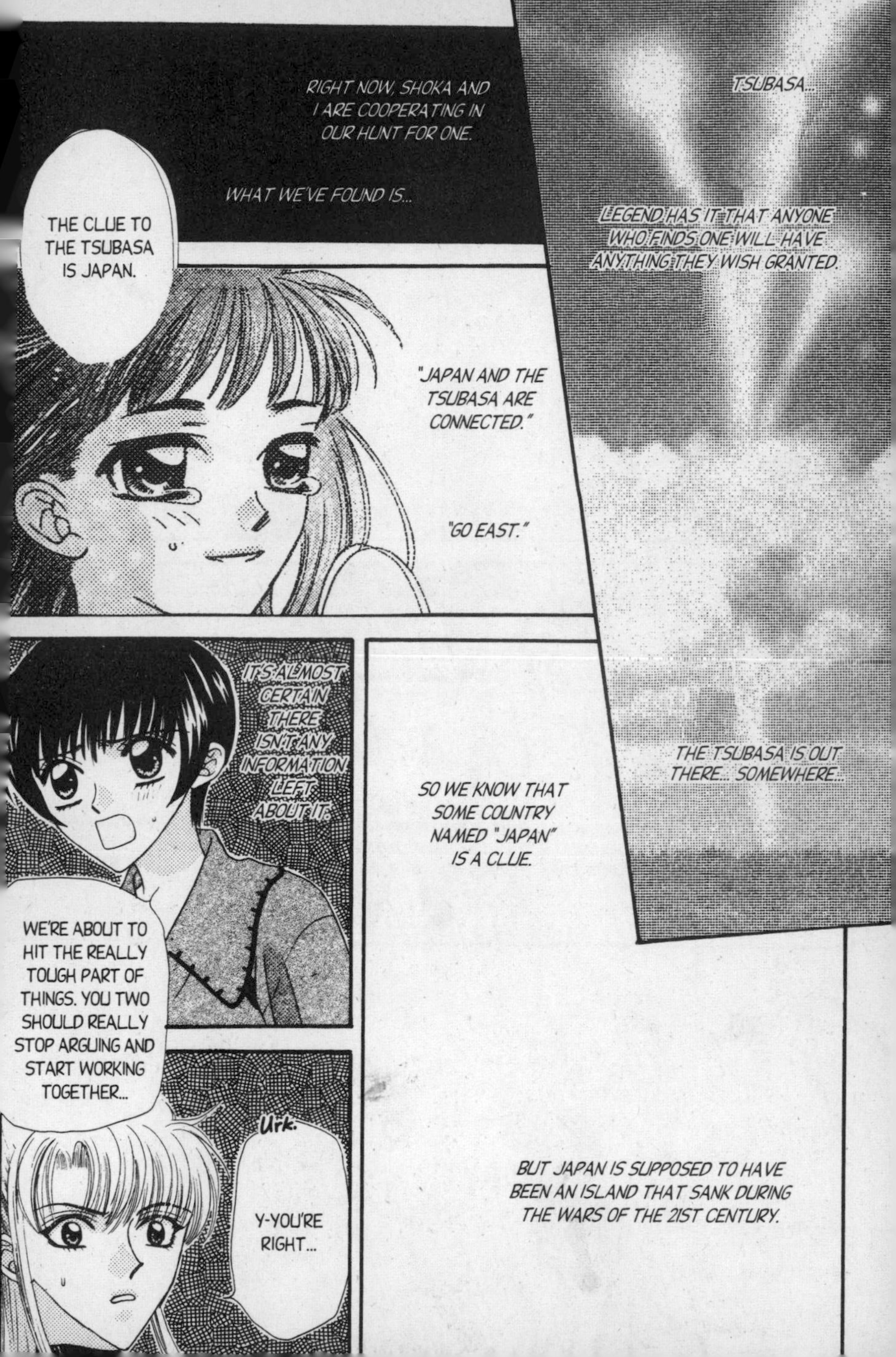
TSUBASA...
LEGEND HAS IT THAT ANYONE WHO FINDS ONE WILL HAVE ANYTHING THEY WISH GRANTED.
THE TSUBASA IS OUT THERE... SOMEWHERE...
RIGHT NOW, SHOKA AND I ARE COOPERATING IN OUR HUNT FOR ONE.
WHAT WE'VE FOUND IS...
THE CLUE TO THE TSUBASA IS JAPAN.
"JAPAN AND THE TSUBASA ARE CONNECTED."
"GO EAST."
SO WE KNOW THAT SOME COUNTRY NAMED "JAPAN" IS A CLUE.
BUT JAPAN IS SUPPOSED TO HAVE BEEN AN ISLAND THAT SANK DURING THE WARS OF THE 21ST CENTURY.
IT'S ALMOST CERTAIN THERE ISN'T ANY INFORMATION LEFT ABOUT IT.
WE'RE ABOUT TO HIT THE REALLY TOUGH PART OF THINGS. YOU TWO SHOULD REALLY STOP ARGUING AND START WORKING TOGETHER...
Urk.
Y-YOU'RE RIGHT...

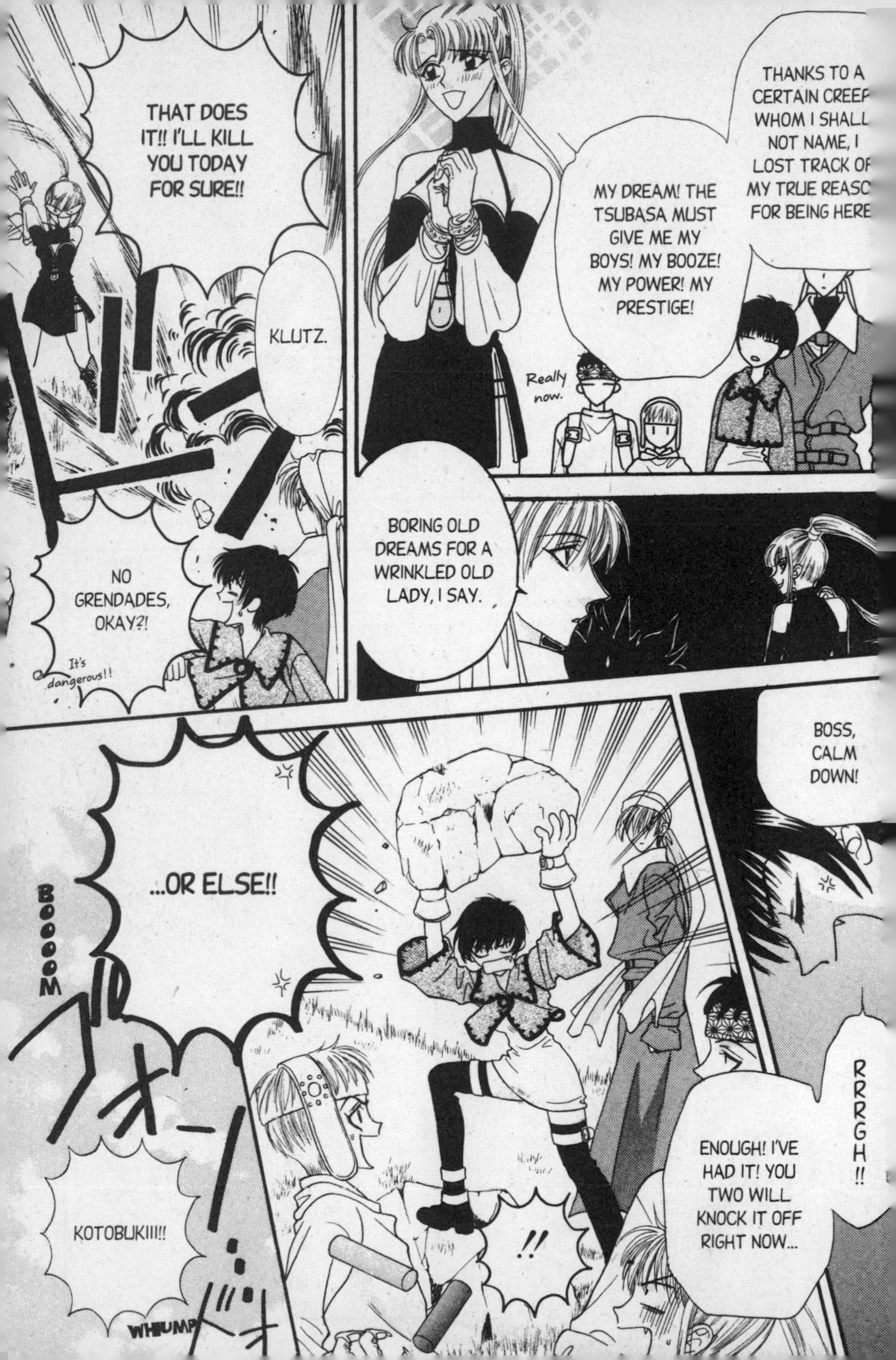

THANKS TO A CERTAIN CREEP WHOM I SHALL NOT NAME, I LOST TRACK OF MY TRUE REASO FOR BEING HERE
MY DREAM! THE TSUBASA MUST GIVE ME MY BOYS! MY BOOZE! MY POWER! MY PRESTIGE!
Really now.
BORING OLD DREAMS FOR A WRINKLED OLD LADY, I SAY.
THAT DOES IT!! I'LL KILL YOU TODAY FOR SURE!!
KLUTZ.
NO GRENDADES, OKAY?!
It's dangerous!!
BOSS, CALM DOWN!
RRRGH!!
ENOUGH! I'VE HAD IT! YOU TWO WILL KNOCK IT OFF RIGHT NOW...
...OR ELSE!!
BOOOOOM
!!
KOTOBUKIII!!!
WHUMP

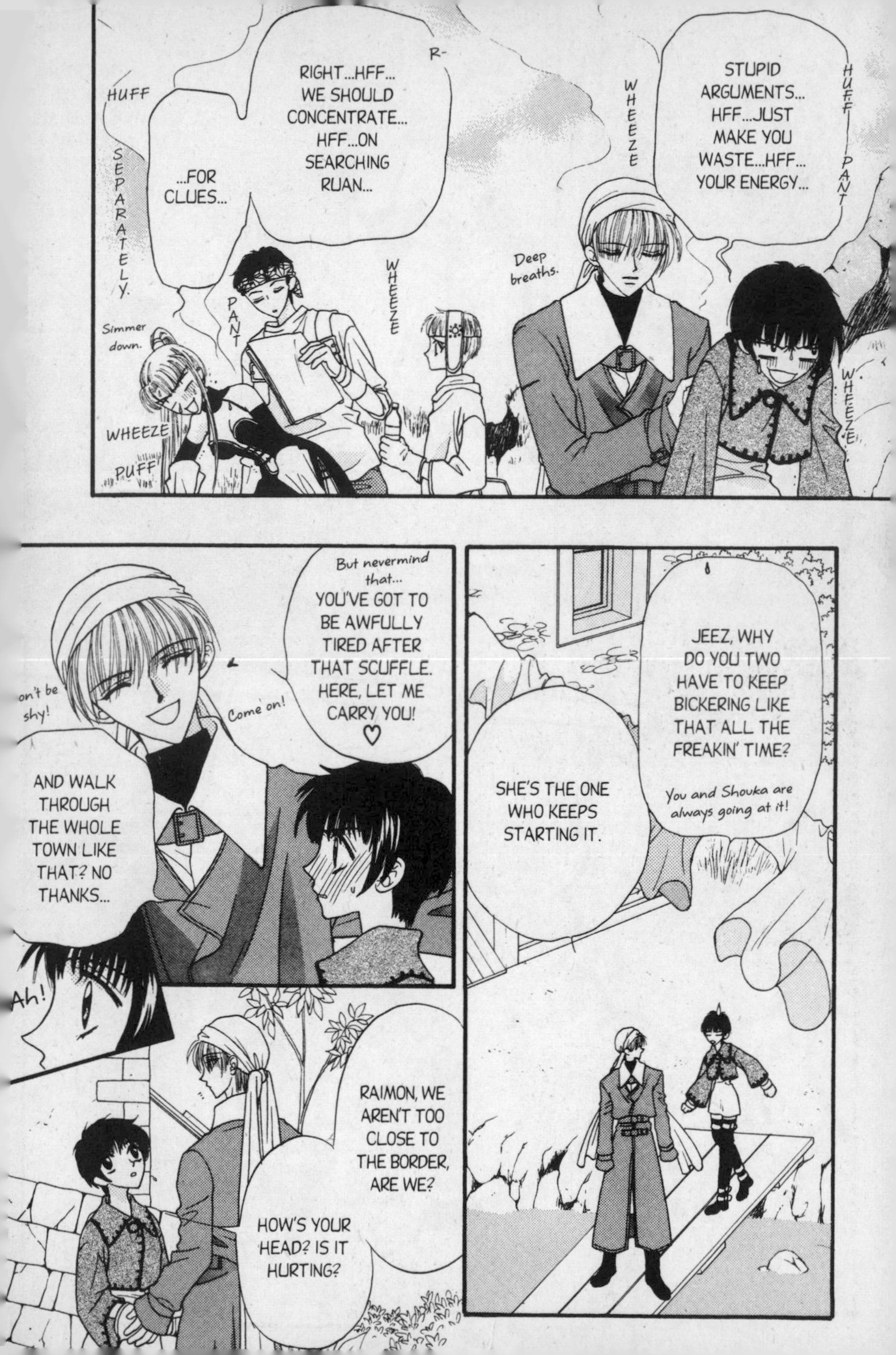
STUPID ARGUMENTS... HFF...JUST MAKE YOU WASTE...HFF... YOUR ENERGY...
HUFF PANT
WHEEZE
WHEEZE
Deep breaths.
R-
RIGHT...HFF... WE SHOULD CONCENTRATE... HFF...ON SEARCHING RUAN...
...FOR CLUES...
SEPARATELY.
HUFF
WHEEZE
PANT
Simmer down.
WHEEZE
PUFF
JEEZ, WHY DO YOU TWO HAVE TO KEEP BICKERING LIKE THAT ALL THE FREAKIN' TIME?
You and Shouka are always going at it!
SHE'S THE ONE WHO KEEPS STARTING IT.
But nevermind that... YOU'VE GOT TO BE AWFULLY TIRED AFTER THAT SCUFFLE. HERE, LET ME CARRY YOU! ♡
Come on!
on't be shy!
AND WALK THROUGH THE WHOLE TOWN LIKE THAT? NO THANKS...
Ah!
RAIMON, WE AREN'T TOO CLOSE TO THE BORDER, ARE WE?
HOW'S YOUR HEAD? IS IT HURTING?

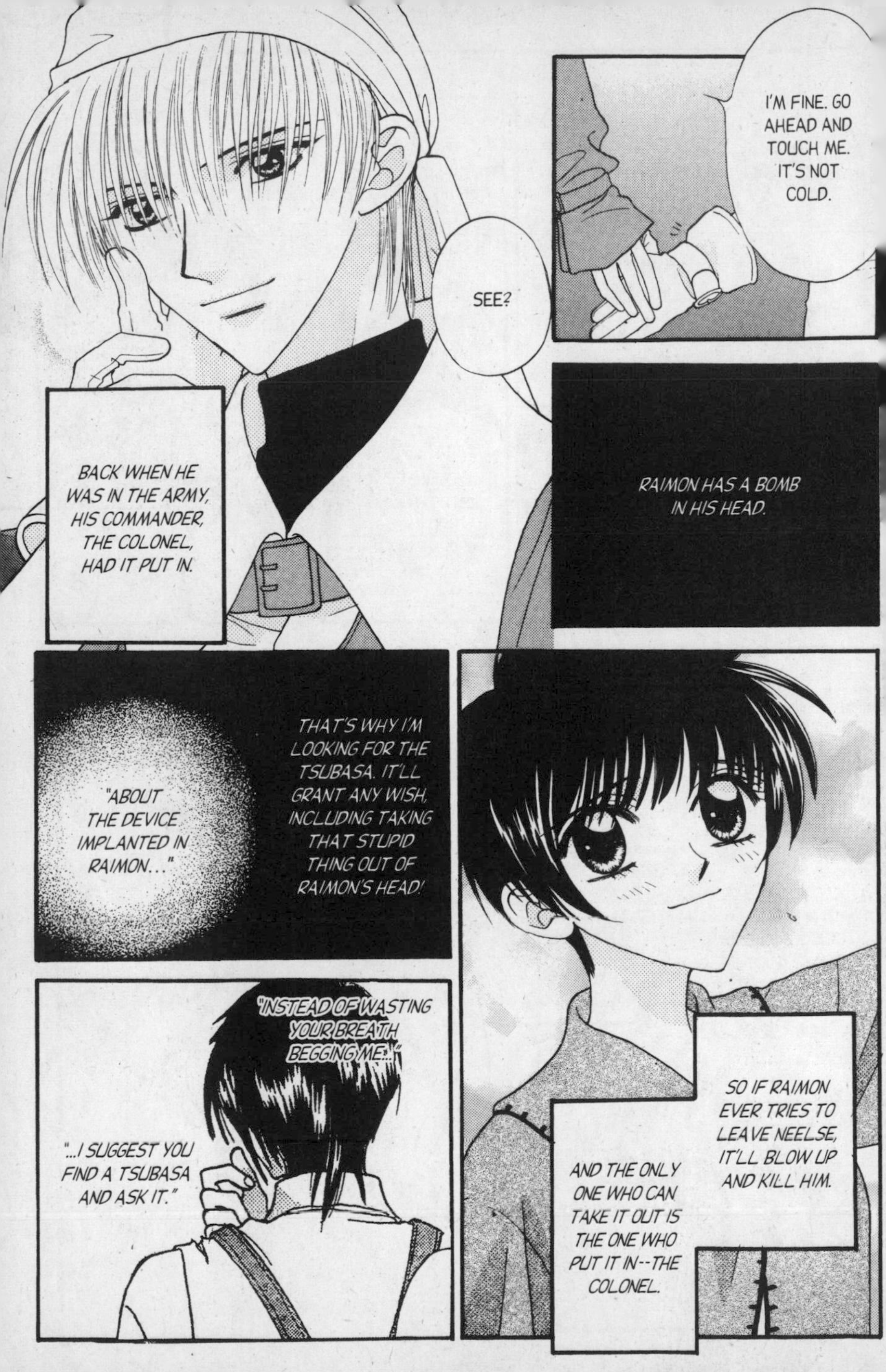
I'M FINE. GO AHEAD AND TOUCH ME. IT'S NOT COLD.
SEE?
RAIMON HAS A BOMB IN HIS HEAD.
BACK WHEN HE WAS IN THE ARMY, HIS COMMANDER, THE COLONEL, HAD IT PUT IN.
SO IF RAIMON EVER TRIES TO LEAVE NEELSE, IT'LL BLOW UP AND KILL HIM.
AND THE ONLY ONE WHO CAN TAKE IT OUT IS THE ONE WHO PUT IT IN--THE COLONEL.
THAT'S WHY I'M LOOKING FOR THE TSUBASA. IT'LL GRANT ANY WISH, INCLUDING TAKING THAT STUPID THING OUT OF RAIMON'S HEAD!
"ABOUT THE DEVICE IMPLANTED IN RAIMON..."
"INSTEAD OF WASTING YOUR BREATH BEGGING ME..."
"...I SUGGEST YOU FIND A TSUBASA AND ASK IT."

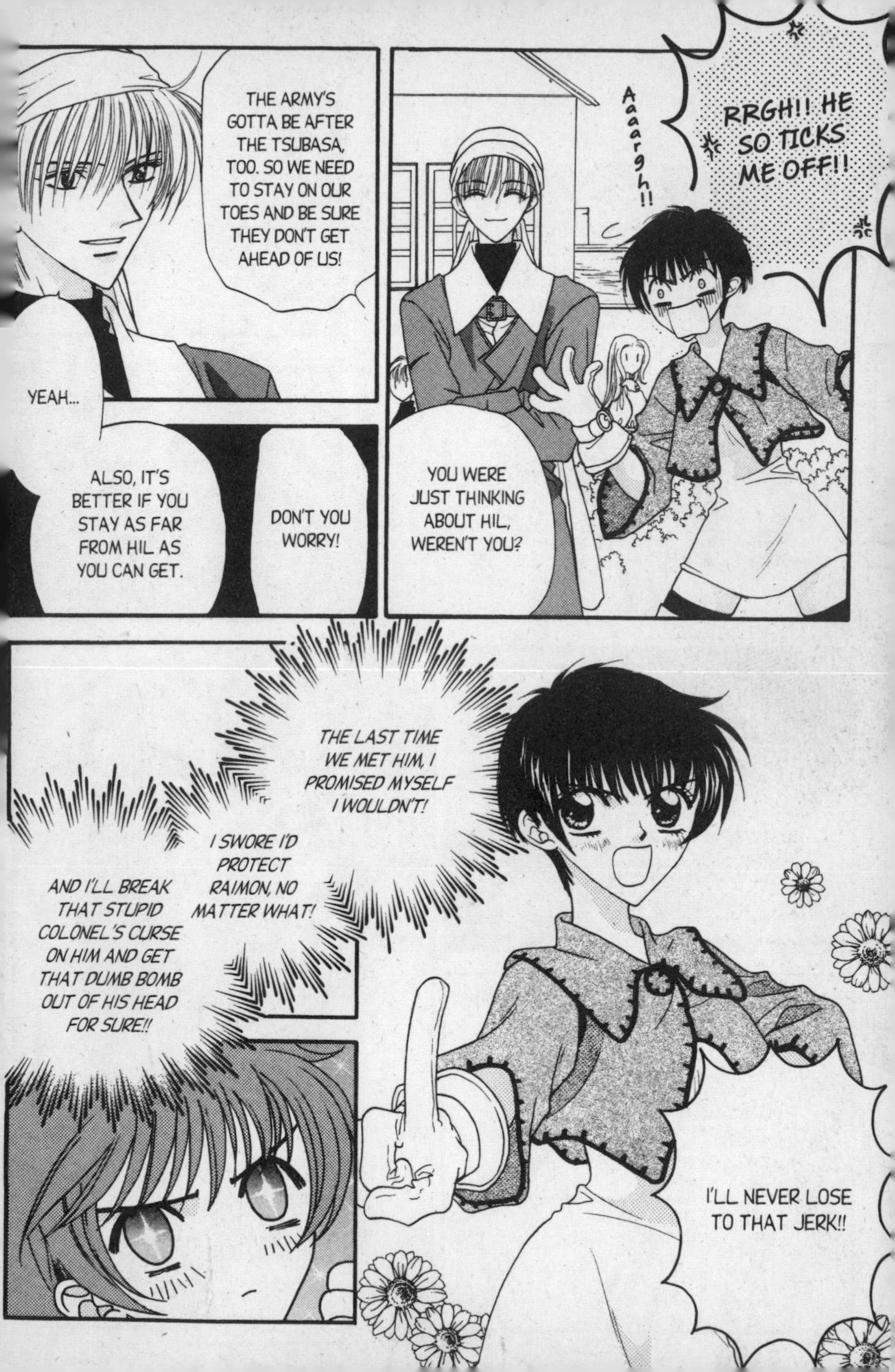
RRGH!! HE SO TICKS ME OFF!!
Aaaargh!!
YOU WERE JUST THINKING ABOUT HIL, WEREN'T YOU?
THE ARMY'S GOTTA BE AFTER THE TSUBASA, TOO. SO WE NEED TO STAY ON OUR TOES AND BE SURE THEY DON'T GET AHEAD OF US!
YEAH...
DON'T YOU WORRY!
ALSO, IT'S BETTER IF YOU STAY AS FAR FROM HIL AS YOU CAN GET.
THE LAST TIME WE MET HIM, I PROMISED MYSELF I WOULDN'T!
I SWORE I'D PROTECT RAIMON, NO MATTER WHAT!
AND I'LL BREAK THAT STUPID COLONEL'S CURSE ON HIM AND GET THAT DUMB BOMB OUT OF HIS HEAD FOR SURE!!
I'LL NEVER LOSE TO THAT JERK!!

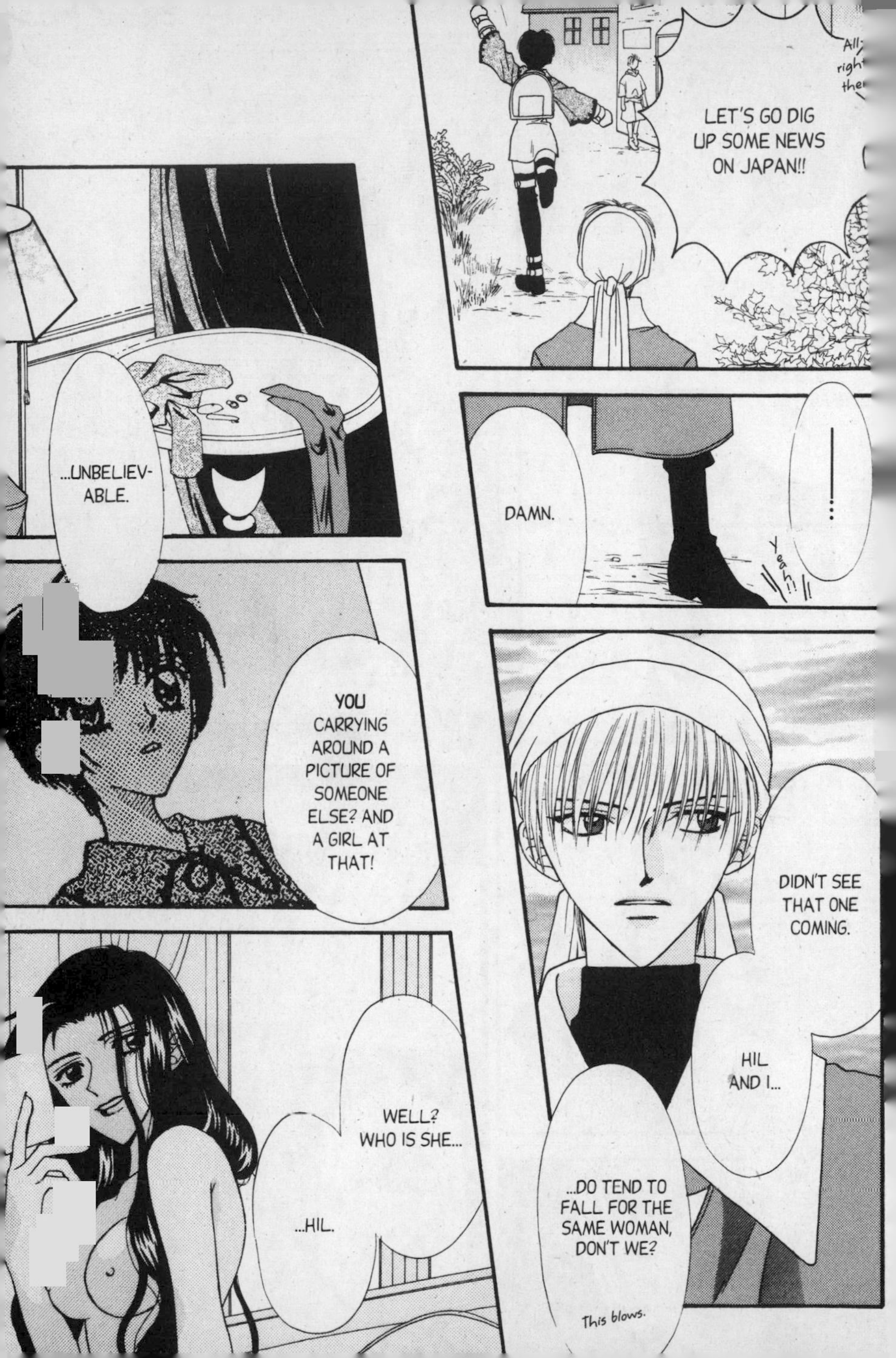
All right
LET'S GO DIG UP SOME NEWS ON JAPAN!!
...!
Yeah!!
DAMN.
DIDN'T SEE THAT ONE COMING.
HIL AND I...
...DO TEND TO FALL FOR THE SAME WOMAN, DON'T WE?
This blows.
...UNBELIEV-ABLE.
YOU CARRYING AROUND A PICTURE OF SOMEONE ELSE? AND A GIRL AT THAT!
WELL? WHO IS SHE...
...HIL.

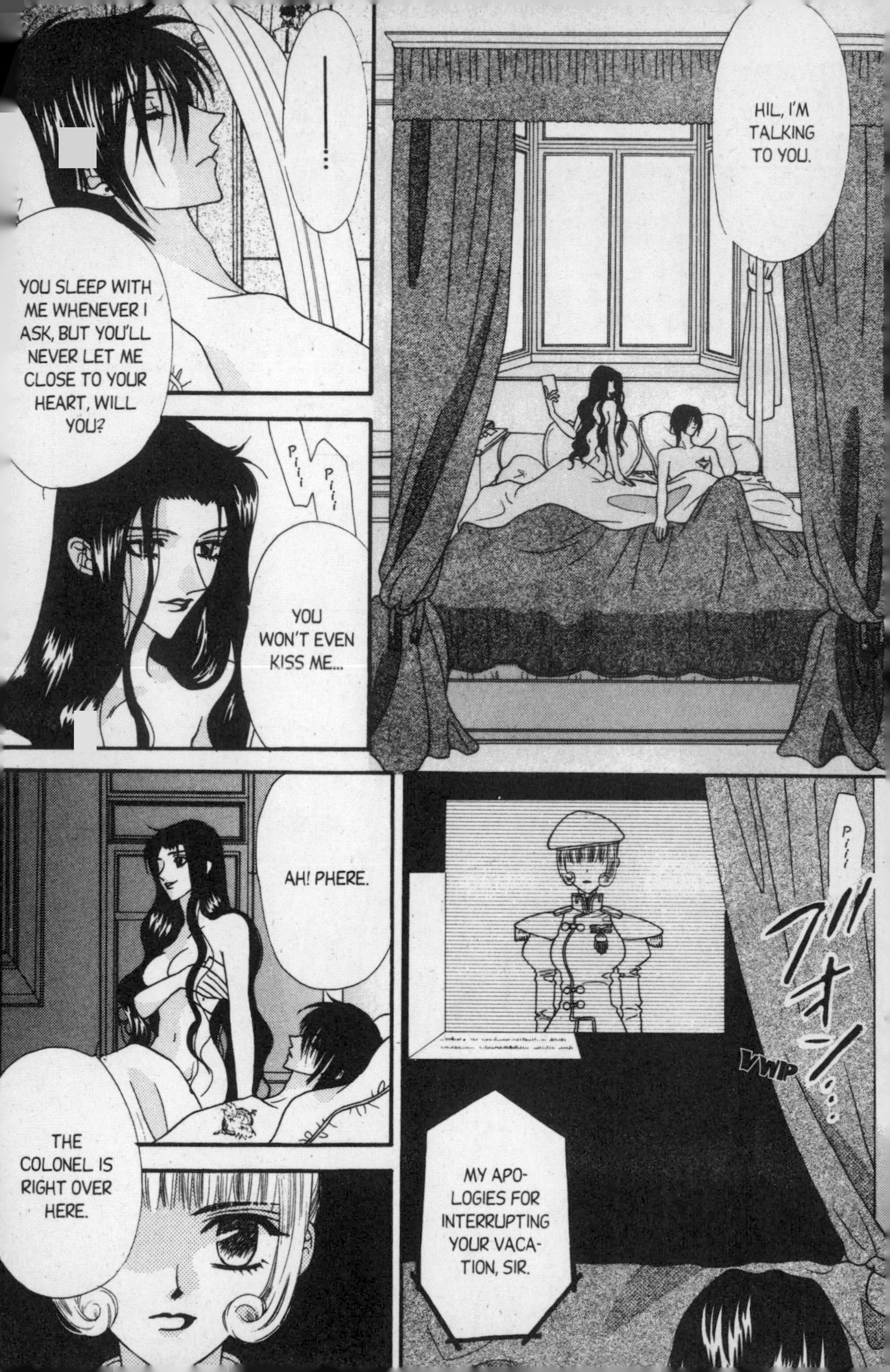
HIL, I'M TALKING TO YOU.
—......
YOU SLEEP WITH ME WHENEVER I ASK, BUT YOU'LL NEVER LET ME CLOSE TO YOUR HEART, WILL YOU?
Piii
Piii
YOU WON'T EVEN KISS ME...
Piii
ブォン...
VWIP
MY APOLOGIES FOR INTERRUPTING YOUR VACATION, SIR.
AH! PHERE.
THE COLONEL IS RIGHT OVER HERE.

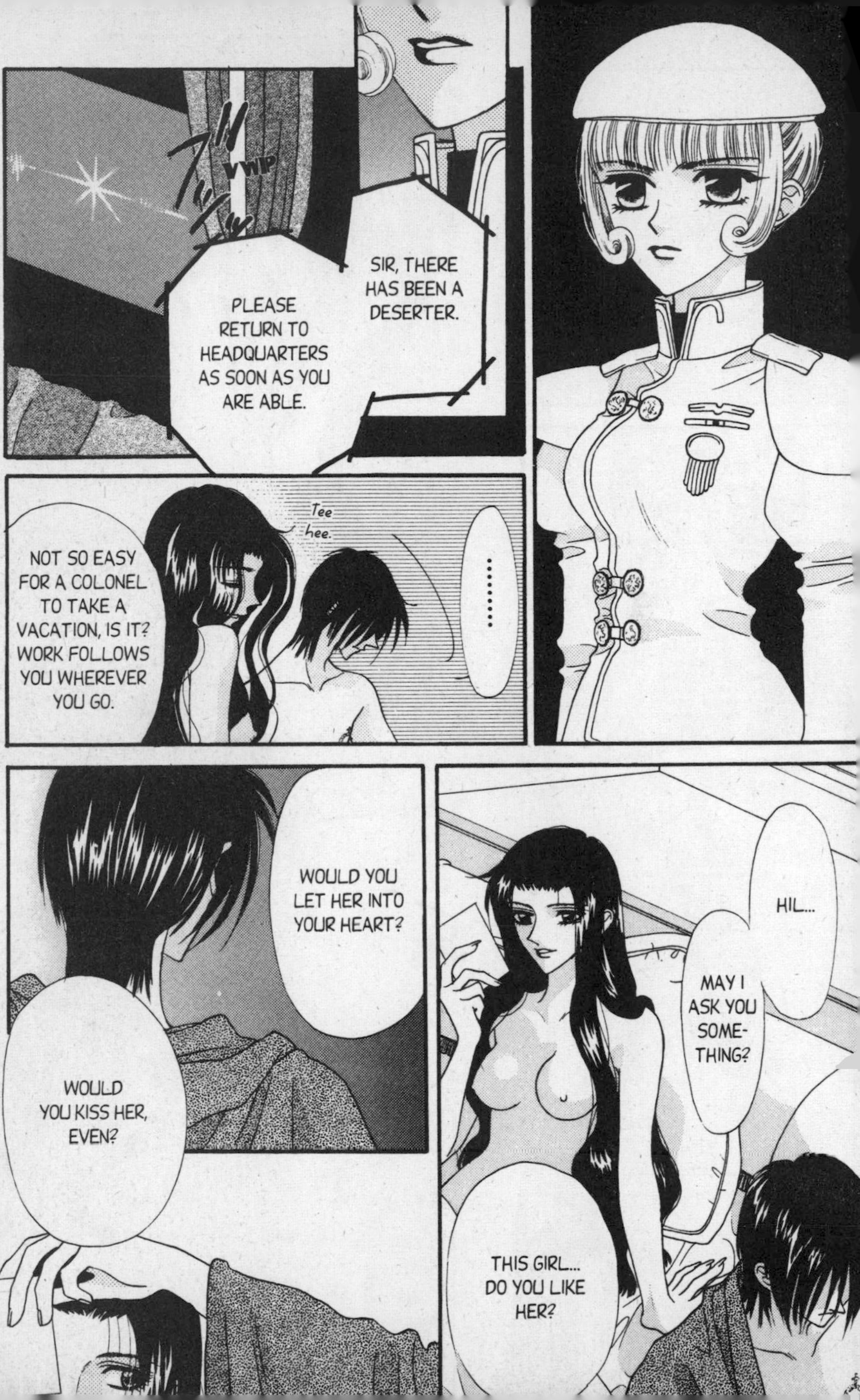

SIR, THERE HAS BEEN A DESERTER.
PLEASE RETURN TO HEADQUARTERS AS SOON AS YOU ARE ABLE.
VWIP
......
Tee hee.
NOT SO EASY FOR A COLONEL TO TAKE A VACATION, IS IT? WORK FOLLOWS YOU WHEREVER YOU GO.
HIL...
MAY I ASK YOU SOME-THING?
THIS GIRL... DO YOU LIKE HER?
WOULD YOU LET HER INTO YOUR HEART?
WOULD YOU KISS HER, EVEN?

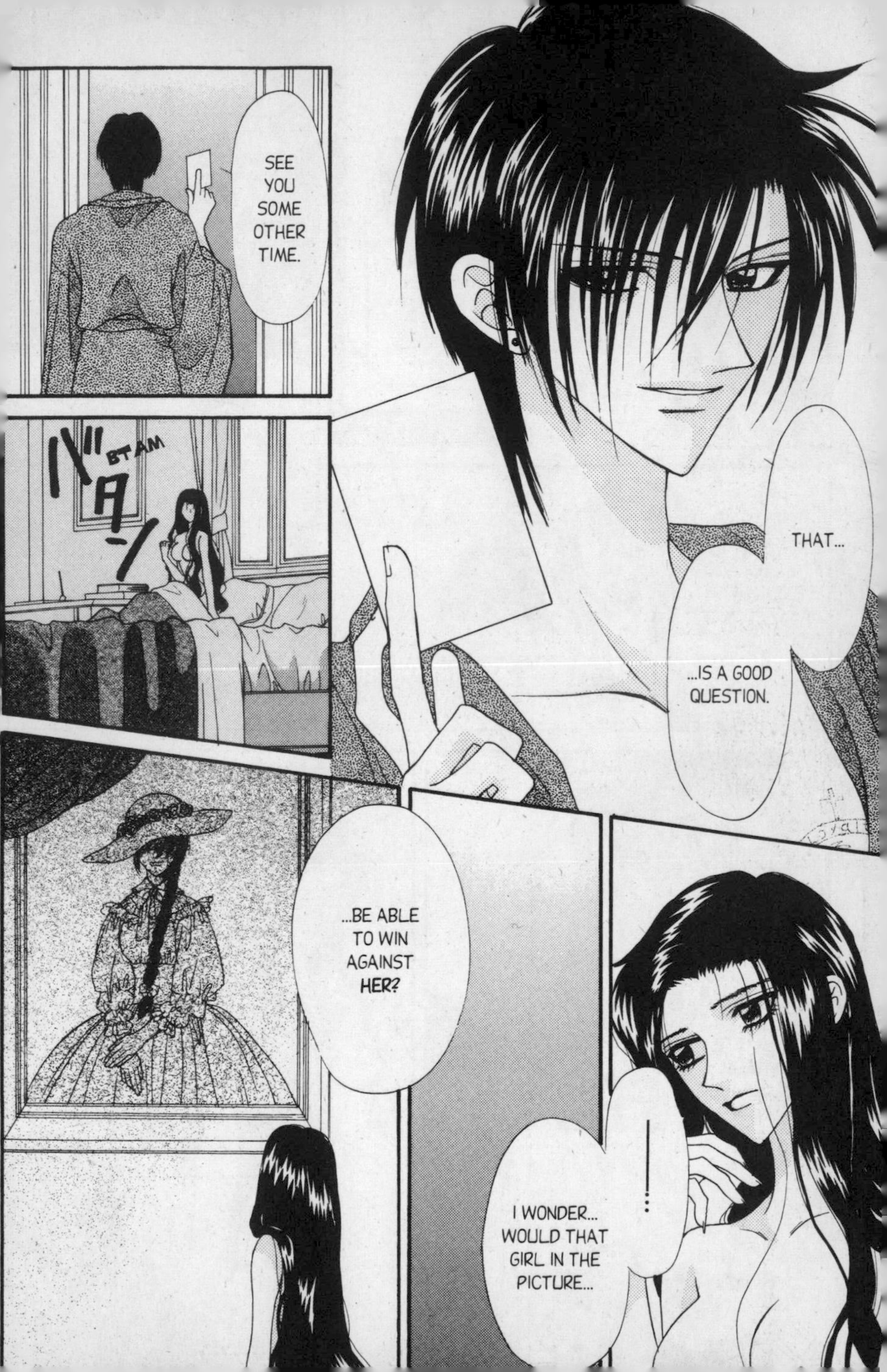
THAT...
...IS A GOOD QUESTION.
SEE YOU SOME OTHER TIME.
BTAM
...
I WONDER... WOULD THAT GIRL IN THE PICTURE...
...BE ABLE TO WIN AGAINST HER?

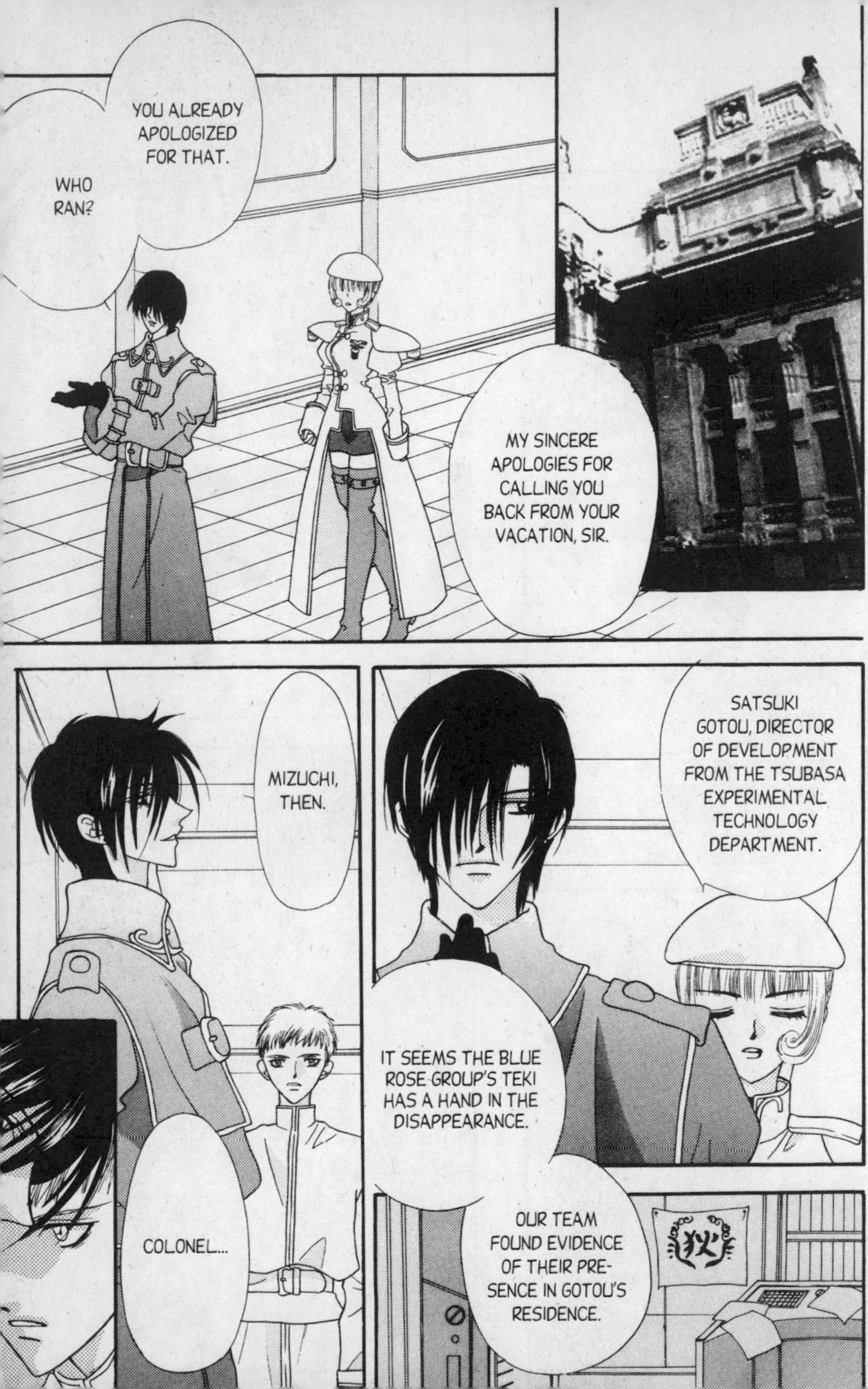
MY SINCERE APOLOGIES FOR CALLING YOU BACK FROM YOUR VACATION, SIR.
YOU ALREADY APOLOGIZED FOR THAT.
WHO RAN?
SATSUKI GOTOU, DIRECTOR OF DEVELOPMENT FROM THE TSUBASA EXPERIMENTAL TECHNOLOGY DEPARTMENT.
IT SEEMS THE BLUE ROSE GROUP'S TEKI HAS A HAND IN THE DISAPPEARANCE.
OUR TEAM FOUND EVIDENCE OF THEIR PRE-SENCE IN GOTOU'S RESIDENCE.
MIZUCHI, THEN.
COLONEL...

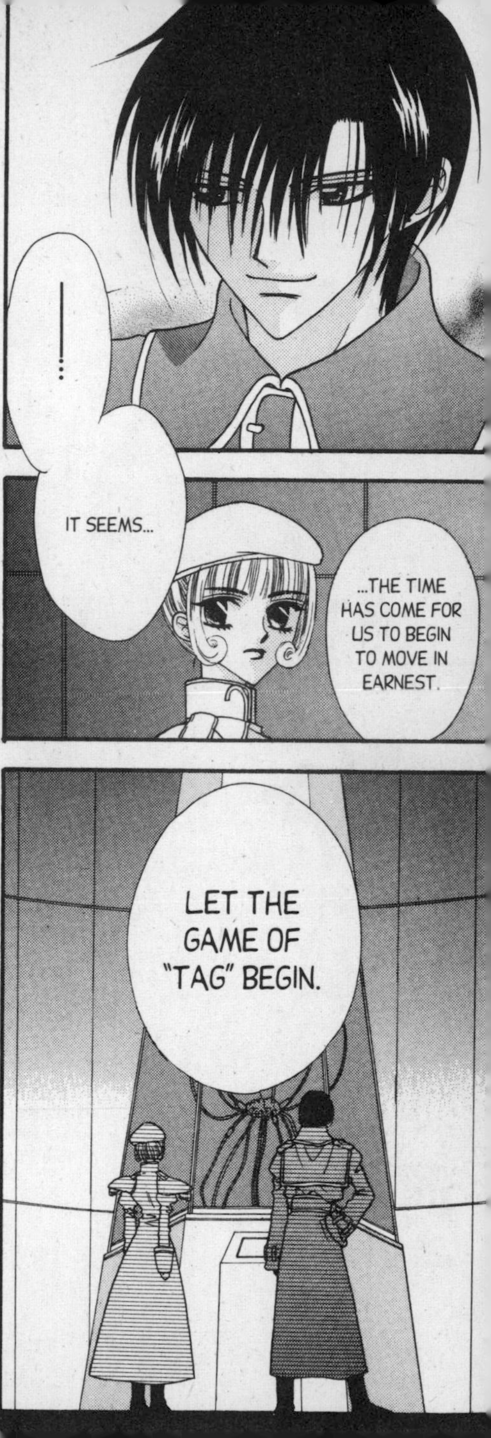
......
IT SEEMS...
...THE TIME HAS COME FOR US TO BEGIN TO MOVE IN EARNEST.
LET THE GAME OF "TAG" BEGIN.
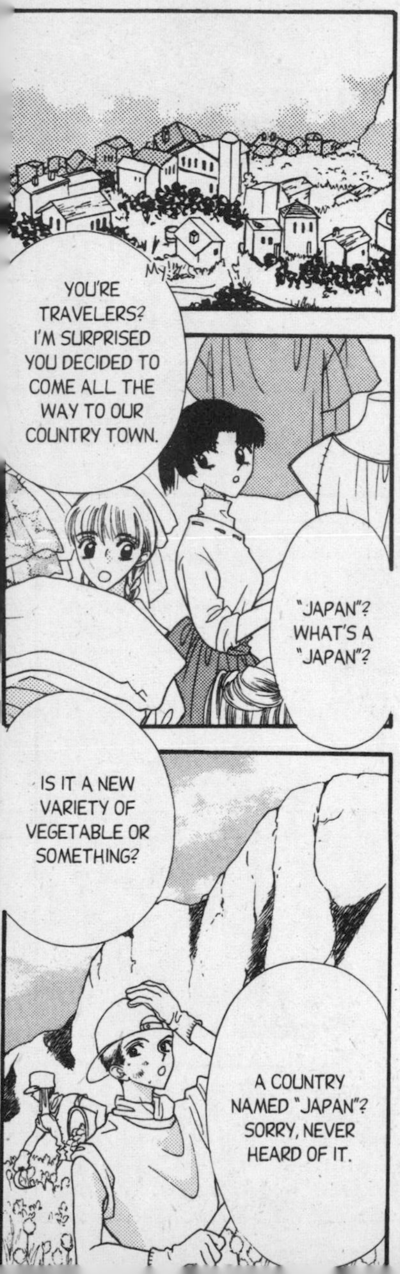
YOU'RE TRAVELERS? I'M SURPRISED YOU DECIDED TO COME ALL THE WAY TO OUR COUNTRY TOWN.
"JAPAN"? WHAT'S A "JAPAN"?
IS IT A NEW VARIETY OF VEGETABLE OR SOMETHING?
A COUNTRY NAMED "JAPAN"? SORRY, NEVER HEARD OF IT.

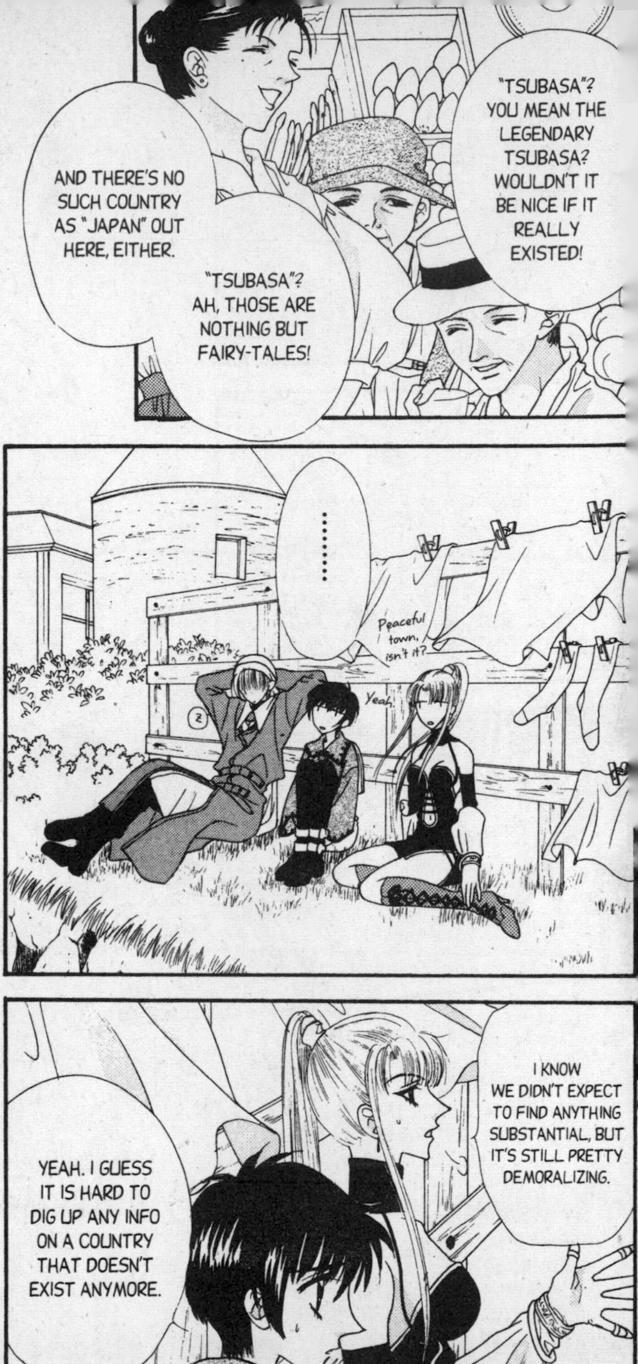
"TSUBASA"? YOU MEAN THE LEGENDARY TSUBASA? WOULDN'T IT BE NICE IF IT REALLY EXISTED!
"TSUBASA"? AH, THOSE ARE NOTHING BUT FAIRY-TALES!
AND THERE'S NO SUCH COUNTRY AS "JAPAN" OUT HERE, EITHER.
......
Peaceful town, isn't it?
Yeah.
z
I KNOW WE DIDN'T EXPECT TO FIND ANYTHING SUBSTANTIAL, BUT IT'S STILL PRETTY DEMORALIZING.
YEAH. I GUESS IT IS HARD TO DIG UP ANY INFO ON A COUNTRY THAT DOESN'T EXIST ANYMORE.
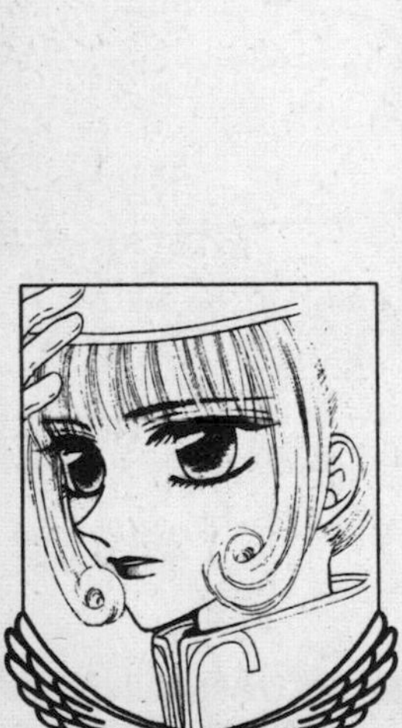

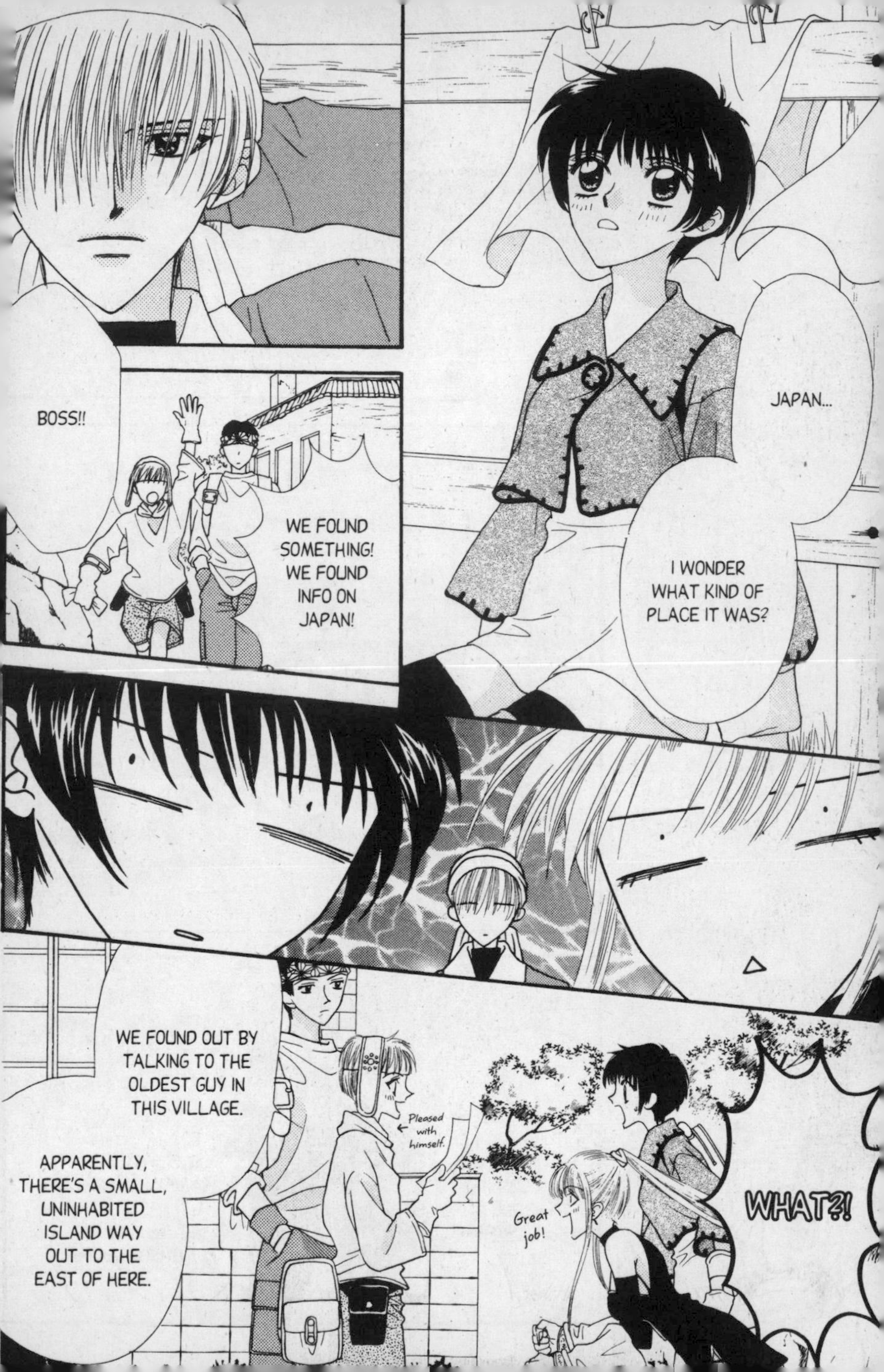
JAPAN...
I WONDER WHAT KIND OF PLACE IT WAS?
BOSS!!
WE FOUND SOMETHING! WE FOUND INFO ON JAPAN!
WHAT?!
Great job!
WE FOUND OUT BY TALKING TO THE OLDEST GUY IN THIS VILLAGE.
Pleased with himself.
APPARENTLY, THERE'S A SMALL, UNINHABITED ISLAND WAY OUT TO THE EAST OF HERE.

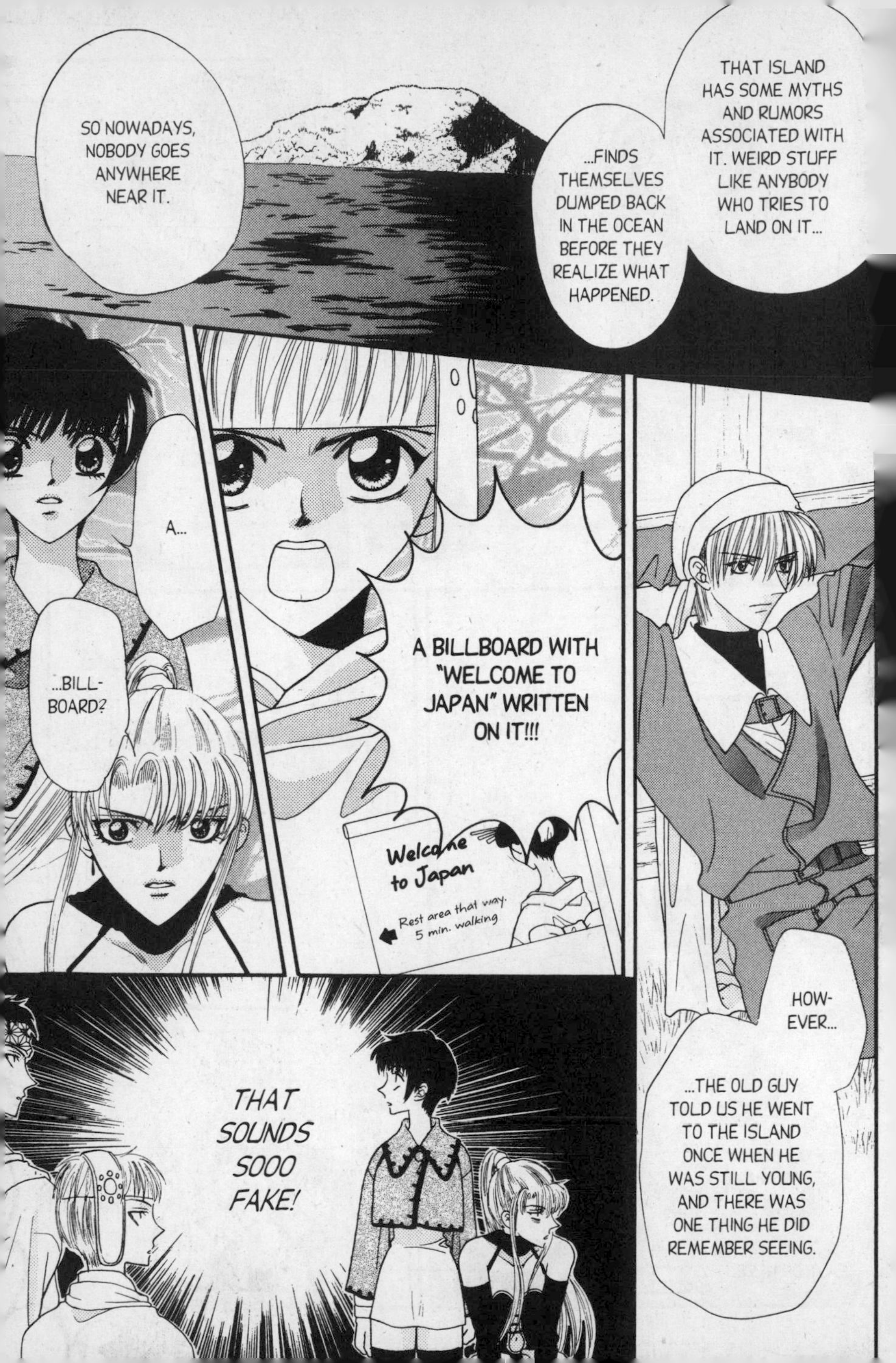

THAT ISLAND HAS SOME MYTHS AND RUMORS ASSOCIATED WITH IT. WEIRD STUFF LIKE ANYBODY WHO TRIES TO LAND ON IT...
...FINDS THEMSELVES DUMPED BACK IN THE OCEAN BEFORE THEY REALIZE WHAT HAPPENED.
SO NOWADAYS, NOBODY GOES ANYWHERE NEAR IT.
HOW-EVER...
...THE OLD GUY TOLD US HE WENT TO THE ISLAND ONCE WHEN HE WAS STILL YOUNG, AND THERE WAS ONE THING HE DID REMEMBER SEEING.
A BILLBOARD WITH "WELCOME TO JAPAN" WRITTEN ON IT!!!
Welcome to Japan
Rest area that way. 5 min. walking
A...
...BILL-BOARD?
THAT SOUNDS SOOO FAKE!

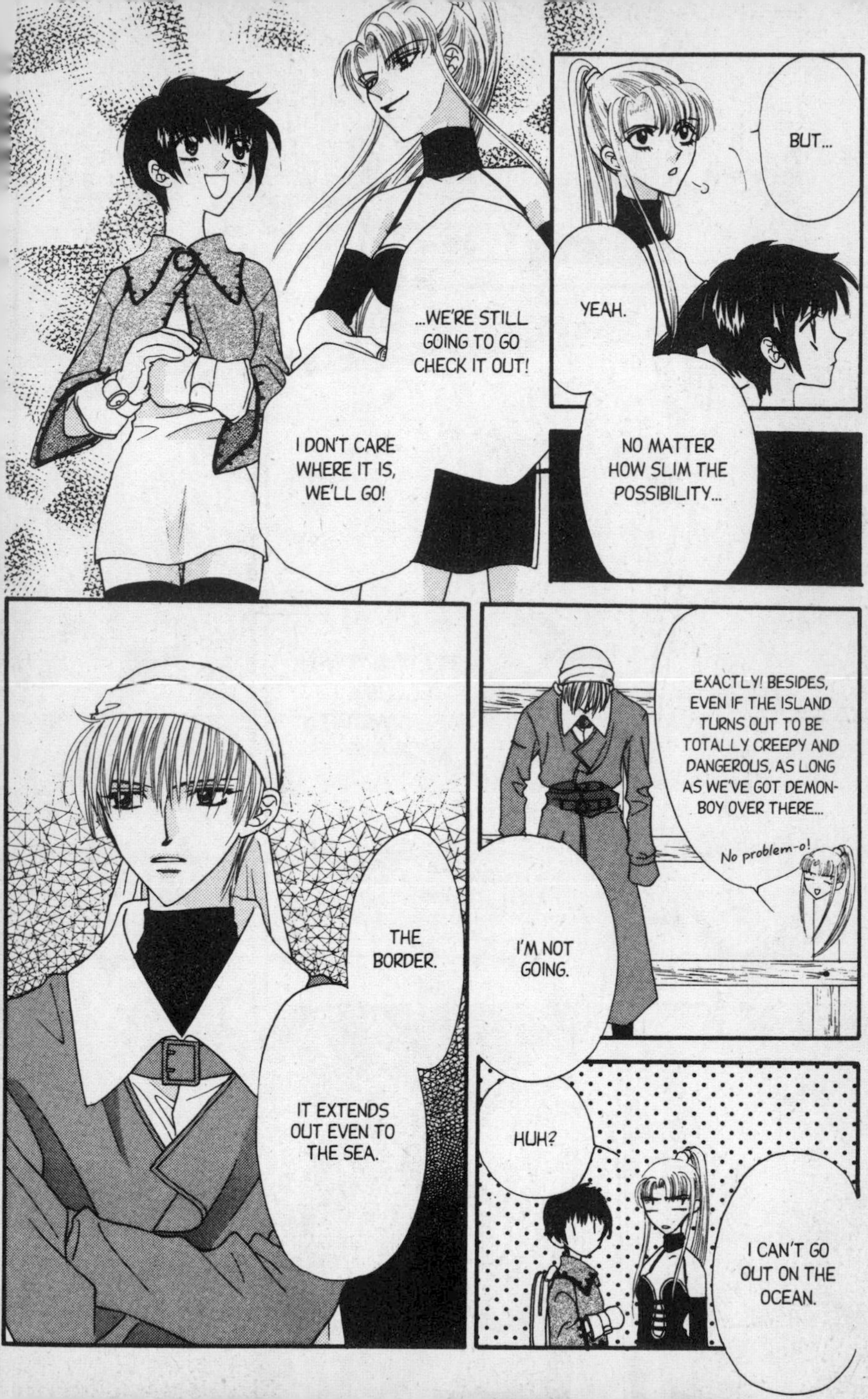
BUT...
YEAH.
NO MATTER HOW SLIM THE POSSIBILITY...
...WE'RE STILL GOING TO GO CHECK IT OUT!
I DON'T CARE WHERE IT IS, WE'LL GO!
EXACTLY! BESIDES, EVEN IF THE ISLAND TURNS OUT TO BE TOTALLY CREEPY AND DANGEROUS, AS LONG AS WE'VE GOT DEMON-BOY OVER THERE...
No problem-o!
I'M NOT GOING.
HUH?
I CAN'T GO OUT ON THE OCEAN.
THE BORDER.
IT EXTENDS OUT EVEN TO THE SEA.

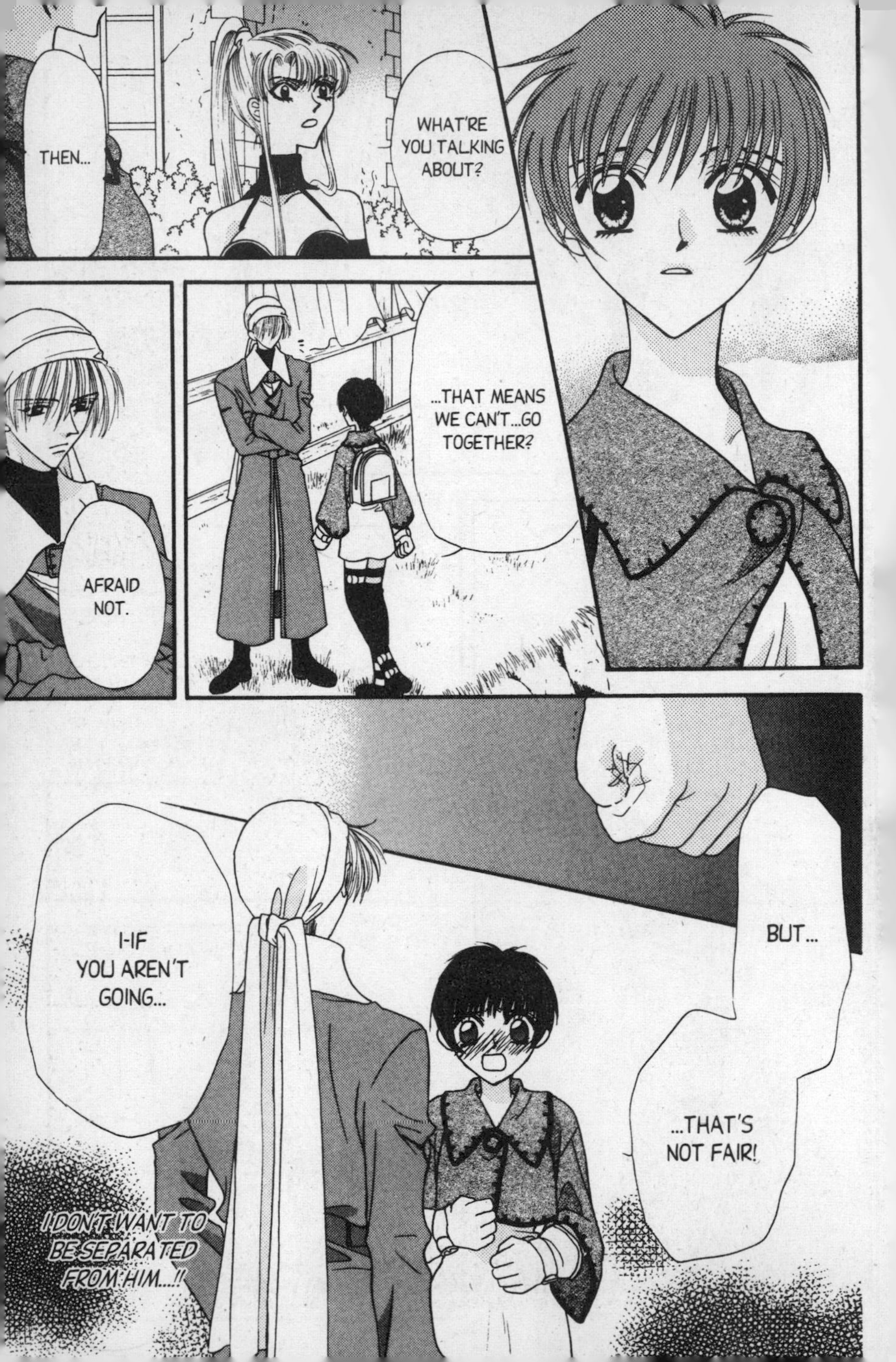
WHAT'RE YOU TALKING ABOUT?
THEN...
...THAT MEANS WE CAN'T...GO TOGETHER?
AFRAID NOT.
BUT...
...THAT'S NOT FAIR!
I-IF YOU AREN'T GOING...
I DON'T WANT TO BE SEPARATED FROM HIM...!!

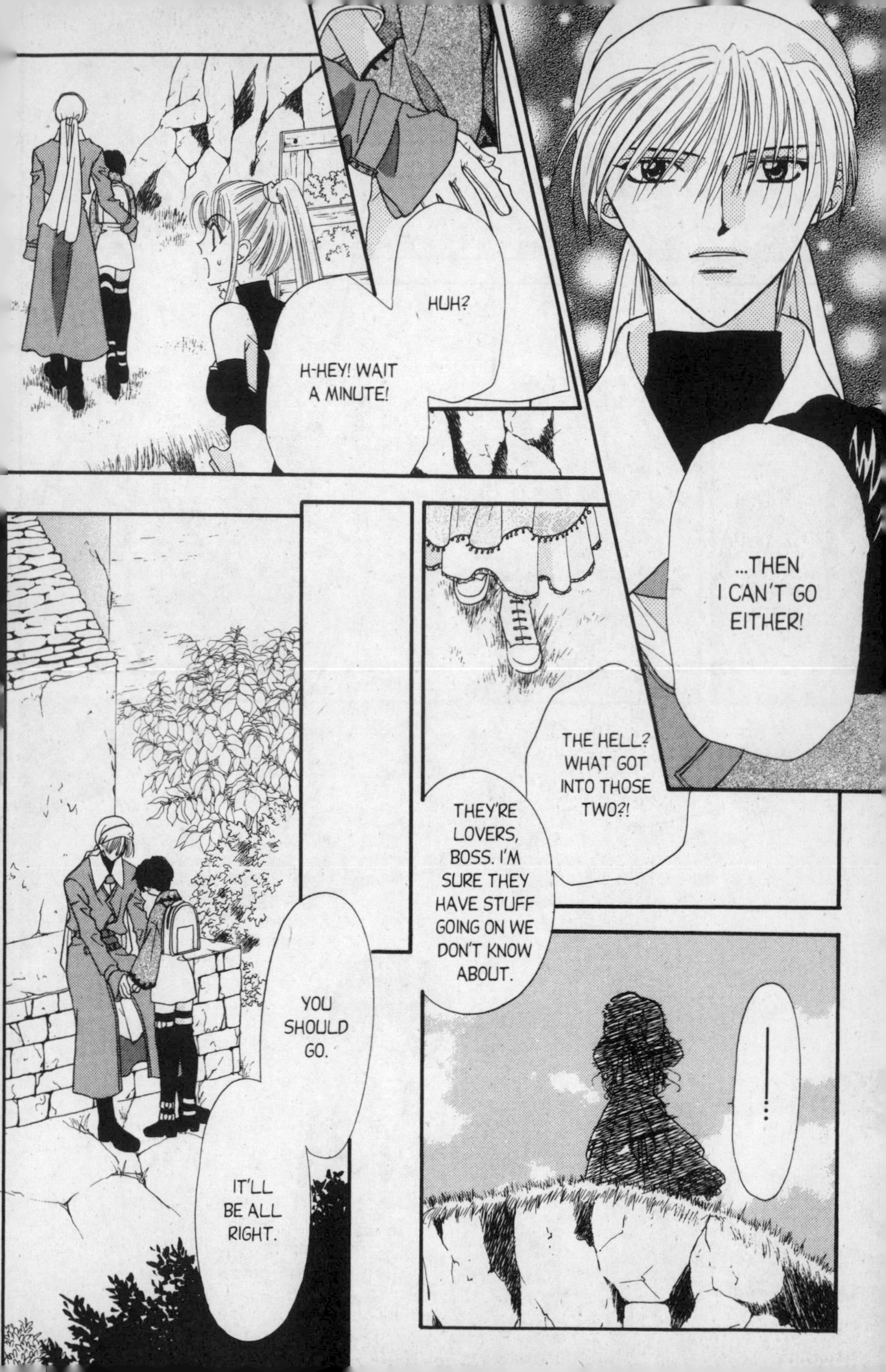
...THEN I CAN'T GO EITHER!
HUH?
H-HEY! WAIT A MINUTE!
THE HELL? WHAT GOT INTO THOSE TWO?!
THEY'RE LOVERS, BOSS. I'M SURE THEY HAVE STUFF GOING ON WE DON'T KNOW ABOUT.
—......
YOU SHOULD GO.
IT'LL BE ALL RIGHT.

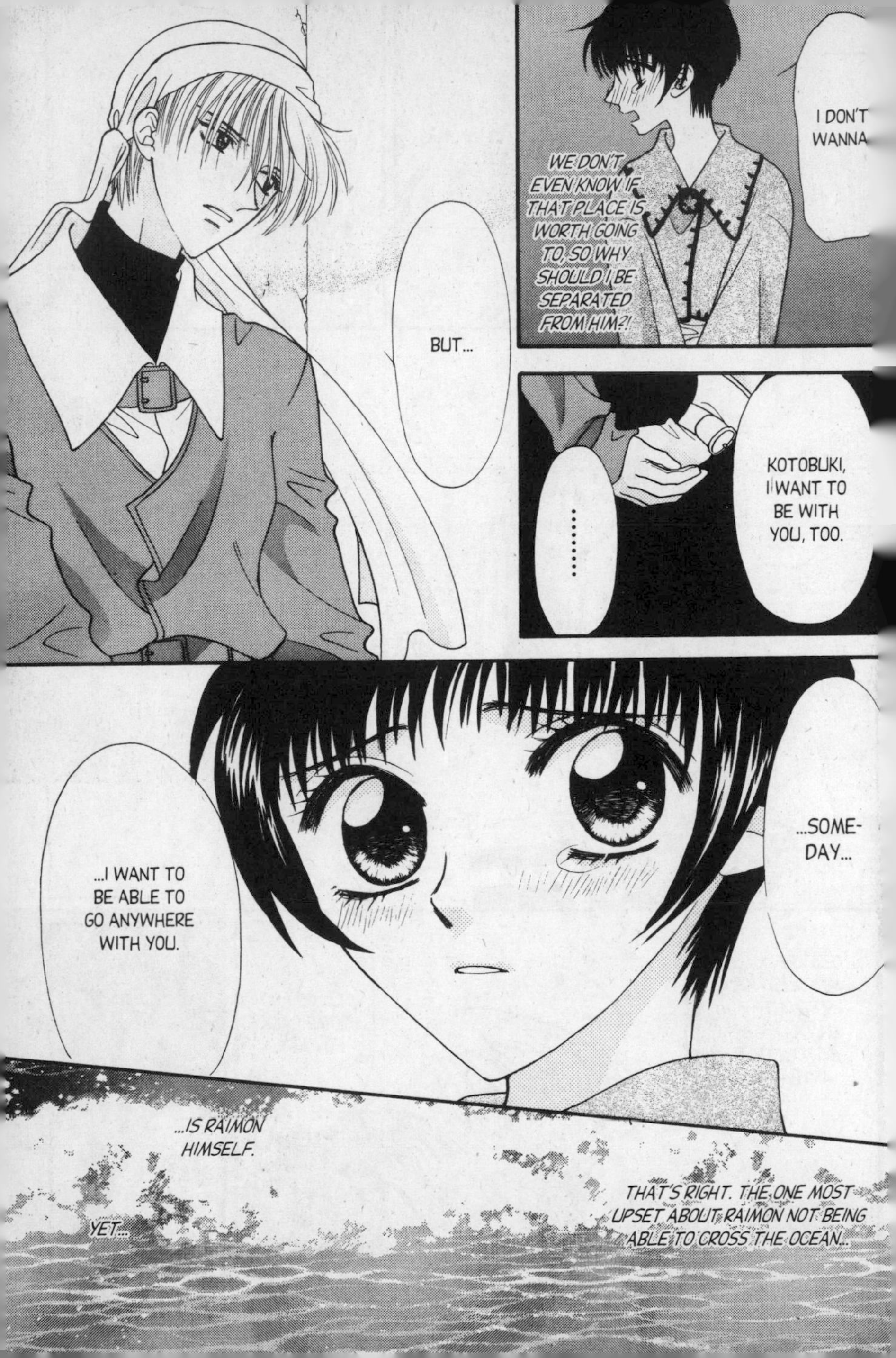
I DON'T WANNA
WE DON'T EVEN KNOW IF THAT PLACE IS WORTH GOING TO, SO WHY SHOULD I BE SEPARATED FROM HIM?!
KOTOBUKI, I WANT TO BE WITH YOU, TOO.
......
BUT...
...SOME-DAY...
...I WANT TO BE ABLE TO GO ANYWHERE WITH YOU.
THAT'S RIGHT. THE ONE MOST UPSET ABOUT RAIMON NOT BEING ABLE TO CROSS THE OCEAN...
...IS RAIMON HIMSELF.
YET...

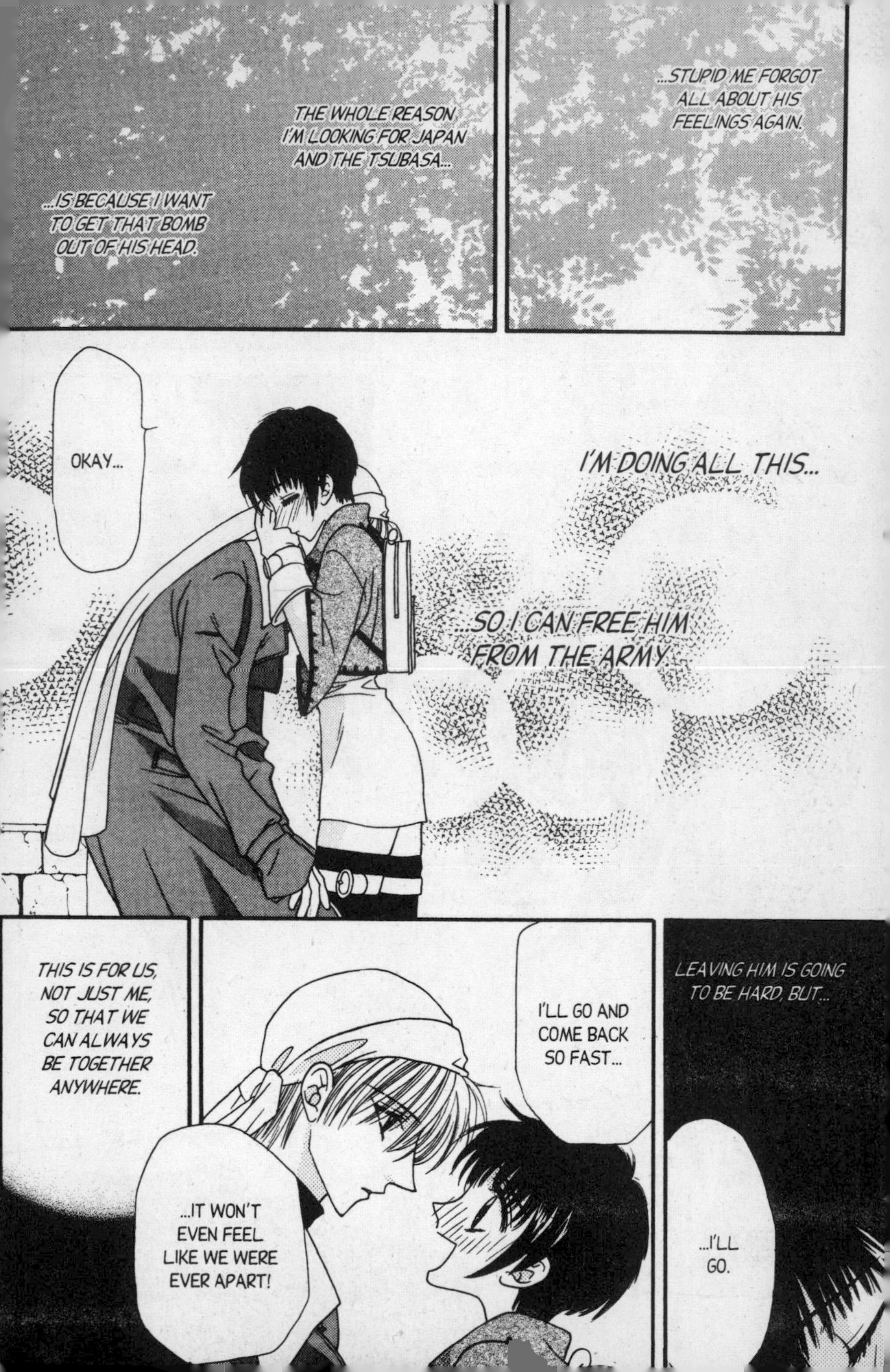
...STUPID ME FORGOT ALL ABOUT HIS FEELINGS AGAIN.
THE WHOLE REASON I'M LOOKING FOR JAPAN AND THE TSUBASA...
...IS BECAUSE I WANT TO GET THAT BOMB OUT OF HIS HEAD.
I'M DOING ALL THIS...
...SO I CAN FREE HIM FROM THE ARMY.
OKAY...
LEAVING HIM IS GOING TO BE HARD, BUT...
...I'LL GO.
I'LL GO AND COME BACK SO FAST...
...IT WON'T EVEN FEEL LIKE WE WERE EVER APART!
THIS IS FOR US, NOT JUST ME, SO THAT WE CAN ALWAYS BE TOGETHER ANYWHERE.

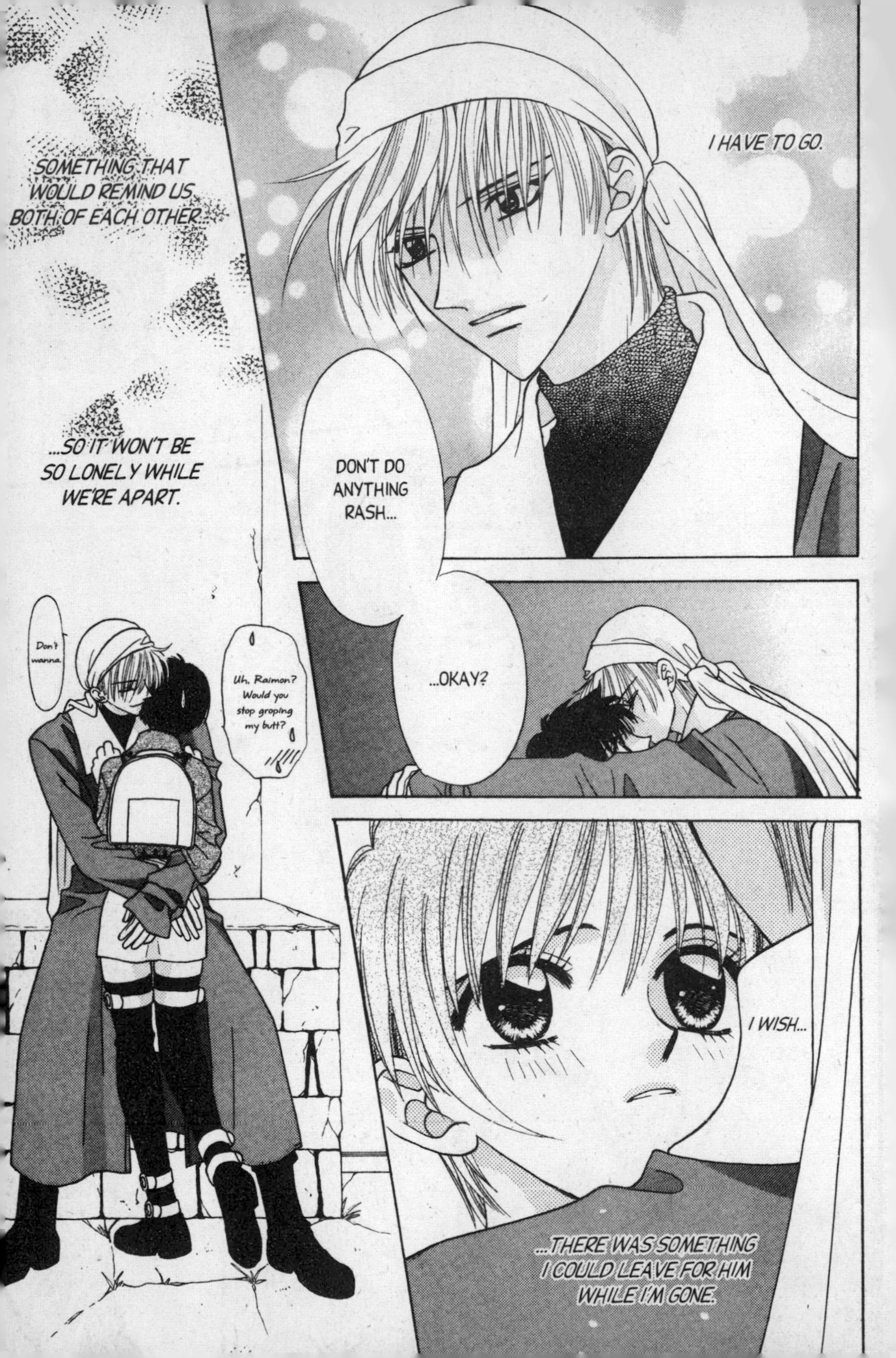
I HAVE TO GO.
DON'T DO ANYTHING RASH...
...OKAY?
I WISH...
...THERE WAS SOMETHING I COULD LEAVE FOR HIM WHILE I'M GONE.
SOMETHING THAT WOULD REMIND US BOTH OF EACH OTHER...
...SO IT WON'T BE SO LONELY WHILE WE'RE APART.
Uh, Raimon? Would you stop groping my butt?
Don't wanna.

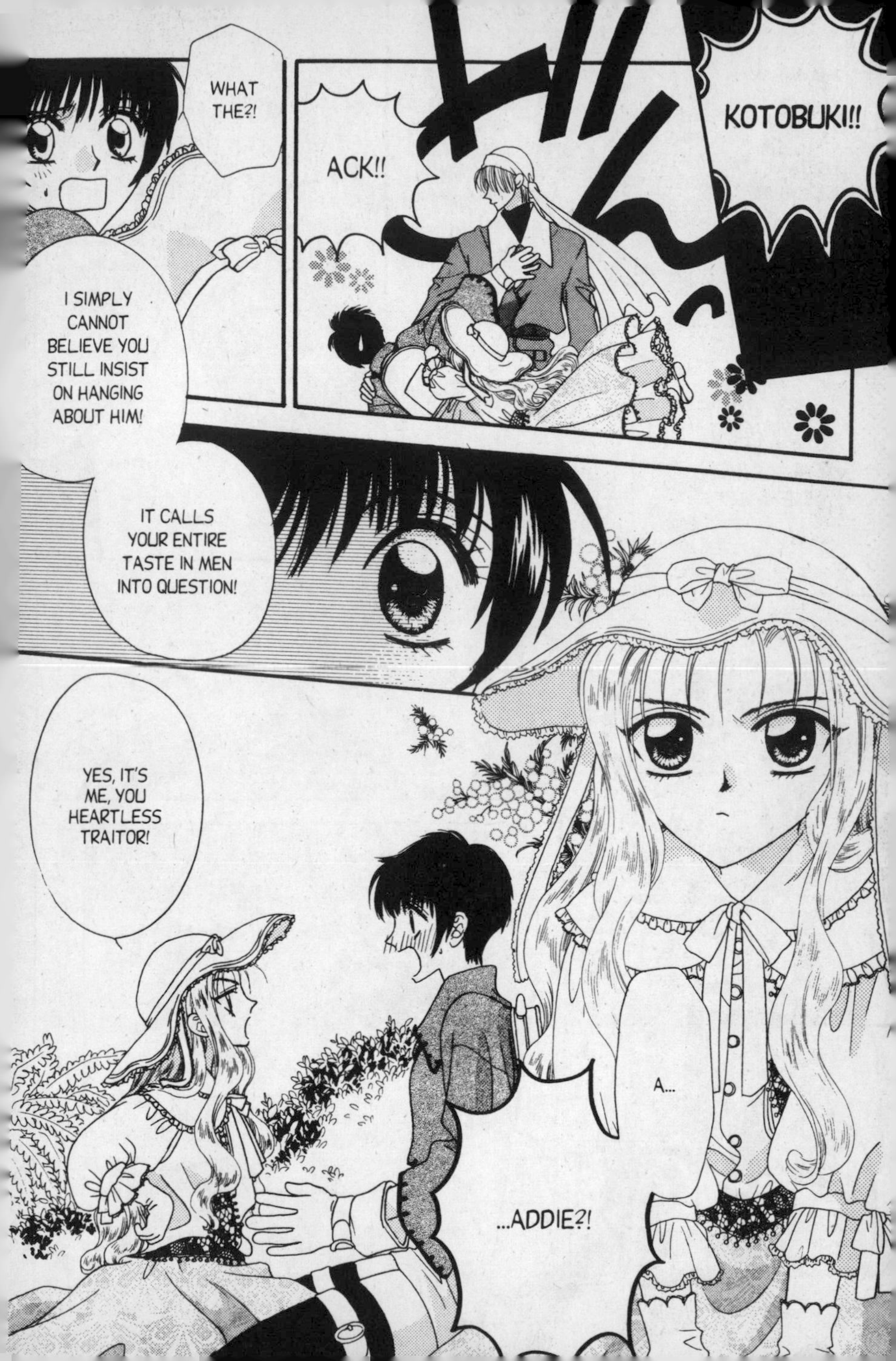
KOTOBUKI!!
ACK!!
WHAT THE?!
I SIMPLY CANNOT BELIEVE YOU STILL INSIST ON HANGING ABOUT HIM!
IT CALLS YOUR ENTIRE TASTE IN MEN INTO QUESTION!
YES, IT'S ME, YOU HEARTLESS TRAITOR!
A...
...ADDIE?!

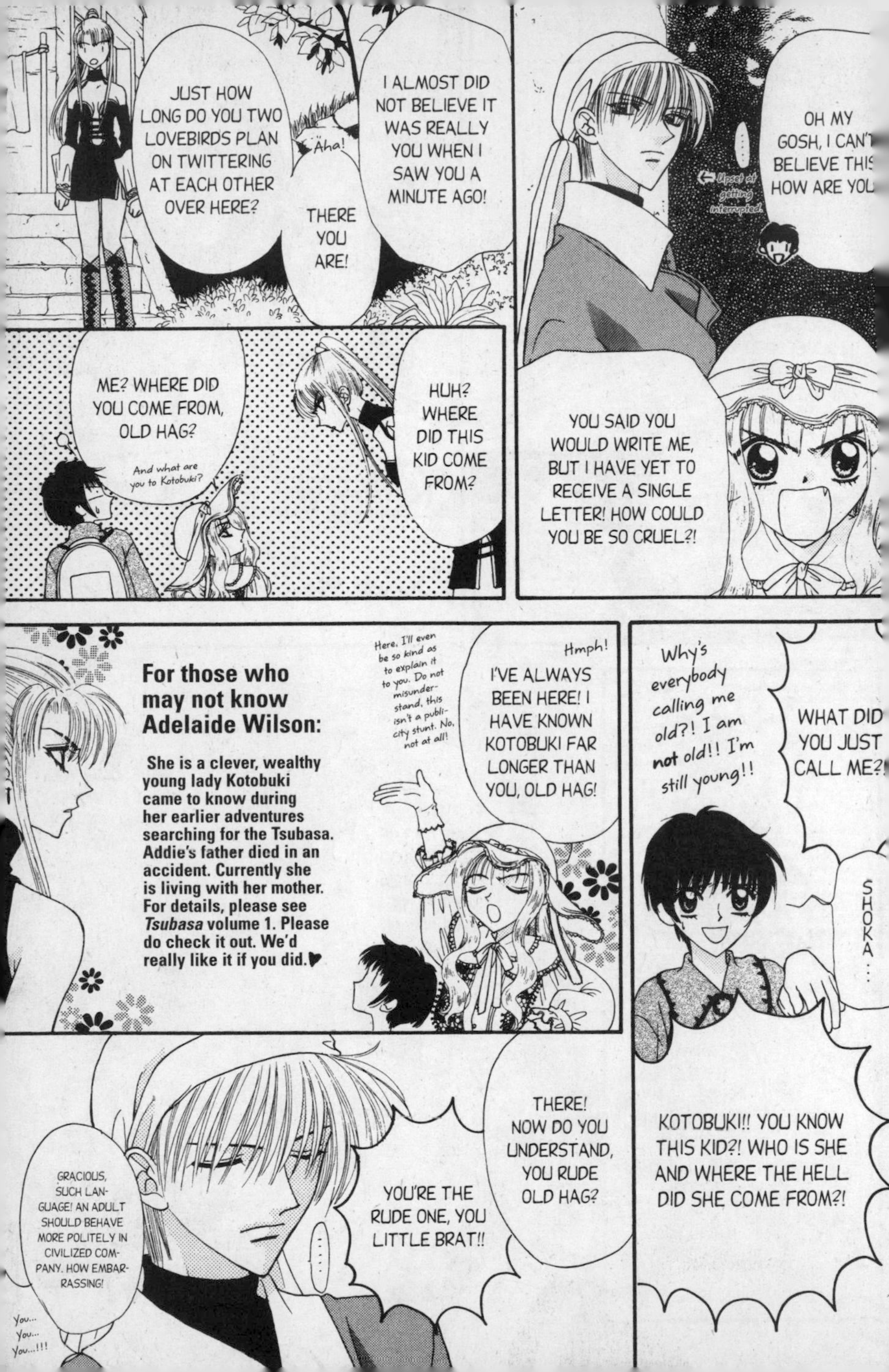
OH MY GOSH, I CAN'T BELIEVE THIS HOW ARE YOU
...
Upset at getting interrupted.
YOU SAID YOU WOULD WRITE ME, BUT I HAVE YET TO RECEIVE A SINGLE LETTER! HOW COULD YOU BE SO CRUEL?!
I ALMOST DID NOT BELIEVE IT WAS REALLY YOU WHEN I SAW YOU A MINUTE AGO!
THERE YOU ARE!
Aha!
JUST HOW LONG DO YOU TWO LOVEBIRDS PLAN ON TWITTERING AT EACH OTHER OVER HERE?
HUH? WHERE DID THIS KID COME FROM?
ME? WHERE DID YOU COME FROM, OLD HAG?
And what are you to Kotobuki?
WHAT DID YOU JUST CALL ME?!
Why's everybody calling me old?! I am not old!! I'm still young!!
SHOKA...
KOTOBUKI!! YOU KNOW THIS KID?! WHO IS SHE AND WHERE THE HELL DID SHE COME FROM?!
Hmph!
I'VE ALWAYS BEEN HERE! I HAVE KNOWN KOTOBUKI FAR LONGER THAN YOU, OLD HAG!
Here, I'll even be so kind as to explain it to you. Do not misunderstand, this isn't a publicity stunt. No, not at all!
For those who may not know Adelaide Wilson:
She is a clever, wealthy young lady Kotobuki came to know during her earlier adventures searching for the Tsubasa. Addie's father died in an accident. Currently she is living with her mother. For details, please see Tsubasa volume 1. Please do check it out. We'd really like it if you did.♥
THERE! NOW DO YOU UNDERSTAND, YOU RUDE OLD HAG?
YOU'RE THE RUDE ONE, YOU LITTLE BRAT!!
...
GRACIOUS, SUCH LANGUAGE! AN ADULT SHOULD BEHAVE MORE POLITELY IN CIVILIZED COMPANY. HOW EMBARRASSING!
You... You... You...!!!

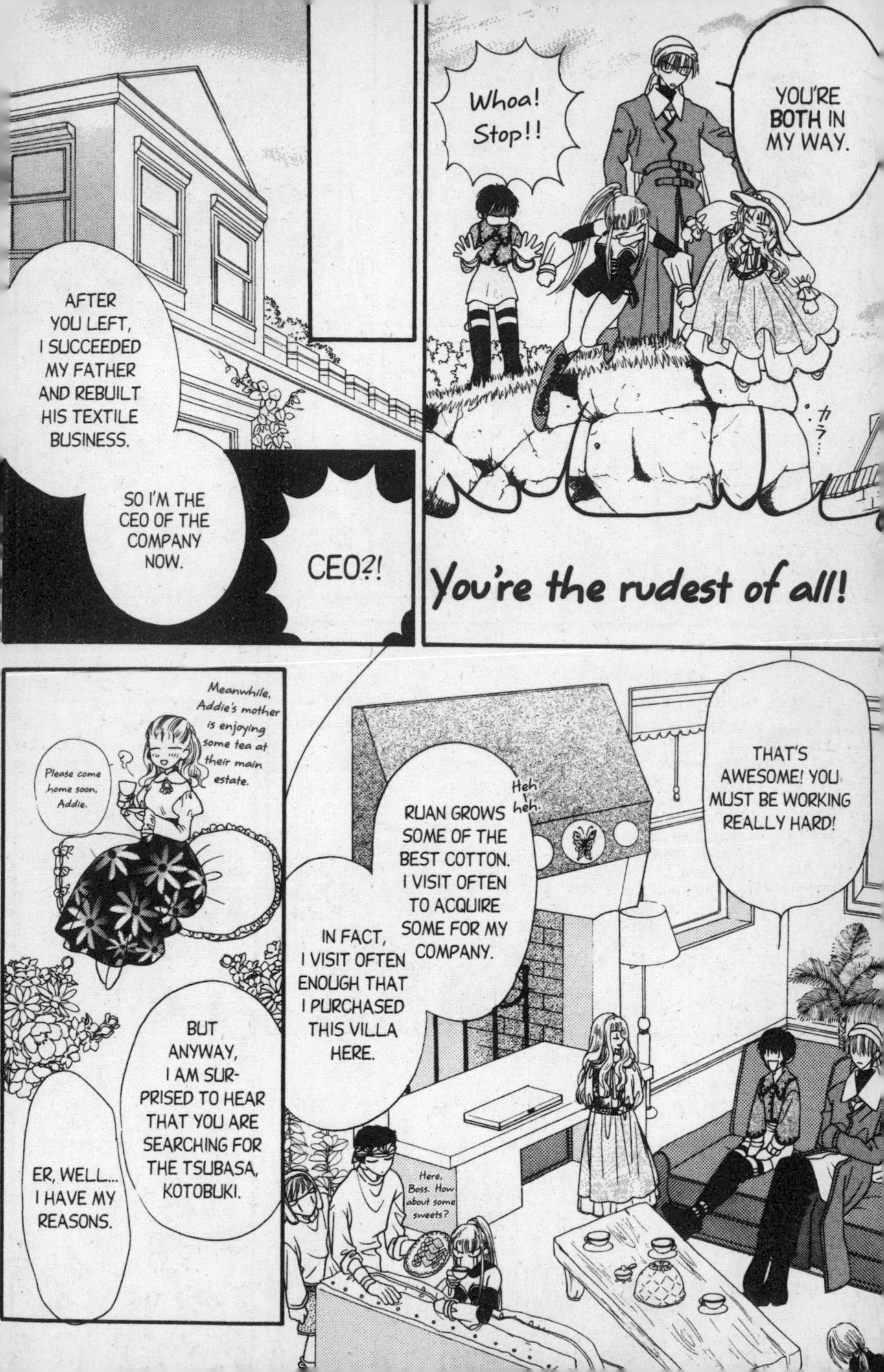
YOU'RE BOTH IN MY WAY.
Whoa! Stop!!
You're the rudest of all!
AFTER YOU LEFT, I SUCCEEDED MY FATHER AND REBUILT HIS TEXTILE BUSINESS.
SO I'M THE CEO OF THE COMPANY NOW.
CEO?!
THAT'S AWESOME! YOU MUST BE WORKING REALLY HARD!
Heh heh.
RUAN GROWS SOME OF THE BEST COTTON. I VISIT OFTEN TO ACQUIRE SOME FOR MY COMPANY.
IN FACT, I VISIT OFTEN ENOUGH THAT I PURCHASED THIS VILLA HERE.
BUT ANYWAY, I AM SURPRISED TO HEAR THAT YOU ARE SEARCHING FOR THE TSUBASA, KOTOBUKI.
ER, WELL... I HAVE MY REASONS.
Here, Boss. How about some sweets?
Meanwhile, Addie's mother is enjoying some tea at their main estate.
Please come home soon, Addie.

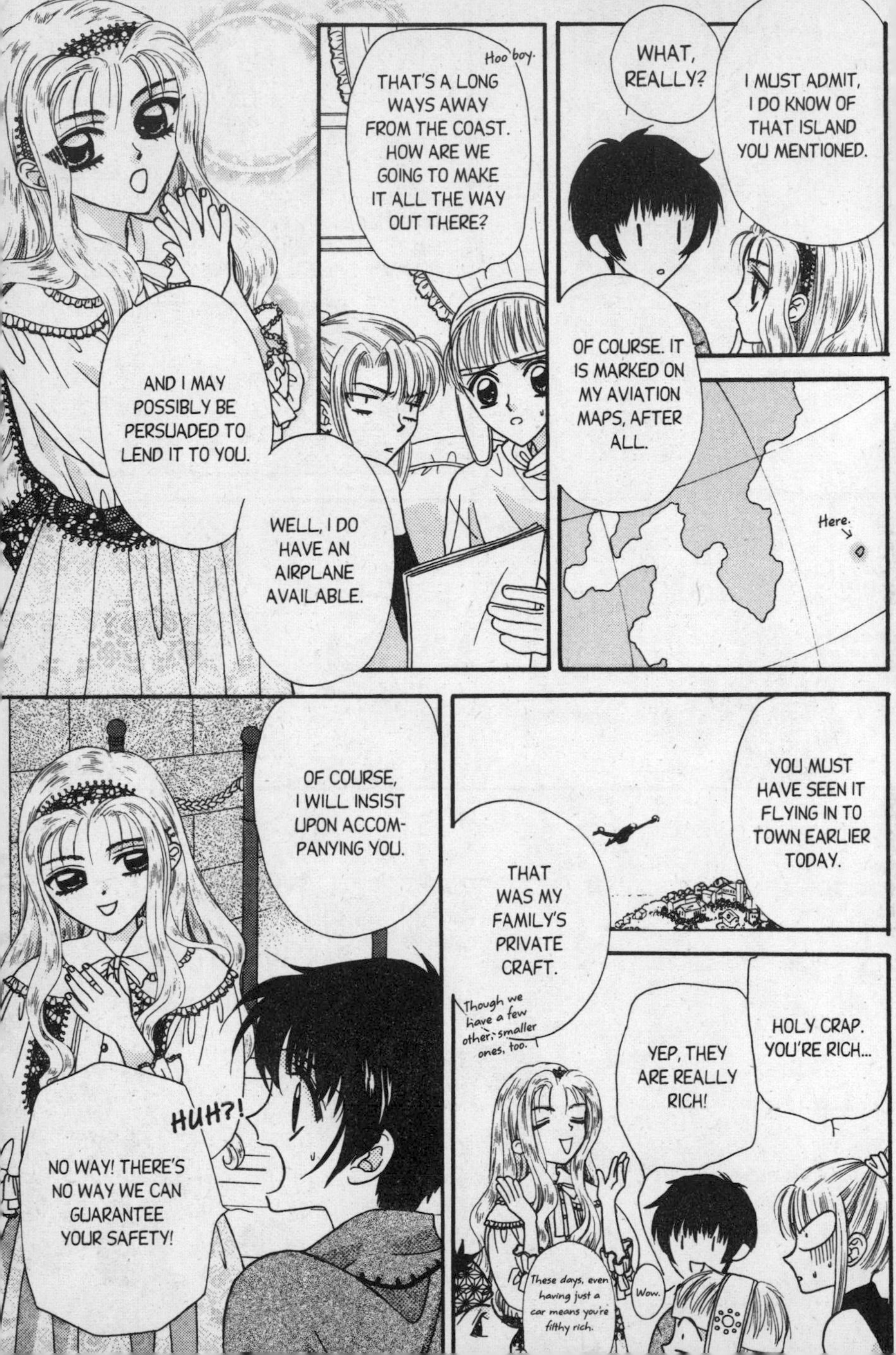

I MUST ADMIT, I DO KNOW OF THAT ISLAND YOU MENTIONED.
WHAT, REALLY?
THAT'S A LONG WAYS AWAY FROM THE COAST. HOW ARE WE GOING TO MAKE IT ALL THE WAY OUT THERE?
Hoo boy.
OF COURSE. IT IS MARKED ON MY AVIATION MAPS, AFTER ALL.
Here.
WELL, I DO HAVE AN AIRPLANE AVAILABLE.
AND I MAY POSSIBLY BE PERSUADED TO LEND IT TO YOU.
YOU MUST HAVE SEEN IT FLYING IN TO TOWN EARLIER TODAY.
THAT WAS MY FAMILY'S PRIVATE CRAFT.
Though we have a few other, smaller ones, too.
HOLY CRAP. YOU'RE RICH...
YEP, THEY ARE REALLY RICH!
Wow.
These days, even having just a car means you're filthy rich.
OF COURSE, I WILL INSIST UPON ACCOM-PANYING YOU.
HUH?!
NO WAY! THERE'S NO WAY WE CAN GUARANTEE YOUR SAFETY!

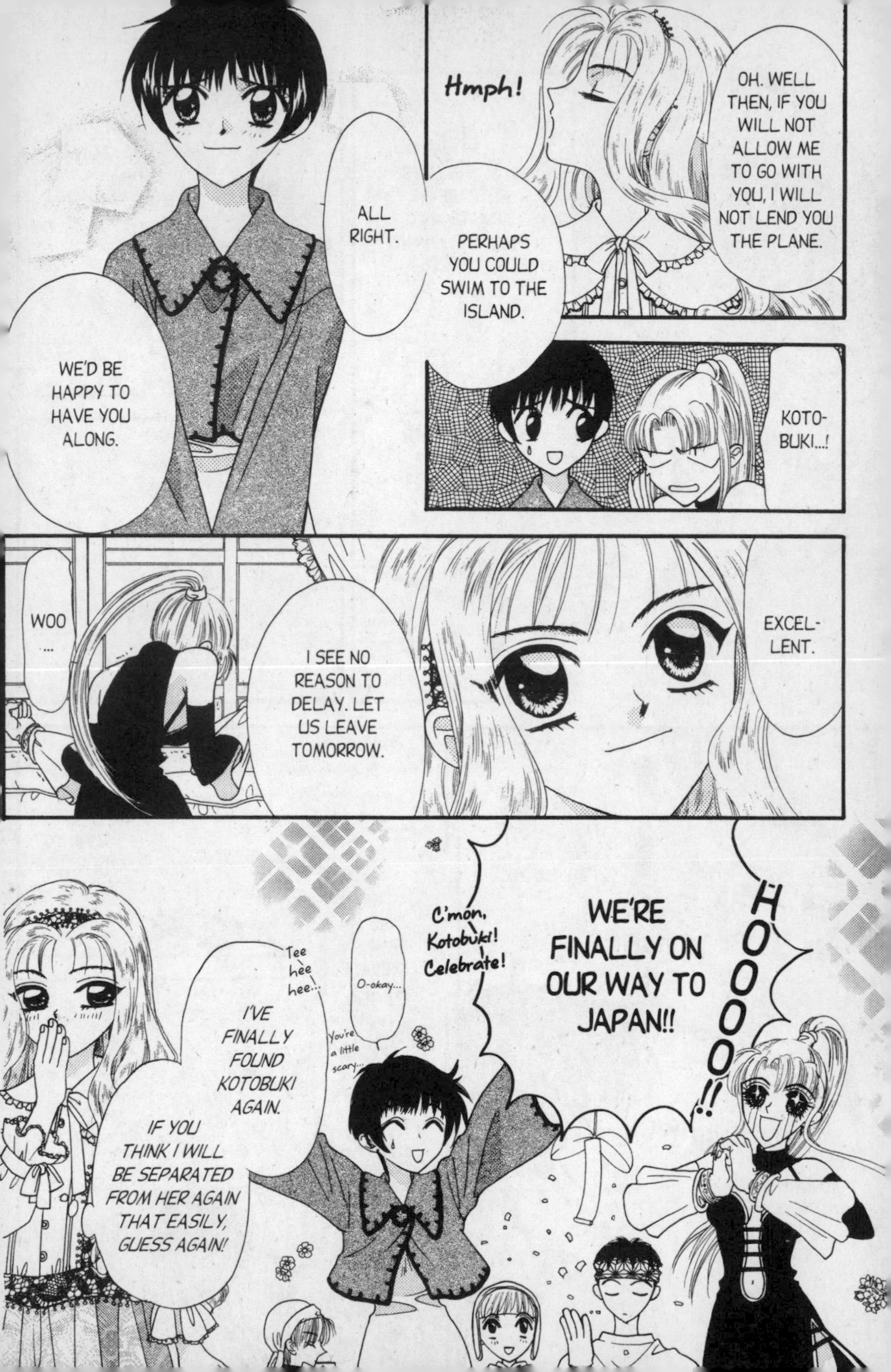
OH. WELL THEN, IF YOU WILL NOT ALLOW ME TO GO WITH YOU, I WILL NOT LEND YOU THE PLANE.
Hmph!
PERHAPS YOU COULD SWIM TO THE ISLAND.
KOTO-BUKI...!
ALL RIGHT.
WE'D BE HAPPY TO HAVE YOU ALONG.
EXCEL-LENT.
I SEE NO REASON TO DELAY. LET US LEAVE TOMORROW.
WOO...
HOOOOO!!
WE'RE FINALLY ON OUR WAY TO JAPAN!!
C'mon, Kotobuki! Celebrate!
O-okay...
You're a little scary...
Tee hee hee...
I'VE FINALLY FOUND KOTOBUKI AGAIN.
IF YOU THINK I WILL BE SEPARATED FROM HER AGAIN THAT EASILY, GUESS AGAIN!

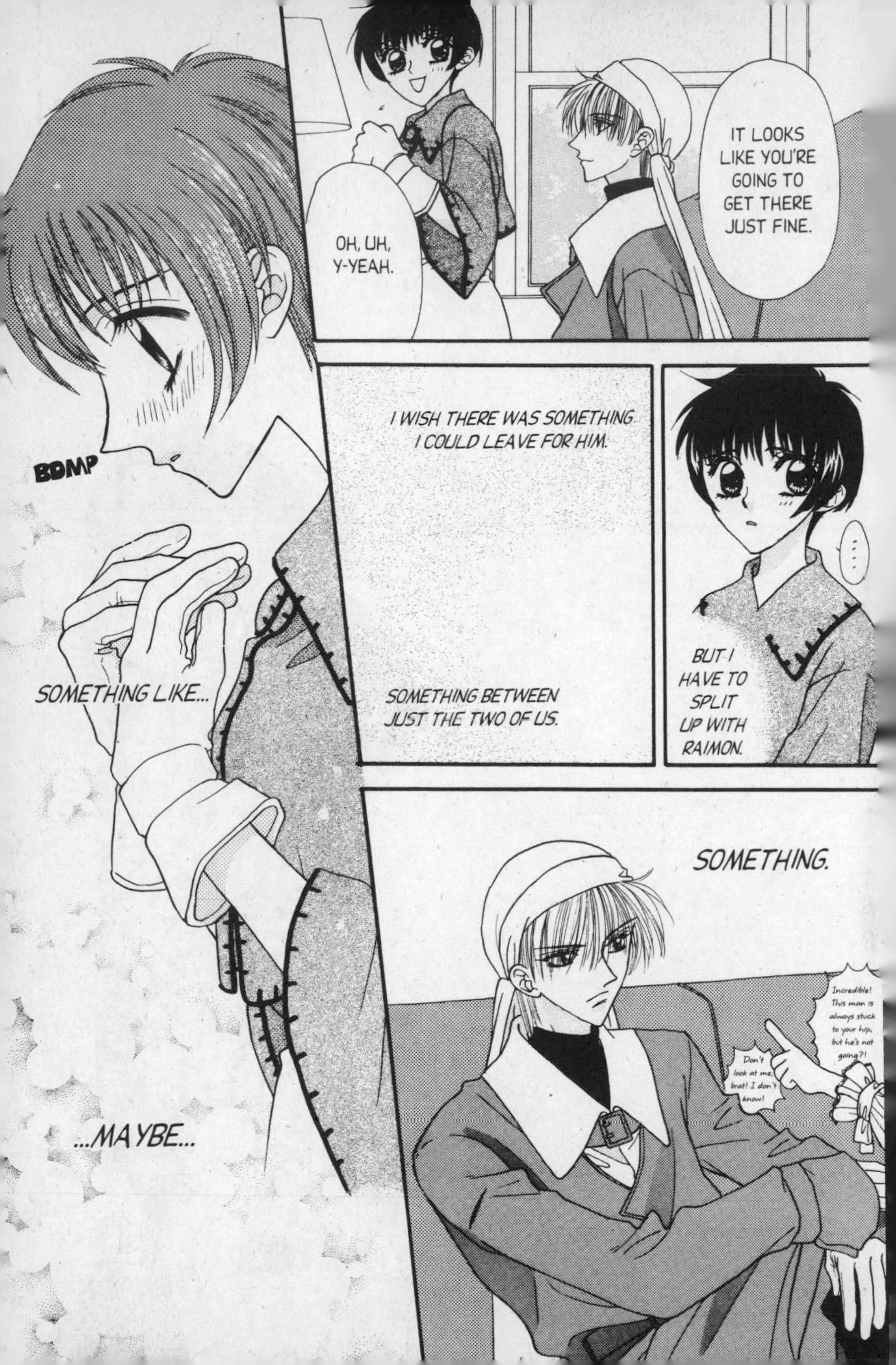
IT LOOKS LIKE YOU'RE GOING TO GET THERE JUST FINE.
OH, UH, Y-YEAH.
....
BUT I HAVE TO SPLIT UP WITH RAIMON.
I WISH THERE WAS SOMETHING I COULD LEAVE FOR HIM.
SOMETHING BETWEEN JUST THE TWO OF US.
SOMETHING.
Incredible! This man is always stuck to your hip, but he's not going?!
Don't look at me, brat! I don't know!
BOMP
SOMETHING LIKE...
...MAYBE...

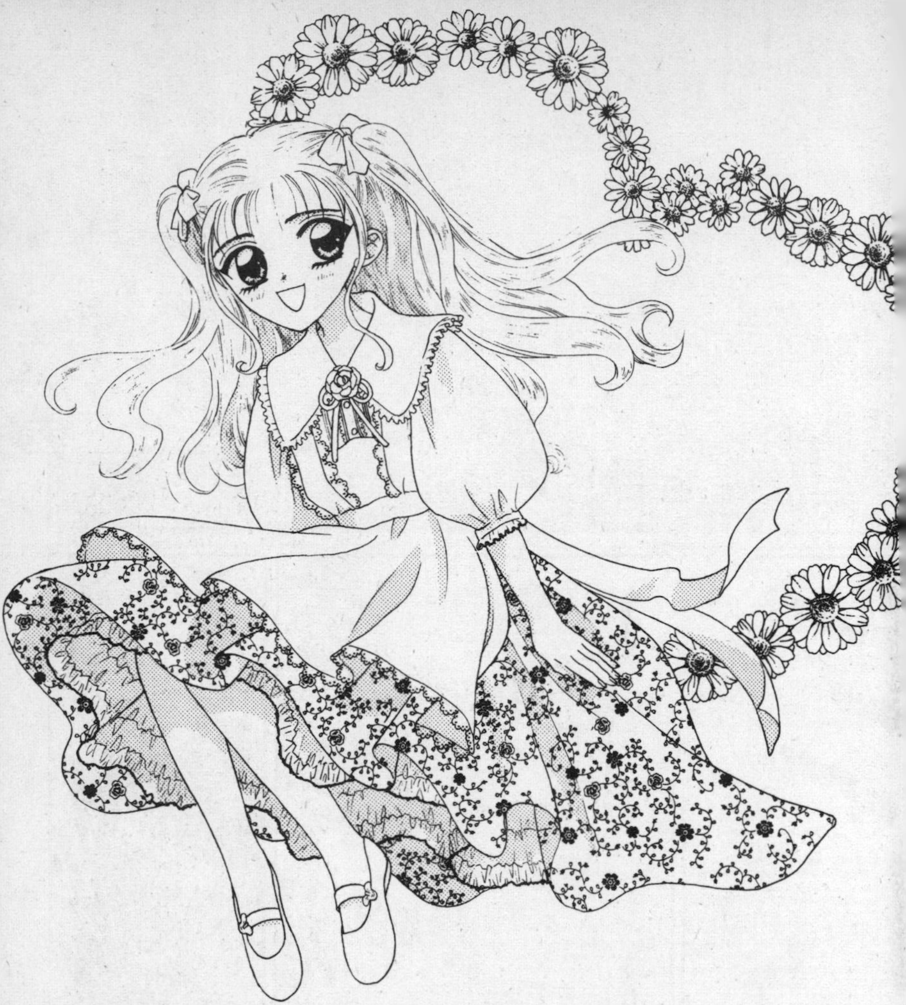

Tsubasa: Those With Wings

翼を持つ者

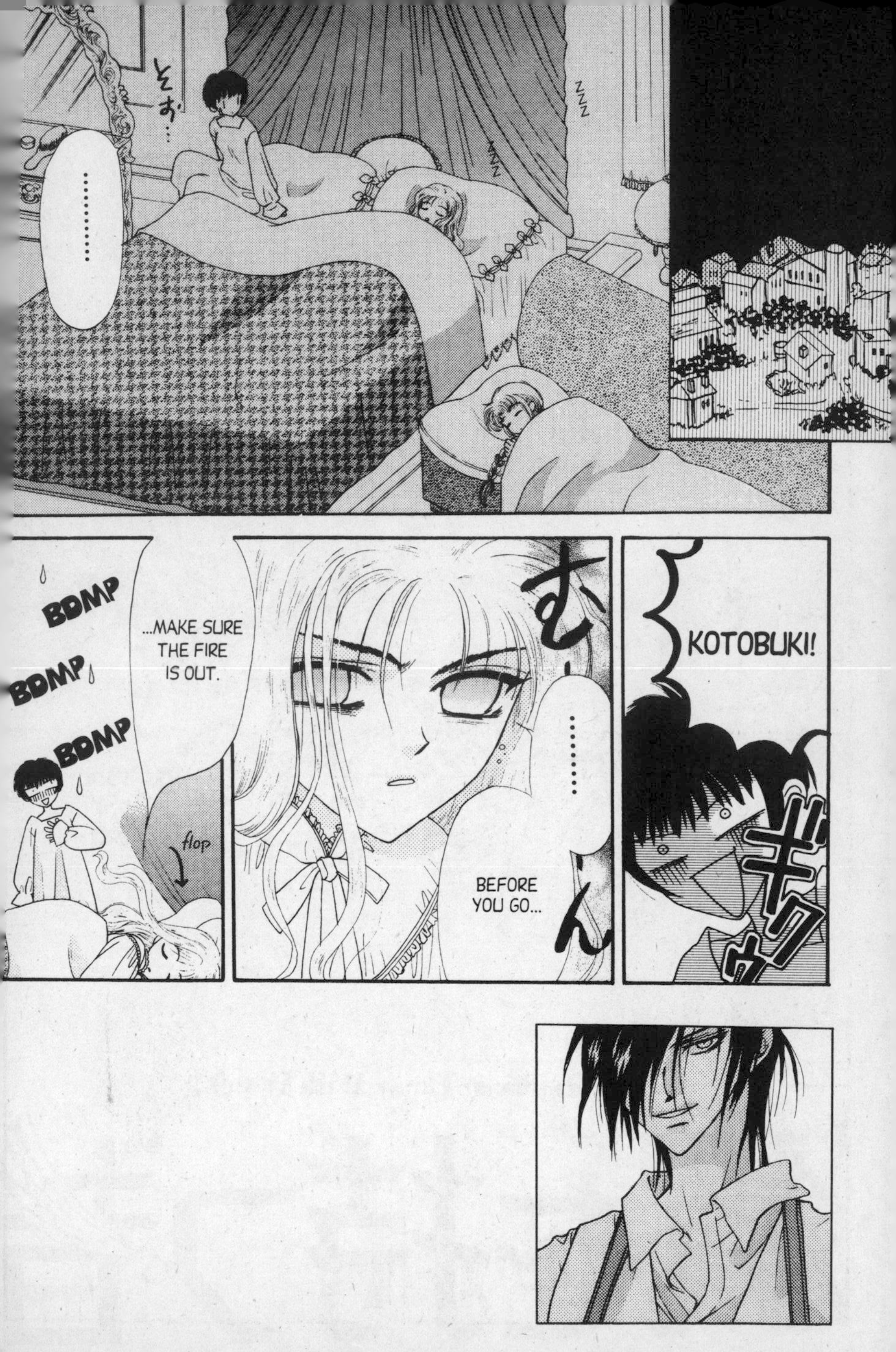
ZZZ
ZZZ
....
KOTOBUKI!
ギクゥ
....
BEFORE YOU GO...
...MAKE SURE THE FIRE IS OUT.
BDMP
BDMP
BDMP
flop

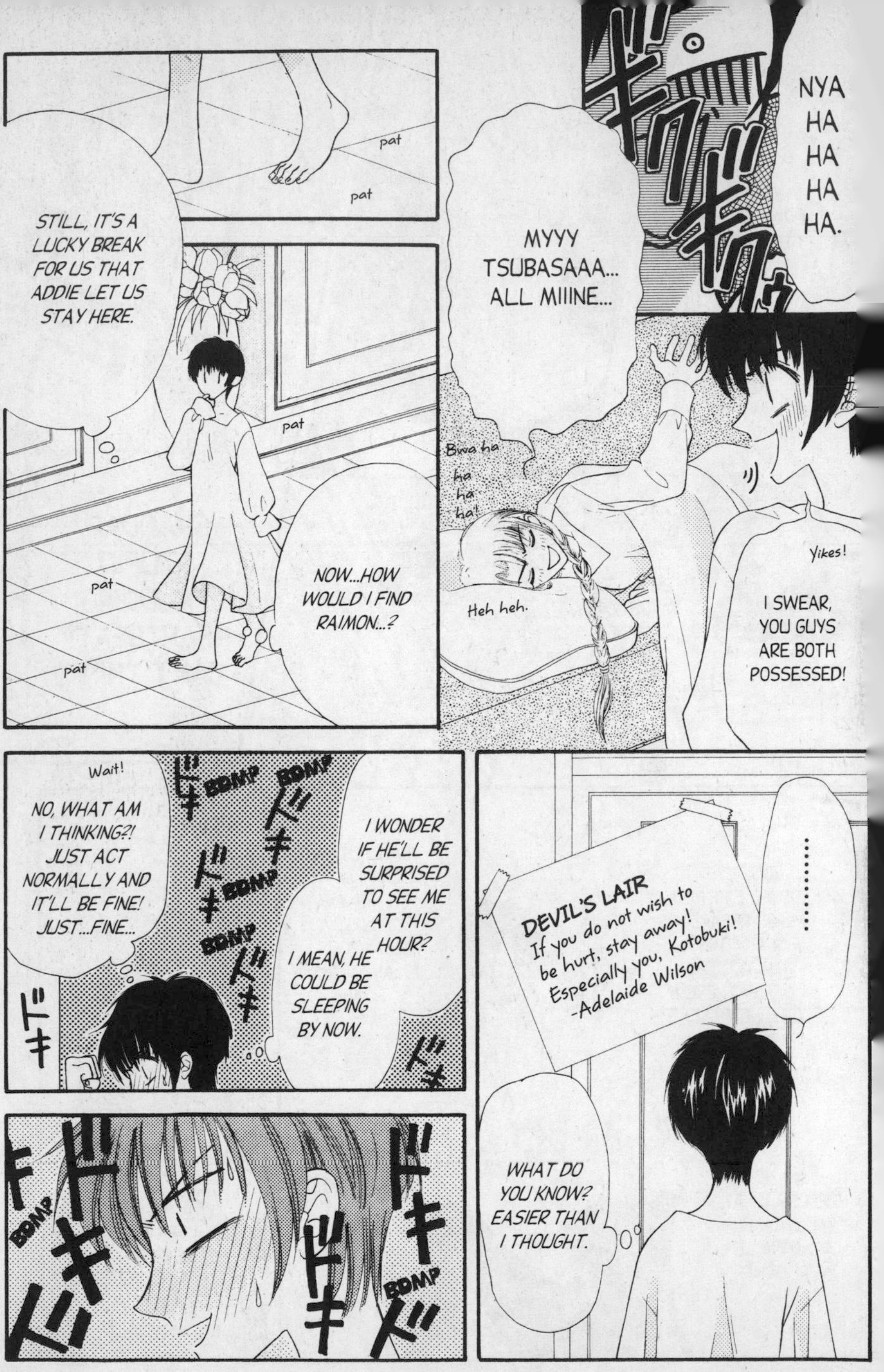
NYA HA HA HA HA.
MYYY TSUBASAAA... ALL MIIINE...
Yikes!
I SWEAR, YOU GUYS ARE BOTH POSSESSED!
Bwa ha ha ha ha!
Heh heh.
pat
pat
STILL, IT'S A LUCKY BREAK FOR US THAT ADDIE LET US STAY HERE.
pat
NOW...HOW WOULD I FIND RAIMON...?
pat
pat
......
DEVIL'S LAIR
If you do not wish to be hurt, stay away! Especially you, Kotobuki!
-Adelaide Wilson
WHAT DO YOU KNOW? EASIER THAN I THOUGHT.
I WONDER IF HE'LL BE SURPRISED TO SEE ME AT THIS HOUR?
I MEAN, HE COULD BE SLEEPING BY NOW.
BDMP
BDMP
BDMP
BDMP
Wait!
NO, WHAT AM I THINKING?! JUST ACT NORMALLY AND IT'LL BE FINE! JUST...FINE...
BDMP
BDMP

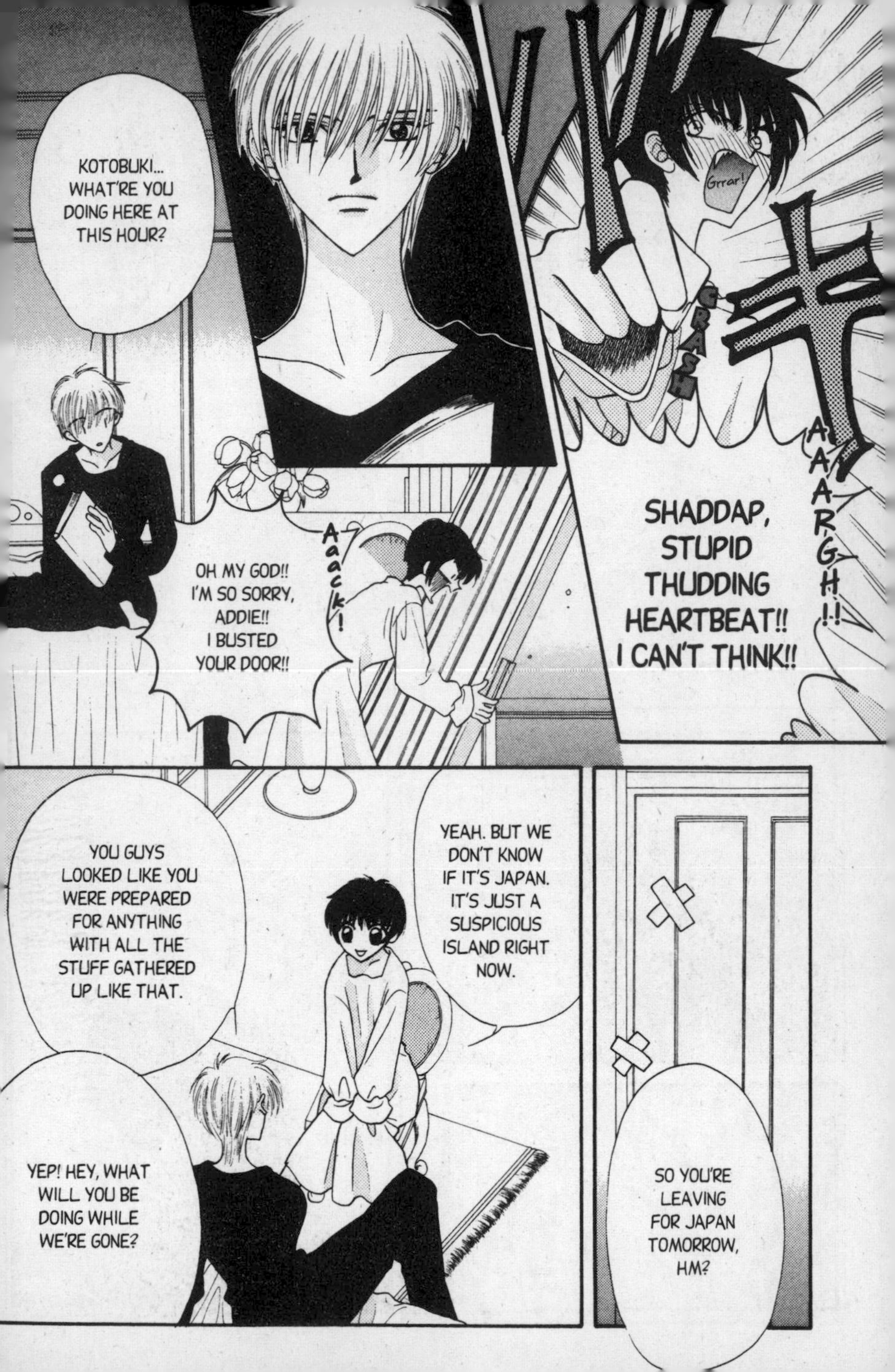
Grrar!
CRASH
SHADDAP, STUPID THUDDING HEARTBEAT!! I CAN'T THINK!!
AAAARGH!!
KOTOBUKI... WHAT'RE YOU DOING HERE AT THIS HOUR?
Aaack!
OH MY GOD!! I'M SO SORRY, ADDIE!! I BUSTED YOUR DOOR!!
SO YOU'RE LEAVING FOR JAPAN TOMORROW, HM?
YEAH. BUT WE DON'T KNOW IF IT'S JAPAN. IT'S JUST A SUSPICIOUS ISLAND RIGHT NOW.
YOU GUYS LOOKED LIKE YOU WERE PREPARED FOR ANYTHING WITH ALL THE STUFF GATHERED UP LIKE THAT.
YEP! HEY, WHAT WILL YOU BE DOING WHILE WE'RE GONE?

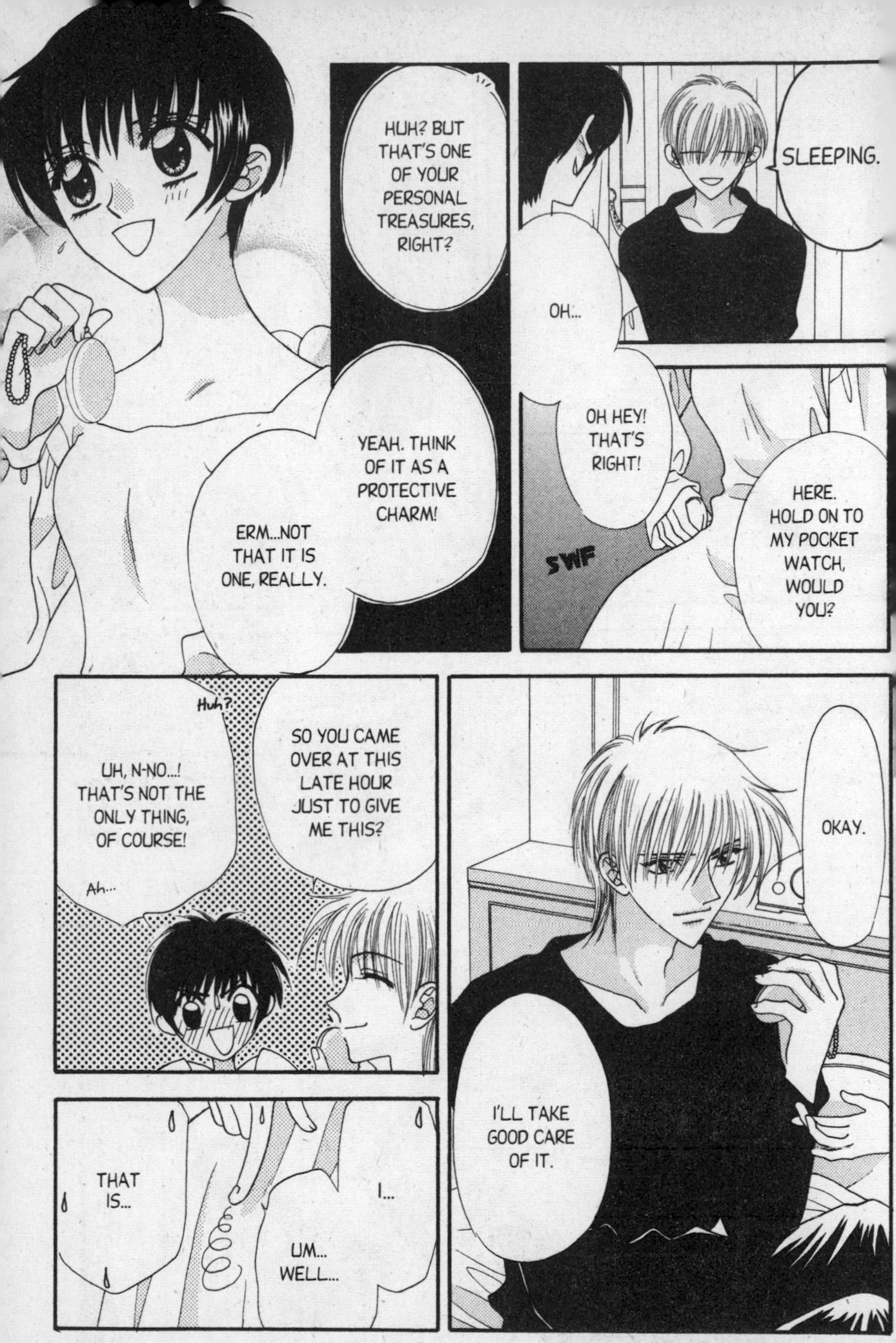
SLEEPING.
OH...
HERE. HOLD ON TO MY POCKET WATCH, WOULD YOU?
OH HEY! THAT'S RIGHT!
SWF
HUH? BUT THAT'S ONE OF YOUR PERSONAL TREASURES, RIGHT?
YEAH. THINK OF IT AS A PROTECTIVE CHARM!
ERM...NOT THAT IT IS ONE, REALLY.
OKAY.
I'LL TAKE GOOD CARE OF IT.
SO YOU CAME OVER AT THIS LATE HOUR JUST TO GIVE ME THIS?
Huh?
UH, N-NO...! THAT'S NOT THE ONLY THING, OF COURSE!
Ah...
I...
UM... WELL...
THAT IS...

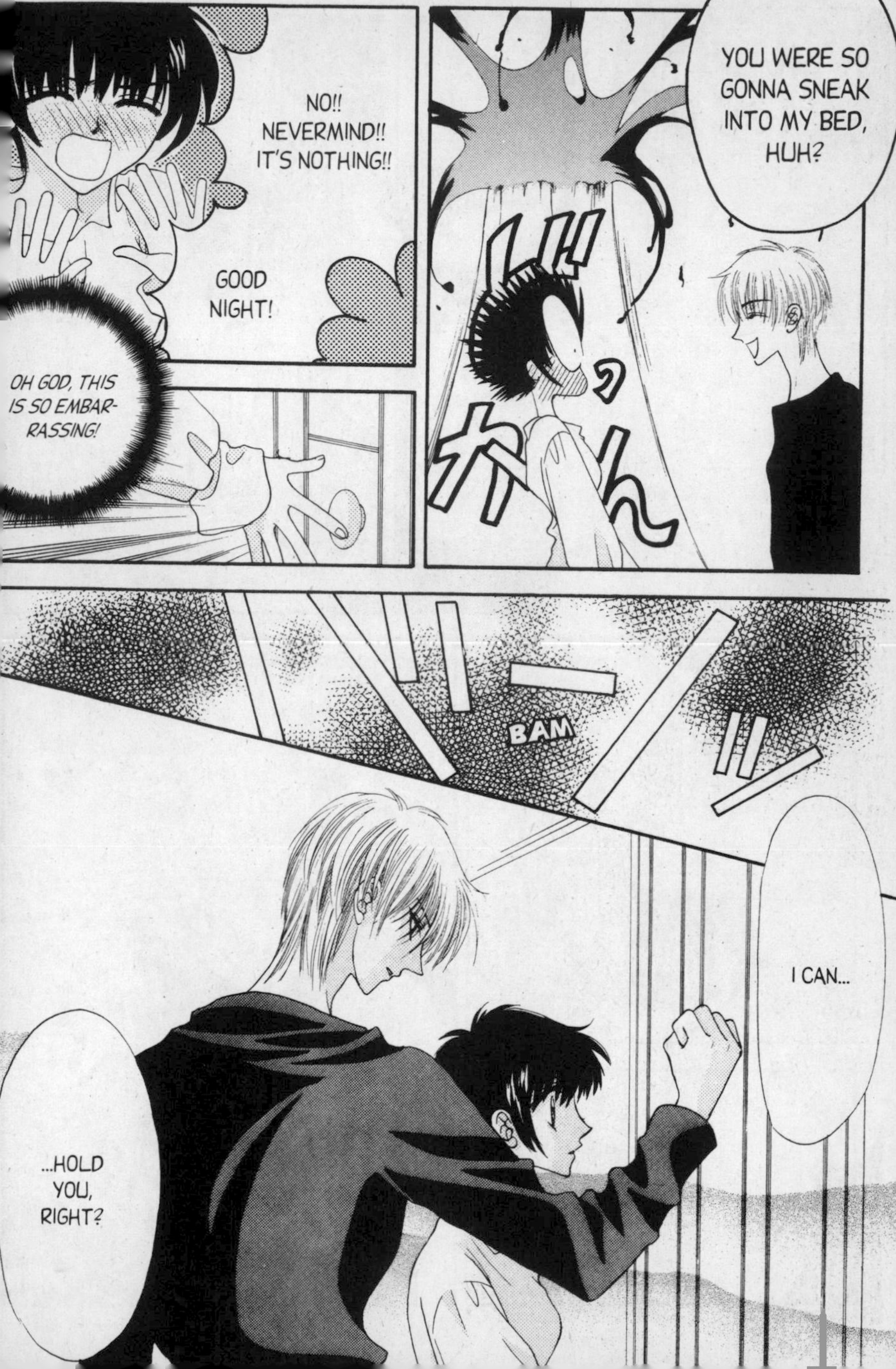

YOU WERE SO GONNA SNEAK INTO MY BED, HUH?
NO!! NEVERMIND!! IT'S NOTHING!!
GOOD NIGHT!
OH GOD, THIS IS SO EMBAR-RASSING!
BAM
I CAN...
...HOLD YOU, RIGHT?

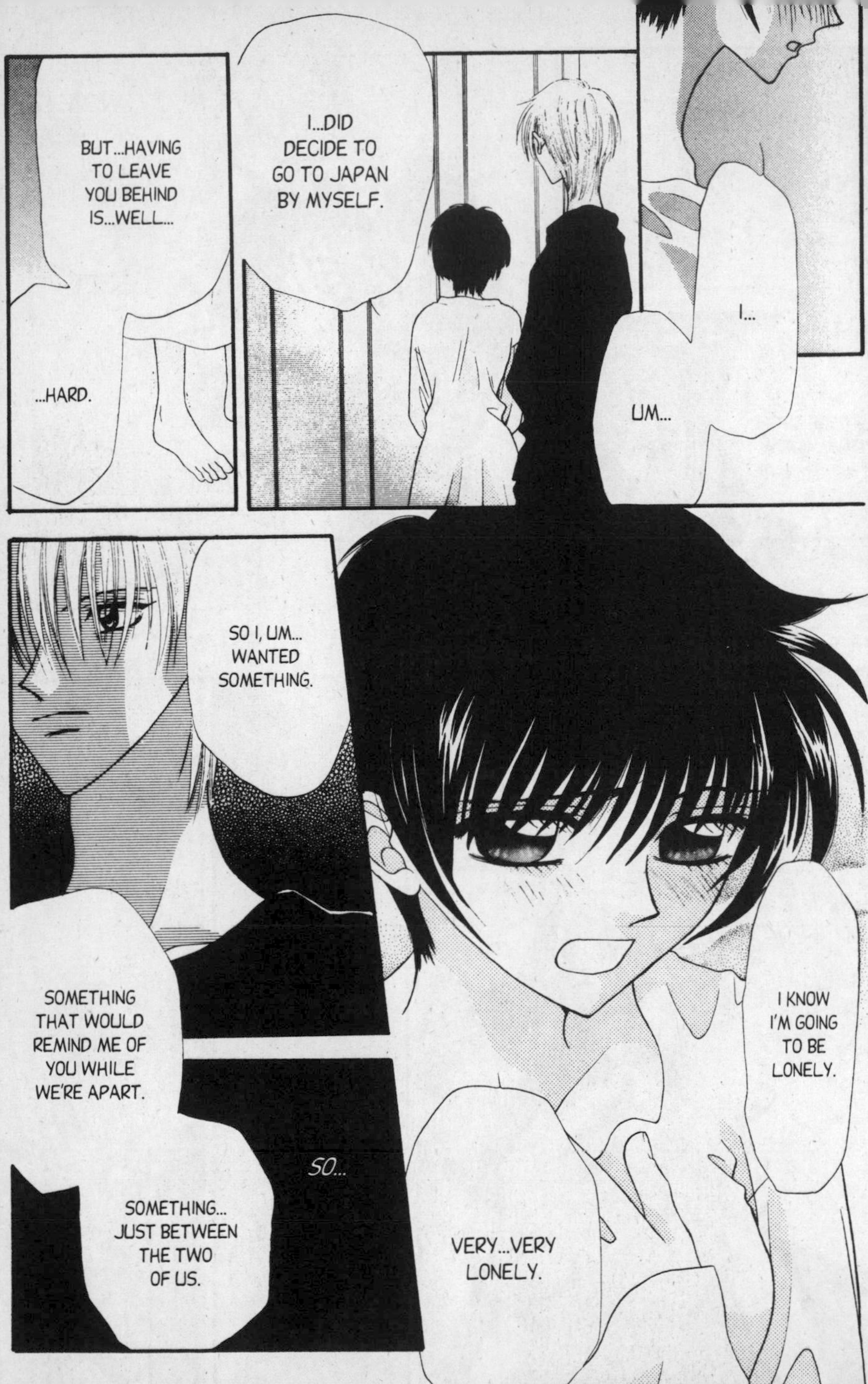
I...
UM...
I...DID DECIDE TO GO TO JAPAN BY MYSELF.
BUT...HAVING TO LEAVE YOU BEHIND IS...WELL...
...HARD.
I KNOW I'M GOING TO BE LONELY.
VERY...VERY LONELY.
SO I, UM... WANTED SOMETHING.
SOMETHING THAT WOULD REMIND ME OF YOU WHILE WE'RE APART.
SO...
SOMETHING... JUST BETWEEN THE TWO OF US.

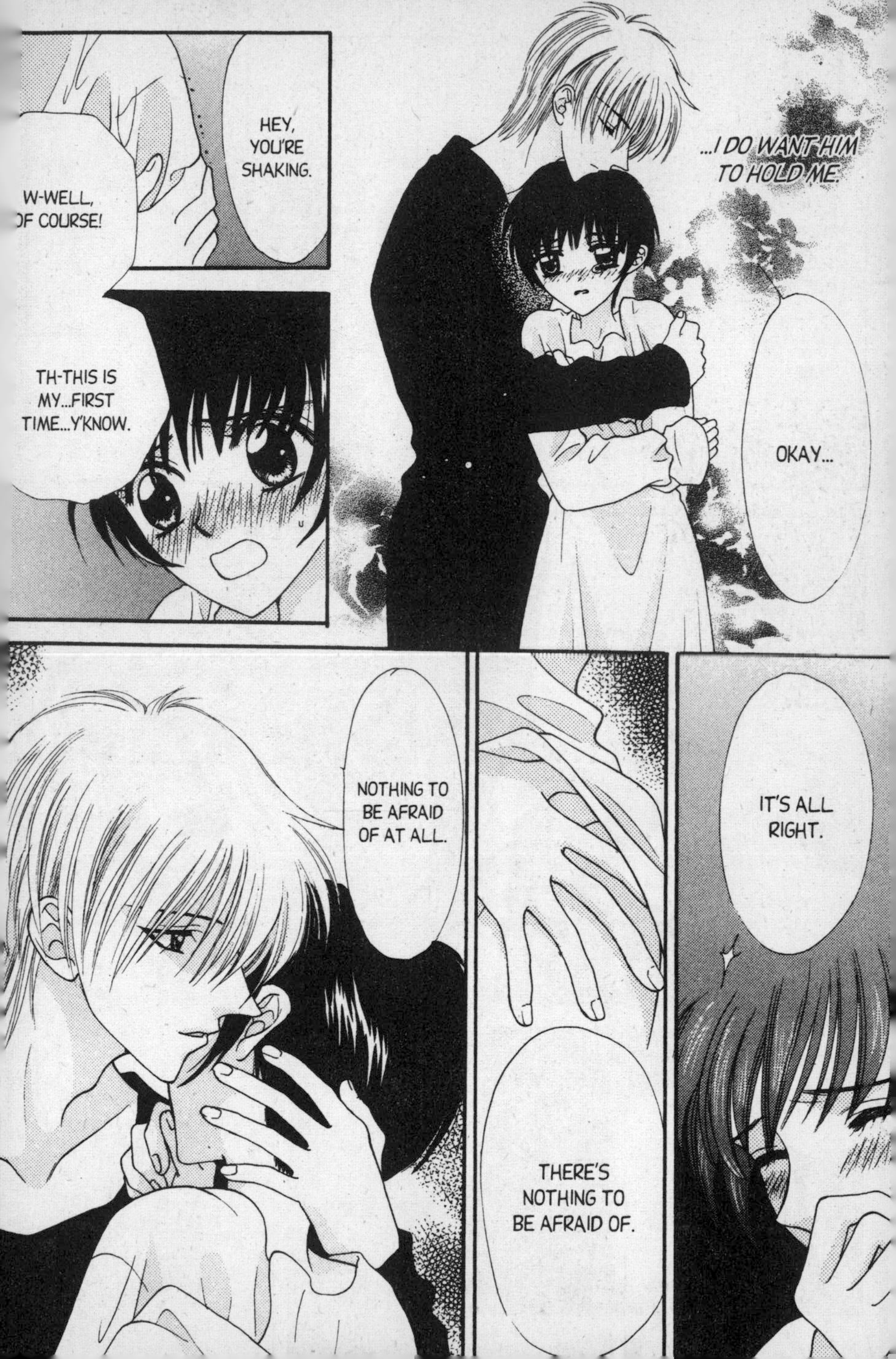
...I DO WANT HIM TO HOLD ME.
OKAY...
HEY, YOU'RE SHAKING.
W-WELL, OF COURSE!
TH-THIS IS MY...FIRST TIME...Y'KNOW.
IT'S ALL RIGHT.
THERE'S NOTHING TO BE AFRAID OF.
NOTHING TO BE AFRAID OF AT ALL.

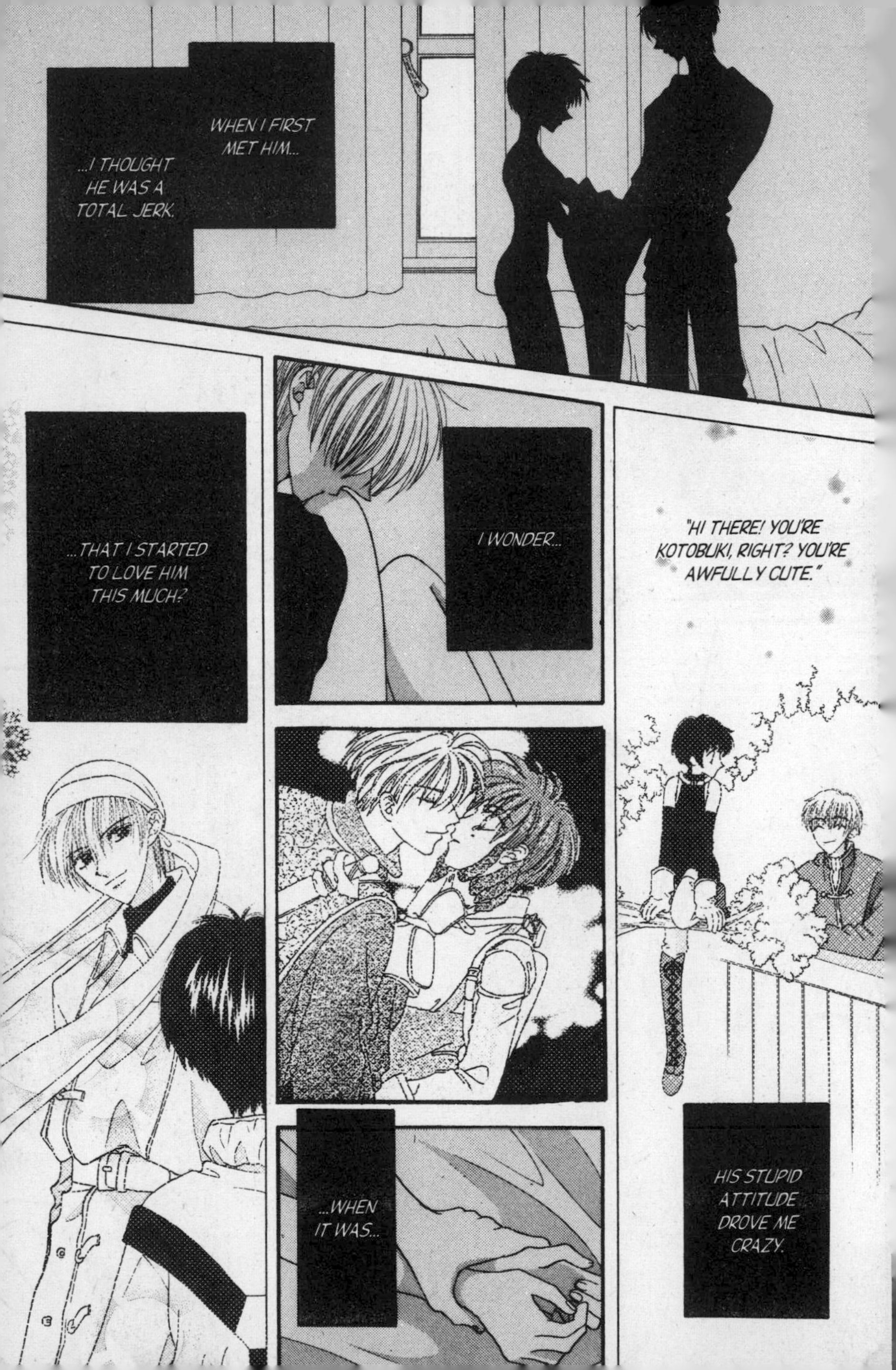
WHEN I FIRST MET HIM...
...I THOUGHT HE WAS A TOTAL JERK.
"HI THERE! YOU'RE KOTOBUKI, RIGHT? YOU'RE AWFULLY CUTE."
HIS STUPID ATTITUDE DROVE ME CRAZY.
I WONDER...
...WHEN IT WAS...
...THAT I STARTED TO LOVE HIM THIS MUCH?

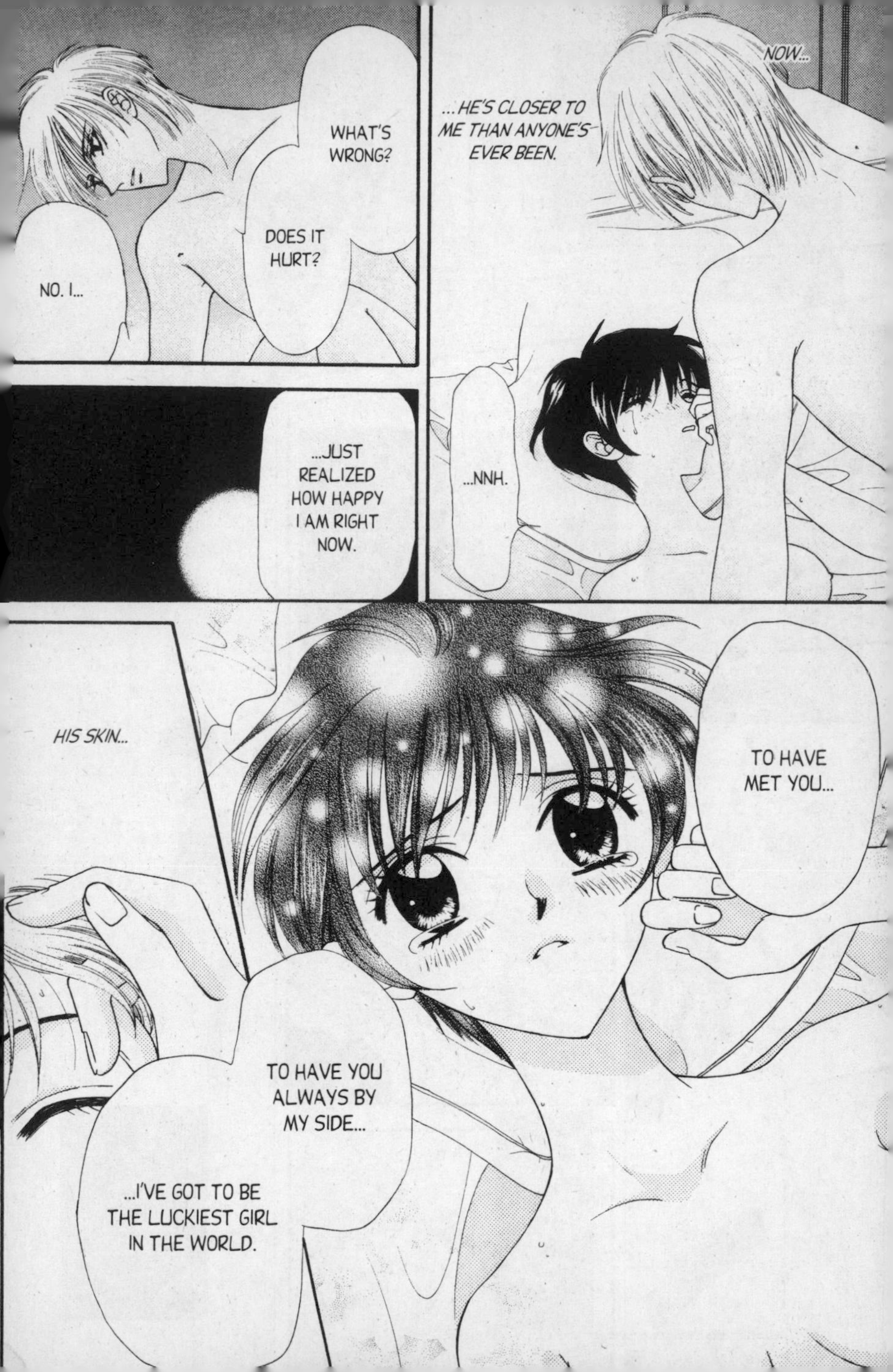
NOW...
...HE'S CLOSER TO ME THAN ANYONE'S EVER BEEN.
...NNH.
WHAT'S WRONG?
DOES IT HURT?
NO. I...
...JUST REALIZED HOW HAPPY I AM RIGHT NOW.
TO HAVE MET YOU...
HIS SKIN...
TO HAVE YOU ALWAYS BY MY SIDE...
...I'VE GOT TO BE THE LUCKIEST GIRL IN THE WORLD.

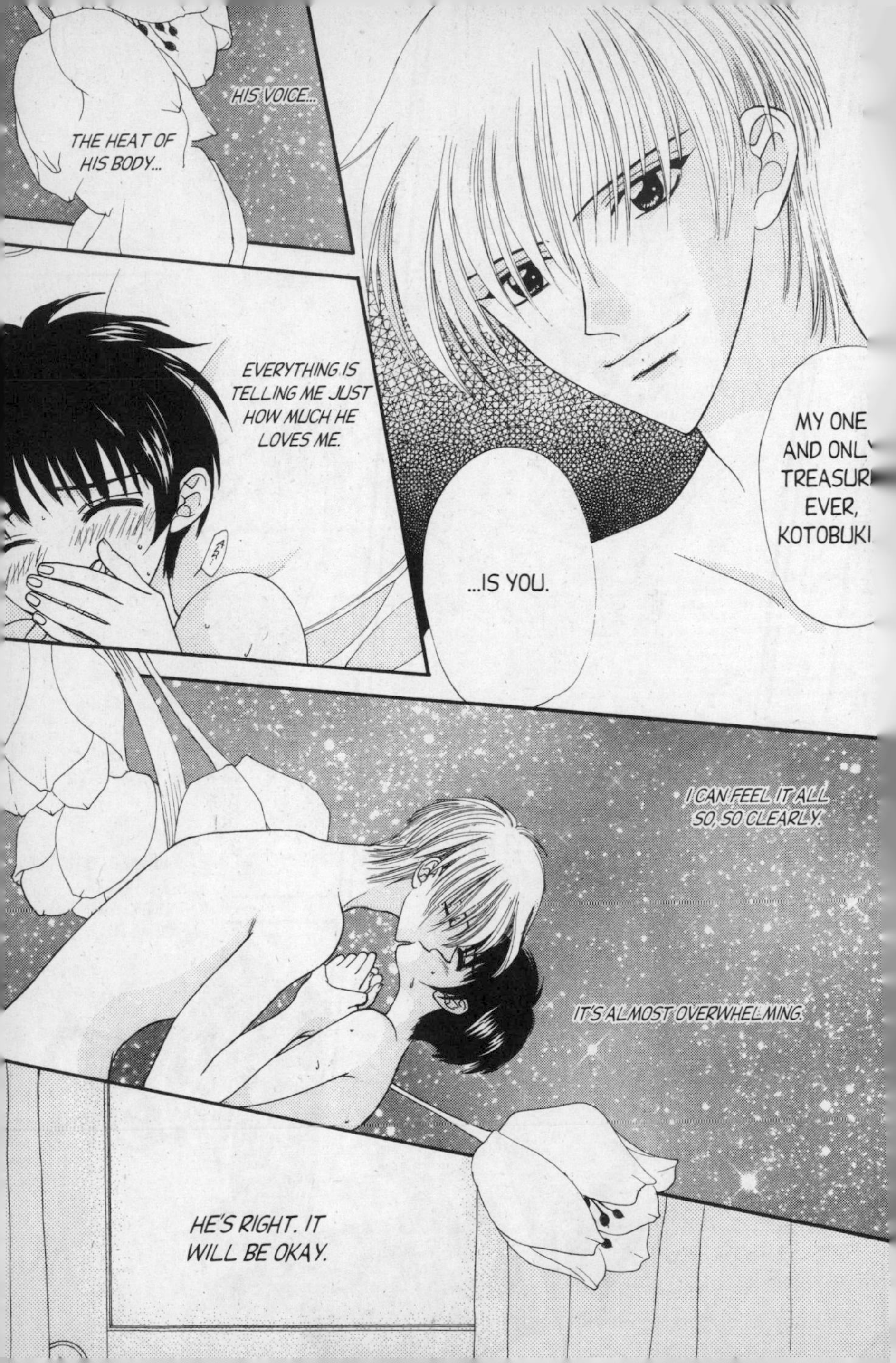

MY ONE AND ONL TREASUR EVER, KOTOBUKI
...IS YOU.
HIS VOICE...
THE HEAT OF HIS BODY...
EVERYTHING IS TELLING ME JUST HOW MUCH HE LOVES ME.
I CAN FEEL IT ALL SO, SO CLEARLY.
IT'S ALMOST OVERWHELMING.
HE'S RIGHT. IT WILL BE OKAY.

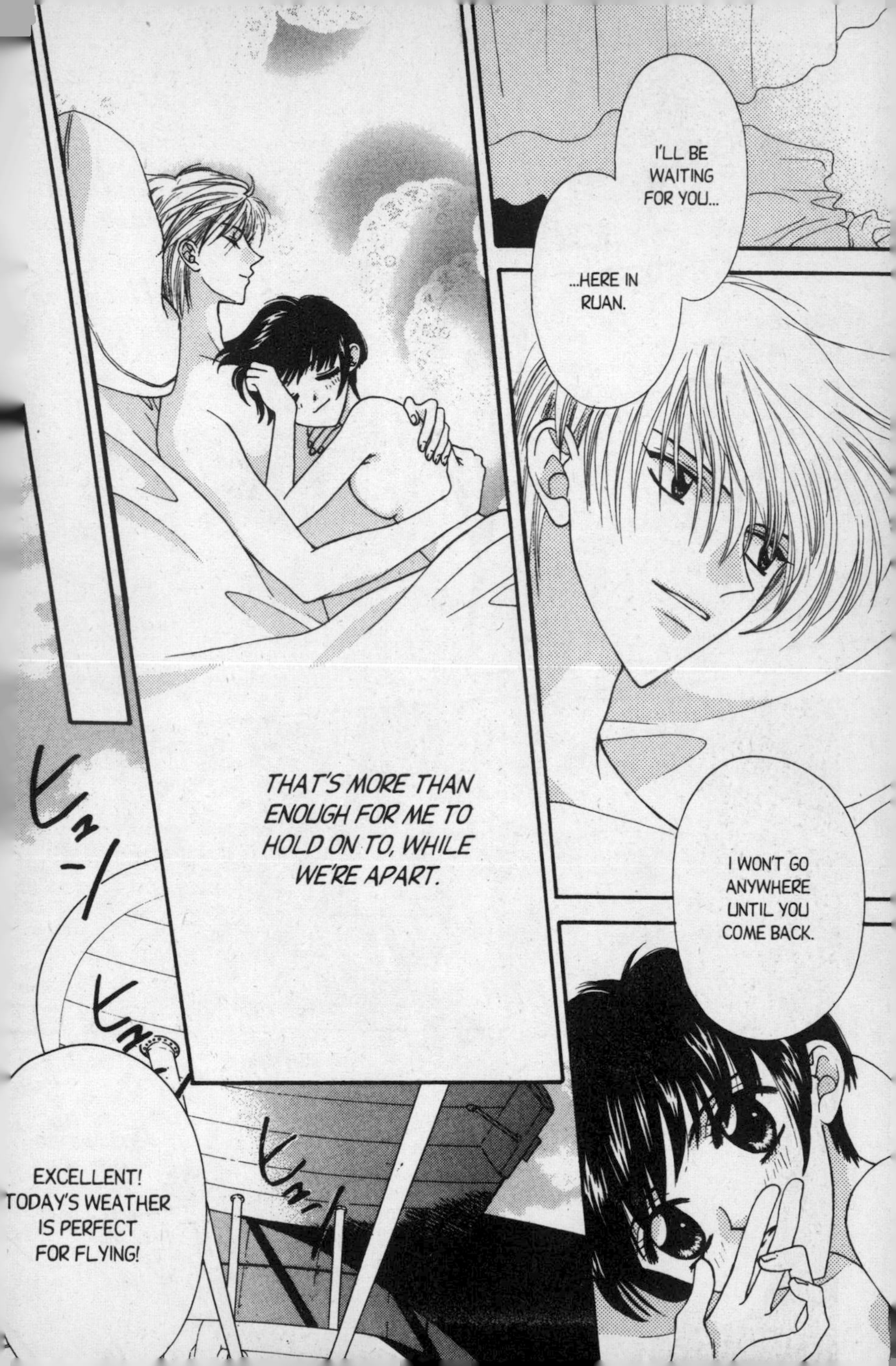
I'LL BE WAITING FOR YOU...
...HERE IN RUAN.
I WON'T GO ANYWHERE UNTIL YOU COME BACK.
THAT'S MORE THAN ENOUGH FOR ME TO HOLD ON TO, WHILE WE'RE APART.
EXCELLENT! TODAY'S WEATHER IS PERFECT FOR FLYING!

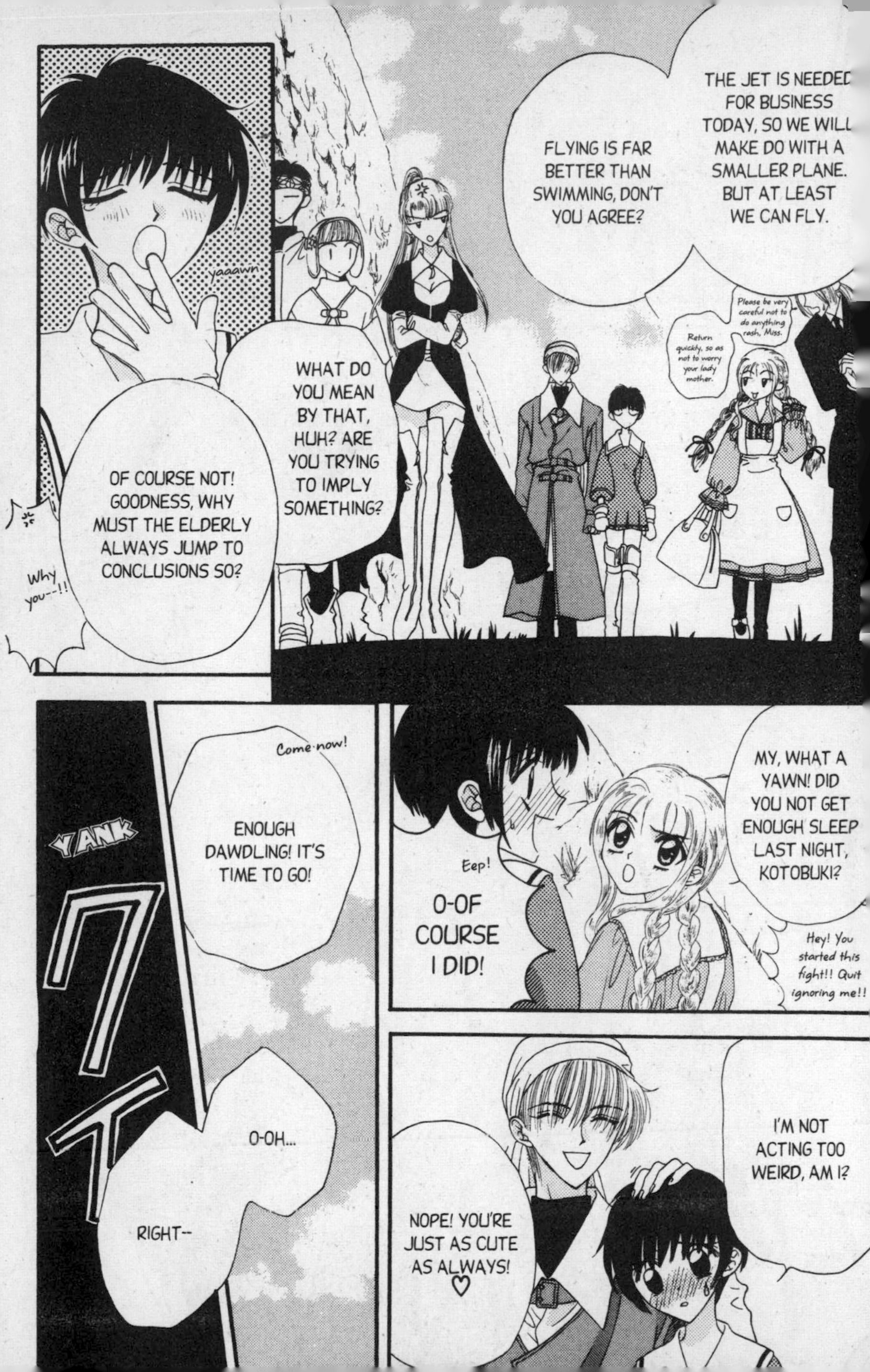
THE JET IS NEEDED FOR BUSINESS TODAY, SO WE WILL MAKE DO WITH A SMALLER PLANE. BUT AT LEAST WE CAN FLY.
FLYING IS FAR BETTER THAN SWIMMING, DON'T YOU AGREE?
Please be very careful not to do anything rash, Miss.
Return quickly, so as not to worry your lady mother.
WHAT DO YOU MEAN BY THAT, HUH? ARE YOU TRYING TO IMPLY SOMETHING?
yaaawn
OF COURSE NOT! GOODNESS, WHY MUST THE ELDERLY ALWAYS JUMP TO CONCLUSIONS SO?
Why you--!!
MY, WHAT A YAWN! DID YOU NOT GET ENOUGH SLEEP LAST NIGHT, KOTOBUKI?
Hey! You started this fight!! Quit ignoring me!!
Eep!
O-OF COURSE I DID!
I'M NOT ACTING TOO WEIRD, AM I?
NOPE! YOU'RE JUST AS CUTE AS ALWAYS! ♡
Come now!
ENOUGH DAWDLING! IT'S TIME TO GO!
O-OH...
RIGHT--
YANK

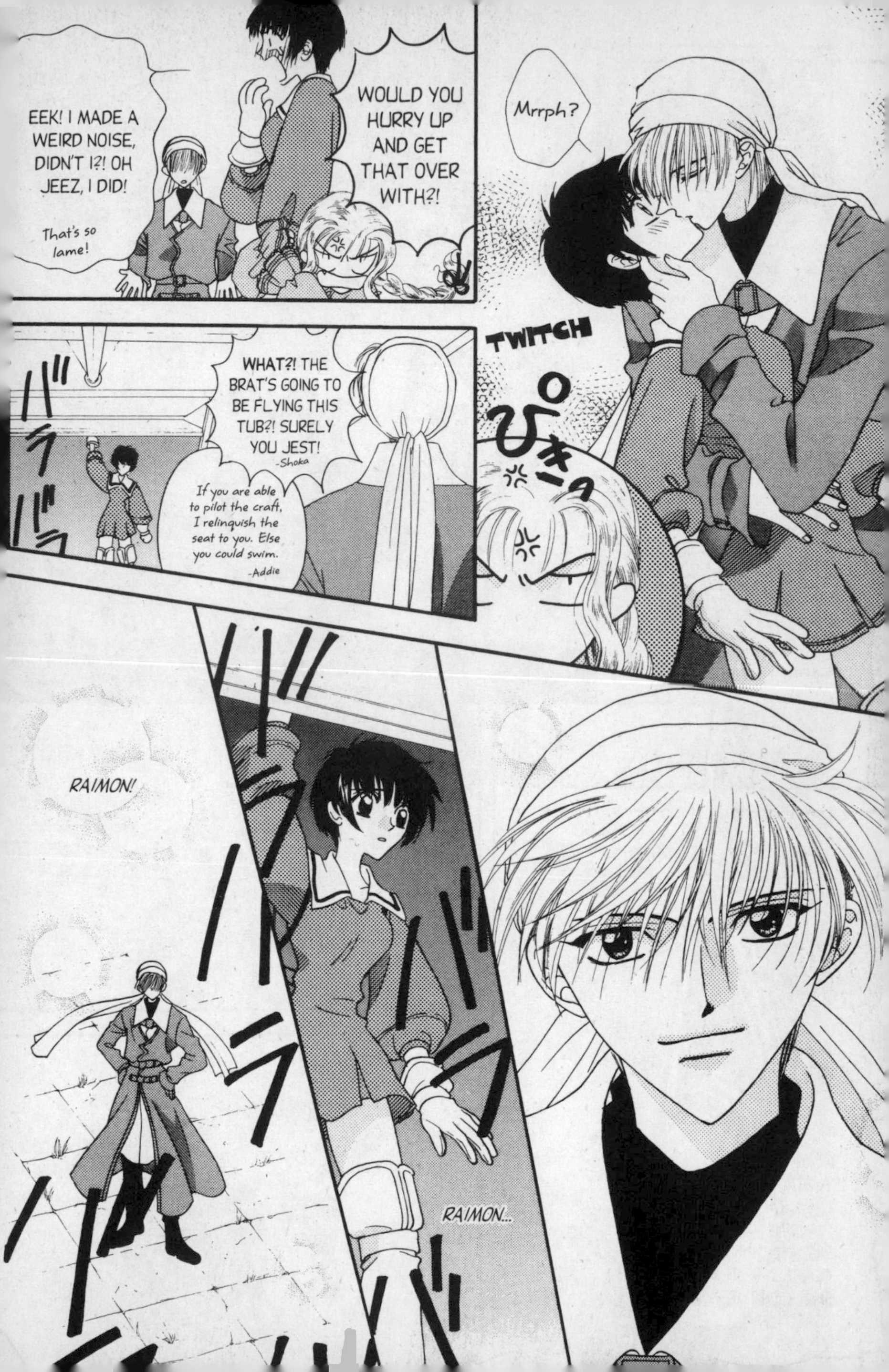
Mrrph?
TWITCH
ぴきっ
WOULD YOU HURRY UP AND GET THAT OVER WITH?!
EEK! I MADE A WEIRD NOISE, DIDN'T I?! OH JEEZ, I DID!
That's so lame!
WHAT?! THE BRAT'S GOING TO BE FLYING THIS TUB?! SURELY YOU JEST!
-Shoka
If you are able to pilot the craft, I relinquish the seat to you. Else you could swim.
-Addie
バラバラ
RAIMON...
RAIMON!

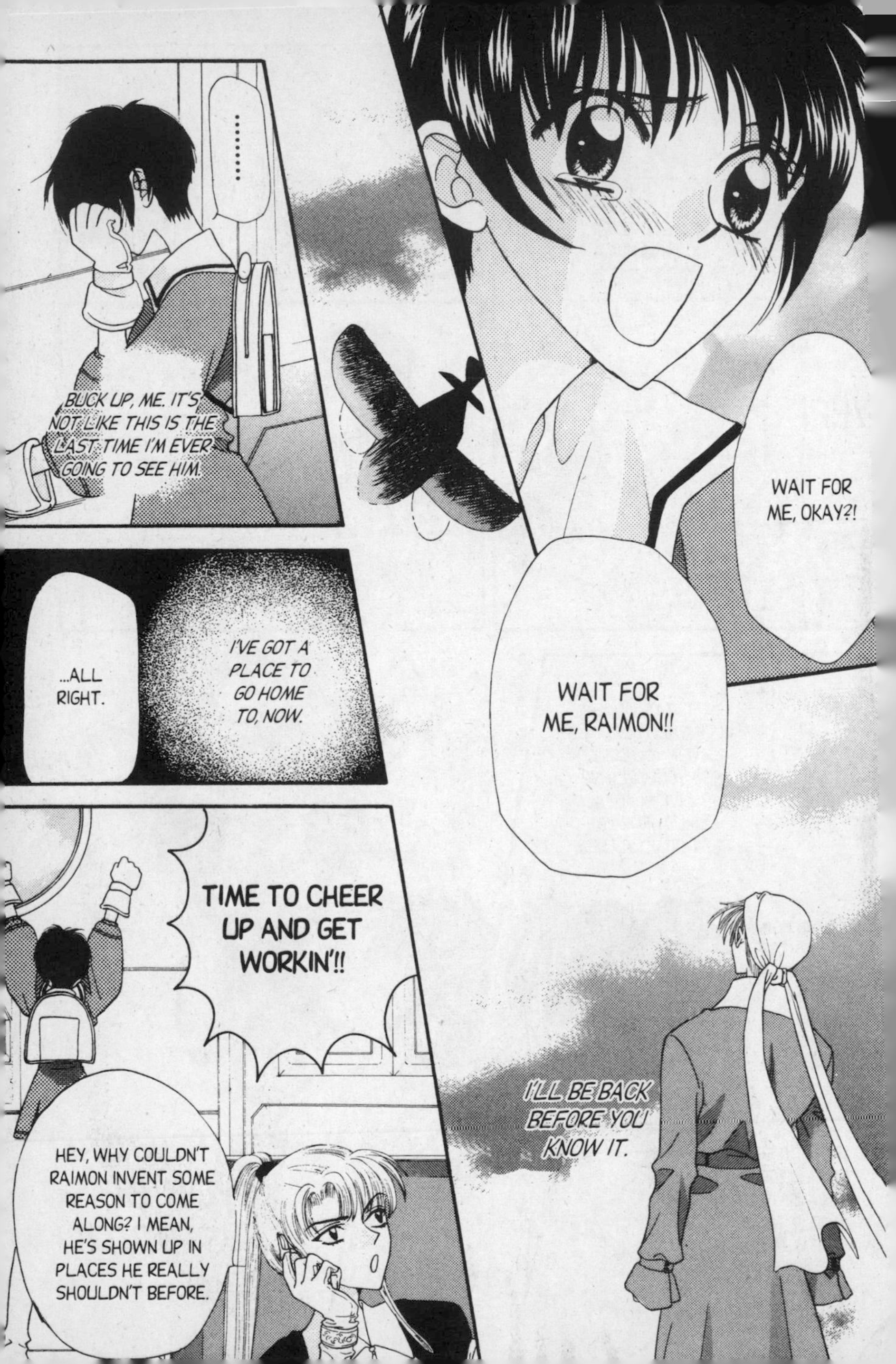
WAIT FOR ME, OKAY?!
WAIT FOR ME, RAIMON!!
I'LL BE BACK BEFORE YOU KNOW IT.
......
BUCK UP, ME. IT'S NOT LIKE THIS IS THE LAST TIME I'M EVER GOING TO SEE HIM.
I'VE GOT A PLACE TO GO HOME TO, NOW.
...ALL RIGHT.
TIME TO CHEER UP AND GET WORKIN'!!
HEY, WHY COULDN'T RAIMON INVENT SOME REASON TO COME ALONG? I MEAN, HE'S SHOWN UP IN PLACES HE REALLY SHOULDN'T BEFORE.

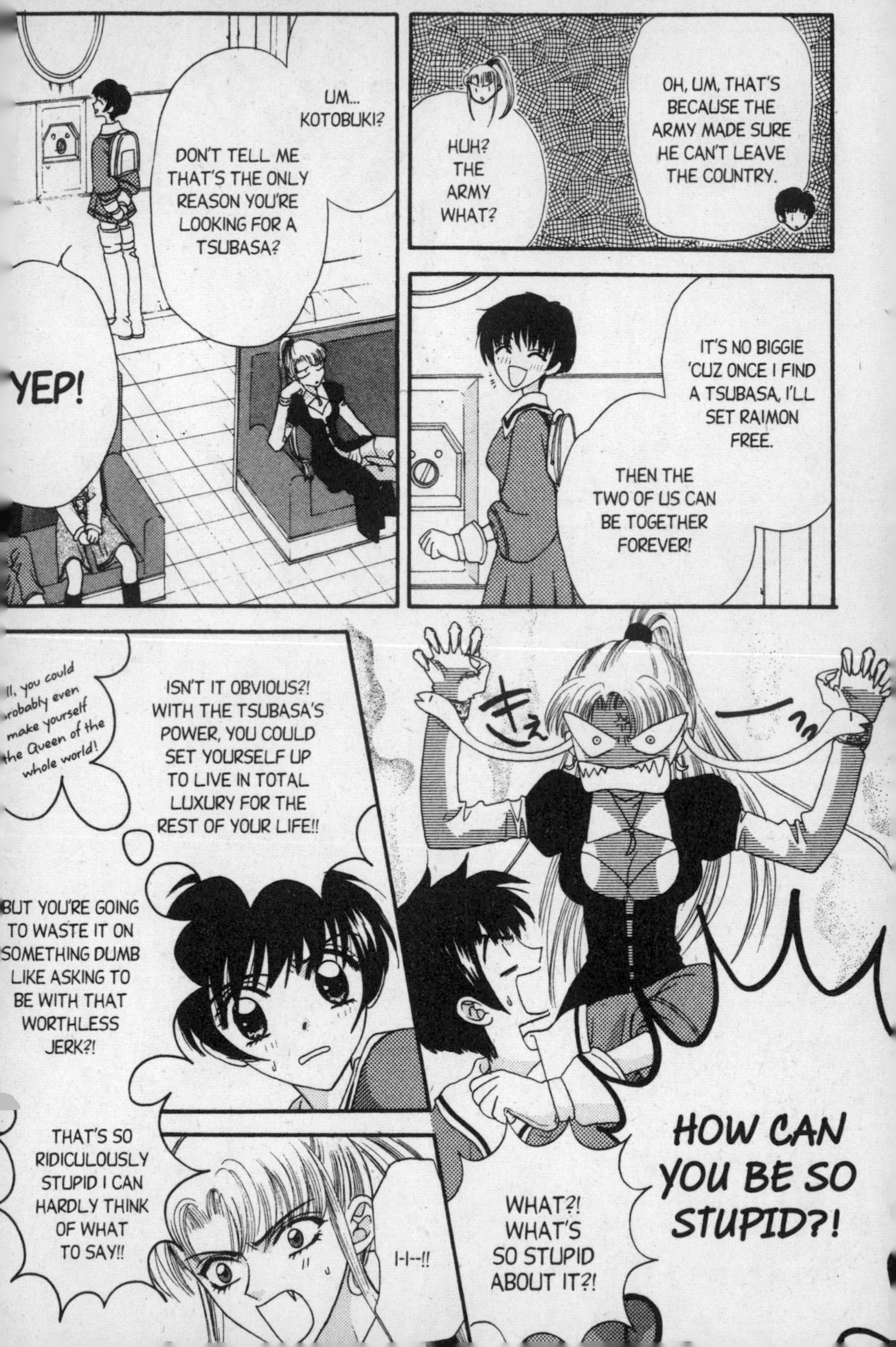

OH, UM, THAT'S BECAUSE THE ARMY MADE SURE HE CAN'T LEAVE THE COUNTRY.
HUH? THE ARMY WHAT?
IT'S NO BIGGIE 'CUZ ONCE I FIND A TSUBASA, I'LL SET RAIMON FREE.
THEN THE TWO OF US CAN BE TOGETHER FOREVER!
UM... KOTOBUKI?
DON'T TELL ME THAT'S THE ONLY REASON YOU'RE LOOKING FOR A TSUBASA?
YEP!
きぇ
HOW CAN YOU BE SO STUPID?!
WHAT?! WHAT'S SO STUPID ABOUT IT?!
ISN'T IT OBVIOUS?! WITH THE TSUBASA'S POWER, YOU COULD SET YOURSELF UP TO LIVE IN TOTAL LUXURY FOR THE REST OF YOUR LIFE!!
ll, you could robably even make yourself the Queen of the whole world!
BUT YOU'RE GOING TO WASTE IT ON SOMETHING DUMB LIKE ASKING TO BE WITH THAT WORTHLESS JERK?!
THAT'S SO RIDICULOUSLY STUPID I CAN HARDLY THINK OF WHAT TO SAY!!
I-I--!!

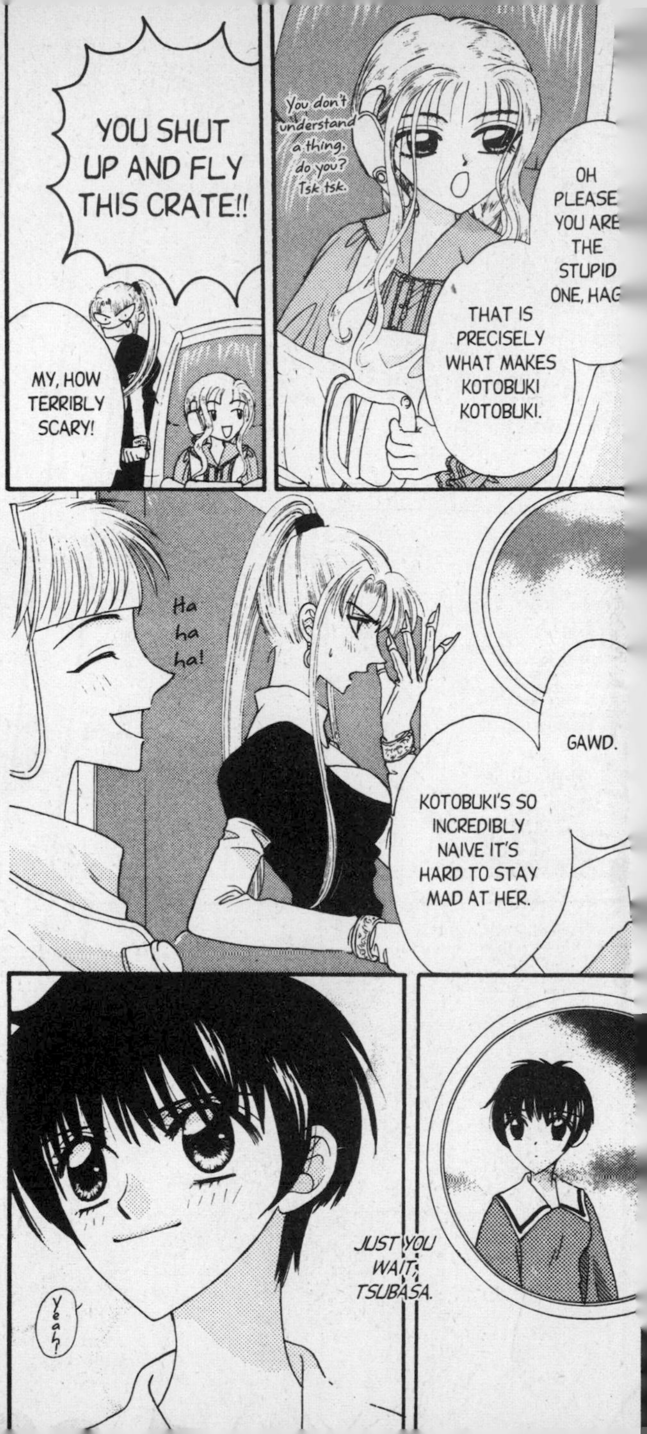
OH PLEASE YOU ARE THE STUPID ONE, HAG
THAT IS PRECISELY WHAT MAKES KOTOBUKI KOTOBUKI.
You don't understand a thing, do you? Tsk tsk.
YOU SHUT UP AND FLY THIS CRATE!!
MY, HOW TERRIBLY SCARY!
GAWD.
KOTOBUKI'S SO INCREDIBLY NAIVE IT'S HARD TO STAY MAD AT HER.
Ha ha ha!
JUST YOU WAIT, TSUBASA.
Yeah?

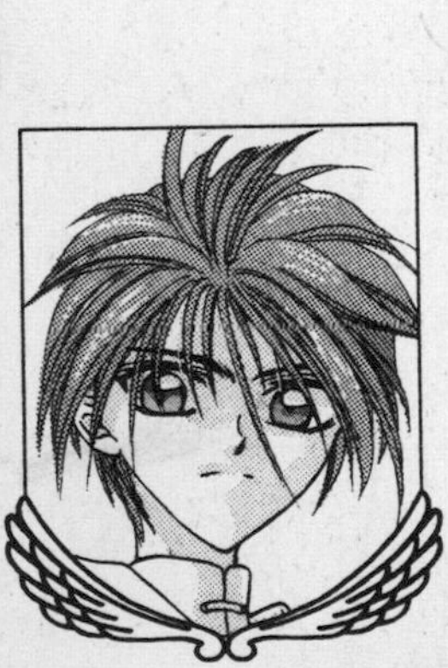

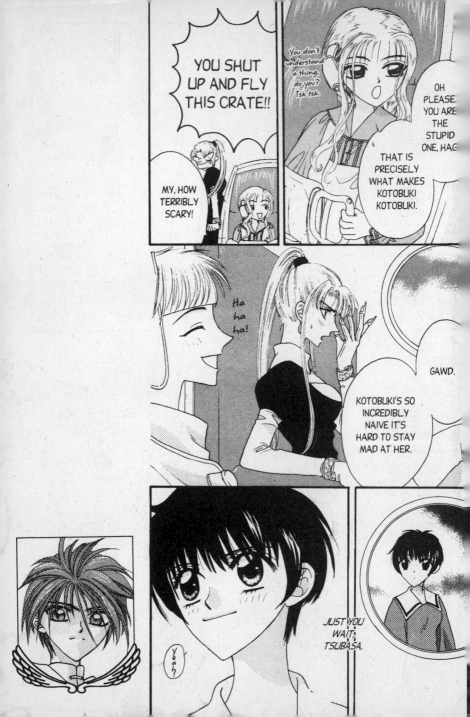

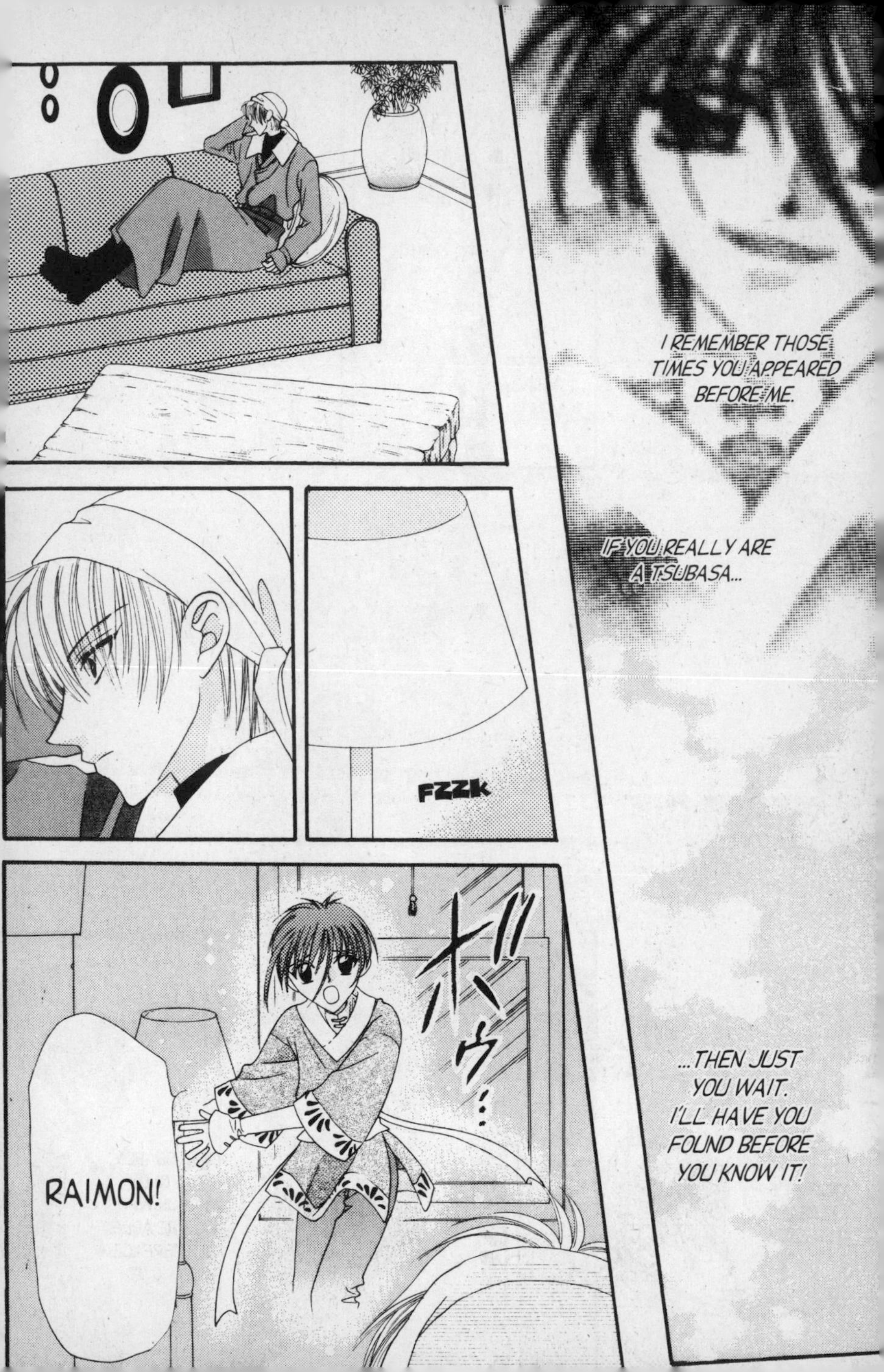
I REMEMBER THOSE TIMES YOU APPEARED BEFORE ME.
IF YOU REALLY ARE A TSUBASA...
...THEN JUST YOU WAIT. I'LL HAVE YOU FOUND BEFORE YOU KNOW IT!
FZZK
RAIMON!

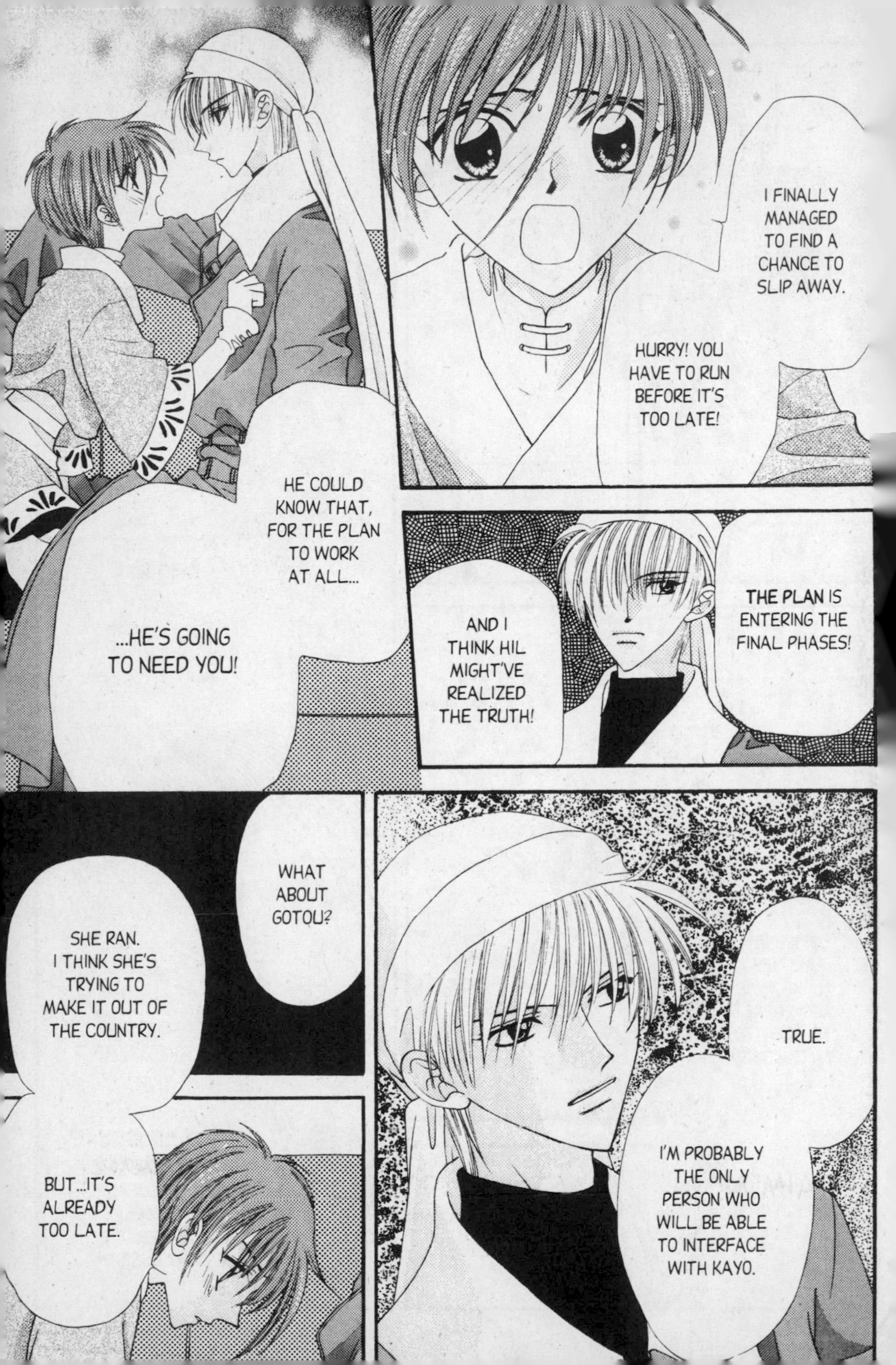
I FINALLY MANAGED TO FIND A CHANCE TO SLIP AWAY.
HURRY! YOU HAVE TO RUN BEFORE IT'S TOO LATE!
THE PLAN IS ENTERING THE FINAL PHASES!
AND I THINK HIL MIGHT'VE REALIZED THE TRUTH!
HE COULD KNOW THAT, FOR THE PLAN TO WORK AT ALL...
...HE'S GOING TO NEED YOU!
TRUE.
I'M PROBABLY THE ONLY PERSON WHO WILL BE ABLE TO INTERFACE WITH KAYO.
WHAT ABOUT GOTOU?
SHE RAN. I THINK SHE'S TRYING TO MAKE IT OUT OF THE COUNTRY.
BUT...IT'S ALREADY TOO LATE.

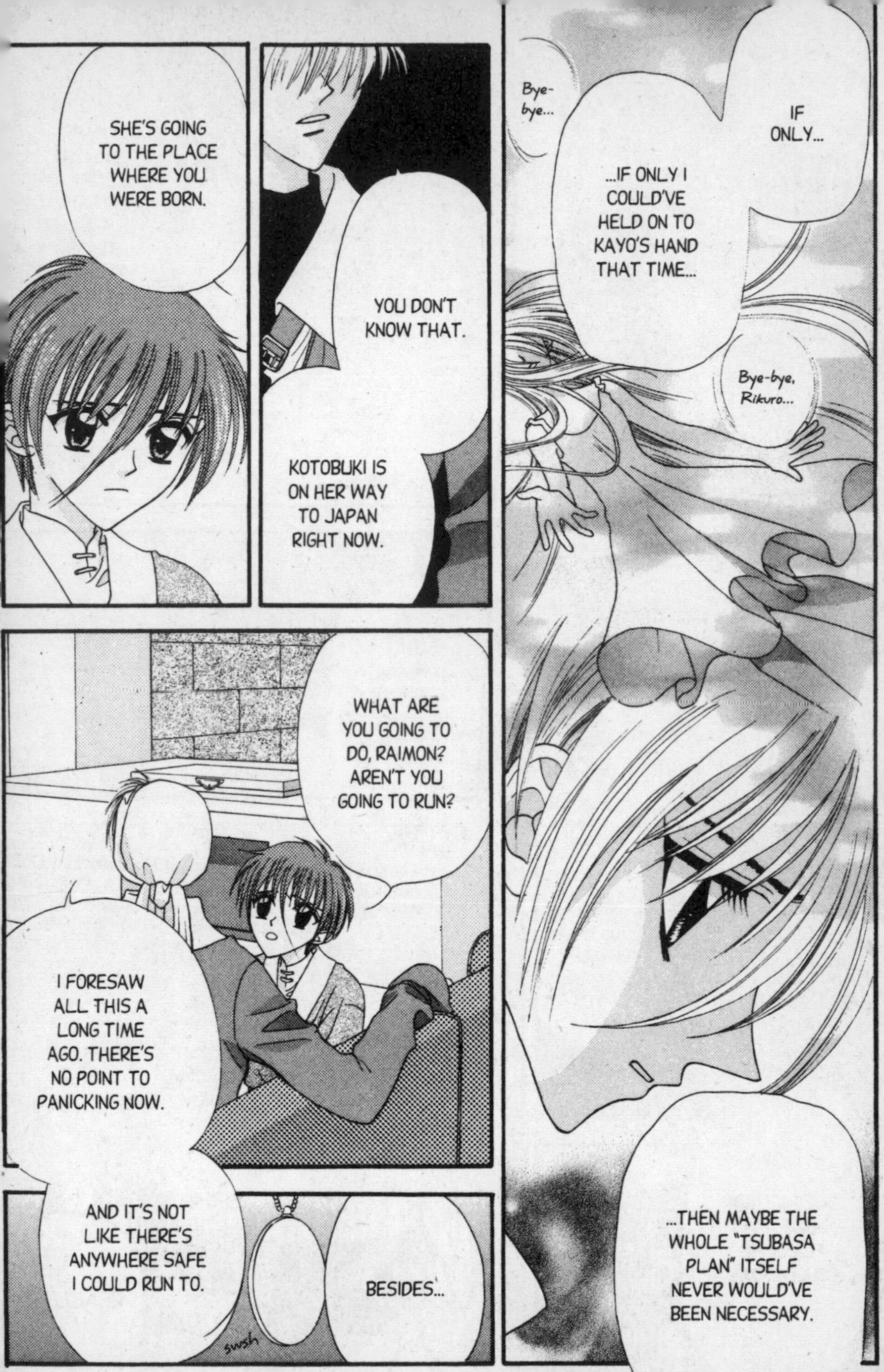
IF ONLY...
Bye-bye...
...IF ONLY I COULD'VE HELD ON TO KAYO'S HAND THAT TIME...
Bye-bye, Rikuro...
...THEN MAYBE THE WHOLE "TSUBASA PLAN" ITSELF NEVER WOULD'VE BEEN NECESSARY.
YOU DON'T KNOW THAT.
KOTOBUKI IS ON HER WAY TO JAPAN RIGHT NOW.
SHE'S GOING TO THE PLACE WHERE YOU WERE BORN.
WHAT ARE YOU GOING TO DO, RAIMON? AREN'T YOU GOING TO RUN?
I FORESAW ALL THIS A LONG TIME AGO. THERE'S NO POINT TO PANICKING NOW.
BESIDES...
AND IT'S NOT LIKE THERE'S ANYWHERE SAFE I COULD RUN TO.
swsh

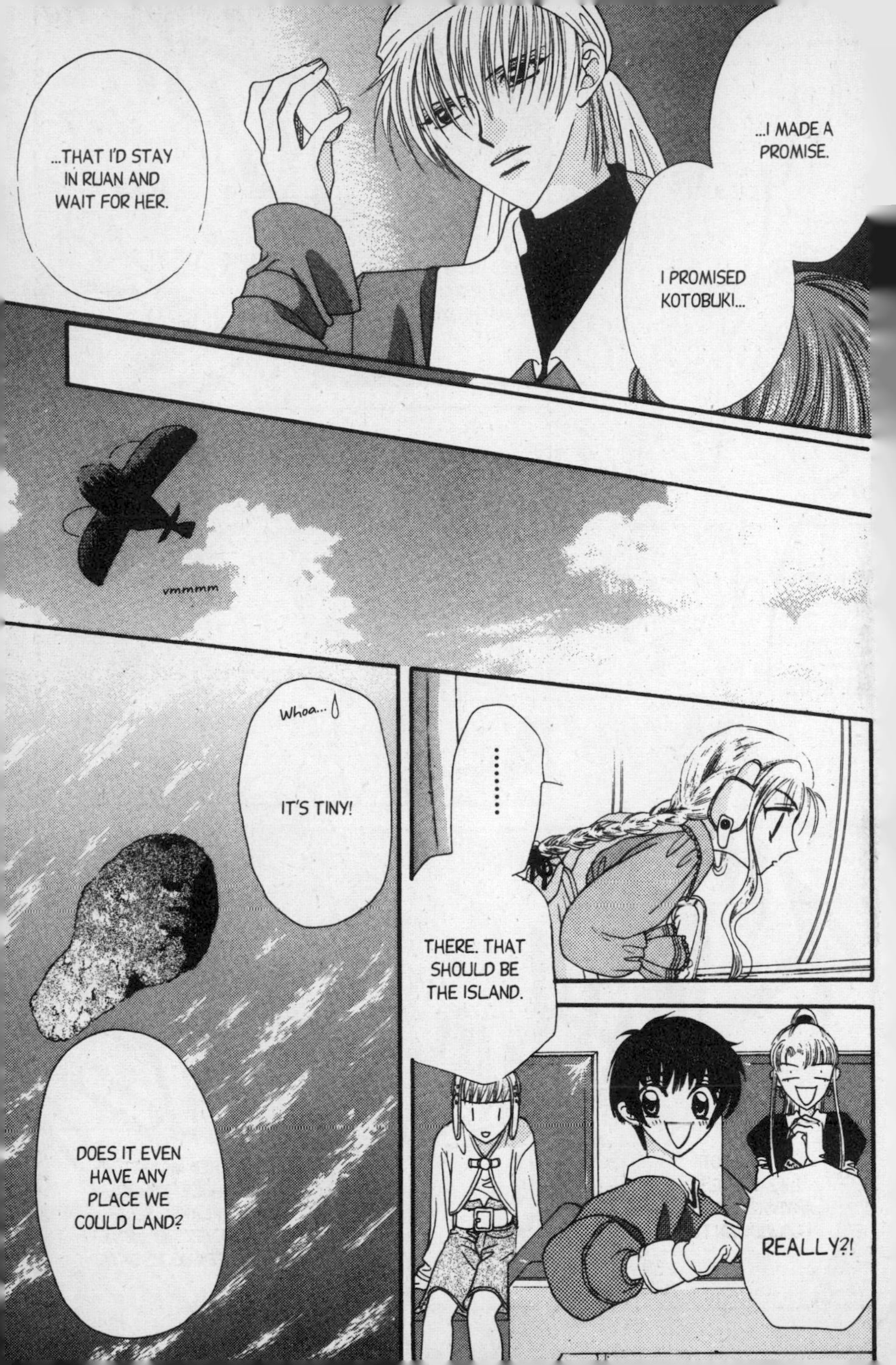
...I MADE A PROMISE.
I PROMISED KOTOBUKI...
...THAT I'D STAY IN RUAN AND WAIT FOR HER.
vmmmm
......
THERE. THAT SHOULD BE THE ISLAND.
REALLY?!
Whoa...
IT'S TINY!
DOES IT EVEN HAVE ANY PLACE WE COULD LAND?

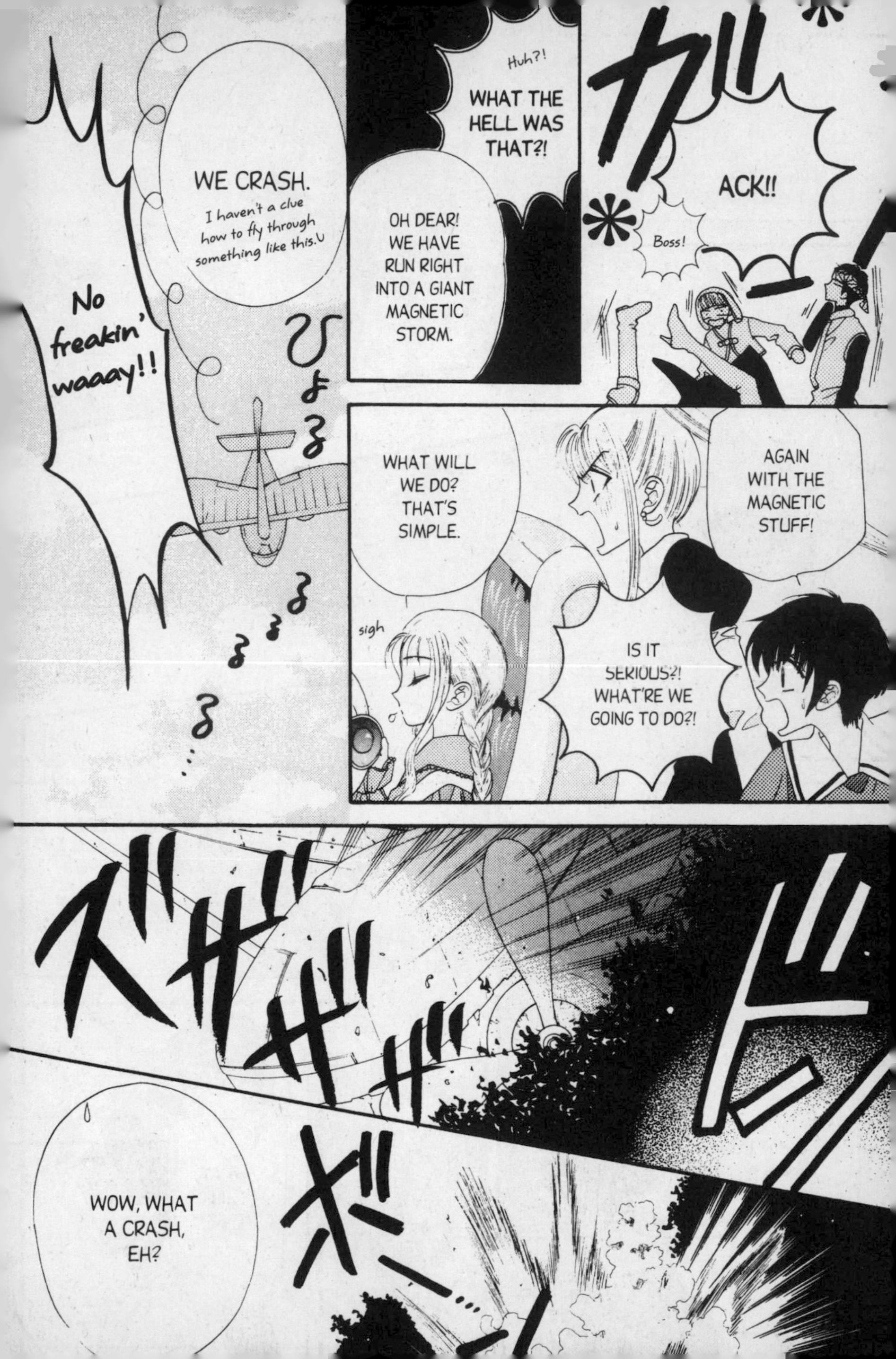
ACK!!
Boss!
Huh?!
WHAT THE HELL WAS THAT?!
OH DEAR! WE HAVE RUN RIGHT INTO A GIANT MAGNETIC STORM.
AGAIN WITH THE MAGNETIC STUFF!
IS IT SERIOUS?! WHAT'RE WE GOING TO DO?!
WHAT WILL WE DO? THAT'S SIMPLE.
sigh
WE CRASH.
I haven't a clue how to fly through something like this.
No freakin' waaay!!
WOW, WHAT A CRASH, EH?

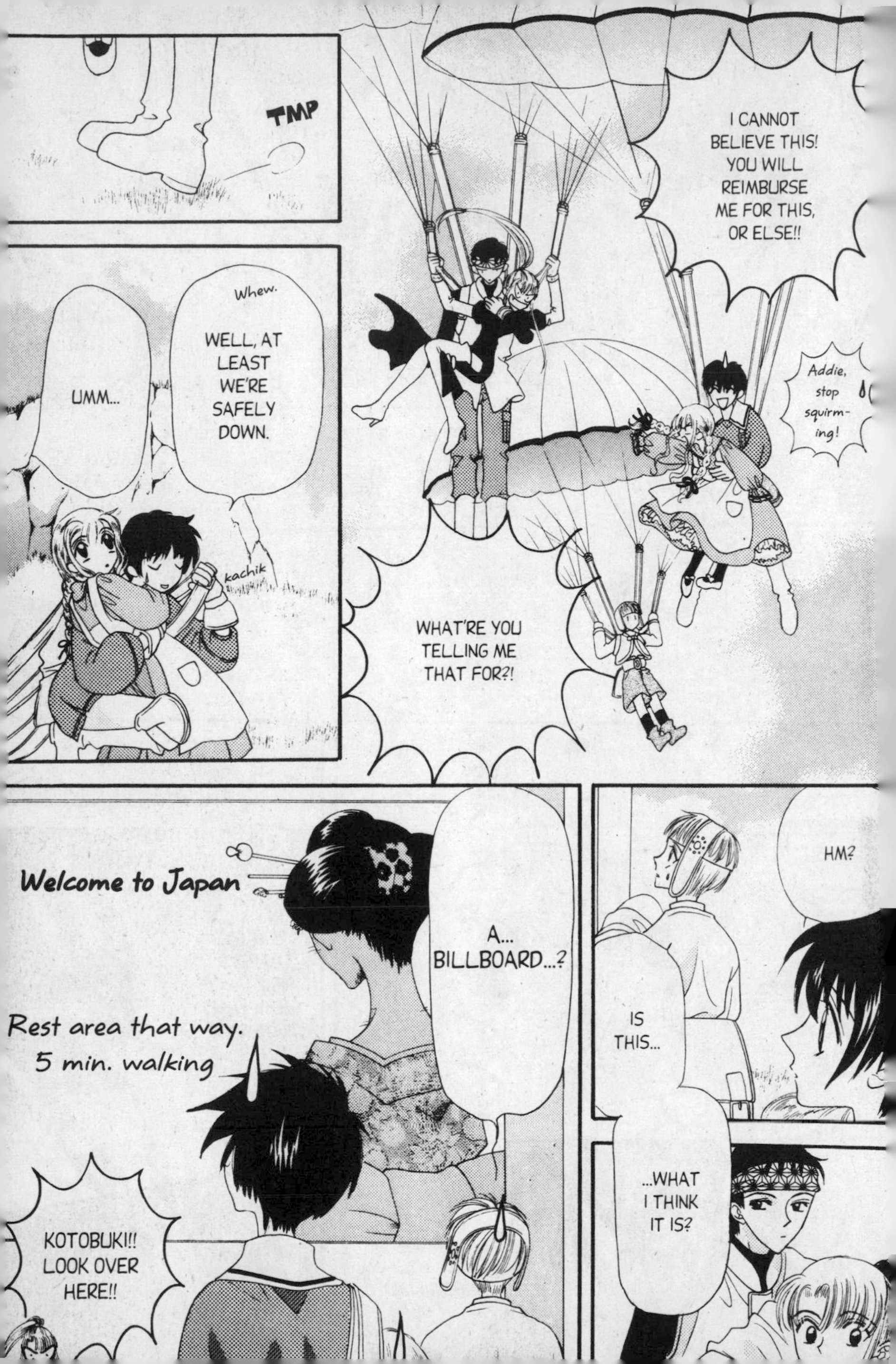
I CANNOT BELIEVE THIS! YOU WILL REIMBURSE ME FOR THIS, OR ELSE!!
Addie, stop squirm- ing!
WHAT'RE YOU TELLING ME THAT FOR?!
TMP
Whew.
WELL, AT LEAST WE'RE SAFELY DOWN.
UMM...
kachik
HM?
IS THIS...
...WHAT I THINK IT IS?
A... BILLBOARD...?
Welcome to Japan
Rest area that way. 5 min. walking
KOTOBUKI!! LOOK OVER HERE!!

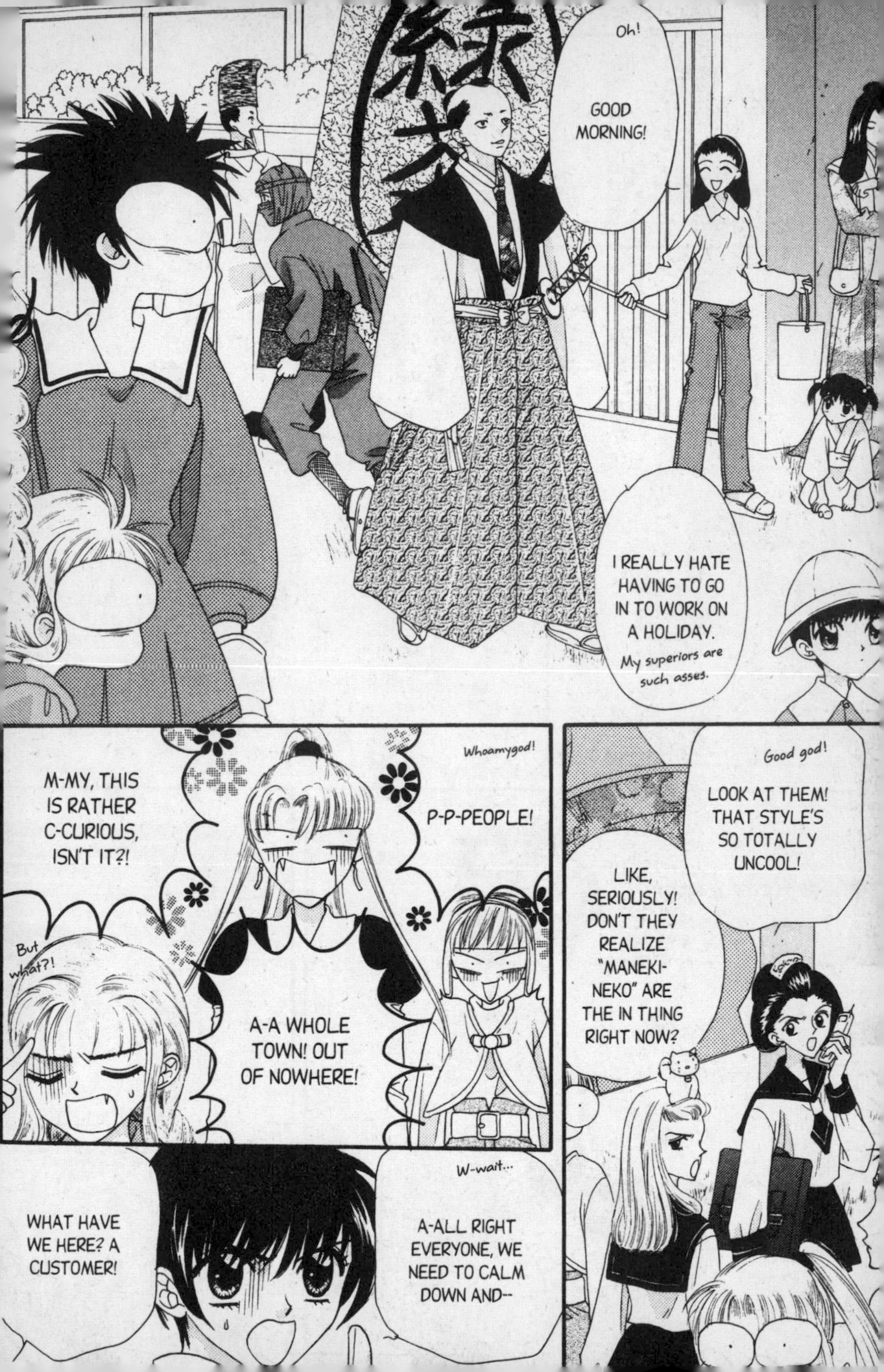
Oh!
GOOD MORNING!
I REALLY HATE HAVING TO GO IN TO WORK ON A HOLIDAY.
My superiors are such asses.
Good god!
LOOK AT THEM! THAT STYLE'S SO TOTALLY UNCOOL!
LIKE, SERIOUSLY! DON'T THEY REALIZE "MANEKI-NEKO" ARE THE IN THING RIGHT NOW?
Whoamygod!
P-P-PEOPLE!
M-MY, THIS IS RATHER C-CURIOUS, ISN'T IT?!
A-A WHOLE TOWN! OUT OF NOWHERE!
But what?!
W-wait...
A-ALL RIGHT EVERYONE, WE NEED TO CALM DOWN AND--
WHAT HAVE WE HERE? A CUSTOMER!

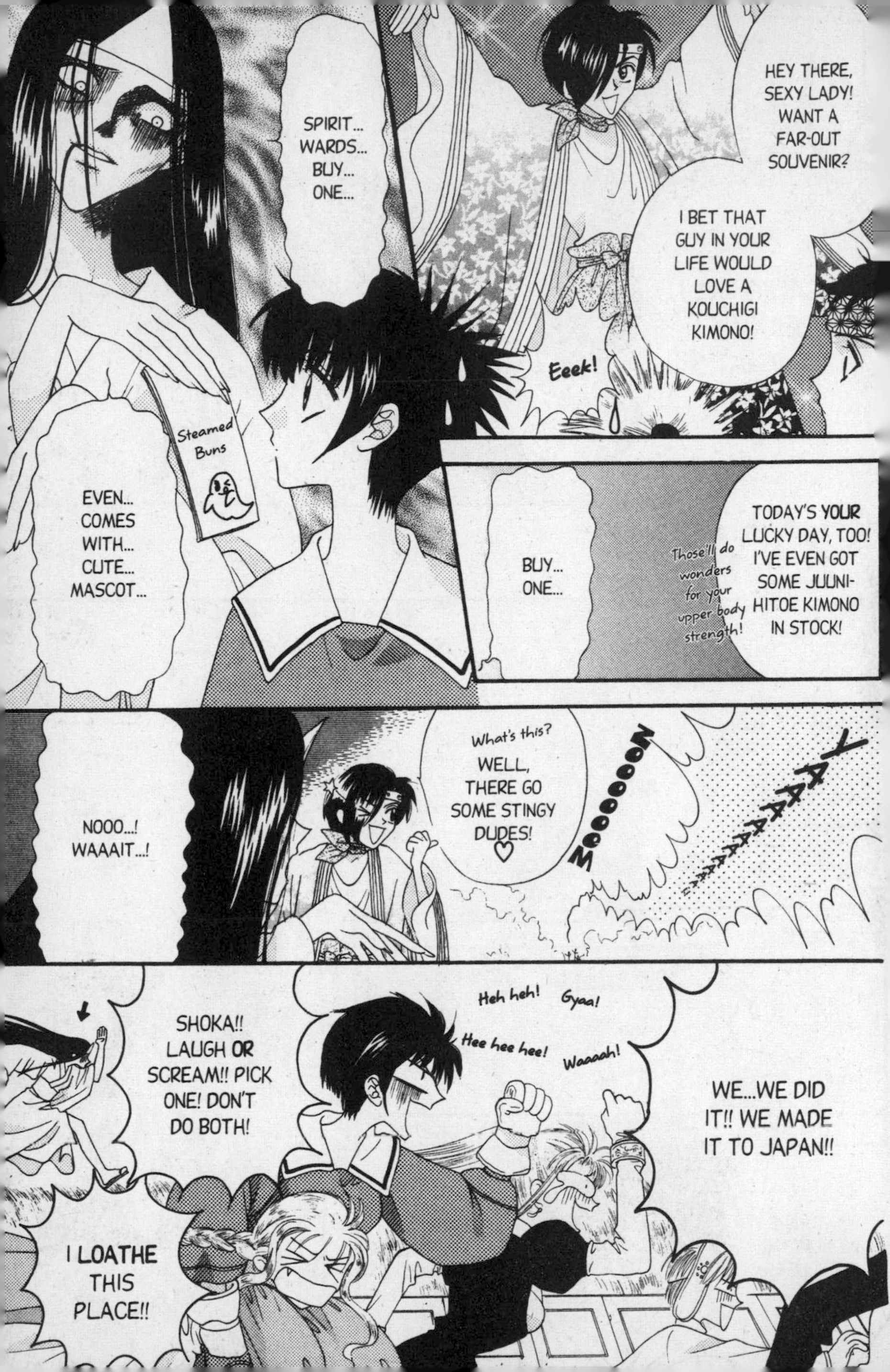
HEY THERE, SEXY LADY! WANT A FAR-OUT SOUVENIR?
I BET THAT GUY IN YOUR LIFE WOULD LOVE A KOUCHIGI KIMONO!
Eeek!
TODAY'S YOUR LUCKY DAY, TOO! I'VE EVEN GOT SOME JUUNI-HITOE KIMONO IN STOCK!
Those'll do wonders for your upper body strength!
BUY... ONE...
SPIRIT... WARDS... BUY... ONE...
Steamed Buns
EVEN... COMES WITH... CUTE... MASCOT...
YAAAAAAAAAA
NOOOOOOOW
What's this? WELL, THERE GO SOME STINGY DUDES! ♡
NOOO...! WAAAIT...!
WE...WE DID IT!! WE MADE IT TO JAPAN!!
Gyaa!
Heh heh!
Waaaah!
Hee hee hee!
SHOKA!! LAUGH OR SCREAM!! PICK ONE! DON'T DO BOTH!
I LOATHE THIS PLACE!!

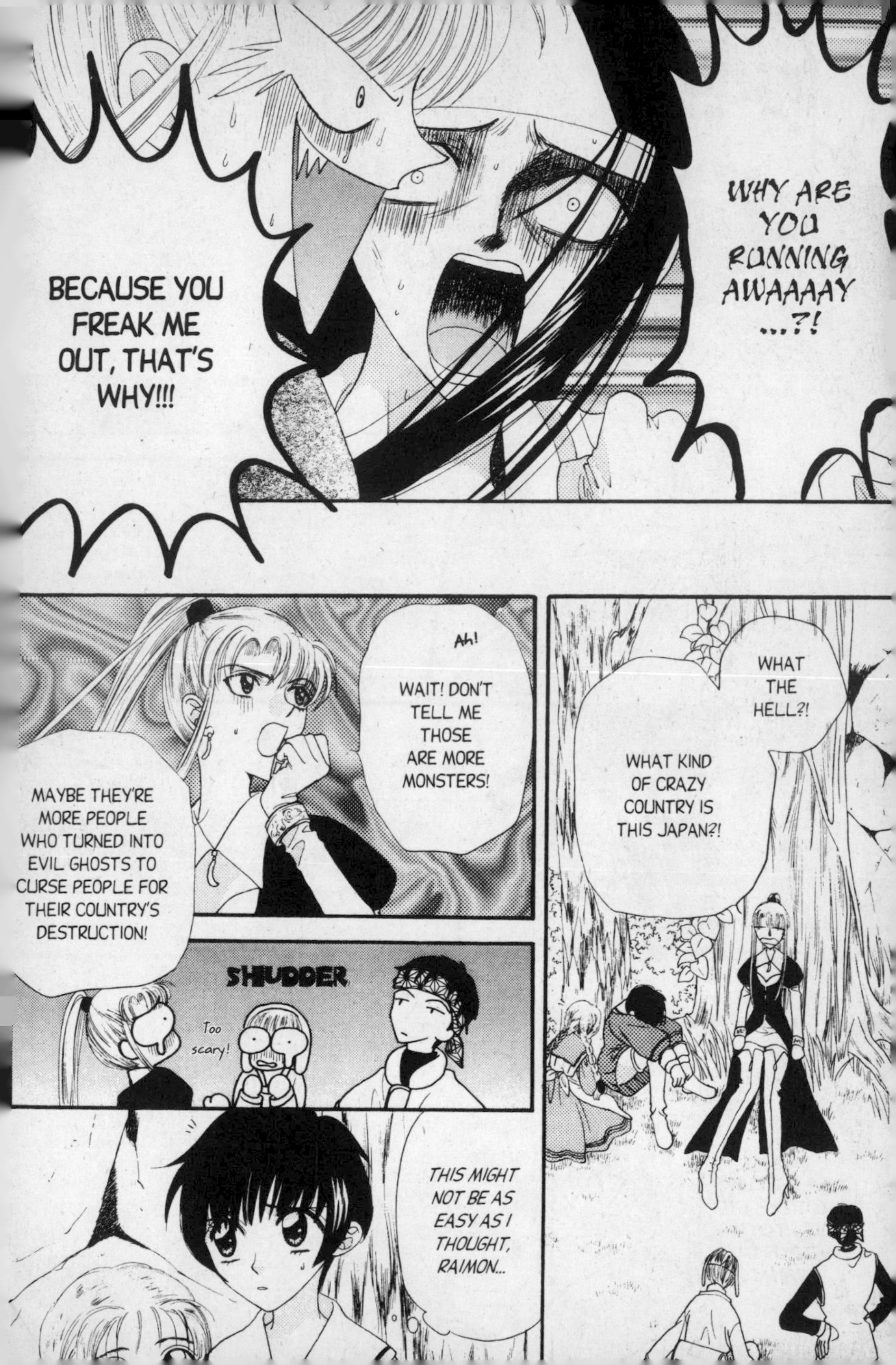
WHY ARE YOU RUNNING AWAAAAY ...?!
BECAUSE YOU FREAK ME OUT, THAT'S WHY!!!
WHAT THE HELL?!
WHAT KIND OF CRAZY COUNTRY IS THIS JAPAN?!
Ah!
WAIT! DON'T TELL ME THOSE ARE MORE MONSTERS!
MAYBE THEY'RE MORE PEOPLE WHO TURNED INTO EVIL GHOSTS TO CURSE PEOPLE FOR THEIR COUNTRY'S DESTRUCTION!
SHUDDER
Too scary!
THIS MIGHT NOT BE AS EASY AS I THOUGHT, RAIMON...

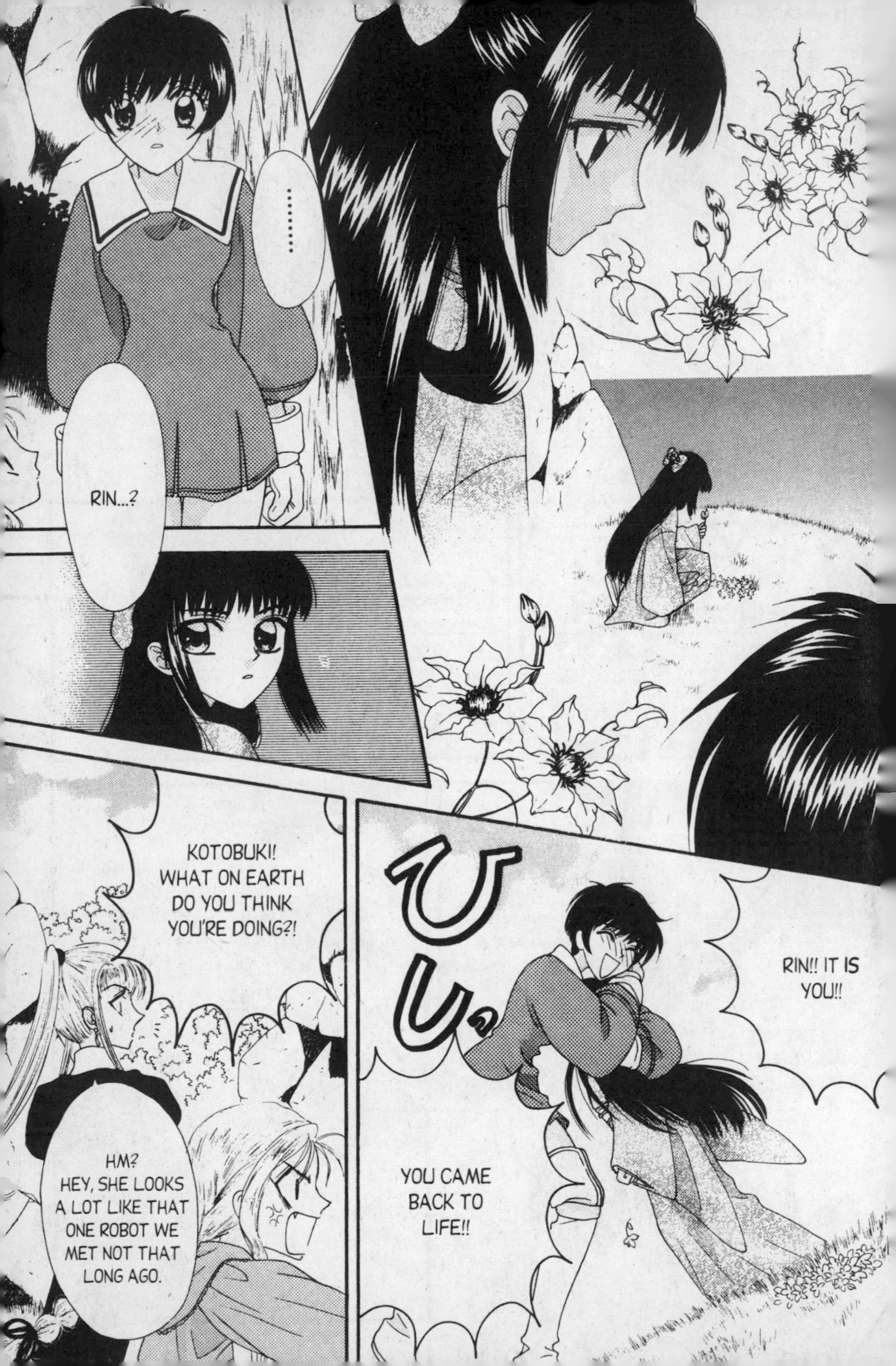
......
RIN...?
ひしっ
RIN!! IT IS YOU!!
YOU CAME BACK TO LIFE!!
KOTOBUKI!! WHAT ON EARTH DO YOU THINK YOU'RE DOING?!
HM? HEY, SHE LOOKS A LOT LIKE THAT ONE ROBOT WE MET NOT THAT LONG AGO.

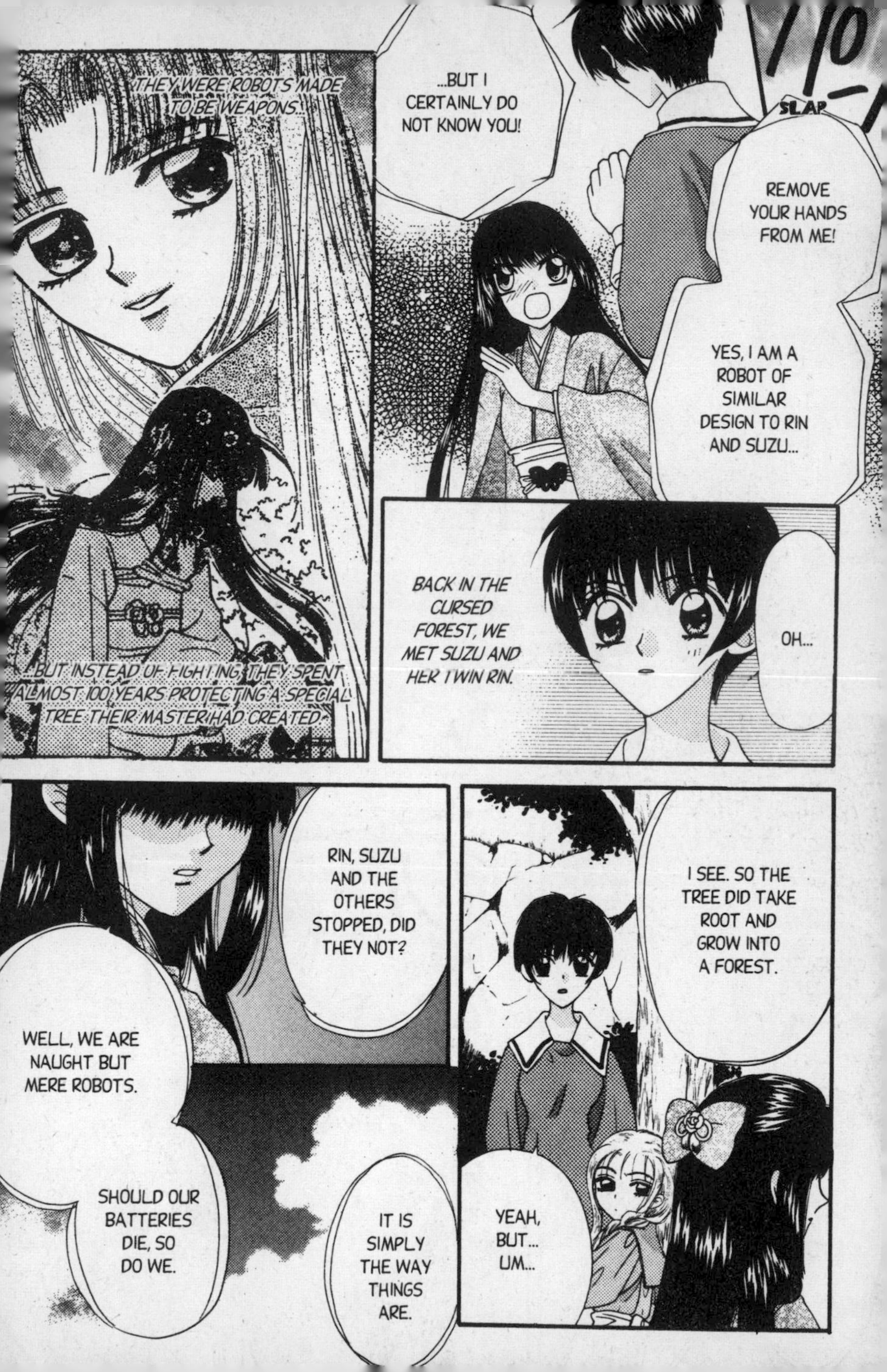
YES, I AM A ROBOT OF SIMILAR DESIGN TO RIN AND SUZU...
...BUT I CERTAINLY DO NOT KNOW YOU!
SLAP
REMOVE YOUR HANDS FROM ME!
OH...
BACK IN THE CURSED FOREST, WE MET SUZU AND HER TWIN RIN.
THEY WERE ROBOTS MADE TO BE WEAPONS...
...BUT INSTEAD OF FIGHTING, THEY SPENT ALMOST 100 YEARS PROTECTING A SPECIAL TREE THEIR MASTER HAD CREATED.
I SEE. SO THE TREE DID TAKE ROOT AND GROW INTO A FOREST.
YEAH, BUT... UM...
RIN, SUZU AND THE OTHERS STOPPED, DID THEY NOT?
WELL, WE ARE NAUGHT BUT MERE ROBOTS.
SHOULD OUR BATTERIES DIE, SO DO WE.
IT IS SIMPLY THE WAY THINGS ARE.

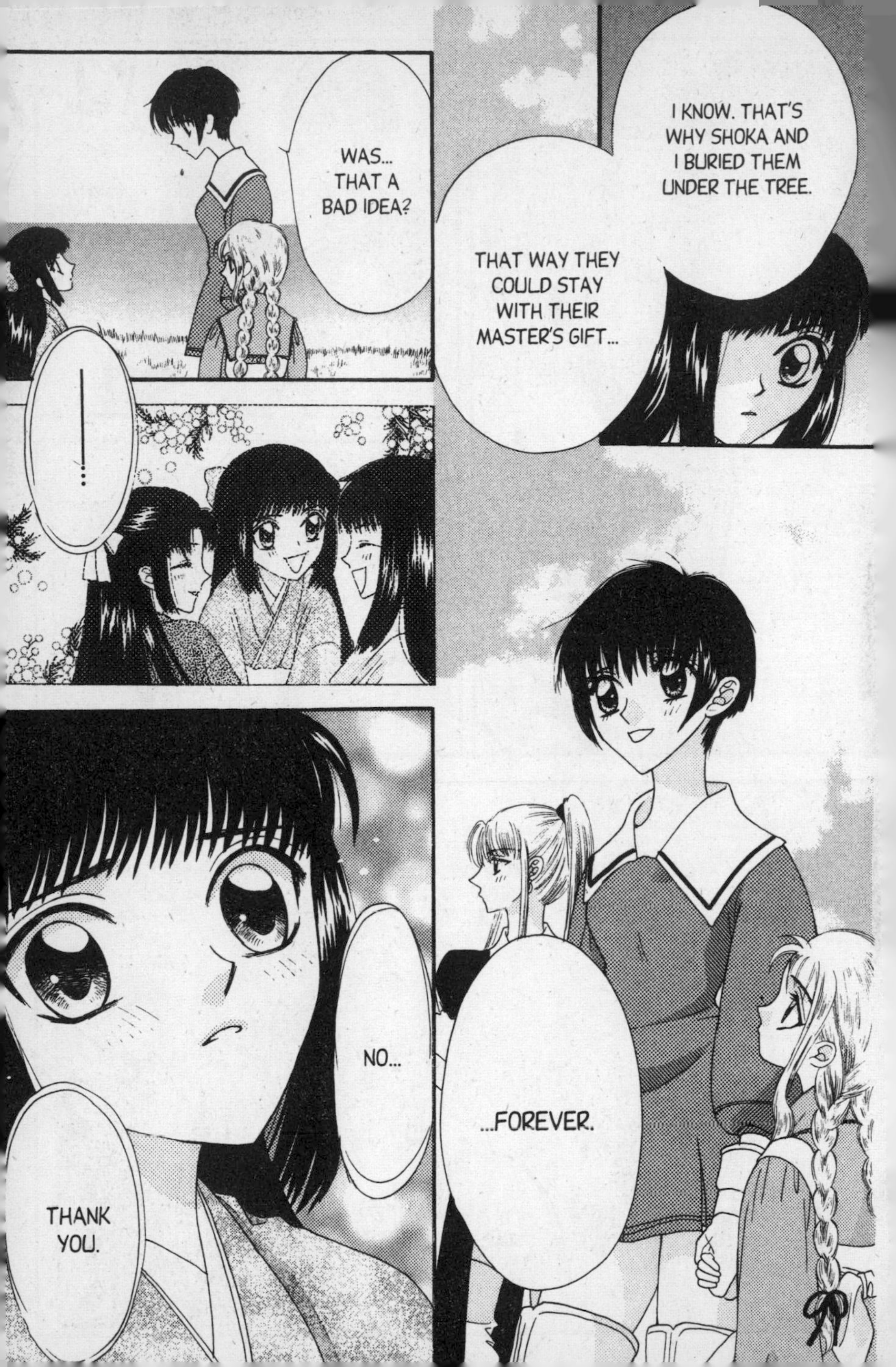
I KNOW. THAT'S WHY SHOKA AND I BURIED THEM UNDER THE TREE.
THAT WAY THEY COULD STAY WITH THEIR MASTER'S GIFT...
...FOREVER.
WAS... THAT A BAD IDEA?
!
NO...
THANK YOU.

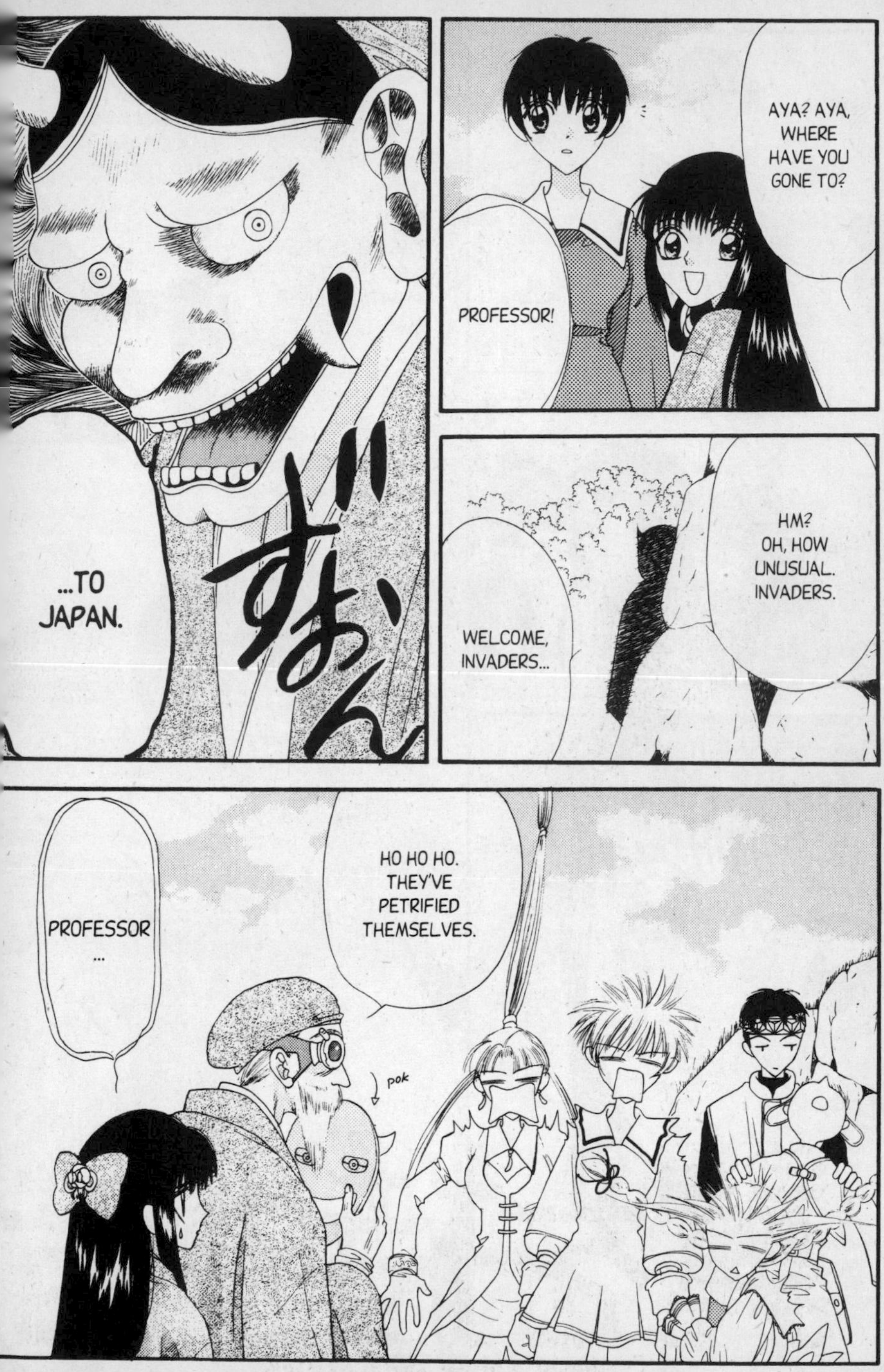

AYA? AYA, WHERE HAVE YOU GONE TO?
PROFESSOR!
HM? OH, HOW UNUSUAL. INVADERS.
WELCOME, INVADERS...
...TO JAPAN.
HO HO HO. THEY'VE PETRIFIED THEMSELVES.
pok
PROFESSOR ...

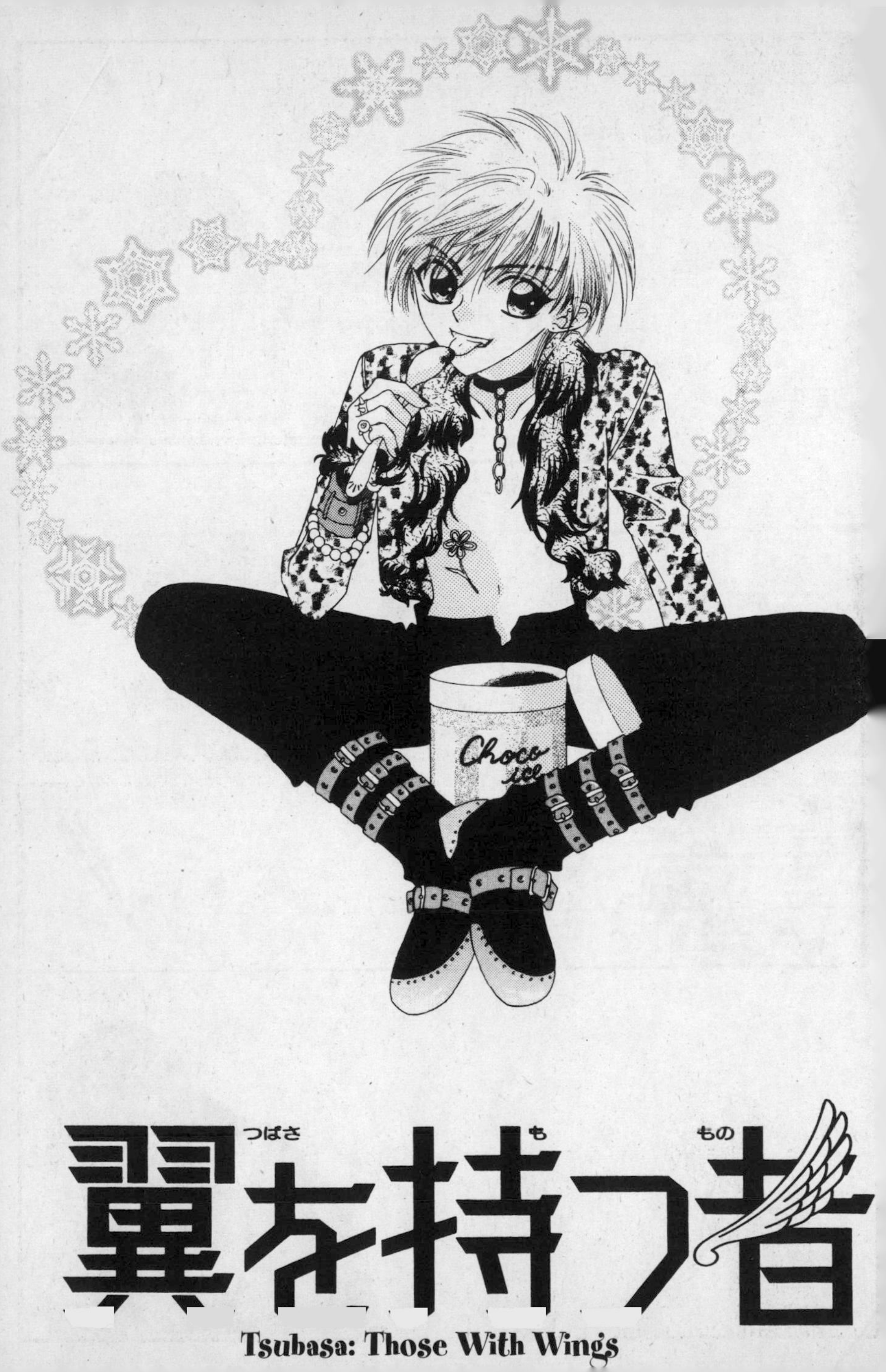
Choco ice

翼を持つ者

つばさ も もの

Tsubasa: Those With Wings

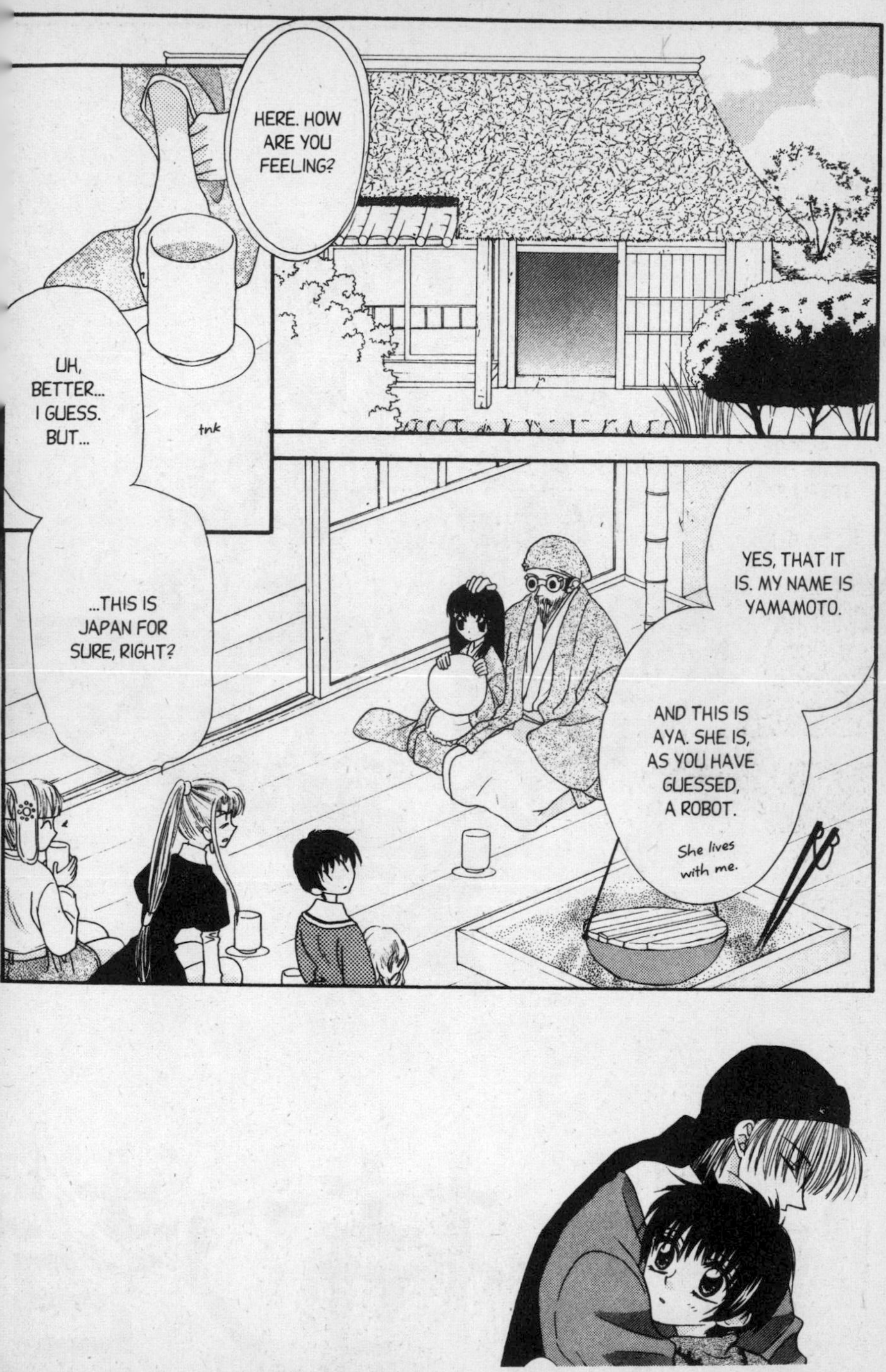
HERE. HOW ARE YOU FEELING?
tnk
UH, BETTER... I GUESS. BUT...
...THIS IS JAPAN FOR SURE, RIGHT?
YES, THAT IT IS. MY NAME IS YAMAMOTO.
AND THIS IS AYA. SHE IS, AS YOU HAVE GUESSED, A ROBOT.
She lives with me.

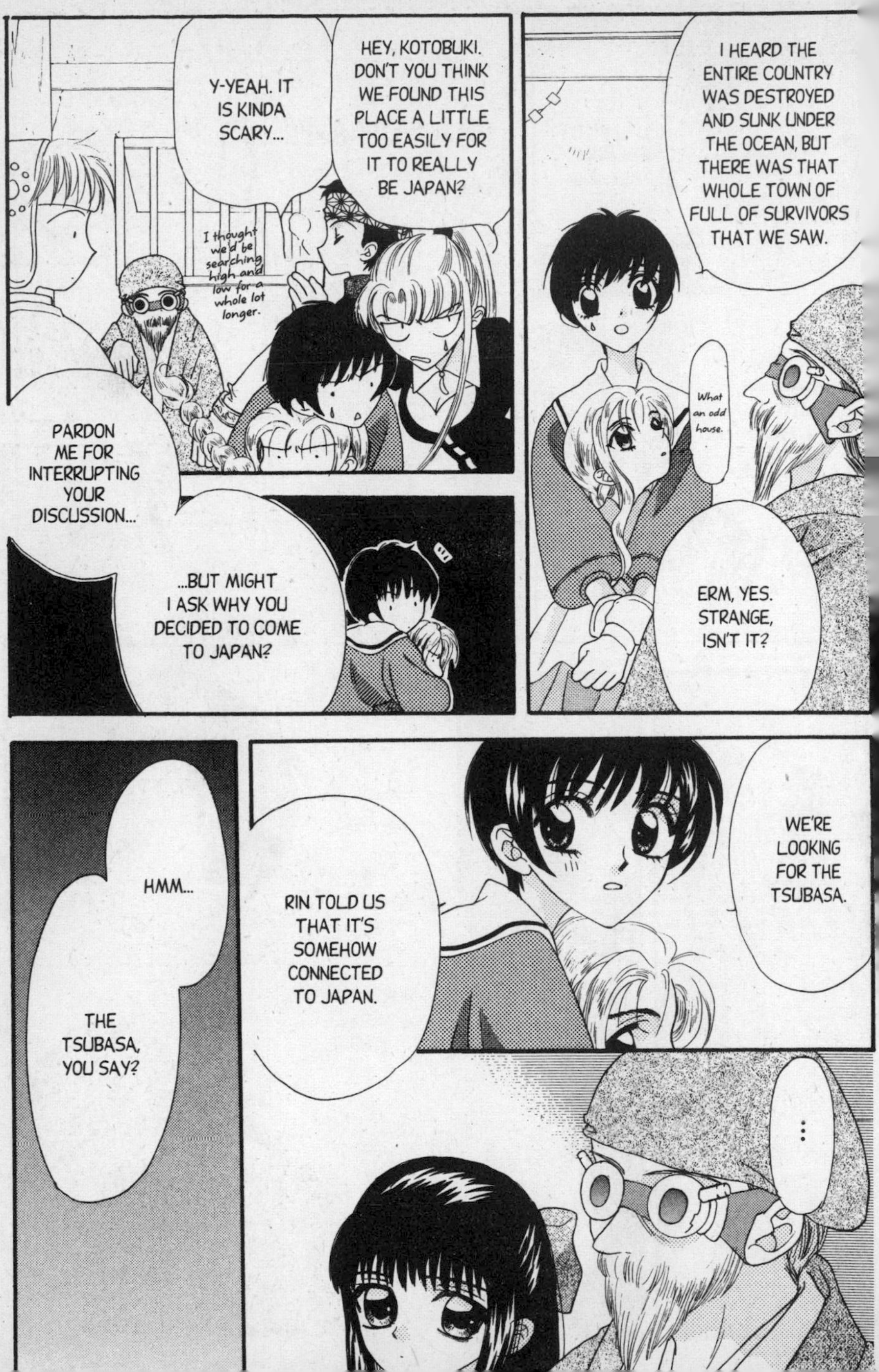
I HEARD THE ENTIRE COUNTRY WAS DESTROYED AND SUNK UNDER THE OCEAN, BUT THERE WAS THAT WHOLE TOWN OF FULL OF SURVIVORS THAT WE SAW.
What an odd house.
ERM, YES. STRANGE, ISN'T IT?
HEY, KOTOBUKI. DON'T YOU THINK WE FOUND THIS PLACE A LITTLE TOO EASILY FOR IT TO REALLY BE JAPAN?
Y-YEAH. IT IS KINDA SCARY...
I thought we'd be searching high and low for a whole lot longer.
PARDON ME FOR INTERRUPTING YOUR DISCUSSION...
...BUT MIGHT I ASK WHY YOU DECIDED TO COME TO JAPAN?
WE'RE LOOKING FOR THE TSUBASA.
RIN TOLD US THAT IT'S SOMEHOW CONNECTED TO JAPAN.
...
HMM...
THE TSUBASA, YOU SAY?

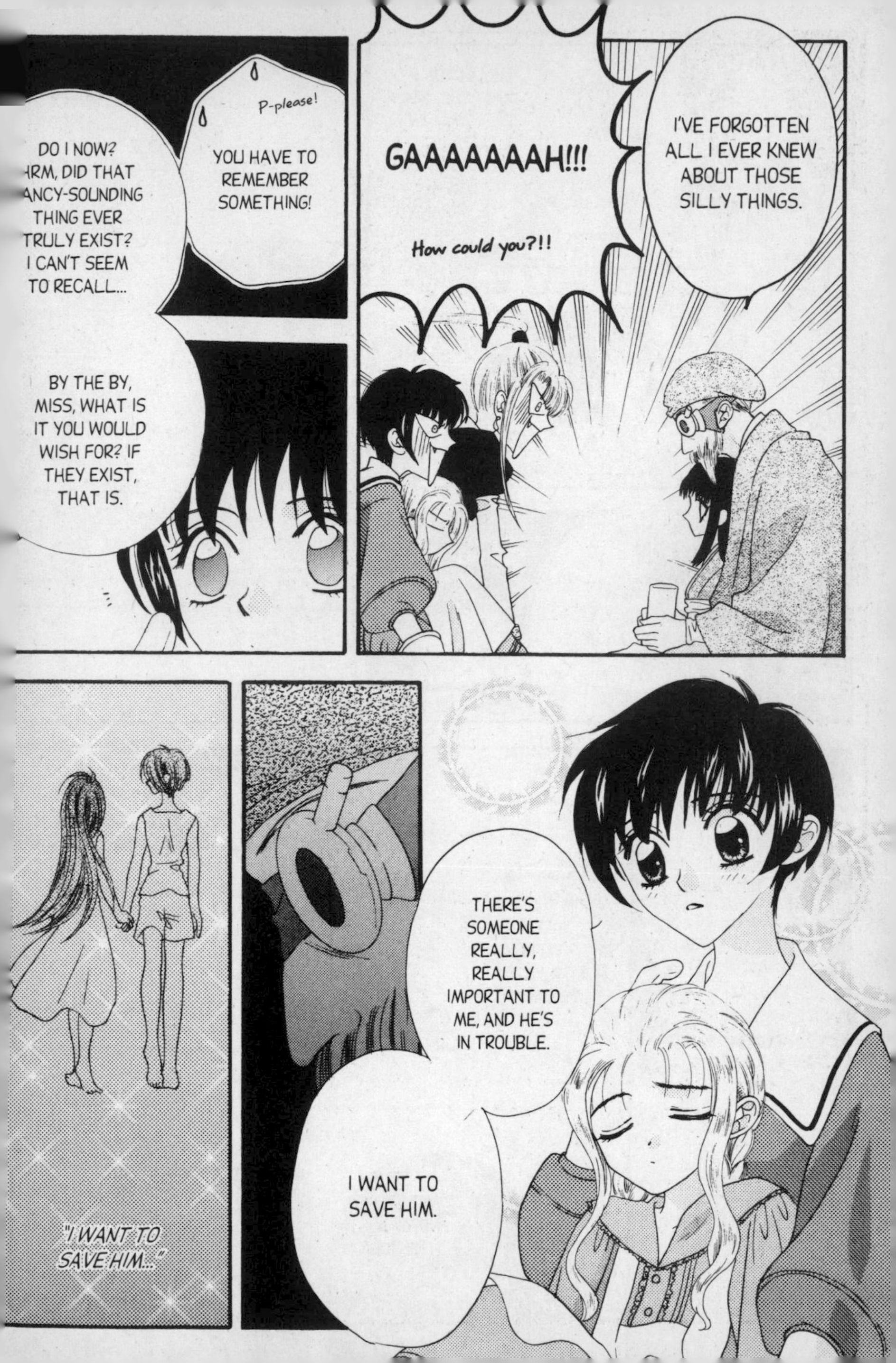
I'VE FORGOTTEN ALL I EVER KNEW ABOUT THOSE SILLY THINGS.
GAAAAAAAH!!!
How could you?!!
P-please!
YOU HAVE TO REMEMBER SOMETHING!
DO I NOW? HRM, DID THAT ANCY-SOUNDING THING EVER TRULY EXIST? I CAN'T SEEM TO RECALL...
BY THE BY, MISS, WHAT IS IT YOU WOULD WISH FOR? IF THEY EXIST, THAT IS.
THERE'S SOMEONE REALLY, REALLY IMPORTANT TO ME, AND HE'S IN TROUBLE.
I WANT TO SAVE HIM.
"I WANT TO SAVE HIM..."

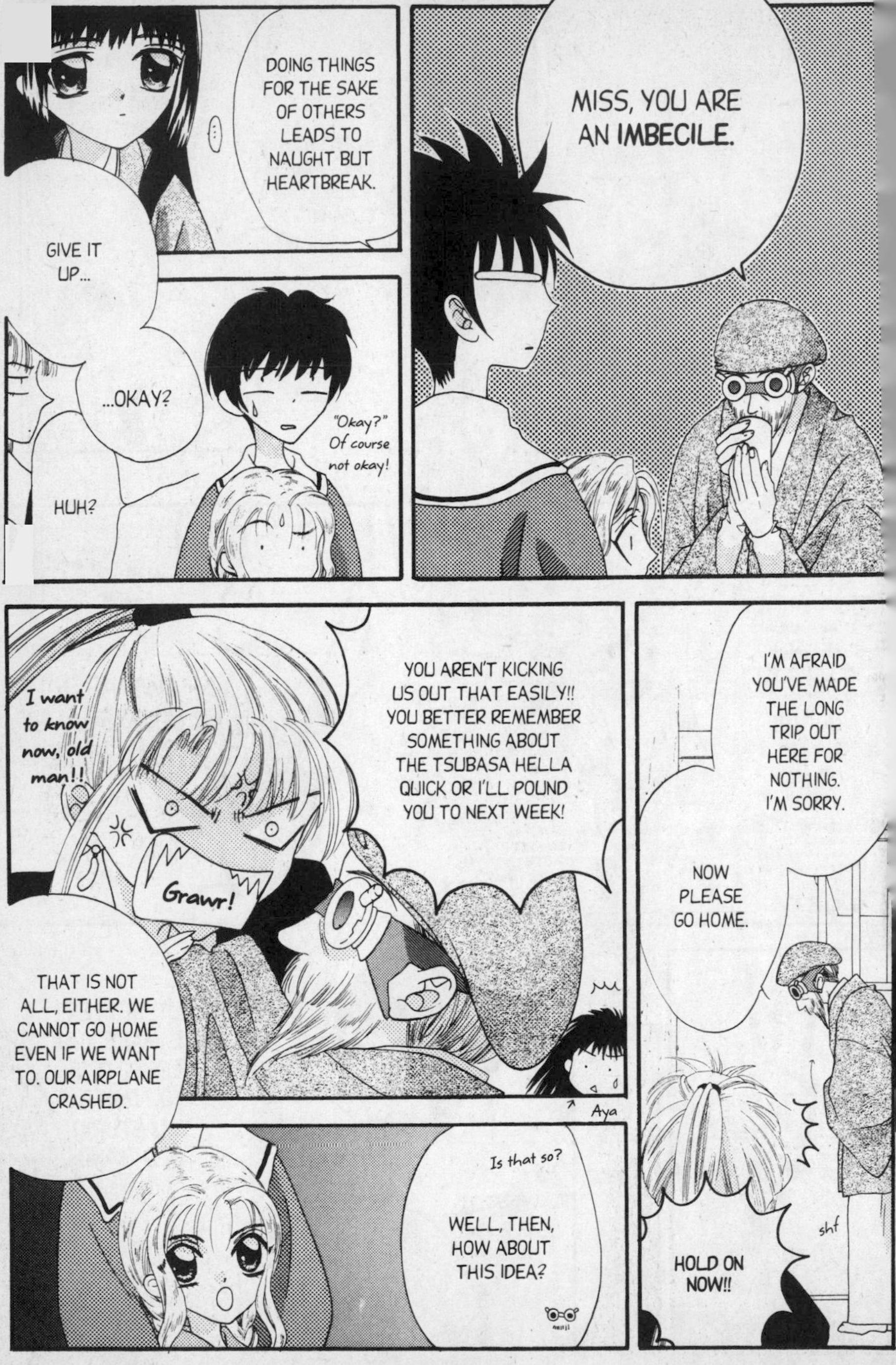
MISS, YOU ARE AN IMBECILE.
DOING THINGS FOR THE SAKE OF OTHERS LEADS TO NAUGHT BUT HEARTBREAK.
GIVE IT UP...
...OKAY?
"Okay?" Of course not okay!
HUH?
I'M AFRAID YOU'VE MADE THE LONG TRIP OUT HERE FOR NOTHING. I'M SORRY.
NOW PLEASE GO HOME.
shf
HOLD ON NOW!!
YOU AREN'T KICKING US OUT THAT EASILY!! YOU BETTER REMEMBER SOMETHING ABOUT THE TSUBASA HELLA QUICK OR I'LL POUND YOU TO NEXT WEEK!
I want to know now, old man!!
Grawr!
THAT IS NOT ALL, EITHER. WE CANNOT GO HOME EVEN IF WE WANT TO. OUR AIRPLANE CRASHED.
Aya
Is that so?
WELL, THEN, HOW ABOUT THIS IDEA?

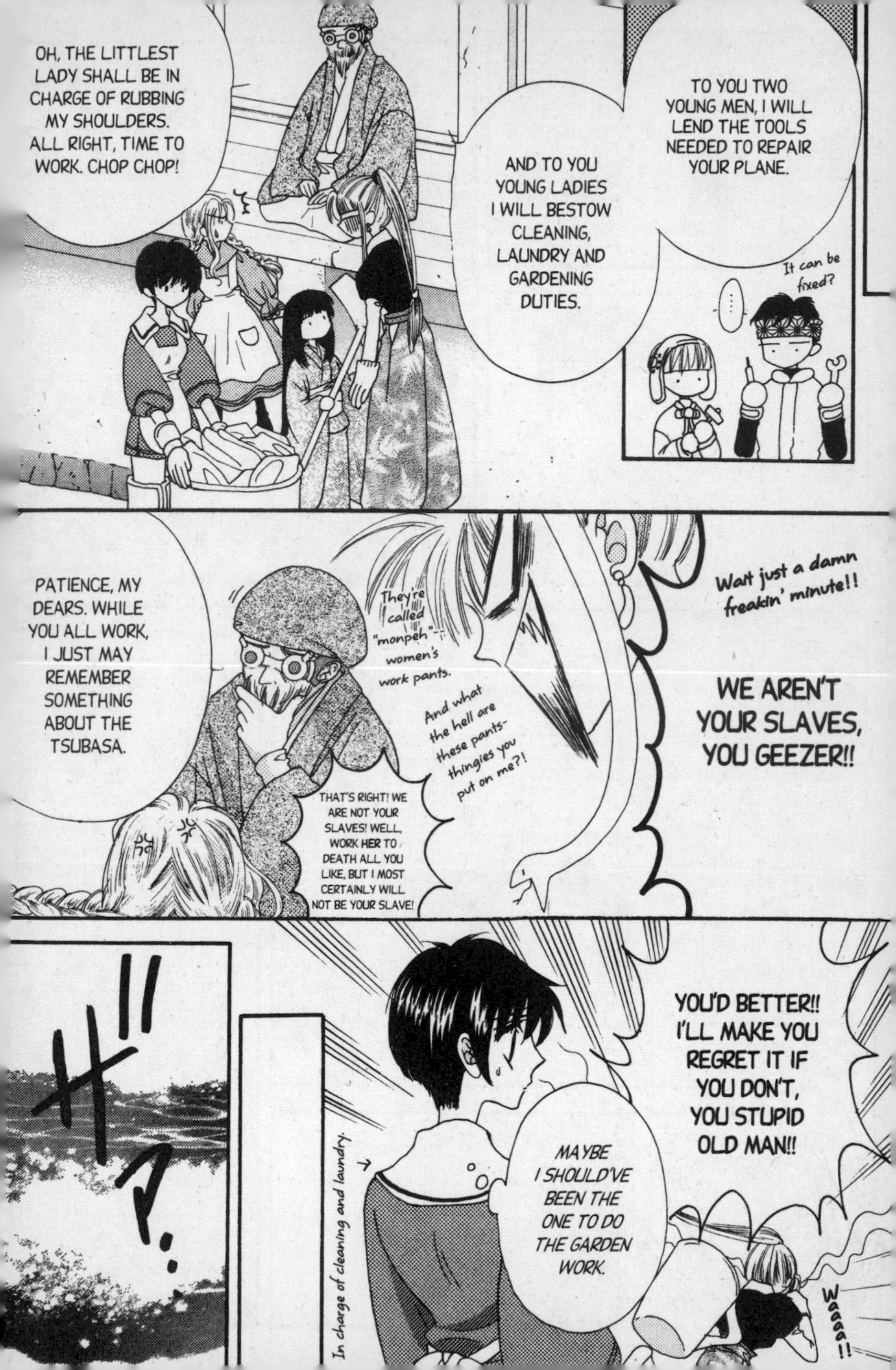

TO YOU TWO YOUNG MEN, I WILL LEND THE TOOLS NEEDED TO REPAIR YOUR PLANE.
AND TO YOU YOUNG LADIES I WILL BESTOW CLEANING, LAUNDRY AND GARDENING DUTIES.
It can be fixed?
......
OH, THE LITTLEST LADY SHALL BE IN CHARGE OF RUBBING MY SHOULDERS. ALL RIGHT, TIME TO WORK. CHOP CHOP!
Wait just a damn freakin' minute!!
WE AREN'T YOUR SLAVES, YOU GEEZER!!
And what the hell are these pants-thingies you put on me?!
They're called "monpeh"-- women's work pants.
THAT'S RIGHT! WE ARE NOT YOUR SLAVES! WELL, WORK HER TO DEATH ALL YOU LIKE, BUT I MOST CERTAINLY WILL NOT BE YOUR SLAVE!
PATIENCE, MY DEARS. WHILE YOU ALL WORK, I JUST MAY REMEMBER SOMETHING ABOUT THE TSUBASA.
YOU'D BETTER!! I'LL MAKE YOU REGRET IT IF YOU DON'T, YOU STUPID OLD MAN!!
Waaaa!!
MAYBE I SHOULD'VE BEEN THE ONE TO DO THE GARDEN WORK.
In charge of cleaning and laundry.

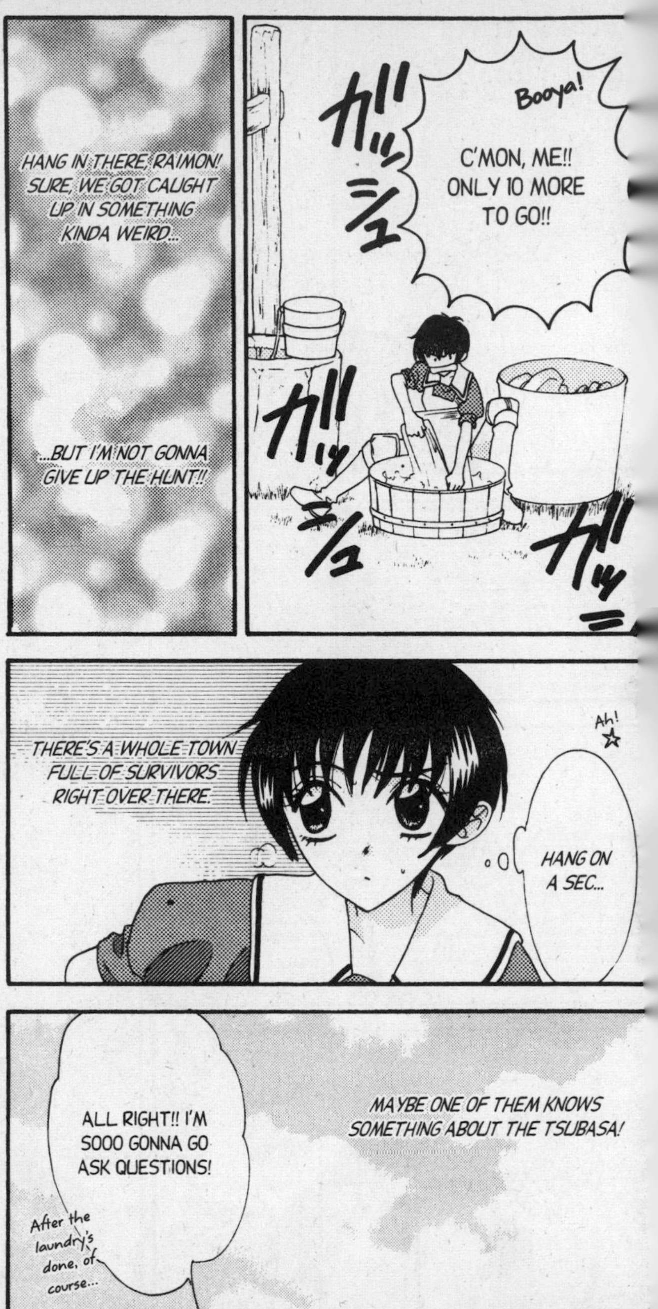
Booya!
C'MON, ME!! ONLY 10 MORE TO GO!!
ガッシュ
ガッシュ
ガッ
HANG IN THERE, RAIMON! SURE, WE GOT CAUGHT UP IN SOMETHING KINDA WEIRD...
...BUT I'M NOT GONNA GIVE UP THE HUNT!!
Ah!
HANG ON A SEC...
THERE'S A WHOLE TOWN FULL OF SURVIVORS RIGHT OVER THERE.
MAYBE ONE OF THEM KNOWS SOMETHING ABOUT THE TSUBASA!
ALL RIGHT!! I'M SOOO GONNA GO ASK QUESTIONS!
After the laundry's done, of course...

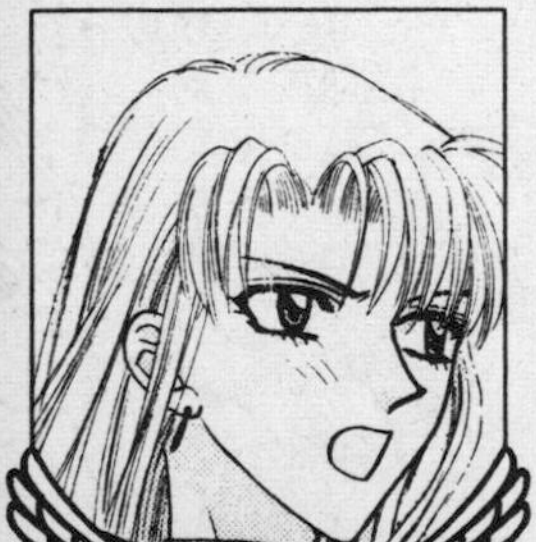

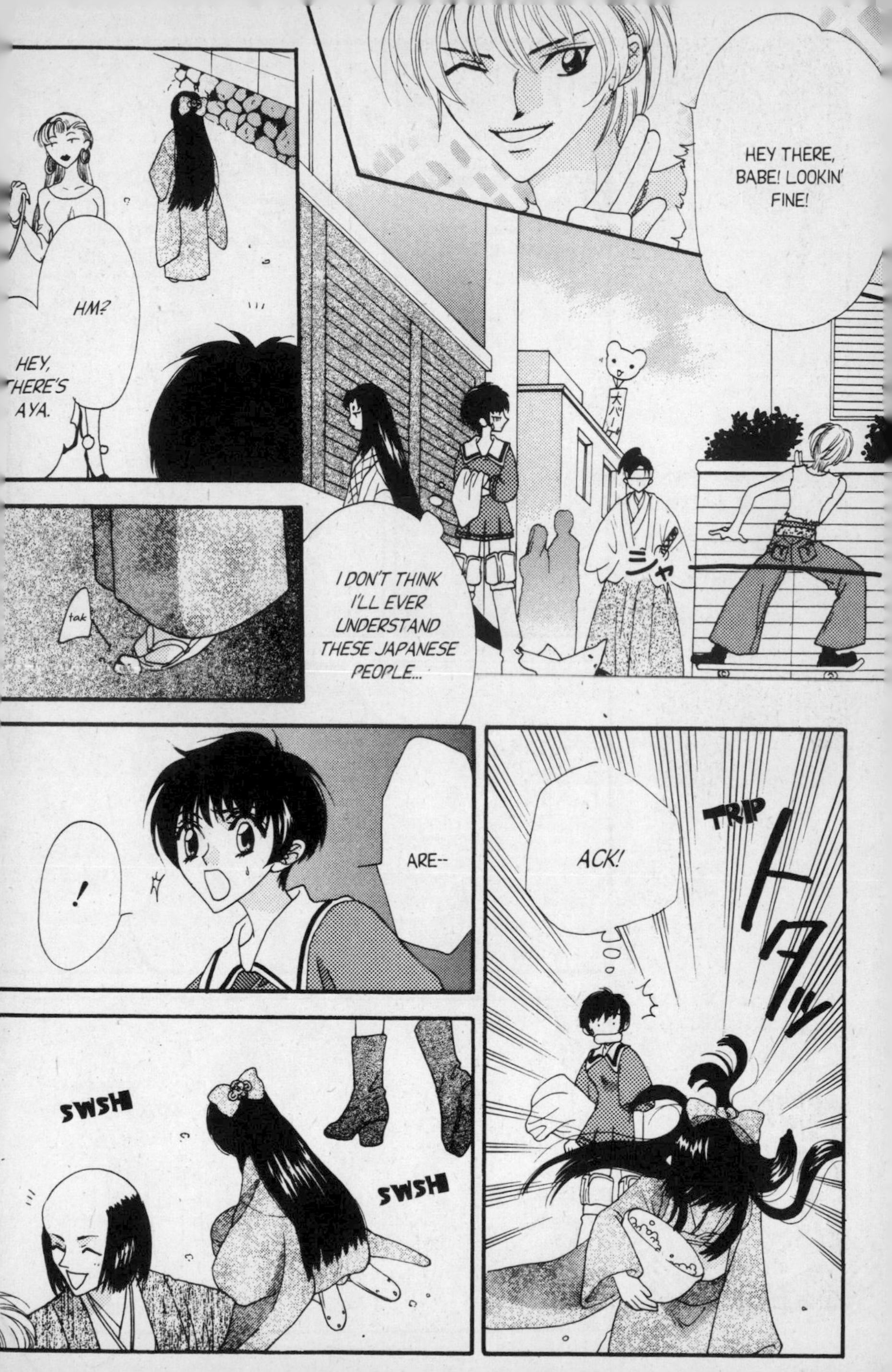

HEY THERE, BABE! LOOKIN' FINE!
シャ
I DON'T THINK I'LL EVER UNDERSTAND THESE JAPANESE PEOPLE...
HM?
HEY, THERE'S AYA.
tak
ACK!
TRIP
トタッ
ARE--
!
SWSH
SWSH

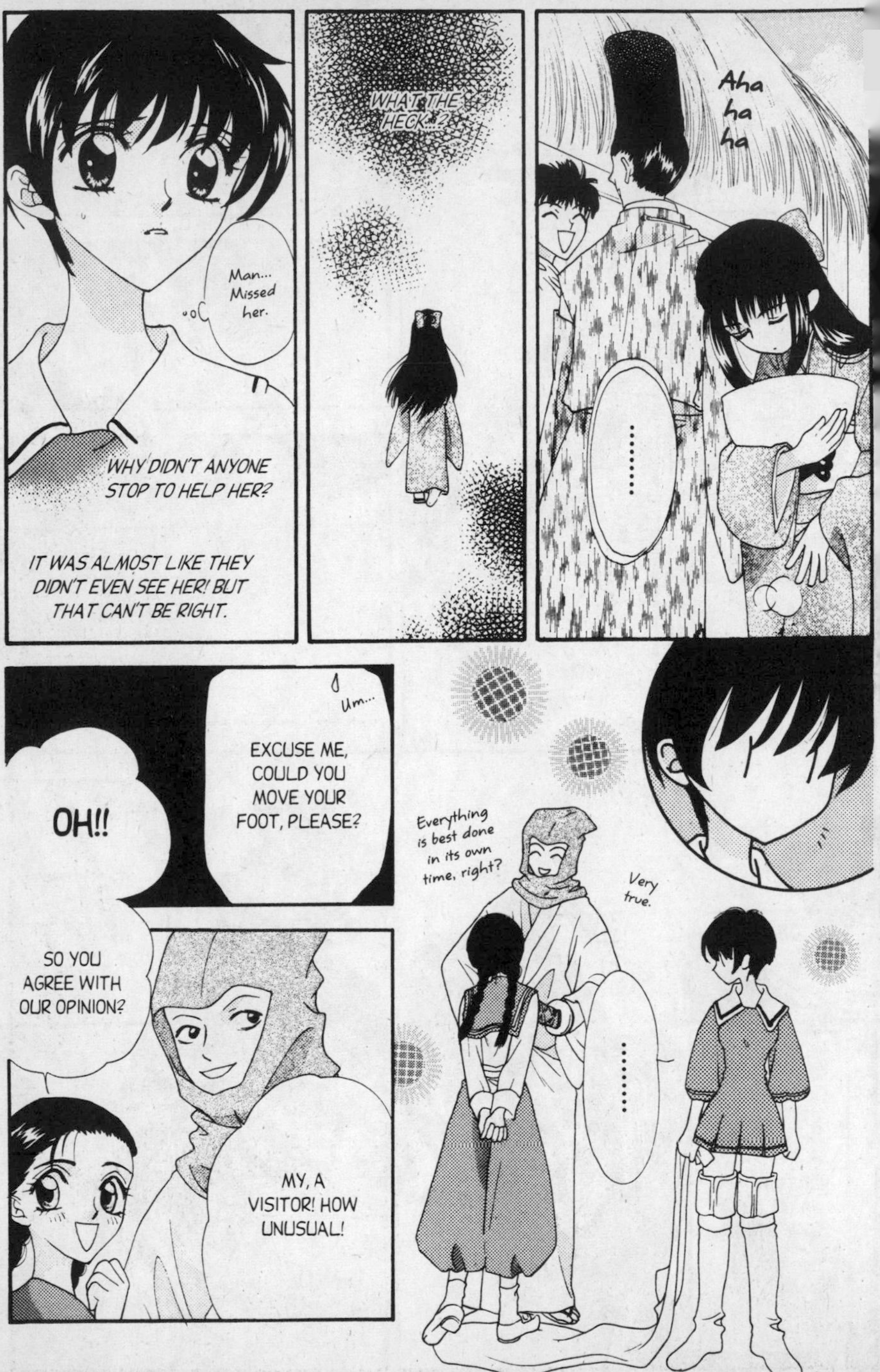
Aha ha ha
......
WHAT THE HECK...?
Man... Missed her.
WHY DIDN'T ANYONE STOP TO HELP HER?
IT WAS ALMOST LIKE THEY DIDN'T EVEN SEE HER! BUT THAT CAN'T BE RIGHT.
Everything is best done in its own time, right?
Very true.
......
Um...
EXCUSE ME, COULD YOU MOVE YOUR FOOT, PLEASE?
OH!!
SO YOU AGREE WITH OUR OPINION?
MY, A VISITOR! HOW UNUSUAL!

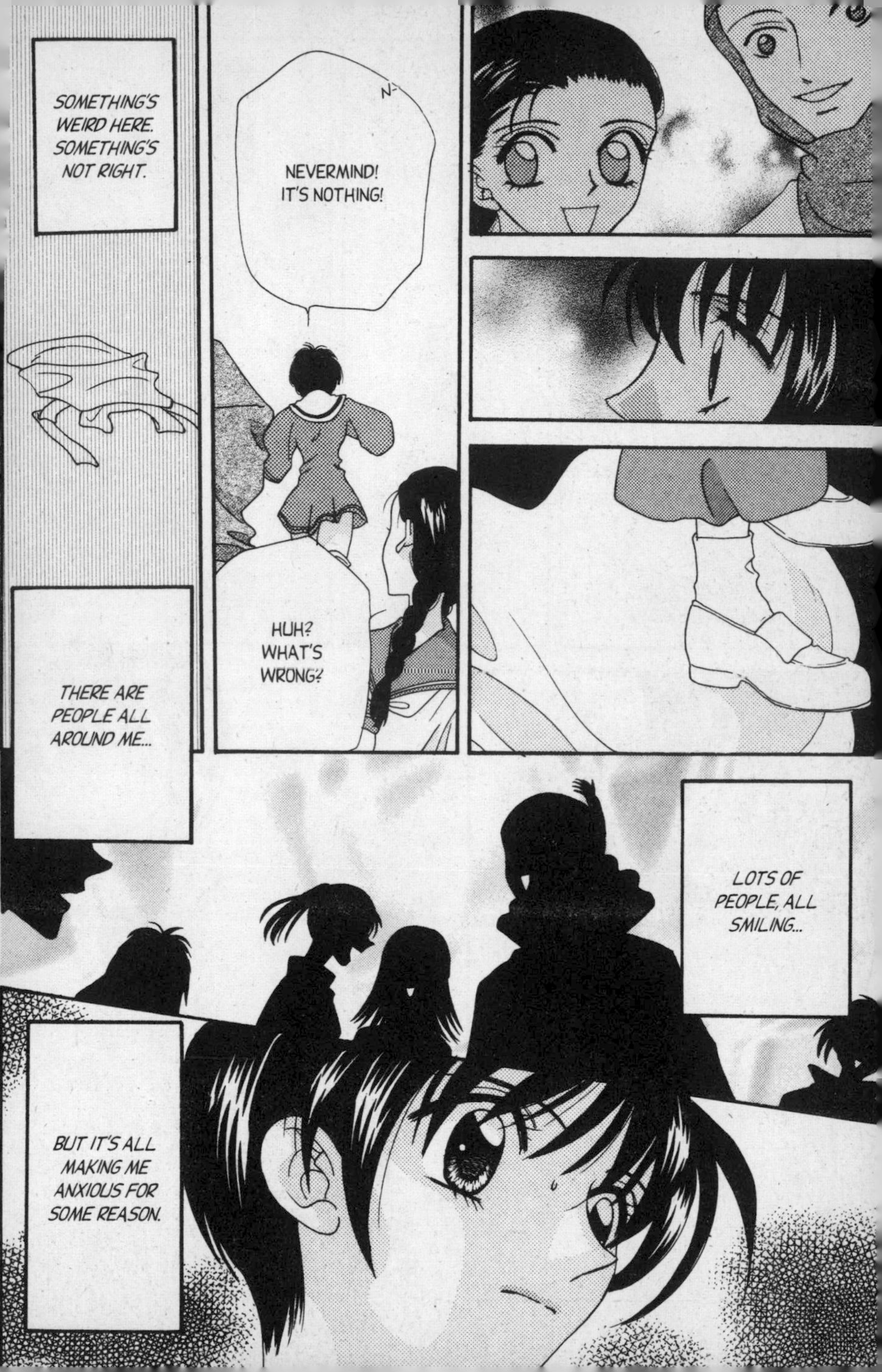
N-
NEVERMIND! IT'S NOTHING!
HUH? WHAT'S WRONG?
SOMETHING'S WEIRD HERE. SOMETHING'S NOT RIGHT.
THERE ARE PEOPLE ALL AROUND ME...
LOTS OF PEOPLE, ALL SMILING...
BUT IT'S ALL MAKING ME ANXIOUS FOR SOME REASON.

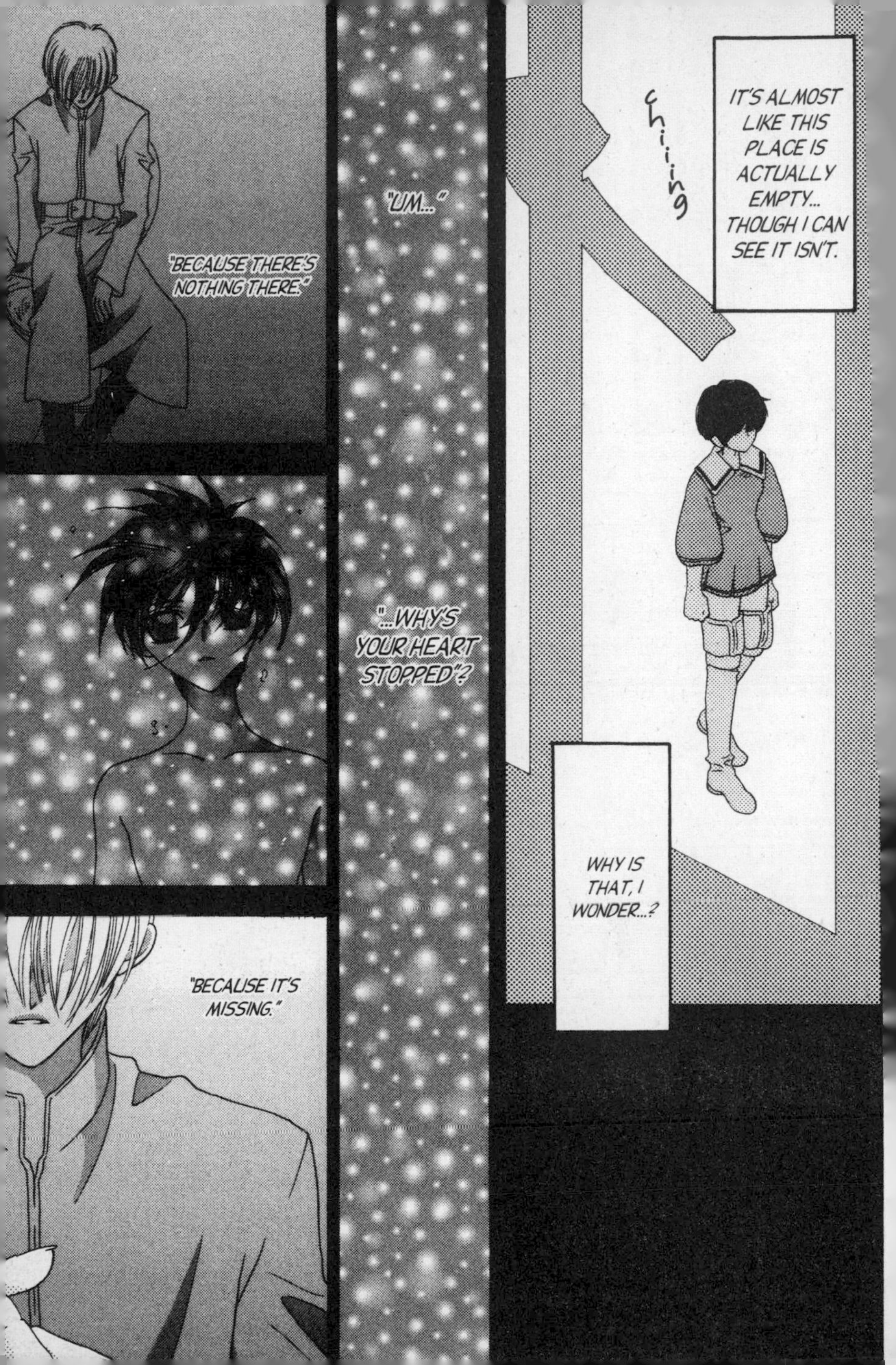
chiiing
IT'S ALMOST LIKE THIS PLACE IS ACTUALLY EMPTY... THOUGH I CAN SEE IT ISN'T.
WHY IS THAT, I WONDER...?
"UM..."
"...WHY'S YOUR HEART STOPPED"?
"BECAUSE THERE'S NOTHING THERE."
"BECAUSE IT'S MISSING."

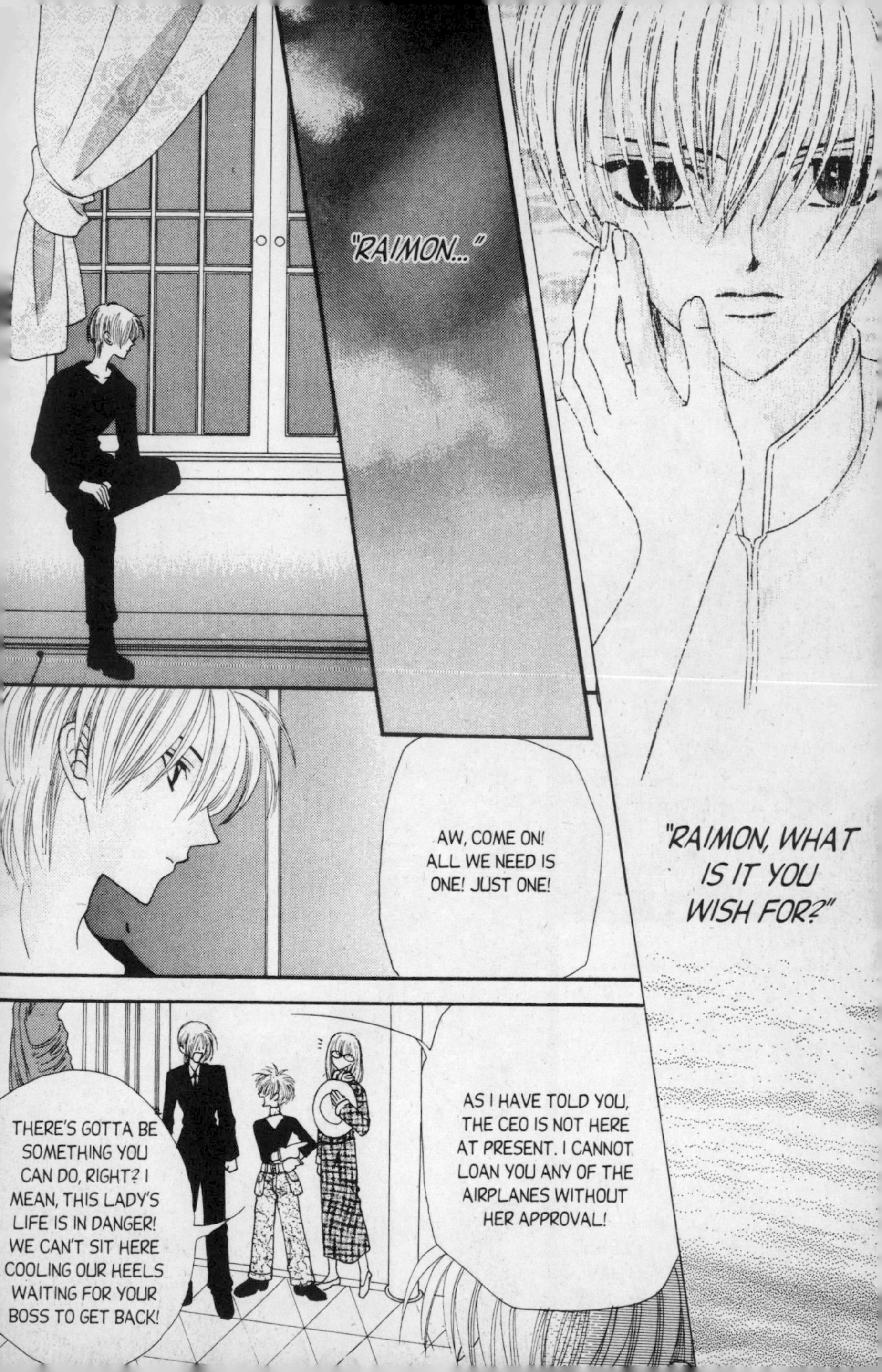
"RAIMON, WHAT IS IT YOU WISH FOR?"
"RAIMON..."
AW, COME ON! ALL WE NEED IS ONE! JUST ONE!
AS I HAVE TOLD YOU, THE CEO IS NOT HERE AT PRESENT. I CANNOT LOAN YOU ANY OF THE AIRPLANES WITHOUT HER APPROVAL!
THERE'S GOTTA BE SOMETHING YOU CAN DO, RIGHT? I MEAN, THIS LADY'S LIFE IS IN DANGER! WE CAN'T SIT HERE COOLING OUR HEELS WAITING FOR YOUR BOSS TO GET BACK!

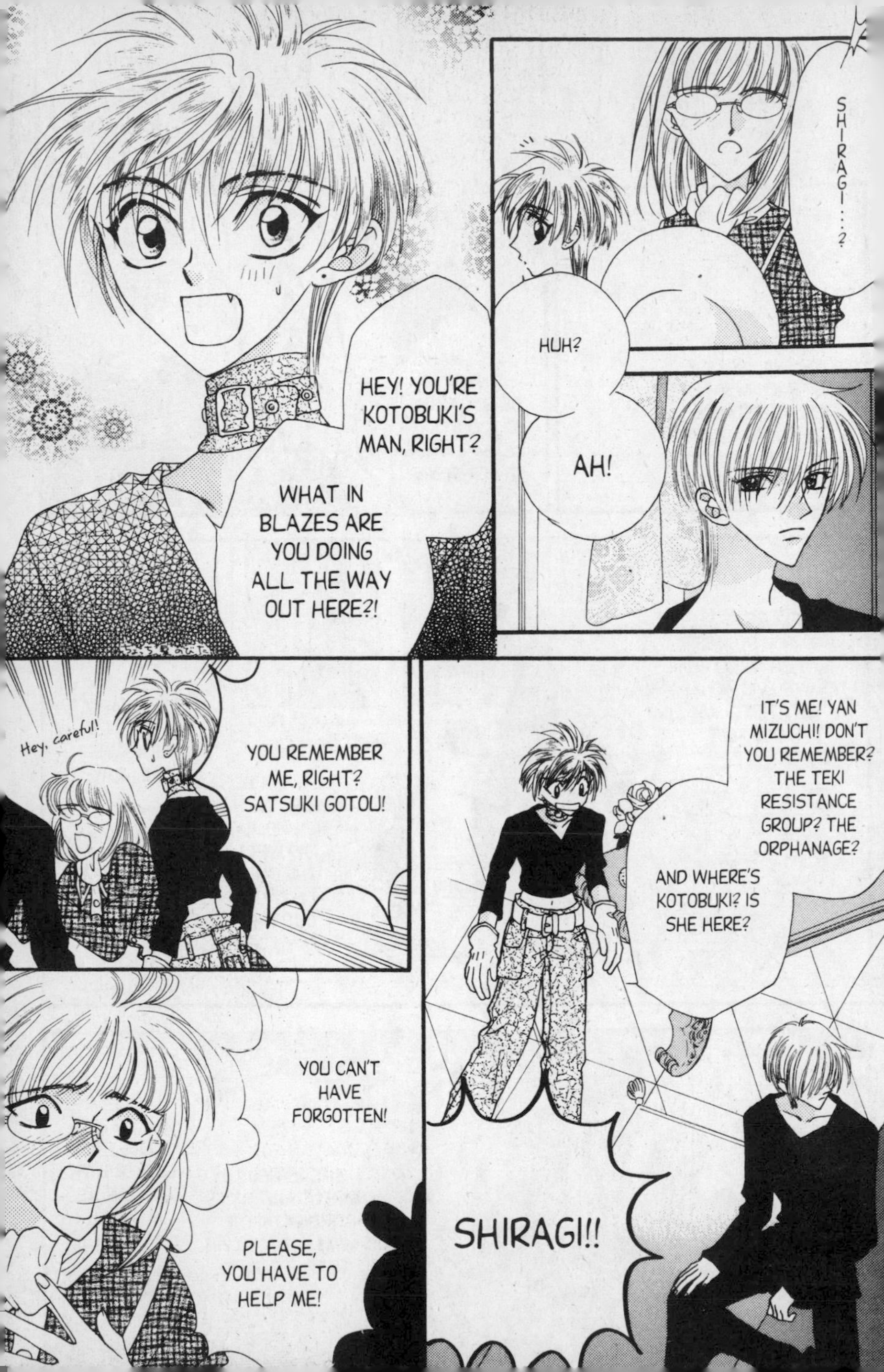
SHIRAGI...?
HUH?
AH!
HEY! YOU'RE KOTOBUKI'S MAN, RIGHT?
WHAT IN BLAZES ARE YOU DOING ALL THE WAY OUT HERE?!
IT'S ME! YAN MIZUCHI! DON'T YOU REMEMBER? THE TEKI RESISTANCE GROUP? THE ORPHANAGE?
AND WHERE'S KOTOBUKI? IS SHE HERE?
SHIRAGI!!
Hey, careful!
YOU REMEMBER ME, RIGHT? SATSUKI GOTOU!
YOU CAN'T HAVE FORGOTTEN!
PLEASE, YOU HAVE TO HELP ME!

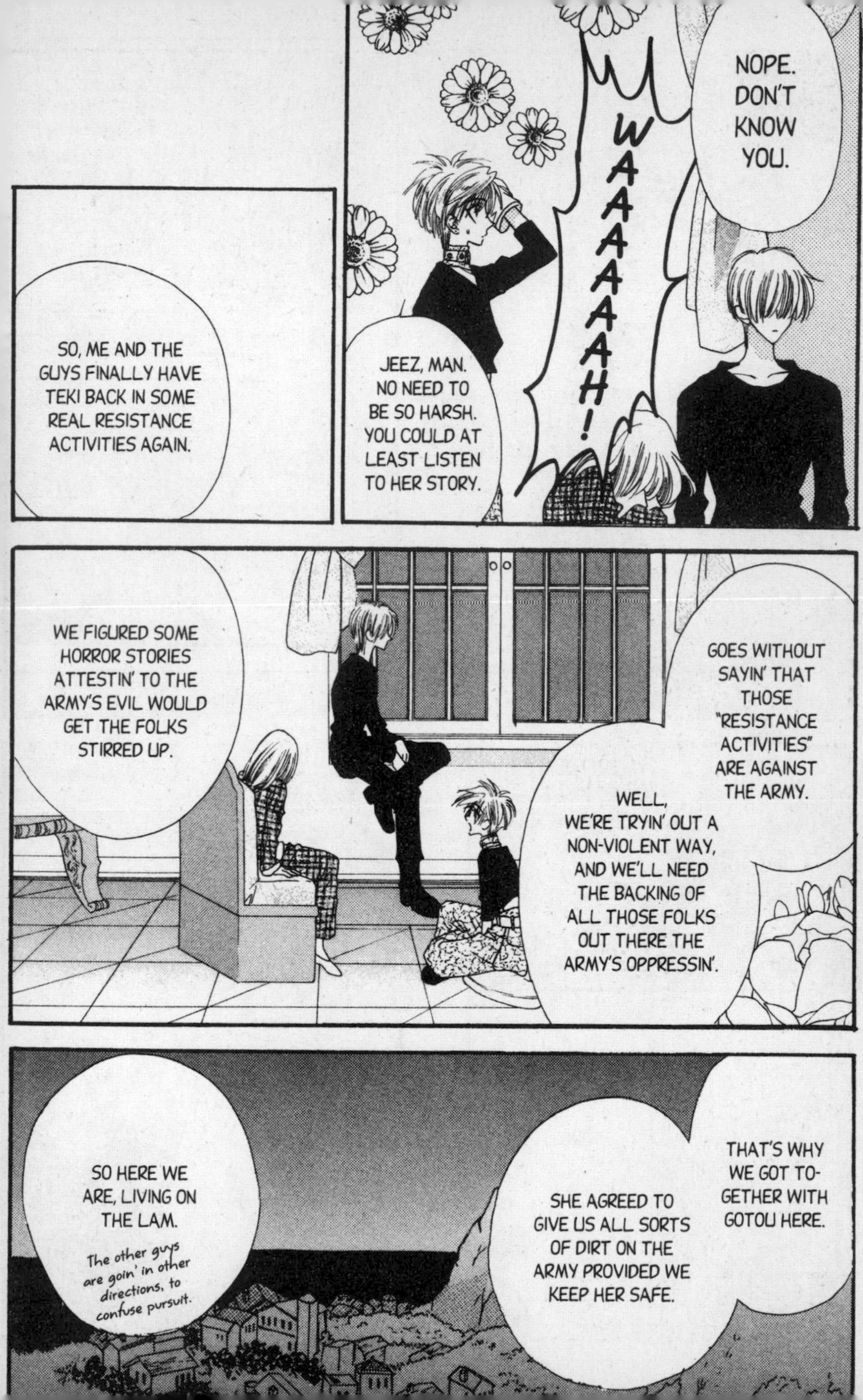
NOPE. DON'T KNOW YOU.
WAAAAAAAH!
JEEZ, MAN. NO NEED TO BE SO HARSH. YOU COULD AT LEAST LISTEN TO HER STORY.
SO, ME AND THE GUYS FINALLY HAVE TEKI BACK IN SOME REAL RESISTANCE ACTIVITIES AGAIN.
GOES WITHOUT SAYIN' THAT THOSE "RESISTANCE ACTIVITIES" ARE AGAINST THE ARMY.
WELL, WE'RE TRYIN' OUT A NON-VIOLENT WAY, AND WE'LL NEED THE BACKING OF ALL THOSE FOLKS OUT THERE THE ARMY'S OPPRESSIN'.
WE FIGURED SOME HORROR STORIES ATTESTIN' TO THE ARMY'S EVIL WOULD GET THE FOLKS STIRRED UP.
THAT'S WHY WE GOT TO-GETHER WITH GOTOU HERE.
SHE AGREED TO GIVE US ALL SORTS OF DIRT ON THE ARMY PROVIDED WE KEEP HER SAFE.
SO HERE WE ARE, LIVING ON THE LAM.
The other guys are goin' in other directions, to confuse pursuit.

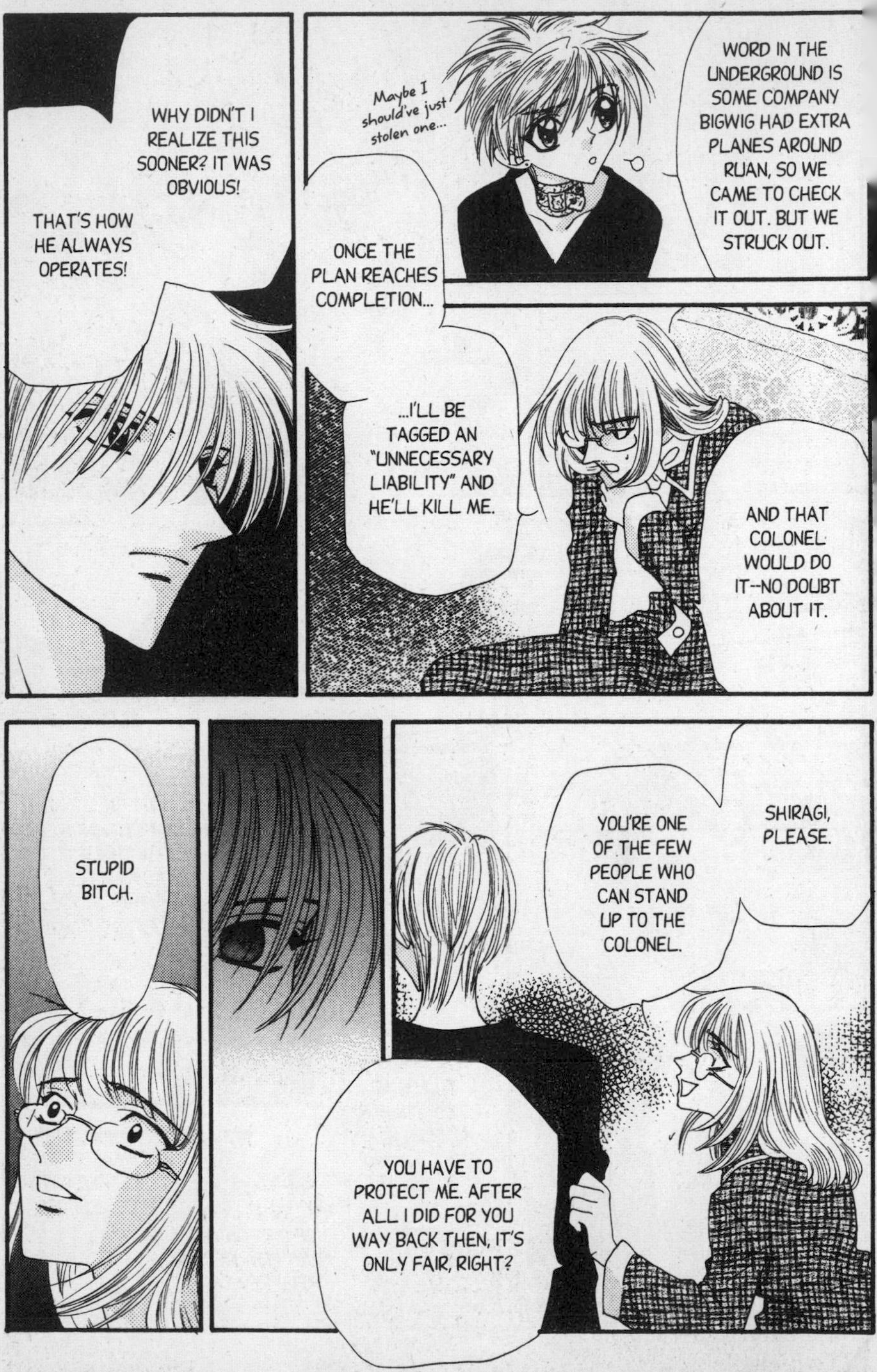
WORD IN THE UNDERGROUND IS SOME COMPANY BIGWIG HAD EXTRA PLANES AROUND RUAN, SO WE CAME TO CHECK IT OUT. BUT WE STRUCK OUT.
Maybe I should've just stolen one...
ONCE THE PLAN REACHES COMPLETION...
...I'LL BE TAGGED AN "UNNECESSARY LIABILITY" AND HE'LL KILL ME.
AND THAT COLONEL WOULD DO IT--NO DOUBT ABOUT IT.
WHY DIDN'T I REALIZE THIS SOONER? IT WAS OBVIOUS!
THAT'S HOW HE ALWAYS OPERATES!
SHIRAGI, PLEASE.
YOU'RE ONE OF THE FEW PEOPLE WHO CAN STAND UP TO THE COLONEL.
YOU HAVE TO PROTECT ME. AFTER ALL I DID FOR YOU WAY BACK THEN, IT'S ONLY FAIR, RIGHT?
STUPID BITCH.

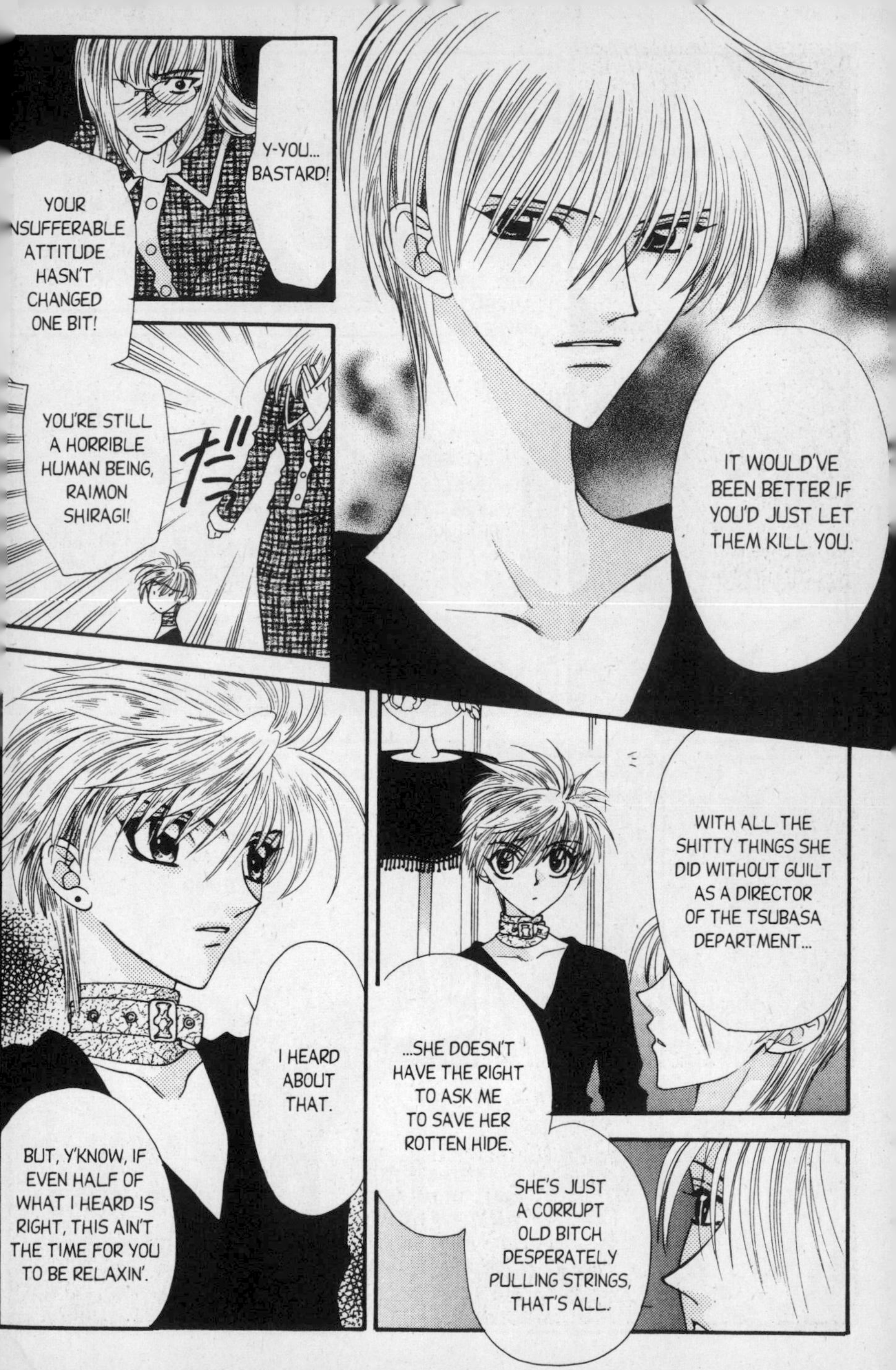
IT WOULD'VE BEEN BETTER IF YOU'D JUST LET THEM KILL YOU.
Y-YOU... BASTARD!
YOUR INSUFFERABLE ATTITUDE HASN'T CHANGED ONE BIT!
だっ
YOU'RE STILL A HORRIBLE HUMAN BEING, RAIMON SHIRAGI!
WITH ALL THE SHITTY THINGS SHE DID WITHOUT GUILT AS A DIRECTOR OF THE TSUBASA DEPARTMENT...
...SHE DOESN'T HAVE THE RIGHT TO ASK ME TO SAVE HER ROTTEN HIDE.
SHE'S JUST A CORRUPT OLD BITCH DESPERATELY PULLING STRINGS, THAT'S ALL.
I HEARD ABOUT THAT.
BUT, Y'KNOW, IF EVEN HALF OF WHAT I HEARD IS RIGHT, THIS AIN'T THE TIME FOR YOU TO BE RELAXIN'.

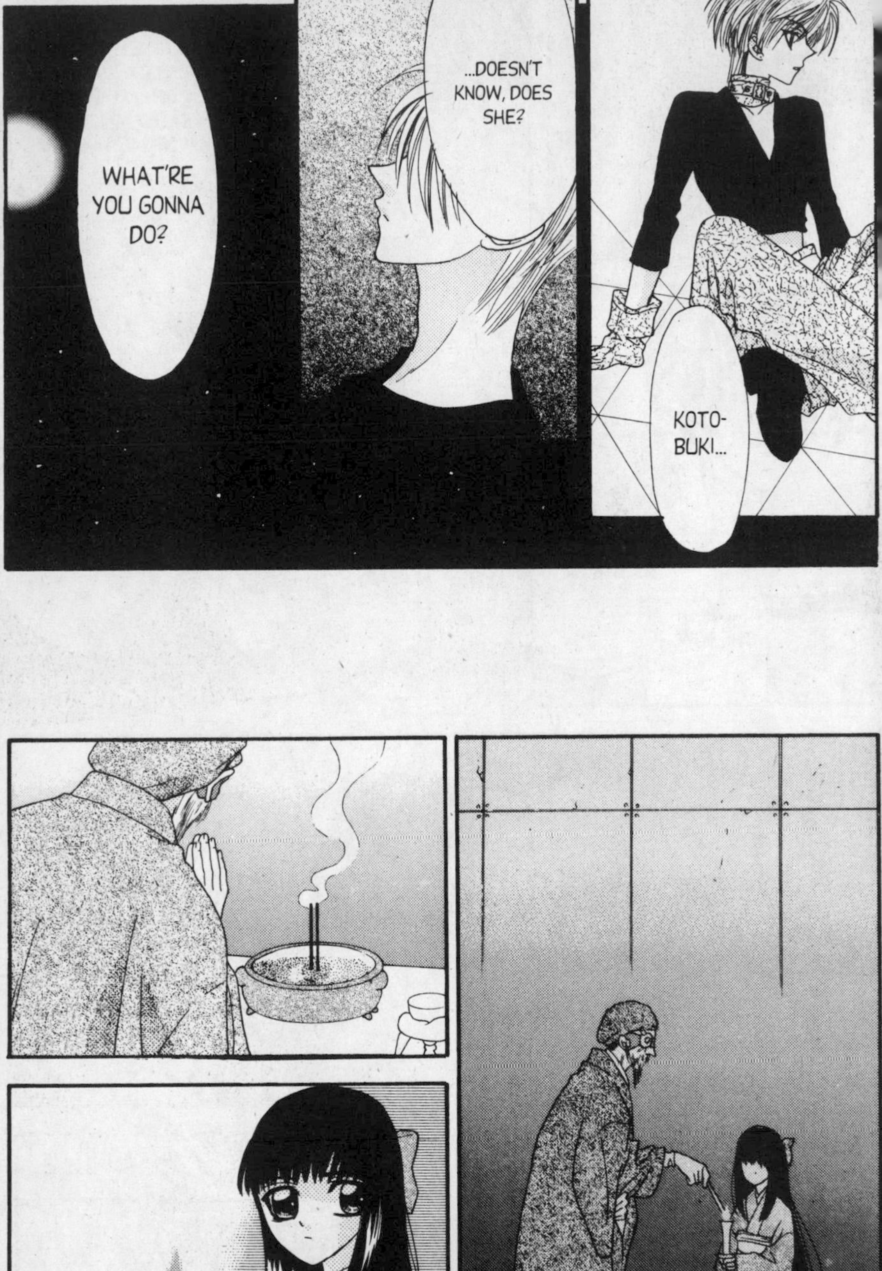
KOTO-BUKI...
...DOESN'T KNOW, DOES SHE?
WHAT'RE YOU GONNA DO?

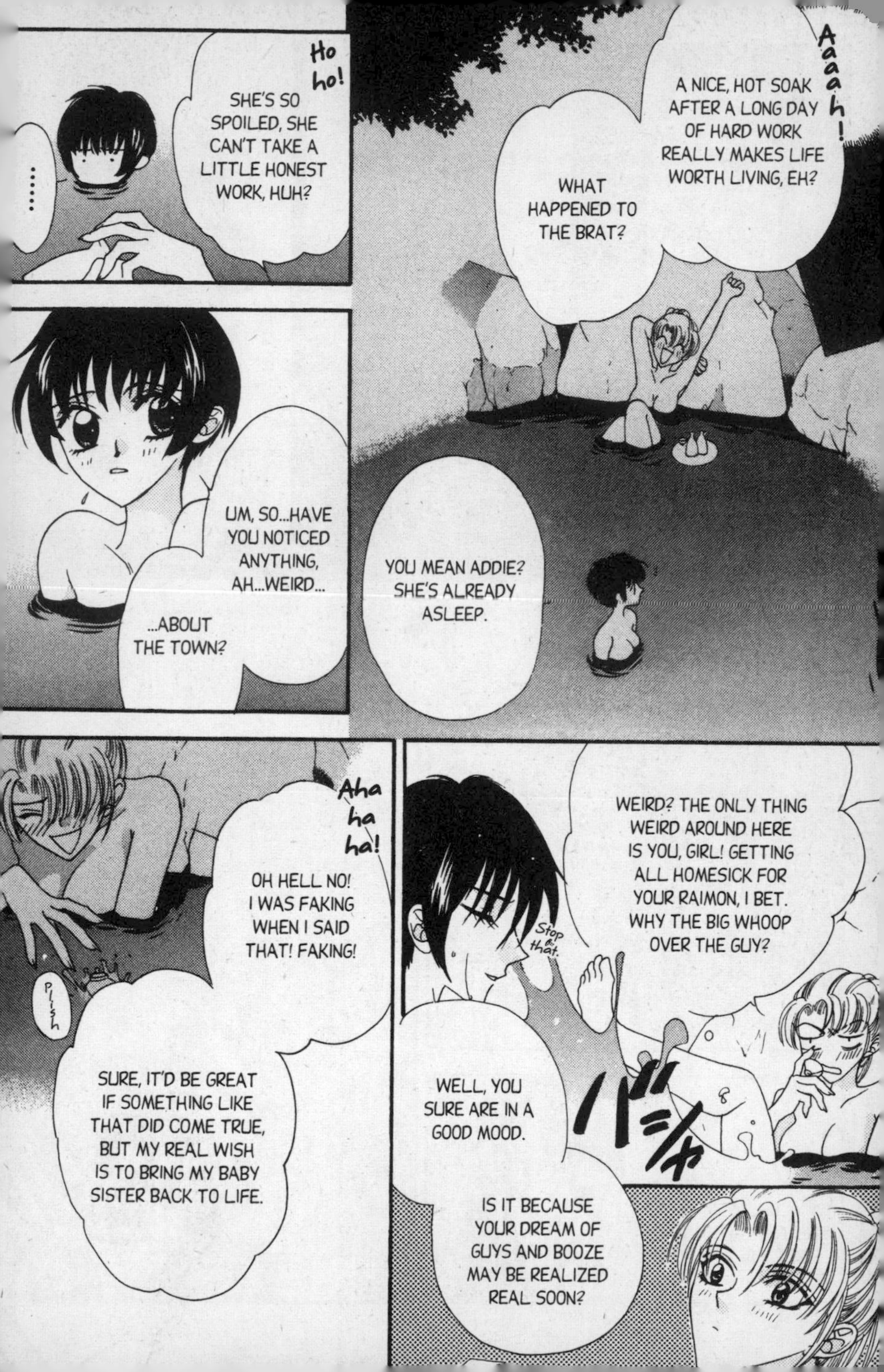
Aaaah!
A NICE, HOT SOAK AFTER A LONG DAY OF HARD WORK REALLY MAKES LIFE WORTH LIVING, EH?
WHAT HAPPENED TO THE BRAT?
YOU MEAN ADDIE? SHE'S ALREADY ASLEEP.
Ho ho!
SHE'S SO SPOILED, SHE CAN'T TAKE A LITTLE HONEST WORK, HUH?
......
UM, SO...HAVE YOU NOTICED ANYTHING, AH...WEIRD...
...ABOUT THE TOWN?
WEIRD? THE ONLY THING WEIRD AROUND HERE IS YOU, GIRL! GETTING ALL HOMESICK FOR YOUR RAIMON, I BET. WHY THE BIG WHOOP OVER THE GUY?
Stop that.
WELL, YOU SURE ARE IN A GOOD MOOD.
IS IT BECAUSE YOUR DREAM OF GUYS AND BOOZE MAY BE REALIZED REAL SOON?
Aha ha ha!
OH HELL NO! I WAS FAKING WHEN I SAID THAT! FAKING!
Plish
SURE, IT'D BE GREAT IF SOMETHING LIKE THAT DID COME TRUE, BUT MY REAL WISH IS TO BRING MY BABY SISTER BACK TO LIFE.

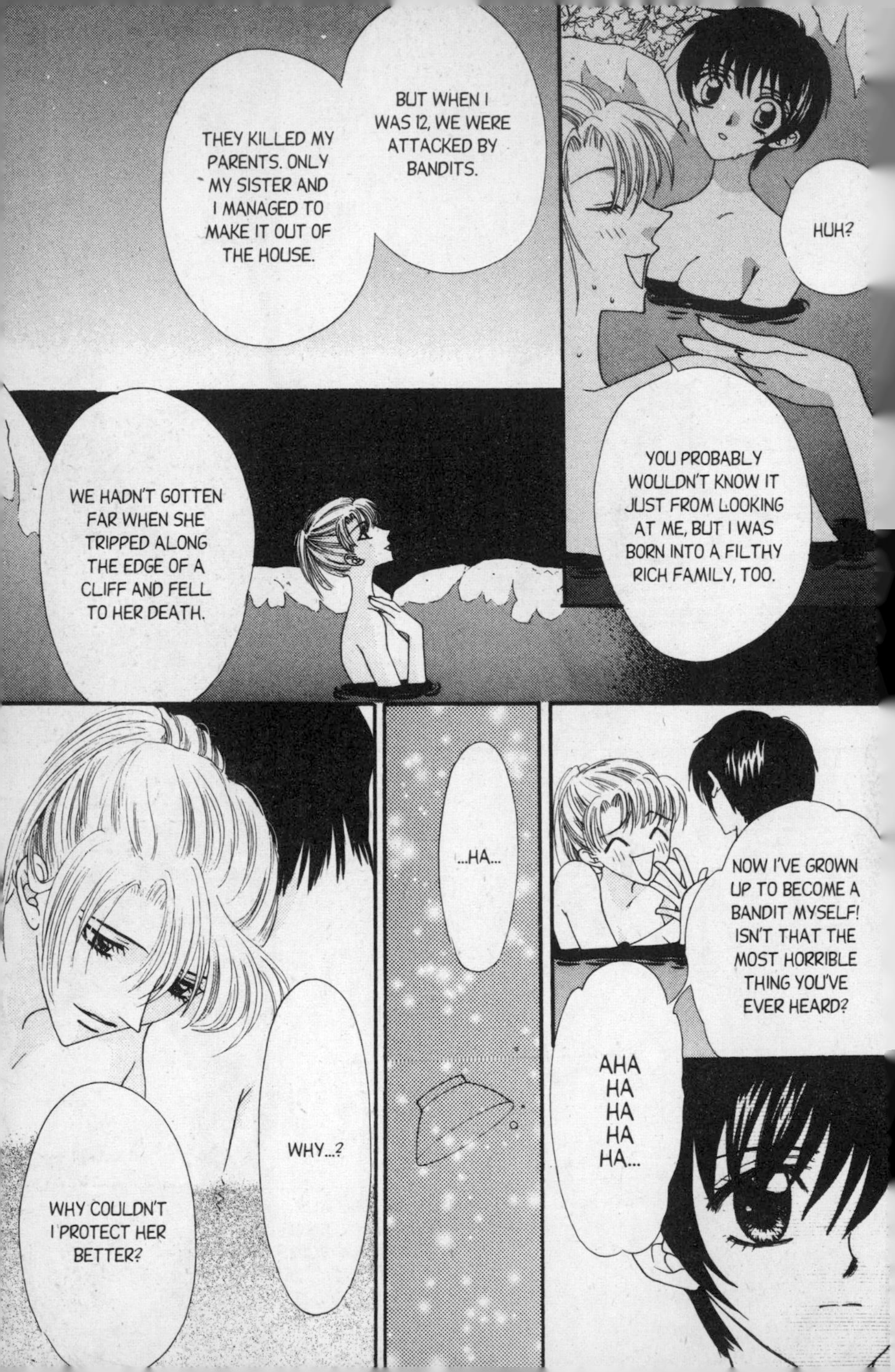
HUH?
YOU PROBABLY WOULDN'T KNOW IT JUST FROM LOOKING AT ME, BUT I WAS BORN INTO A FILTHY RICH FAMILY, TOO.
BUT WHEN I WAS 12, WE WERE ATTACKED BY BANDITS.
THEY KILLED MY PARENTS. ONLY MY SISTER AND I MANAGED TO MAKE IT OUT OF THE HOUSE.
WE HADN'T GOTTEN FAR WHEN SHE TRIPPED ALONG THE EDGE OF A CLIFF AND FELL TO HER DEATH.
NOW I'VE GROWN UP TO BECOME A BANDIT MYSELF! ISN'T THAT THE MOST HORRIBLE THING YOU'VE EVER HEARD?
AHA HA HA HA HA...
...HA...
WHY...?
WHY COULDN'T I PROTECT HER BETTER?

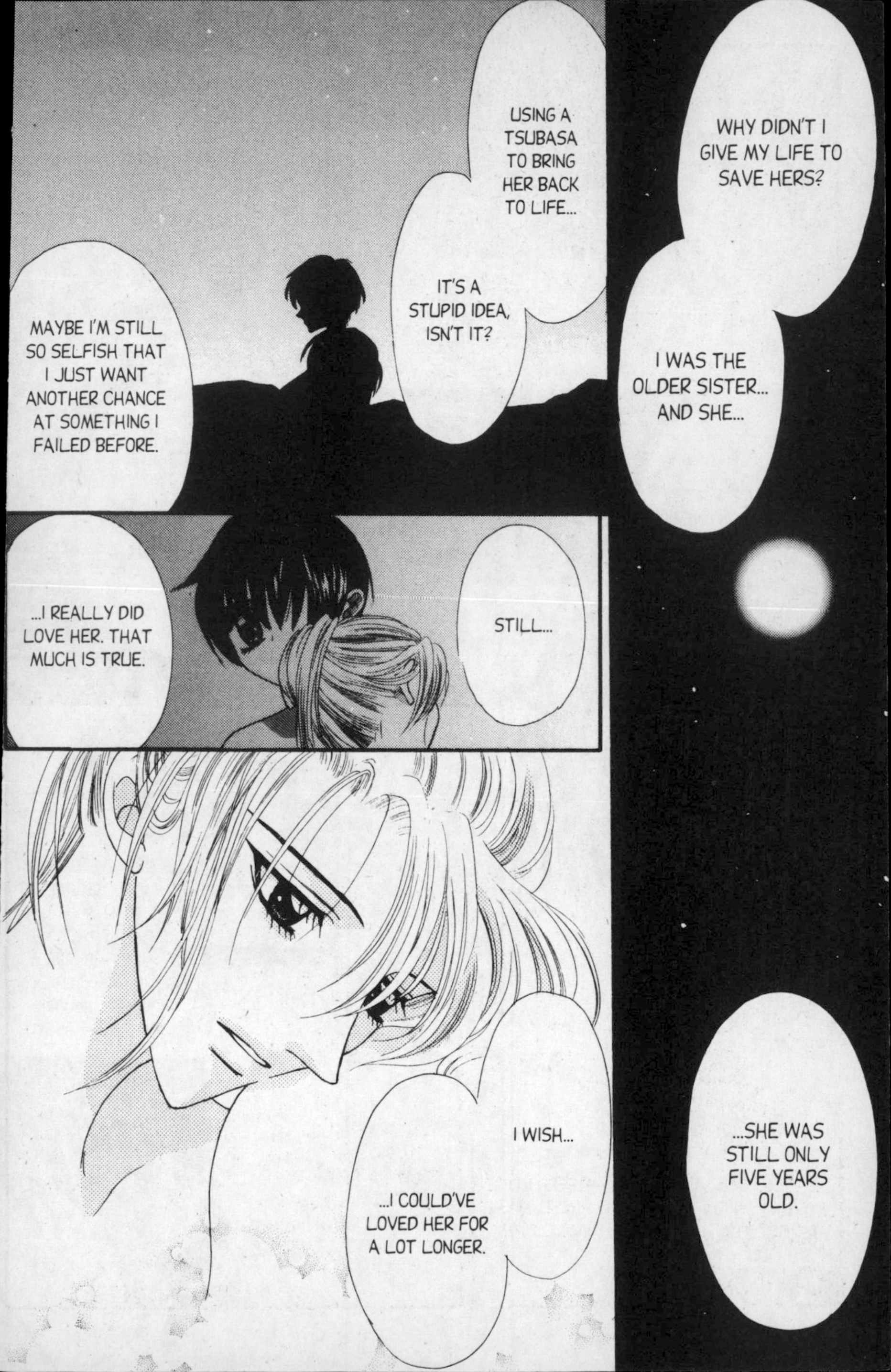
WHY DIDN'T I GIVE MY LIFE TO SAVE HERS?
I WAS THE OLDER SISTER... AND SHE...
...SHE WAS STILL ONLY FIVE YEARS OLD.
USING A TSUBASA TO BRING HER BACK TO LIFE...
IT'S A STUPID IDEA, ISN'T IT?
MAYBE I'M STILL SO SELFISH THAT I JUST WANT ANOTHER CHANCE AT SOMETHING I FAILED BEFORE.
STILL...
...I REALLY DID LOVE HER. THAT MUCH IS TRUE.
I WISH...
...I COULD'VE LOVED HER FOR A LOT LONGER.

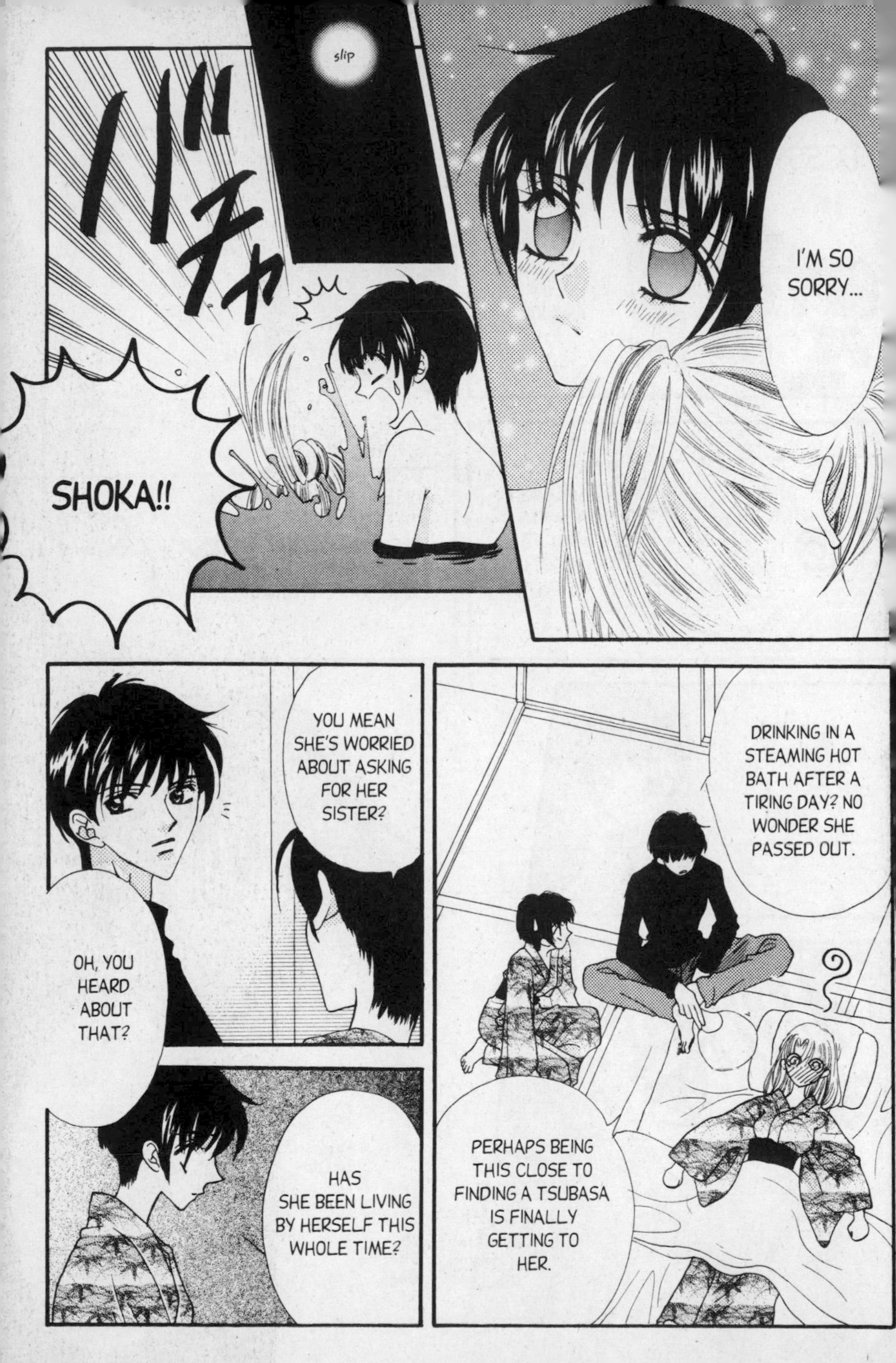
I'M SO SORRY...
slip
バチャ
SHOKA!!
DRINKING IN A STEAMING HOT BATH AFTER A TIRING DAY? NO WONDER SHE PASSED OUT.
PERHAPS BEING THIS CLOSE TO FINDING A TSUBASA IS FINALLY GETTING TO HER.
YOU MEAN SHE'S WORRIED ABOUT ASKING FOR HER SISTER?
OH, YOU HEARD ABOUT THAT?
HAS SHE BEEN LIVING BY HERSELF THIS WHOLE TIME?

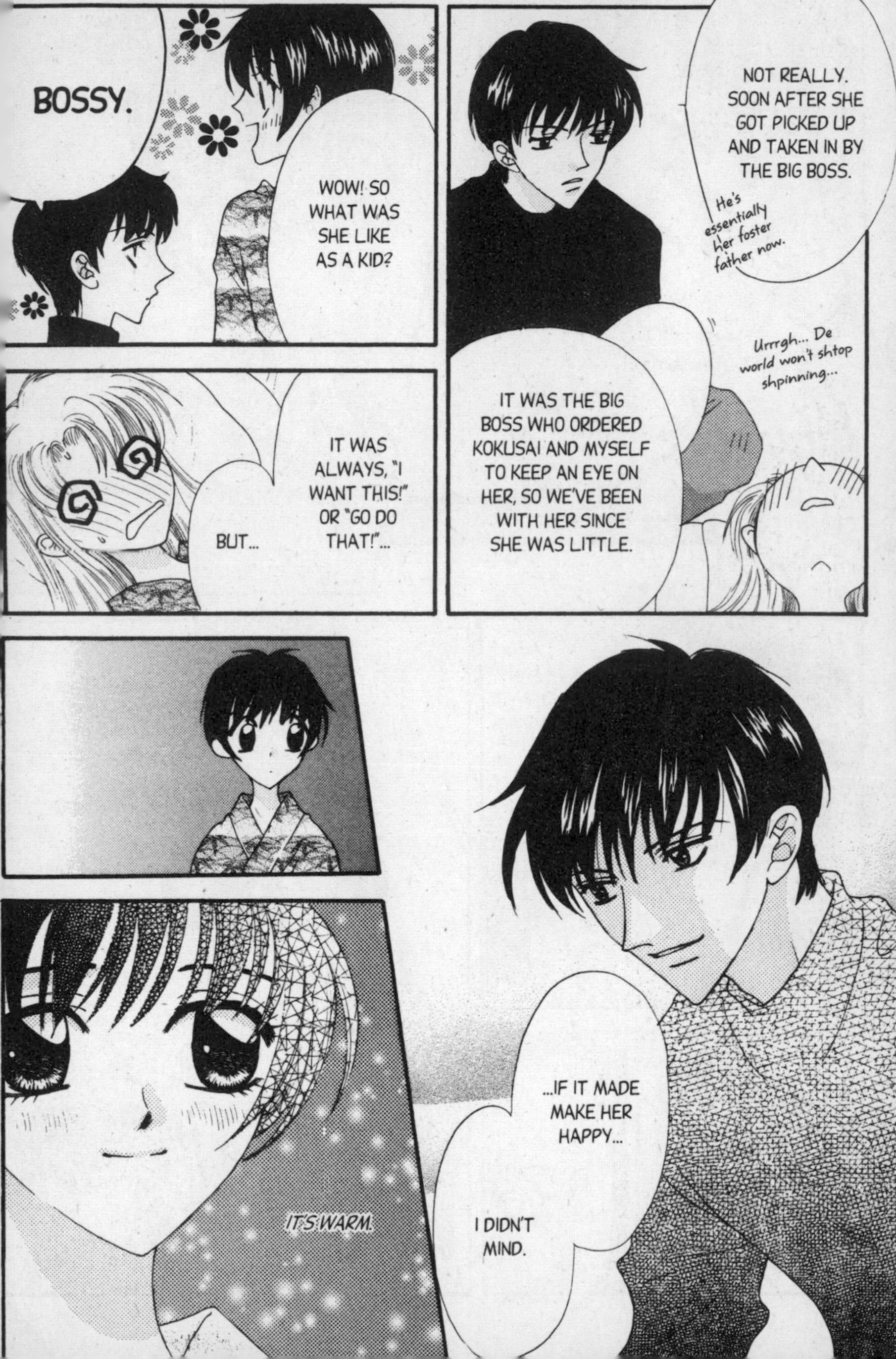
NOT REALLY. SOON AFTER SHE GOT PICKED UP AND TAKEN IN BY THE BIG BOSS.
He's essentially her foster father now.
Urrrgh... De world won't shtop shpinning...
IT WAS THE BIG BOSS WHO ORDERED KOKUSAI AND MYSELF TO KEEP AN EYE ON HER, SO WE'VE BEEN WITH HER SINCE SHE WAS LITTLE.
WOW! SO WHAT WAS SHE LIKE AS A KID?
BOSSY.
IT WAS ALWAYS, "I WANT THIS!" OR "GO DO THAT!"...
BUT...
...IF IT MADE MAKE HER HAPPY...
I DIDN'T MIND.
IT'S WARM.

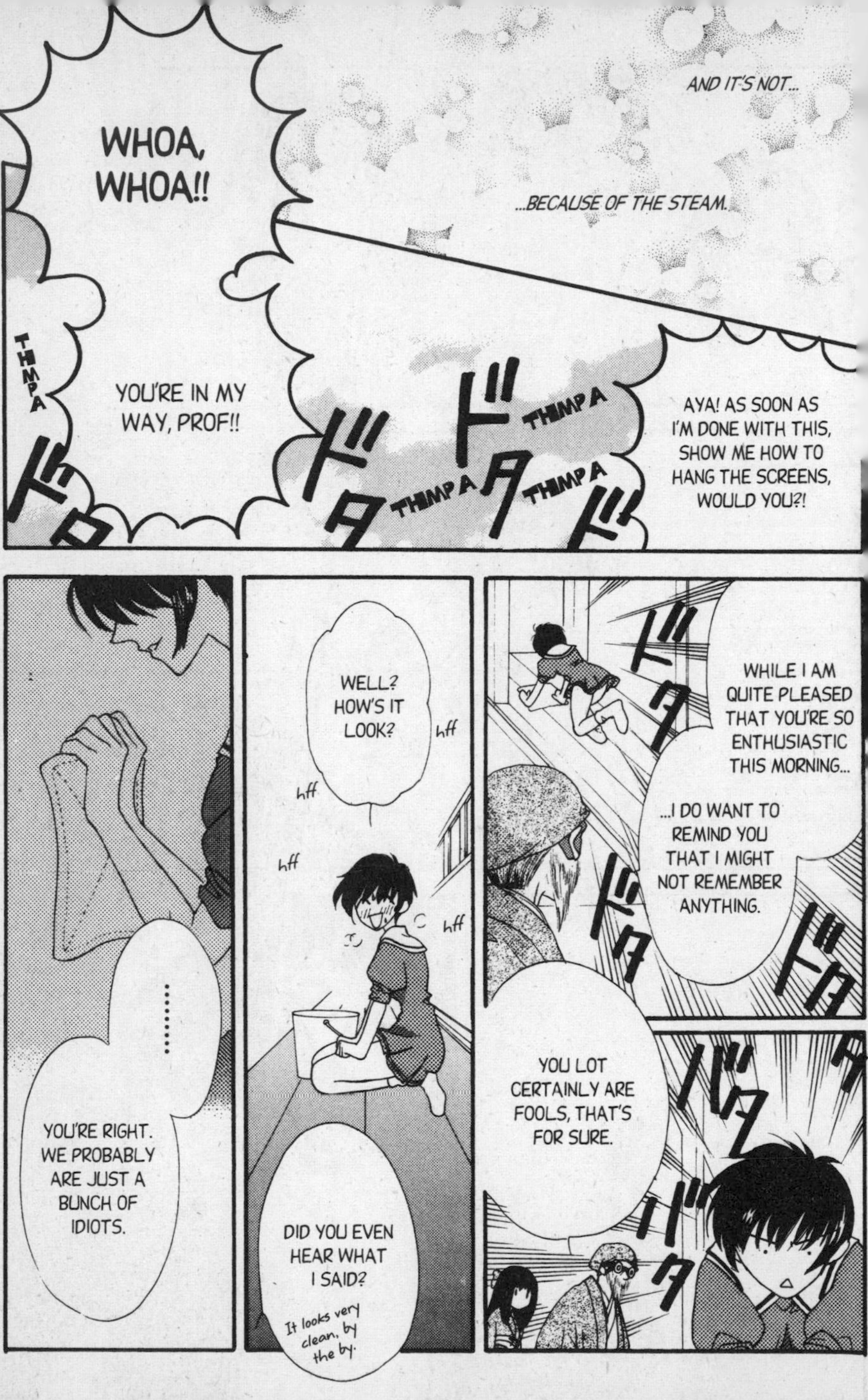
AND IT'S NOT...
...BECAUSE OF THE STEAM.
AYA! AS SOON AS I'M DONE WITH THIS, SHOW ME HOW TO HANG THE SCREENS, WOULD YOU?!
ドタ THIMPA
ドタ THIMPA
ドタ THIMPA
YOU'RE IN MY WAY, PROF!!
ドタ THIMPA
WHOA, WHOA!!
ドタ
WHILE I AM QUITE PLEASED THAT YOU'RE SO ENTHUSIASTIC THIS MORNING...
...I DO WANT TO REMIND YOU THAT I MIGHT NOT REMEMBER ANYTHING.
ドタ
ドタ
バタ
YOU LOT CERTAINLY ARE FOOLS, THAT'S FOR SURE.
バタ
WELL? HOW'S IT LOOK?
hff
hff
hff
hff
DID YOU EVEN HEAR WHAT I SAID?
It looks very clean, by the by.
......
YOU'RE RIGHT. WE PROBABLY ARE JUST A BUNCH OF IDIOTS.

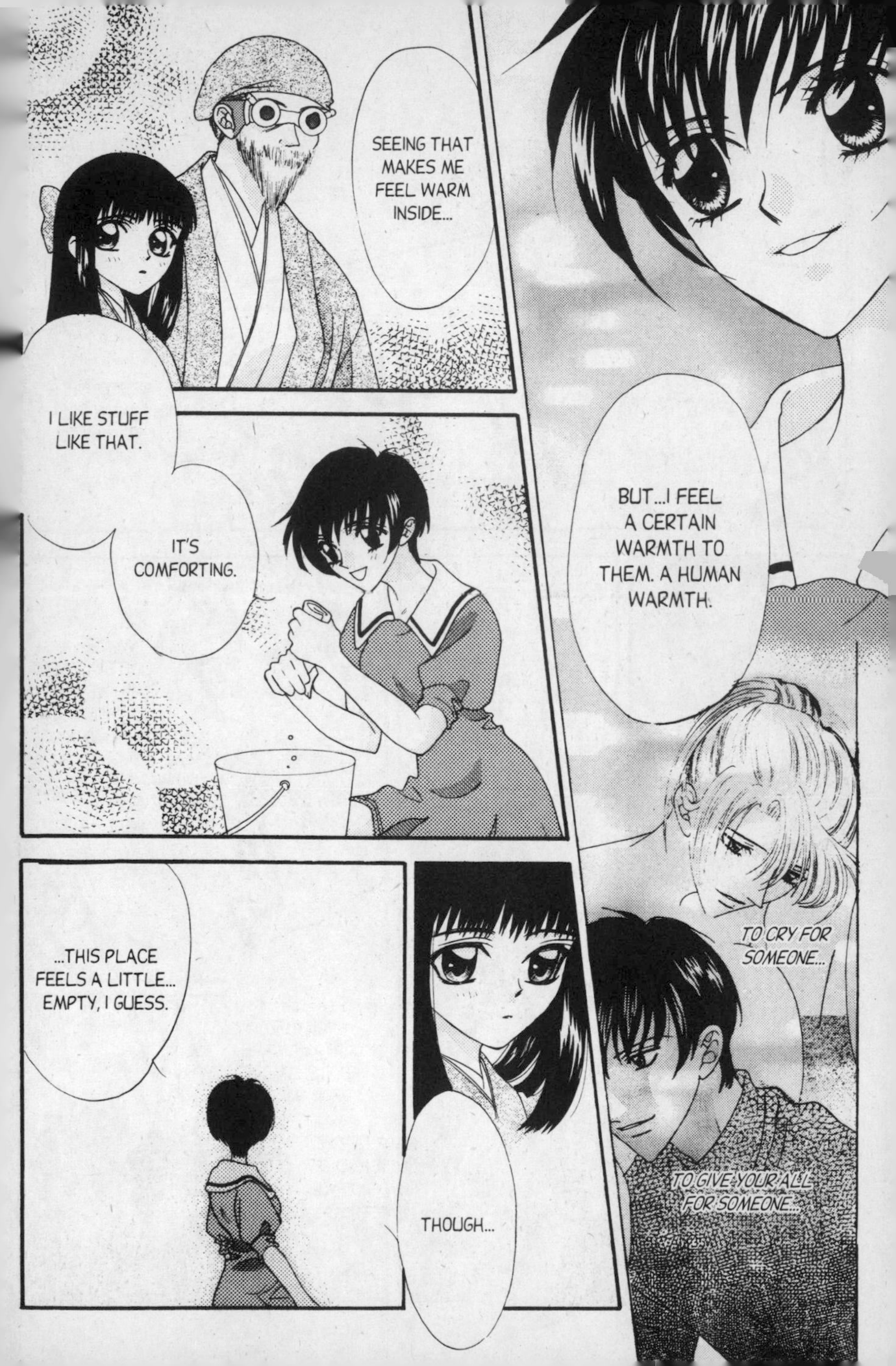
BUT...I FEEL A CERTAIN WARMTH TO THEM. A HUMAN WARMTH.
TO CRY FOR SOMEONE...
TO GIVE YOUR ALL FOR SOMEONE...
SEEING THAT MAKES ME FEEL WARM INSIDE...
I LIKE STUFF LIKE THAT.
IT'S COMFORTING.
THOUGH...
...THIS PLACE FEELS A LITTLE... EMPTY, I GUESS.

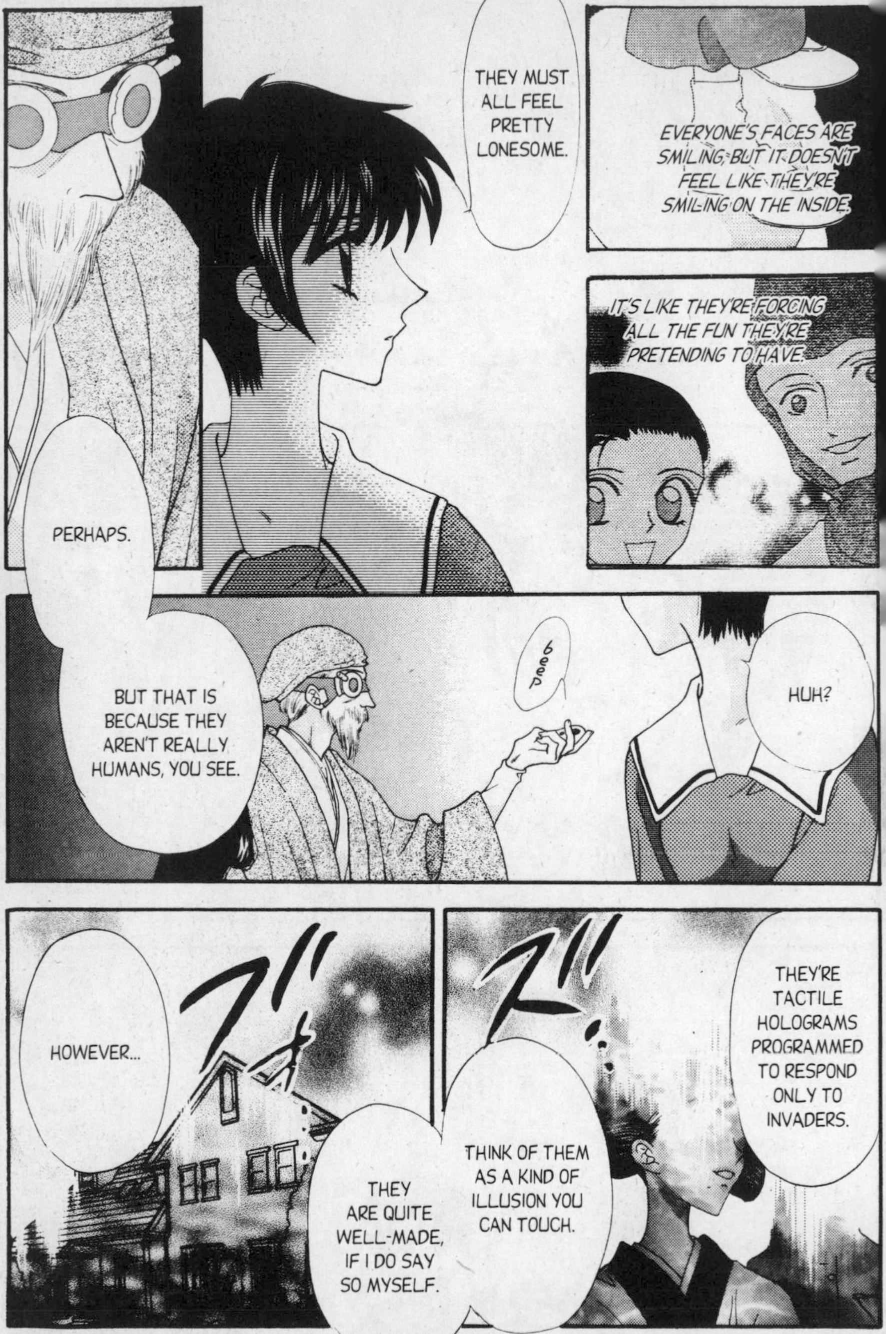
EVERYONE'S FACES ARE SMILING, BUT IT DOESN'T FEEL LIKE THEY'RE SMILING ON THE INSIDE.
IT'S LIKE THEY'RE FORCING ALL THE FUN THEY'RE PRETENDING TO HAVE.
THEY MUST ALL FEEL PRETTY LONESOME.
PERHAPS.
HUH?
beep
BUT THAT IS BECAUSE THEY AREN'T REALLY HUMANS, YOU SEE.
THEY'RE TACTILE HOLOGRAMS PROGRAMMED TO RESPOND ONLY TO INVADERS.
THINK OF THEM AS A KIND OF ILLUSION YOU CAN TOUCH.
THEY ARE QUITE WELL-MADE, IF I DO SAY SO MYSELF.
HOWEVER...

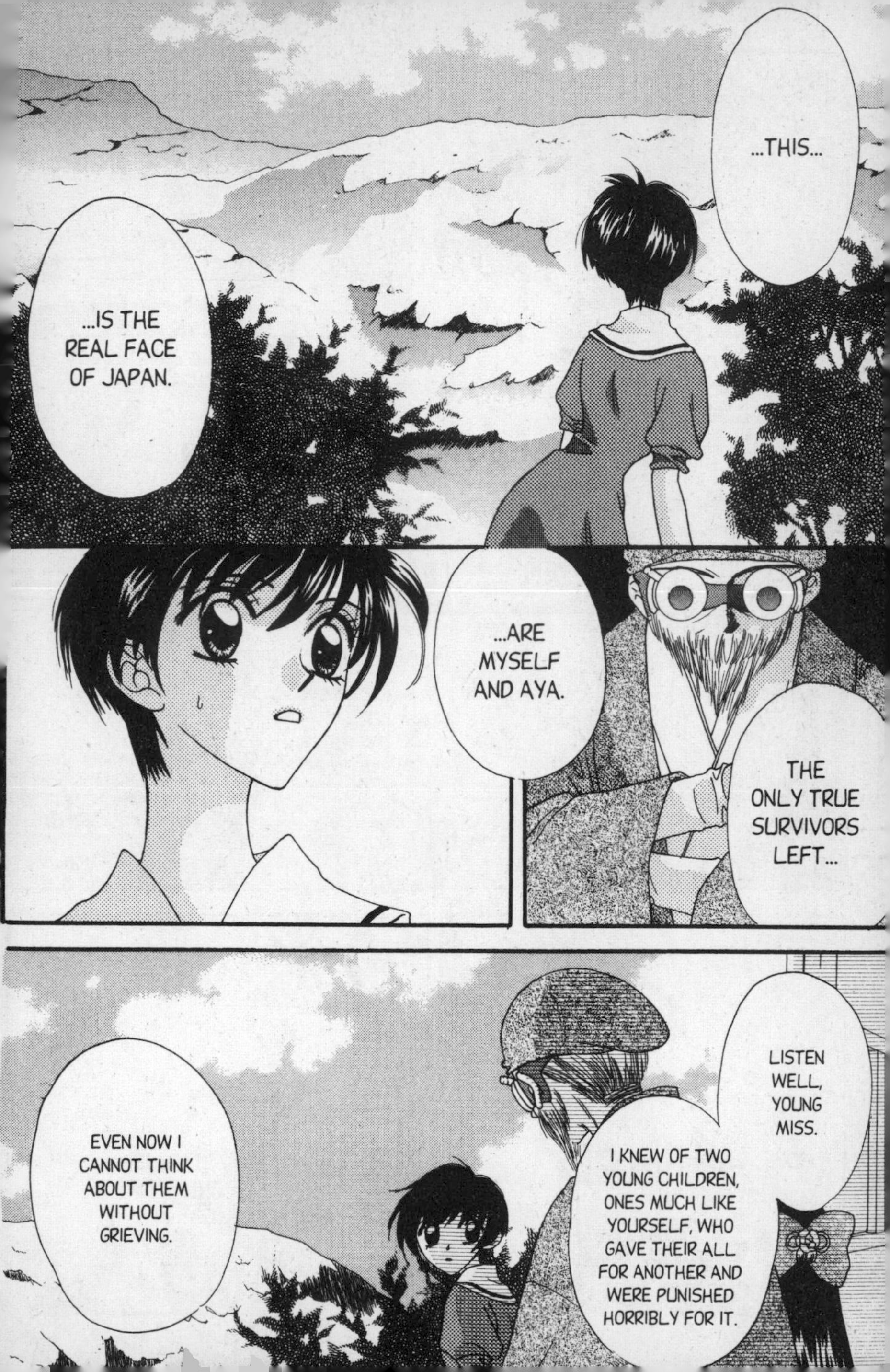
...THIS...
...IS THE REAL FACE OF JAPAN.
THE ONLY TRUE SURVIVORS LEFT...
...ARE MYSELF AND AYA.
LISTEN WELL, YOUNG MISS.
I KNEW OF TWO YOUNG CHILDREN, ONES MUCH LIKE YOURSELF, WHO GAVE THEIR ALL FOR ANOTHER AND WERE PUNISHED HORRIBLY FOR IT.
EVEN NOW I CANNOT THINK ABOUT THEM WITHOUT GRIEVING.

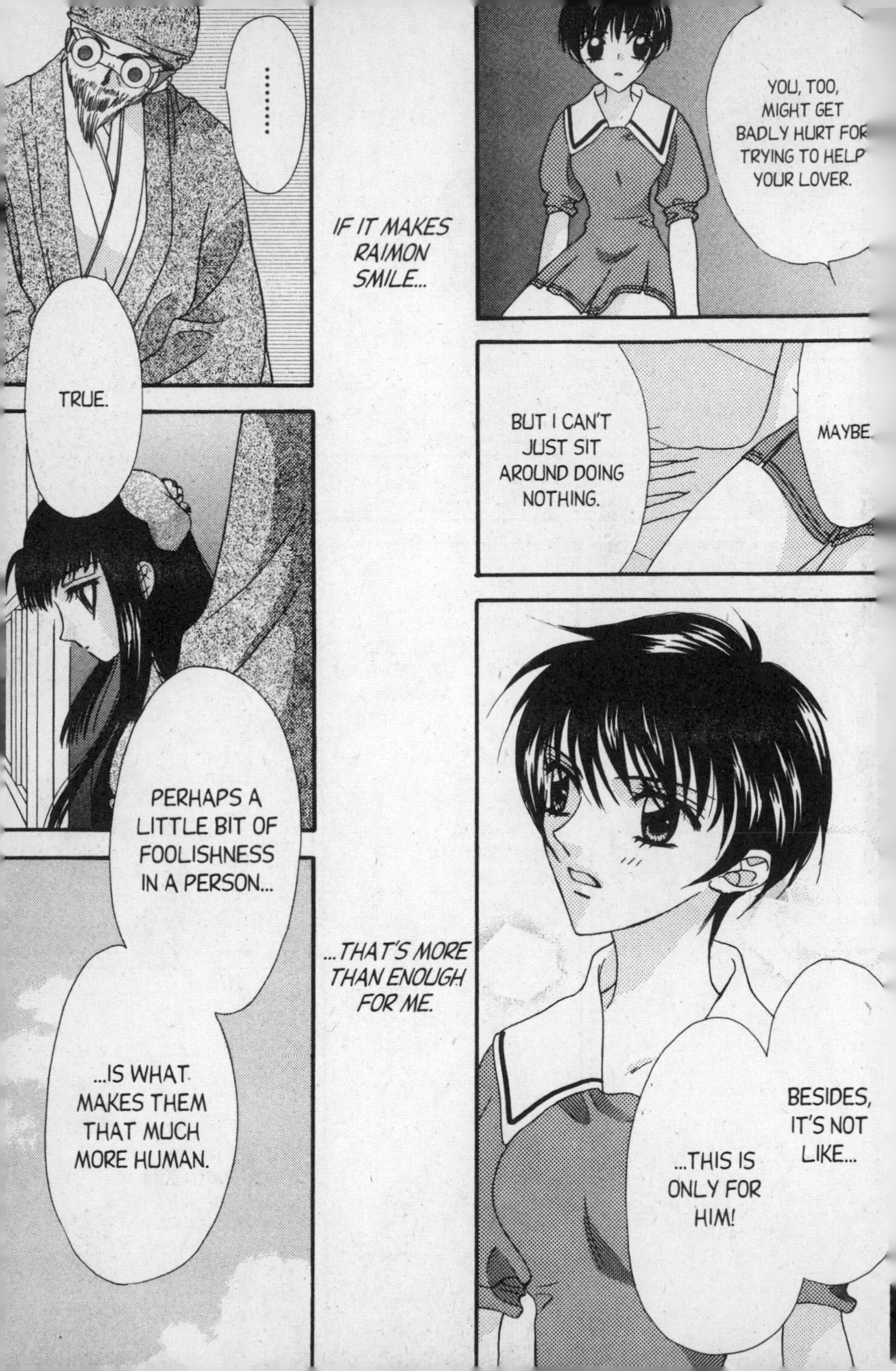
YOU, TOO, MIGHT GET BADLY HURT FOR TRYING TO HELP YOUR LOVER.
MAYBE.
BUT I CAN'T JUST SIT AROUND DOING NOTHING.
BESIDES, IT'S NOT LIKE...
...THIS IS ONLY FOR HIM!
IF IT MAKES RAIMON SMILE...
...THAT'S MORE THAN ENOUGH FOR ME.
......
TRUE.
PERHAPS A LITTLE BIT OF FOOLISHNESS IN A PERSON...
...IS WHAT MAKES THEM THAT MUCH MORE HUMAN.

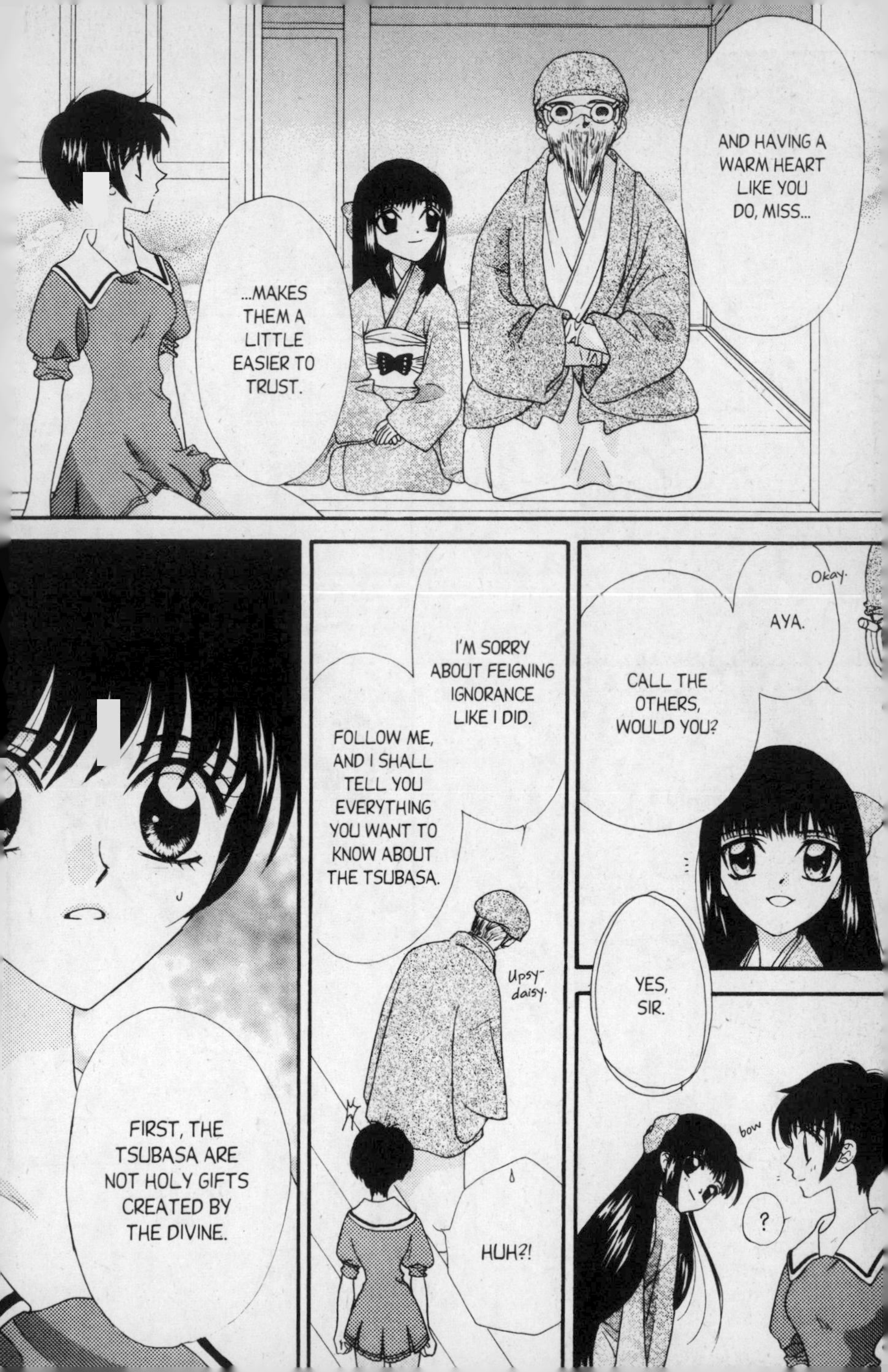
AND HAVING A WARM HEART LIKE YOU DO, MISS...
...MAKES THEM A LITTLE EASIER TO TRUST.
Okay.
AYA.
CALL THE OTHERS, WOULD YOU?
YES, SIR.
bow
?
I'M SORRY ABOUT FEIGNING IGNORANCE LIKE I DID.
FOLLOW ME, AND I SHALL TELL YOU EVERYTHING YOU WANT TO KNOW ABOUT THE TSUBASA.
Upsy-daisy.
HUH?!
FIRST, THE TSUBASA ARE NOT HOLY GIFTS CREATED BY THE DIVINE.

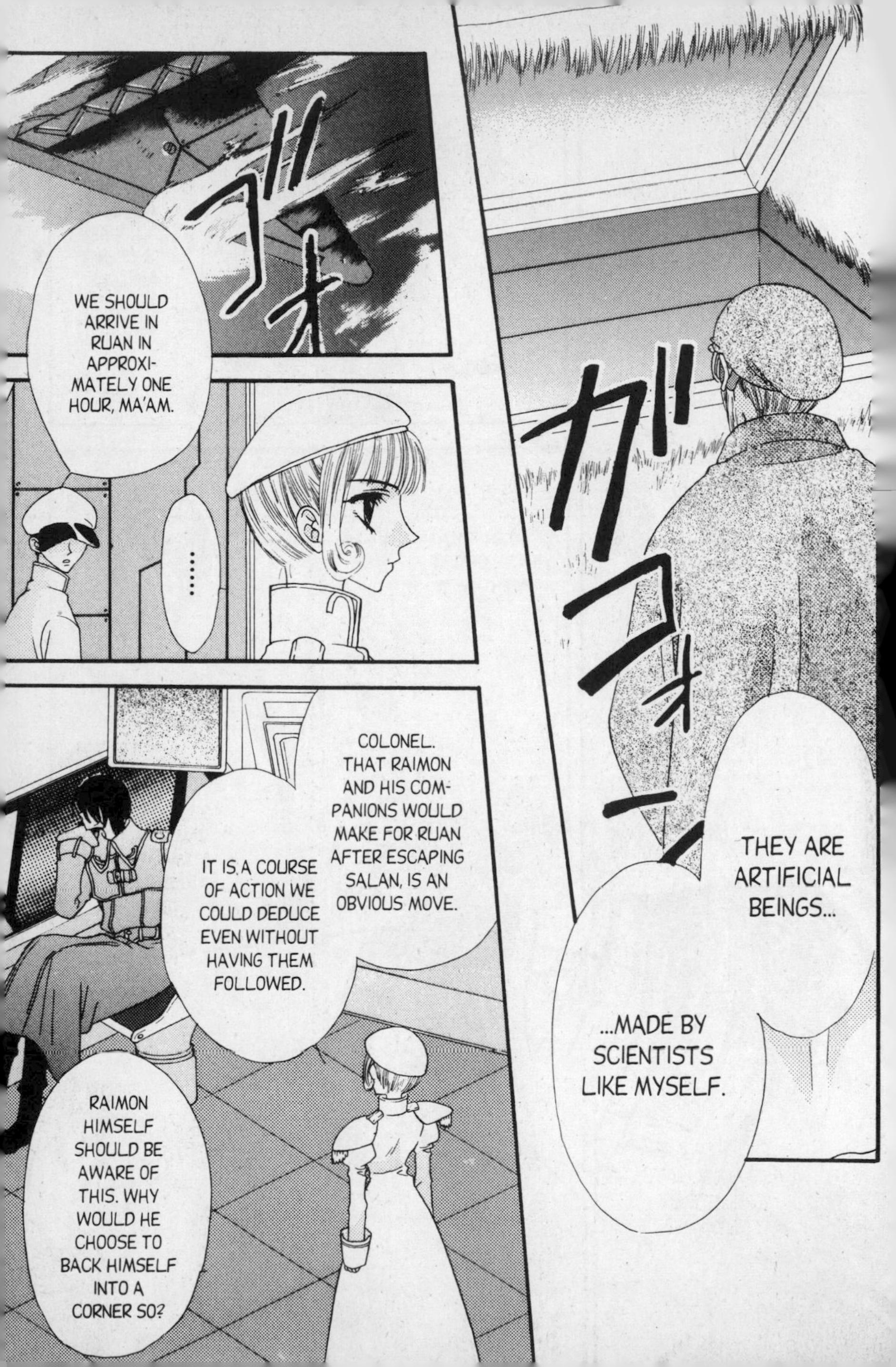
ガコォン
THEY ARE ARTIFICIAL BEINGS...
...MADE BY SCIENTISTS LIKE MYSELF.
ゴォ
WE SHOULD ARRIVE IN RUAN IN APPROXI-MATELY ONE HOUR, MA'AM.
......
COLONEL. THAT RAIMON AND HIS COM-PANIONS WOULD MAKE FOR RUAN AFTER ESCAPING SALAN, IS AN OBVIOUS MOVE.
IT IS A COURSE OF ACTION WE COULD DEDUCE EVEN WITHOUT HAVING THEM FOLLOWED.
RAIMON HIMSELF SHOULD BE AWARE OF THIS. WHY WOULD HE CHOOSE TO BACK HIMSELF INTO A CORNER SO?

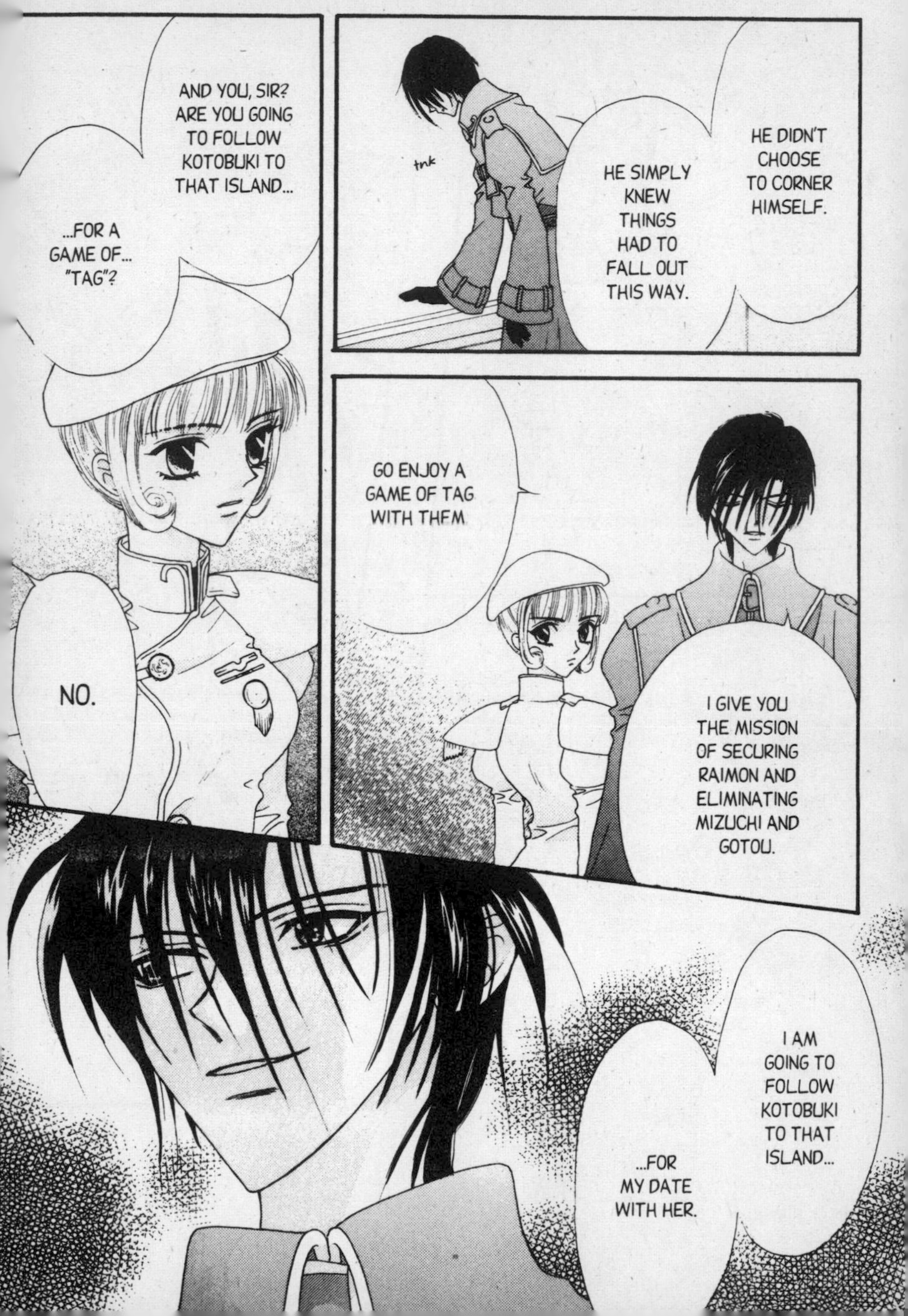
HE DIDN'T CHOOSE TO CORNER HIMSELF.
HE SIMPLY KNEW THINGS HAD TO FALL OUT THIS WAY.
tnk
I GIVE YOU THE MISSION OF SECURING RAIMON AND ELIMINATING MIZUCHI AND GOTOU.
GO ENJOY A GAME OF TAG WITH THEM.
AND YOU, SIR? ARE YOU GOING TO FOLLOW KOTOBUKI TO THAT ISLAND...
...FOR A GAME OF... "TAG"?
NO.
I AM GOING TO FOLLOW KOTOBUKI TO THAT ISLAND...
...FOR MY DATE WITH HER.

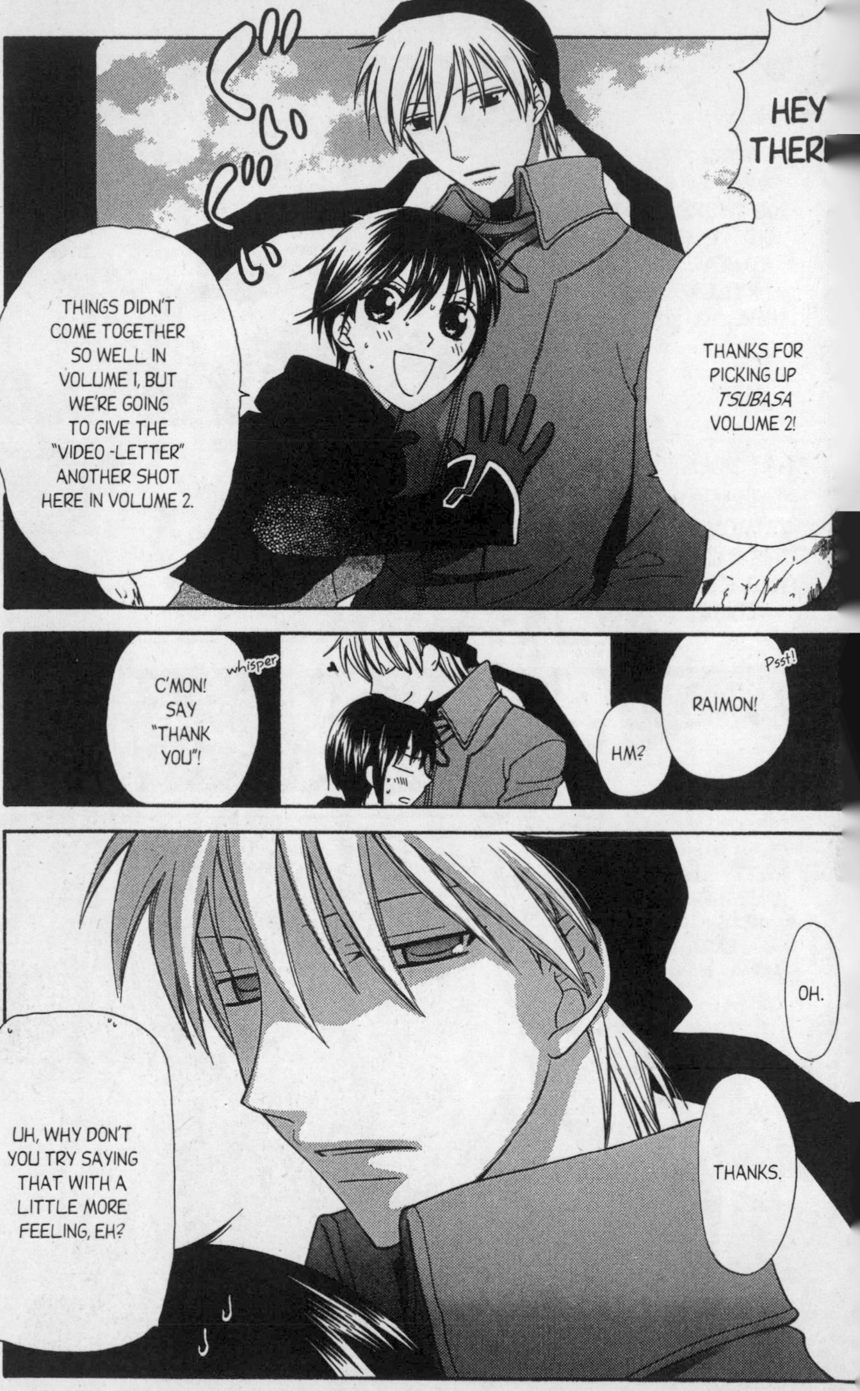
HEY THER
THANKS FOR PICKING UP *TSUBASA* VOLUME 2!
THINGS DIDN'T COME TOGETHER SO WELL IN VOLUME 1, BUT WE'RE GOING TO GIVE THE "VIDEO -LETTER" ANOTHER SHOT HERE IN VOLUME 2.
Psst!
RAIMON!
HM?
whisper
C'MON! SAY "THANK YOU"!
OH.
THANKS.
UH, WHY DON'T YOU TRY SAYING THAT WITH A LITTLE MORE FEELING, EH?

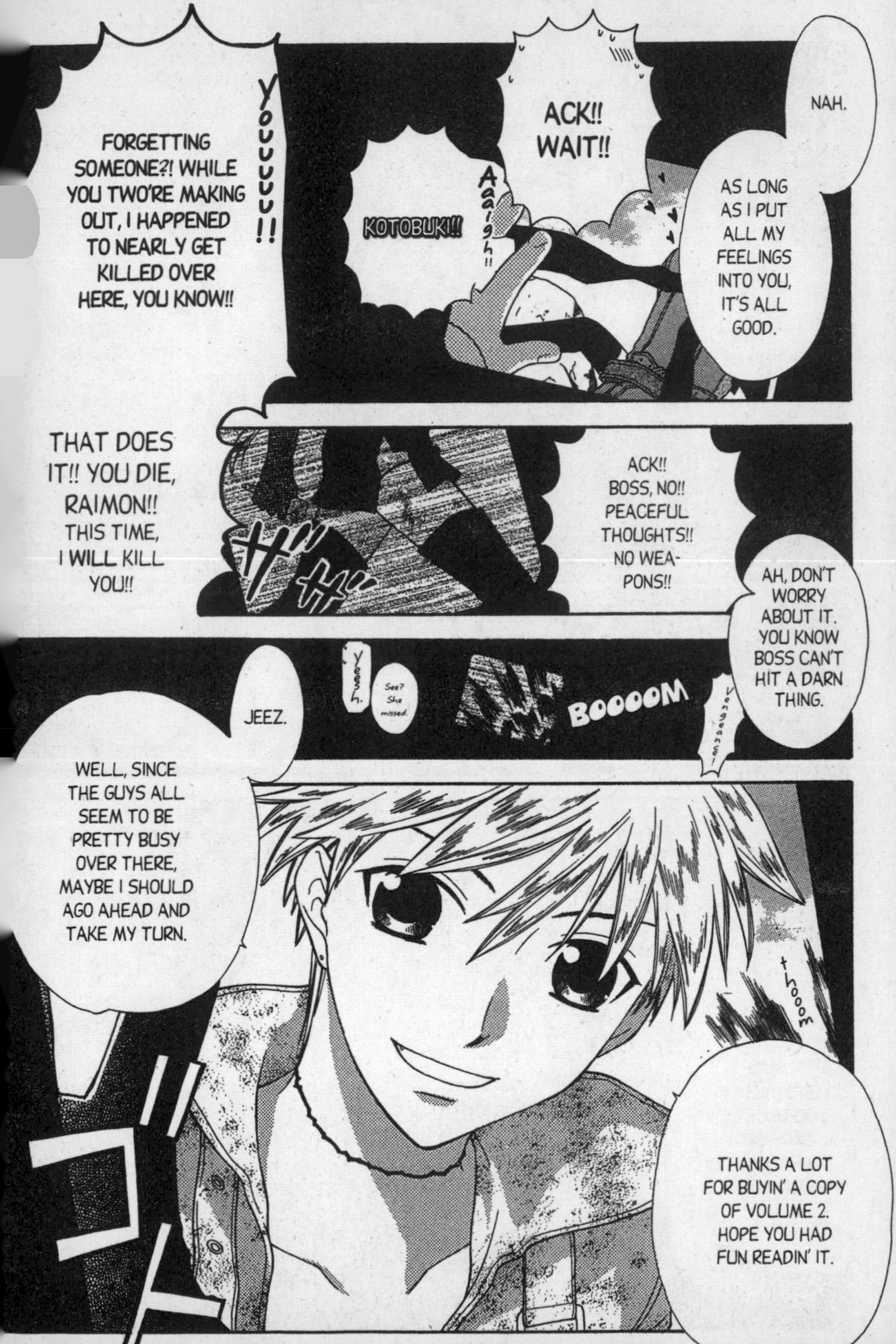
NAH.
AS LONG AS I PUT ALL MY FEELINGS INTO YOU, IT'S ALL GOOD.
ACK!! WAIT!!
Aaaigh!!
KOTOBUKI!!!
Youuuuuu!!
FORGETTING SOMEONE?! WHILE YOU TWO'RE MAKING OUT, I HAPPENED TO NEARLY GET KILLED OVER HERE, YOU KNOW!!
ACK!! BOSS, NO!! PEACEFUL THOUGHTS!! NO WEA-PONS!!
THAT DOES IT!! YOU DIE, RAIMON!! THIS TIME, I WILL KILL YOU!!
AH, DON'T WORRY ABOUT IT. YOU KNOW BOSS CAN'T HIT A DARN THING.
Vengeance!
BOOOOM
See? She missed.
Yeesh.
JEEZ.
thooom
WELL, SINCE THE GUYS ALL SEEM TO BE PRETTY BUSY OVER THERE, MAYBE I SHOULD AGO AHEAD AND TAKE MY TURN.
THANKS A LOT FOR BUYIN' A COPY OF VOLUME 2. HOPE YOU HAD FUN READIN' IT.

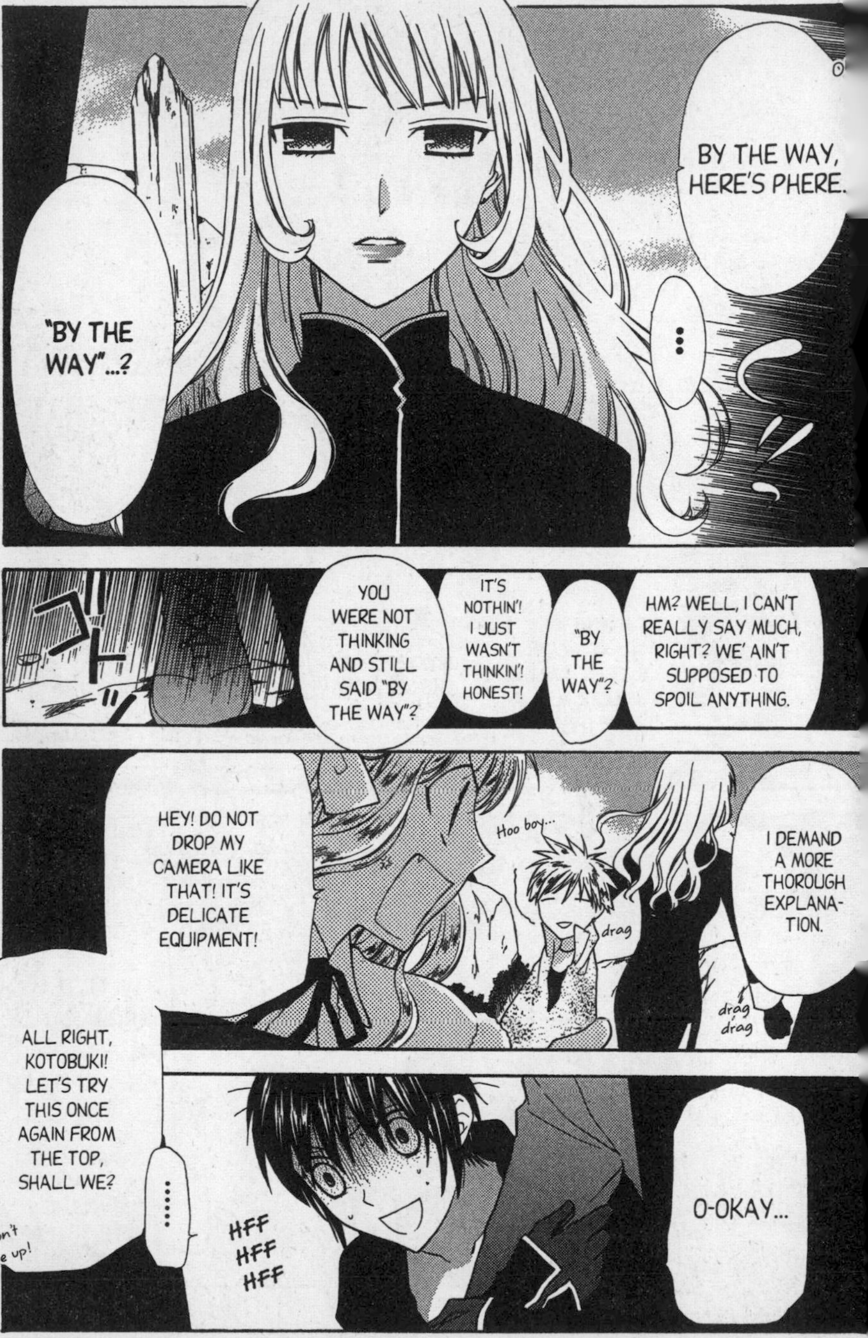
BY THE WAY, HERE'S PHERE.
...
"BY THE WAY"...?
HM? WELL, I CAN'T REALLY SAY MUCH, RIGHT? WE' AIN'T SUPPOSED TO SPOIL ANYTHING.
"BY THE WAY"?
IT'S NOTHIN'! I JUST WASN'T THINKIN'! HONEST!
YOU WERE NOT THINKING AND STILL SAID "BY THE WAY"?
I DEMAND A MORE THOROUGH EXPLANA-TION.
drag drag
drag
Hoo boy...
HEY! DO NOT DROP MY CAMERA LIKE THAT! IT'S DELICATE EQUIPMENT!
O-OKAY...
HFF HFF HFF
......
ALL RIGHT, KOTOBUKI! LET'S TRY THIS ONCE AGAIN FROM THE TOP, SHALL WE?
Don't give up!

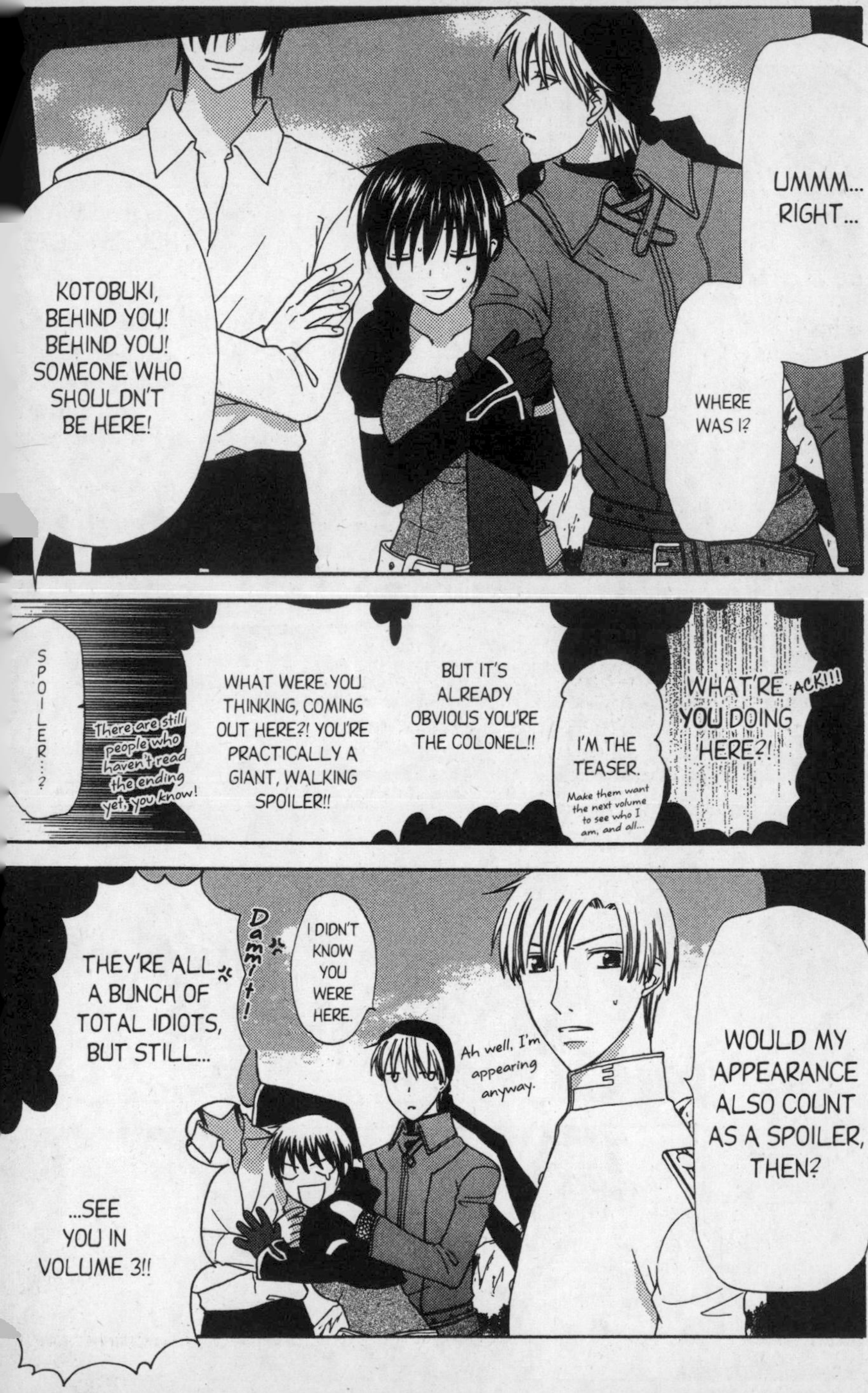

UMMM... RIGHT...
WHERE WAS I?
KOTOBUKI, BEHIND YOU! BEHIND YOU! SOMEONE WHO SHOULDN'T BE HERE!
WHAT'RE YOU DOING HERE?!
ACK!!!
I'M THE TEASER.
Make them want the next volume to see who I am, and all...
BUT IT'S ALREADY OBVIOUS YOU'RE THE COLONEL!!
WHAT WERE YOU THINKING, COMING OUT HERE?! YOU'RE PRACTICALLY A GIANT, WALKING SPOILER!!
There are still people who haven't read the ending yet, you know!
SPOILER...?
WOULD MY APPEARANCE ALSO COUNT AS A SPOILER, THEN?
Ah well, I'm appearing anyway.
I DIDN'T KNOW YOU WERE HERE.
Dammit!
THEY'RE ALL A BUNCH OF TOTAL IDIOTS, BUT STILL...
...SEE YOU IN VOLUME 3!!

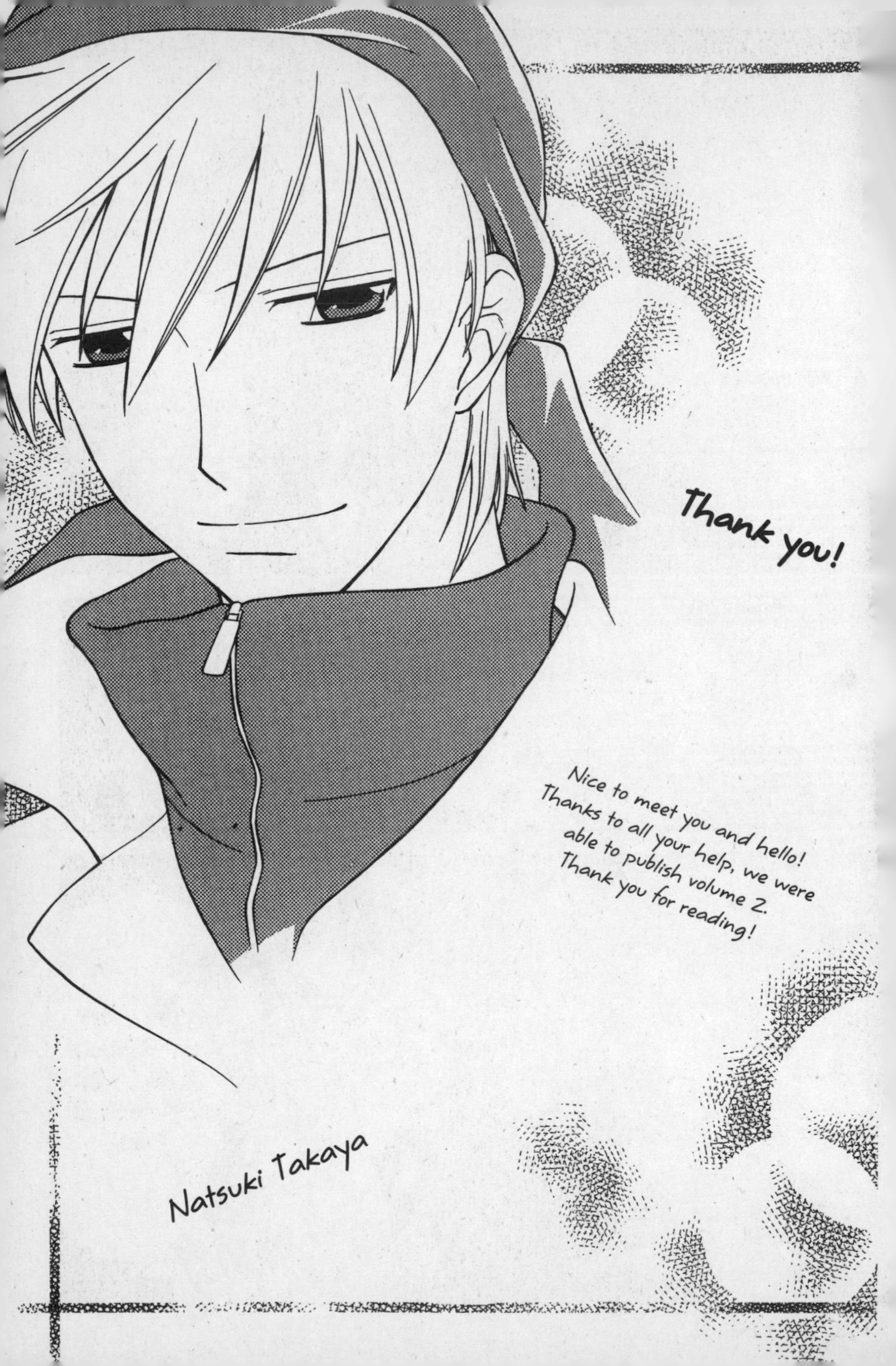

Thank you!
Nice to meet you and hello!
Thanks to all your help, we were
able to publish volume 2.
Thank you for reading!
Natsuki Takaya

In Volume 3 of

TSUBASA

THOSE WITH WINGS

• From the creator of FRUITS BASKET •
TSUBASA
THOSE WITH WINGS
3
Natsuki Takaya

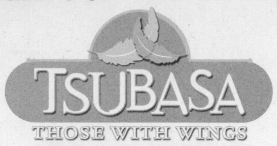

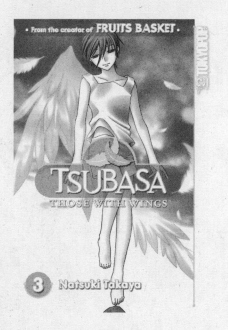

At long last, the truth behind the Tsubasa is revealed! The legendary wish-granting artifact is-- a pair of artificially created human brains?! Scientists experimenting in neuro-science in the 21st Century created two artificial human brains with extraordinary powers, including flight, teleportation and the power to take human shape... and one of them looks very familiar! Unfortunately, without the pair of them together, the "Tsubasa" power will not work, and one has been missing for decades.

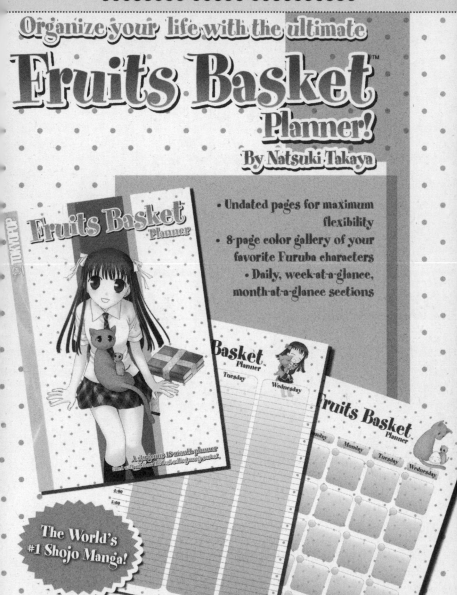

STOP!

This is the back of the book.
You wouldn't want to spoil a great ending!

This book is printed "manga-style," in the authentic Japanese right-to-left format. Since none of the artwork has been flipped or altered, readers get to experience the story just as the creator intended. You've been asking for it, so TOKYOPOP® delivered: authentic, hot-off-the-press, and far more fun!

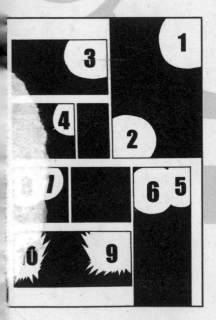

DIRECTIONS

If this is your first time reading manga-style, here's a quick guide to help you understand how it works.

It's easy... just start in the top right panel and follow the numbers. Have fun, and look for more 100% authentic manga from TOKYOPOP®!